THE MAKING OF A GREAT POWER

Late Stuart and early Georgian Britain
1660–1722

General editor: *Geoffrey Holmes*

THE TRANSFORMATION OF MEDIEVAL ENGLAND
1370–1529
John A. F. Thomson

THE EMERGENCE OF A NATION STATE
The commonwealth of England 1529–1660
Alan G. R. Smith

THE MAKING OF A GREAT POWER
Late Stuart and early Georgian Britain
1660–1722
Geoffrey Holmes

THE AGE OF OLIGARCHY
Pre-industrial Britain, 1722–1783
Geoffrey Holmes and *Daniel Szechi*

THE FORGING OF THE MODERN STATE
Early industrial Britain 1783–1870
Eric J. Evans

THE ECLIPSE OF A GREAT POWER
Modern Britain 1870–1975
Keith Robbins

THE MAKING OF A GREAT POWER

Late Stuart and early Georgian Britain 1660–1722

Geoffrey Holmes

LONGMAN
LONDON AND NEW YORK

Longman Group UK Limited,
Longman House, Burnt Mill,
Harlow, Essex CM20 2JE, England
and Associated Companies throughout the world

Published in the United States of America
by Longman Publishing, New York

© Geoffrey Holmes, 1993

First published 1993

ISBN 0582 48438 3 CSD
ISBN 0582 48439 1 PPR

British Library Cataloguing-in-Publication Data

A catalogue record for this book is
available from the British Library

Library of Congress Cataloging in Publication Data
Holmes, Geoffrey S., 1928–
    The making of a great power: late Stuart and early Georgian
Britain. 1660–1722 / Geoffrey Holmes.
        p. cm. – (Foundations of modern Britain)
    Includes bibliographical references and index.
    ISBN 0–582–48438–3. – ISBN 0–582–48439–1 (pbk.)
    1. Great Britain – History – 1660–1714. 2. Great Britain – History –
George I, 1714–1727. I. Title. II. Series.
DA435.H614 1993
941.06 – dc20   92–13685
                                                                                   CIP

Set 9A in 9½/12 Linotron 202 Times
Produced by Longman Singapore Publishers (Pte) Ltd.
Printed in Singapore

Contents

Contents

List of maps

Editor's foreword

So prodigious has been the output of specialised work on British history during the past twenty years, and so rich its diversity, that scholars and students thirst continually after fresh syntheses. Even those who read for the pure pleasure of informing themselves about the past have become quite reconciled to the fact that little can now be taken for granted. An absorbing interest in local situations, as a way to understanding more general ones; a concern with those processes of social change which accompany economic, educational and cultural development, and which often condition political activity too: these and many other strong currents of modern historiography have washed away some of our more comfortable orthodoxies. Even when we know *what* happened, there is endless scope for debate about *why* things happened and with what consequences.

In such circumstances a new series of general textbooks on British history would not seem to call for elaborate justification. However, the six volumes constituting *Foundations of Modern Britain* do have a distinct rationale and they embody some novel features. For one thing, they make a serious attempt to present a history of Britain from the point at which 'Britain' became first a recognisable entity and then a Great Power, and to trace the foundations of this state in the history of pre-eighteenth-century England. The fact that five of the six authors either have taught or are teaching in Scottish universities, while one has held a chair in the University of Wales, should at least help to remind them that one aim of the series is to avoid excessive Anglo-centricity. The first two volumes, spanning the years 1370–1660, will certainly concentrate primarily on the history of England, emphasising those developments which first prepared the way for, and later confirmed her emergence as an independent 'Commonwealth', free from Continental trammels whether territorial or ecclesiastical. But the reader should also be aware, as he reads them, of England's ultimate rôle as the heart of a wider island kingdom in which men of three nations came to be associated. During the period covered by volumes 3, 4 and 5, 1660–1870, this 'United Kingdom of Great Britain' became not only a domestic reality but the centre of an Empire and the possessor of world-wide influence. Space will allow only limited treatment of Ireland and of Anglo-Irish relations until after the Union of 1801. It is appropriate, however, that in the final volume of the series reasserted nationalism should figure almost as strongly as the erosion of imperial status in the story of Britain's slide down the slippery slope from palmy greatness to anxious mediocrity. The terminal date of volume 6, 1975, is deliberately chosen: the year in which Britain, tortured once again by her Irish inheritance and facing demands for Scottish devolution, or even independence, belatedly recognised that the days of complacent self-sufficiency as regards Europe, too, were past.

As well as paying more than mere lip-service to its own title, the present series adopts an irreverent attitude to time-honoured chronological divisions. Those lines of demarcation between volumes which dominated virtually every English history series conceived before 1960 (and, with a few exceptions, have displayed a remarkable capacity for survival subsequently) are seen as a quite unnecessary obstacle to readers' understanding of the way modern historiography has reshaped whole vistas of our island's history in the past forty years. Years such as 1485, 1603, 1689, 1714, 1760 or 1815 established themselves in textbook lore at a time when they accurately reflected the heavily political and constitutional emphasis of traditional history teaching. Even on those terms they have become of limited utility. But equally seriously, the conventions which such divisions perpetuate often make it extremely difficult for authors to accommodate fundamental aspects of social and economic development within their allotted compass. The brutal slicing off of 'Tawney's century' (1540–1640) at 1603 is perhaps the worst of these atrocities; but it is not the only one.

All dates are to some extent arbitrary as lines of division, and all present their own difficulties. It is hoped, none the less, that those selected in this series to enclose periods which are in any case a good deal longer than average, may prove less inhibiting and confusing than some of their predecessors and much more adaptable to the needs of British history courses in universities and colleges.

In one further important respect the authors have kept in mind the practical requirements of students and teachers. Their approach eschews lengthy narrative wherever possible and concentrates, within chapters short enough to be rapidly absorbed, on the development of themes and the discussion of problems. Yet at the same time they attempt to satisfy their readers' need for basic information in two ways: by providing, at appropriate stages, skeletal 'frameworks' of events, chronologically ordered, within which the subsequent analysis and interplay of argument can be set; and by placing at the end of each volume a 'compendium' of factual data, including statistics, on a scale much greater than that of normal textbook appendices.

These compendia are essential companions to the texts and are designed for ready and constant use. The frequent references to them which punctuate so many chapters in this series will be found within square brackets, e.g. [B]. They should be easily distinguishable from the numerous arabic numbers within round brackets inserted in the text, e.g. (117). These refer readers to the Bibliography, in which most items are thematically arranged and serially numbered. Where necessary, specific page numbers (in italic) follow the main reference in the round brackets. In references to articles page numbers are not usually given. References to statutes, also in round brackets, are by regnal year and chapter. Superior numerals are for the references which appear at the end of the relevant chapter. The place of publication of books is London unless otherwise indicated.

Geoffrey Holmes

Preface

This book has had rather a chequered history. I was originally contracted to write a single volume, on a similar scale to the other volumes in the *Foundations of Modern Britain* series, covering the period 1660–1783, and began work on it in 1981. Unfortunately, the book ran to excessive length; and a decade of serious and worsening health problems have made it impossible for me to undertake the difficult task of rewriting and cutting it down to scale. I am exceedingly grateful to Longman for deciding, in the circumstances, not to send the whole thing to the shredder, but to issue two separate books instead of one to cover the period, with the division in the early 1720s. The next book *The Age of Oligarchy*, covering the years roughly from 1722 to 1783, in the writing of which Daniel Szechi collaborated, will appear simultaneously. These two volumes are thus on a larger scale than the other four in the series.

Because the original single-volume treatment was organised in a number of substantial but discrete sections, arranged broadly chronologically, dividing it to make two related but independent volumes, each self-sufficient and convincing in its own right, proved less arduous in practice than we might have feared. Nevertheless, a few rough edges remain. The division at 1722, like so many chronological clean cuts, is more justifiable in terms of politics (with the election of 1722, which ushered in the long period of Whig oligarchy) than economic or social terms. Scotland and Ireland are other cases in point. Neither the traditional dividing date, 1714, nor the present division at 1722, makes much sense for either country. This book, therefore, deals with the Union of 1707 and its aftermath down to 1727; a close scrutiny of the 'Fifteen and 'Forty-Five Jacobite rebellions, as well as the later implications of the Union, follow in *The Age of Oligarchy*. Ireland up to 1688 figures incidentally in this volume, but the extensive treatment of Ireland from the Williamite settlement to Grattan's Parliament follows in chapter 16 of *The Age of Oligarchy*. While these methods of solving my problems may not be ideal, I can only plead that they were the best possible in the circumstances. It has also proved impracticable to divide either the original Prologue, which appears in this book, or the Conclusion, which will appear in the next. For these solutions to my difficulties I must beg the reader's indulgence.

There has been another unfortunate result of the way the book has had to be written: the textbook-writer's nightmare, a rush of relevant material appearing at a late stage in the book's production, has afflicted me not once but several times over the past decade. For all my efforts, I have not been able to incorporate all recent work in the finished book.

I am happy to acknowledge much valuable help which I have received from various friends and colleagues: Bill Speck made pertinent comments on chapters

11 and 13. Daniel Szechi, my co-author in *The Age of Oligarchy*, was responsible for several parts of the Compendium, helped me with the Bibliography, and with some sections of the Framework of Events and also helped with the proof-reading. I am exceedingly grateful to him. I must also thank the British Academy for awarding me a Small Grant which enabled me to spend time in London looking at some important primary sources; and the University of Lancaster, for making me a grant from its Research Fund, thanks to which I was able to employ for a few months two part-time research assistants, Stuart Handley and Alan Marshall, who did excellent spadework on the Framework of Events and some sections of the Compendium, respectively. Stuart has also given valuable help by checking references and quotations in London which I was not able to do myself. And I must acknowledge with special warmth the encouragement, sympathetic assistance and understanding shown me over many years by Andrew MacLennan of Longman.

More than ever before, my greatest debt has been to my wife, Ella. Without her scholarly and secretarial assistance, encouragement and nursing care, this book would never have been completed, let alone seen through the press. Any errors, of course, which escaped the net of her and my friends' scrutiny are my responsibility alone.

Geoffrey Holmes
Burton-in-Lonsdale,
March 1992

Acknowledgements

The publishers would like to thank the following for permission to reproduce copyright material: Cambridge University Press for table L.1 from W.A. Cole's chapter in *The Economic History of Britain since 1700: I, 1700–1860*, R.C. Floud and D.H. McCloskey, eds, (1981); and Oxford University Press for the figure in M.1 from *Crime and the Courts in England 1660–1800*, J.M. Beattie (1986).

Note on dating and quotations

At this period, England still used the Julian calendar ('Old Style' or O.S.) when much of the rest of Europe used the more accurate Gregorian calendar ('New Style' or N.S.). Old Style dating was 10 days behind New Style until 1700, and 11 days behind thereafter, and this discrepancy continued until 1752, when the New Style calendar was finally adopted in England. In this book all dates, except where otherwise noted, are given in Old Style; the New Year is, however, taken to begin on 1 January, although in England the Julian New Year began on 25 March. In a few cases, both Old Style and New Style dates are given, thus : 15/25 January 1698, or 15/26 January 1704.

In original quotations, spelling and punctuation have been modernised.

List of abbreviations

The following abbreviations are used in end-notes, compendium and bibliography.

Add.MSS	Additional Manuscripts, British Library
AgHR	*Agricultural History Review*
BIHR	*Bulletin of the Institute of Historical Research*
BL	British Library
EcHR	*Economic History Review*, 2nd series
EHR	*English Historical Review*
HJ	*Historical Journal*
HMC	Historical Manuscripts Commission
JBS	*Journal of British Studies*
JEH	*Journal of Ecclesiastical History*
Parl. Hist.	*Parliamentary History: A Yearbook* (1982–6) or *Parliamentary History* (1987–)
P & P	*Past and Present*
RO	Record Office
TRHS	*Transactions of the Royal Historical Society*, 5th series

To my former pupils
John Beckett
and
Peter Borsay
in whose achievements
I rejoice

PART ONE

Restoration to Revolution, 1660–1688

1660   Monck enters England with the Army of Scotland (Jan); reconvenes the Long
        Parliament, including the 'secluded members' of 1648 (Feb); establishment of New
        Model Army reduced to 28,342 (27th). Self-dissolution of Long Parliament; writs
        issued for new election (Mar). Conciliatory Declaration issued by Charles II from
        Breda (4 Apr).
            First meeting of the Convention; Presbyterian Speaker elected (25 Apr). Both
        Houses vote the government to be 'by King, Lords and Commons' (1 May);
        Charles proclaimed King (8th), lands at Dover (25th). Convention declares itself
        full and legal Parliament; Act for Confirming Judicial Proceedings passed; Land
        Sales Bill introduced (June). Crown – but not Church or delinquent – lands
        excluded from Bill of Sales (July – bill lapsed Dec). Act of General Pardon,
        Indemnity and Oblivion – only 33 living persons exempted from pardon, of whom
        a third executed (Aug). Act confirming Ministers of Religion in possession –
        except Baptists, notorious republicans and those who had replaced rejected
        Anglicans; new Navigation Act, regulating trade and shipping; disbandment of
        New Model Army begins; first session of Convention Parliament ends (Sept).*
            Earl of Southampton appointed Lord Treasurer (Sept); Lord Hyde (E. of
        Clarendon 1661) Lord Chancellor since appointment in exile, 1658. Land commis-
        sion, to settle compensation for dispossessed, begins work; Worcester House
        Conference between Anglican and Presbyterian divines; King's conciliatory
        'Worcester House Declaration' (Oct). Convention's second session (Nov–Dec);
        Presbyterian attempts to embody Worcester House Declaration in legislation fails
        by 28 votes. Irish land settlement announced in royal declaration (Nov).
            Samuel Pepys begins his diary (Jan); 'College' established in London (Nov) for
        'physio-mathematical learning' – incorporated, 1662, as 'The Royal Society';
        publication (by Robert Boyle) of 'Boyle's Law'.
1661   Meeting of first post-Revolution Scottish Parliament; minor rising of Fifth Monarchy
        Men in London under Thomas Venner (Jan). First General Election of the new reign
        (Jan–Feb) [E.1(i)]. Paying-off of New Model Army – 31 regiments and garrisons –
        completed; Charles II's own army – initially c. 3,000 infantry and cavalry (excluding
        Dunkirk garrison) £122,000 p.a. – formally established (Jan–Feb).
            Anglican-Presbyterian conference opens at the Savoy palace (Apr).
            First meeting of 'Cavalier' Parliament (8 May); spiritual peers readmitted to
        Upper House; Quaker Act [N.2(ii)]; Act 'to preserve the person and government
        of the King' (May). Irish Parliament, with entirely Protestant House of Commons,
        called (8 May) to effect the land settlement – the only such Parliament to meet
        1660–85. Fear of further republican/sectarian plots in England; dispute between
        Commons and Lords over constitutional exercise of powers to purge municipal
        corporations (June – see also Dec).
            Treaty of Alliance and Marriage (Charles and Catherine of Braganza) signed
        with Portugal (23 June) [H(i)]. Charles's army establishment ['guards and garri-
        sons'] completed – 4 regiments of foot and horse guards, 28 garrisons, c. 6,000
        men, £190,000 p.a. (June). Failure of Lords' bill to secure greater toleration for
        Catholics; Militia Act – giving crown supreme control of armed forces and militia
        (July).
            Savoy Conference ends in deadlock, without 'Comprehension' in state church
        for Puritans (July). Bishops reintroduced into Scottish Church and parliament; Act
        Rescissory negatives all proceedings of Scots Parliaments, including religious

* For precise dates of parliamentary sessions, where not given, see E.2.

changes, since 1633 (Sept). At Westminster the '18 Months' Assessment' (£1.2 m.) granted as emergency aid to Charles (Nov); Corporation Act ultimately passed as desired by Commons (Dec).

Robert Boyle's *Sceptical Chemist* published.

1662   Uncompromising revised Prayer Book accepted by Convocation (Dec 1661), Council (Feb) and Parliament (Mar). Amid continued anxiety over security (Feb–Mar) Court plans for new militia rouse parliamentary fear of standing army; Lords accept but Commons reject inclusion of a royal dispensing power, in favour of Presbyterian ministers, in Church Uniformity Bill (Mar).

Hearth Tax imposed – 2s. p.a. per hearth; King voted £70,000 p.a. to strengthen *existing* county militias; Act of Uniformity [N.2(iii)] passed – all ministers refusing new Prayer Book and 39 Articles to be deprived (May); first session of Cavalier Parliament (1 year 11 days) ends (19 May). King fails in attempt to suspend Uniformity Act (June). St Bartholomew's Day (24 Aug): 'the Great Ejection' of just under 1,000 nonconforming ministers.

Scottish Parliament prorogued after ratifying restoration of episcopacy and imposing anti-covenanting test on office-holders (Sept). Anglo-Dutch Treaty of 'amity' papers over outstanding disputes. Charles II's English army increased to 8,000 (Sept–Oct). Sale of Dunkirk to France; beginning of Scotland's 'great ejection' – of ministers elected by congregations without lay patronage; Sir Henry Bennet, later Lord Arlington, becomes principal English Secretary of State – a Court setback for Clarendon (Oct). Charles's 'First Declaration of Indulgence' proposes relief to English dissenters by royal dispensations (Dec – see Feb 1663).

Irish Act of [Land] Settlement, setting up commissions to adjudicate rival claims of Cromwellians and dispossessed royalists (Apr). All English publications subjected to pre-printing censorship by Licensing Act. Royal Society incorporated, with Charles II patron and Brouncker President (July).

1663   Cavalier Parliament reassembles; Crown's claims to a dispensing power in religion rejected by Commons (Feb) and abandoned by Charles (Mar); first attempt to assert Parliament's right to scrutinize public spending (April/May).

Attempted republican rising in Ireland, under Blood, in protest against land settlement (May). Gilbert Sheldon, bishop of London, nominated archbishop of Canterbury on death of Juxon (June). Unsuccessful attempt by earl of Bristol to impeach Clarendon; Parliament prorogued (July). Republican conspiracies uncovered in Yorkshire and Durham (Aug). Scottish Parliament dissolved after voting Crown £40,000 p.a., re-establishing the Lords of the Articles (Chs. 1, 13) and approving Scottish army of 22,000 (Sept – not recalled until 1669). Yorkshire 'rebellion' nipped in the bud by militia (Oct).

'Navigation' system extended to make England a two-way trading entrepôt (Staple Act); Royal African Company founded to trade in slaves, ivory and gold (cf. 1672); founding of first post-Restoration colony in [North] Carolina.

King's company of actors settled at Drury Lane; Samuel Butler's *Hudibras*; Isaac Newton discovers the Binomial Theorem.

1664   Treason trials in the North – 24 executions (Jan–Aug). New session of Parliament opens; King's Speech stresses danger of further insurrection (Mar); bill repealing and revising Triennial Act of 1641 passes Commons by 57 and Lords *nem.con.* – provision for automatic summons of a Parliament after 3 years dropped (Mar/Apr); Act, for 4 years, against Dissenting Conventicles [N.2(iv)] passes smoothly, owing to King's anger against northern conspirators.

Anti-Dutch grievances of English merchants rehearsed in Parliament (Apr);

New Amsterdam in N. America seized from Dutch (Aug); force under Prince Rupert attacks Dutch stations on Guinea Coast, W. Africa (Sept); De Ruyter leads Dutch counter-attacks (Dec). Parliament reassembles and Commons vote £2.5 million to be raised by direct taxation for anticipated war against United Provinces (UP).

Sheldon begins reform of Church courts; prompts Convocation to vote to end separate clerical taxation (Nov). New Amsterdam granted to duke of York, renamed New York. Foundation of French *Compagnie des Indes* inaugurates new phase in French colonization of Canada.

1665   Dutch (Feb) and English (Mar) declarations of war launch Second Anglo-Dutch War. Naval battle off Lowestoft (June) – 26 Dutch ships destroyed or crippled, heavy casualties; Louis XIV's attempt to mediate between England and his ally, UP, fails (Aug); 3-week blockade of Thames by reconstructed Dutch fleet (Oct).

Fifth session of Cavalier Parliament at Oxford because of plague (9–13 Oct); additional war supply (£1.5 m.) voted and for first time 'appropriated' in Supply Act; 'Five Mile Act' passed [N.2(v)] against dissenting preachers and teachers, despite opposition by Clarendon and other ministers; Clarendon's 'Non-Resisting Oath' – dictating absolute loyalty to the constitution in church and state – narrowly rejected by Commons; first Commons bill to prohibit import of lean Irish cattle opposed by King and Clarendonians, aborted in Lords.

Outbreak of Great Plague in London (Apr); mass exodus of well-to-do (July). Plague peaks in London and widespread in provinces (Sept); dies down in London after causing 68,000 recorded, and many unrecorded, deaths (Nov).

Founding in Oxford of what became (1666) the *London Gazette*. 'Act of Explanation' completes Irish land settlement.

1666   France enters war on side of Dutch (Jan); Denmark adheres to Franco-Dutch alliance; Charles II returns to Whitehall Palace after the Plague (Feb). English West Indian islands of St Kitts and Antigua fall to the French (Apr, Nov); half Rupert's battle fleet defeated in Channel in 'The Four Days' Fight' (May); naval victory by Rupert and Albemarle over Dutch, North Foreland (July) paves way for 'Holmes's Bonfire' (Aug) – 250 Dutch merchantmen burnt by Sir Robert Holmes's ships and men.

Great Fire of London (3–6 Sept); Parliament reassembles (18th); war supply of £1.8 m. voted, only after Commons' demand to inspect Navy accounts accepted (Oct). Bitter parliamentary strife over ways of raising supply, 2nd Irish cattle bill and Garraway's Commission of Accounts bill; growth of opposition to Court in Lords – Buckingham – as well as of a 'Country interest' in Commons (Oct–Dec).

Pentland Rising of Presbyterian dissentients in Scotland defeated at Rullion Green (Nov); but led to greater influence of Lauderdale and belated concessions to religious dissent. Dissolution of only Irish Parliament of Charles II's reign after passage of Irish Act of Uniformity and deprivation of Ulster Presbyterian ministers.

Bunyan's autobiography, *Grace Abounding*, published.

1667   Charles forced to accept 2nd Irish Cattle Act (see below p. 6) as price of getting taxes through and Garraway's bill dropped (Jan); sixth session of Parliament ends in mood of acrimony; duke of Buckingham dismissed for his parliamentary opposition; government decides to 'lay up the big ships' and send to sea only cruisers for commerce protection (Feb). Death of Lord Treasurer Southampton, succeeded by a Treasury Commission of five headed by Albemarle and including Ashley and Sir William Coventry (May).

Secret Anglo-French treaty (Apr); Louis XIV's troops overrun much of Spanish Netherlands, claiming them by 'Devolution' through his wife; tentative Anglo-Dutch peace talks (May); Medway Disaster – Dutch fleet under De Ruyter burns English battleships laid up in the river and captures the *Royal Charles* (June). Harman defeats French fleet off Martinique, saving English West Indies from French annexation (20th). Peace of Breda brings to an end Second Dutch War (July) [H(ii)].

Dismissal of Clarendon; meeting of Parliament; impeachment proceedings against Clarendon initiated (Oct); flight of Clarendon to France (29 Nov); Act setting up first parliamentary Accounts Commission – to investigate government war finance (Dec).

Import of Irish cattle into England illegalized (see Jan) – later to be extended to mutton, lamb, butter, cheese – severe damage to Irish economy despite widespread evasion (not repealed until 1759). Failure of Charles II's attempt to promote Anglo-Scottish economic union; tariff war begun by England's main European customer – French duties on imported textiles doubled by Colbert; Anglo-Spanish Commerce Treaty (May) gives England favoured treatment in Spanish trade.

Milton's *Paradise Lost* 'stole into the world almost unperceived' (K. Feiling); Acts regulating the re-building of London passed (1667–8); Christopher Wren appointed 'Surveyor-General and principal architect'.

1668   Condé conquers Franche-Comté; Anglo-Dutch alliance signed to counter French aggression (Jan); limited war preparations – hamstrung by inadequate parliamentary supply (Mar–Apr); Anglo-Dutch alliance expanded to Triple Alliance with adherence of Sweden (Apr) [H(iii)]; Treaty of Aix-la-Chapelle ends Louis's War of Devolution – extends French frontier well into, and along coast of, Spanish Netherlands.

Lords' hearing of *Skinner* v *East India Company*, begun Oct 1667, challenged by Commons as breach of privileges (Apr); 1st Conventicles Act lapses when session terminates in mutual acrimony between the Houses (9 May) – Parliament kept prorogued until Oct 1669.

Colbert de Croissy sent to London to propose Anglo-French alliance, but official negotiations fail (Aug–Dec); ciphered private correspondence begins between Charles and duchess of Orleans re. French alliance (Dec). Sir Thomas Osborne, MP for York – later Danby – appointed to office as client of Buckingham of the *Cabal* (see Ch. 7).

Setbacks for Archbishop Sharp and the hard-line episcopal party in Scotland.

1669   Duke of York converted to Roman Catholicism; Charles reveals Catholic, pro-French sympathies at secret meeting with York, Arundel, and Clifford and Arlington of the Cabal (Jan); clandestine negotiations with France soon after begun. Dismissal of High Anglican Ormonde, Lord Lieutenant of Ireland, and Sir William Coventry (Feb).

Charles's First Letter of Indulgence issued in Scotland, though only *c.* 40 ejected ministers accepted episcopacy on its moderate terms; beginning of the Cabal's negotiations for an Anglo-Scottish legislative union (June). New Scottish Parliament summoned in hope of forwarding Union; Lauderdale of the Cabal goes to Scotland as Lord Commissioner to the Parliament (Oct); but opposition delays appointment of Scottish Union commissioners – until 1670. French ambassador at last informed of the secret Anglo-French negotiations (Oct).

Cavalier Parliament begins 8th session (19 Oct); renewed battle over *Skinner* v *the East India Company* and other uncooperative behaviour quickly confirms King in his French designs; merchants' petitions against French commercial policies. Sudden prorogation by Charles, blocking a new Conventicles Bill (11 Dec). First draft of a secret treaty with France completed (18th).

Burnet, archbishop of Glasgow, forced by Lauderdale to resign, after protests from Scottish church hierarchy against new Supremacy Act subordinating the Kirk to royal authority (Dec).

Pepys's diary ends (31 May). Newton appointed Professor of Mathematics at Cambridge (1669–1701).

1670 Death of Albemarle; Ashley [-Cooper] now senior Commissioner of Treasury; King accepts need to sanction tough measures against dissenters in return for cooperation of parliamentary 'cavaliers' (Jan). New session of Parliament; Charles begins to attend Lords' debates; valuable additional duty on wines granted for royal ordinary revenue for 8 years (Feb). Passage of Second Conventicles bill – Commons accepting Lords' amendment reaffirming royal prerogatives in ecclesiastical affairs (Feb–Mar). Commissioners of Accounts abandon work (Mar); session adjourned until Oct (Apr).

Duchess of Orleans meets King at Dover (16 May); Secret Treaty of Dover [H(iv)] (15, *I*, *344–5*) between Charles and Louis XIV signed by Arlington, Clifford, Arundel, Bellings, Colbert de Croissy (22nd); death of duchess of Orleans (June).

Parliamentary session resumed; Triple Alliance policy endorsed by Commons (Oct); new spirit of financial generosity again in evidence over autumn and winter. Second (sham) Treaty of Dover between England and France – Catholic clauses omitted – anti-Dutch offensive alliance with date of attack on UP fixed for Spring 1672 (21 Dec).

Collapse of negotiations for Anglo-Scottish Union (Sept–Oct). Hudson's Bay Company chartered; English settlement of South Carolina and establishment of log-cutting base off Honduras Bay.

John Ray's *Catalogue of Plants* published.

1671 Auxiliary Excise bill – additional duties on ale and beer for 6 years to swell ordinary revenue – passes Commons (Feb); Commons accept bill to exclude Catholics from office; royal proclamation against Jesuits and Romish priests (Mar); anti-Catholic bill still before the Lords when Parliament prorogued (Apr) – not reconvened until Feb 1673.

Osborne becomes Treasurer of the Navy (Sept). Farming of Customs revenue ends (Oct) – Customs commissioners appointed under Treasury Secretary, Sir George Downing, to supervise direct collection. Right of Irish ports to receive 'enumerated' goods direct from colonies abolished.

Milton's *Paradise Regained* published.

1672 'Stop of the Exchequer', suspending for a year all capital repayments to government creditors, ordered against Ashley's advice (Jan). Second Declaration of Indulgence published – penal laws suspended, freedom of worship for dissenters and (privately) for Catholics (Mar) [N.1(iv)]. Declaration of War on UP, on shallow commercial pretexts (15th) – begins 'Third Dutch War' (1672–4).

Battle of Sole Bay – Anglo-French naval setback at hands of De Ruyter, death of Admiral Lord Sandwich; Henry Coventry, Anglican Cavalier, made a Secretary of State as counterweight to the Cabal (May). French troops capture Utrecht, leading to fall of De Witt brothers and appointment of William of Orange as Stadhouder (June); allied fleets dispersed by storm off the Texel (July).

Clifford created Baron and made Lord Treasurer; Ashley created earl of Shaftesbury and Lord Chancellor (Nov); alarm caused by duke of York's absence from Christmas Communion.

Some opposition to war taxation in Scottish Parliament – William Moir, MP, imprisoned. Conflict of policy between Scottish Parliament – Acts punishing nonconformity – and Privy Council, issuing second Scottish Declaration of Indulgence. Royal African Company (see 1663) reconstituted after early problems.

John Banister starts in Whitefriars first regular series of *public* concerts in Europe.

1673   William of Orange begins subversive diplomacy to detach England from the war (Jan). 10th session of Cavalier Parliament begins (4 Feb); in his *Delenda est Carthago* speech, Shaftesbury, supporting request for ample war revenue, declares the Dutch 'England's eternal enemy'; Commons vote 'penal statutes in matters ecclesiastical cannot be suspended but by an Act of Parliament'; advocate relief bill for Protestant dissenters; vote £1.2 m. for war but hold up supply bill pending attention to their religious grievances (Feb).

Moulin [William's agent]'s *England's Appeal from the Private Cabal* insinuates government's popish sympathies and Dutch War as part of popish conspiracy; with Cabal divided, King abandons Indulgence policy; assents to 1st Test Act [N.5A(i)]; ends parliamentary session (Mar). As result of Test York resigns from office of Lord High Admiral and Clifford from Treasury – succeeded as Lord Treasurer by Osborne [E. of Danby, 1674] (June).

Failure of Cologne Peace Conference; naval setbacks (28 May–11 Aug), culminating in battle of the Texel, frustrate Anglo-French plans for descent on Holland; Emperor, Spain and Lorraine ally with Dutch against France (Aug). Marriage of duke of York with Catholic Mary of Modena (Sept). New York falls to Dutch (restored at peace of 1674).

Parliament reassembles for brief unruly session (27 Oct–4 Nov); violent anti-Catholic, anti-war, anti-Court feeling; refusal to vote supply; Commons address against York's marriage. Dismissal of Shaftesbury; disintegration of Cabal ministry (Nov). New session of Scottish Parliament – Lauderdale faced with 'such a spirit as I thought never to see here' (Nov–Dec). No further Parliament called in Edinburgh 1674–81.

Rebuilding of St Paul's begun by Wren (1673–5) – choir not opened until 1697. Foundation of a mathematical school in Christ's Hospital. Temple's *Observations upon the United Provinces of the Netherlands* published.

1674   Parliament recalled (12th session): clamour for peace; after Commons' attacks on Arlington, Buckingham and Lauderdale, Buckingham dismissed (Jan). Country opposition vote 'the continuing of any standing force other than the militia . . . a great grievance', and introduce a Habeas Corpus bill and a bill to eliminate Catholics from the Lords; Lords' bill for bringing up York's children as Protestants. Parliament prorogued to kill hostile bills (24 Feb) – not to meet again until April 1675.

Treaty of Westminster [H(v)] brings profitless end to third Dutch War (19 Feb); Shaftesbury expelled from Council (May); retirement of Arlington to honorific office (Sept) removes last obstacle to Danby's ascendancy.

Archbishop Burnet of Glasgow (see 1669) restored, marking end of phase of religious tolerance in Scotland (Sept); Danby and other English ministers added to

Scottish Privy Council – Court–Lauderdale influence in Scotland now impregnable (Dec).

Death of John Milton. Formation of Green Ribbon Club.

1675 Implementation of Danby's political and religious policies begins: announcement of new measures against Catholics and dissenters (Jan). Cavalier Parliament meets for first time in 15 months (Apr); abortive attempt to impeach Danby, begun by Russell (Apr–May). Court's attempt to carry a 'non-resisting test' (on MPs and freeholders [A]) into law defeated after protracted struggle in both Houses (Apr–June). Prorogation, a week after abandonment of non-resisting bill (June).

Shirley v *Fagg* upholds right of House of Lords to hear appeals, overriding MPs' privileges (May–Nov). Danby's Court Party cemented by 'influence' – 34 MPs given or promised pensions (June–Oct). By secret agreement Louis XIV promises subsidy to Charles II in return for keeping Parliament prorogued (Aug).

Autumn session of Parliament dominated by financial issues. Commons narrowly reject Danby's proposals to re-settle the ordinary revenue in order to deal with the King's debts; resolves, after voting small Navy supply, 'that no other charge be laid upon the public this session'. Opposition build-up in Lords – proposed address calling for dissolution of Cavalier Parliament lost by only 50–48. Parliament prorogued for 15 months (22 Nov). Charles proposes to Louis new secret treaty (Dec).

Greenwich Royal Observatory founded. Lord Rochester's *Satyr against Mankind* published.

1676 Archbishop Sheldon, at Danby's request, instructs Bishop Compton of London to organize a religious census of the kingdom (Jan). New secret treaty concluded between Charles II and Louis XIV – Danby refuses to countersign (Feb). York refuses King's plea to take Anglican Easter Communion. Compton census completed (Ch. 2, p. 45). Danby uses census returns to defeat York's proposal for a dissolution to procure a more tolerant Parliament.

French successes against Dutch alarm English opinion (July–Aug).

1677 Parliament recalled; Shaftesbury, Buckingham, Salisbury and Wharton sent to Tower for arguing in Lords that Parliament had no longer legal existence; Danby's Court party rejects opposition motion alleging illegality of last prorogation (Feb); also secures large supply for Navy and renewal of additional excise of 1671 (Feb–Mar). After more French successes in Netherlands both Commons and Danby urge vigorous anti-French foreign policy on King (Mar–Apr). Commons move, 182–142, to address Charles for a Dutch alliance; Danby's bill to limit ecclesiastical power of a future Catholic monarch killed by Parliament's adjournment, commanded by King (May).

Bentinck's mission to England; Danby urges Charles to invite William of Orange over and to mediate for peace from basis of a Dutch alliance (June). Parliament re-adjourned amid disorder; release of Buckingham, Salisbury and Wharton (July). After negotiations begun by Ralph Montagu and unwillingly – and for him disastrously – assented to by Danby, Charles given 2 m. French livres in return for keeping Parliament prorogued until April 1678 (Aug). Laurence Hyde – Clarendon's son – sent to Nijmegen to represent England at peace conference (Sept).

Betrothal (Oct) and marriage (Nov) of Princess Mary to William of Orange – great public rejoicing in London and boost for Danby. Anglo-Dutch treaty, laying down peace terms to be put to France, concluded (Dec). Sancroft, Dean of St

9

Paul's, chosen to succeed Sheldon at Canterbury, in preference to Danby's nominee, Compton (Dec).

Beginning of 11 years of unprecedented prosperity for English trade (Ch. 3); Purcell appointed Court composer, aged 18. First publication of Andrew Marvell's *Account of the Growth of Popery and Arbitrary Government in England*: £100 reward offered for discovery of author.

1678   King ratifies Anglo-Dutch treaty (full alliance to follow in Mar) – but uses it to try to screw more money out of Louis; Barillon orchestrates French diplomatic and bribery campaign to counter the new alliance and seduce the country party in the Commons by rousing fears of standing army etc. (Jan). When Parliament meets (28 Jan) organized obstruction of government business ensues, but Court party carry votes for 30,000 troops and £1 m. war supply for six months (18 Feb); Shaftesbury released and returns to House of Lords.

Commons call for immediate declaration of war on France but sudden fall of Ghent and Ypres to French attack leads to irresistible demands for peace in Holland, frustrating Danby's foreign policy schemes (Mar). Mistrust of Court's intentions grows – some desert from Court party, others tied to it by payments from Secret Service fund (Mar–Apr). Further secret subsidy treaty between Louis and Charles (May). Commons abandon hope of war against France, vote (inadequate) money for disbanding the new army, renew for three more years the additional Customs of 1670 but flatly refuse a permanent increase of ordinary revenue from £1.2 to £1.5 m. (June). Parliament prorogued; Montagu dismissed and conspires with opposition leaders to destroy Danby (July). Separate Franco-Dutch peace concluded at Nijmegen (31 July) – Emperor, Spain and remaining confederates make peace subsequently.

Israel Tonge and Titus Oates reveal 'Popish Plot' to murder the King and exterminate Protestantism (Aug–Sept); Oates interrogated by Privy Council and Coleman's papers seized; Oates's 'revelations' widely known and accepted by mid-October; murder of Sir Edmund Berry Godfrey (17 Oct) – panic in London.

Cavalier Parliament begins its 16th session (21 Oct); resolutions affirming existence of 'damnable and Hellish' plot carried *nem.con.* in both Houses (1–2 Nov); 2nd Test Act passed [N.5], excluding Catholics from Parliament; clause making exception for James (York) in House of Lords passes Commons only by 158–156; Coleman, James's former secretary, convicted of treason (Nov); Montagu reveals Danby's involvement in secret deal with France (1677) and Danby impeached by the Commons (Dec). Despite much support for Danby in Lords, Charles prorogues Parliament (30th).

Bunyan's *Pilgrim's Progress* published and Dryden's *All for Love* first performed; Narcissus Luttrell starts his diary of public affairs (ended 1714); Britten's weekly concerts begin in Clerkenwell.

1679   Dissolution of Cavalier Parliament (24 Jan); General Election, resulting in rout of Danby's Court party and heavy majority for Country opposition [E.1(i)] – majority 2–1. Deteriorating situation in Scotland – Highland Host unleashed by Lauderdale on Lanarkshire and Ayrshire, but fails to provoke rebellion that would justify permanent standing army (Jan–Feb); Sunderland becomes Secretary of State and a leading adviser to Crown (Feb); York sent into precautionary exile in Brussels (3 Mar).

First Exclusion Parliament opens (6 Mar); Danby, in hiding, resigns – replaced by a Treasury Commission headed by Essex, lately a prominent critic of the Court (Mar). Privy Council remodelled with admission of Shaftesbury, as Lord President, and other leaders of Opposition, and Finch as 1st Lord of the Admiralty; Danby, assured of royal pardon, committed for safety to the Tower until 1681 (Apr). Sir Thomas Player MP, City ally of Shaftesbury, moves for a bill to exclude York from succession; passes at the 2nd Reading by 207–128; but Parliament prorogued, killing the bill (11–27 May). Habeas Corpus Act ('Shaftesbury Act') to protect liberty of subject passed on last day of this Parliament.

Murder of Archbishop Sharp of St Andrews prompts Covenanter rebellion in Western Scotland (May). Covenanters defeat royal troops under Graham of Claverhouse at Drumclog (1 June); duke of Monmouth appointed Captain-General in Scotland; insurgents defeated by Monmouth's troops at Bothwell Brig (22nd) – leads to fall of Lauderdale (Oct).

Royal army raised in 1678 finally disbanded; English Parliament dissolved (July); King's serious illness and James's temporary return from Brussels (Aug); General Election [E.1(i)] – large majority of Exclusionists returned (Aug–Sept); James sent to Scotland as King's Commissioner to the Estates; Shaftesbury dismissed; 2nd Exclusion Parliament prorogued before meeting (Oct); Parliament later prorogued six further times to Oct 1680, provoking the great petitioning campaign of the first Whigs (see below).

Mass pope-burning processions in London (Nov). Hyde and Godolphin (along with Sunderland known as 'the Chits') appointed to office: Hyde as 1st Lord of Treasury vice Essex, and Godolphin as member of Treasury Board (21st). Monmouth returns from Holland unauthorized and is stripped of his offices. Beginning of the Whigs' great petitioning campaign aimed at securing the meeting of Parliament: purge of Whigs from local office begun (Dec 1679–mid–1680s).

Edmund Halley, astronomer, elected a FRS, aged 23.

1680   First *monster* petition (Westminster and Southwark) presented to King (21 Jan); resignation of Exclusionists, Russell, Cavendish, Capel and Powle from Privy Council and firm commitment to opposition (31st); James, allowed to return from Scotland, arrives in London (Feb). First of the 'abhorring' addresses, the 'Tory' reply to the 'petitioners', presented (Apr).

'Cameronians' – irreconcilable Covenanters – in South-West Scotland declare holy war on Charles II (Sanquhar declaration [N.7(ii)]); Anglo-Spanish alliance (June). Monmouth's triumphant 'Western Progress' strengthens his case in many Whig eyes to be named Protestant successor to the throne (Aug–Sept). James once more sent into exile, by vote of the Council (Oct).

Second Exclusion Parliament allowed to meet at last (21 Oct); 2nd Exclusion Bill introduced, passes Commons in nine days (2–11 Nov); defeat of Bill in Lords, 63–30 (15th). Shaftesbury revives proposal for a parliamentary bill divorcing Charles II from Queen Catherine. Both Houses discuss 'limitations' on James's powers if he succeeded (Nov–Dec). Finch's bills for the Comprehension and Toleration of dissenters progress in the Commons; Lord Stafford, imprisoned in Tower as a Plot suspect since 1678, impeached, convicted and executed (Dec).

Sir Robert Filmer's *Patriarcha* published (Ch. 9).

1681   Parliament prorogued, then dissolved – nipping Comprehension in the bud (Jan). Whigs hold ground at General Election [E.1(i)]; Sunderland replaced as Secretary of State by Conway (Feb). French subsidy to Charles II renewed (Mar); 3rd Exclusion Parliament's brief session at Oxford (21st–28th).

Execution of Plunket, Primate of Ireland, as a 'Popish plotter' and Fitzharris, first victim of 'the Stuart revenge' (1 July); Shaftesbury sent to Tower on charge of treason. Meeting of Charles's 3rd Scottish Parliament, with James as Commissioner

– first session since 1674; James's rights of succession safeguarded; oaths of loyalty to state and church establishment imposed on Scots office holders; dismissal of marquess of Argyll (July). Massive pro-Tory changes in English commissions of the peace (July–Aug).

Treason charge against Shaftesbury rejected by Middlesex grand jury (Nov). Argyll sentenced to death for treason but escapes to Holland (Dec).

French troops enter Strasbourg (Sept), beginning Louis XIV's *Réunions* encroachment on the Empire (1681–4). Founding of Pennsylvania by proprietory grant to William Penn; much of Locke's *Two Treatises of Government* written; publication of Dryden's political satire, *Absalom and Achitophel*.

1682   Surrender of Thetford's charter inaugurates Crown's *quo warranto* campaign against Whiggery in borough corporations (Feb). Duke of York's return to England from Edinburgh (Apr–May). Governmental and judicial changes reflecting York's new ascendancy – influence of Halifax (though appointed Privy Seal in autumn) eclipsed by that of York and Hyde (Rochester); readmission of Sunderland to the Council, Sir George Jeffreys made LCJ of King's Bench (May–Oct).

Court-rigged shrieval elections in London won by Tories (July). A further 'progress' by Monmouth, in the North West, feeds government's suspicion of widespread conspiracy and likely rebellion (Aug–Sept). Political control of city of London wrested from the Whigs (Oct); Shaftesbury, confronted again with arrest for treason, flees to Holland (Nov).

Whitelocke's *Memories of the English Affairs*; Grew's *Anatomy of Plants* and Ray's *Methodus Plantarum* landmarks in study of botany.

1683   *Quo Warranto* writ issued against London corporation; Shaftesbury dies in exile; Sunderland reappointed principal Secretary of State (Jan).

Charter of London declared forfeit (June). Whig plot – 'Rye House' – to assassinate King and York uncovered (June), along with plans for Whig insurrection in Scotland, where Baillie of Jerviswood later sentenced to death for complicity; 'Oxford Resolutions' passed by University Congregation – affirmed sinfulness of resistance and duty of unconditional obedience (passive, at least) to authority (July); execution of Whig leaders Russell (July) and Algernon Sidney (Dec) for alleged involvement in Rye House Plot; suicide of Essex in prison (July).

Marriage of Princess Mary's sister Anne to Lutheran Prince George of Denmark (July). John Locke, under suspicion of treason, flees to Holland (Aug–Sept). Evacuation of Tangier (Aug) and return of 3,000 Tangier garrison to swell Charles II's army in England. In Scotland savage repression begins, autumn 1683, culminating in summary execution of *c.* 100 Covenanters in 'the killing times' of 1684.

Settlement of Delaware begins. Habsburg forces raise siege of Vienna by the Turks.

1684   Danby and the three surviving aristocratic victims of the Popish Plot released from the Tower (Feb); Charles ignores Triennial Act and omits to summon a new Parliament (Mar); invests James again with power – but not title – of Lord High Admiral and restores him to Privy Council in defiance of Test Act (May).

Trial of Titus Oates – found guilty of *scandalum magnatum* against James (June). Truce of Ratisbon ratifies most French *Réunions* seizures in Germany since 1681 (Aug). Rochester, formerly Hyde, 1st Lord of Treasury since 1679, 'kicked upstairs' to Lord Lieutenant of Ireland; Godolphin succeeds at Treasury (Aug–Sept).

'Great Persecution' of English dissenters and Scottish Cameronians reaches climax; Massachusetts charter annulled – start of an aristocratic reaction in the American colonies. Formation of a Holy League, to aid Austria against the Turks.

1685 Death of Charles II: accession of James II as King of England and Ireland and as James VII of Scotland (6 Feb). Rochester returns to key office, as Lord Treasurer (16th); General Election – Whigs, with only 57 members, routed (Mar–Apr); Scottish Estates meet under the moderate Queensberry as Commissioner (Apr) – in subservient first session vote James life excise and implement his wishes for swingeing penal laws. James's first and only English Parliament meets (May); grants the King the same life revenue as Charles II but in July adds further ordinary supply; prorogued due to state of emergency (2 July).

Earl of Argyll lands in Western Scotland and raises rebellion (May); rebellion fails, earl executed (June). Monmouth lands at Lyme and starts rebellion in West Country (11 June); proclaimed King at Taunton; county militias fail to check him, regular forces under Feversham sent to the West ; crushing defeat of rebels at Sedgemoor and execution of Monmouth (July); 'Bloody Assizes' conducted by Judge Jeffreys – 300 executions and many more transportations (Aug–Sept).

Ireland falls under Catholic influence of Tyrconnel, despite appointment of High Anglican Clarendon as Lord Deputy (Aug). Revocation of Edict of Nantes by Louis XIV (Oct); preceded and followed by flood of Huguenot (French Protestant) refugees into England – between 40,000 and 70,000 by 1688. Dismissal of Halifax, LPS, for opposition to James II's plans to appoint Catholic army officers (Oct). 2nd session of English Parliament (9–20 Nov); Commons protest against breaches of Test Act in granting army commissions; King in pique cuts short the session by prorogation.

Halifax's *Character of a Trimmer* published; press Licensing Act renewed.

1686 Tyrconnel appointed marshal of Irish army; begins purge of Protestant officers and men (Jan). James by prerogative grants freedom of private worship to Catholics, and Quakers, in Scotland (Feb); 2nd session of Scottish Parliament opens (Apr); supremacy of Drummonds enhanced – Melfort named Commissioner – but Protestant resistance to proposed Toleration legislation stiffens. Sharp, rector of St Giles, London, begins a notable series of sermons against Roman Catholicism (May).

Case of *Godden* v *Hales*: judges' verdict in favour of royal dispensing power (June); four Catholic peers admitted to Privy Council; Ecclesiastical Commission under Jeffreys – now Lord Chancellor – established to strengthen prerogative control over Anglican Church (July); Catholic penetration of Oxford University begins – John Massey elected Dean of Christ Church (July); Bishop Compton of London suspended by Ecclesiastical Commission for refusing to silence anti-Catholic preaching in diocese (Sept); Lord Rochester dismissed after protests against King's ecclesiastical policies (Dec).

Defensive League of Emperor and German princes (League of Augsburg) formed to protect Germany from further French intrusion; East India Company base first established at Calcutta.

1687 Godolphin returns to Treasury, but Catholic Lord Belasyse becomes First Lord (Jan). James's first Declaration of Indulgence in Scotland: complete toleration and admission to office for Catholics, rights of private worship and relaxation of penal laws for Presbyterian 'conventiclers' (Feb). Tyrconnel, now Lord Deputy, intensifies Catholic attack on the 'Ascendancy' in Ireland (Feb). Catholic Lord Arundel made Privy Seal in England (Mar).

James first English Declaration of Indulgence issued [N.1(v)]; King begins attack on Magdalen College, Oxford, by declaring its new President, Hough, deposed; Magdalen rejects royal nominee and supports Hough (Apr); Cambridge Vice-Chancellor deprived after University's refusal to award degree to Benedictine monk (May); James's state visit to Oxford – further stage in his bid to break Anglican monopoly there (Sept).

The 'Three Questions' on the repeal of the Test Acts tendered to county JPs and militia (Oct–Dec); Jesuit Father Petre made privy councillor; Queen Mary's pregnancy confirmed; 25 Fellows of Magdalen expelled; 'Board of Regulators' set up to remodel corporations (Nov); first tour of boroughs by professional agents of the Board (Dec).

Charter of Connecticut annulled; Halifax's *Letter to a Dissenter* and Newton's masterpiece, the *Principia*, published.

1688   King demands return of Anglo-Dutch brigade from Dutch service (Jan and Mar) – refused; Catholic President of Magdalen appointed by royal mandate (Mar); Second Declaration of Indulgence issued, embodying promise to call a Parliament in autumn (Apr). Order-in-Council requiring Declaration to be read in all churches; petition of Archbishop Sancroft and six bishops begging to be excused giving this directive (May); 'Seven bishops' indicted on a charge of seditious libel, i.e. questioning the royal dispensing power; birth of son (Prince James Edward) to James and Mary; William of Orange's envoy, on mission to England, contacts opposition leaders (June). Trial and triumphant acquittal of Seven Bishops (29–30 June); invitation to William to intervene by force in England sent by seven opposition notables [Danby, Shrewsbury, Devonshire, Lord Lumley, Bishop Compton, Edward Russell, Henry Sidney] (30 June).

Death of 'Great Elector' of Brandenburg – succeeded by pro-Dutch son, Frederick III (Apr); death of Archbishop-Elector of Cologne and subsequent defeat of Louis XIV's candidate inaugurates new European crisis (May); Louis's offer to transfer French ships to Channel to reinforce James II's navy declined (May–June); James refuses Louis's second offer of protection against invasion (Aug); Louis's fateful decision to invade the Palatinate, relieving military pressure on the Dutch (Sept).

James calls a General Election – but then withdraws writs on ground of imminent invasion (21–8 Sept); William of Orange's *Declaration*, justifying his coming expedition (30th); frantic concessions by James to Anglican churchmen and Tories – policies on Church, universities, JPs, charters, etc. put into reverse (Oct); William's first invasion attempt repelled by storms (19th); Sunderland dismissed (26th).

Invading force reaches Torbay (5 Nov); William at Exeter, joined by Devonshire Tories under Seymour (8–21st); William marches east but General Churchill deserts James and royal army retreats from Salisbury without engagement (21st–24th); York seized by Danby and rebels (22nd); James back at Whitehall (26th); his commissioners contact William to negotiate terms (8 Dec); James's first abortive flight (11–15th); anti-Catholic riots in London (11th–12th); King's second, successful flight to France (18th–22nd); a Convention (Parliament) summoned by William's letters (28th).

1.   The Restoration of Charles II

In 1649 the King of England, Scotland and Ireland was beheaded on a scaffold in Whitehall, the English monarchy was abolished and a republic inaugurated. Like Ireland – mercilessly crushed and ravaged by a republican army in 1650 – Scotland declined at first to follow England's example. In February 1649 the late monarch's eldest son was proclaimed her rightful and lawful king; but after the third civil war in nine years and the loss of two decisive battles Scotland too succumbed to the military power of the Puritan Commonwealth. Although the Commonwealth gave way to a Protectorate in 1653 and the republicans found the search for a settled constitution singularly frustrating, the chance of the house of Stuart being restored still seemed extremely remote nine years after the death of Charles I. In October 1651 its head, then a young man of 21, had left England in humiliation after the battle of Worcester: a hunted fugitive ('a long dark man, above two yards high') with a price of £1,000 on his head. Indeed, Charles II had been exceedingly lucky to escape at all. Even so, the 'Miraculous Providence' to which royalists later came to attribute his good fortune seemed for many years unlikely to guarantee its recipient anything more than a continuing succession of dispiriting Continental 'travels'.

There were certainly few signs in England in the first half of 1658 of a vast tide of popular reaction building up against the Puritan republic. The kind of spontaneous revulsion against its instability, against its supposed oppression and allegedly gloomy, suffocating moral atmosphere, which once figured prominently in traditionalist accounts of the republic's fall, was barely in evidence. Even Scotland, which had accepted the enforced union of 1654 resentfully and where a large army of occupation remained a permanent necessity, had settled by 1658 into grudging but orderly pacification. A measure of partnership between the military and the Scots' 'natural' rulers had been achieved and the alarms of Glencairn's Highland rising of 1655 had receded.[1] South of the border in that same year more ordinary citizens in the West Country had turned out to oppose rather than to support Penruddock's royalist rising, which hardly suggests a country crying out for liberation. Anxiety among the propertied classes about the continuing failure of Oliver Cromwell to produce a stable framework of government that would command widespread acceptance was clearly in evidence; but even after the abrupt dismissal of the Second Protectorate Parliament in February 1658 it had not yet reached neurotic levels. Taxation in the 1650s had been heavy beyond all precedent; but as Queen Anne's ministers were to find fifty years later, English taxpayers would grumblingly disgorge so long as they could see tangible dividends. And even when the war with Spain, begun with éclat by

Cromwell in 1657, began to turn sour, with heavy losses of merchant shipping and the piling up of a ruinous government debt, few of the Protectorate's opponents felt disposed to argue with the New Model Army. The army was certainly resented, along with high taxes and Thurloe's spy network; but it must also be stressed that there was much that was notably *un*oppressive about the Cromwellian regime. Its religious policies, for instance, its attitudes to freedom of speech and of the press, and its administration of the criminal law were liberal and humane by contrast with those of the century before the 1650s.

In June 1658 the seasoned veterans of the Protectorate's army, fighting for the first time on the continent, co-operated with Turenne to decisive effect in defeating the Spanish army at the battle of the Dunes; and the capture and cession to England of Dunkirk which soon afterwards followed was in general regarded as a proud achievement. It certainly appeared to have made Charles Stuart's long-term prospects of repossessing his lost kingdoms more dismal than ever. And yet in less than two years he was to find himself, to his astonishment, restored to his throne and with good grounds for anticipating a reasonably secure occupancy.

It is no purpose of this prologue to give a detailed account and explanation of Charles II's restoration. But three major contributory factors must be briefly stressed because of the deep implications which all were to have both for the shaping of the Restoration Settlement (Ch. 1) and for the subsequent course of political and religious events.

The most obvious factor was the glaring inability of any individual or group to fill the enormous vacuum left after the death of Oliver Cromwell in September 1658. At that time it is probable that only a minority of Englishmen desired Charles Stuart's return, and certain that only a few indestructible optimists expected it. But first Richard Cromwell, who succeeded as hereditary Lord Protector under the 1657 constitution, and then the restored Rump Parliament failed signally to resolve the intractable problems of political instability and constitutional confusion. What was worse for the Good Old Cause, they were utterly unable to give the traditional political class of Tudor and Stuart England, the landed gentry, any sense of security. Towards the end of his protectorate Oliver Cromwell's exceptional personal authority and self-evident political and institutional conservatism had managed to instil in them some measure of confidence, to judge from the increasing numbers from the older county families prepared to accept local office again at that time (33, *17*; 124, *18*). But in the great uncertainty which followed in 1659, how could they continue to believe in the republic's capacity to preserve their political and social predominance in the face of a military power which could seemingly break any government at will, as it had Richard's? And how could they trust it to control the profoundly disturbing, 'overturning' influence of extreme Puritan sects such as the Fifth Monarchists, the Baptists and (most feared of all) the Quakers, towards whom many officers of the New Model Army appeared unduly indulgent? By the end of 1659, as they observed not merely the confusion at the centre of government but the continuing infiltration of their old local strongholds, the militias and commissions of the peace, by 'persons of no degree or quality',[2] the county communities of England and Wales – including many of those landed families which had stood firm to the republic, as well as those who had remained warily neutral – were fast approaching despair (cf. 124, *32–4*).

These were civilians, however. And however deep their disillusionment, no return was possible to kingly rule or to other traditional political institutions and values as long as an army of more than 40,000 men and an officer corps permeated by independency or rank sectarianism stood in the way. A second and crucial stage along the road to the Restoration was thus the divisions which rent the New Model in 1659. The fissures were complex. Even before the enforced dissolution of the Rump in October they had set conservative grandees in the English army at loggerheads with radical, republican junior officers. Then in the autumn they threatened a confrontation between the army in England, dominated not by its official leader, Fleetwood, but by the engineer of the October *coup*, General John Lambert, and George Monck's large force stationed north of the border to keep the Scots in awe. From Charles Stuart's point of view, the outcome – a bloodless victory for Monck (33, *71–84*) – was vital. Monck was more than a good general. He was a crafty politician who had already changed sides once since 1642, from royalist to parliamentarian, and who, after declaring against the arbitrary dissolution of the Rump, marched south in January 1660 with his mind not entirely closed to the possibility of changing sides again. No doubt his rôle as *deus ex machina* over the next few months has been much exaggerated: he was more indecisive and manipulable than is often thought; and it is certainly a moot point whether his decision to pitch for a Restoration could have been taken in 1660 without the agitation and financial backing of the City of London, which in recent months had lost all confidence in the republic.

The third major factor, the one which transformed the Restoration from a possibility into a certainty, was Charles's own flexibility in response to the approaches made to him by Monck and others. His conciliatory temper and political acumen were most evident in the Declaration he issued from Breda in Holland on 4 April 1660 [N.1(i)]. Among many shrewd promises it contained, not the least telling was an undertaking to meet in full the arrears of pay of the army. The Declaration could not have been more skilfully timed. It neatly coincided with the elections to the first freely chosen Parliament to assemble at Westminster, undoctored, since the Long Parliament had begun its first session in November 1640. In the House of Commons of this so-called 'Convention' Cromwellians, Rumpists and army officers were reduced to the merest handful. Some fifty Cavaliers (men, or the sons of men, who had actually fought for the King) were allowed to sit, in spite of a supposed ban on their election, and twice as many again who came from royalist families. The largest single group were probably the 'Old Presbyterians', including numerous veterans who had opposed Charles I from 1642 to 1646 but who had broken with the radicals and independents in the turmoil of 1647–8 and had almost all become, by now, anti-republicans. But this party was neither as strong nor as determined as its leaders in the Lords, such as Manchester, Northumberland and Clare, could have wished, and in particular, not strong or united enough to insist on the return of the monarchy being made contingent on the acceptance of preconditions by the restored King (25, *I, 13, 27, 31–2*; 13, *131*); [E.1(i)].

Early in May 1660, therefore, both Houses of the Convention carried a vote that 'according to the ancient and fundamental laws of this kingdom, the government is and ought to be by King, Lords and Commons'. On the 22nd Charles and his entourage sailed for Dover from Scheveningen in the *Naseby*, tactfully rechristened the *Royal Charles*. On the 29th he made his triumphal entry into London. Not everyone huzzaed, danced round maypoles or threw flowers to welcome the exile home. 'A pox on all kings', yelled one woman as he rode by; a Captain Southwold was heard to threaten that if he laid hands on Charles he would chop him up 'as small as herbs in a pot'; and a Lincolnshire parson personally stamped out his parishioners' bonfire. But over much of England, and in London especially, the mood was in general one of clamorous jubilation and relief. It was a reception that could hardly fail to stir the weary King's ironic sense of humour. 'How foolish of me', he is said to have remarked to one of his retinue, 'not to have come home long before'.[3]

2. England, Wales and Scotland at the Restoration

This volume is concerned with the history of *Britain* from 1660 to 1722. But at the time of the Restoration of Charles II 'Britain' was still a term that could only be used with some artificiality. Things might by then have been very different had James VI of Scotland, after his succession as James I of England in 1603, succeeded in recommending to his two kingdoms in the years 1604–7 the plan for their Union that was dear to his heart. His schemes were never put to the test, however, and for the rest of James's reign Scotland (or 'North Britain', as seventeenth-century Englishmen often called her) had gone much her own way, except that the independence of her Parliament was shackled by the control of royal nominees, the 'Lords of the Articles', and her Presbyterian Church had to accept from 1610 onwards the grafting on to it of a half-hearted episcopacy. After 1625 Charles I had undermined and finally destroyed this compromise by trying to subject Calvinist Scotland to the heavy hand of prerogative, to an Arminian prelacy and finally to a Prayer Book which seemed to most Scots the symbol of Rome, and by 1638 his northern kingdom was in revolt. However, the involvement of the Scots in the first English Civil War in 1643 had produced a chain of events that can hardly have been anticipated by the men who forged the Covenant in 1638. It ended in Scottish Presbyterian armies fighting for the very king against whom they had first revolted, in their ultimate crushing defeat, and in the enforcement on the country of the Cromwellian Union of 1654. The price the Scots had to pay for representation by 30 members in a united Parliament, for the restoration of order to an exhausted land and for the preservation of her Presbyterian Kirk from anarchic sectarianism was military occupation by an army of over 10,000 men and high taxation. Although many Lowlanders in later years came to look back on the years 1655–60 with a tinge of nostalgia, the first Union was too shallowly rooted, as we shall see (Ch. 1), to survive the *bouleversement* of May 1660.

Meanwhile, England and Wales had been a political and administrative unit for well over a century. Most of the great castles built in the Middle Ages to keep the Welsh in awe had either succumbed to the attrition of time and neglect or (like Pembroke) had been pulverised in the 1640s by parliamentary cannon. The electors of Wales returned their knights and burgesses to the common Parliament at Westminster: 24 members sat for Welsh constituencies in the 'Cavalier Parliament', which had its first meeting in January 1661. The Welsh subjects of the Crown paid their taxes and duties into the Exchequer, exactly like their English counterparts: and when the Customs and the Excise went over to direct collection in 1671 and 1683 Wales acquired its network of centrally-appointed customs officers and excisemen, just as England did. Of the other civil and military institutions which were either reinstated or continued after the Restoration, perhaps the most influential – and certainly the most omnipresent – in the provinces were the amateur bureaucracies and militia establishments staffed by the justices of the peace, the lords lieutenant and the deputy lieutenants. The Principality shared them. The Council in the Marches of Wales, often an active instrument of royal policy under the Tudors and early Stuarts, had disappeared into oblivion in 1641. But this was no cruel discrimination: the King's Council in the North had gone the same way and for the same reasons, along with all the hated machinery of Stuart prerogative government and jurisdiction.

Parliamentary and governmental institutions were perhaps the most tangible and the strongest of the links holding Wales and England together, but they were by no means the only ones. In both kingdom and principality the English system of common law held sway (Scottish justice was based on Roman law). The 'Grand Sessions in Wales' were only assizes in another form, the main difference being that the 'Justices' who presided over them twice yearly were not chosen from the twelve common law judges at Westminster who went on assize in the English counties. The 'Welsh Judges' were political appointees who for the rest of the year pleaded in the Westminster courts, but it is doubtful whether the Welsh felt themselves second-class judicial citizens in consequence; for the hearing of criminal cases the County Palatine of Chester shared the very same system.

Ecclesiastically, likewise, Wales was to all appearance thoroughly absorbed into the Anglican Church again by 1661. Her four bishops, though among the poorest of the twenty-six [N.4], sat with the rest in the House of Lords. Welshmen were often, but not invariably, appointed to Welsh sees in the fifty years after 1660.[4] Those old enough to recall the 1620s had not forgotten that one William Laud, born in Reading, had first worn the mitre at St David's, and if James I had had his way he would have stayed there, bringing stern enlightenment to a people then considered by the English to be only a step or two away from paganism. Although Anabaptism of a peculiarly radical kind, and Independency too, had made some progress in the Marches in the 1650s, Dissent was found to be, numerically speaking, relatively weak among the Welsh in surveys carried out both in 1676 and 1715–16 [N.6]. Wales had after all been the most solid of royalist strongholds in the First Civil War. As late as Anne's reign her counties and boroughs were returning overwhelming majorities of Tories – stalwarts of 'the Church Party' – to Westminster. It has been plausibly claimed that 'by sheer diligence, application and enthusiasm, dissenting ministers of the period 1660–1730 exercised an influence which was entirely disproportionate to their numbers.'[5] Nevertheless, the great age of Welsh nonconformity and evangelism still lay well ahead in 1660 (*The Age of Oligarchy*, Ch. 8).

Although the restored Church in Wales used the Book of Common Prayer, it did so more often than not in Welsh translations. The first Welsh version of the revised Prayer Book of 1662 was explicitly authorised in the Act of Uniformity (Ch. 1) and published in 1664, and between then and 1730 there were at least 15 more issues including four revised editions.[6] The overwhelming majority of parish clergy in the Principality in the generation after 1660 were Welsh by birth and in speech, a fact which says much for the prevalence of Welsh speaking among their flocks in the late seventeenth century. When the fiery High Church preacher Dr Sacheverell, a Wiltshire man (Ch. 21), was presented in 1710 to the living of Sellatyn, on the Shropshire side of the Welsh border, the Whig bishop Fleetwood of St Asaph found his excuse – perhaps a trifle disingenuously – for at first refusing to institute in the plea that

> as soon as the last incumbent died, I was applied to by some of the parish to take care that the poor people of it might have a minister who could understand them, and be understood by them . . . This was the cause why I refused Mr Lloyd's clerk and why I would have refused the Queen herself had she presented a mere Englishman to a Welsh cure.[7]

In fact the clergy were probably the only section of educated Welsh society in the 1660s to use the native language regularly, though most merchants, tradesmen and lawyers were bi-lingual as were many of the parish gentry, like the cock-fighting gentlemen of Anglesey in Queen Anne's reign whose 'scolding was all in Welsh and civilities in English'.[8]

The Anglicisation of the middling and upper gentry and of the urban pseudo-gentry, on the other hand, was already becoming more marked than in the early seventeenth century; and it was to be still more pronounced by the early eighteenth century when clergy in St Asaph diocese were rebuked by their bishop for an undue 'respect and complaisance' because they prayed and preached in English once a month when 'the best families in the parish' attended their churches.[9] Wales had almost no *resident* aristocracy by the second half of the seventeenth century. In fact, when Edward Chamberlayne began compiling the early editions of his *Angliae Notitia* in Charles II's reign, there were seven of the twelve Welsh counties in which he could learn of no aristocratic seat of any note at all, let alone one that was regularly lived in. The best families in Welsh landed society could therefore be effectively equated with the gentry, and it is possible that one feature of the Welsh gentry at the beginning of our period which did distinguish it from its English counterparts was its relative stability. Of Glamorgan, at least, it has been shown that the group of squirearchal families which dominated the shire in 1660 had remained largely unchanged since the sixteenth century and they continued thus for several more decades until, after 1700, a period of remarkable flux began (190).[10] There is no English county, so far as we can tell from modern research, of which the same can be said.

In 1660 the population of Wales is unlikely to have much exceeded 350,000, which was under seven per cent of that of England, with Monmouthshire [B.1]. But although the country's notoriously difficult terrain was obviously a factor in the sparseness of her population, and the standard of living of most of its heavily rural population was low by the standards of southern England, the economy of Wales in Charles II's reign was by no means uniformly backward. There were few travellers there who did not express surprise at the fertility of the valleys that lay between her rugged mountains, and many who commented on the richness of her mineral wealth – coal and copper in the south and lead in the north. There were already many valuable economic links between Wales and England. Much of the coal produced on such Glamorgan or Pembrokeshire estates as those of the Mansels of Margam or later from the mines of the great 'Adventurer', Sir Humphrey Mackworth of Neath, was despatched to London or Bristol from the developing ports of Neath, Swansea, Tenby and Milford (3, *II, 55, 57, 59*; 218b); black cattle from Brecknockshire and Radnorshire were sent to Smithfield; and the chief market for Welsh cloth and flannel was Shrewsbury. As well as merchants and superior tradesmen, the small urban bourgeoisie of Restoration Wales also contained a significant nucleus of lay professional men. Carmarthen, for instance, was one of a number of Welsh towns which already had not simply the odd attorney but a small colony of lawyers. In this respect, as in others, the differences between Wales and England were differences of scale more than of character.

This was not so, as we have already seen, with Scotland. It seems possible that there were at least three times as many Scots as Welshmen living in Britain at the time of the Restoration [B.3(ii)]. What we know of the effects of disastrous famine and exceptionally heavy mortality in the 1690s strongly suggests that in spite of terrible epidemics in the years 1644–8 the population of Scotland might well have been higher in the middle of the seventeenth century than at the end. It was a population frighteningly dependent on the land. Nine Scots in every ten either worked the land or lived on it, possibly a third of this 90 per cent being inhabitants of the wild fastnesses north and west of the Highland line. By contrast, between two and three Englishmen out of ten at the Restoration already lived in towns, even if most of the towns were very small (Ch. 2). Such urban population as there was in Scotland was largely distributed among the country's royal burghs, some sixty-five of them, the majority dotted about a relatively small area comprising the Central Lowland belt, Perthshire and Fife, with outposts in the east and north-east coastal strip and in the far south-west. Although Scotland's capital city, Edinburgh, was the second largest urban centre in the British Isles, after London, no other Scottish town had more than 10,000 inhabitants in 1660 [B.3(iii)]. The overwhelming majority of the country's urban settlements housed hundreds rather than thousands of inhabitants (274, *157*; 276, *100–1*).

The rural landscape of Restoration England was pocked by innumerable small market towns and villages. In Scotland, on the other hand, villages on the English model were a rarity. Most seventeenth-century Scots lived out peasant lives in tiny hamlets, some of them settlements so small that there could be as many as ten or fifteen within a single parish. The key to this significant difference between the two kingdoms was the ancient system of land tenure which still held sway in Scotland. Down to the Union of 1707, and indeed long after it, Scotland was a *feudal* country – something her neighbour, apart from a few anachronistic survivals, had long since ceased to be: she was feudal not just in her social relationships, in which 'lordship', and *kin* as well as clan, enjoyed a continuing importance that was only slowly being eroded by economic realities (268, *243*; 276, *2–6*), but also in the strictest sense of her land law. Both the social and economic implications of this were vast. Although there was a small class of Scottish land-holders, holding directly from the crown as tenants-in-chief, who were sometimes called 'freeholders', there were virtually no freeholders in Scotland to parallel the English 'yeomanry', those several hundred thousand farmers with unencumbered rights in their property (Ch. 4; 277a, *71–2*). Leaving aside the great numbers of crofters and landless labourers so characteristic of the Scottish rural scene, the small acreages, and above all the short leases, of the country's peasant farmers (most of them annually at the mercy of their landlords) were a desperate drag on enterprise. 'Without those long and kind leases the tenants of England have', as one contemporary observer was to put it in Queen Anne's reign, 'they are not encouraged by their lords in [enclosures] and . . . other improvements'.[11] Recent scholarship has been at pains to stress that all was not doom and gloom in later seventeenth-century Scottish agriculture. Improving landlords have been identified in the lowland counties; and a slow trend towards longer leases and single tenancies was in evidence. Nevertheless, the interest in new crops and methods of cultivation of which travellers through late seventeenth-century England found such ample evidence (Ch. 2) left large parts of open-field Scotland, even of the Lowlands, relatively untouched until well after the Union (Ch. 20; *The Age of Oligarchy*, Ch. 15).

If the social structures of the two kingdoms are thought of in pyramidical terms, Scotland's formed much the flatter pyramid. The number of great families who dominated social, and much political, life there in the seventeenth century has been estimated at about 100 (274, *135*), and with relatively few exceptions they were the families of hereditary noblemen and Highland chieftains. Although in the restored Scottish Parliament, which resumed its old life in Edinburgh's 'Parliament House' early in Charles II's reign, the 'Nobles' sat and voted, as by tradition, in the same chamber as the representatives of the other two Estates, the 'Barons' (county members) and the 'Burgesses' (borough members), it was they who normally governed its debates, along with a few of the wealthiest lairds and the odd lawyer, and it was they who were the natural leaders of its factions. There were few counterparts to the hundreds of great landed commoners who in England were able to maintain a lifestyle, and sometimes exert a degree of political influence, scarcely distinguishable from that of the majority of peers. Below the small élite in Scottish society there may have been 1,500 landlords – almost certainly no more – who in English parlance could claim to be considered 'gentry', in the sense that they maintained themselves and their families not by their own labour but by that of their tenant farmers. It is now generally agreed that in terms of local influence, as opposed to central power, the better-off lairds were gaining ground at the expense of the magnates in the seventeenth century. But in living standards, at least, the typical Scots laird, remote in his gaunt and spartan 'towerhouse', maintaining what appearances he could on a rent roll that often fell as low as £20 to £50 sterling, was half a world removed from the thousands of country gentlemen who were the pillars of English rural society and county government. As for the 8,000-odd 'Bonnet lairds', as they later came to be called, who made up the rest of the landowning sector in Scotland, the great majority held no more than a single farm which, like the English yeomen, they worked themselves (276, *80*).

In the middle sections of the Scottish social pyramid there was an urban patriciate, mainly entrenched in the merchant guilds of the more important royal burghs, though stiffened, especially in Edinburgh, by the wealthiest members of a growing corps of lawyers servicing Scotland's indigenous legal system. These bourgeois might well cut a figure locally, and in a few cases on a national stage, through Parliament and the courts, as they did in England. But compared with England's urban middle orders, Scotland's were by 1660 not only far less numerous, but, as yet, much more resistant to penetration, whether from the professions, the superior crafts or domestic traders; and their interest both in the land market and in intermarriage with the landed gentry probably less pronounced. (Recent research, however, suggests that their culture was becoming more cosmopolitan and that both their permeability and their interest in 'gentrification' were increasing [267].)

Foreign trade was the lifeblood of this urban élite; and the mid-seventeenth century had proved a less than fruitful era for most Scottish ports and overseas merchants. The traditional major markets in Holland and France and secondary outlets in Germany and Scandinavia grew less receptive, on the whole, to Scotland's very limited range of exports; unlike England (Ch. 3), she had no colonies to provide alternatives or supply cheap imports, while political and religious disorders at home seriously disrupted her economy after 1639. Apart from fish, and some coal and grain, Scottish merchants sold little of notable value abroad apart from three basic commodities – raw wool, salt and linen, 'the most noted and beneficial manufacture of the kingdom',[12] to which a good deal of Scottish agriculture was subordinated through the growing of hemp; and although the linen trade with England continued to expand despite the reimposition of customs duties at the border in 1660, it was already very clear that Scottish commerce lacked the resilience and adaptability of that of England, quite apart from its relative poverty in capital reserves. To make matters worse, the three wars with the Dutch (1652–72), into which Scotland was dragged on England's coat-tails, further damaged both her trade and her shipping (282, *18–19 passim*). As late as 1692 a mere 10,000 tons of merchant shipping was based in Scottish ports – less than a thirtieth of the tonnage registered in England – and although Glasgow had by then made more progress than any other trading town since the Restoration, she still boasted a mere fourteen ships.

In both England and Scotland internal communications remained in 1660 a serious handicap to economic development. Yet there were massive differences of degree. In England the maintenance of roads still represented a formidable problem, making winter travel frequently unpleasant and wagon transport slow and expensive. The Cromwellian road ordinance of 1654 did achieve temporary improvements to some major arteries, but it was not until the 1660s that the turnpike system of raising tolls for the upkeep of roads, which was to be the eighteenth century's solution to the problem, made its first beginnings – and very modest they were. Nevertheless, England did at least possess at the time of the Restoration an extensive road complex, with London at its hub – a fact of which Ogilby's justly celebrated road maps, or gazetteer, of 1675 leaves us in no doubt.[13] And the existence of thousands of 'carriers' by the mid-seventeenth century, many working remarkably systematically, as well as of an army of pedlars and packhorse men testifies to its equally extensive use.[14] In Lowland Scotland, on the other hand, 'roads' – in the basic sense of thoroughfares that could be used by wheeled traffic in dry weather – were rare enough to merit a special remark from travellers fortunate enough to come across them; and by the same token there were virtually no roads at all in the Highlands until General Wade's men began their building work there in 1726. Economically this would still have been seriously inhibiting to Scotland, even supposing she could have rivalled England's already valuable network of navigable rivers. But north of the border only the Tay, the Forth and the Clyde, with their broad estuaries, were navigable for any distance from their mouths. It was very different in the south where great rivers such as the Thames, Severn, Trent, Great Ouse and Yorkshire Ouse penetrated deep into the English heartland, making inland ports of such towns and cities as Oxford, Gloucester, Shrewsbury, Nottingham, Bedford and York (218; 173, *279*). England's existing waterways were still capable of great improvement, as numerous late seventeenth- and early eighteenth-century projectors were to demonstrate, but in 1660 they were already one essential guarantee of the flow of trade, the other being a very large coastal shipping fleet for handling the bulkier commodities. Scotland, too, had her coasters, but except along parts of the east coast they were far too few to compensate for the gross deficiencies of her roads and rivers.

For a long time modern social historians have tended on the whole to echo Macaulay's view of the insularity and frequently extreme isolation of the average Briton of the seventeenth century. They do so no longer. Even in Scotland it should not be assumed that 95 per cent of the population lived out their whole lives within a three- to four-mile radius of their own cottages. People rode, and indeed (as with many poor students of Scotland's four universities) walked, staggering distances. Peter Clark has provided some extraordinary evidence of physical mobility in late Stuart England, even among the humblest classes. Immigration into London proceeded on a vast scale throughout the century, and surviving records (for example, of apprenticeships) make it clear that tens of thousands made their way to the capital in search of work, from distances ranging from 20 to over 200 miles (177; 188a). It is surely significant, too, that provincial England already seethed with inns by 1660, and that they were to multiply still

more impressively over the next century (247b). The earliest stage-coach services
to and from London had begun over very unambitious distances in the 1630s, but
by 1655–7 there were services to Exeter, Chester, York and Newcastle, and in
fair conditions the new six-horse 'flying coach' plying to Chester in 1657 reckoned
to cover the 182 miles in three days. Scotland was less fortunate. The serious
inadequacy of her roads, even in good weather, is highlighted by the fact that the
country's first regular stage-coach service – Glasgow to Edinburgh – was not
introduced until 1749. Even the coaches of their great men, it was said in 1702,
could only proceed with 'much caution' and with horse-power supplemented by
the muscles of 'lusty running footmen'.[15]

Communication does not, of course, depend solely on travel. Nothing is more
efficacious than literacy in breaking down the barriers of isolation. Although
levels of literacy in late seventeenth-century England and Wales have been much
disputed (see *The Age of Oligarchy*, Ch. 12), it is beyond question that the
proportion of their population able to read with some proficiency had risen
steeply between 1560 and 1660; Scotland, with its statutory parish and burgh
schools throughout the Lowlands, was by Charles II's reign enviably literate for
a poor country. How news was transmitted commercially in our period is
discussed in *The Age of Oligarchy* (Ch. 13). In 1660 word of mouth and private
letters were still the main disseminators. Tentative Tudor and early Stuart
attempts to lay the foundations of something like a postal system in England had
been taken appreciably further in the 1630s, and further still, through a state-
regulated postal farm, under the Commonwealth and Protectorate. In one way
or another, therefore, most Britons at the time of the Restoration, except in the
remoter highland regions, were conscious of a wider world than the parish pump,
if in many cases only vaguely. And unless we accept that this was so, there will
be many aspects, especially of England's history, in the late Stuart and early
Hanoverian period covered by this book which will not make much sense to us.
So it was, most notably, with the exceptional vigour of the country's political life,
its periodic waves of nationwide religious passion or phobia, and the ever-growing
range and sophistication of its economy.

---

1. F.D. Dow, *Cromwellian Scotland 1651–1660* (Edinburgh, 1979).
2. Clarendon's words: *The History of the Great Rebellion*, 6 vols, (Oxford, 1888, repr. 1958), VI, p. 176.
3. Quoted in paraphrase in A. Bryant, *Charles II* (1930), p. 83.
4. The proportion of English-born appointees rose quite sharply after 1714.
5. G.H. Jenkins, *Literature, Religion and Society in Wales 1660–1730* (Cardiff, 1978), p. 26.
6. *Ibid*, pp. 38, 67–8.
7. William Fleetwood [to Henry Prescot], 22 Apr 1710: Cheshire RO Prescot Correspondence (by courtesy of Mr John Addy).
8. J. Macky, *A Journey through England*, II (1722), p. 149.
9. [W. Fleetwood], *The Bishop of St. Asaph's Charge to the Clergy of that Diocese in 1710* (1712), pp. 11–12.
10. J.P. Jenkins, 'The Demographic Decline of the Landed Gentry in the Eighteenth Century', *Welsh Hist.Review*, **11** (1982).

11. Rev. Thomas Morer, *A Short Account of Scotland* (London, 1702), p. 4. (This account was based on notes taken during a visit 14 years earlier.)
12. Morer, op.cit., p. 3.
13. John Ogilby, *Britannia . . . or An Illustration of the Kingdom of England and Dominion of Wales: by a Geographical and Historical Description of the Principal Roads thereof* (London, 1675).
14. J.A. Chartres, 'Road Carrying in the 17th Century', *EcHR*, **30** (1977); M. Spufford, *The Great Reclothing of Rural England* (1984), Ch. 1.
15. Morer, op.cit., p. 24.

CHAPTER 1

The Restoration Settlement: State, Church and Land

When Charles II resumed kingly government in May 1660 there was a formidable range of problems requiring settlement. The three most taxing were all matters of urgency. Most obviously, there was the constitutional problem. There would have been no Restoration at all but for the expectation that a monarchical regime would succeed in re-establishing a stable, acceptable system of government, both central and local. Then there was the religious problem: how could the now widespread desire for a state church in both England and Scotland be reconciled with the need to heal the religious wounds which had periodically tortured the republic? How, in particular, could the natural aspirations of the long-suffering Anglicans be realised without alienating the Presbyterians, who had done so much to make the Restoration possible? Thirdly, there was the land question: what was to happen to the countless acres of land which had changed hands since 1646, either through confiscation or obligatory sales? There were many interested parties, understandably, to whom this last seemed the most acute question of the three. But these were by no means the only matters calling for prompt and politic action. The armed forces, which many times in the past thirteen years had threatened to develop into a separate estate, had been another indispensable instrument of the return of monarchy. For the maintenance of a large navy there was likely to be strong support; but what was to become of that Frankensteinian monster, the New Model Army? Although much reduced from its peak strength of 70,000 in 1652, it still numbered over 42,000 officers and men at the end of the Protectorate, and a further reduction planned in February 1660 had so far had little effect. A further problem was that of the sectarian political enemies of the restored monarchy: was there to be an amnesty for republican irreconcilables, or were the royalists to be allowed to purge away all their indignities in the bloodshed of a judicial massacre? Finally, as we shall observe in due course (Chs. 2, 3), there were major economic and social decisions to be taken: how far, for example, would the Convention feel committed to the mercantilist trade and shipping policies instituted by the Rump in 1651?

An essential point to bear in mind is that what historians have labelled the Restoration Settlement was a long time in the making, and that in making it, in England, King Charles and his ministers acted through two Parliaments, radically different from each other in character: the Convention (April-December 1660) and the so-called 'Cavalier' Parliament, which first met in May 1661. Charles had committed himself at Breda to some of the broad principles of a settlement while promising to accept the details as 'shall be determined in Parliament'. He also took the view that Parliament might as well share the opprobrium for any policies that might misfire. But what, more than anything, made full parliamentary cooperation inescapable was the fact that a return to legality was the overriding aim of the entire settlement. The idea of re-establishing *legitimacy* within a secure constitutional and legal framework, a goal that had tantalised but always eluded Cromwell, obsessed the minds of most Restoration politicians. It impregnated much of what was done in Parliament between 1660 and 1662. In particular it underlay two acts, among the first to be touched by the sceptre in both the Convention and Cavalier Parliaments, which explicitly embodied basic guidelines for the making of the Settlement. The first was the Convention's Act for Confirming Judicial Proceedings (7, *371–4*), which established that no judgements arrived at by due processes of law since May 1642 (with the pointed exception of sales of land 'by ordinance of pretended Parliaments') could be set aside on the plea that the authority of the courts was in question. What was asserted in principle here – nothing less than the validity of all private acts and transactions conducted legally during the Civil Wars and the Interregnum – obviously had implications of the first importance to the settlement; not least, in confirming the hundreds of private land conveyances of that period. But the vital corollary which it silently assumed, of the *in*validity of all the *public* acts of 1642–60 which had never received a king's consent, was more important still. And while it is clear that most members of the Convention consistently proceeded on the basis of this assumption, it was left to the next Parliament in its opening weeks to endow it with statutory authority through an Act 'to preserve the person and government of the King' (above, p. 3). This included the provision that all 'pretended orders and ordinances of both or either houses of parliament . . . to which the royal assent was not expressly had or given . . . are and so shall be taken to be null and void'.[1] The import of this second principle was utterly fundamental. For once it was accepted that the last valid legislation was that of 1641, so that nothing enacted subsequently (with one notable exception (p. 30 below)) was thought to require annulment, the strong likelihood was that the constitutional settlement of 1660–1 would take shape with the very minimum of formal consideration, while any attempt to devise a written constitution was effectively ruled out.

Looking back to the *status quo ante bellum*, rather than forward to a future which could come to terms with the legacy of the immediate past, was a sore temptation even to many members of the Convention. However, to the Anglican cavaliers who flooded back to Westminster in May 1661, outnumbering the genuine Presbyterians and other Puritans in the Commons by possibly ten to one (38),[2] the extremism of the whole period 1642–60 seemed like a protracted nightmare which they desired only to blot out. Hence the strength of the feeling that grew up in the twelve months following Charles's return that the only secure basis for a lasting settlement would be one wiped as clean as possible of the traces of the previous eighteen years. As we survey the Restoration Settlement in the rest of this chapter, therefore, two major questions must be kept in mind: how far did the Settlement involve in practice an attempt to 'put back the clock' and eradicate the recent past? And in so far as this was the intention, how successfully was it carried out? But with the future rather than the past in mind, there is a further question we shall also need to be aware of. What problems were created for the next generation by the propensity of the old generation in the years

1660–62 to look backward rather than forward, and by its inability in the process even to take a realistic view of the present?

In its two sessions in 1660 the Convention (created a legal Parliament *ex post facto* in June) produced a clear-cut solution to one of the five main problems which faced the restored regime, the indemnity, and made good progress with another, the armed forces. It was also much occupied with laying the financial and political foundations of a stable system of government based on the assumed virtues of the 'ancient constitution'. But of the three most crucial issues dropped into its lap by the Breda Declaration [N.1(i)] one, the land question, was partly side-stepped, and with a second, religion, no headway was made at all. Consequently there was no lack of scope for the newcomers elected early in 1661 or for the many peers created by Charles in 1661–2 to put their own mark on the settlement.

I

The New Model Army had made itself generally obnoxious, a financial as well as a political embarrassment. That it should be disbanded, and the county militias revived as the bases of England's future land defence, was thus a matter of overwhelming consensus and one of the plainest indications of a prevailing wish to remove the scars of the previous decade and a half. However, the past has a way of refusing to die quietly, and in three respects was this so in the case of the army. In the first place, because of the threat of continued republican unrest, seemingly confirmed by Venner's insurrection (above, p. 3), establishment was provided in 1661 for the small English standing army planned by Charles II in September 1660 (139a, *16–17*; 139b, *xviii*). The fact that numbers were initially very small (above, p. 3) should not obscure the fact that this was a break with pre-Civil War tradition: a break still further emphasised by the 1661 treaty with Portugal [H(i)] which enabled Charles to raise further regiments, including Cromwellian veterans, for overseas service in Tangier and the Peninsula, and by the maintenance of some 1,200 troops in Scotland and 7,500 in Ireland at no cost to the English taxpayer (139a, *197, 204*). Just how significant the break was would not be fully revealed until the 1680s. In the second place, the Cavalier Parliament's Militia Act (1661) placed all regular troops, as well as county militia, firmly under royal control. This turned the clock back to 1640 rather than to 1641–2, and, although swayed in the end by rumours of intended coups by disbanded Cromwellians, many parliamentarians were uneasy at committing themselves to a step which the Convention had pointedly refused to take in 1660.[3] Had they been possessed of a crystal ball they would have been unhappier still. Finally, because the Convention badly miscalculated the cost of paying off the New Model Army, the King was saddled with a further unfortunate addition to his debts – a matter of no trivial consequence (Ch. 5).

At Breda Charles had promised 'a free and general pardon' to all republicans, other than those whom parliament chose to except. The passing of the Act of Oblivion, though not without its unedifying features, can fairly be regarded as a genuine, statesmanlike and above all successful attempt to heal the nation's self-inflicted wounds. The number excluded from the general pardon, mostly notorious regicides, was small, and fewer still were executed (above, p. 3). That it was so humane owed much to the personal determination of the King, backed by his chief adviser Sir Edward Hyde (Lord Hyde, November 1660, earl of Clarendon, 1661), to prevent a bloody royalist revenge. The Convention gave the bill a rough ride, especially in the House of Lords. But in the end wisdom prevailed.

II

The successful settlement of the constitution after the Restoration hinged on the decisions that were taken in five principal problem areas. These can be briefly summarised as: the constitutional relations of the three kingdoms; the powers of the restored monarchy; the place of Parliament in the English system of government, including the question of who was to be represented in it as well as the extent and limitations of its influence; the settlement of the public finances; and the relationship between central and local authority. Recalling the political turmoil of 1640–2, and more recently the agonisings of the republicans over constitutional schemes in the 1650s, it may appear strange that in many respects such problems seemed to the politicians of 1660–1 the most straightforward of all they had to deal with. Yet it is not so strange in the light of the basic assumptions which, as we have seen, governed so much of their thinking. Put at its very simplest, two things happened in consequence.

On the one hand, all the constitutional innovations of the Interregnum were scrapped: the most significant being the parliamentary unions of England, Scotland and Ireland, the changes made to the electoral system in the 1650s which had taken account of some new towns and shifts in population, and the attempts either to dispense with a second chamber or experiment with a new kind of second chamber. Only one of these reversions to the status quo needed formal legislation. The Convention had voted on the eve of the Restoration for a return to 'government . . . by King, Lords and Commons' (above, p. 3); but although the House of Lords had been, in its eyes, illegally abolished in 1649, the bishops had been excluded from it by an act to which Charles I had assented, at the very beginning of 1642. This act was repealed. However, while one side of the constitutional coin rested on the conviction that all subsequent changes in government between 1642 and 1660 were illicit, it had another and equally vital reverse side. The gains made by the Long Parliament during the year 1641, in other words virtually all the major changes to which Charles I had given his formal consent before the first Civil War broke out, were accepted by the restored regime. It was not pre-ordained that this would be so. Many of the Cavaliers of 1661 had a mind to reverse the changes, probably by an act similar in nature to the Scottish Parliament's Act Rescissory, passed in September (pp. 3–4 above); but in the event the sense of legality, not unmixed with a sense of caution, prevailed.

Simple and conservative though these steps seemed to be as solutions to the immediate problem of how the three kingdoms were to be governed, their implications in practice were anything but simple and their consequences in many cases far-reaching. The latter was self-evidently true of the end of the brief essays in parliamentary union. In the case of Ireland the experiment had followed the protracted rebellion of the 1640s and Cromwell's brutal conquest, leading to the entrenchment of a new Protestant ruling class.[4] The Irish had sent 30 elected members to each of the three Westminster Parliaments of 1654, 1656 and 1659, and in the latter had exerted, as a group, some influence (269, *111–112*). But Charles II's appointment of a Lord Lieutenant (Albemarle) in 1660 and of three Lords Justices to lead the council in his absence signalled a return to the old constitutional order and Ireland's reversion to quasi-colonial status. The King reluctantly called one Irish Parliament early in his reign (1661–6), to vote a revenue and advise on a land settlement: there was no successor until 1685. As for the land settlement in Ireland, embodied in Acts of 1662 and 1665 (above, pp. 4, 5) it involved much painful redistribution of estates as between Cromwellian planters and dispossessed royalists (and in a manner wholly satisfactory to neither), but it did nothing to reverse the fundamental change of the 1650s. By the mid-Sixties Roman Catholics held a mere 22 per cent of the kingdom's land, compared with almost 60 per cent in 1641 (273a, *13–17*; 269, *118–21*).

For two more decades, nevertheless, the new Irish order appeared to be assuming an air of permanence. From the English government's point of view, at least, it seemed to be well justified by the fact that Ireland survived the crucial years of the Exclusion Crisis (Ch. 8) without serious trouble. For this and much else Charles and his ministers were indebted to the management of the Protestant duke of Ormonde, the success of whose fourteen years as Viceroy [D.6] was largely due to his policy of judiciously strengthening the foundations of a new Anglo-Irish governing class while at the same time treating the Catholics mildly and avoiding controversial measures which would have made a new Irish Parliament necessary. When he did finally urge the calling of such a Parliament for financial reasons Whitehall (perhaps wisely) rejected his advice (268a). How hollow was the sense of security induced by Ireland's passivity was, however, to be dramatically exposed in 1687 when the earl of Tyrconnel began to change Ormonde's ground-rules fundamentally. Within two years the Kingdom was convulsed by its third major eruption of the seventeenth century; the anti-Catholic backlash which this was to produce, the most severe yet, would ensure that by contrast with post-Revolution Scotland, Ireland's constitutional position would remain unchanged for a further 90 years (Ch. 13; *The Age of Oligarchy*, Ch. 16).

The Scottish nobility and gentry had made no contribution to the Restoration, so in contrast with the situation in 1689, they were in no position to make terms with a new monarch and a new regime. And although few bitter tears were shed at the time over the dissolution of the Cromwellian Union, there was some ambivalence even then about the Scottish attitude and this increased when it became clear that the return of Scotland to the 'traditional' constitution, with government effectively in the hands of the Edinburgh privy council in nominal consort with the Scottish Estates, had by no means restored the northern

Kingdom to her position in 1641. This was not, of course, without its compensations for the country's nobility and gentry, for the years immediately preceding the Civil Wars had seen the Covenanters riding high politically as well as in religion. Theocracy, at least, went for good in 1660. But although historians are right to point to the restored authority of the aristocracy as an important feature of the settlement in Scotland, that authority, as its possessors soon found, was heavily trammelled by the more decisive power re-acquired by the Crown and its servants. The ultimate effect of the events of 1660, therefore, was to condemn Scotland to all but thirty years of political frustration, aggravated by damaging economic rivalry with her infinitely richer neighbour. The membership of the privy council from the start was moulded from London; the revived Scottish Parliament voted such an extravagantly loyal annual supply that it could be dissolved in 1663, leaving the Edinburgh Estates with far less leverage than the English House of Commons and inevitably vulnerable when they did assemble to the manipulations of 'the Lords of the Articles', restored in 1663 (above, p. 4).

One must be careful, all the same, not to exaggerate their plight. The settlement of 1660–3 did not reduce the Scottish ruling class to abject subordination. It has been emphasised, for instance (275, *Ch. 19*), that the Committee of Articles was no longer as omnipotent in managing parliamentary business as it had been under James VI; that the Scottish privy council could not be kept entirely insulated from dissident influences; and that in the second Scottish Parliament of Charles II (1669–74) vigorous parliamentary opposition sprang up from time to time. It usually proved ineffectual, but was to cause particular alarm to the government in the sessions of 1673–4 when an organised opposition party were to claim for the Estates, in Burnet's words, 'still an entire authority to examine into the state of the nation' (1, *II, 36*). Ironically the chief casualty of this Parliament's attempts at self-assertion proved to be the negotiations for a new Union, for which Charles II had called in 1669 and which petered out in 1670 (above, pp. 6–7). Not until the Revolution of 1688–9 had gone far to correct the constitutional imbalance created by the Restoration Settlement in Scotland would the chance recur (Chs.13, 20).

The rejection in 1660 of the two other major constitutional initiatives of 1649–58, a unicameral legislature and electoral reform, both had repercussions at least as important through the late seventeenth and eighteenth centuries as the abandonment of the parliamentary unions. By restoring the House of Lords unchanged, with the twenty-six bishops back on their bench again, the Commons of 1660 were re-instating a body which was soon to reveal greater potential power than at any time since the fifteenth century. By locking horns over the Act of Oblivion in 1660 (39b, *224*; 33, *132–5*) and then by virtually rewriting the Corporation and Uniformity bills sent up to them from the Commons (1661–2), the Lords soon showed that they were determined to play both a vigorous and vigilant rôle in legislation. They resisted privy councillors' control, in the 1660s at least, fought jealously for their privileges, especially in the bruising battles with the Lower House over the cases of *Skinner* v. *the East India Company* (1668–70) and *Shirley* v. *Fagg* (above, p. 9), and many times in the years 1679–1714 they were to succeed in frustrating the political aspirations of the

Commons.[5] It was not until the bishops as a whole were brought permanently to recognise an obligation, as royal nominees, to support the King's ministry of the day in all but the most exceptional circumstances – something that (except for an interval from 1675–81) did not happen until the 1720s – that the Lords became notably more susceptible to Court control, and more docile an instrument of party oligarchy than was the Lower House (*The Age of Oligarchy*, Ch. 2). As for the restored House of Commons itself, the lower house of Parliament could hardly have become the landowner's paradise that it was throughout the Hanoverian period without the revival of the old constituencies and franchises in 1660 (96, *13–20*). Especially significant in that respect was the restoration of the county vote (determining the return of 92 members) to 150–200,000 forty-shilling freeholders, most of them *very* small proprietors, and the resuscitation of 81 small boroughs laid low in 1654, many of them near-moribund, and all ripe sooner or later for gentry domination (see also Ch. 21).

Of more immediate constitutional moment, however, than the return to an unreformed electoral system was the acceptance in 1660 that what Charles I had legally surrendered in the first year of the Long Parliament had gone for good. The legislation of 1641 had had three vital effects. It had abolished Star Chamber and other prerogative courts and councils which had caused so much offence before the Civil Wars, especially to the common lawyers and the gentry. It had prohibited all non-parliamentary taxation – all those devices, such as benevolences, 'impositions' (trade duties) and Ship Money, by which the first two Stuart kings had raised revenue by virtue of their prerogative alone. And it had rendered illegal a protracted period of Personal Rule, such as that of 1629–40, by stipulating in the Triennial Act of 1641 that a parliament must be called at least once in every three years. It is worth noting that this last condition was to be significantly modified in 1664, when there was a reissue of the Triennial Act (above, p. 4), which dropped its original provision for an automatic summons of Parliament if the King failed to comply with the law. For all but the last year of Charles II's reign the practical effects of this change were to be nil, but it was nevertheless of great potential importance, as the 1680s would show. With this one exception, however, the Crown was restored in 1660 to the constitutional territory it had legally occupied in the late autumn of 1641: to prerogative powers, in fact, that remained very considerable. Theoretically Charles II enjoyed absolute discretion in the appointment and dismissal of ministers; an unquestionable responsibility for controlling the executive power, maintaining the security of the state and both devising and directing foreign policy; and the freedom – subject only to the limitation of the Triennial Act – to call, prorogue and dissolve Parliaments as he thought fit. Indeed, in one respect he was much better off than his father: in that he was granted a life revenue which, once granted, could not be subsequently cut off (Ch. 5).

What had been restored, therefore, was not so much the 'balanced constitution' venerated by early seventeenth-century politicians and political writers as a system of government condemned to remain for over twenty years in a state of instability, yielding at best an uneasy equilibrium. While the capacity of the

English monarchy for authoritarian rule had been severely limited, it had not been conclusively destroyed. Equally, while its control over administration and over the shaping of policy was still unfettered by any restrictions written into the statute book, that control was subject to various practical constraints. One key factor here was the restored system of local government. The two great provincial councils, those for the North and for the Marches of Wales, had fallen under the 1641 axe; the county committees, too, were no more; and there was a return to the old order of amateur administration in which the main instruments, the lords lieutenant and the justices of the peace, regarded themselves as servants of their county communities no less than as servants of the Crown. The restoration of this pre-civil war order *per se* was not difficult, since neither Parliament nor Cromwell since 1649 had made fundamental changes in the actual structure of local government: commissions of the peace and municipal corporations, though purged of anti-republicans, had continued to function, as had local courts and parish officials, the whole still punctuated by the twice yearly descents of the judges on assize.[6] The Major-Generals had caused deep dismay, but their intensive presence had not lasted. The system had sometimes creaked and groaned, as in the early months of 1660 when many Quarter Sessions and some corporations failed to meet (125, *30*), but it had never utterly broken down. The Restoration therefore meant drastic changes of personnel in local government, but very little institutional upheaval. New commissions of the peace were issued which turned out 'Oliverians' and sectaries in droves from most county benches, and brought back hundreds of royalist-Anglican squires to share the responsibilities of magistracy with a minority (generally, but not invariably, small) of survivors from the Interregnum (125, *31*; 124, *18–19*). The new justices at once took up their traditional duties and braced themselves to shoulder such fresh burdens as the King's early Parliaments might impose on them, soon forthcoming, indeed, in the shape of a new poor law (Settlement Act, 1662) and a string of measures against religious dissent(see below, p. 41). The municipalities could not be purged of their undesirables quite so easily; but the Cavalier Parliament provided an effective solution to that problem through the Corporation Act of 1661 [N.2(ii)]. The only significant pre–1649 local institutions which had to be virtually resurrected in 1660 were the county lieutenancies, to which the Militia Acts of 1661–3 gave effective responsibility for policing the provinces. The parliamentary tussles over the new militia system, endowing the King with formal authority, but the leading local gentry with real power, over the county 'trained bands', illustrate vividly that even the euphoric cavaliers had not forgotten all the constitutional lessons of the 1620s and 1630s (148, *3–17*; 33, *155–6*; 125, *42*).

Arguably the most serious single element of imbalance in the working of the pre-Civil War constitution had been the poverty of the Crown, for it had meant that without resort to dubious and unpopular forms of taxation the executive was unhealthily dependent on parliamentary charity. Charles II's first two Parliaments, down to 1662, did show some awareness of the seriousness of the problem, as we shall see (Ch. 5), but as in other fields, their thinking was too deeply coloured by past conventions and the appeal of the status quo to produce the radical solutions which, in this instance, were called for. Thus the time-honoured distinction between 'ordinary' and 'extraordinary' revenue – so often a cause of friction – was duly revived, and with it the idea that the King ought again to 'live of his own'. In practice the politicians were forced to concede that adjustments to the basic position of 1641 would have to be made, since the sources of the ordinary revenue enjoyed by Elizabeth and James I, let alone by Charles I, could not be expected in themselves to yield the restored monarchy an adequate peacetime income. At the very least the Crown would have to be compensated for the loss of two 'vexatious' sources of revenue, those from wardship and feudal tenures; these had been abolished unregretted in 1643 and 1646, and in 1660 their demise was quickly confirmed by statute. The outcome was two expedients designed to boost the ordinary revenue by permanent taxes, both representing departures of principle (Ch. 5) and one of them, the excise, of great future import. They helped to patch up the old system temporarily, but they did not alter the fact that Charles II had been saddled with a financial settlement that was badly outmoded, and which could only compound one of the most basic unsolved constitutional problems of Restoration, as of early Stuart, England – how to re-establish a harmonious working relationship between executive and legislature.

III

At Breda Charles had smartly passed to Parliament the responsibility for procuring 'the just satisfaction' of all parties concerned in the 'many grants and purchases of estates . . . to and by many officers, soldiers and others' during the turbulent years of the Interregnum. It needed no genius to appreciate that this was bound to be one of the most sensitive aspects of the Restoration Settlement. Historians of the seventeenth century were at one time fairly unanimous in their belief that, despite the obvious hopes and wishes of the royalists, and contrary to the clear private sympathies of Charles and Hyde (235a), many of those who had newly come into possession of their lands were preserved in their gains. This belief led to the natural assumption that there was an important injection of fresh blood into the landowning class after 1650,[7] a phenomenon that it was tempting to connect with the emergence of Whiggery later in Charles II's reign (15, *I, 163*). There is now only very limited support for this view; but despite much illuminating research, notably by Thirsk, Habakkuk and Holiday,[8] there remains some uncertainty about how far the practical realisation of the land settlement squared with what was intended either by the Convention or by the Cavalier Parliament, as they edged their way towards the inevitable compromise (235c, *81–102*).

It is plain enough from the terms of both the Judicial Proceedings Act and the Act of Oblivion that the Convention intended a basic distinction to be made between confiscation, as public acts of an illegal regime, and private sales by due process, even when transacted under varying degrees of duress. Nor is there anything in the King's attitude to either Act to suggest he opposed this principle. Other things, however, are less clear. Did either Charles and his ministers or Parliament, for example, regard all categories of confiscated land in the same way? Charles professed to do so; the Convention House of Commons, to judge from its debates, did not. We can distinguish three main categories: Crown lands appropriated by the republicans and then put on the market, frequently to be bought by officers of the New Model Army; Church lands similarly seized and sold, but to owners who (especially if they had been formerly leaseholders of ecclesiastical property) attracted more sympathy than the state's beneficiaries;[9] and private lands of 'delinquent Cavaliers' who had been unable to 'compound', that is, retain their estates by paying a fine. In each case the situation was complicated further by the fact that scores of the original buyers had subsequently re-sold, at market prices. The evidence that the first two categories of forfeited estates were in general restored, despite the ultimate failure of the Convention to proceed by firm legislative action, is powerful, although few owners of *Church* lands were dispossessed without some measure of compensation, thanks to the activity of a special land commission. A good deal more haze surrounds the confiscated lands of the private non-compounders. But it would seem that former owners bent on recovery had normally no alternative – if private agreements were not forthcoming – but to resort to law-suits, to petitions, or, if they could afford them, to private parliamentary bills. The early stages of the Cavalier Parliament, especially, saw a predictable rash of such legislation, for instance the private acts promoted by Lord Culpeper and the marquess of Newcastle (235b).

The most important revisionist conclusion of modern research, now generally accepted, is that, in one way or another, a majority of the main royalist families whose estates had been at risk in the 1640s and 1650s were in possession of most of their lands again by the early 1660s. But how they succeeded in doing this, and indeed when they did it, remain intricate problems. Local studies have revealed that even private sellers of land, to whom (as we have seen) the new regime could offer no kind of official comfort, had a remarkable recovery record – not only after the Restoration but in many cases even before it. The older families, in particular, often showed a notable determination and resilience in this respect. What is not so evident is how extensive private land sales by royalists had been during the Civil Wars and the Interregnum. Some scholars take the view that most cavalier families had had to sell at least some land (13, *135*), either to pay their fines, or to meet the penal tax demands of the republic, or to discharge debts which were not infrequently grievous. Others disagree, Habakkuk, especially, arguing that fines alone led to few sales; that the bulk of the royalists contrived to get by either by mortgaging properties, helped enormously by a dramatic cut in interest rates to 6 per cent in 1651, or by leasing them; that some of the most crippling debts were of long standing and not primarily attributable to sacrifices in the King's cause; and indeed, that there were possibly more sales after the Restoration than before it (211, *II, 145–50* [Habakkuk]).[10]

However, none of this should beguile us into imagining that the casualties of the Civil Wars among the landowning classes were relatively few. They were very numerous. A sizeable minority of royalists, especially among the lesser gentry families, either failed to get their estates back at all or failed to recover more than a part of their former holdings. Even recovered lands were often bought back only at great sacrifice, as many a numbing mortgate debt bore witness for a generation after 1660. Moreover it was not only fines and high taxes which had taken their toll, but the free quartering of troops, the indiscriminate plunder of farms, the pillaging of country houses, the accumulation of heavy rent arrears. The unluckiest families were those already financially embarrassed, and possibly with encumbered estates, in 1642, who then committed themselves heavily to the losing side. They not only had to sell to pay delinquency fines but often had to unload estates to stay afloat at all. Charles II's personal generosity subsequently to hard-pressed cavaliers, through the distribution of offices, pensions and royal bounty, is well known (Ch. 5), though possibly exaggerated. What is still very little known are the effects, and above all the political effects, of the hardships of those who, in the end, had nothing but sympathy to show for all their sacrifices, and sometimes not even that. Their number must have run into hundreds – thousands, if we include sons as well as heads of families. How far their misfortunes contributed to the growth of disenchantment with the restored monarchy, and even, by the 1670s, to the hardening of opposition to the Court, remains an open question.

IV

The settlement of religion in England[11] after the Restoration involved issues that were very different in character both from the constitutional questions calling for solution and from the heterogeneous nature of the land problem, and it has proved more difficult to reach a historical consensus over their interpretation. The assumption of all main parties that there must be a return to a state church, together with the expectation of the loyalist moderate Puritans that their freedom of conscience would be fully safeguarded, presupposed a settlement in this field that would have to be *made*, and not simply allowed to emerge piecemeal. There was no self-evident basic formula to apply, as with the civil government; neither was there scope here for the complex of private initiatives or deals which characterised the land settlement. It was not possible for Charles or his leading advisers to abdicate responsibility – the King had, after all, inherited with his crown the mantle of Supreme Governor of the Church of England. Nor was it possible for Parliament to stand aside, even to the partial extent it chose to do in dealing with land questions: a state church would sooner or later have to be cemented and buttressed by legislation, as it had been in the 1530s, in 1549–52 and in 1559.

About the central facts of the Restoration ecclesiastical settlement there is no room for dispute. Between 1660 and 1662 the Church of England was re-established in a form which, on the surface, appeared to bear a close affinity with its early Stuart predecessor. It was a Church to which the allegiance of all the King's English and Welsh subjects was legally bound by a state-imposed policy of uniformity. It had episcopally ordained ministers and a traditional system of ecclesiastical government and discipline. It was furnished with a Prayer Book in obvious line of descent from that of Cranmer and Parker, with church courts, and with most of the other external trappings of the Church of 1641. The one prominent exception was the prerogative Court of High Commission, whose statutory abolition by the Long Parliament was accepted in 1660 with as little apparent regret as that of the Star Chamber. But if the main institutional facts of the settlement seem unassailable enough, vital aspects of its making and intrinsic character have been diversely interpreted. For instance, divining the motives and intentions of leading protagonists, especially those of the King, of Edward Hyde, and of the restored and newly-appointed Anglican bishops, is far from straight-forward, for the line between camouflage and reality is rarely obvious. When and why did the religious settlement begin to part company from the model foreshad-owed in the royal declarations of April and October 1660, and how far did accident or design dictate this divergence and its outcome? Even then, was there not a good deal more to the religious situation of 1662–5 than a simple 'turning back of the clock' to 1641?

On various occasions in 1660 Charles II indicated willingness to go a long way to meet the religious scruples of the moderate Puritans. This he did initially at Breda, where the commitment to a 'liberty to tender consciences' was drafted by Hyde, his chief minister in exile, primarily to reassure the Presbyterians that there would be a place for them within the restored state church. Subsequently King and Chancellor sponsored the summer and autumn meetings between Anglican and Presbyterian leaders, culminating in October at Worcester House [N.1(ii)]. Most explicit was the royal declaration issued at the end of that final conference at Hyde's London residence, for it hinted broadly at latitude in matters of ceremony and announced agreement in principle on a scheme for 'reducing' episcopacy by associating synods and presbyters with the exercise of some of the bishops' powers.[12] Although note must be taken of arguments to the contrary (13, *137–8*), a thoroughly convincing case has now been built up for taking these pronouncements at something like face value (156b; 156a; 14 [Beddard]). It should be remembered that the committed Presbyterian clergy, though a small minority (perhaps no more than ten per cent) of the parish ministry by the end of the Interregnum, had powerful champions in the King's first Privy Council. And while political heavyweights such as Manchester, Annesley and Holles – all prominent in the 'reconciling' moves of June-October – accepted that a restoration of episcopacy and a service book in some form was inevitable, they seriously believed that Charles was just as opposed as they themselves were to a revival of that exclusive, persecuting type of Church establishment that had given such offence under Laud. About the King personally they were unquestionably right. Their confidence in Hyde, whose sincerity is more often questioned (156a) was not misplaced either, for he shared both their wish for a religious settlement based on 'comprehension' and their unease about a policy of 'indulgence' towards the separatists, who would continue to resist absorption in *any* new state church. In this he differed from his royal master, whose mischievous encouragement of Quakers and evident tenderness towards Catholics equally alarmed him (14 [Beddard]; 33). Just as encouraging was the early attitude of many leading Anglican divines. Of those present at Worcester House only Cosin, Dean of Peterborough, refused to sign the agreement. Furthermore, when the bench of bishops was at last re-stocked, September-

November 1660, it became apparent that favour had fallen in particular on clergy in the moderate 'Jacobean' tradition of the Church, such as Morley, Sheldon, Sanderson and Henchman, along with no fewer than three ex-Covenanters (Reynolds, Gauden and Monck), who would have numbered five had Edmund Calamy and Richard Baxter chosen to accept the sees they were offered. Of all those appointed or promoted at this crucial time only one committed Laudian could be identified.[13]

In spite of the failure of an attempt in the Convention to give legislative teeth to the October declaration (above, p. 3), prospects for the achievement of a compromise settlement still looked bright in December 1660. Eighteen months later they had become dim, almost to the point of extinction. The change was a momentous one and it defies simple explanation, but three reasons can be heavily underlined. One was the inability of both the King and the Anglican hierarchy to act independently of Parliament; the second was the fatal tendency of the Presbyterians to overplay a fair but far from invulnerable hand, and the third was a spontaneous Anglican reaction out in the dioceses – a reaction so powerful in its flow, among the laity in particular, that events in London were at length left swirling in its wake.

Very possibly because he had the relief of Roman Catholics ultimately in mind, Charles II was palpably anxious to assert his ecclesiastical prerogatives in the shaping of the settlement; both he and Hyde would have preferred to hold off any major parliamentary initiatives on religion until the legislature could be presented with a *fait accompli*, down to the small print, worked out synodically by Anglican and Presbyterian divines. This is the most plausible explanation for the successful, but in retrospect unwise, blocking tactics used by the Court against the Worcester House Bill in the Convention (156a; but cf. 150). In practice, however, there was never a realistic prospect that Members of Parliament would refrain from involving themselves in what the vast majority regarded as a matter of the highest concern. And this involvement seemed far less likely to favour the cause of reconciliation from the time the Convention gave way to the Cavalier Parliament, elected against the macabre backcloth of Venner's London rising, a brief interlude of terror which revived all the old fears of Puritan fanaticism. It is all the more extraordinary, therefore, how little anxiety or sense of urgency seems to have afflicted the spokesmen of the Presbyterians as they prepared for the national synod due to meet in the spring of 1661. This synod, with its equal representation of Anglican and Presbyterian clergy, had been promised by Charles at Worcester House as the means of resolving outstanding major problems, such as the validity of non-episcopal ordinations, and in particular, it was commissioned to work in detail on the revisions of the Prayer Book necessary to deliver Comprehension. The Savoy Conference duly convened in April, and its failure after months of wrangling was primarily due to the obduracy of the Presbyterian negotiators, foremost among whom in inflexibility and negative tactics was Richard Baxter. At the start of the conference a majority of bishops was still sincerely disposed to make concessions. Some had already put a great deal of labour into preparing their own moderate revised version of the Prayer Book. But none could accept the virtually rewritten liturgy astonishingly produced by the other side as late as July, any more than they could embrace the Laudian book proposed by Cosin and Wren. Moderate comprehensionists such as Gilbert Sheldon, bishop of London, were exasperated and departed for their summer visitations aware that the new Parliament would now go on to dictate its own settlement. Such an outcome did not at this stage unduly alarm them, for in the early months of their first session the Cavalier Commons had tempered their Anglican zeal and intolerance with some restraint, while a strong voice for moderation was still to be heard from the Lords.

Any prospect that this temperate mood might persist to the end of a year-long session was, however, destroyed by the situation – rapidly developing its own momentum – which the bishops found awaiting them in the country. The collapse of the Puritans outside London, long before the legal enforcement of a uniformity policy, surprised even opponents who had chafed under their supremacy for years, though its extent ought to be less startling to historians now that we have a better understanding of the tenacity with which Anglican traditions and practices had survived during the dark years from 1646 to 1660.[14] Between May and December 1660 almost 700 incumbents not in Anglican orders are known to have abandoned their livings under various degrees of local pressure. The process continued at a slower rate in 1661. The counterpart of this Puritan exodus was the 'irresistible Anglican reflex' (14 [Beddard], *163*), which in parishes, dioceses and cathedral chapters up and down the land had unofficially achieved a partial restoration of dispossessed clergy, liturgical worship and Church rights even before the opening of the Savoy Conference (33, *171–3*; 14 [Beddard]). At this local level, too, the firm resistance of many of the country gentry, as justices of the peace and holders of advowsons, to an eirenic settlement had become increasingly evident; in fact, one historian of the settlement considers 'that the most important single influence upon its shape was the zeal of the gentry for the episcopal Church of England' (156a, *200*). The pre-war errors and excesses of the episcopalians were forgotten by a traditional ruling class in the grip of a nostalgic yearning for familiar ways and for the old social, as well as religious, certainties. Charles II and Hyde, it has been argued, returning from exile, grossly underestimated the strength of this reaction, which made nonsense of their initial calculations (14, *155–63*). That it impressed the bishops, too, we cannot doubt, but the sheer confusion of practice at parish level to which it led made a greater impact still on them. The urgency of obtaining an enforceable legal settlement as quickly as possible was now clear to Anglican leaders, and in December 1661 they did their part in Convocation where they secured approval of the new Prayer Book, steered through by the moderate Bishop Sanderson: a book which, despite several hundred minor amendments, was substantially in 'the old method' of 1604.[15] But their chances of embodying this in a Uniformity bill which would contain enough concessionary clauses to draw in all but the most doctrinaire Presbyterians, were destroyed over the next few months; partly by the mounting intransigence of the Cavalier gentry in the Commons, but partly too by alarm at the signs, early in 1662, that a pro-Catholic party at Court, headed by the earl of Bristol and bent on a wide measure of toleration for all non-Anglicans, might be advancing in interest at the expense of Hyde (now earl of Clarendon).

In such circumstances the House of Commons' solution to the problems of the hour was predictably uncompromising. Despite opposition in the Lords, led by the strong phalanx of Presbyterian peers, and the moderating attempts of Clarendon and those bishops who still supported comprehension,[16] a Uniformity Act passed in May 1662 [N.2(iii)], enforcing on all ministers of religion unqualified subscription to the new Prayer Book and to the Thirty-Nine Articles of Religion. This led in August, on the black day of St Bartholomew, to 'the Great Ejection', when 936 more parish ministers, including the most distinguished of the Presbyterians and one-third of the London clergy, were added to the roll of those already deprived. The full tally of Puritan victims from 1660–62, including town lecturers and college fellows, has been calculated by Michael Watts at 2,029 (150, *219*).

Meanwhile, the passing of the Corporation Act and the Quaker Act (December-May 1661–2) [N.2(i, ii)] had already launched the series of repressive laws against dissenters (laity as well as clergy) which history has totally mislabelled 'the Clarendon Code'. But if Clarendon's rôle in the religious settlement has often been misinterpreted, so too has that of Sheldon, who was soon to succeed the aged Juxon as Primate of all England. Much has been made by some scholars of the skill and determination shown by this undeniably great churchman in devising and driving through a settlement very much after his own heart. Yet he can be found supporting moderate policies in and out of Parliament down to the very spring of 1662, and his period of staunch leadership should probably be dated rather from the time the Uniformity bill, which he had striven to amend, became law (156a, *e.g. 23*; 14 [Beddard], *167*). Thereafter his record speaks for itself: in his pugnacious opposition to the King's suspending manoeuvres in August 1662 (Ch. 7, p. 109); in drafting and urging through Parliament the Conventicles Act of 1664; in the wake of the Yorkshire 'rebellion' of the sectaries the previous autumn (33, *204–9*); and in sponsoring the Five Mile Act (1665), the last penal addition to the 'Code' for this decade at least, and effectively the coping-stone on the statutory settlement of religion [N.2(v)]; (see also above, pp. 4–5).

Sheldon's lack of dogmatism from 1660 to 1662, however, and later, as archbishop, his shrewd and conscious courting of parliamentary support and of a clerical-gentry alliance, illustrates one essential feature of this church settlement which it remains to underline. It is distorting to think of the Acts of the Cavalier Parliament as bringing about a return to the pre-Civil War religious situation. They did of course restore an episcopal state church, *in general* hostile to religious dissidence. Yet it was very far from being the Laudian Church of the 1630s that was being recreated. Doctrinally, the influence of Arminianism among its leaders was not strong. Liturgically, and in other ways, at least a third of the bishops' bench of the early 1660s retained some sympathy with moderate Presbyterianism and continued to hope for a broader church than that which had emerged in 1662: seven years later nine of them were to support a Comprehension bill in the Lords.[17] As the swift appearance of a 'latitudinarian' party among its divines shows, the Restoration Church was not untouched even from the start by the early stirrings of the rationalist and scientific spirit in the mid-seventeenth century (306; Chs. 10, 24). Laud would have been equally displeased by its lack of theocratic pretensions and the pragmatism with which it viewed its ties with the secular order; and he would have been shocked by the attitude towards it of its Supreme Governor, at best detached and at worst subversive, far removed from that of the zealously supportive Charles I. But what would have appalled Laud most of all was the fact that the legislators of 1661–5 had created for the first time a legally-acknowledged division in the Protestant religious fabric of the kingdom, a schism between an established church and Dissent, in addition to the existing division between Protestants and Roman Catholic recusants. Nonconformity did, of course, pay a heavy price for acknowledgment, being called upon to shoulder a burden of disabilities which condemned it for most of the period 1662–87 to harassment and at times to stern persecution (Ch. 10). Nevertheless, an historic demarcation was made in England in the years 1661–5, and the implications of this demarcation, not simply for the country's religious life, but for its political, economic and cultural life, were incalculable.

All these differences between the religious situation of the mid-1660s and that of 1640–1 illustrate very well what is perhaps the most fundamental underlying theme of the Restoration Settlement. Legally it was not impracticable to 'put back the clock', and much of the legislative activity (or, in the case of the constitution, non-activity) of the early 1660s gives the impression of having been inspired with this purpose. But England between 1640 and 1660 had been through a deeply disturbing experience, with intangible repercussions which had gone far beyond its institutional framework and which neither the statute book nor the law courts had power to obliterate. So it was with the survival of religious 'independency' and sectarianism; with Parliament's experience since 1642 of the mysteries of government; and with the concepts of political contract, popular sovereignty and natural rights, disseminated during the Interregnum by the Levellers and James Harrington, and destined to enjoy a remarkable reflorescence under the first Whigs (Ch. 9). Perhaps the most awesome of these intangible legacies was the fact that in 1649 an English king had been judicially tried and executed for treason. However vehemently disavowed and emotionally expiated thereafter, this remained a shattering event which was to have an immense effect on the outlook and fortunes of the restored regime, and no amount of loyalist-Anglican political theorising later in Charles II's reign could fully repair the insidious damage it had wrought to the sanctity of monarchy. In this, as in many other ways, those Cavaliers who at the Restoration nostalgically sought to recapture not simply the institutions but the very essence of a society which had been eighteen years in the melting-pot were destined for disillusionment.

---

1. C.G. Robertson, ed., *Select Statutes, Cases and Documents . . . 1660–1832* (8th edn, 1947), p. 22.
2. There was, however, a middle group of *conforming* ex-Presbyterians (and some ex-Independents) in the Cavalier House of Commons, which amounted to roughly 13% of its total membership, 1661–79. B. D. Henning, ed. (25), I, p. 13).
3. 'Men not being forward to confirm such perpetual and exorbitant powers by a law . . .',

H.H. Margoliouth, ed., *The Poems and Letters of Andrew Marvell* (Oxford, 1927), II, p. 7, quoted in D. Hirst (39b), p. 225).

4. For a lucid brief account see A.G.R. Smith, *The Emergence of a Nation State* (1984), Ch. 38.

5. A. Swatland, 'The Role of Privy Councillors in the House of Lords, 1660–81' in C. Jones, ed., *A Pillar of the Constitution: the House of Lords in British Politics, 1640–1784* (1989), pp. 66–74; C. Jones and G. Holmes, 'The House of Lords in the Early 18th Century' in *idem*, eds, *The London Diaries of William Nicolson, Bishop of Carlisle, 1702–1718* (Oxford, 1985). About one third of all the Acts of Parliament passed in the years 1660–81 were initiated by the House of Lords.

6. J.S. Cockburn, *A History of English Assizes, 1558–1714* (Cambridge, 1972), *passim*.

7. See, e.g. H.E. Chesney, 'The Transference of Lands in England 1640–1660', *TRHS*, 4th ser., **15** (1932).

8. J. Thirsk (235b); Sir H.J. Habakkuk, 'Landowners and the Civil War', *EcHR*, **18** (1965); *idem*, (235a); P.G. Holiday, 'Land Sales and Repurchase in Yorkshire after the Civil Wars, 1650–70', *Northern History*, **5** (1970).

9. See Habakkuk (235a), pp. 203–5 for the Presbyterian MPs who had bought church land before Pride's Purge.

10. H.J. Habakkuk, 'Public Finance and the Sale of Confiscated Property during the Interregnum', *EcHR*, **15** (1962–3).

11. For the Scottish religious settlement see Ch. 10.

12. Based, according to Richard Baxter, a leading clerical negotiator for the Presbyterians, on Archbishop Ussher's compromise proposals for Church government of 1641.

13. Viz. Cosin, appointed to Durham. Two antique survivors from the bench of the 1630s, Juxon and Duppa, received high promotion – Juxon to Canterbury – but they were too decrepit to influence Church policy. I am indebted for this analysis of the Restoration episcopate, and for several other points in this treatment of the religious settlement of 1660–2, to the late Dr G.V. Bennett, whose unpublished Birkbeck Lectures (1983) on The Restored Church of England I was privileged to read in typescript, with the permission of his literary executor.

14. J.S. Morrill, 'The Church in England, 1642–9', in *idem.*, ed., *Reactions to the English Civil War* (1982), pp. 89–114; cf. C. Cross, 'The Church in England, 1646–1660', in G.E. Aylmer, ed., *The Interregnum* (1972).

15. G.J. Cuming, 'The Prayer Book in Convocation, November 1661', *JEH*, **8** (1957).

16. A. Swatland, 'The House of Lords in the Reign of Charles II, 1660–1681', (Birmingham Ph.D. thesis, 1985), pp. 202–8, 217.

17. Swatland, op. cit., pp. 202–13, *passim*.

CHAPTER 2

Population, agriculture and industry in England, 1660–1688

I

Until recently it was possible to make only the roughest of guesses at the size of England's population in 1660. Self-confessed uncertainty among historians was an appropriate reflection of the bemused state of seventeenth-century opinion on matters demographic. Ironically, the later Stuart period is associated with the emergence of a select breed of Britons who helped to revolutionize English government by their insistence that in order to be efficient, administration must be fully and carefully informed about the people it was governing. John Graunt, Sir William Petty, John Adams and Peter Pett down to the late 1680s, John Houghton, Charles Davenant, William Culliford and, pre-eminently, Gregory King in the early and mid-1690s, were the chief pioneers of a new science which Petty christened 'political arithmetic', and most of them had a natural concern with basic demographic data. Moreover, from the time Parliament first imposed a Hearth Tax on England and Wales in 1662 (Ch. 5), enquiring minds were alive to the fact that in the records of the number of houses kept by the new Hearth Office, there lay a key to opening the door to the mystery of mysteries, how many people there were in the kingdom. Unfortunately there was an inner as well as an outer door, and for this a quite separate key was needed, one which could unlock the question, how many persons on average lived in each house? Between the 1660s and the early 1690s, a variety of keys were groped for and produced, all of them crude, and they yielded an equal variety of uneasy assertions about the size of the population of England and Wales ranging from 6 million (in Petty's *Verbum Sapienti*, 1667) to 7.8 million (in Davenant's *Essay upon Ways and Means*, 1695). On the whole, Petty's second thoughts of the 1680s, based on the assumption of six persons per house and suggesting a population of 7–7.4 million, gained widest credence.[1] But it was still possible for two MPs to use a figure of 8 million to calculate the yield of a new salt duty and (*graduated*) poll tax in 1692 without provoking a murmur of dissent from the Commons.[2]

It was in the hope of dispelling this fog that in 1695 the government of William III, faced with the problem of collecting new duties on baptisms, marriages and burials, called for a complete enumeration of every parish in the country. As a national operation this first planned census proved a disaster. Nevertheless, enough good returns were made to enable the most ingenious of the 'computers' of the day, Gregory King of the College of Heralds, to find the elusive key to the inner door of the political arithmeticians. By using something akin to a modern 'sampling' technique, he evolved not a blanket ratio of people to houses for the country at large, but a quite sophisticated series of ratios appropriate to different types and sizes of community; and in this way he arrived at a figure of 5.42 million for the settled population of England and Wales in 1695, pushed up to the golden number of 5.5 million by a somewhat arbitrary addition for 'transitory people' [B.1].[3] It was a figure far lower than any recent reputable estimate or count (with the sole exception of the 1676 'Bishops' Survey' of persons over 16, now known as the Compton Census (Ch. 10)[4]) had led King's countrymen to expect. It was one that many politicians of his day found hard to stomach. Yet by contrast with contemporary resistance to King's formidable logic, modern historical demographers have in general applauded him warmly for his pioneering work. As the subsequent (and appreciably higher) estimates for the year 1701, made by late nineteenth- and early twentieth-century scholars, lost conviction through their dependence on the discredited 'P.R.A.' method of calculating the eighteenth-century population backwards from 1801 (176a, *5*; 195a), so Gregory King's work grew in stature.

Unfortunately, little of value could be deduced from King about what had been happening to the population in the course of the century before he wrote. It has been agreed for a long time that throughout the sixteenth century the general trend of England's population had been very steeply upwards, exhibiting great resilience in weathering periodic demographic squalls. And with their sights set on King, historians were equally confident that the seventeenth century saw a further significant growth. However, the view of J.D. Chambers, made posthumously known in 1972 (194, *22–3*), was that 'the long upward movement of population' had ended 'by the middle of the century' and that the brakes then went on for several decades before a renewed thrust began in the 1680s. Tempered as it was by evidence which suggested more vigorous growth in the late seventeenth century in certain economically-advancing regions, it seemed authoritative, but it was hard to put any statistical flesh on this or any other hypothesis.

The publication in 1981 of Wrigley and Schofield's *Population History of England* (196), crowning two decades of sustained attack on the registers of over 400 parishes by the Cambridge Group for the History of the Population (196, *esp. Table A3.3*), has gone far to resolve some of the most salient problems. It has confirmed Chambers's belief that around 1657 England was falling into the throes of a demographic recession, and likewise the fact that by the end of James II's reign a slow recovery had just begun [B.1; Ch. 19]. We must, of course, accept that statistical certainty about the population in the pre-census era is always going to be unattainable; and not all historians have been entirely happy either about the representative nature of the 'sample' parishes selected by the Cambridge Group, or about the mind-bending technique of 'back projection' used to arrive at total population figures (169, *37*; 189a). Nevertheless, the latter certainly represent the most scientific and well-founded estimates yet produced and they enable us to proceed fairly securely on the basis of certain assumptions about seventeenth-century England and Wales. We may be reasonably sure that the previous century's sharp rise in population continued apace for about four more decades after 1600 [B.1]; that thereafter the kingdom's population edged more slowly up to a seventeenth-century peak in the mid-1650s; that by the time of the Restoration it had fallen back to about 5.5 million, and that the next quarter of a century saw a further slight decline (of 5–6 per cent) to a lowest point reached in 1686. By 1696, however, the most sophisticated modern computation begins to converge impressively on the most ingenious contemporary one, that of Gregory King [B.1].

Before we look at some of the economic implications of this demographic pattern (Ch. 4, pp. 80–1), we must try to understand why the mid- to late seventeenth-century slump took place, what exceptions there were to it, and how, very broadly speaking, the static or declining population of England in the first thirty years of our period was distributed. In the first place, it is now well established that there was, as Laslett first argued in 1965, a general decline in fertility in Stuart England, and that this was not arrested until William III's reign (219; 196, *420*). Even aristocratic marriages were producing fewer children at the end of the century than at the beginning; of labouring families this seems to have been emphatically true in most (but significantly, not in all) parts of the country down to the 1680s. The major cause of lower fertility seems clear enough: couples were marrying later than they had in Tudor England, while a far higher proportion of both men and women were not marrying at all. The implication is hard to resist that many men delayed or renounced marriage for economic reasons – because a century of demographic expansion and inflation had put great pressure on land and jobs down to the 1640s – and that the change in social habits thus brought about then became ingrained, persisting for decades after real wages [M.2] had begun to climb again (170a, *Ch. 1, esp. 23–4*). A pioneering study in 1966 of Colyton in Devon showed that whereas from 1560 to 1646 the average age of marriage for the females of the parish was 27, it rose to nearly 30 from 1647 to 1719. The national pattern, however, was less startling than this, and it changed fundamentally after 1700.[5] Yet it would be distorting to put over-heavy emphasis on fertility and the birth rate, or even on what demographers inelegantly term 'nuptiality'. Most married women continued to bear surprisingly large numbers of children. The trouble was, they did not bear enough to cope with a very high rate of mortality and, above all, with the waves of serious epidemic disease which were the scourge of seventeenth-century England. From the mid-1640s to the mid-1680s such waves followed each other with exceptional frequency [B.4].

The most dreaded of these epidemics – though not in fact the most destructive over the century as a whole – was bubonic plague, the terrible 'pestilence'. It began from the 1590s once again to hit England periodically with great savagery. 1593, 1603, 1625, 1636 and 1645 (in the North) were all bad years, and if the 'Great Plague' of 1665 was arguably not the worst of all, relative to the total population, London's 68,000 recorded plague deaths (and almost certainly many others that went unrecorded) represented a horrendous toll. Although no one knew it at the time, the plague bacillus was transmitted through flea-bites, and the black rats which hosted the fleas had a liking for the crowded, insanitary houses and cellars of the typical early Stuart town. This explains why London was more vulnerable than anywhere else in Britain to attacks of the plague.

Although it is recognised that the disease was on the retreat in Europe generally in the second half of the seventeenth-century, it is still something of a mystery why there was no repetition of the 'Great Plague' of 1665 in England. No single explanation that has been offered, biological or otherwise, carries complete conviction, although Paul Slack has made a plausible case for the importance of a more effective quarantine policy at the ports.[6] It would be surprising, however, if the rebuilding of London after the Great Fire (1666) and the general tendency for new building in provincial towns after 1660 to be in brick and stone, tile and slate (*The Age of Oligarchy*, Ch. 14) did not have a marked influence in inhibiting and localising the minor outbreaks that still did quite frequently occur. Unfortunately for Restoration England, environmental changes, slow as they were, were powerless to check other epidemics spread in ways entirely different from the plague. And for at least two decades after 1665 the country was frighteningly exposed to other mass killers [B.4]: chronic influenza; enteric and other fevers; smallpox, a notorious child-killer (like those two endemic scourges, diphtheria and tuberculosis) and as likely to carry off the highest as the lowest in the land, and perhaps worst of all, the deadly typhus, carried by lice, and despite its reputation as a 'hunger' disease, fully capable of striking in years of plenty. Indeed, it was the typhus epidemic of the mid-1680s which was the main demographic landmark of the later Stuart England [B.4] (194, *91*), the end of a series of great decimating waves and the herald, as events proved, of well over thirty years of equally unaccountable epidemic recession [B.4; Ch. 19].

There is, however, another side to the general demographic scene so far depicted, a scene where the heavy losses over the years 1658–88 were attributable not only to frequent mortality rises but to the high rate of emigration, especially to the New World, which had begun before and during the Civil Wars (196, *185–6, 223–33 passim*). Whereas over the country at large the population level was at best struggling to hold its own, in some places, notably in London and a few of the largest provincial towns and cities (Norwich, Bristol, Newcastle and a relative newcomer, Birmingham) growth remained buoyant throughout, while other and wider areas discovered a fresh impetus in the 1670s and 1680s. Most expanding towns owed their growth to immigration, and in London, chronically unhealthy, yet still increasing its inhabitants so fast after 1650 that by 1700 it housed one Englishman in every ten [B.2(i)], the influx was on a spectacular scale (177; 188a, *9–10, 40–9*; 188b). But in some towns – Liverpool, for one – there are signs of 'natural increase' by the late seventeenth century, and such evidence is more impressive still in certain regions with a particular economic identity. Local research in these regions has revealed a quite different demographic pattern from that of the rest of the country, with a birth-rate resilient enough to resist the buffetings of frequent epidemics and high infant mortality. Parts of the East Midlands and the Vale of Trent formed one such area by the second half of Charles II's reign; Staffordshire and the Black Country to the west of Birmingham another; south Lancashire yet another (194, *136–7*; 170a, *28*; 189a, *60ff*). It is likely that east Norfolk, Tyneside and parts of the West Riding of Yorkshire can be added to the list.[7] Wherever there were groups of towns or clusters of industrial villages engaged in some thriving branch of the economy – be it textile or metal manufacture, frame knitting or coalmining – where labour was in demand, wages or piece-rates competitive, or where some small pastoral farming was available to supplement resources, there were incentives present to immigration, earlier marriage and chances for greater fertility. If one is to understand the regional development of Britain, not only in the late seventeenth century but in the whole century from 1660 to 1760, this is a point essential to bear in mind, for it remained generally true throughout, applying as much to the disease-ridden 1720s and 1730s as to the 1670s and 1680s.

It has recently been suggested that by 1700 'the counties north of the line from the Severn to the Humber probably contained between a third and two fifths of the population' (170a, *28*). Thanks to the levying of the Hearth Tax from 1662 to 1689 we know far more about the broad regional distribution of the English and Welsh population in that period than would otherwise be the case.[8] By 1689 the four south-eastern counties of Middlesex, Surrey, Kent and Sussex contained roughly a million men, women and children, the capital itself accounting, with Southwark, for half of them. More surprising to modern students is the revelation that as many people again inhabited the six south-western counties of Cornwall, Devon, Somerset, Gloucestershire, Wiltshire and Dorset: almost 450,000 of them lived in Devon and Somerset. The three seaboard counties between the Thames and the Wash, of which Norfolk was the most populous and boasted, in Norwich, by far the largest provincial city in the kingdom, contained about half a million inhabitants; so too did south and east Lancashire combined with the West Riding of Yorkshire, a region cut in two by the Pennines but united by a mutual involvement in textile industries. It is no coincidence that three of those four principal concentrations of late seventeenth-century Englishmen were also the country's leading areas of textile production, for outside the land, with which it was closely connected, cloth manufacture remained the chief employer of labour (below, p. 54).

II

Although industry, and still more overseas trade (Ch. 3), are rightly held to have provided many of the sinews from which England's remarkable access of strength in the late seventeenth and early eighteenth century derived [L.1], a great majority of the largest family incomes between 1660 and 1688 were land-based: in other words, their size largely depended, in the final reckoning, on the profitability of the farms from which the big landowners drew their rents.

The face of agrarian England was changing, slowly but perceptibly, in the first three decades after the Restoration. At one time it was a commonplace of history textbooks that an 'agricultural revolution' began somewhere about the middle of the eighteenth century. That was indeed to be an important period for the agrarian economy (*The Age of Oligarchy*, Ch. 9). But now that seventeenth-century agriculture has been the focus of many years of close research, many economic historians find it more logical to think of a much longer-term process of improvement and to date its origins from nearer 1650 than 1750 (216a; 216b;

215a, *Intro and Ch. 6*; 212). It is true that the course of progress was uneven, a series of short, localised spurts rather than a broad frontal advance, and that across it lay formidable barriers of conservatism and ignorance. But two basic facts of life were common to most of the country for most of the time between the Restoration and the Glorious Revolution. Firstly, because population growth was continually being pruned back, while harvests, especially in the 1680s – a decade of 'marvellous bounty' from the land – were generally very good (214), this was a period of far lower farm prices than early seventeenth-century England had experienced [K.1; K.2(ii)]. Secondly, as towns increasingly responded to a more euphoric commercial climate, the demand for home-produced food became steadily more concentrated, with London's requirements inevitably exerting a unique influence, and thus the pressures to farm – and also to garden – for the market rather than for family subsistence became more insistent than they had ever been (222b; 211 [Thick]). And to make a profit, perhaps even to survive at all, through farming for a market of growing sophistication (211, *255* [Chartres]), in an era of low-prices, efficiency was of the essence. There was, in other words, the strongest incentive to 'improve' wherever capital, soil and climate allowed it. Additional incentives were provided for farmers in the eastern corn-growing counties, from Suffolk to the East Riding, by the beginning of grain exports to the Continent in the 1670s (216b), and for the big grazier farmers of such counties as Herefordshire, Lincolnshire, Leicestershire and Wiltshire by the unprecedented demand of clothiers for English long staple wool, used in serges, worsteds and other 'medley' cloths.

That Restoration England should have seen an acceleration of earlier seventeenth-century trends towards higher levels of efficiency in farming is not, therefore, surprising. The lead came from above, and from none more strongly than from those numerous former royalist landlords who urgently needed to recoup the losses of the Civil Wars in a period plagued by falling rents and failing tenants. They were often among the keenest students of 'improvements'.[9] The placing of the home farms of the wealthier gentry and aristocratic proprietors in the care of full-time stewards or bailiffs grew commoner between 1660 and 1690 (225, *162* [D. Hainsworth]). More important still was the way more efficiency-minded or professional management encouraged the larger agricultural units, in which alone serious improvements could be attempted. This was a slow progress, and the squeeze it imposed on small farmers was still relatively light in the 1680s, compared with the great bear hug into which it had developed by the second half of the next century. But copyholders and small peasant proprietors did find it much harder to survive than before 1640; and to an extent this was true of the small tenant farmer, too, for landlords had a strong motive, at a time when rents were hard to raise, to consolidate two or more farms into one when leases fell in or when tenants prematurely gave up the unequal struggle.

Apart from the continuing process of land reclamation, the agrarian advances which characterised this period were in four main areas : enclosure, animal feeding, soil fertilisation and grain supplies. The natural tendency of economic historians to concentrate on the tangible evidence either of vociferous opposition to enclosure or of enclosure acts on the statute book has, until very recently, obscured the strong claims of the seventeenth century to have been the most active century of all in the long history of England's enclosure movement [K.3]. The years 1650–90 were almost certainly one of those phases of maximum activity in land enclosure by private agreement which occurred periodically from the early sixteenth to the late eighteenth century (217a; 170a, *123–4*). Significantly, they were also important in signalling an unequivocal change of attitude from Westminster. A generally laissez-faire attitude characterised Restoration Parliaments, and governments, in their approach to many aspects of the domestic economy, in sharp contrast to their attitude to overseas trade. No attempt was made to renew or even properly enforce the existing anti-enclosure legislation which had gone on to the statute book between the reign of Henry VII and the 1590s. There were no more commissions of enquiry into the practice on the earlier Stuart paternalist model, and no further government prosecutions of enclosing landlords. The defeat in 1656 of the last parliamentary attempt to regulate enclosures set the tone for the new era. Social conscience and fear of unrest caused by rural depopulation had finally given way to hard-headed recognition of the economic benefits of a practice which so obviously encouraged convertible husbandry and vastly improved the quality of pasture land. Midlands graziers were among the major groups of owners and farmers who were to benefit significantly from the new climate.

One example of parliamentary intervention did, however, have most important effects for domestic agriculture. The Irish Cattle Act (above, p. 6) provided a valuable stimulus for cattle rearers, in relatively backward areas like the North-West, though it was less popular among prosperous southern graziers (10, *155–9, 806–7*; 211, *II, 349–55*). Yet what counted in the end was home demand. Higher real incomes, as labour grew scarcer and its value rose, substantially increased meat consumption in the second half of the seventeenth century. By the 1690s England had become celebrated all over Europe (perhaps exaggeratedly so) as a nation of meat-eaters.[10] Not only for the big cattle graziers, such as those of the Essex and Kentish marshes, but for lesser men too, the ability to rear fatter stock, to feed more and more of it on the same acreage, and to get as many beasts as possible successfully through the winter, became the key to profit. Hence the attractiveness of new meadow crops, like the clovers and sainfoin introduced from the Continent around 1650, and of root crops for winter fodder. The turnip, whose introduction into Suffolk again dates from the 1650s, found its way into Norfolk in the 1670s and became thereafter inseparably associated with 'Norfolk husbandry'. What fodder crops were to the go-ahead grazier and dairy farmer, better fertilisation was to the progressive arable farmer. The soil of Restoration England was fed as never before. Vast quantities of human as well as animal ordure found their way back to Mother Earth: there was, for example, a flourishing demand among Hertfordshire farmers for London dung. But the merits of lime, and to some extent also of seaweed, ashes and soot were also explored. All were grist to the mill of families like the Verneys, zealous improvers of their Buckinghamshire estates (211, *II, 561–2*). Mixed farming areas discovered their good fortune: for the more cattle that could be pastured, the more manure could be spread on neighbouring fields. Other areas, limestone wolds or chalk downs which for centuries had been regarded as nothing but vast sheep runs, could for the first time be ploughed up, enriched and made to yield reasonable grain crops; a quarter of Salisbury Plain, for example, was converted in this way from 1660 to 1685 (170a, *110–11*).

More fertile soils meant better crops of every variety, including the green and root vegetables for the table that were in mounting demand after the Restoration. But in particular it enabled farmers to grow more corn. The manifest prosperity of King's Lynn and Yarmouth by the late 1680s and 1690s, a prosperity in which wheat and barley exports to the Continent already had some part, is often cited as evidence of the success of the big grain farmers of East Anglia. But it is important to remember that England's solution in this period of an age-old problem – that of raising agricultural productivity to the point at which a population of little more than 5 million was not only guaranteed a comfortable surplus in an average year but at least a bare sufficiency in a bad one – was contingent on much more than an expansion of wheat output in her more favoured regions. At least as significant was the success of her farmers, including those in less favoured counties, in increasing production of the lesser or coarser grains, rye and oats, as well as barley, on which the poor still so heavily depended.

No picture, however brief, of the development of English agriculture between 1660 and 1690 would be complete without reference to two other features. A marked characteristic of this period, and one that was to spill over into post-Revolution England, was the extent to which the improving ideas just mentioned, and many others besides (for instance, the flooding of water meadows, crop rotation and a more scientific approach to fruit growing), were propagated by an assiduous generation of agricultural propagandists. The Royal Society (above, pp. 3, 4), founded in 1660, had an active agricultural and horticultural committee (211, *II, 562–8*). Of various innovations for which it is given much credit, perhaps the most important was the commercial growing of the potato in the north of England and the Fenlands as an insurance against grain harvest failures. Individual proselytisers whose writings had well-documented influence in promoting change and breaking down local traditionalism included Evelyn, Yarranton (*Treatise on Clover*, 1668), Worlidge, and, above all, Houghton (see below, 9n.). The second feature is necessary to redress the balance of what has so far been said. Despite the efforts of the literary improvers, the forward thrust of the Agrarian Revolution, in this first stage as in later stages, had a heavily localised bias. Especially as far as arable farming was concerned, its benefits were mainly concentrated down to 1690 in two regions which partly overlapped: those counties with ready access, by sea, river or land, to the vast London market and to the new Dutch and German grain buyers; and the light-soil areas – mostly in the south, as far west as Dorset and the Cotswolds, in the south Midlands, and in parts of eastern England. The lands of owners and farmers on the great Midlands clay belt, however, were far from untouched by the hand of progress, for this was the prime enclosing region of seventeenth-century England, a fact which had vital implications both for its big sheep and cattle raisers and for the spread of convertible husbandry (210).

III

The years from 1660 to 1688 have not, on the whole, been singled out as one of those special periods of enterprise and expansion in English industry which punctuated the long prologue to the late eighteenth-century birth of the world's first industrial nation. The Elizabethan age, the years from 1690 to *c*. 1720, and the period from the 1740s to the 1760s, have all attracted attention in this respect; Restoration England, much less by comparison. Yet bearing in mind the dislocation which industry had suffered in the 1640s, and the subsequent effects of a serious trade depression from 1658 to 1663, the achievements of English manufacturers under Charles II and James II were considerable. They could be measured in terms not just of rising output, but of the range and variety of the goods produced and the techniques used in their production.

Markets as usual were the key to performance, and from the late 1660s, at the very latest, they became exceptionally promising in several respects. As we shall see (Ch. 3), changes took place in overseas markets between then and the late 1680s which have justifiably been described as 'revolutionary'. Of late, however, scholars have been disposed to attach equal weight to the buoyancy of the home market at this very same time. With labour scarcer, wages either rising or appreciating in real value [M.2], the prices of many commodities (especially foodstuffs) lower by the 1680s than in living memory [M.1; K.2(ii)], and much new wealth being generated by trade, and as time went on by industry itself, there was some surplus purchasing power even among the humbler classes of the population. From craftsmen in basic trades such as joinery and bricklaying, down through artisans and small farmers to domestic servants and wage labourers, wherever the breadwinners were in fairly steady work, demand for English manufactured goods increased. Families found that they could buy more, and sometimes better, clothing – serges from time to time, for instance, instead of the traditional kerseys; more boots and shoes, or the worsted stockings which for the first time could be cheaply produced on the new stocking-frames; more tobacco and sugar, both of which, though imported raw, had to be industrially processed before being retailed; more hardware, cutlery, household utensils, even clocks; and possibly for the first time – depending on transport costs – coal for their grates. Contemporaries were startled to observe, also, that 'the poorer sort' were beginning to cross the once unthinkable frontier between necessities and minor luxuries: wearing 'Brummagem' [Birmingham] buckles on their shoes, for example, or Manchester ribbons on their hats (175, *173–80*; 186b, *149*; 170b, *30–1*; 173, *186*). On a more specialised level, as the acreage of land reclaimed for or converted to arable use grew, so also did the market for agricultural implements.

Two further ingredients in the late seventeenth-century economy strengthened the pull of domestic demand. The broad middling bands of urban society were manifestly more prosperous in 1688 than in 1660, and in some sectors at least had grown in numbers (see Ch. 4). Their more sophisticated tastes, natural wish to ape the fashions of the social élite, and therefore increased demand for superior and luxury manufactures, gave a significant boost to certain branches of industry. And in the meantime the increased *capacity* to purchase, among both lower and middle orders of Restoration society, was being crucially enhanced by improved *opportunities* to purchase. Retail outlets were multiplying: not only did many new shops open in provincial market towns after the Restoration, but an army of peddlars and a whole irregular cavalry of petty chapmen continued to create a distribution network which 'did indeed cover the remotest areas of the whole Kingdom'. To the chapmen especially has been allotted a key rôle in what Margaret Spufford has called 'the great reclothing of rural England' in the seventeenth century.[11]

Three brief examples illustrate how important was the industrial impact of domestic market forces. The most rapidly expanding branch of the textile industry in the second half of the seventeenth century was the manufacture of Norfolk worsted 'stuffs', commodities aimed mainly at the middle and lower middle range of consumers. Before the Civil Wars, a majority of the cloths finished in Norwich were sent out for export, mostly through London. By 1690, at the end of two decades in which the population of Norwich itself had risen by an estimated 8,000 (equivalent in itself to the population of Salisbury and greater than that of Leeds), an overwhelming proportion of the stuffs, possibly 90 per cent, was absorbed by domestic demand (246 [Corfield], *279–80*). To the west, this was a period of ample work and rising material standards for the metal workers of the Black Country; but the full order books of one group of them, the master scythesmiths of Worcestershire and Warwickshire, put them on a different plane from their neighbours, save the great forgemasters and ironmongers (186b, *31, 41, 48 etc.*). The reaction of the coal industry to home demand can be seen rather more as a development of an earlier seventeenth-century syndrome than the two previous examples, but it is compelling none the less. In the late 1650s Newcastle upon Tyne had shipped coastwise 412,000 tons of coal annually, an increase of 38 per cent in 30 years. By 1682–3 shipments had reached 559,000, all but 29 per cent going to London (168, *84*; 218b, *117*), while the port of Sunderland, reported by Ralph Thoresby in 1682 to have 'of late grown to a considerable repute and resource for coals and salt',[12] was now sending out a further 120–130,000 tons from the Durham mines. But as well as the expansion of the great north-eastern field – roughly 1.1 million tons on average being raised annually through the 1680s, of which an estimated 300,000 tons was consumed by local industries (such as the Shields salt pans) and domestic users[13] – many new mines were opened and existing ones further exploited from 1660–90 in other coal-bearing areas [L.3], such as South Yorkshire and the West Midlands, West Cumberland and South Wales (207a, *I, 52–72*). Some estimates (admittedly speculative) have put the total increase in annual production between 1660 and the 1680s in the region of three quarters of a million tons (168, *167*).

The development of foreign and colonial markets, which will be analysed in the next chapter, was of great moment to the post-Restoration textile industry. Regions which specialised in the lighter-weight and more gaily-coloured cloths profited most, but were not the only centres to benefit. 'Salisbury Whites', along with 'Stroudwater Reds' and other finely dyed and dressed West Country broadcloths, gobbled up a large share of the quality Levant market[14] [J.3.C(iii)], while the Spanish trade offered a lifeline to Essex bays. It was a mark of the exceptional competitiveness of the serge industry of Devonshire, the most flourishing textile region of the period next to Norfolk, that it was able to send most of its exports to traditional homes in Germany and Holland, despite increasingly adverse tariffs. Although British settlers in North America cannot have numbered more than a quarter of a million by 1688, their needs already provided a valuable extra stimulus not only to English clothiers, especially those of Lancashire, but to the hardware and metal-working industries. The nailers of Walsall and other Black Country towns, for instance, had already had cause to bless the operation of the 'Navigation' system (Ch. 3), and they were to have much more in decades to come. Nor was it only as additional export markets that the new overseas territories of the Crown proved their value to post-Restoration industry. They began to make a contribution, though as yet a relatively small one, to that steep rise in the volume of industrial raw materials which was a feature of England's import trade in the last thirty to forty years of the century (170b, *66*; 199a, *151*). The most valuable of all late seventeenth-century imports in terms of its industrial benefits, however, was unrecorded in the Customs books. Well over 50,000 Continental immigrants settled in England between the Restoration and 1689, many of them in the 1680s, and without them domestic industry would have been less successful in responding to market demand. Their particular contribution lay in helping to launch new manufactures and in enabling established industries to increase the diversity of their products. The Walloon settlers of Elizabeth I's reign had been largely responsible for the rise of the New Draperies in England. The Huguenots and other Protestant refugees entering the country under the later Stuarts brought with them skills and techniques far wider in range, and in addition vastly more business capital than their predecessors. Porcelain and fine glass manufacture were among the novel luxury industries which benefited, as did clock and watchmaking and the production of precision instruments. Huguenot or Flemish influence was especially vital, however, to three industries, fine silk, white paper and the manufacture of high quality linen (171, *103–4*). Although still fledglings in 1688 they were poised for flight in the favourable climate of the years 1689–1713, when French competition was eliminated (Ch. 19). The contribution of the Huguenots has sometimes been exaggerated: it was less essential, for example, in the launching of the new white paper industry (1675–86) than in its early technical development, and by no means central in the establishment of calico-printing works in London from the 1670s, one of the major new departures (for England) of this period.[15] Certainly in the cloth industries – still the great bedrock of the manufacturing economy – many of the most notable innovatory achievements were wholly, or largely, indigenous. This was true of the many experiments with new cloth dyes, a matter in which the Royal Society took a keen interest, and a highly important, if unglamorous, aspect of the late seventeenth-century process of diversification. There was also by 1690 a far greater variety of textile 'lines' on offer, to titillate both home and overseas customers, than had been the case in 1660, and they were predominantly the fruits of domestic enterprise. Inventories taken of the stocks of Norwich worsted weavers in 1674 and 1692 included, Dr Corfield tells us, 'damasks, russells, satins, tamines, cheyneys, callimancoes, crapes, camblets, jollyboys, druggets and faringdons'; only the crape, a Huguenot-inspired innovation, was a new type of fabric; the rest were ingenious native refinements on older themes (246 [Corfield], *281–2*). Worsteds had established themselves by the 1680s in the Halifax area and were to transform the prospects of the West Riding cloth industry over the next sixty years. Lancashire fustians, now made from east Mediterranean or West Indian cotton together with Irish or German linen, were beginning to penetrate new markets, as were Manchester smallwares, which had a rather longer pedigree.

The success enjoyed by 'Manchester ware' in the 1680s (for instance, in selling to North America and the West Indies) (189b, *92n.*) illustrates two further aspects of industrial progress in this period which we must touch on in conclusion. In the first place, it was the introduction of Dutch engine looms, and their grouping together in workshops [L.2], which was largely responsible for the cheapness and popularity of Manchester tapes and ribbons, and these looms proved crucial at much the same time in increasing the output of the silk-throwing workers of Spitalfields and Canterbury. Their installation underlines the unaccountable neglect of the post-Restoration decades in many general surveys of industrial technology before the late eighteenth century, for indeed, there was notable technical advance in many quarters. It can be seen in the switch to lead pans in salt-works (173, *201*); in the plant of the new sugar refineries, and in the use of engines rather than knives in the tobacco processing works of Bristol, London and Liverpool (10, *332–3*). It was no less evident in the rapid spread (though not the invention, which was pre–1660) of stocking-frame knitting, a phenomenon that was to be of the utmost importance to the industrial development of the North and East Midlands throughout the later seventeenth and eighteenth centuries, or again in the new techniques of clockmaking, which so lowered production costs as to enable the clock to become a regular feature of the inventories of quite humble households by 1688.[16] In some ways the most significant technical breakthrough of the period was the successful development (1670s-early 1690s) of the reverberatory furnace, which made it possible for coal fuel to be used in the smelting of lead, tin, copper and brass, in much the same way as the earlier invention of the 'closed crucible' had enabled coal to be employed in the glass works of Newcastle upon Tyne, Stourbridge and Lancashire (170b, *44–5, 86*; 173, *202*). Unfortunately, the problem of using coal in the blast furnaces of the much bigger iron industry continued to prove intractable, and with iron-masters still dependent on dwindling charcoal supplies (the old Wealden iron industry virtually collapsed between 1660 and 1689), they were quite unable, despite building much larger furnaces, to keep pace with the rising demand of the ironworkers and smiths for bar and rod iron, and about half the latter's needs had to be met by a rising volume of imported iron, especially from Sweden (170b, *46, 55*; 205).

Finally, we may note a second respect in which the introduction of the Dutch engine loom points to a more general trend in the post-Restoration economy. In common with the large new 'sugar houses' of Liverpool, Bristol and Glasgow, with the tobacco-cutting engines, and indeed with a good deal of successful traditional industry too, it was to be found in an urban setting. The population of Manchester itself, one of the two chief repositories of the looms, increased by 60 per cent in the forty years after the Restoration [B.2(ii)]. Towns like Tiverton as well as cities like Norwich seethed with weavers in the 1680s, as well as accommodating the finishing processes of their industries. Serge-making, at one stage or another, already employed three-quarters of the inhabitants of Exeter. Smiths and grinders had possession of Birmingham and Sheffield, and brewers of Southwark. Of course, country cottage industry was still the norm in many manufacturing regions, and the rural river valley was still the natural habitat of iron smelting and forging, as of the new water-powered paper mills, but a different age was already being foreshadowed (Ch. 19; *The Age of Oligarchy*, Ch. 11).

---

1. *The Earliest Classics: John Graunt and Gregory King* (Pioneers of Demography, 1973), pp. 120, 275.
2. See *The Parliamentary Diary of Narcissus Luttrell* (ed. H. Horwitz, Oxford, 1972), pp. 112–46 *passim*.
3. Gregory King, *Natural and Political Observations* (1696), p. 36, printed in *The Earliest Classics* (see note 1 above).
4. For contemporary reception of the results of this survey, and the general belief that it had *under*estimated those of communicant age even in dioceses which had made full returns, see A. Whiteman, ed., *The Compton Census of 1676: A Critical Edition* (1986), Intro., esp. pp. lxxix–lxxxii.
5. Wrigley and Schofield (196), p. 423, Figure 10.8. For those born between 1700 and 1775, the average age of first marriage fell from almost 28 to under 26 (men) and from 26 to 24 (women).
6. P. Slack, 'The Disappearance of Plague: an Alternative View', *EcHR*, **34** (1981); cf. A.B. Appleby, 'The Disappearance of Plague: a Continuing Puzzle', *EcHR*, **33** (1980). For the classic recent study pre-1660, see P. Slack, *The Impact of Plague in Tudor and Early Stuart England* (1985).
7. Leeds, for instance, was already growing by 'natural increase' in the late 17th century. Hey (185) p. 234.
8. The rough estimates in this paragraph are based partly on the house totals, county by county, included by John Houghton in his *Account of the Acres and Houses, with the proportional Tax, etc. of each County* (1693).
9. John Houghton, *A Collection for . . . Husbandry and Trade*, (ed. Bradley, 1728) IV, p. 56; Thirsk (212), pp. 561–2.
10. John Macky, *A Journey Through England* (1722), II, p. 239.
11. T.S. Willan, *The Inland Trade* (Manchester, 1976), Ch. 3, 'Provincial Shops in the Seventeenth Century'; M. Spufford, *The Great Reclothing of Rural England: Petty Chapmen and their Wares in the Seventeenth Century* (1984), p. 21 and *passim*.
12. J. Hunter, ed., *The Diary of Ralph Thoresby*, 2 vols (1830), I, p. 141, quoted T. S. Willan (218b), p. 117.
13. See J.U. Nef (207a), I, p. 36 for these estimates. Nef gives a shipment figure for the decade 1656–65 as 600,000 tons, and a further 150–200,000 tons may be assumed to have been consumed locally at the time of the Restoration.
14. J. de L. Mann, *The Cloth Industry in the West of England from 1640 to 1880* (Oxford, 1971), pp. 19–21.

15. D.C. Coleman, *The British Paper Industry 1495–1860* (Oxford, 1958), Ch. 3; A.P. Wadsworth and J. de L. Mann (189b), pp.130–7.
16. J.D. Chambers, *The Vale of Trent 1670–1800* (1956), pp. 13–16; Rowlands (186b), p.149.

CHAPTER 3

Trade and colonies:
England's 'Commercial Revolution'

I

When the English republic gave way to the restored monarchy in May 1660 it was not only religion, the constitution and the ownership of land (Ch. 1) over which great question marks hung. Trade had been languishing in the late 1650s; the cloth industry was in the doldrums, afflicted in 1650 by one of those troughs of recession which had periodically checked its progress since 1600. Merchants and manufacturers alike were anxious to know whether that natural reaction against the recent past which coloured so much ministerial and parliamentary thinking in the early months of the new regime would extend to the economy too. One question in particular loomed large. Would there be a reversal of one of the boldest of the initiatives of the Commonwealth, the so-called 'Navigation' policies inaugurated in 1650 and 1651 which had launched England's overseas trade, merchant shipping and colonies on a new course? When the Acts of the Rump automatically lost their legal force after May 1660, what then would become of that grand strategy devised by the Rump which had promised, but not yet yielded, the golden prize of maritime and commercial primacy? (135, *52–8*; 14, *144* [Jackson, 'Trade and Shipping']). The answer came with decisive speed. On 13 September 1660 the King touched with his sceptre a new 'Act for encouraging and increasing of shipping and navigation'. It at one and the same time confirmed, modified and developed the trends set nine years earlier. Only three other public measures in the next eighty years – the offer of regal power to William of Orange in 1689, the great finance acts of 1693–4 and the negotiation of the Grand Alliance in 1701 – contributed as much as the 1660 Navigation Act to the forging of a great power out of the metals of Restoration England.

The Navigation policy of the republicans had had two aims, closely interconnected and both backed by a heavy weight of mercantile opinion. One was to break the dominance which the Dutch had established since 1600 over the world's carrying trade. The other was to build up in the process a very large native merchant fleet, a source on which the navy could draw in wartime both for men and ships. Basically, the Navigation Act of 1651, which put teeth into a declaratory Act of the previous year, prohibited foreign ships from taking part either in the English colonial trade or in the carrying of imports to England. These were to be the preserve of English 'bottoms' and seamen. However, to legislate was one thing; to implement was another. The Act was so rigorous and undiscriminating that even after a successful war with the Dutch, the first true 'trade war' in the English experience (1652–4), it was beyond even the power of Cromwell's Protectorate to enforce the Navigation policy properly. It was only when the provisions of 1651 were refined by the Convention's Act of 1660 that this policy could be fully mobilised in the service of economic nationalism and growth.

The chief architect of that Act was Sir George Downing, an Exchequer official and MP for Carlisle (25, *II*, 224–9). A New Englander by upbringing, though not by birth, his character and manners were a poor advertisement for the new college at Harvard. Pepys, who served under him for a while, loathed him and there were few men in Restoration politics more unpopular. But Downing had the shrewdest economic sense of any Englishman of the 1660s or 1670s and his grasp of the realities of contemporary trade had been sharpened by first-hand observation of Dutch commercial methods while serving as the government's Resident at the Hague,1658–60. A favourable balance of payments was for him the only sure way to economic health, and England in 1660 had a balance of payments problem, the root of which was inadequate shipping resources [J.3.B]. Despite the 1651 Act and the heavy captures of enemy vessels in the First Dutch War, many more merchant ships were needed. Equally important was the need for the right kind of ships. Over decades the Dutch had capitalised on their skills in building capacious but lightly manned and unarmed ships – the 'flyboats'. The English were good at building great East Indiamen, bristling with cannon, or alternatively, small coasters, but not cheap, ocean-going carriers with ample hold space for bulk cargoes. Their ships, which vainly tried to compete with the Dutch for the coveted Baltic trade were, Downing contemptuously told Clarendon, 'rather tubs than ships' (135, *42*, *95*). Ships alone, however, could not remedy the current economic depression. The largest merchant fleet in the world could not bring succour to the cloth industry, for instance, simply by carrying its products to those traditional markets in western and northern Europe which had once been so profitable but were now fast shrinking and highly competitive. Everything possible, therefore, must be done to encourage further the already promising trade with other parts of Europe, and with countries far beyond Europe. But the best remedy for revival and the surest guarantee of future health, Downing argued, lay in developing London, and even other English ports, as entrepôts. Another of Holland's immensely profitable rôles since the early seventeenth century had been to act as an intermediary through which both imports and exports passed. England, by exploiting her colonies with her own merchant ships, must steal the Dutch thunder. The produce of North America, the West Indian islands and the East, and in the other direction, those continental manufactures which the transatlantic colonies needed and could not obtain direct from England, must be the lifeblood of a great English re-export trade.

In framing the Navigation Act of 1660 and its ancillary statutes down to 1663 it was such practical considerations as these, rather than theoretical mercantilism, which Downing and his collaborators kept in mind.[1] The Navigation Act itself was complex and extraordinarily wide-ranging [J.1(i)]. But it was in two major refinements of the precedents of 1651 that its principal significance for the future lay. In place of the unworkable prohibition of *all* imports carried in foreign ships there was now introduced selective prohibitions or deterrents. About half Europe's trade to England was affected by these provisos, which included double customs duties specified on 'alien' goods if they were not imported in English-owned or -manned ships. And, significantly, most of the commodities fully discriminated against were bulk cargoes [see J.1 (*i*), cl. (5), (6)], which would stimulate demand at home for sheer tonnage and which so far had been mainly carried by the Dutch. Even more important were the changes in the 1651 provisions relating to the transatlantic 'Plantations' and the trade with the Asian and African trading stations. Not only were all imports into England and Ireland from these quarters reserved for English ships (with a concession to Irish and colonial vessels only if their captains and the bulk of their crews were English); in addition, all the most important colonial goods, including industrial raw materials like dyestuffs and cotton-wool, [ibid. cl. (8)], could only be shipped *directly* either to England and Ireland or to another English plantation. Here we see both the shipping and the entrepôt purposes of the legislation being equally served.

As Charles Wilson has observed, 'the Act of 1660 was not the end of the new policy: it was only the beginning' (135, *101*). Other measures quickly followed. The most notable was the Staple Act (1663), which completed the main framework of the 'Old Colonial System' by stipulating that the colonists must purchase all the European goods they needed (principally manufactures) in England [J.1(ii)]. So from now on the Mother Country would serve as an entrepôt in both directions, importing those manufactures she herself could not produce (for example, fine linens from Holland) in order to re-export them, at a profit and at prices high enough to ensure an advantageous position in the transatlantic market for English native products (14, *145* [Jackson]). To the mercantile stronghold erected between 1660 and 1663 Ireland, as a valuable economic appendage, was given a third-class ticket of admission, partly cancelled in 1671 (above, p. 7). The more competitive Scots, on the other hand, were almost totally shut out by a thoroughly nationalist Westminster parliament. The repercussions were not for many years disastrous: indeed, enterprising Glasgow merchants were able to exploit the grudging concessions made to Scottish salt and fish to work up a small but prized illegal trade in tobacco and other colonial goods. But the exclusion rankled; it provoked retaliatory measures from Edinburgh, and eventually, as Scotland's Continental markets shrank, it became very serious (282). Although Charles II's own hankerings after an economic union between his two kingdoms proved premature, the Navigation policies did give Scotland a powerful shove along the later stretches of the road which led to the union of Parliaments and the state of 'Great Britain' in 1707.

For England their effects were obviously more direct and, despite ten years of widespread evasion of the Staple Act by colonial merchants (14, *146*), infinitely more dramatic. During the first part of the eighteenth century many English writers and politicians were to look back on the closing decades of the seventeenth century as a period of both economic and social transformation, certainly as a period when England's merchants and manufactures had first seized the commercial leadership of the world. Daniel Defoe's *Compleat English Tradesman* is redolent with such assumptions, and so are other writings of his in the 1720s, such as *The Plan of an English Commerce* and even parts of the famous *Tour through . . . Great Britain.* Soon afterwards the term which modern historians have eagerly borrowed to convey the scale and consequences of these changes, 'Commercial Revolution', was first anticipated by contemporaries. To the spacious mind and epigrammatic pen of a Bolingbroke such a concept seemed wholly appropriate to describe England's upsurge of prosperity before the French wars of 1689–1713. The danger, of course, for the historian in appropriating words such as 'revolutionary' and applying them to phenomena of an economic, social or institutional nature is that they can too easily obscure evolutionary and comparative developments that are essential to understanding them. Critical though the Navigation policies of 1651–63 clearly were in stimulating the unprecedented commercial activity of the next quarter of a century, many of the preconditions of rapid economic growth were already present at the Restoration. Some had already been anticipated by the United Provinces, while in England itself one has to go back almost a hundred years before the first Navigation Act to find the earliest seeds of the late-seventeenth century 'Commercial Revolution' being sown.

II

The disastrous slump in the heavy woollen cloth industry in the later years of Edward VI's reign and the drying up of its Antwerp market necessitated a painful period of reappraisal and reorientation in the English economy. Out of this, between the reign of Mary Tudor and the last years of Elizabeth I, emerged a complex of essentially new developments which prepared the ground, first for a gusty, uneven phase of economic expansion under the early Stuarts, and ultimately for the spectacular growth of the 1670s and 1680s. Four of these developments are of particular relevance to us: the search for and opening up of new markets for English goods; the rise of the 'New Draperies'; the foundation of new trading companies, and the beginnings of colonisation.

Partly through voyages of discovery, partly by following trails already laid by others, markets were sought both in the remoter parts of Europe and much further afield. By the early seventeenth century attention had come to focus on four areas in particular: on Spain and other parts of southern Europe, which appeared to offer the most enticing prospects of all; on the east Mediterranean seaboard – Turkey and the Levant; on America, and on India. And it was on trade with these areas – supplemented by contacts with Northern Europe and Africa – that England's commercial achievements after 1660 largely hinged. Of supreme importance to the initial penetration of all these markets were the lessons learned by the English cloth industry in the second half of Elizabeth's reign, with the introduction of the 'New Draperies' by Protestant immigrants from the Continent. These were lighter, cheaper types of fabric than the old broadcloths and kerseys, more adaptable to changing European fashions, but above all more appropriate to the next century's new markets in the Iberian and Mediterranean lands, in the Orient and, later, in the warmer-climed transatlantic colonies. Significant too, in the longer term, for English commerce was the greater diversification of English manufactures in the late sixteenth and early seventeenth centuries and the technical progress made in non-textile branches, such as coalmining, glassmaking and metallurgical crafts (170b, *64–6*).

Meanwhile, new trading companies had appeared to meet the challenges and exploit the opportunities of far-flung markets [J.3.A(i), (ii)]. The most vital development for the future was the rise of the joint-stock company between 1553 and 1601. The Muscovy and Levant Companies pioneered the new model, and in turn inspired the East India Company, which was chartered towards the end of Elizabeth's reign and inside two decades became a major force in world trade. No longer need investment in overseas trade be confined to merchants alone: anyone with capital could buy his shares. Furthermore, long and dangerous voyages could now be financed by big capital, company capital, capable of securing the trade by establishing 'factories' or trading stations at the other end. And round the more powerful trading companies[2] political pressure-groups gelled, to whose promptings much of the so-called economic 'policy' of seventeenth-century English government was probably related.

Finally, the idea that Englishmen might establish not just trading posts but *colonies* overseas, having first taken root in the second half of the sixteenth century, began to be translated into reality in the first half of the seventeenth [J.2]. The settlement of the North American seaboard, begun with the foundation of Virginia in 1606–7, continued apace, and the heavy Puritan emigration of the 1630s increased its impetus. The colonisation of the West Indies began with the appropriation of St Kitts and Barbados in 1624–5. When the civil wars broke out in 1642, therefore, England and her new overseas possessions, with their 50,000 transatlantic settlers, and her Mediterranean and Indian trading stations, already formed a very promising springboard from which a more dramatic leap forward might be made at some time in the not-too-distant future. And while economic progress was held back in the 1640s by acute political instability, events in the 1650s, quite apart from the Rump's commercial legislation, ensured that long-term prospects would be brightened rather than dimmed by the Interregnum. The English merchant fleet, for instance, was augmented by heavy captures in the First Dutch War of 1652–4 [J.3.B];[3] and in 1655 Jamaica, a large island of great potential profit in the inner Caribbean, was seized from Spain. It has been estimated that by 1660 the population of the English West Indian islands had reached 55,500, of whom already over 22,000 were negro plantation slaves shipped in from Africa (201).

III

The first great phase of the English 'Commercial Revolution' (alternatively we can think of it as the *seventeenth*-century revolution, as distinct from its eighteenth-century successor after 1745) started in the late 1660s, when a trade revival began which, with only occasional setbacks, lasted until about 1690. Except for one outstanding feature that had scarcely any genuine precedent – a massive boom in re-exports that was to surpass Downing's wildest dreams – it was characterised mainly by a rapid acceleration of trends already in evidence before 1660. The Navigation policy, as soon as conditions were right after the second Dutch War of 1665–7, supplied the sudden pressure on the accelerator. But what kept the accelerator down for more than two decades, with some help from further government or parliamentary measures [e.g. J.1(iii)], was two factors which crucially governed supply and demand in these years. One was a fresh burst of colonisation (1663–82) , initiated by the acquisition of the Carolinas and accompanying the rapid economic development of the existing colonies [J.2]. The other was that changing pattern of home demand in Restoration England already noted (Ch. 2).

The unquestionable rise in real incomes in England after 1660, as cereals and some staple manufactures grew cheaper, had knock-on effects that were by no means confined to stimulating domestic industry. It also helped to create mass demand for certain imports, especially colonial and 'Company' imports; so much so that Donald Coleman has characterised the transformation of English trade from the 1670s to the 1740s as essentially "an 'import-led' advance" (168, *137*). But consumer habits at home did much, indirectly, to encourage exports too, since, for example, the new textile fabrics that were produced initially to satisfy the changing tastes of the home market, such as Norfolk 'stuffs' (above, p. 53), soon proved highly attractive to foreign and colonial customers. Even the cold countries round the Baltic seaboard rediscovered their liking for English cloths when Devonshire serges and perpetuanos came on to the market (170b, *148*). Lady Fashion was a capricious creature, however, not easily tamed. There were some domestic tastes, like the increasing use of fine linen among the 'middling sort' and the passion for silks, brocades and velvets among the wealthy, which simply could not be satisfied as yet by English manufacturers. And so, at some peril to Downing's 'balance of payments', the linens had to be shipped in large quantities from Holland and Germany (by the end of the century the linen import bill was not far short of £1 million a year) (170b, *Table XVI*) and the fine silks either from France (except in years of trade embargo), from Italy, or latterly even from India, where they had to be paid for usually by bullion (14, *151* [Jackson]).

It was a source of chagrin to most writers on economic affairs between 1660 and 1690 that the balance of trade with France, particularly after Colbert's tariff walls went up, remained seriously unfavourable to England. Quoting a string of figures produced by Samuel Fortrey, Dr Edward Chamberlayne came to the gloomy conclusion in 1694 that before the Glorious Revolution 'the nation was yearly impoverished by the French trade, £1,600,000 per annum. Thus our gold and silver was exported to fetch from thence strong drink and fripperies, to the debauching and emasculating our bodies and minds.'[4] Significantly, no contemporary made a similar complaint about Italy. The spectacular part played in the Commercial Revolution by trade with southern Europe exemplifies very well how trends already set in a more modest way before 1640 became of decisive importance after 1660. Of all the changes in traditional trading patterns pioneered before the Civil Wars few had become so prized by the second half of the seventeenth century as the exploitation by English manufacturers and merchants of new markets south of the Alps and the Pyrenees; farther afield, in Asia Minor and, through Iberia, in the Spanish and Portuguese colonies. Devonshire and East Anglia owed much of their late seventeenth-century prosperity (Ch. 2) to the popularity of serges, 'stuffs' and bays with their southern European customers. In 1600 only one-tenth of English cloth sent abroad had gone to southern Europe and the East Mediterranean, but by 1640 the proportion was already approaching one-third. The further substantial increase after 1660, therefore [J.3. C(ii)] has to be seen as a natural progression, as was the parallel growth in the coveted cargoes, including essential industrial raw materials such as Levantine silk and dyestuffs, Turkish cotton and Spanish short wool which English merchants brought back from these same countries in their ships' holds.

Up to a point the same can be said of a second outstanding feature of the Commercial Revolution, the expansion of trade beyond Europe. To label this crudely 'the colonial trade' would be very misleading, for two essentially different streams of commerce were involved: trade with 'the Plantations' – the colonised lands in North America and the West Indies – and trade with the various 'stations' in Asia and, later, West Africa. Dominating the Asian stream was India, where the East India Company had its principal trading posts but where only Bombay (ceded by Portugal in 1661) was a Crown possession. All these transoceanic areas, India as yet excepted, afforded consumer markets of growing importance for English exports, but it was not until the second great wave of commercial growth began to build up in the eighteenth century that this rôle became premier. It was imports and re-exports from across the Atlantic and from the Orient which made the great impact after the Restoration, dramatically so in the years between 1670 and 1690, when it was reinforced by the African slave trade. Manifestly a child of the Navigation Act, which illegalised the activities of the Dutch slavers who had hitherto supplied the labour needs of the British planters, the slave trade was not just a two-way affair between Africa and Barbados or Jamaica; it was normally a 'triangular' venture in which the slave ships carried metals or textiles to Africa before transporting their all-too-perishable human cargo across the Atlantic, and finally carrying sugar back from the Caribbean to England.[5]

Sugar was one of three extra-European commodities that were far ahead of all others in the van of late seventeenth-century commercial change. The other two were tobacco and East Indian fabrics. The first oriental products to find a serious market in England were spices, pepper and drugs, which began to trickle into the country via the Levant in the late sixteenth century. Under James I pepper began to be shipped in bulk in the holds of the East Indiamen until eventually, by 1675–81, an average of 4.6 million pounds of it was coming into London annually. New drugs, some of them opiates, also figured increasingly prominently on their bills of lading. But in terms of sheer quantity these imports were as nothing to the flood of cheap, attractively coloured Indian textiles, mainly calicoes and chintzes, with which the Company deluged the home market after 1660. Such imports had been negligible before the Civil Wars. They took off in the 1660s, to reach an average of 240,000 cloths a year by 1663–9. By the 1680s even that figure was to seem tiny [J.3.D].

The cultivation of tobacco in Virginia had begun as an experiment in 1614. By

1630 the product was still an aristocratic luxury in England. But so massively did output increase in the second half of the seventeenth century in response to an explosive European demand [J.3.E] that by 1700 tobacco, close on 34 million pounds of it, from Maryland as well as Virginia, was available to almost everyone in the kingdom who desired it. Sugar too had been a scarce commodity at the start of the century, most of it being Brazilian, imported at considerable cost through Portugal. It was not until the 1640s that English colonists in Barbados began to turn land over to the growing of sugar cane. The big profits they soon made encouraged planters in the much larger island of Jamaica to follow suit after 1660. So began the vast sugar boom of the late Stuart period [J.3.F], stimulated by a demand in which two other new 'Company' imports, tea from China and coffee from (at this stage) Arabia, played a significant part, for most Englishmen and women who became snared by the tea and coffee habit would have shuddered at the thought of drinking them unsweetened (292, *45*). Sugar and tobacco lined the pockets not only of the planters, and of the Barbados, Jamaica and Virginia merchants of London, but of the slave traders. By the 1680s the call for ever more slaves to work the sugar plantations had become clamorous; one estimate has put the number of blacks arriving in the English West Indies in the final quarter of the century at 174,000.[6] Much of the eventual success of the Royal Africa Company, the most important joint-stock foundation of Charles II's reign [J.3.A(ii)], clearly stemmed from this, though its members also traded direct from the Guinea coast to London in ivory and gold, as well as carrying on a flourishing export business.

Just over a third of all the imports shipped into English ports in 1700 came from either Asia, the West Indies or North America – another remarkable change in trade patterns, only very faintly foreshadowed before the mid-century upheavals [J.3.D-F]. Yet imports were only part of the story. Above all else it was the *re-export* trade in goods from these different lands which entitles us to discuss commercial changes in the late seventeenth century in terms of 'revolution'. The transatlantic colonies and the Far Eastern trading stations by the last two decades of the century were supplying infinitely more of their prime consumer goods than the English public could possibly absorb. Nine-tenths of the record shipments of pepper coming into London by the late 1670s ended their travels in European warehouses and shops. Most of the coffee followed the same routes (197, *23*). Much more important commercially was the fact that home consumers, despite their rising expectations and purchasing power, could only take one-third of the massive quantities of tobacco being imported by 1700; the other two-thirds were shipped out again to appease a now insatiable continental craving. It was likewise with sugar and with textiles; one-third of the vast English sugar import was being passed on to Europe by the end of the seventeenth century, and of the average of 860,000 East Indian calicoes which came into the port of London annually in the years 1699–1701, two-thirds were re-exported. The entrepôt Downing had dreamed of when the second Navigation Act was being hammered out in 1660 was now an established fact, worth more than £1.6 million a year to England in non-European goods alone (199a; 167).

It has been possible here to highlight only the dominant features of the two decades of unprecedented commercial expansion and change which preceded the Glorious Revolution. Other aspects, less spectacular at the time but at least as important in their long-term significance for the British economy, should not be overlooked, however. The flourishing export trade in manufactures other than woollen and 'medley' cloths is a clear case in point, for that trade almost doubled in value between the late 1660s and the end of the century, responding to an upsurge in demand, especially from the colonies, for such commodities as metalware, hats and clothes, earthenware, paper and leather (199a). The overseas territories and stations also played a growing part in meeting the swelling demand for imported raw materials which marked the same period. During the vigorous trade revival which followed the ending in 1697 of the first great war against France, and which wrote a dynamic epilogue to the first phase of the Commercial Revolution, the volume of such transatlantic and oriental imports for the first time touched a value of over £2 million a year, approximately three-quarters being commodities vital to the progress of the textile industries.

IV

It remains briefly to consider what major implications this 'Revolution' had for later seventeenth-century England. We shall note four particular consequences here, although as subsequent chapters will show, the full catalogue is far more voluminous. In the first place, as one of the foundations of her swift rise to Great Power status between 1689 and 1713 (Ch. 14), England now possessed the most broadly-based economy in the world; her booming entrepôt and re-export business having for the first time, by the end of the century, pushed cloth below 50 per cent of the value of the country's *whole* export trade (a proportion that would have been unimaginable half a century earlier).[7] The second major consequence of the Commercial Revolution that must be emphasised also became one of the instruments of national greatness. To satisfy the needs of an ever-burgeoning commerce English shipbuilders (with much help, prior to 1674, from further wartime captures from the Dutch) had equipped the country by the beginnning of James II's reign with the largest merchant fleet in Europe. Total tonnage had virtually trebled between 1629 and 1686, and had probably doubled since the Restoration [J.3.B]; and those bulk cargo carriers which had been in such short supply at the time of the Restoration were now plentiful (198). Moreover, thanks to the Navigation Acts England had acquired by 1688 by far the most plentiful supply of trained seamen any country could boast.

A third consequence, very different in character but unquestionably profound, stemmed from the capacity of England's overseas trade in the three decades after 1660 to stimulate and to satisfy a whole new range of domestic consumer habits. It needs to be stressed once again that the standard of life which the average Englishman of modest means or better – and even many of the relatively poor – could aspire to by the end of the seventeenth century was on a different plane from that of a hundred, or even sixty years before. A more efficient and productive agriculture certainly had something to do with this (Ch. 2). But for much of the variety and quality in matters of diet and dress it was the Commercial Revolution that was responsible. The south European and east Mediterranean lands, for example, so important economically as markets for English exports, made a telling contribution *socially* with their imports. From Portugal came the new Madeira wine; from Spain came raisins, figs and oranges; from Italy, manufactured silks and olive oil; from Asia Minor, dyestuffs, as well as mohair, raw silk and cotton. It was the transatlantic and East India trade, however, whose social effects were most widely felt. Tobacco was selling in England in the late 1690s at a mere twentieth of what it had cost in 1620: the pipe had become an indulgence which even the very poor could occasionally afford. Tea-drinking was still a relatively expensive habit, but late Stuart London saw coffee-houses spring up literally by the hundred and provincial towns already beginning to ape the capital. The new beverages, as we have seen, along with the greatly increased consumption of both fresh and dried fruit, increased the already heavy demand for sugar. The price of sugar was halved between 1650 and 1688. By 1700 every man, woman and child in England was consuming on average 5 pounds of sugar each year per head, and the average adult almost double that amount. As for the light-weight and gaily-coloured Indian calicoes and chintzes, these first took the fashionable world by storm and then, towards the century's end, 'descended [in Defoe's words] into the humours of the common people' (3, *I, 165*). So extraordinary was their popular success that even the well-established Devon serges and Norwich stuffs began to feel the pinch of their competition and their manufacturers' repeated cries of anguish were eventually to extract discriminatory legislation from Parliament in 1701.

Finally, the Commercial Revolution brought an access of wealth to the merchant class the importance of which can hardly be over-estimated. Naturally much of this new wealth was concentrated in the city of London: after all, the East India Company, the Royal African and the Levant Companies were essentially London monopolies. And it was above all London merchants who, protected by the government's Navigation policies from Dutch competition where it mattered most, were best placed to exploit as middlemen the unprecedented entrepôt possibilities of the new era. None the less, by the 1680s more and more transatlantic goods were finding their way into western ports, particularly into Bristol and (though as yet on a relatively small scale) into Liverpool. From the early 1690s, as will later appear (Ch. 19), this trend was to be sharply accentuated. At the same time Exeter merchants grew rich on serge exports, Hull and Newcastle were able to appropriate an increasing share of the trade with the Baltic and Germany, and other east coast ports further south, especially Yarmouth and King's Lynn, were enjoying a renaissance. At Lynn the harbour front and civic buildings were completely and impressively rebuilt between 1660 and 1690.[8]

There were few, therefore, who failed to reap some benefit from England's Commercial Revolution. Economists might still fret about the balance of trade; politicians and independent merchants might still grumble about the over-dominant rôle of the monopoly companies and strive – as did the interlopers in the slave trade – to undermine it. But no one could rationally deny that England was a far richer country in the late 1680s than she had been in 1660, for the evidence was everywhere palpable: in the conspicuous consumption of her gentry and 'middling sort'; in the rising living standards of yeomen, artisans, craftsmen and even many labourers, and not least, in her possession of a business community which in capital resources and potential for investment was now second to none in Europe. The existence of such a community remained a partially neglected asset in the 1670s and 1680s. It was left to the testing years of war with the mighty power of France after 1689 to reveal its critical importance (Ch. 17).

---

1. Cf. J.O. Appleby, *Economic Thought and Ideology in Seventeenth-century England* (Princeton, 1978); D.C. Coleman, 'Mercantilism Revisited', *HJ*, **23** (1980).
2. Including the Levant Company, even though by the 1590s its members had ceased to 'joint their stocks' [J.3. A(i)].
3. Against these gains must be set the losses caused by the Spanish War later in the decade.
4. Dr Edward Chamberlayne, *Angliae Notitia: or the Present State of England* (1694 edn.), p. 68.
5. See K.G. Davies, *The Royal Africa Company* (1957).
6. P.D. Curtin, *The Atlantic Slave Trade: A Census* (Madison, Wisconsin, 1969), pp. 54–5, cited in C.G.A. Clay (170b), p. 175.
7. In 1640 its share had been well over 80 per cent.
8. V. Parker, *The Making of King's Lynn* (Chichester, 1971), e.g. pp. 152–4.

CHAPTER 4

English society after the Restoration:
stability and change

The five and a half million men, women and children who inhabited England and Wales at the time our period opens lived within a social order which in the previous 120 years had undergone some momentous changes. This fact has been firmly established by an abundance of work directed over the past three to four decades towards the study of society between 1540 and 1640 – 'Tawney's century'[1] – and by exhaustive attention, notably through regional studies, to the period of the Civil Wars and the Interregnum.[2] The basic 'frame' of Tudor and early Stuart society may have been less drastically affected than that of early nineteenth-century England was to be under the impact of industrialisation, but all modern scholars have agreed that many of the component parts of its structure between 1540 and 1660 were unstable, subject to degrees of tension and mobility, rapid expansion or pressurised contraction to which there had been no counterpart in the late Middle Ages. There is much less consensus, however, about what happened to England's social structure after 1660. This is hardly to be wondered at, since it is only in recent times that serious groundwork has been done on the social history of the last century before industrialisation. That *relative* stability returned to English society after the Restoration is not in doubt. This was what the governing classes fervently desired, and for a generation, at least, they were not unduly disappointed. On the other hand, how secure that stability was, how far the social framework of post-Restoration England – and later of Britain – was forced to accommodate itself to new changes, and how successfully it contrived to do so over the next century and a quarter, are all questions which remain more open and which will concern us from time to time in the course of this book.

One thing we can be sure of: changes did take place. Even before the wars with France, beginning in 1689, exposed society once again to exceptional pressures, stability was by no means synonymous with stasis. As for the belief, once widely entertained, that after the Restoration the main social groups settled into a mould that survived more or less unaltered until it was broken by the Industrial Revolution, this no longer bears examination. Why such an orthodoxy proved so durable is hard to explain without reference to the dependence of twentieth-century historians on one fascinating seventeenth-century document – Gregory King's famous table of the social structure of England in 1688, with its 'Scheme of the Income and Expense of the Several Families'. This was drawn up, originally in 1696 and in a revised form in 1698, while King was engaged on his pioneering enquiries into population and national wealth (Ch. 2). And because there exists no comparable contemporary source – none, that is, with serious pretensions to statistical analysis – between 1600 and 1760 (when Joseph Massie attempted an up-dated version of King's table), the 'Scheme' has offered an alluring point of departure for numerous streams of theory and generalisation about pre-industrial society [for both see B.5].

Unfortunately, both the sources on which King's social statistics were based and his methods of deduction from them have turned out on close scrutiny to be highly dubious. This does not mean that all his estimates of the numbers and incomes of families in the various groups identified are automatically invalidated. An attitude of healthy scepticism towards them, however, is the very least that is called for, and even the neat social classifications themselves must be seen for what they were – deliberately simplified to serve the purely practical fiscal ends for which King's table was devised (227, repr. in 16). This said, these same 'social categories, and the seemingly deliberate status-order in which they are arranged . . . [clearly] reflect how the pre-industrial Englishman of a traditionalist cast of mind preferred to think his social order was constituted' (227). An arch-conservative, who had taken part in the last two heraldic visitations ever held in England, in 1684 and 1687, may not have been the man to divine for the historian's benefit the organic social changes still in progress at the time he wrote; but he did, of course, take due account of that great metamorphosis in English society which had already taken place between the later years of Henry VIII, with the release of the monastic lands on to the market, and the restoration of the monarchy in 1660. And it is in the retrospective light it throws on that period – fundamental, of course, to comprehending our own – that the main value of King's table lies.

Movements of seismic scale affected three major social strata prior to 1660, producing respectively the so-called 'rise of the gentry', a prolonged squeeze on the small peasant proprietor and a swelling of that host of landless labourers and 'poor cottagers' at the base of rural society. Changes at three other levels, the post-Tudor expansion of the peerage, the development of the professions, and the growth and diversification of the commercial sector of society, involved smaller numbers but held implications hardly less important for late Stuart and Hanoverian Britain. We shall attempt in this chapter first to view each process with a brief backward perspective from 1660, and then to take a forward glance at the significance of each over the next thirty years.

'The rise of the gentry' has been a matter for strenuous argument since R.H. Tawney identified and labelled the phenomenon almost fifty years ago, designat-ing it one of the great dynamic forces at work in the century before the English civil wars. Debate has ranged over all conceivably relevant ground, from the definition of the gentry and the validity of the evidence deployed to demonstrate its 'rise', to the constructions that ought to be placed on it.[3] But that such a phenomenon did take place, in the sense that despite many goings as well as comings, there was between 1540 and 1640 an extraordinary multiplication of gentry families as well as important structural developments within the gentry class, there can be no possible doubt. Had there been a Gregory King alive to serve Thomas Cromwell in the 1530s, able to analyse and quantify the social groupings of that time, he would certainly not have written down 800 baronets,

600 knights, 3,000 esquires and 12,000 gentlemen; nor would he have given them a joint income remotely near £5 million per annum, or indeed one that, even in the currency of Henry VIII's reign, was some ten times as large as the collective income of the lay peerage.

The creation of the rank of baronet, although in one sense a reflection of James I's financial embarrassments, can also be seen as a symbolic act, a public recognition of the rise of the gentry. A new top rank of commoners came into being in 1611, the only hereditary rank under the peerage. Ownership of land worth at least £1,000 a year – a substantial income in the early seventeenth century – and three generations of armigerous credentials were the minimum qualification for entry, not forgetting the down payment of £1,095 into the Exchequer which was required of the original beneficiaries. Three bursts of reckless creations went some way to debase the honour between 1618 and 1641. But from 1660 to 1688 it became once again a natural aspiration among the wealthiest squires to seek this rank as a signal of their territorial eminence and social superiority. That it did not at once reassert its true status after the Restoration is clearly attributable to Charles II's over-exuberance in distributing his favours to win political support (304 English baronetcies were created from 1660–65) and his scant regard for pure landed pedigrees in the process. What Charles did not do, however, except in rare cases, was bestow the honour on loyalists of self-evidently stricken fortunes.

Indeed, as Dr Roebuck has demonstrated in Yorkshire, the strong demand for baronetcies from families of recent, or even current, commercial stock, ensured a rising not a declining level of wealth among the baronets of the late seventeenth century (241a, *31, 289*; 243a, *Intro.* and *19–20, 29 (Table), 19–42 passim*). So when Gregory King put the mean income of the 800 English baronets of 1688 at £880 he was being quite unrealistic (16, *295* and *n. 61*). It is known that by the early eighteenth century, even in the two most notoriously poor counties in England, Cumberland and Westmorland, £1,000 was a low annual income for a baronet. The hard-pressed cavalier baronets of the late 1640s and 1650s showed a remarkable capacity for recovery: the Hothams of Dalton, for instance, struggling on less than £700 a year after the execution of the first baronet and his son in 1645, had hoisted their annual rental to £1,900 by 1680 (243a, *66, 68*). By then, moreover, trade and, to a minor extent, the law and government office, had pumped into the order a good deal of red financial blood. The wealthiest of the new 'business baronets' by the 1680s were possibly Sir John Banks (£7,500 a year by the second half of the decade), and Sir Josiah Child, the 'sordidly avaricious' Midas of the East India Company;[4] though Sir William Blackett of Newcastle (bart. 1685) must have run them close through the rich harvest of his coal and lead mines. Banks and Child were heavy investors in land, like Blackett's elder brother Edward, heir to a coal fortune and a baronetcy, who built on his great estate at Newby, near Ripon, what Fiennes was to call 'the finest house I saw in Yorkshire' (4, *84–5*). These were exceptional cases, but not unique. By 1688 there was a sizable cluster of major landowners among the baronets whose rent-rolls of £3,000–£6,000 a year made them indistinguishable, save in their lack of formal nobility, from scores of peers. Indeed the West

Country Tory grandee, Sir Edward Seymour, considered himself the equal of a duke.

At the time of the dissolution of the monasteries the cream of the gentry class consisted, as it traditionally had, of the knights and the esquires, perhaps 1,300 in all by 1540; in addition, there were several thousand other recognised gentlemen with landed estates who were armigerous [A]. That was the situation when the great land mania started in the later years of Henry VIII. By 1660 the gentry class had, at the very least, trebled in size; placing the most generous construction on its constituents it may well have quadrupled. There is a school of thought which now argues that, in numerical terms, 'the rise of the gentry' was checked after the Restoration: that by the end of the seventeenth century the number of landed gentry in England and Wales was already lower than it had been in 1660, the result of a combination of adverse demographic factors and a rent famine caused by years of cheap grain (Ch. 2), which affected especially the smaller gentry of comparatively recent vintage (170a, *158–9*; cf. 236b, *65–9*; 190). The question of numbers is virtually certain to remain insoluble. Careful modern estimates of the tally of esquire and gentry families on the eve of the Civil Wars range from 17,000 to 23,000, and there is evidence of an official nature from the beginning of Anne's reign which could indicate a total of (at least) over 25,000.[5] It would, therefore, be folly to build too much on the contemporary estimate of Gregory King for 1688 (16,600 esquires, gentlemen *and knights*), and would seem likely that even the later comparable figure arrived at by Joseph Massie in 1760 (*c.* 18,000) is too low. However, even if there was a slight shrinking of the size of the gentry class between 1660 and 1690, with replacements failing to offset all losses, we can be certain that in three respects its remarkable development in the period 1540–1660 was not reversed.

For one thing, the combined estate holdings of the gentry, which one calculation has put at nearly 50 per cent of the entire acreage of England's cultivated land around 1690 – possibly twice as much as in the mid-fifteenth century – held more or less firm after the Restoration (220a). Secondly, the evolution of the gentry into a much more diffuse and economically complex amalgam than its early Tudor counterparts was confirmed. At the top, the superior esquires now formed, together with the baronets and *some* of the knights, a social élite of commoners in most English and Welsh counties for which it is hard to find a precedent, in terms of size, wealth or political influence, in the magnate-dominated county communities of the fifteenth and early sixteenth centuries. The one group difficult to place in the new order of landed society which had emerged under the Stuarts were the knights, a strangely heterogeneous body. Charles II created a startling number of knights bachelor in the course of his reign, almost half of them from 1661–5 (241a, *492–4*), but among the many London tycoons, provincial merchants and businessmen, and professional men or government officials who received knighthoods from him and later from his brother James were a high proportion who, if they dabbled in the land market at all, did so mainly for residential purposes or to fulfil electoral ambitions (25, *II*, *84–5* – case of Sir R. Clayton). Their involvement in county affairs was usually quite small. There were some spectacular exceptions. Sir Stephen Fox, Paymaster-General to Charles II, having started with virtually nothing, had spent over £100,000 on land, much of it in Wiltshire, by the mid-1680s, and the odious Sir Charles Duncombe, after acquiring manors in the same county, disgorged some £90,000 shortly after the Revolution on the famous Villiers property in Yorkshire, inspiring in the process one of Pope's immortal couplets:

> Fair Helmsley, proud Buckingham's delight,
> Sold to a scrivener or city knight.[6]

At the opposite end of the scale, on the other hand, were the true 'country knights', dozens of representatives of solid county families such as the Goughs of Staffordshire or the Wartons of East Yorkshire. The Wartons indeed were *grands seigneurs* in the East Riding; Sir Michael (knighted in 1666), even when plain 'Mr Warton of Beverley', was 'frequently called the rich Warton, because he was the richest man, for to be a gentleman only, that was in all England, for he was worth fifteen thousand pound a year.'[7]

In any event, it was well below the level of the landed élite, among the ordinary, run of the mill gentlemen, that the biggest long-term social change had taken place since early Tudor times, and this was a change which continued unchecked after 1660. The 'gentry' of Restoration England included many thousands of families which were not armigerous but whose right to gentle status was nevertheless not seriously challenged. Before the Civil Wars the heralds in their visitations of the counties had rejected the claims of such families in droves, but they were fighting a hopeless battle. An integral place in the social structure of late seventeenth-century England was thus held by men whose liberal education, genteel life-style and ability to support a leisured existence entitled them to be styled 'gentlemen', regardless of formal qualifications. Gregory King, like the Westminster legislators who identified them in a series of finance acts passed between 1689 and 1694, referred to these men as 'reputed gentlemen'. Modern historians have called them the pseudo-gentry (221; 222a; 222b, *44–6*). Not all of them were *landed* gentlemen in the traditional mould. The urban gentry, though relatively new arrivals on the social scene in 1660, grew steadily more prominent over the next twenty years for a variety of reasons, of which the difficulty of supporting large families on small or moderate landed estates was only one.

By contrast with the gentry, the numbers and fortunes of the select group of families which by rank stood at the head of landed society between the Restoration and the Revolution are less open to debate, in that period at least. The hereditary peerage had expanded strikingly since the mid-sixteenth century. At the end of 1559 there were only sixty-two English peers, and by the time Elizabeth I died in 1603 the number had fallen into the mid-fifties. As a result of the unprecedented crop of creations in the early Stuart period that number more than doubled, and many Irish peerages were granted too, about thirty of which went to Englishmen whose connections with Ireland were either tenuous or non-existent. Lawrence Stone has stressed how much, between the mid-sixteenth and the mid-seventeenth centuries, the titled aristocracy lost ground, economically as well as politically, before the irresistibly advancing tide of the gentry. All the same, he estimates the mean gross income of 121 English peers in 1641 at £6,060.[8] Between 1660 and 1688 the peerage acquired a net reinforcement of roughly forty new members, with few lean kine among them; the *haute noblesse* of the 1680s, with their often great acreages, increasing recourse to specialised steward- ship, and ability to attract lucrative jobs and marriages in a Restoration world which placed conscious stress on the re-assertion of traditional values and hierarchies, had plainly left far behind whatever traumas they had suffered, as an order, between the late sixteenth century and the closing years of the Republic. Some ex-royalist peers took longer than others to slough the embarrassments incurred from 1642–60. The extravagance of life at Charles II's court inevitably produced a few fresh casualties. But, as landowners, the peers at large proved more resilient than the bulk of the lower and middling gentry or the yeomanry to the buyers' market conditions which prevailed by the 1670s and 1680s (Ch. 2). The equivocations of many of the nobility at the time of the 1688 Revolution (55) were indicative of how much they had to lose by taking a wrong step. Even if we include among the peers at this time, as we should, the thirty-odd holders of Scottish and Irish titles whose main estates and chief residences lay in England, their average gross income must have been at least double Gregory King's cautiously revised estimate of £3,200 a year for 1688.

After the rise of the gentry, no feature of Gregory King's table more firmly signalises a fundamental change in the social order since the early sixteenth century than the importance given to the professions. He rightly picks out five major groups as the architects of this change: holders of government offices; lawyers and legal officials; clergymen; officers in the armed forces; and 'persons in the liberal arts and sciences', made up for the most part of medical prac- titioners, university dons and teachers in grammar schools or other 'secondary' institutions of education [B.5]. If 1540–1640 saw the rise of the gentry, 1580–1680 saw the emergence of the professions as a widening pool of respectable employ- ment, and it was a pool in which not only the sons of the gentry but, still more, those of the bourgeoisie and the prosperous yeomanry could find refreshment, and which was not wholly inaccessible to the upwardly mobile clambering up from more plebeian levels (225, *8–11 and passim*).

By the 1680s every major profession except the ministry of the Established Church had expanded notably in size in response to a steady long-term growth in demand for its services; in the Anglican ministry an equally striking change had taken place – its transformation since the Reformation into a body dominated, by 1680 overwhelmingly, by *graduate*, *preaching*, career clergy, a body which had developed 'a sense of corporate identity' that was unmistakably 'professional' (157, *46–9*; cf. 158a, *42–3*). It was around 1680 that a more spectacular period of expansion in the professions, accompanied by greater diversification and moder- nisation, was just beginning, one that was to continue well into, and ultimately through, the eighteenth century. During that time, also, the rôle of the profes- sions as vehicles of social advancement increased emphatically in importance (226a and b). Yet the foundations of almost every later advance had been laid in the previous century and a half. In 1500 England was still a preponderantly non- literate society. The printing press was a recent novelty; education was conducted by and predominantly for the clergy, and even among laymen of high birth there were still not a few who were barely lettered, let alone 'educated'. Yet seventeenth-century England, as Keith Thomas has written, was able to sustain 'one of the greatest literary cultures ever known and witnessed an unprecedented ferment of scientific and intellectual activity' (149, *4*). A country which had by Charles II's reign a Locke, a Newton, a Wren, a Dryden and a Purcell ready to occupy a stage traversed since 1600 by giants of the stature of Shakespeare, Bacon, Milton and Hobbes was richly endowed indeed. Although England had only her two ancient universities still to set against Scotland's four, they teemed with students well into the 1670s (296c, *37–57*); and a far higher proportion of the country's boys attended grammar schools in the middle decades of the seventeenth-century than was the case in the early twentieth. Basic literacy rates were remarkably high, and the argument that they declined in the later Stuart period is not yet proven (see Ch. 13).

This 'educational revolution', as it has been aptly called (295a) – a process which, so far as the schools at least were concerned, was not over until the late 1720s (226a; also *The Age of Oligarchy*, Ch. 13) – was what basically made possible the flowering of the professions. But of course there were powerful stimuli of a more direct kind. One of these, of prime importance for the future as well as the present by the 1680s, was the needs of the state. On the one hand, government became more ambitious once the watershed of the Henrician Reformation was reached. The 1530s proved to be only the first of several periods of growth, over the next century and a half, in the numbers of those who looked to make *careers*, as opposed to temporary profit, in the administrative service of the state. When much of the Republic's handiwork in this respect perished at the Restoration, it seemed a serious setback to the prospects of such a profession, but in the event, by the 1680s lasting (if still very partial) foundations for a permanent bureaucracy were already being securely laid. There was useful ground to build on from the 1660s and 1670s (Ch. 16), but it was a reforming Treasury from 1679–87, dedicated to the task of making the Stuart monarchy financially viable and inspired by constructive and farseeing ministers such as Rochester and Godolphin [D.1], which played the key governmental rôle in the advance of the late seventeenth-century professions. It is possible to quibble over the use of the term 'civil service' within the context of what Professor Aylmer aptly describes as the 'extraordinary patchwork' of eighteenth-century adminis-tration, with its illogical mixture 'of old and new, useless and efficient, corrupt and honest'. But there can surely be no question that none of the early landmarks on the road to the institutionalised civil service of the nineteenth and twentieth centuries was more important than the creation by Rochester and his colleagues of England's first truly large-scale government department, the Excise (1683) (121; 118; 122).

The decade 1678–88 was a vital one, too, for the professional armed forces of the Crown. A century earlier these had scarcely existed, in the sense of forces guaranteed the continuity on which secure vocational hopes could be based. Little changed before 1640, but much between 1640 and 1660. At the end of Charles I's Personal Rule there was still no standing army, and the fleet of great

East Indiamen built in the past four decades offered far better career prospects for seamen, officers and petty officers alike, than did the King's tiny Ship Money navy. Yet in the 1660s, despite the disbandment of the New Model Army, its officers were able to carry something of their traditions into the new age (Ch. 1); more significantly for the future, there was sufficient continuity between the personnel of the large republican navy and the new Royal Navy, of which Charles II and James II were proud, if not always provident, custodians, for us to regard the reforms of Pepys and the Admiralty after 1677 as consolidating rather than initiating the growth of a professional naval officer corps. Even the army officer – 'the military man' – was considered enough of a permanency in society by 1688 to be accorded separate recognition by the ultra-conservative Gregory King, a fact which reminds us how far the allegedly unconstitutional army which James II maintained from 1685–88 was, in fact, built round the nucleus of his brother's Guards and Tangier regiments (226a, *Ch. 9*; 139a and b; 225 [I. Roy]).

Where it owed nothing directly to the necessities of the state, the rise of the professions owed almost everything, in one way or another, to the changing character and needs of society itself in the late sixteenth and seventeenth centuries. Most obviously, an increasingly educated society needed trained men to educate it. The fellows and professors of Oxford and Cambridge approached 1,000 in numbers by the time of the Glorious Revolution. The mushrooming of public or 'free' grammar schools in the century after 1550, already referred to, created the first recognisable 'teaching profession' of any size, though one that was inchoate and, apart from an élite minority, lowly in status. Its members were heavily supplemented after 1660 by those who taught, not merely in the new and often liberally endowed public foundations of the later Stuart period and in the private schools and academies which this period produced in abundance, but also in the forerunners of those charity schools, elementary institutions dispensing the 'three R's', on which early eighteenth-century society lavished much care and philanthropy (*The Age of Oligarchy*, Ch. 13). At a rough guess, schoolmasters and ushers staffing the grammar schools (some 70 per cent of them still clerics), the private school teachers (increasingly laymen) and those who made a career of teaching in elementary schools of various kinds, totalled somewhere near 10,000 by the end of the 1680s (226a, *Ch. 3*).

If schoolmasters were close to the bottom of the professional pile, lawyers were much more likely to be near the top. The emergence between the early sixteenth and the late seventeenth centuries of a society which was not only literate but highly competitive and economically dynamic had far-reaching implications for the ancient profession of the law. It engendered an extraordinary amount of litigation, especially before 1650; it also produced – in this case more emphatically after than before 1650 – mounting demand for a sophisticated range of non-litigious legal services. Even by the outbreak of the Civil Wars calls to the bar had risen by roughly forty per cent in forty years. But even this rate was outstripped in the clamour of young men to train for the bar in the first decade after the Restoration. The pressure was maintained, though at a rather lower level, almost down to the Revolution, by which time leaner times were in store for the Inns, for, indeed, by 1688 the upper apartments of the common lawyers' profession were bulging at the seams and the number of those actively practising at the bar in the Westminster Courts was already beginning to decline from its seventeenth century peak of 400–450 (226a, *Ch. 4 and 288–9*; 225, [Prest, 'Lawyers']). On the other hand, the 'lesser degrees' of the law, recruited on the whole from more modest social backgrounds, were expanding even faster and with, apparently, no ceiling in sight. Attorneys and solicitors, and in smaller measure notaries and scriveners, had been busily making themselves for a century or more the indispensable factotums of an increasingly complex social order,[9] and both the range and profitability of their activities extended progressively, decade by decade, after 1660 (226b; 226a, *Ch. 4*). Taking in the full gamut of the profession, from judges down to copying clerks and minor court officials, King's estimate of 10,000 'persons in the law' in 1688 may well have been too low. Top barristers could by now earn up to £3–4,000 a year and leading attorneys might aspire to as much as £1,500 or even £2,000.

Finally, it was of great significance to the professions that Stuart England, especially over the second half of the seventeenth century, while maturing culturally and aesthetically was also become increasingly conscious of its comforts and amenities, and less passive in the face of the whims of Fate. The implications of this for the future of, for example, professional architects and musicians had barely been glimpsed by 1688. But in one field, medicine, the consequences were already striking. The boom in the practice of medicine dates from the late sixteenth century. A modern attempt to compile 'A Directory of English Country Physicians'[10] has come up with the names of 814 legally qualified physicians in the provinces alone as early as the period 1603–43. However, the real turning point for the old profession of 'Physic' was to come after 1700, as first the more prestigious Continental medical schools and then the new school in Edinburgh (founded in the 1720s) began to attract very large numbers of British students. Far more numerous in the later seventeenth century were the apothecaries, whose remedies were the resort of middle-class or humbler people, those who could not afford physicians' fees but who came to expect the new remedies, especially the 'exotic' pain-killing drugs from the Orient, which apothecaries could by now offer. In London and its suburbs, where the legal practice of medicine was supposedly confined to the fellows and licentiates of the Royal College of Physicians (136 by 1695), the number of apothecaries' shops had reached almost a thousand by 1704, compared with 104 in 1617,[11] and wealthy apothecaries' houses had by then become a noted feature of many of the larger provincial towns. Though apothecaries still kept their shops, their claim to be an integral part of 'the profession of medicine' was underlined by the action of their London Company in changing its name to 'Society' in the early 1680s. By then there were many licensed surgeons, too, in the provinces (where many already acted as 'general practitioners') as well as in the capital, where the London Company of Barber Surgeons still held sway. The surgeons' image as the 'saw-bones', of whose attentions everyone lived in terror, was slowly changing. As their instruments, techniques and training went through a vital period of development under the last two Stuarts and the early Hanoverians, surgeons grew not only in numbers but in status and made the important transition from superior craft to accepted profession. By the 1720s William Cheselden, a wizard at 'cutting for the stone', was able to charge his wealthier patients £500 an operation, and Thomas Rentone was granted £5,000 from the Secret Service money for developing and publicising new surgical techniques for treating ruptures (226b, *329–30*; 226a, *165–204 passim*).

When seventeenth-century Englishmen referred collectively to 'the middling sort of people' in their society they commonly had in mind, not so much those whom we would now call members of the professions, as men involved, above the level of mere artisans and small retailers, in the various processes of trade and of manufacture. There, as elsewhere, they recognised fine gradations of status, but who occupied the apex of the business hierarchy was in no doubt. Unreliable though Gregory King's statistics are, there is no mistaking the confidence with which he places 'eminent merchants and traders by sea' next in order behind 'gentlemen' and office-holders in the general status-table. Equally significantly, he places them fifth as a group, only narrowly behind the esquires and well ahead of the gentlemen, in terms of average income (£400 p.a.). But at the same time he recognises a much larger body of 8,000 'lesser' overseas and coastal merchants, four times as numerous as their 'eminent' colleagues, though with mean incomes only half as high [B.5]. The Commercial Revolution had brought a great access of wealth since the 1660s to what was already the second richest merchant class in Europe (Ch. 3). How widely this wealth was shared is another matter. Modern research on seventeenth-century merchants (248a and b) suggests two conclusions that are especially relevant here: first, that a large majority of them, even in London, were not men of big fortunes, even at a time when £20,000 marked a man out as a 'rich merchant' (indeed, it is abundantly clear that overseas trading, even in the golden 1670s and 1680s, remained a precarious venture); but also that the rewards of the very successful were princely enough to tempt even wealthy landowners to continue paying high premiums to place their younger sons in prestigious London merchant houses, and occasionally to apprentice them in one of the larger outports. Provincial merchants like a Turner of Lynn, a Maister of Hull or a Colston of Bristol were, after all, major figures in local society, living in the grand style and often marrying into the county gentry. However, in the late as in the early seventeenth century, merchant houses trading abroad recruited much more from within their own class than from any other source.

Because of the diverse ways in which late seventeenth-century industry was organised, men who were described, correctly, as 'merchants' were often to be found involved in the making as well as the marketing of commodities. This was particularly true of textiles. Through the 'putting-out' system fustian merchants, along with 'linen drapers', organised much of the flourishing industry of south Lancashire. Leeds and Exeter merchants were the key figures in the West Riding heavy woollen and the Devonshire serge industries and they usually owned the workshops and mills used in the finishing processes. But whereas many Leeds and Exeter merchants sold cloth directly overseas, the Manchester men, like those in Norwich who marketed Norfolk stuffs, were essentially domestic traders (187b; 189a; 246 [Corfield, on Norwich]). There were, on the other hand, plenty

of industrialists who were patently not merchants: they concentrated on organising and financing manufacture but left the marketing to others. This was generally
true of brewers;[12] of many ironmasters, from great operators like the Foley
brothers, Philip and Paul, to the owners or lessees of modest blast furnaces; of
Gloucestershire and Wiltshire clothiers; or of the Spitalfields silk manufacturers,
the biggest of whom employed 500–600 workers (189b, *106*). The same could be
said of those entrepreneurs (including an appreciable number of immigrants)
responsible for the newer minor growth industries of post-Restoration England
(Ch. 2), among them glassmakers, paper-makers and sugar boilers, operations
which often involved considerable investment in premises and plant.

The hopeful entry '40,000 shopkeepers and tradesmen', to which is attached
an equally speculative average income of £45 a year, is Gregory King's only
remaining concession to 'the middling sort'. It could hardly be more opaque and
unhelpful. It is not just that it conceals the existence of most manufacturers,
given that the line between small manufacturer and superior craftsman was often
a hazy one. It also masks the great variety of men and of levels of wealth involved
at all levels of domestic trade and grossly underestimates their numbers [cf. B.5
for Massie, 1760]. Internal as well as external commerce flourished between 1670
and 1688, and there were no easy classifications to cover those who enjoyed its
prosperity. Their range spanned, for example: London goldsmith bankers of
great fortune, such as Edward Blackwell and the Viners in the 1660s; middlemen
between industry and trade, potentially a highly lucrative occupation, as Blackwell Hall cloth factors and Birmingham 'ironmongers' could testify; the coal
dealers or 'crimps' who distributed Newcastle coal from their Thames-side
wharves; entrepreneurs in agricultural produce, as for instance, Cheshire cheese-
factors or East Anglian butter factors (228; 222b, *38–41*. Later Stuart England
was also a happy hunting ground for wholesalers of all kinds – mercers and
ironmongers frequently figuring among the richest – while tens of thousands of
retailers ran the gamut from exclusive London tobacconists, drapers and book-
sellers to the smallest country shopkeepers. And if there was one invaluable link
between so many of the social and occupational groups we have been reviewing,
it was surely the innkeeper, in himself an epitome of the diversity of the social
order in this period and of the counterpoint of change and continuity. Inns were
multiplying, or at least being rebuilt and extended, at an unprecedented rate
between 1650 and 1700. Great establishments like the *Three Cranes* in Doncaster,
the *George* in Northampton or the *Bull* in Stamford were now kept by men of
substance well fit to rank with the minor gentry.[13] Yet there were also a host of
'inn-holders', keeping the meaner houses, who would be lucky to leave estates
worth £20–£50 in capital value.

However intrigued they were by the progress of industry and trade, none of
the social observers or political arithmeticians of late seventeenth-century England doubted that the bedrock of the social structure was composed of those who
owned and worked the land. The century from 1540 to 1640 had seen a good deal
of flux throughout landed society as a whole, and not only at gentry level. By
contrast, after 1660 stability may appear to be the order of the day, at least until
the French wars at the end of the seventeenth century, possibly until the great

79

spate of parliamentary enclosures began in the middle of the eighteenth. Certainly this was once a commonly-held view among historians. It is so no longer. One of the most basic long-term changes in the balance of English society since the early sixteenth century was very far from having run its course by 1660, or indeed by 1688. This was the process which historians have labelled 'the decline of the small landowner' (244). It was as evident to Gregory King as to any informed Augustan that a great segment of the country's population in their day – well over a quarter of the whole, King speculated, counting their families – still farmed the land, either as freeholders or tenants [B.5]. Both groups varied vastly in substance. Their incomes might be as high as £150 or even £200 at one end of the scale, and as low as £15 or £20 at the other. King's own revised average income figure for the upper yeomanry, at £91 a year, is by no means unrealistic, though the odds are it was arrived at by pure guesswork. But what is more instructive is that in his second thoughts of 1698 he raised the numbers of those who farmed as tenants, without significant freehold, or even customary and copyhold, land of their own, from 45 per cent to almost 50 per cent of all farmers above the level of mere cottagers. This may fairly be taken as a recognition by one who was professionally knowledgeable about county society that a process which had begun well over a century before the start of our period was continuing. The minor yeoman, the small owner-occupier or peasant proprietor, call him what we will, the figure who had dominated the agrarian scene from end to end of the country in the fifteenth century (often referred to as 'the golden age of the English peasant') was palpably on the way out by the second half of the seventeenth. The steep rise in population down to 1650, and the demand for food to feed more and more mouths, and therefore for increased efficiency of farming methods within more commercialised units (Ch. 2), had sealed his fate, though his disappearance was to be stubbornly protracted and its pattern much dictated by regional differences. Between 1660 and 1688 mixed farmers on Midland clays and the smaller arable farmers of the South and East seem to have been the chief victims of the price depression of the 1670s and 1680s (244; 213, *170–99*; 170a, *92–101*).

Prosperous or modestly prosperous yeoman families were still to be counted in tens of thousands at the time England entered a long period of warfare in 1689. The big squeeze on them was yet to come. All the same, there were already fewer such families in proportion to the population than would have been found early in the century, and there certainly appears to have been less pressure now from this quarter to break into the ranks of the country gentry, though we must not assume that there was none (243b). Of the families of the 'lesser freeholders', however, countless thousands had by now drifted into pure tenant status, or alternatively, and of even greater moment for the future, had dropped to the very bottom of the pecking order of rural society, among the labourers and cottagers, or taken up by-employment (as, say, weavers or nail-makers), or even moved permanently into towns. Beckett has rightly stressed the gradualness and geographical patchiness of this process, and it could not be argued that 1660 was a particularly significant watershed in it. But the 1680s, when the correspondence of landlord after landlord reads like a threnody on the loss of tenants broken by arrears and debts, were a traumatic time which left some parts of the social landscape of rural England permanently changed (238b; 170a, *92–3*).

The gauntest feature of that landscape in 1688 to stand out from King's 'Scheme' is the great army of landless labourers. Over the next 100–150 years that army was to go on multiplying. Yet the rural pattern of the future, the nineteenth century's 'tripartite pattern [as Stone has put it] of . . . landlord, prosperous tenant farmer and landless labourer',[14] was already foreshadowed in 1688 when King labelled 364,000 out of his total of 1,350,000 families as 'labouring people and [living-]out servants'. In one of his unpublished notebooks King recorded his belief that those labourers in rural employment now totalled some 300,000. Whether he was right or wrong, there can be little doubt that the ranks of the agricultural labourers, combined with those (in all probability at least as numerous) who as cottagers and smallholders provided most of the casual labour force of late Stuart and early Hanoverian farming, and who (if they were lucky) helped to sustain much of rural industry as well in later Stuart England, included a large proportion of families whose forebears had been small freeholders making an independent living from the land.

It is equally apparent that it was these same groups, especially those lacking by-occupations, who were responsible for a good deal of the drain on the overworked poor relief system of late-seventeenth century England and which touched the Christian social conscience of the day far more than is often thought (224a). In the sixteenth and earlier seventeenth centuries, owing largely to demographic forces, mass poverty had become for the first time a major social problem and a periodic cause of anxiety to Parliaments and governments. By the 1670s and 1680s, as rating and taxation records show, *rural* poverty was not alone in causing alarm. An unregulated economy ensured that the towns too made a substantial contribution to the situation Gregory King tried to depict with graphic clarity – albeit with statistical licence – in 1695. It was his belief (one not necessarily shared by all modern scholars)[15] that over half the population of his day lived so close, much of the time, to the barest subsistence level that only periodic dependence on public or private charity could guarantee them against disaster; in his own striking words, they 'decreas[ed] the wealth of the kingdom'.[16] That there was abundant prosperity in Restoration England, and that its benefits were shared widely by those in regular work as well as by the leisured, is not in question. But equally it is plain that the economic gulf between the 'haves' in the country's social order and the 'have nots' was a good deal wider than it had been within the less complicated economy of 150 years before, as indeed was the corresponding gulf in social attitudes, perceptions and values in every community where the favoured and the unfavoured co-existed. For 'the relative social tranquillity of the later seventeenth century [as Keith Wrightson warns us] must not be mistaken for a reversal of the social forces active in the preceding three generations' (172, *228*).

---

1. Recent general surveys which synthesise this work admirably include K. Wrightson (172), Chs. 1, 5; C.G.A. Clay (170a), Chs. 5, 6; and J.A. Sharpe (169), Chs. 6–8.
2. See, e.g. B.G. Blackwood, *The Lancashire Gentry and the Great Rebellion* (Manchester 1978); A.G.R. Smith, *The Emergence of a Nation State* (1984), bibliography entries 156, 157, 252, 253.
3. For a good brief summary of these arguments and a useful bibliographical guide, see G.E. Mingay (236b), pp. 50–61. For a more recent contribution to the debate, on a broader canvas, see Habakkuk, (233c): 'Did the Gentry Rise?'
4. D.C. Coleman, *Sir John Banks, Baronet and Businessman* (Oxford, 1963), pp. 172ff, 186; E.S. de Beer, ed., *The Diary of John Evelyn* (abridged edn, 1959), p. 738.
5. For example G.E. Aylmer, *The King's Servants* (1961) has an upper limit of 23,000 and a lower limit of 17,000 for esquires and 'gentlemen'. For 1702 see Holmes (227), pp. 57–8 or (16), pp. 297–8.
6. C.G.A. Clay, *Public Finance and Private Wealth, the Career of Sir Stephen Fox 1627–1716* (Oxford, 1978), pp. 191–7; E.S. de Beer, ed., *Evelyn Diary* (abridged edn.), p. 1009: 11 June 1696.
7. *The Diary of Abraham de la Pryme* (Surtees Soc. No. 54, 1870), p. 83: 10 Mar 1696.
8. L. Stone, *The Crisis of the Aristocracy 1558–1641* (1st edn, Oxford, 1965), p. 762.
9. C.W. Brooks, *Pettyfoggers and Vipers of the Commonwealth: the 'Lower Branch' of the Legal Profession in Early Modern England* (Cambridge, 1986).
10. J.H. Raach, *A Dictionary of English Country Physicians, 1603–1643* (1962).
11. Robert Pitt, M.D., *The Antidote* (1704), Preface.
12. P. Mathias, *The Brewing Industry in England, 1700–1830* (Cambridge, 1959).
13. Thomas Baskerville, 'A Journey into the North' [*c.*1675], printed in HMC *Portland MSS.*, II [p. 310 for Doncaster];, A. Everitt, 'The English Urban Inn, 1560–1760', in *idem*, ed., *Perspectives in English Urban History* (1973).
14. L. Stone, *The Causes of the English Revolution* (1972), p. 68.
15. It may be noted, however, that T. Arkell, in 'The Incidence of Poverty in England in the later Seventeenth Century'(*Social History*, **XII**, (1987), pp. 23–47), suggests that the true figure in late 17th-century England was nearer 15 per cent of the population receiving 'some form of charity in the course of a year', but that 5 per cent of the population required only *intermittent* support from the poor rates.
16. Holmes (227), p. 68 or (16), p. 308.

CHAPTER 5

Personality and penury:
King Charles II and his finances

I

The prosperity of Restoration England was not matched by the affluence of its kings and governments. It is possible for historians to detect the seeds of greatness implanted even in the soil of a country that remained a continued prey to political instability for much of the three decades after 1660. A handful of contemporaries, most notably William of Orange (Ch. 12), had the perception to do likewise, without benefit of hindsight. But the vast majority of Englishmen themselves, accustomed for most of the 110 years before 1660 to see their country picking its way warily, and sometimes ingloriously, round the periphery of European politics, were more coy about its potentialities and prospects. They preferred, it seemed, a monarchy too hard-up to threaten their liberties to one endowed with the capacity for heroics; the more so since, *ipso facto*, that monarchy's subjects remained for the most part ridiculously under-taxed. Many were genuine sceptics. Right through the 1690s – the Revolution notwithstanding – stern voices such as that of Charles Davenant warned against the folly of the nation over-extending itself in foreign affairs and war, convinced that England's recent economic upsurge was precariously based and that ruin would attend a protracted struggle against the might of France. Gregory King was one who often elaborated in his writings on the theme of 'the vanity of over-valuing our own strength'.[1]

Even while King wrote, one of the most critical steps in the emergence of early-eighteenth century Britain as a great power was being taken: the private and public wealth of England was being slowly brought, if not into balance, then at least into a far more rational relationship than had existed hitherto (Ch. 16). Yet certainly down to 1685, and to a lesser extent from 1685 to 1688, the *im*balance between the wealth of the Crown and the state and that of the crown's subjects had been almost as marked as in the years before 1642. Indeed, for twenty-one of the twenty-five years of Charles II's reign that imbalance had been so gross that, so far from being a cause for national self-congratulation, it had threatened once again to undermine the constitution.

We shall see in the course of this chapter, and later (Chs. 7, 8, 9, 11), how the state of the royal finances can provide one with an ever-serviceable key for unlocking nearly all the deepest political problems, as well as for understanding many of the lesser conundrums of the years 1660–85. But since so much of Restoration politics hinged on Restoration kingship, any attempt to study and analyse both must logically begin with the persons of the ruling monarchs. Our starting-point here, therefore, will be King Charles II himself, for it can surely be argued that with him, as later with his brother James, the kind of man he was, no less than the priorities which directed his rule, profoundly influenced the course of his reign in matters both of high politics and religion.

Despite a penchant for dissimulation and a gift for staging elaborate charades, Charles's character and personality, though not always of a piece with the facade he loved to present to the world, were straightforward enough to set him apart from all the rest of the Stuarts who ruled in England from 1603 to 1714, who as a breed would comfortably have filled a modern psychiatrist's notebook. From his letters, speeches and recorded *bon mots* (he was, to his infinite satisfaction, a much-quoted sovereign), Charles is unmistakably the 'sport' of his line: clear-sighted and realistic where his father and brother fell prey to ruinous illusions; supple where other Stuarts were obstinate; nimble-witted where they were either limited in intelligence or, as with James I, pedantically clever and rather too wise in his own conceit. In his manifest normality, especially, Charles II might have stepped straight out of the Tudor stable. Like Elizabeth I and Henry VIII, he had an innate talent for human relationships. Unselfconscious and affable, a tireless conversationalist and witty raconteur who once provoked Gilbert Burnet (himself no Trappist) to complain that he 'runs out too long and too far',[2] an athlete of some prowess, a strenuous lover, a king who delighted in shrugging off the stuffy formalities of kingship and flouting protocol – Charles was indeed as great a social extrovert as ever sat on the throne of England. William III, who matched him in native ability and far surpassed him in determination and self-discipline, fell sadly short of his uncle in the priceless gift of getting on with his fellow mortals.

William apart, Charles II was beyond argument the cleverest of the Stuarts. The cutting edge of his grandfather's mind was ultimately destroyed by physical excess and premature senility; not so with Charles. A king who pottered enthusiastically in his own laboratory and who found the discoveries of the scientific revolution more congenial than state-paper drudgery was a not inappropriate first patron of the new Royal Society (Ch. 10; above pp. 3, 4). What was more to the point in the free-for-all of post-Restoration politics and court intrigue, Charles wedded to his intellectual gifts shrewd judgement of men and appraisal of human motive. The harsh years from 1649 to 1660 had done much to whet those particular skills. Unfortunately, the squalid manoeuvrings of the exiled court, following his humiliating experiences at the hands of the Scottish Covenanters (35, *33ff.*), also bred in him a cynical outlook on politicians and on politics. Worldly wisdom by 1660 had come seriously close to disillusionment, tainting his delight in character-reading with an acceptance of deceit and double-dealing as a natural, if not inevitable, part of all political relationships. This was to cloud both his foreign policy and his relations with Parliament for much of his reign. Placing no genuine trust in others, he came to inspire little himself. His ministers, Halifax remarked, learned to watch his face when he talked, judging it 'of more importance to see than to hear what he said'.[3]

*

84

Charles, who had little time for humbug, never claimed to be custodian of any noble political, religious or moral principle, not, at least, until his family's legitimate rights of succession came under attack in 1679 (Ch. 8). Political aptitude meant to him pragmatism, not infrequently to the point of shiftiness. The high-toned qualities with which certain historians, mainly of an inter-war vintage,[4] have tried to endow Charles are hard to detect in the cold light of the evidence. Although lack of principle is particularly striking in his conduct of foreign affairs, where even common patriotism is at times glaringly absent, and in his less-than-frank management of Parliament, it permeated other aspects of royal policy too, notably religion. Charles has been credited both with a genuine commitment to religious toleration and, by some, with covert zeal for the Catholic faith. To do him justice he pretended to neither. His gestures on behalf of religious minorities, frequent enough down to the 1670s, were not insincere, but sprang from a naturally tolerant nature rather than from any deep well of principle. His deathbed conversion to Catholicism in 1685 may possibly have been a belated recognition of what he had secretly practised for some time (though there can be no certainty even about that); but more significant are Charles's maintenance of outward respect for established Anglican forms for twenty-five years before this, and the risks he was *not* prepared to take for religion's sake. He took care to be adequately informed on religious matters and he read his Bible sufficiently to be able to quote it to the discomfiture of more sanctimonious opponents, but he had little sympathy with theological disputation and, in common with many of his generation, regarded most religious zealotry with a mixture of amusement and contempt. He slept contentedly through the sermons which assailed him week by week in the Chapel Royal, and never more peacefully than when the preacher threatened hell-fire for the dissolute.

There is, however, a paradox in Charles II's character which has to be taken into account when assessing some of the most important events of his reign. For while he would rarely stick out for a principle, and plainly mistrusted the generality of politicians and placemen who angled for his favours, he was not without a sense of personal obligation. He showed this conspicuously within his family circle, not only in affection for congenial spirits like his favourite sister, Henriette, but by loyalty in the direst crisis of his reign (1679–81) to a brother with whom he had scarcely a shred of temperamental affinity. But he could show it too, more than he is often given credit for, to ministers who had served him faithfully. To say that he treated his ministers ungenerously and dismissed them lightly is not altogether fair. He put up with Clarendon's badgering and moralising for seven years, long after his Chancellor had lost almost all support in the Council and at Court. He then, it is true, dismissed him and subsequently encouraged the impeachment proceedings against him when the earl refused to appease the parliamentary opposition by retiring quietly; yet he also connived at his escape abroad (Ch. 7) and subsequently bestowed the royal favour on his two sons (33, *276–84*; cf. 40a, *60*). After the passing of the Test Act in 1673, he was powerless to keep Lord Treasurer Clifford in his post (cf. 14, *20*). In 1679 he also bowed to the inevitable when dismissing Clifford's successor, Danby, but enabled him to evade the wrath of Parliament – which spelled certain ruin and probable death – by lodging him securely in the Tower. Such incidents are worth comparing with the betrayal of Strafford in 1641 by his father, a man of honour to whom loyalty was supposedly sacred.

A greater handicap to Charles II than lack of principle was the difficulty he found in sharing a common wavelength with his English subjects. He was essentially a cosmopolitan. He lacked that gut feeling for English aspirations and prejudices which Elizabeth I had had in abundance, and which even his niece Anne was to make into a queenly asset. It was one thing to promote French fashions, in food, dress, music and the arts, among his courtiers; it was a very different matter to allow his admiration for French forms of government and for 'Gallican' churchmanship to obscure his political vision. There seems little doubt that Charles right down to 1679 misjudged the strength of national feeling over such traditional bugbears as Popery and arbitrary government.

This was not his only basic misreading of the situation in his new kingdom. He was convinced for much of his reign that radical Puritanism and republican sentiments were much stronger than they really were. Recently historians have rightly stressed how much more insecure Charles felt for many years than was once commonly assumed, but Dr Miller's argument that the King's experiences with the plots of the early 1660s and with the panic of 1667 made mere survival his overriding priority for the rest of his reign (14, *33ff* [Miller]) has not found general support. It will be argued later (Chs. 7, 11) that a combination of persistent frustrations at home in the first decade of his reign and admiration for his powerful cousin, Louis XIV, made the notion of benevolent authoritarianism a seductive one for Charles. A constitution in which kingly power would be liberated from some of the shackles his predecessors had forged, in which Parliament would play a minor and preferably largely ornamental role, but in which the established Church – preferably Anglican, but conceivably Roman Catholic if circumstances should ever prove ripe for such a change – would be an essential pillar of authority and hierarchy: such an ideal was rarely out of Charles's sights after 1669. What is more, England's experiences in Charles's last years, 1682–5, and indeed Scotland's for much of the 1670s and 1680s (above, pp. 7–14, *passim*), were to provide proof enough that it was no idle pipe-dream.

One of the most intriguing questions for the historian about the first quarter-century after the Restoration is therefore this: why was it not until the 1680s that Charles, a dangerously clever man unencumbered by principle, began to advance in an authoritarian direction with anything approaching consistency and calculation? There was menace in some of his moves from 1669 to 1673, notably the French alliance (below, pp. 95–6), but they were not sustained. His financial plight was a powerful restraining factor, as we shall presently see, and the political circumstances to which he had to adapt his game in the years 1670–81 also held him in check in various ways. But it was also a question of character. Charles was a prudent man, and his innate realism and shrewd judgement rarely permitted him to stray far outside the limits which reasonable prudence dictated. But above all, temperamentally, Charles II was not cut out to wear the tyrant's mantle. The requisite toughness of fibre and consistency of purpose seem to have been lacking. Resembling the Tudors in many respects (among other things, he shared Elizabeth I's penchant for balancing rival factions and ventilating disagreements in the Council) (42a, *17*), in this respect he differed from them strikingly. Although Charles was capable of acts of cynical callousness, which seem to belie the myth of 'the Merry Monarch', there was nevertheless a warm and generous streak in his nature. Open-handed to the point of soft-heartedness in his early years towards down-and-out royalists, he was also generous, well beyond the point of prodigality, to his array of mistresses, both current and discarded. Money he desperately needed to make himself a freer constitutional agent was gaily splashed out on objects which, however unworthy in the eyes of his critics, hardly presented a threat to national liberties. Energy, too, which might have been single-mindedly applied to politics, was squandered elsewhere. Charles was not a lazy man, but he was a lazy king. Desk-work, for instance, was a penance he expected his ministers to suffer on his behalf, and he carefully rationed the amount of time he would allot even to talking business. 'He walked by his watch', one of his ministers later recalled, 'and when he pulled it out to look upon it skilful men would make haste with what they had to say to him'.[5] The objects of his competing activities were diverse; one can only conclude that to a king determined to enjoy to the full those regal pleasures which had been so long withheld from him, they seemed more compelling at the time than any impulse towards absolutism and the effort and self-sacrifice needed to satisfy it.

A final paradox concerning Charles II's character and its political implications remains, and it is one about which students of the period sharply disagree. How far did his live-and-let-live temper, his addiction to the soft option, his preference for the expedient over the long-term solution, survive the traumatic experiences of the Exclusion Crisis of 1679–81? The present writer's interpretation of the politics of the last years of the reign, as will be seen (Ch. 11), hinges on a very decided answer to this question. In the meantime, the view of a leading contemporary civil servant and political writer is worth pondering:

> We are to consider that King Charles [in 1660] was a young Prince, more inclined to taste the pleasures of power than willing to feel its weight. He had undergone many troubles, which he intended to recompense with great ease and luxury; so that the rugged work of subverting the laws suited neither with his age nor temper. Had he lived longer, as time and opposition began to sour his blood, what he might have attempted is very doubtful.[6]

Although it seems clear that for almost twenty years after the Restoration Charles II was not prepared to accept the financial sacrifices which single-minded exploitation of his prerogatives entailed, it is possible to argue that even the adoption from the start of a stern, austerity-model court and style of kingship might still not have been enough, before the 1680s, to yield that degree of financial independence which a prospective authoritarian ruler required. To test this hypothesis, and to help us to evaluate much that actually did take place, both in domestic and foreign affairs during Charles II's reign, we must return to, and examine in greater depth, the financial dilemma of the restored monarchy which was briefly touched on earlier.

II

The fundamental problem, one that was present from the very start, stemmed from the decision of the Convention to revert in the Restoration Settlement to a traditional system of public finance (Ch. 1). A parliamentary committee calculated in 1660 that for the Crown to carry out the regular functions of government, once the New Model Army and part of the Cromwellian navy had been paid off, would necessitate an 'ordinary' (i.e. permanent) revenue of £1.2 million. This was not in itself an unrealistic sum, bearing in mind that prices had now begun to level out. But to translate it into a realistic revenue there had to be some guarantee that the permanent grants made by the Commons at the beginning of the reign would produce what they were supposed to produce.

These grants were of three kinds. To begin with, there were the usual customs grants: the old tonnage and poundage, voted for life. But they were followed by two expedients which represented more of a break in practice with pre-Civil War thinking. In 1660, to compensate the Crown for the loss of its feudal revenues, the Convention made a life grant to Charles of the excise on liquors, a lucrative parliamentary innovation of the 1640s subsequently maintained under the Republic. Two years later, while the Cavalier House of Commons was still on good terms with the King, Parliament voted him a new tax, the Hearth Tax or 'Chimney Money'. For the first time a direct impost had become part of the ordinary revenue of the English Crown, as distinct from the land or property taxes (first subsidies, later 'assessments') which were to be voted to provide the King with extraordinary supplies in the emergencies of his reign. The Hearth Tax, however, was supposed to make up a tax deficit of £300,000: in the first year, 1662–3, it brought in £87,700 and only once before 1678 was it to yield as much as £200,000 (110a, *348–57 passim*). Its very imposition, moreover, was an acknowledgement that the basic life grants of customs and excise were thoroughly unpredictable instruments which could not ensure the King the income he had a right to expect. In devising an ordinary revenue for Charles, Parliament had saddled him with a seriously inflexible system. Less excusable and almost as damaging was its attitude to the royal debts. It took the view that Charles's personal debt, incurred since 1649, was his own responsibility, declined to take notice of the debts the King had inherited from his father, and seriously misjudged the cost of paying off the republican forces, so that by the time the new reign was a few months old the restored monarchy found itself £800,000 in the red – an unenviable incubus, given the uncertainty of its revenue.

Storm clouds gathered round the Restoration financial settlement, therefore, almost from the start. The new grant of 1662 did little to disperse them and between 1665 and 1667 they produced a cloudburst which left the settlement virtually in ruins and the monarch bitterly aggrieved. On the rickety structure of the settlement four heavy blows fell. One was royal extravagance or otherwise wasteful use by the Crown of its own resources. This was a factor exaggerated by the opposition in the Commons at the time, and one that has been both overplayed and underplayed by historians. Professor Chandaman's authoritative conclusion is that it was not a negligible factor in Charles's early penury but that it was less important, relatively, in the mid- and late 1660s than it was to become in the 1670s. More damaging in the opening years of the reign was the state of the economy. As the trade depression of the late 1650s spilled over into the new decade, affording little hint as yet of the boom years to come (Ch. 3), the ordinary revenue showed just how sensitive it was, given its heavy dependence on customs and excise, to the economic climate. During the period 1660–64 its actual return fell short by on average almost £400,000 a year, or more than 30 per cent of its theoretical yield. There were timely windfalls, in the shape of the Portuguese dowry and the more controversial proceeds from the sale to the French of Cromwell's capture, Dunkirk (above, pp. 3–4), but despite these, and two very valuable parliamentary supplements (1661–3) through special 'one-off' tax levies, notably the so-called 'Eighteenth Months' Assessment' (110a, *332*) in not one of these four years did the Crown succeed in balancing its books. These accumulated deficits served further to aggravate the third important factor in the demolition of the settlement, the size of the debt. This had already passed the £1 million mark by 1664, and Charles could justly claim that most of it had been incurred through no fault of his own.

However, with trade and industry slowly returning to health and duty yields increasing, the outlook was not hopeless. Then came catastrophe, in the shape of the Second Dutch War of 1665–7 (Ch. 6), its evils being compounded first by the Great Plague, then by the Fire of London. The ordinary revenue slumped to its nadir, £700,000 per annum over these two years; a war debt of £1.5 million, much of it incurred at inflated interest rates, left the King with a total debt burden which on his current income was simply insupportable. In the three years after the end of the war the Restoration monarchy had to live with a financial problem which was nothing short of desperate. Although the ordinary revenue painfully recovered, so that by 1670 it was bringing the Treasury some £950,000, it was impossible to finance out of this even the standard expenses of court and administration, let alone the government's crippling debt obligations: interest payments to the London goldsmith bankers, who enjoyed in the mid- and late 1660s what D.C. Coleman has called a 'financiers' paradise',[7] and repayments of loan capital, as and when these became due. The advent of a vigorously reforming Treasury Commission in 1667, guided by Sir George Downing (its Secretary) and Sir Thomas Clifford, with able assistance from Sir William Coventry and Lord Ashley, prevented total disaster (111a; 118). But it is easy to understand, nonetheless, how Charles grew increasingly irritated and impatient with his position, caught in a poverty trap all the more frustrating in the light of the growing affluence of the kingdom at large. It was determination to break out of this trap which almost certainly supplied the chief incentive behind the most dramatic policy change of the entire reign – Charles's decision in 1669 to embark on the negotiations which led to the Secret Treaty of Dover with France (110a, *222–3*) (Ch. 6).

That treaty was signed in May 1670. By 1671 a marked change for the better in the financial fortunes of the King and his government, in some respects at least, was clearly in progress, and despite occasional setbacks in the next few years it was not until 1678 that this revival was seriously checked. The first instalment of a French pension worth around £150,000 a year in peacetime (it was augmented from 1672–4 by a war subsidy of £225,000 a year) was paid to Charles early in 1671. The price paid by Louis XIV for the doubtful privilege of having Charles II for an ally was not a huge one, but for one in Charles's Micawberish position it was very significant, as was the sum of some £160,000 promised to him (but not all paid) under a renegotiated agreement of 1675 for keeping Parliament in abeyance during 1676 and 1677 (110a, *134–5, 237*). More valuable in financial terms, however, than the controversial change in foreign policy was a change in the government's parliamentary policy. In 1668 Clifford had begun to gather together and organise on the Crown's behalf a body of Court supporters in the House of Commons. In the session of 1670–1 this policy paid handsome dividends when Parliament approved easily the most generous additional supplies of the reign, as a supplement to the ordinary revenue (above, p. 88). Country gentlemen who ventured to ask for details of the royal debts before granting extra revenue to relieve them 'were run down with calling "to the question"',[8] and a new excise on ale, beer and other excisable liquors (110a, *45–6*), plus extra customs on wine were voted for periods of six and eight years respectively. Between 1671 and 1674 they brought in an average of £285,000 a year, the excise, voted from June 1671 to June 1677, being especially productive.

In such circumstances it may seem astonishing that the Crown should in January 1672 have declared itself bankrupt: for this is what in effect it did in the so-called 'Stop of the Exchequer'. But the circumstances of 1672 were wholly exceptional. In that year some £1 million of capital owed to the bankers, who had done so well out of Charles's embarrassments since 1665, was due for redemption. It was a vast sum; but even so the Crown might have been able to meet a large part of the obligation had Charles and his ministers not been aware at the beginning of 1672 that a further war with the Dutch, in fulfilment of the Dover commitment to France, was immediately at hand, and had they not regarded the anticipated plunder of this war as a source of certain gain to the Exchequer as well as to the country (110a, *224, 227*). The 'Stop' was thus not so much a genuine bankruptcy as a calculated device, of Clifford's devising, designed to ease the Crown's short-term financial difficulties and to facilitate the fighting of a war for its long-term profit. Charles did not repudiate his debts, but he did postpone indefinitely repayment of the 1672 obligations, paying the bankers 6 per cent thereafter on the Stop Debt. It was a dubious measure, much criticised even by prominent members of Charles's own government, notably Ashley, Chancellor of the Exchequer (42b, *295–6*), but financially it proved profitable, especially as Parliament ultimately guaranteed funds from taxation for meeting the interest payments.

If these three circumstances turned the financial tide in favour of the Restoration monarchy in the early 1670s, three more factors helped to keep that tide flowing. One was the decision to take the administration of the Customs directly into government hands in 1671. A second was the appointment of the future earl of Danby as Lord Treasurer in 1673, though Danby was a careful steward rather than an inspired finance minister and in some respects – for example, his handling of the Excise farm – his policies were misguided. The third, and much the most important, was Charles's enforced decision to pull out of the Third Dutch War in 1673 (above, p. 8; Ch. 7), a decision which yielded far more substantial benefits to English trade by neutrality over the next four years than had accrued as a result of the war itself. For one reason or another, the total income of the Crown in the years of peace from 1674–7 averaged no less than £1.4 million, with customs revenues rising in one bumper year (1674–5) to £730,000. Thus endowed, a less indulgent – and self-indulgent – king than Charles II could conceivably have worked himself by 1677 into a very formidable political position. The fact that Charles was not by then out of the wood and in a position to get a firm upper hand in his tussle with Parliament was mainly his own fault. The benefits accruing from rising income in the 1670s were partly wiped out by a renewal of Court extravagance. This now reached levels that were nothing less than sinful, although the heavy cost of oiling the machinery of parliamentary management in the House of Commons was one new commitment that was certainly defensible.

In the winter of 1677–8 the tide turned once more and from then until 1681 the royal and public finances again became a matter for acute concern. The basic reason for the deterioration was mounting anti-French feeling in Parliament (above, pp. 9–10; also Ch. 6), which Charles's ministers were unable to stifle and which had three embarrassing financial consequences. In 1677 most of the King's French pension was cut off after he had failed to carry out his undertaking to Louis (above, p. 9) to keep Parliament prorogued. In 1678 Charles found himself embroiled, under parliamentary pressure, in expensive war preparations which raised the Debt to a record £2.5 million. Later the same year Parliament imposed a three-year ban on trade with France which seriously affected customs revenue. In fact, it is doubtful whether Charles would have had the financial resilience to come through the most testing period of his reign, the years of the great Exclusion struggle when he faced three new and hostile Parliaments in succession (Ch. 8) but for two things. Firstly, in the last two sessions of the old Cavalier Parliament Lord Treasurer Danby's carefully-drilled following mustered enough votes to secure a three-year renewal both of the Additional Excise of 1671–77 and of the auxiliary wine duties of 1670–78. This was a critical *coup*, for it meant that instead of being forced to exist from 1678–81 with absolutely no margin for manoeuvre on a permanent ordinary revenue of only fractionally over £1 million, the Crown had another £214,000, on average, to play with. Secondly, Charles was at last persuaded by the new Treasury regime which succeeded Danby in 1679 [D.2] to accept a policy of retrenchment, which enabled the Crown – just – to live within its means (110a, *249–50*).

During the course of 1681 Charles II emerged not only from his greatest political crisis but from his financial troubles as well, and he did so without that permanent parliamentary settlement of his revenue for which he had always hoped. The lifting of the French trade embargo in 1681 signalled the zenith years of the Commercial Revolution, so that, despite the expiry in this year of the last of the auxiliary duties, the basic ordinary revenue touched £1.29 million in 1681–2, by far its highest yield of the reign, and had reached £1.37 million by

1684–5. Since he also enjoyed a new, though modest, French subsidy (110a, *250, 324, 332*), had accepted at last, at Rochester's insistence, the need to continue to curb his extravagance, and resolutely steered clear of foreign commitments, even to the point of abandoning Tangier, the King was unquestionably better off than at any time in his reign. Like every other phase of the monarchy's financial situation since 1660, this last period of unaccustomed solvency had important political implications. For the only protracted period since 1660 Parliament became dispensable. This not merely facilitated the Stuart reaction of Charles II's closing years. It also goes far to explain the reckless confidence with which a new king, less adroit by far than his brother, careered after 1685 down the path to revolution.

---

1. Charles Davenant, 'Memorial Concerning Credit', BL Harleian MSS. 1223, ff.115–56, *passim*; Davenant, *Political and Commercial Works*, ed. C. Whitworth (1771), I, p. 135; G. King, 'Burns Journal', p. 240, printed in *The Earliest Classics: John Graunt to Gregory King* (1973).
2. H.C. Foxcroft, ed., *A Supplement to Burnet's History of My Own Time* (Oxford, 1902), p. 48.
3. J.P. Kenyon, ed., *Halifax: Complete Works* (1969), p. 252.
4. E.g. A. Bryant, *King Charles II* (1931); C.H. Hartmann, *Charles II and Madame* (1934), *The King my Brother* (1954), *Clifford of the Cabal* (1937).
5. *Halifax: Complete Works*, p. 261.
6. Charles Davenant, *Essay upon . . . the Balance of Trade* (1699).
7. D.C. Coleman, *Sir John Banks: Baronet and Businessman* (Oxford, 1963), p. 41.
8. Add. MSS 36916, f.167: Newsletter to Sir Willoughby Aston, 22 Feb 1670. See also ff. 165–7, 199–213, *passim*.

CHAPTER 6

The Restoration monarchy and Europe: isolation without splendour, 1660–1688

Despite the unprecedented prosperity which England achieved by the second half of Charles II's reign and the firm, stable government the country enjoyed in his last four years, there are few signs that she was a more effective or more highly regarded force in Europe in 1685 than she had been in the 1660s: rather the contrary. In the summer of 1688 Louis XIV's invasion of the Palatinate, the preliminary to the bloodiest European war of the seventeenth century, was to be launched with little more than a momentary calculation of how James II's crisis-ridden kingdoms might react. Such a decline in standing since Cromwell's time cannot be completely understood until the domestic politics of 1660–1688 have been adequately analysed. But many of the clues to it can be found through an examination of the foreign policy of the Restoration monarchy, set in the context of the financial constraints under which Charles, at least, operated (Ch. 5).

England's relations with Europe in the quarter century following the Restoration have been much debated and diversely interpreted. By contrast it has been hard for scholars to work up great interest, let alone controversy, over James II's dealings with his neighbours after February 1685, for these were so heavily overshadowed by his obsessive preoccupation with his religious and constitutional objectives that historians have often felt justified in assuming that he had no foreign policy worthy of the name. This is erroneous. A king who built up his navy, and paid such careful attention to diplomatic intelligence, as James did (47; 50) was hardly indifferent to external relations. Although his thinking was mainly negative, prompted chiefly by determination not to get involved in a war that would wreck his domestic schemes and not to alienate the power he judged most likely to help him in any extremity, France, James's attitudes to Europe are of interest, if only as a further reflection of the priorities and patterns already established by his brother. It is on the latter, nevertheless, that the discussion in this chapter must mainly focus, with a particular emphasis on the reasons why England's foreign policy took the course it did from 1660 to 1685 and on the effects those policies had on the nation's interests.

Basic to an understanding of the whole field of foreign affairs under the later Stuarts is an appreciation of how foreign policy was made. Whose policies were they? And what influences shaped them or governed their execution? The key question is the first one. For the greater part of the period between the Restoration and the Revolution the foreign policy of England was to all intents and purposes equatable with the personal policy of the King. This was both a question of constitutional powers and of practical realities. Under the Restoration Settlement Charles II's prerogative right to formulate and carry through foreign policy was theoretically unchallengeable. Although early Stuart Parliaments had occasionally put the Crown under some pressure to adopt a more Protestant stance abroad, as they did with James I in the early 1620s, not even the Long Parliament in the revolutionary atmosphere of 1641 had claimed more than the right to be consulted and to tender advice. Sovereignty in this particular area was never disputed. Similarly between 1660 and 1688: there was frequent parliamentary grumbling, and sometimes sharp sniping, at royal foreign policy, yet at no time did this amount to a direct confrontation with the King's lawful prerogatives. When in February 1668 'Sir Richard Temple and Mr Seymour moved that the league made with the Dutch [see below p. 99] should be brought in read *(sic)* openly in the House, . . . it was opposed as an unreasonable motion, and the Solicitor made a very good speech against it, affirming that it was an unreasonable thing to question the league, as if foreign princes should not enter into and make a league with the King of England without the approbation and consent of the House of Commons. These gentlemen then retracted and said they did not mean any such thing . . .'[1] Indeed only very occasionally, for example in the long and turbulent session of 1677–8, can the Commons be said to have mounted even an oblique challenge in this area (39b, *230*).[2] These constitutional niceties would not have been so vital had either Charles II or James II displayed a less proprietory attitude to their rights. But foreign policy was one field where even Charles showed intense jealousy of his prerogative and maintained his interest and control very closely. This was just as true of Scotland, where the Estates were more docile than the Westminster Parliament. Scotland dutifully engaged, along with England, in the two short wars of the period, 1665–7 and 1672–4, paying her share of taxes and suffering her share of merchant shipping losses, with less than the English to hope for in the way of compensation.

A critical factor in translating royal foreign policy into an effective reality was the role of the Secretaries of State [D.2]. These two ministers, one with responsibility for the 'Southern department' of Europe, the other for the North,[3] had a brief which included instructing English diplomats abroad and keeping contact, and where necessary negotiating, with foreign representatives in London. In theory here were the two politicians capable of exercising ministerial supervision over the actual execution of foreign policy and best equipped to advise the King on its formulation. In practice this responsibility was almost completely undermined after the Restoration, partly by the lack of any united 'cabinet voice' in the royal councils (the so-called Committee for Foreign Affairs and its successor, the Committee of Intelligence, had an advisory function but they advised as collections of individuals or *ad hoc* factions, and their advice was frequently ignored) (118, *105–7*; 138, *297* and *passim*). But what did most to erode secretarial authority was the attitude of Charles and his brother towards the two offices concerned. Politicians who combined real political stature with unquestioned administrative ability were rare birds among the Secretaries of 1660–88; significantly, the only two (with the fleeting exception of Sidney Godolphin) who clearly satisfied both criteria, Arlington and Sunderland, were men whose sympathy with royal views and loyalty in implementing the King's policies were not in doubt. Sir Henry Bennet, later Lord Arlington, served Charles II as his chief (Southern) Secretary in an exceptionally long stint

(1662–74), while Robert Spencer, 2nd earl of Sunderland, held secretarial office under both monarchs, from 1679–81 and subsequently from 1683–88. Among the rest, Sir William Morice, an 'old Presbyterian' with more interest in theology than diplomacy, held the Northern office for eight years at the start of the reign, mainly, it seems, on the strength of his staunch support for the Restoration; Sir Joseph Williamson and Sir Leoline Jenkins were able men with some diplomatic experience, and in Williamson's case outstanding executive gifts,[4] but both lacked political muscle; Sir John Trevor and Henry Coventry, brother-in-law to Lord Shaftesbury, were adroit politicians but little trusted by Charles and therefore allowed no effective power, while men such as Lords Conway and Middleton were almost embarrassingly anonymous.

Not only were such incumbents generally unable to exercise any creative influence on foreign policy, they were often in the dark about what was going on, by-passed at times even in formal negotiations as well as by the two kings' own closet diplomacy. Lord Treasurer Danby frankly admitted that the English peace initiatives of 1678, which preceded the Treaty of Nijmegen between France and the United Provinces, were carried out so secretively 'that the Secretaries of State themselves [Williamson and Coventry] know nothing of it'.[5] Danby himself was one of only two of Charles II's leading ministers – Clarendon being the other – who can be credited with any significant influence on the King's foreign policy decisions, and even that was strictly limited. Arlington had ample interest in foreign affairs, yet except in 1668 (see below, p. 99) little trace of his personal pro-Spanish and pro-Dutch instincts can be found in the policies he formally endorsed and at times administered. It is surely revealing that a first minister as gritty as Danby, and one whose distinctive concept of foreign policy, essentially anti-French, was an integral part of a general political strategy conceived entirely in the King's own long-term interests (Ch. 7), should have made so little headway in recommending it from 1673 to 1677. Charles was remarkably impervious to advice on foreign affairs which ill accorded with his own wishes.

He could afford to be. For one thing, both he and his brother, secure in their prerogative, had non-ministerial channels of negotiation open to them which were invulnerable against any kind of supervision, let alone control, and from the late 1660s, especially, they plied them insatiably. The most notorious outcome of this personal diplomacy was the Secret Treaty of Dover. It was concluded in May 1670 after lengthy clandestine negotiations between the King and his sister, the duchess of Orléans, who acted as proxy for Louis XIV of France (above, p. 7). Apart from Charles's brother, only one prominent minister, Clifford, took part at Dover in the final negotiations, and only one other, Arlington, was apprised of the full terms [H.(iv)] after the event, in order to secure his countersignature (42b, *281–5*; 138, *308, 313–14*; 129, *61, 77*; 130); the rest of the ministry, Parliament and the country were duped by a later bogus treaty (above, p. 7).

Yet Dover was only the first of a string of undercover royal agreements with France down to 1688, most of which King Louis salted with a financial bribe. By a pact concluded in 1675, for example, Charles agreed to dissolve the Cavalier Parliament if it became antagonistic to France. Letters secretly exchanged between November 1675 and February 1677 bound each king to secure the other's prior consent before entering into a treaty of alliance with any other power. In May 1678, in blithe disregard of an alliance with the Dutch, concluded only the previous December and aimed against France (below, p. 101), Charles made yet another secret subsidy agreement with Louis, selling his new freedom of manoeuvre for 6 million livres (134, *133*). When the French pension was renewed in April 1681 after three years' intermission (110a, *324*), it was at the price of further undertakings. At home Charles bound himself to summon no other Parliament after the dissolution of the Oxford Parliament on 28 March, while abroad he promised to renege on existing treaty obligations to Spain or Holland if they threatened to involve England actively in Continental affairs (14, *21*).

There was a second major reason why both Charles II and James II could afford to ignore unpalatable advice from their ministers on relations with Europe and go their own way. Provided they kept clear of wars there was not a great deal Parliament could in this field do to constrain them. Quite apart from the lack of theoretical authority already noted, it was simply not practical politics in the circumstances which prevailed between 1660 and 1688 for any effective parliamentary oversight of foreign policy to be sustained. In the first place, Parliament met far too irregularly to be able to impose for long any serious limitations on the executive's freedom of action. During the ten years from January 1679 to January 1689 there was a Parliament in session for a mere seven and a half months *in toto*. Even before 1679, although there were only two years (1672 and 1676) in which the Cavalier Parliament failed to meet at all, sessions were sometimes very brief [E.2] and the Houses frequently stood prorogued for many months while important diplomatic developments were in progress. In the second place, the Parliaments of this period never commanded enough firm information to aspire to anything more than spasmodic criticism of the government's relations with foreign powers. Unless the King and his ministers chose for tactical or other reasons to admit them into their confidence, there was not much that members or peers could do about it, except when, as in 1678 (below, p. 101), they had a financial lever to operate. Information was the key to the performance of an adequate watchdog rôle; lack of it was responsible not only for crippling Parliament (or, ironically, making opposition MPs themselves vulnerable to foreign diplomatic blandishments) but also for inhibiting the emergence of an effective public opinion 'out of doors' on European issues. Stuart censorship of the press may have been inconsistently applied, but it was tough enough at times, notably in the 1680s, to hinder both the dissemination of news and the publication of opinion about what was going on abroad. The educated public in the Restoration period had lusty prejudices about Europe, but, as J.R. Jones has explained (130), they had astonishingly little knowledge or understanding of Continental politics for much of Charles II's reign, and even in the 1680s could scarcely be described as 'well informed'. The merchant community knew more than the gentry, but even their information tended, naturally enough, to be localised.

Because of the way foreign policy was made under the Restoration monarchy, because of the ramshackle ducts through which it was conducted, and because of the inability of Parliament or public opinion, or indeed of most ministers of the Crown, to influence the shape it took, or even to appreciate some of the basic implications – least of all the financial implications – of the options that were on offer (130, *51–3*), it inevitably bore a highly personal stamp and frequently an irresponsible one. Only in wartime was the King's freedom of action seriously curtailed: he could not persist with an unpopular war if the House of Commons was prepared to cut the lifeline of supply, a fact which Charles II had to recognise in 1674 (above, p. 8) when, much against his will, he accepted Danby's advice and extricated his kingdoms from the Third Dutch War (Treaty of Westminster [H.(v)]). Otherwise there was simply no guarantee that royal policy would serve truly national interests. Notwithstanding this, some historians have claimed that Charles II's foreign policies did not neglect these interests. At very least, J.L. Price has argued, because 'the gains made by France in this period were relatively minor, and no harm came to England's interests despite her neutrality' from 1674–88, the policy which both he and his brother 'pursued for their own interests may well have served their country better than they knew' (134, *135*). How justified are such claims?

Two points may be made at the outset which admit of little argument. One is that Charles began his reign with some important advantages in terms of European relations. He had succeeded in England to a kingdom whose prestige in Continental eyes was still high, in spite of some weathercock shifts of direction following Oliver Cromwell's death; yet he was patently not committed to republican policies if they were unacceptable to him, and he was equally unencumbered by obligations to fellow monarchs, since he had regained his throne without powerful foreign support. On the other hand, to take on a serious European rôle for any length of time cost money: even in peacetime it involved at least the maintenance of an adequate diplomatic corps (something Charles II never had). If Charles is to be charged with failing to exploit his initial assets, it must at least be said in extenuation that no government as financially precarious as his was, especially in the 1660s, could have afforded an ambitious foreign policy in more than fits and starts. The burden of the charge against him remains, however, that these problems did not absolve Charles from at least *conceiving* his policies in the best interests of his kingdoms, as these were generally envisaged at the time, rather than as tools for serving personal ends or pursuing domestic political advantage. Neither did they necessarily disqualify him and his ministers from safeguarding or promoting at least some of these interests, even in the difficult first decade of his reign.

One of the few political achievements of the Commonwealth and Protectorate that had been both concrete and popular was an active policy in support of commercial and colonial expansion (Ch. 3). The restored monarchy was undoubtedly expected to keep the same objectives high in its own priorities, even though national resources were no longer as fully mobilised as they had been in the 1650s. Cromwell had wielded a large and feared standing army; Charles had only a small one, though there were enough seasoned ex-officers and men available for years after 1660 to make its swift expansion in any emergency perfectly feasible. Cromwell's power, too, had rested on full coffers, supplied largely by permanent and heavy direct taxation; Charles's penury was in sharp contrast. Nevertheless, England's navy remained large and respected; the scale of her trade and the sheer length of her commercial arm gave her ample scope to offer economic inducements or apply economic sanctions; and in other respects too she was well-equipped to further her objectives in Europe and the wider world by diplomatic manoeuvre and combination.

Commerce and colonisation were never seen as the be-all and end-all of these objectives. From the 1570s right through to the 1650s English and Scottish governments, royal or republican, had been expected by both parliamentary opinion and popular sentiment to identify themselves with 'the Protestant interest' in Europe. That interest was mainly on the defensive from the 1660s and was to become more beleaguered thereafter. Protestant rulers or governments now controlled no territory of significance west and south of the Rhine, except for the southern United Provinces and the Swiss cantons. Lutheran regimes held sway round much of the Baltic seaboard, but the death of Charles X in 1660 marked the end (though the fact was not at once apparent to the Habsburgs in Vienna) of Sweden's pretensions to be a major force in Germany. The Protestant Hohenzollerns of Brandenburg-Prussia aspired to such a rôle and their defeat of the Swedes at Fehrbellin (1675) was an important pointer to the future, but 'the rise of Prussia' was an eighteenth-, not a seventeenth-, century phenomenon (*The Age of Oligarchy*, Ch. 4). The position of the Dutch, above all, was critical to the Protestant cause. Re-invigorated by their recovery of 1654–60, they retained their commercial ascendancy and their old economic aggressiveness through the first decade of our period, but politically, their internal tensions and deep concern about their vulnerability to attack from the Netherlands, on which the French were soon casting a proprietary eye, led them to adopt a posture that was increasingly defensive. Of course the interests of Protestant and mercantilist states did not always coincide, and this was a dilemma which recent Anglo-Dutch relations, and in particular the war of 1652–4, had acutely emphasised. But from England's point of view it was not impossible, as Oliver Cromwell had shown, to get something of the best of both worlds; and Charles II had only to look back to the reigns of his father and grandfather, and to the history of the Thirty Years War, to be aware how unpatriotic and offensive to public sentiment in Britain was any suspicion of sympathy to the Catholic cause.

For decades a spectre which had haunted Protestant Britons was the achievement of a massive preponderance of power on the Continent by one of the great Catholic giants, Spain, France, or the Austrian Habsburgs, who in addition to their own vast territories in Central Europe, including Bohemia, Moravia and part of Hungary, held by election the throne of the Holy Roman Empire. Habsburg Spain had been the chief bogey ever since Elizabeth I's reign and had only recently been at war with Cromwell's England. The Peace of Westphalia, ending the Thirty Years War (1648) and the Treaty of the Pyrenees (1659) had allayed apprehensions on her account but had not entirely removed them. The

Emperor Leopold I was believed (rightly) to be too preoccupied with the threat from the resurgent Ottoman Turks after the Austro-Turkish War of 1661–4 to be able to indulge in serious aggression in the West. But France, the victor of 1648, had since emerged from the troubles of the Fronde with the absolute powers of her monarchy confirmed; given her great resources of men and wealth, and a vigorous twenty-year-old king, poised in 1660 to take over personal control from the veteran Mazarin, she undoubtedly had the capacity to fulfil the Austrian diplomat Lisola's prophecy of 1643 that she would henceforward present the gravest threat to European equilibrium. Granted the many uncertainties in the European situation of the early 1660s, Protestantism and interest alike seemed to dictate to Restoration England a vigilant attitude to the Balance of Power and a readiness to apply necessary counterweights, not through any major involvement in land wars but through diplomatic initiatives and, where unavoidable, limited armed intervention based on sea power.

The sober fact is, however, that as a *principle* of foreign policy – as opposed to an occasional tactical ploy – the Balance of Power was virtually ignored by English governments for almost thirty years after the Restoration. In practical terms, from the time of Louis XIV's military successes in the Spanish Netherlands in the War of Devolution against Spain in 1667–8 (above, p. 6), a Balance of Power policy meant an anti-French policy. France was by then plainly the dominant, as well as the most aggressive, power on the Continent, and further-more, this dominance threatened concrete English interests. French designs on the whole of the Low Countries, known to Charles II as early as 1669 through his pre-Dover negotiations, and militantly confirmed in 1672, were a standing menace to national security, aimed at what had traditionally been England's most sensitive Continental spot. At the same time, England's commercial and even colonial interests were placed in potential jeopardy through the economic policies pursued by Louis's great minister, Colbert, in particular after the erection of the hostile French tariff of 1667.

Charles can be excused for being slow to grasp the full import of these earliest symptoms of French aggression. He was not alone among Englishmen in that respect. In the mid-1660s memories of old struggles with Spain and preoccupation with past and present disputes with the Dutch over colonial, African and Far Eastern trades seemed more real to most politicians and merchants than vague presentiments about France. France had, after all, been the ally of the Republic in the 1650s, and a new dynastic link had been forged with her in March 1661 through the marriage of Charles's sister, Henriette, to Louis's brother, the duke of Orléans. The aid Louis XIV gave to the United Provinces in the Anglo-Dutch War of 1665–7 (the two states had been defensively allied since 1662 (above, p. 5)) was relatively unobtrusive. The brief interlude of the Triple Alliance policy in 1668 [H.(iii)] when, following the spectacular success of the French army in Flanders, England joined with the Protestant United Provinces and Sweden to bring pressure on Louis to end the War of Devolution, must not be taken at face value. However much Charles may have *appeared* to be responding to a threat to the Balance of Power, to be heeding the warnings of the alliance's distinguished diplomatic architects, Sir William Temple – a noted advocate of a balancing rôle for England – and John de Witt,[6] or even to have experienced full conversion to a popular, 'national' policy, in fact he was doing none of these things. Admittedly, the 'League' or 'Triple Bond' was initially popular in England, a sign that feeling against France was beginning to harden, and Charles reaped some mostly undeserved credit for the resulting Franco-Spanish peace settlement. Yet he himself frankly regarded the diplomacy of 1668 as a means of extorting money from a Cavalier Parliament which for some years had grown increasingly grudging with the purse-strings, and which at the end of the Second Dutch War had shown scant sympathy for the Crown's desperate financial plight. This was not the first emergence of that financial *leitmotif* which was to permeate the King's relations with European powers, and there were to be many more such manifestations to the reign's end. Nothing better illustrates the basic irresponsibility of Restoration foreign policy than the way Charles II related almost every major policy decision, at some point, to his own domestic difficulties, usually to the state of his Treasury.

From 1669, the year in which merchants and cloth manufacturers orchestrated a noisy series of complaints in Parliament and the press against Colbertism (129b, *120–1*), the mounting antagonism towards France became unmistakable. In December 1669 Charles's prorogation of the legislature was greeted with undisguised relief by the French ambassador (39a, *97*). And yet at this very time the King's secret negotiations with Louis that were to end in the Dover alliance were already far advanced. Whatever might be said on Charles's behalf, therefore, to excuse his initial complacency in reacting to the new shifts in the Continental power structure, it is impossible to exonerate him for being prepared after 1670 positively to assist France to crush and dismember the United Provinces. His apologists' plea that most of his 'Cabal' ministers (Ch. 7) favoured a new trade war with England's old Dutch rivals at the start of the 1670s does not alter the case. With the prominent exception of Sir Thomas Clifford, none of them envisaged the creation of a huge power vacuum in Western Europe through the outright destruction of the Dutch Republic (42b), and it is significant that most of the merchants who had been so enthusiastic about the Second Dutch War in 1665 were far cooler about the Third in 1672. Charles II's blinkered attitude towards the flood tide of French power persisted for almost the whole of the last fifteen years of his reign. In the years 1681–85, for instance, he was happily to stand aside and draw his pension while Louis XIV, in his policy of *Réunions*, systematically encroached on Germany in a barely disguised bid to secure from the embattled Habsburgs the throne of the Holy Roman Empire.[7] It was isolationism with a vengeance which involved such shameless indifference to 'the balance of Europe'. As the marquess of Halifax wrote in the last weeks of the reign: 'instead of weighing in a wise balance the power of either crown [Bourbon or Habsburg], it looketh as if we had learnt only to weigh the pensions and take the heaviest'.[8]

Just once between 1669 and 1685 did Charles seem to be sincerely, if very belatedly, responding to years of growing anti-French hysteria, and to be genuinely concerned at the inability of a large coalition, headed by William of Orange, the Emperor and Spain, to subdue Bourbon ambitions that were now backed by easily the largest professional army Western Europe had seen. In 1677, in an abrupt change of front, he precipitately arranged a marriage between the Prince of Orange and his own niece, the elder daughter of his brother James. Parliament was as startled as Princess Mary, and a good deal more gratified – especially when the King followed this in December 1677 by concluding a formal Anglo-Dutch alliance [H(vi)], with the avowed end of enforcing on France a European peace, and by putting the armed forces on a war footing. Peace duly followed at Nijmegen the following year, but it was a peace much to Louis's liking, and in view of Charles's new secret deal with him a mere five months after the Dutch alliance was signed (above, p. 10), it seems unlikely that English pressure contributed materially towards it (134). Indeed, it does not require minute scrutiny of the evidence to reveal motives in the uncharacteristic digression of 1677–8 which hardly match the picture of either a good patriot or a good European. They were, in fact, compounded of a mixture of family and dynastic concerns, domestic political calculation (Ch. 7) and, as so often, financial necessity. From 1669 to 1677 Charles had been consistently selling either his alliance or his neutrality to France to make himself more independent financially of Parliament. The most plausible explanation, therefore, of the brief *volte face* of 1677–8 is that he had at last realised what Danby had been urging since 1674, that the Commons would never agree to a generous permanent settlement of the Crown's revenue until their now obsessive anxiety about the Franco-Popish menace was taken heed of.[9] In the event such a settlement proved unattainable in 1678 (Ch.7). But Danby did secure for Charles that priceless extension of the auxiliary grants of 1670–71 which was to be largely instrumental in seeing him through the Exclusion Crisis (Ch. 5), and but for the promise, and later the brief achievement, of an anti-French alliance it may be doubted whether even that would have been possible.

Mercenary or tactical considerations apart, however, the irresponsibility with which Charles II conducted relations with his European neighbours from 1669 to 1685 can only be fully understood by taking into account those pro-French personal sympathies we earlier observed. Realist though he was, Charles may well have been more dazzled by the Sun King than he would have cared to admit. This is not to say he was subservient or sycophantic. Even with Louis he could drive a hard bargain (though Louis's views on this were less comforting to Charles's self-esteem than the latter's over-inflated conceit of his own cleverness). But the bargain was a personal one at all times. The one period of which it can fairly be said that he did not sell his favours to France primarily for money or personal advantage was from 1679 to 1681, and then it was a French guarantee, at a time of acute domestic crisis, of his Catholic brother James's right of succession to the English throne which principally concerned him.

Throughout all this, inevitably, the popular or 'Country' view of England's rôle as a leading supporter of 'the Protestant interest' in Europe was reduced for most of the time to little more than a sick joke. It may even be that Charles II's own religious sympathies, already touched on (Ch. 5), are of some relevance here as well as his personal admiration for his cousin and for the ideal of authoritarian kingship which Louis XIV pre-eminently embodied. At all events,

Charles was patently prepared in the early 1670s to see – and contribute to – the elimination of the Continent's major Calvinist power; if the 'Catholic' clause of the Secret Treaty of Dover [H(iv) cl.(1)] has any meaning at all, it can only suggest that he was even prepared to make use of a foreign army, if the opportunity arose, to re-establish the Roman religion in England itself.

Most historians, however, have questioned the sincerity of the religious undertakings Charles made at Dover. The period of the Dover policy sees him at his most inscrutable and it seems unlikely now that any new evidence will come to light conclusive enough to settle the long-standing debate about his motives and objectives. Authoritative modern opinion favours the line that the secret religious clauses were either totally insincere, and deceived no one in the know, least of all Louis, or that they were an optimistic gesture designed to gain Louis's confidence but ignored as soon as it decently could be (40b, *110–16*; 36; but cf. also 136). The historian can only try to test the probabilities against what is known for certain. It seems beyond doubt that when Charles embarked on the Dover negotiations he was already attracted by the *political* aspects of Catholicism; that he knew of his brother's private conversion to the old faith in 1669, and that by this stage of his reign he was more totally disillusioned than at any other time before 1680 with the frustrations of dependence on Parliament. So some form of Catholic-absolutist deliverance from his problems must have seemed like an oasis to a parched desert traveller. From May 1670 until the outbreak of war in 1672, most of the evidence shows Charles fertile with excuses for delaying his conversion, yet he did sign a secret article in the *traité simulé* of December 1670 confirming the 'Catholic' clause and both Clifford and his brother James continued to take his commitment seriously. However murky the truth, one thing that seems unlikely is that on this occasion, at least, his objectives were purely mercenary: the Dover treaty differs entirely in scope and complexity from all the other secret agreements made subsequently with France, in particular the clauses that bound Louis to send a small army to Charles's aid at a time of the latter's choosing and bound Charles to commit his kingdoms to war against the Dutch at a time of Louis's choosing. There is also the very material point that if it was solely the French pension that the King sought he had no need to give final agreement to a document which, at very least, committed him for several years to walking a highly dangerous political tightrope. For although when the negotiations were initiated Charles was chronically hard-up – his much vaunted Triple League policy having yielded only a niggardly parliamentary supply in 1668 – before they were concluded the Commons had already shown signs of responding to Clifford's blandishments,[10] promising that new mood of generosity that was to yield the vital auxiliary duties of 1670–1 (Ch. 5).

Kenneth Haley has argued that as Charles looked ahead in 1670 to the certainty of a fresh war against the United Provinces, English naval and commercial interests were probably uppermost in his mind, rather than plain financial advantage to the Crown (36, *16–17*). It has to be said that the two strands of advantage in this case, the national and the personal, are (as with the Second Dutch War) hard to disentangle. The whole basis of the Crown's peacetime revenue was such that any long-term benefits to English trade, arising from war or negotiation, were bound to swell customs income and ultimately increase the excise yield too. Whether there was any genuine altruism behind the Dover policy can only be judged, therefore, in the context of Charles II's overall record as a promoter of trade, colonisation and naval power. His apologists have usually claimed that however selfish Charles's foreign policy may have been in other respects, it was at least designed to further English commercial and colonial interests, wherever the opportunity arose. How persuasive is their case?

The 1661 marriage treaty with Portugal [H(i)] is sometimes cited as one important piece of evidence in its support, and it is true that Charles received, along with Catherine of Braganza, two Portuguese possessions – Tangier in North Africa, a base useful for commerce protection, despite its vulnerability to attack from the Moors, and Bombay, whose long-term importance was far greater. Yet it is probable that the two factors which in the end swayed the decision were the lure of Catherine's dowry and pressure from Louis XIV, whose own interests would be clearly served by buttressing Portuguese independence against Spain (138, *46–8*). The argument that England's entry into the Second Dutch War in 1665 was essentially prompted by the King's staunch championing of the nation's economic interests against those of its chief trade rival seems superficially more plausible, until we remember that most modern scholarship now sees this as very much a 'merchants' war', and that Charles was to begin with almost as uneasy as Clarendon about getting involved in full hostilities, as opposed to the brash sabre-rattling of 1664 (135; 33, *214–19*). In the light of such evidence as this, is it feasible that one of the prime motives behind the signing of the Secret Treaty of 1670 was France's undertaking to cede to England two small islands in the Scheldt that were of some commercial importance, or even the expected capture of Dutch naval vessels?

All this is not to say that Charles was uninterested in commercial affairs; there is enough evidence of the encouragement he, like his brother, gave from time to time to the colonial ventures of his reign (Ch. 3) to set against the fact that he sold the crown colony of Bombay to the East India Company and reserved his most sustained enthusiasm for the attack on colonial charters in the 1680s (15, *Ch. 18*). It is probably true that *other things being equal* he was ready to use both defence and foreign policies, where practicable, to further such interests. His shrewdly-informed interest in the Royal Navy – best exemplified in his encouragement of Pepys's reforms (47) – would appear to point in this direction. But was he ever prepared to give such interests priority over his own, often short-term, personal, financial and political objectives? That he was not, over the reign as a whole, seems to be proved by the sheer inconsistency with which commercial advantage was pursued. In the mid-1660s an anti-Dutch policy could still be equated with the national interest, and Charles espoused such a policy, once he was convinced its advantages to himself might outweigh the obvious disadvantages to a penurious Crown. But when Colbert in the late 1660s and during the 1670s was busy transforming France into a far more serious economic competitor and ultimately a more formidable naval rival, than the Dutch, with their limited resources, could ever hope to become, Charles ignored for years the anti-French clamours of the City, the politicians and the nation as a whole, and his response when it came lasted less than six months.

Some major economic advantages did, of course, accrue to England as a direct or indirect result of foreign policy decisions taken by the Crown between 1660 and 1688, but it is not without significance that easily the most important of these – the great trade boost her merchants enjoyed as a result of English neutrality after the Treaty of Westminster [H(v)] – was a fortuitous, not a calculated bonus. On the other hand, the inability of ministers, Parliament and public opinion materially to affect the course of royal policy had one fundamental consequence of great gravity: the depressing phase of disengagement from Europe to which over time it inexorably led. The country's standing held up tolerably well in the 1660s, but except for the brief sally of 1677–8, the period after 1674 and especially that from 1679 to 1688 was characterised by low national prestige and an isolation from the mainstream of European politics that was the reverse of splendid. It was indefensible, and by the 1680s demeaning, that only twice in twenty-eight years was England able to intervene diplomatically on the Continent to any real effect in the interests of the Balance of Power. As for the only two wars in which Charles and his brother engaged, both were fought on a very limited scale, and confined almost entirely to maritime operations, and both fell well short of the achievements of the Republic's war against the Dutch. The second was mainly an expensive waste of time. The first (which the Commons financed generously to begin with) did bring in a valuable prize haul of Dutch merchant shipping, but the formal fighting contained only one victory of significance – the battle of the North Foreland, leading to 'Holmes's bonfire' (above, p. 5) – and thereafter almost everything went wrong. English trade suffered heavy damage, ground was lost to the French in the West Indies, and the war ended with the shameful spectacle of prime English men-of-war being burnt at their own anchorages in the Medway by the intrepid Dutch and in the unseemly panic in London graphically recorded in the diary of Samuel Pepys (9, *VIII, 261–9 passim*). Understandably, few exulted at the time at the North American gains made by England at the subsequent Peace of Breda. [H(ii); J.2(i)]

To sum up: by his own criteria Charles II's foreign policy may not have been a failure, financially, and in the great succession crisis of his reign, it brought him short-term rewards. One may even admire the dexterity with which at times he picked his way along a very slippery path. But one must be careful not to confuse political agility with patriotism or genuine statesmanship. Charles's claims to both are more dubious, if anything, than those of his successor.

---

1. C. Robbins, ed., *The Diary of John Milward* (Cambridge, 1938), pp. 191–2.
2. Add. MSS. 28091, ff.62–3: Commons' debate of 5 Feb 1678, speeches of Littleton, Lee, Meeres, Cavendish, Garraway, etc.
3. As yet (till 1688) an unofficial division of duties, but well understood: see M.A. Thomson, *The Secretaries of State, 1681–1782* (Oxford, 1932); *Handbook of British Chronology* (3rd edn, 1986), p. 118.
4. My pupil, Alan Marshall, has demonstrated Williamson's abilities conclusively in his

Lancaster Ph. D. thesis, 'Sir Joseph Williamson and the Development of the Government Intelligence System in Restoration England, 1660–1680' (1991).
5. Danby to R. Montagu, Feb 1678, quoted in F.M.G. Evans, *The Principal Secretary of State 1558–1680* (Manchester, 1923), pp. 139–40.
6. K.H.D. Haley, *An English Diplomat in the Low Countries: Sir William Temple and John de Witt, 1665–1672* (Oxford, 1986); M. Sheehan (137), pp. 28–9.
7. From 1682 the Emperor Leopold was engaged in a life-and-death struggle with the invading Turks (Ch. 15). In the following year Louis withdrew from Luxemburg after apparent remonstrances from Charles, but the claim that this was cause and effect cannot be justified (J.L. Price, 134, p. 133). In any case Luxemburg was reoccupied by French troops in 1684.
8. *Character of a Trimmer*, in J.P. Kenyon, ed., *Halifax: Complete Works*, p. 88.
9. For example, Add. MSS 28091, ff. 46, 59: MP's notes on debates of 16 and 20 Mar 1677.
10. Add. MSS 36916, ff. 151–7: newsletters to Sir Willoughby Aston, 11 Nov–9 Dec 1669; Add. MSS 28052, f. 72: Charles to Sir Wm. Godolphin, 12 Apr 1670: '. . . his Majesty declaring himself well pleased with what they had done both for himself and the public'.

CHAPTER 7

The constitution under stress, 1661–1678

I

The apparent equipoise achieved in England in 1660–1 between the two main arms of the constitution, Crown and Parliament, soon proved illusory. From 1663, at the latest, recurring stresses of mounting severity began to disrupt the harmonious working of the settlement accepted after the Restoration. By the 1670s the pressures on it had grown so acute that its validity was brought into serious question, until in the winter of 1678–9 England was once again facing the nightmare of total constitutional breakdown.

It will be recalled that the frustration of Englishmen's hopes of stable government during the 1650s had led the bulk of the political nation by 1660 to put its faith in traditional solutions. The result was the restoration of both the executive and the legislature to the territory they had occupied immediately before the Civil Wars (Ch. 1). Inevitably, therefore, there remained between the two sides after 1660, as at the end of 1641, a wide stretch of no-man's-land, sketchily defined, and an invitation to encroachment from both camps. It included, for example, a particularly contentious sector of the field of legislation, for while accepting that law-making was the province of the King-in-Parliament, the Crown still claimed for its own prerogative both the power to *suspend* the operation of existing laws for certain periods at the royal discretion and the power to *dispense* particular subjects from the penal provisions of statutes. Legal opinion was divided about the validity of the latter but almost unanimous that the 'suspending power' was unconstitutional (120a). In the area of law execution, too, the Crown retained powers which were capable of abuse. The Restoration Settlement had confirmed the victory of Common Law and Equity over prerogative jurisdiction. Yet the judiciary, whose job it was to interpret and administer the law, was left in a vulnerable position, with judges still open to dismissal at the royal whim if the monarch chose (as Charles II did after 1667) to have the words *durante bene placito* [A] written into their commissions (cf. Ch. 11). These were not the only grey areas, by any means. Thus the King's right to choose his ministers was nowhere legally circumscribed, yet early Stuart precedents, especially that of impeachment, had revealed Parliament's power to challenge his right to hold on to such advisers if the Commons deemed them 'evil counsellors' (109, *1–41; but cf. 77–119*).

It would have been too much to expect the Cavalier parliamentarians of 1661, buoyed up by loyalty and optimism, to anticipate such problems. In any case few of them, then or later, claimed to recognise anything basically unsound in the constitution itself; it became customary, as it had been under the early Stuarts, for them to blame everything that subsequently went wrong during this seemingly interminable Parliament on bad ministers and bad policies or on the failure of the Crown to redress reasonable grievances (41a, *16–17*). It does not follow, however, that they were always right: that, as one recent student of late Stuart politics has argued, 'the Restoration constitutional balance was not in itself unworkable' and that 'one can explain [its breakdown] in terms of Charles's political errors and of the fears which they aroused in his subjects' (41a, *2, 5*). Beyond question, much of the course of Restoration politics did hinge, as it has in every age, on the quirks of individuals, their policies, their prejudices and their mistakes. And yet, taking a realistic view of the years 1661–78, the possibilities of future trouble in Charles II's reign were latent from the very start in the indeterminate constitutional boundaries of 1660. The fact that the revenue settlement reached at that time left members of the Cavalier House of Commons with an unhealthy potential for political blackmail (Ch. 5) only served to increase the risk of friction and, ultimately, serious conflict.

This is far from saying that, even in the Commons, those who opposed the King and his ministers were constantly spoiling for a fight; in the restored House of Lords, with its 'dead weight' (in Shaftesbury's words) of Court dependants and bishops, the determination to keep the wagon on the rails was still stronger. But the Commons did become more aggressive in the 1670s, as attitudes hardened, and the Lords did not always act as a stabilising force. They rarely intervened in rows over finance, and when religion was at issue their docility could not be relied upon. Moreover, the acute sensitivity of the peers to encroachments by the Commons on their privileges led to fierce inter-House disputes which, especially in 1668–9 and 1675 (above, pp. 6–7, 9), further aggravated political and constitutional tensions by bringing parliamentary sessions to a premature and frustrating end (42a, *24–7*; 39b, *224–5*).

II

Early signs of squalls ahead in the relations between Crown and Parliament appear, at least in retrospect, in 1662. Threats to the security of the new régime seemingly posed by a series of sectarian-republican plots from the spring of 1661, to the autumn of 1663 (above, pp. 3–4), produced a strained atmosphere in which government proposals effectively to professionalise part of the militia aroused Commons' fears of a new standing army. Amity was restored by the second Militia Act, but Charles's attempt to draw the sting of the Act of Uniformity by various devices (below, p. 109) caused renewed irritation, much of which was vented against Lord Chancellor Clarendon (33, *175–6*). The sale of Dunkirk in the interval between Parliament's first and second sessions provoked a far heavier salvo from disgruntled members in 1663, and again Clarendon bore the brunt. There was even a bungled attempt to impeach him, led by the earl of Bristol. After the 1663 session the honeymoon air which had helped at first to sweeten relations between Crown and Parliament became still harder to detect. The King had grown resentful of the Chancellor's growing intractability towards the unreconciled dissenters and possibly saw him as a resolute opponent of any future plans to indulge the Catholics. Yet although he never again invested complete confidence in him after 1663, Charles still expected the earl to manage Parliament on his behalf, a thoroughly unsatisfactory position (156a, *227–30*; 25, *I, 33*). Bickering between the two partners in government, Court and Commons, became more frequent; eventually, in the autumn of 1667, with members smouldering over the failures of the Second Dutch War, the stability of that whole partnership was for the first time threatened, until Clarendon's flight offered the chance to rebuild it on safer foundations.

It would be wrong, however, to over-personalise the strained parliamentary relations of 1663–7. Certainly Clarendon's unpopularity was an extra embarrass-ment to Charles. He had many enemies, and his opponents within the ministry, above all Secretary Arlington, probably did more by their faction feuds to upset the parliamentary apple-cart than those outside it. In the process they even used their privileged position on the Chancellor's management group in the Commons to undermine him (25, *I, 33*; 44a, *51–2*). Yet there was much more than personalities and ministerial rivalries behind the Cavalier Parliament's deteriorat-ing relations with King Charles II down to 1667. Finance, for one thing, proved an abrasive issue. For two sessions the Commons showed a certain sympathy with the King's straitened position, but thereafter members began to display a growing scepticism about the problems of the ordinary revenue, as the conviction grew that misuse of funds was at the root of them (Ch. 5). Battles over supply, though not invariably lost by the Court's supporters (see 39a, *28–33* for 1664) were protracted and galling, and the suspicious mood they engendered in the Commons is reflected in two significant constitutional departures of the years 1665–7: the practice of appropriation, that is, of tying grants of money to specific purposes spelt out in the bills of extraordinary supply, and the appointment of the first Commons' Commission of Public Accounts (above, pp. 5–6). There were distant precedents for these measures as far back as Henry IV's reign, but in a Tudor and Stuart context both were entirely novel, and the latter, in particular, challenged the King's prerogative right to manage his own revenue. Charles proved too slippery to be bound by such constraints, much helped by the impenetrability of the Exchequer procedures, and by 1670 the poor accounts commissioners had shot their bolt.[1] But while the main importance of these innovations lay ahead, after the 1688 Revolution, they nevertheless signify a clear incursion from Parliament's side into that constitutional no-man's-land referred to above (41a, *7–11*; 39b, *228*).

In his study of the Cavalier House of Commons Dr Witcombe makes much of religion as a major contributor to political instability down to 1674; but in the years from 1661 to 1667, as he correctly points out, Charles's flexibility on the question of toleration for minorities outside the Established Church acted as an effective safety-valve (39a, *173*). Above all, he was not yet widely suspected of any sinister Catholic design. He was known to be grateful to his Catholic subjects both for supporting his father and contriving his own escape in 1651. Privately he freely admitted his hopes of rewarding them with a measure of relief, but a feature of the 1660s is that *publicly* this intention was kept securely battened down. After the failure of the Savoy Conference and the hopes of Protestant comprehension (Ch. 1), Charles's main priority, in the spirit of Breda, was to temper the severity of the Uniformity Act of 1662 and of future harassing legislation against Protestant nonconformists which he rightly foresaw. To do this he was prepared to use his suspending and dispensing powers, a fact which with hindsight invests the skirmishes of 1662–3 over the religious settlement with a more ominous air than was generally apparent at the time. For it was characteristic of Charles that, aware of the controversial nature of these powers, he rested his case for using them not on the prerogative (as James II was later to do) but on the discretionary power, and the responsibility to all his subjects, which he enjoyed as Supreme Governor of the Church of England.

His first step could not have been faulted for propriety. With the help of Clarendon and several bishops he pushed for the inclusion of a dispensing clause, tender of Presbyterian susceptibilities, in the Uniformity bill:[2] it passed the Lords but met a brick wall in the Commons. In June 1662 Charles tried a more serious gambit. He floated before the Privy Council a scheme to suspend the new Act's operation, initially for a period of three months. When episcopal counsellors, rallied by Bishop Sheldon, combined with government lawyers to oppose this move, the King backed down – but only to try a different tactic six months later. In what historians have traditionally described as his 'First Declaration of Indulgence' [N.1(iii)], but what is now seen as more 'a declaration of intent' (40a, 45), Charles proposed, by proclamation, to fulfil his obligations to the Puritans by using his dispensing power, 'that power . . . which he conceived to be inherent in him', to relieve certain individuals convicted under the penal laws. Acting with great caution, however, he added a caveat: he would not exercise this right until he had sought and received the consent of Parliament at its next meeting (2, *IV, 257–8*). Despite a spirited defence of his dispensing power, however, in the Speech from the Throne in February, and the encouragement of the Lords, this consent was not forthcoming. In vigorously denying the legality of dispensations the Commons' precedents were shaky, but their financial muscle was, from Charles's point of view, only too firm. By the end of the 1663 session it was clear that he had decided to accept their rebuff.

For the next few years religion was not a prominent constitutional issue. This was mainly because, as one can see from the passage of the Conventicles and Five Mile Acts (1664–5) [N.2(iv,v)], Charles kept his head down on the toleration front; but it owed something too to the changing membership of the Cavalier House of Commons and the changing climate that induced. During the 17-year life of this Parliament in the region of 350 by-elections were held, and already before the end of 1667 deaths (which were plentiful) and promotions to the Lords had led to 112 seats changing hands (25, *I, 36, 125–522 passim*). Only 15 per cent of the 345 new members returned between 1661 and 1678 had had previous parliamentary experience (25, *I, 27*), and even in the 1660s many of the remainder belonged to a different political generation from those Puritan and royalist veterans who had crammed the Commons' benches after the 1661 General Election. Their piety and religious loyalties (anti-Popish prejudices apart) were by and large less obsessive, and their interest in material matters such as finance and the pursuit of 'place' more marked, than those of their predecessors. Of the 1661–7 entry a large majority were initially predisposed to the Court. But as time went by about a quarter of these reinforcements began to take up a less accommodating posture on supply and other government business (25, *I*, *36*), and this drift from the Court, together with the election in the years 1665–7 of a number of committed 'Country' members, such as Sir Thomas Clarges and Sir Trevor Williams, may be taken to reflect growing discontent with the government's administrative record in wartime, with the Crown's financial extravagance, and with the atmosphere of sleazy irresponsibility at Court which was shocking even to a loyal official like Pepys (9, *VI*, *167–8*, *VIII*, *361*).

The changing complexion and mood of the Commons put an additional premium on effective parliamentary management by the government, but Clarendon's ministry rarely seemed capable of supplying it. Following the clash over the dispensing power in 1663, further retreats by Charles took place on almost every occasion when serious Commons' opposition arose. Though admittedly he was handicapped by the parliamentary intrigues of factious colleagues, Clarendon's own attitude to Parliament was disastrously archaic. His ideas on government had coagulated back in 1641, when he was active in the debates of the Long Parliament. Then he was 32; twenty years later he was as convinced as ever that Crown and Parliament each had its legitimate sphere; that Parliament should not pressurise the King, and the King's ministers should not manipulate Parliament, and that the harsh experience of the 1640s would be enough to guarantee harmonious cooperation. With attendance in the House of Commons surprisingly low throughout the period 1661–81, and lowest of all in the 1660s, only organisation or a truly powerful emotive issue could guarantee the Court a working majority, however favourable the general disposition of members. Yet Clarendon's gentlemanly concept of the dignity of politics, which favoured daily *pourparlers* with a group of leading loyalist MPs, 'without any noise',[3] to smooth the path of government business, did not allow him to contemplate *permanently* marshalling a party of 'King's Friends' in the Lower House: at least, not by the coarser methods advocated (and ultimately used against him) by less scrupulous younger ministerialists, such as Arlington, Clifford and Coventry. Sadly he failed to learn even from the government's very few successes of the mid-1660s. Both in forcing through the important revision of the Triennial Act in 1664 (Ch. 1, p. 33) and in extracting an unprecedented emergency war supply of £2.5 million from the Commons in the same year, some measure of *ad hoc* organisation was successfully imposed on the Crown's supporters. The pressure, however, was not kept up, at least not by Clarendon. Thus, while the great supply of 1664 was voted in one day, the means of raising it, by reversion to the 'Assessment' used during the Interregnum, was only agreed to by the House weeks later and 'after great conflicts' (110a, *145–6 [qu. p. 146]. See also* 42a, *32*; 25, *I*, *33*; 44a, *51*).

Only with the earl's fall did the opportunity for a basic change of management arise. In 1667, with the active encouragement of some of Charles's leading ministers, the Commons worked off its anger at the failures of the recent Dutch War (Ch. 6) by projecting the impeachment of Clarendon, who ironically had disapproved of entering it. As we have seen, the King's respect for his old mentor had already evaporated. He made no bones about dismissing him, and later harrying him, though it is likely that he connived at Clarendon's escape from the country before the final attack on him could be pressed home (Ch. 5). Clarendon's friend, the long-ailing Lord Treasurer Southampton, had died six months before. The removal of the two veterans allowed a reconstruction of the ministry and ushered in that phase of Charles II's reign, from 1668 to 1673, which historians have dubbed 'the period of the Cabal'.

'The Cabal' was the label which came in time to be attached to the loose confederacy of five leading ministers which, after a confused political entr'acte, replaced the regime of Clarendon. They were a strangely mixed bunch. Sir Thomas Clifford, a concealed Roman Catholic, and Arlington, a Catholic sympathiser, were counter-balanced in religious terms by Lord Ashley, Chancellor of the Exchequer since 1661, and the duke of Buckingham, the new Master of the Horse. Ashley (the former Anthony Ashley Cooper) was an ex-Cromwellian who had gone into opposition to the Protectorate in the mid-1650s, and had friends both among Presbyterians and Independents. Buckingham, another man of Puritan sympathies, was a former royalist – the son of Charles I's favourite – who had later made his peace with the republic and married Fairfax's daughter. The group was completed by one of the King's personal cronies, Lauderdale, the Secretary for Scotland. The term 'Cabal' was coined from the initial letters of their names.

The work of Professors Lee and Haley in the 1960s put paid for good to the traditional notion of the Cabal as an unhealthy conspiracy of ministers hand-in-glove with one another in their determination to monopolise and dictate policy.[4] It is clear beyond any doubt that the five men were frequently at cross purposes, and sometimes intrigued to undermine each other's place in the King's favour, as Arlington schemed (successfully) against the volatile and dangerous Buckingham in 1669. It is also apparent that other ministers were at times at least as influential as they – notably Sir William Coventry and the duke of Ormonde, until their fall in 1669, and that indeed, the great power attributed to the group at the time was largely a myth. The real power behind the throne in these years was the power *on* the throne, Charles himself, fully liberated at last from Clarendon's tutelage, and not those sinister figures whom contemporary imaginations had by 1673 transformed into such bogies. The fears vividly expressed in the popular jingle of the day,

> How can this nation ever thrive,
> Whilst 'tis governed by these five,
> The Formal Ass, the Mastiff Dog,
> The Mole, the Devil and the Hog,

never bore much relation to reality.

Initially the only alliance which existed within the Cabal was a negative one. Arlington, Clifford and Buckingham had worked together before the autumn of 1667 to destroy Clarendon, though it is typical of the confused state of politics in the late 1660s that the other leading hatchet-man was not Ashley but Coventry. Subsequently, more positive agreement on policy matters proved elusive. The

Cabal was more or less united in a determination to achieve financial recovery for the Crown, Ashley and Clifford being prominent in the reforming Treasury Commission of 1667–72 (Ch. 5, p. 89), and also in an attempt to conclude a parliamentary union with Scotland in 1669–70 (42b, *271–2*; above, pp. 6–7). But the emphasis they all placed on religious toleration (a not unnatural one in view of their own diverse religious backgrounds) was the only major area of common ground they consistently shared; this became more marked after the failure of a second attempt at Protestant comprehension, in 1668–9, and especially after the 'Clarendonians' (hard-line Anglicans) in Parliament forced through the Second Conventicles Act in 1670 [N.2(vi); Ch. 10].

On the other hand, the five ministers did share a similar *attitude* to politics. Idealism was a scarce commodity among them. They understood the business mentality and could identify themselves with commercial interests, and their initial support for the French alliance and the Third Dutch War should be seen partly in this light. More lasting in its effects was the cynical way they conducted political relationships, setting the tone in many ways for some of the worst features of politics over the next three decades. Specifically, to win support for the King in Parliament the Cabal had no reservations about using blatant management, and even corruption, in a way that would have revolted Clarendon. Their morality was that of a new generation, the post-Restoration generation, now entrenched at the centre of influence.

It was logical, therefore, that one of the two outstanding developments in the constitutional arena which mark the period 1668–73 should be the building of a 'Court party' in Parliament. As noted earlier (Ch. 5) a key figure in this achievement was Clifford, dubbed for his pains 'the Bribe Master General'. Apart from the capture of a number of major figures from the ranks of the Commons' opposition in the autumn of 1670, apparently through the lure of office or straight financial reward,[5] not a lot is known about Clifford's tactics. The Crown had a plethora of minor working offices and antique sinecures in its gift, and when the supply of these ran dry, support could still be wooed by the judicious allocation of pensions, funded from the King's secret service money, or by the distribution of other kinds of royal bounty. It would appear that, in exploiting these assets to mobilise a numerous corps of parliamentary supporters for the King, Clifford chose to concentrate the Court's attention in particular on those Cavaliers with financial embarrassments. Although his methods had been partially anticipated by Arlington and others in 1664, Clifford can properly be regarded as the true inaugurator of the 'influence of the Crown' in the House of Commons, which was to come under heavy attack periodically from the 1690s until the middle years of George III, but which was to remain an essential cog in the constitutional machinery of Britain for almost a century and a half after 1670.

Ironically, the Cabal's most notable legacy was not able to preserve the ministry itself from destruction. The seeds of Clifford's strategy were slow to germinate. It was February 1670 before an acute 'Country' observer conceded that 'the face of affairs are much altered; the Courtiers now carry all before them in the House of Commons'.[6] The auxiliary supply votes of 1670 and 1671 (Ch. 5) brought in the first harvest. And they came too late to prevent the King embarking on his Dover policy (Ch.6), the very policy which was to delude, divide and finally wreck the Cabal. The road to Dover led on inescapably to the revival and culmination of Charles II's policy of toleration. The final devastating defeat of the Dover policy destroyed not only the prospects of toleration for years to come; it also destroyed the Cabal.

In the Clarendon period religion had only intermittently, and down to 1663, led to tension between Crown and Parliament. But by 1672–3 it had become easily the most important cause of what was by then a manifestly unstable constitutional situation. Not until Charles was bound to fulfil his military commitment to assist Louis XIV in a new war against the Dutch, in March 1672, did he also feel prepared to fulfil the first stage of his Dover commitment to Catholicism. His second Declaration of Indulgence [N.1(iv)] was a much more ambitious and determined one than that of ten years earlier. That had merely reconnoitred Charles's right to make dispensations on behalf of dissenters. Now, with the firm backing of the Cabal, the full weight of the royal suspending power was used to nullify the operation of the penal laws against *all* non-Anglicans. Charles paid calculated lip-service in his Declaration to the privileged position of the Church of England, and he drew a cunning distinction between Catholics, who were to be allowed freedom of *private* worship only, and non-conforming Protestants, who were to have the liberty of worshipping publicly under licence. But militant Protestants were not to be deceived. Too many ill omens had been detected of late: the presence of known Catholic fellow-travellers in the Cabal; the permeation of the Court by many outright Papists, from the Queen down-wards, and above all, the insistent rumours that the King's own brother and leading privy councillor, the duke of York, had been converted to the Roman faith.

By the time the Commons re-assembled in February 1673, after twenty-one months in cold storage, its members were in no mood to acquiesce in the Indulgence. In the debate on the King's Speech they proceeded by a large majority on a procedural vote to a resolution 'that penal statutes in matters ecclesiastical cannot be suspended but by an act of Parliament'.[7] When the King showed some signs of resistance there was a scarcely-veiled threat from the opposition to delay supplies for the war. Charles was also under pressure from Louis, who urged that he should on no account sacrifice £1 million of revenue for the sake of the Catholic cause; early in March, disregarding the pleas of both Clifford and the earl of Shaftesbury (formerly Ashley) that he should stand firm on his constitutional rights, he abandoned the Indulgence. The fact that Shaftes-bury, who had all along endorsed the Indulgence policy, soon afterwards came out vehemently in the House of Lords in favour of a new bill imposing the Anglican sacramental test on office-holders has seemed to some historians a *volte face* so dramatic as to presuppose that the secret clauses of the Dover Treaty had been privately revealed to him, possibly by Arlington. Professor Haley, however, has argued against the likelihood of such a leak at this stage, stressing that Shaftesbury saw William Sacheverell's Test Bill of 1673 as entirely anti-Catholic in its intent and therefore consistent with a continued championship of freedom of worship for Protestant nonconformists; and that his true parting of the ways with the Court over the issue of Popery came during the summer, when a huge wave of anti-Catholic hysteria flooded the nation (42b, *323–6*).

What is certain is that the Test Act [N.5A(i)] played a decisive part in building up that wave and so proved to be one of the great landmarks in the constitutional history of Restoration England. It is important to distinguish between the Act's long-term and short-term consequences. Ultimately it made the position of *all* non-Anglicans decidedly worse than it had been before; since its operation was eventually to be felt most cruelly by conscientious *Protestant* dissenters, it is correct to see it in retrospect as signalling the conclusive defeat of Charles's toleration policies. But initially the imposition of the Test, with the declaration against transubstantiation which accompanied it, was aimed at making a clean sweep of all Roman Catholics currently in office. (Witness the fact that the Commons sent up to the Lords at the same time as the Test bill a 'bill of ease' which, had it passed into law, would have made to Protestant nonconformists concessions not far short of those that were to be written into the Toleration Act in 1689 [Ch.23]). All-important about the immediate impact of the Test Act was that, among its first victims, it smoked out James, duke of York, who gave up the post of Lord High Admiral rather than take the Anglican communion, and Lord Clifford, who surrendered the Treasurer's white staff and went into immediate political retirement for the same reasons.

The effect of these resignations on public opinion was electric; the more so because suspicion and anxiety had just been heightened by the insinuations in a widely circulated pamphlet, *England's Appeal from the Private Cabal*, to the effect that the whole drift of government policy had for some time been dangerously pro-Catholic. By the time Parliament assembled again in October 1673 its relations with the King had for the first time in the reign become totally dominated by one overpowering emotion, fear of Popery. It was heightened not only by the recent revelations and rumours, but by the fact that Queen Catherine, after twelve years of marriage, had failed to match Charles's strapping fecundity, so that York was still heir to the throne. The peak of the Popish phobia, on this occasion, was soon passed, but while it lasted it inflicted damage on the already unstable foundations of the Restoration constitution, which could never be fully repaired thereafter, for all the determined efforts made in the mid-1670s and early 1680s to shore them up. Politically, its most obvious effect was to complete very swiftly the disintegration of the Cabal, which Clifford's resignation began. During the summer and autumn of 1673, using the weight of his new office as Lord Chancellor, Shaftesbury engaged in bitter opposition to James's intended marriage to the Catholic Mary of Modena, as well as urging a divorce on the King (46, *151*). By now he was totally disenchanted with his rôle in supporting what seemed to him a regime committed to reintroducing Popery and a French alliance, and a war probably intended to foster that design. He was also furious at the deceptions which had been practised on him. Before the end of the year he was dismissed by the King and soon went over to the parliamentary opposition. There he was shortly afterwards joined by Buckingham, also dismissed. Secretary Arlington, his nerve gone, clung on only a few months longer before retiring. Of the Cabal only Lauderdale survived into the new regime, an alliance of convenience. By December 1673, therefore, the second phase of Charles II's relations with Parliament had come to an end with the King's administration in disarray, its war and toleration policies discredited and the prerogative under heavy siege.

For the next five years the survival of the royal government and the Restoration constitution was largely in the hands of Clifford's successor at the Treasury, Sir Thomas Osborne, whom Charles in 1674 created earl of Danby. A more marked contrast to the members of the Cabal it would have been hard to imagine. His background was solidly respectable rather than brilliant, rooted in those South Yorkshire acres which had earned his father a baronetcy, and in a firm commitment to Anglicanism. When he came into the House of Commons in 1665 he was not a wealthy man compared with the great patricians of the Court. His rapid rise to become Joint Treasurer of the Navy (1668), sole Treasurer of the Navy (1671) and Privy Councillor (1672), was due partly to the influence of his patron, Buckingham, but more to sheer ability. Certainly he did not get there by boot-licking the Cabal, for he disapproved of most of their major steps of policy from the 'public' Treaty of Dover in 1670 onwards: the French alliance, the war against the Dutch, the Stop of the Exchequer, and not least the indulgence both to Catholics and dissenters. In fact, Osborne's appointment as Lord Treasurer in June 1673 was a fair measure of the straits to which Charles II had been reduced. He was in no sense a personal favourite of the King's: his canny, cold-blooded nature struck no sympathetic chord with Charles. If the King had not realised by midsummer 1673 that his toleration and foreign policies were both bankrupt and that his damaged relations with Parliament stood in urgent need of repair, Osborne would probably not have got his chance. He was selected for the job partly on his administrative record, but mainly because he commanded the confidence of a considerable section of the House of Commons (43a, *I, Chs. 1–6 passim*). Enemies he had from the start, even in Parliament and certainly at Court. But as keen a judge as Sir William Coventry was prepared to forecast as early as July 1673: 'he . . . will be too hard for them all, as experienced and crafty as they are'.[8]

If stability was to be restored to the Restoration constitution, however, there was need for a total rethinking of government strategy as well as an able new Treasurer and a changed ministry. Mere corruption as practised by Clifford had proved quite inadequate to hold a Court following together in the Commons through a major crisis of confidence. Danby had a well thought-out alternative prescription to offer, with three distinct but dovetailing features (46, *154*). In the first place, he hoped to re-construct a parliamentary majority for the Crown through the appeal of a policy of Anglican supremacy: a policy which initially, like Clarendon's, was broad enough for him to support the second Comprehension bill introduced into the Lords by the bishops in 1674, but which subsequently became strict and exclusive, and one which, more crucially, was reinforced (as Clarendon's had not been) by the full battery of Court techniques for influencing members. Secondly, he aimed to retain the loyalty of this majority, once secured, by pursuing a popular foreign policy which would assuage the anti-French sentiments now so widely apparent. Finally, he planned to use his Court party to bring the constitution into equilibrium, by persuading the Commons to make a radically new approach to the King's financial problems that would make him more solvent and less dependent.

Danby's thinking was sound, but in its short-term prospects, at least, his strategy was undermined by circumstances, in particular Charles II's fairly predictable failure to give his chief minister the whole-hearted support he deserved. For instance, Parliament was central to all Danby's schemes, and after a long prorogation for much of 1674, he intended that it should meet in November and transact business through the following winter. But without consulting his Treasurer, the King pressed a further prorogation on the Privy Council, and not until April 1675 did he permit a new session. In the field of foreign policy, too, as we have seen (Ch. 6), Danby was gravely handicapped by the King's French philanderings. And but for Charles's seemingly incurable extravagance, the Treasurer might have been able to greet Parliament in 1677 with the Crown's financial books at last impressively balanced. Almost as important, however, was the time factor. Even without unforeseen prorogations it would have taken the best part of two years to prepare the ground thoroughly enough in the Commons to put Danby's programme fully into effect, and between 1673 and 1675 the political situation grew decidedly less favourable to its implementation.

In those years a crucial change came over the character of the parliamentary opposition. Thus far, opposition to the Crown had been vigorous and hard to resist when fully roused over front-line issues. But it had not been *sustained* opposition and only to a limited extent, and for brief periods, had it been *organised* opposition. From early 1674 onwards there existed an opposition group in the House of Commons (though not yet in the Lords) sufficiently organised to be capable of achieving continuity from session to session, even across long intervals of parliamentary inactivity (42b, *349–52*). The turning-point is clear enough: the loss by the King of the support of Shaftesbury and Buckingham, and above all the defection of Shaftesbury, a ruthless man of great gifts and a parliamentarian worthy of Danby's steel. From the spring of 1674 onwards his antagonism to the Stuart brothers, particularly to James, became permanent and unrelenting; under his stimulus (it would be misleading at this stage to use the work 'direction' [Ch. 9]), the anti-ministerial and anti-Popish forces in Parliament after April 1675 ceased to be primarily defensive, checking Charles's misdemeanours and getting him back on to the straight and narrow. Aggression replaced defence. The fact that it only rarely succeeded in its objectives should not obscure the nature and importance of this change (42b; cf. 41a, *23*).

Attacks on ministers, for example, were pressed home with concerted virulence. An early attempt to impeach Danby himself failed, it is true, to get the full backing of the 'Country' members (above, p. 9). But an address for the removal of the hated Lauderdale was carried in 1675, and from March to May 1678 the Commons first narrowly failed (by five votes), and then succeeded in votes to address the King to dismiss all ministers who defended the prerogative against Parliament. Such men as the able Lord Keeper (by 1675 Chancellor) Finch, a zealous Church-and-Crown 'Tory' [D.3], were among those in their sights. But Danby himself, rightly recognised by Shaftesbury and his allies as a formidable foe, naturally remained the prime target. However, driven by fear of the Court's intentions, the Opposition in these latter sessions of the Cavalier Parliament assailed powerful citadels of constitutional principle as well as persons. Though lacking as yet any systematic programme 'to fetter the King', as Lord Conway alleged,[9] they did not jib at trying to place fresh restrictions on the powers of the Crown for particular ends (as with the abortive bills of 1674 for Habeas Corpus and judicial independence [42a, *65*; 42b, *359–61*]), and in a prophetic move (1674) they tried to challenge the succession rights of any prince of the blood who made a Catholic marriage unacceptable to Parliament (cf. Ch. 9). They narrowly failed in a bold attempt (1675) to divert parliamentary funds from the Exchequer (46, *162*) and 'tacked' anti-prerogative clauses to bills of supply in a manner which threatened (according to Finch) to 'alter the whole frame and constitution of Parliaments'.[10] They declared the standing army 'a grievance' (1674), and in 1677–8 encroached, more exceptionally, on the royal preserve of conducting foreign relations in a series of votes that were repugnant to Charles (41a, *13–14*) (Ch. 6), undeterred by the fact that the 'word Prerogative [was] made use of on all occasions to hinder us'.[11]

Aggressive disrespect for the prerogative was nowhere more apparent than in the implacable determination of opposition members and peers to secure the dissolution of the Cavalier Parliament. By 1675, when Danby's manipulation of patronage had been perfected, they were well aware that in this perpetual 'Pension Parliament' the scales were now weighted too heavily in Charles's favour. Shaftesbury, in particular, regarded a dissolution henceforward as vital to his whole strategy and was prepared to use fair methods or foul to bring it about. In a powerful speech to the House of Lords in November 1675 he identified 'a standing Parliament' as one of the greatest dangers to the safety of the nation, and only by two votes did the peers reject a motion praying the King to dissolve. An extraordinary motion brought into the Commons in February 1677 asserting that Parliament *was* dissolved (again Shaftesbury's brainchild) actually claimed 142 votes (above, p. 9). By 1678 the opposition was 'drag[ging] into debate everything most vexatious to the Court in order to force a dissolution' (46, *171*).

Such was the magnitude of the change which came over the character of opposition, and for that matter the whole political situation between 1674 and 1678. At its heart lay the transformation of the 'Country' opposition to the Court (as it had styled itself since the mid–1660s) into what seemed, to many contemporaries at least, a permanent 'Country party'. 'The adverse party . . . go on contending and disputing every particular step that is made', wrote one Court supporter, 'having a greater number of able and contentious speakers, though they are outdone in votes.'[12] It was this basic change in both the climate and structure of politics which made Danby's task so much more difficult than it would otherwise have been.

In the four parliamentary sessions between April 1675 and July 1678 the Lord Treasurer marshalled his forces for a determined effort to implement his plan of campaign and, above all, secure for the King a revenue settlement that would make him genuinely solvent. Each time he got some way along the road to success, his most concrete achievement being to prise from the Commons in 1677 and 1678 life-saving extensions of the auxiliary Customs and Excise duties of 1670–1 (Ch. 5). But each time he was thwarted in the end. On one occasion, May 1677, it was Charles himself who foiled him, insisting on an adjournment at a moment singularly inopportune for his ministers, because he resented the Commons' increasing assertiveness on foreign policy which the Francophobe Danby had privately encouraged (above, p. 9). Ironically, one of the casualties of this session was a government-backed bill, reflecting Danby's anti-Catholicism and concern to protect Anglican supremacy, which would have removed Church patronage and control of his children's education from any future Catholic ruler.[13] On at least two other occasions, however, Danby simply found it impossible to cope with the sheer wrecking potential of the new Country party. In 1675, for instance, after appeasing Cavalier prejudices by a period of strict enforcement of both anti-recusant and anti-Puritan laws, he began the Spring-Summer session confident of paving the way for success by imposing a 'Non-Resisting Test' by law [A] on members of both Houses. But the session ended in dismay and frustration, the Test bill bogged down, and the two Houses locked together over the case of *Shirley* v *Fagg*, a dispute deliberately driven on by the opposition. In 1678, following the Dutch alliance of the previous December (Ch. 6), the climate seemed more favourable still to the Court. Yet after winning some early divisions, the Treasurer found himself by May and June with his precious Commons majority crumbling away, the road to a permanent new revenue settlement blocked (above, p. 10) and a blatantly obstructionist opposition – now reinforced by a cool switch of French bribes from the Court to the Country activists – in full cry, 'turn[ing] it all into poison'.[14]

Danby would no doubt have tried again, for his worst enemies could not have charged him with lack of resolution, but he was not to be given the chance. For in the autumn of 1678, before Parliament was due to begin its next (and as events proved its last) session, his own career was threatened with ruin, the political world plunged into turmoil, and the constitution brought to the verge of collapse by the 'discovery' of the Popish Plot.

---

1. Add. MSS 36916, f.165; H.M. Margoliouth, ed., *The Poems and Letters of Andrew Marvell* (1927), II, p. 314.
2. The proviso would have enabled the King to grant a dispensation to any parish minister who objected to wearing the surplice or making the sign of the cross at baptisms.
3. [Clarendon], *The Life of Edward, Earl of Clarendon* (Oxford, 1857), II, p. 197.
4. M. Lee jun., *The Cabal*, (Urbana, Illinois, 1965); K.H.D. Haley (42b).
5. Andrew Marvell records how Sir Robert Howard, Edward Seymour, Sir Richard Temple, Sir Robert Carr and Sir Frescheville Holles 'openly took leave of their former party to head the King's business'. Quoted in Henning (25), I, pp. 33–4.
6. Add. MSS 369165, f.166: Newsletter to Sir Willoughby Aston, 19 Feb 1670. At the adjournment in April Charles expressed himself 'well pleased with what they had done'. Add. MSS 28052, f. 75.
7. *C.J.*, IX, 251 (quoted in 39a, pp. 132–3).

8. Coventry to Thynne, 7 July 1673, quoted in W.D. Christie, *The First Earl of Shaftesbury*, II, p. 149n.
9. O. Airy and C.E. Pike, eds, *Essex Papers* (Camden Soc. 1890), I, p. 168: Conway to Essex, 27 Jan 1674.
10. *L.J.*, XIII, 222–3: 23 May 1678.
11. Add. MSS 28091, f. 62: Lord Cavendish, 5 Feb 1678.
12. Sir Robert Southwell to Duke of Ormonde, 9 Feb 1678: HMC *Ormonde MSS*, NS, IV, p. 399.
13. This bill had considerably discomfited the Country leaders in the Commons, some of whom resorted to delaying tactics. K. Feiling (46), p. 166; Add. MSS. 28091, f. 59: 20 Mar 1677.
14. Southwell to Ormonde, 9 Feb, loc.cit..

CHAPTER 8

Popery and Exclusion

I

The alleged uncovering by Titus Oates in 1678 of the so-called 'Popish Plot' ushered in an episode which combined elements of melodrama, tragedy and pure fantasy to a degree that is almost unique in the history of the British Isles. It involved unworthy men, base motives and discreditable events, yet its political repercussions proved to be momentous. To appreciate the circumstances which produced it, and at the same time gave a bizarre individual the chance to achieve lasting notoriety, we need to go back many decades – at the very least, as far as the year 1605.

It was in November 1605 that a determined group of a dozen English Catholic gentry, with the connivance of two Jesuit priests, had come within an ace of consummating an astonishing conspiracy which had been almost two years in preparation. The Gunpowder Plot was the first occasion on which English Catholics had sought to liquidate members of Parliament *en masse*, but it was not the first time they had conspired either to depose or assassinate their Protestant sovereign. In the 1570s and 1580s the intelligence services of Elizabeth I's ministers had unearthed no fewer than three major plots, each followed by reprisals and the unleashing of much anti-Catholic passion. But none of those attempts became branded on the folk-memory of ordinary Englishmen in the same way as the terrible day of Gunpowder Treason. On every November 5th since 1605 the inescapable association of 'Popery' with violence and terror had been brought home to several million people by bonfires, processions, and sermons preached to captive congregations up and down the land.

One section of these audiences which needed little convincing by the 1660s was the many literate English men and women who had been reared – like three generations of their predecessors – on the strong meat of John Foxe's *Acts and Monuments*. The famous 'Book of Martyrs' catalogued in sanguinary detail the Marian burnings of the 1550s, and in one or other of its nine editions was said to be, after the Bible, the best-thumbed book in the average seventeenth-century household (45a, 5). By the 1670s, however, not only educated but popular minds were at one in their implicit assumption that Popery, as they understood it, was a ruthless, baleful force, which if unchecked would assuredly bring catastrophe in its wake. A foretaste of the blind strength of anti-Popery had been given on the eve of the Civil Wars, in the Irish-inspired panic of 1641. Latent prejudices were equally apparent when the Great Fire swept London in 1666 and was promptly blamed on the machinations of the Papists. With the Pope firmly identified with

Anti-Christ, the hand of his agents could confidently be detected in all manner of misfortunes, natural as well as political.

Anti-Popery, however, would hardly have achieved its enormous potency as an emotional and ideological force in the England of the 1670s if the Stuart family had not lain periodically under grave suspicion of promoting the Catholic cause. The courts of the first two Stuart kings had been tainted with Catholic influences. In particular, it was the coincidence between a Court that was half-Catholicised, half-Laudianised in the 1630s and the Personal Rule of Charles I which did most to implant in Englishmen's minds, thereafter, the association of 'Popery' with 'arbitrary government'. And as John Miller has emphasised (40b, *67–8, 80–4, 90*), the sheer violence of anti-Popery in England in the years 1673–89 is only fully explicable in the light of this reflex association. It is true that in the first decade of the Restoration monarchy the kind of fears that Charles I had aroused before the Great Rebellion had receded, in spite of his son's known exposure to Catholic influences in exile and his subsequent Portuguese marriage. Until the early 1670s not even the court of Charles II appeared in the public mind as suspect as those of the early Stuarts. For once, popular fears actually lagged behind events, for by 1669, as we know, Charles was already discussing with the French measures the like of which his father would never have contemplated, while his brother and heir was being secretly converted to the Old Faith.

The relative complacency of the first half of the reign was shattered for good by the revelations and resulting phobia of 1673 (Ch. 7). Ironically, recusancy in the country at large was probably weaker by then than at any time since 1600. Numerically, as Bishop Compton's religious census was to confirm in 1676 [N.6(a); Ch. 10], the Catholic community was very small. Professor Bossy's estimate suggests that little more than one per cent of the population of England and Wales embraced the faith by 1680 (151, *187–90*), and it is clear that the older Catholic families, in particular, had lost ground, by deaths or conversions. Yet, even if these facts had been appreciated at the time, they would not have brought Protestants much comfort. For what was so feared was not recusancy but *Popery* – the one being seen as a local and essentially religious manifestation, the other as an international phenomenon, which in its English guise was perceived as strongly political and primarily metropolitan. And no-one could deny that Catholicism was flourishing in the 1670s where it attracted most notice, in London, and strongest of all at Court where, it was now revealed, the Queen kept fourteen priests in her household, and the duke of York and his second, Catholic, wife Mary of Modena, maintained several more; where lay Papists were freely employed; and where the leading royal mistress for much of the decade, Louise duchess of Portsmouth, was a Frenchwoman 'of the Roman persuasion'. Under the apprehensive eyes of the Parliament-men who gathered in town for their autumn or spring sessions, masses were regularly said in the private chapels of wealthy Catholic peers, and the King looked on with indifference, if not benevolence, while London recusants flocked to the services held in the chapels of foreign ambassadors. Only very spasmodically – and then, it seemed, more as a public relations exercise than as a demonstration of serious intent – were the numerous anti-Catholic laws on the statute book enforced with even a modicum of rigour (cf. Ch. 10; *The Age of Oligarchy*, Ch. 6). And right through the 1670s, Charles II's opponents could never forget that across the Channel was Louis XIV, with his mammoth army, the ally of their King, and the living embodiment of Popish absolutism on the grand scale. To a Country MP of these years it was axiomatic that the Court Papists were as eager 'to introduce a French slavery' as 'to establish the Roman idolatry'.[1]

Acute alarm, then, was only to be expected once it became public knowledge in 1673 that the heir to the throne, a man of known autocratic temper, 'heady, violent and bloody',[2] was a self-confessed Catholic. When he acquired an Italian wife as devout as himself (1673), there was every reason to fear that James would produce Catholic sons to negate the succession rights of the two Protestant princesses, Mary and Anne, born to him by his first wife. Fears of James, it must be stressed, were not confined to the chilling prospect of a Popish succession. He remained a major force in Charles's Council even after he resigned the Admiralty, and Shaftesbury at least was convinced – as a private memorandum of 1679 makes plain – that 'his interest and design are to introduce a military and arbitrary government *in his brother's time*, which only can secure a man of his religion a quiet possession of his beloved crown.'[3]

The passing of the first Test Act, therefore (Ch. 7), brought only limited reassurance. Even when the anti-Popish fever to which England succumbed in the summer of 1673 had partially abated, the whiff of conspiracy was left in the air and the wildest rumours gained credence. The most insistent of them forced Charles to order all non-householding London recusants to leave the city for the duration of the 1674 parliamentary session. That session lasted only six weeks, and two long prorogations over the next three years, one lasting nearly fourteen months, another fifteen [E.2], fuelled suspicions that the Court had much to hide. When Andrew Marvell's *Account of the Growth of Popery and Arbitrary Government* burst like a bombshell over the country in the autumn of 1677, arguing at length the charge that 'there has now for diverse years a design been carried on to change the lawful government of England into an absolute tyranny, and to convert the established Protestant religion into downright Popery', the silencing of Parliament was seen as especially sinister.[4] By the first half of 1678 there were several hints that things might be coming to the boil. Foreign agents buzzed about the capital, intriguing merrily. There was deep apprehension about the army of well over 20,000 men, much of it raised during the previous winter's war scare (above, p. 10), which the King seemed strangely loth to pay off. By the time Parliament rose in mid-July, a thoroughly nervy, overwrought nation was just about ripe for a plot to end all plots.

That such a plot arrived exactly on cue was not coincidental. Eighteen months earlier the Reverend Titus Oates, having concluded that the Anglican Church offered inadequate scope for a man whose chief gift was a breathtaking talent for mendacity, decided on a new career, as a professional plot-detector. He trained for it assiduously: first joining the household of a Catholic peer, then getting himself received into the Roman Church, and finally securing admittance to Jesuit colleges in Spain and France. He was soon expelled from both institutions, but that was common form for Oates, who had already been expelled from

Merchant Taylors' School, from Cambridge, from the Navy and from Lord Norwich's household. He was not the most prepossessing of students, for his Latin was primitive, his language foul, and he was a homosexual. But he did stay at the colleges long enough to absorb much choice information about the Jesuit order into his phenomenal memory, information which proved priceless to him when he returned to England in July 1678, down and out, to take up his new profession.

Not finding a plot immediately to hand in London, he promptly concocted one out of his own fertile brain. Even the original 'Popish Plot', as revealed by Oates and his ally and dupe, Israel Tonge, was on the grand scale: forty-three articles intricately dovetailed to implicate various persons in high places (even the duke of York, indirectly), along with Jesuits, Benedictines and Dominicans, in a conspiracy supposedly aimed at the assassination of the King and the total extirpation of English Protestantism. Danby was not unimpressed with the revelations (43a, *I, 290–2*), but with the King frankly contemptuous Oates was forced back to the drawing-board. At the second attempt he produced thirty-eight further articles, and to the authenticity of the whole, an amazing tissue of lies stuck together by just a few strips of truth, he duly swore before a prominent London magistrate. He was interrogated at length by the Privy Council, where, despite a wonderfully assured performance, he would probably have been exposed but for two strokes of luck. One was a blind stab under questioning, when he invited the Council to search the papers of Edward Coleman, former secretary to the duke and duchess of York, and the seizures uncovered a treasonable design to overthrow Protestantism and parliamentary government with French help (45a, *70ff.*). The second came when Godfrey, the JP who had taken Oates's affidavit, was found mysteriously murdered. The plot-detector was now home and dry. The murder was unhesitatingly attributed to the Jesuits, and the Cavalier Parliament's sixteenth session began on 21 October in an atmosphere of anti-Catholic hysteria unsurpassed even by this plot-happy nation.

The situation was a godsend to the Country party and to Shaftesbury, and recent parliamentary campaigns had given them the steel to exploit it. A resolution was moved in both Houses 'that there hath been, and still is, a damnable and hellish plot . . . for the assassinating and murdering the King . . . and rooting out and destroying the Protestant religion'.[5] It passed both Lords and Commons without a single dissenting voice – a fair reflection of the extent of the panic. From these votes stemmed almost everything else of significance that happened in the remaining eight and a half weeks of the session, and two events, in particular, that were of immeasurable importance. In the first place, the former ambassador to France, Ralph Montagu, ensnared in the web of intrigue that had been spun between Louis XIV's representative, Barillon, and a small knot of Country extremists, revealed to the Commons letters incriminating Danby in negotiations earlier that year for a French subsidy. The scandalised Commons at once impeached the Treasurer; it soon became plain to Charles that, if he was to save his minister from probable disaster, he must concede what for so long had been the opposition's most persistent demand. Accordingly he first prorogued and then, on 24 January, dissolved the 'Pensioners' Parliament'. Before the prorogation, however, Shaftesbury and his supporters had succeeded in extending the range of their attack, beyond Danby and other ministers, and beyond all Catholics in Parliament [Second Test Act, N.5(ii)], explicitly to the Catholic heir to the throne. And while the attack did not at this stage involve an open attempt to exclude James from the succession to the throne, it was clear from the bids to expel him from the King's counsels and from the House of Lords in November 1678 that the launching of a full-blooded Exclusion campaign was only a matter of time.

II

In the two years between March 1679 and March 1681 English politics was totally dominated by the great Exclusion crisis. This was much more than the culmination of the conflict between Crown and Parliament which had been developing since the 1660s. It was an attempt at a bloodless revolution. The Exclusionists were bent on effecting a truly radical political and constitutional change which would have given Parliament the power to dictate the succession to the throne – a power that was explicit in all three Exclusion bills and was without precedent. The attempt was at least as revolutionary in implication as that of 1688; this does not seem surprising when one considers that among the authors of the campaign of 1679–81 were men of far more extreme political views than the majority of the architects of the 'Glorious' Revolution. Had the campaign succeeded, the political changes which ensued would, without doubt, have gone further than those of 1688–9: secularising the constitution, undermining the whole principle of hereditary kingship, perhaps to the point of inaugurating an elective monarchy, and conceivably placing heavier shackles than those of 1689 on the powers of the Crown, although we should carefully note Dr Miller's argument that most Exclusionist MPs were conservative constitutionalists at heart and did not desire a drastic diminution of the prerogative (41a, *20–2*).

In the remainder of this chaper five questions are considered. What, or who, caused the Exclusion crisis? What made the Exclusionists so formidable, on the national as well as the parliamentary stage? Of what elements were they and their opponents comprised? What objectives did each have and what tactics did each pursue? And why did the Exclusion campaign end in frustration, and eventually pulverising defeat, for its promoters?

The causes of the crisis are not as self-evident as is sometimes assumed. It was not simply the end-product of the Popish Plot, even though the plot provided almost the perfect political terrain for fighting the campaign. Although the Parliament which sat from October to December 1678 unanimously subscribed to the Plot's 'hellish' authenticity, it would never have entertained a measure as radical as the first Exclusion Bill. Proof positive of this is that even in that final, near-hysterical session the Cavalier House of Commons could not agree to exclude the Catholic heir from Parliament, under the second Test Act (above, p. 10), let alone bar him from the throne. The fact that many at the time saw Shaftesbury as the arch-villain of the piece has led some historians to echo them in assuming that he engineered the Exclusion crisis in the winter of 1678–9. Further than that, because the hysteria produced by Oates's revelations, brilliantly exploited by Shaftesbury, so clearly provided the explosive charge behind the initial Exclusion campaign, the earl has been suspected, if not of fabricating the Plot himself, then at least of encouraging Oates and other informers to come forward with spoon-fed testimony. Yet although it is true that he took Oates under his wing during the autumn, and that as chairman of the Lords' investigating committee on the Plot he protected disreputable rogues like Bedloe, whose evidence he must have known to be perjured, there is no hard evidence to support either of these suspicions (42b).

By supreme irony, it was Charles II who succeeded in doing what Shaftesbury alone could not have accomplished – plunging the country into a revolutionary situation, and transforming the Country opposition from the difficult and obstructive force it had been since 1673–4 into the dangerous and subversive force of 1679–81. This he did through the fateful decision to dissolve Parliament. It was the most serious error of political judgement Charles ever made. No doubt the Cavalier Parliament had long outstayed its welcome and would have had to go, sooner or later, but the timing of the dissolution was all-important. Charles's main motive in January 1679, protecting Danby, was commendable. But to allow himself to be stampeded into such a step when it was far from certain that the Lords would have voted Danby guilty (42b, *490–1*), and before the demented mood of the autumn and winter had subsided, was a dreadful mistake. Having raised large forces in the wake of the Dutch alliance he now had to disband them, and financially this was impossible without a fresh parliamentary grant. If, therefore, he sent the existing Parliament packing, the King had no alternative but to send out writs for the election of a new one almost at once, and new elections could not possibly have taken place in an atmosphere less favourable for Court supporters than February 1679. More than anything else, it was the heavy Commons majority [E.1(i)] the Country opposition secured at this General Election – the first for over eighteen years – which allowed the campaign for Exclusion to assume the dimensions of a serious crisis. For without the encouragement this gave him, even Shaftesbury must have hesitated to initiate so revolutionary a measure as the Exclusion bill. Even as things were, its introduction was delayed for many weeks, it was opposed by several of the leading Country stalwarts of the previous Parliament (42b, *519, 521* [re Clarges]), and it had only just passed its second Reading in the Lower House when the brief life of this Parliament was brought in May to a sudden end (above, p. 11). This muzzling of Parliament settled nothing, however, and it remained for the future to determine whether the King, having done much to create a desperate situation by his own uncharacteristic blunder, would prove to have the steel as well as the resource to extricate the monarchy from its consequences.

The magnitude of Charles's task needs to be measured against the strengths, and weaknesses, of his opponents. In the course of the struggle the Opposition was identified for the first time by a new name – the Whigs, and between 1679 and 1681 they became the most highly organised political force yet seen in Britain. This aspect will be examined more closely in Chapter 9. Here, however, it must be emphasised that it was much more than parliamentary cohesion which the Crown and its supporters had to combat. It was thanks largely to their unexampled local organisation that the Whigs were able to secure a substantial majority in the last two of the three Parliaments of the years 1679–81, even when the initial impetus they received from the Popish Plot hysteria had been lost. And this reflects the extent to which the Exclusion struggle – uniquely at this stage of British political development – was an extra-parliamentary one, conducted in the country at large. The three Exclusion Parliaments were indeed in session for only five and a half months *in toto* out of the twenty-four months the crisis period lasted [see pp. 10–12; E.2]. From May 1679 until October 1680 Charles actually succeeded in carrying on the government for almost seventeen months without any sitting Parliament, keeping the members elected in August-September 1679 waiting over a year before they were allowed to convene. And yet through all these long intervals, and even when there was no electioneering in progress, the vehemence of the Whig effort scarcely flagged.

Some clues to this achievement can be discerned by enquiring, what elements made up the Whig opposition, and in particular, what were its objectives and tactics? The aims of the Whigs were not limited to Exclusion. A second object with many was a stringent and permanent restriction of the powers of the Crown (though the Whigs were far from united on this, and it is notable that Shaftesbury himself, who was very far from being the crypto-republican of Tory libel, believed not in destroying the prerogative but in vesting it in the right hands). In the third place, the Whigs aimed, with varying degrees of sincerity, at achieving toleration for the Protestant dissenters: some, like Shaftesbury and Locke, on grounds of principle (42b; 310b, *94–101*), others for pragmatic reasons, since nonconformists supplied such an important constituent of their support. Some Whigs were enthusiastic for parliamentary reform, and a bill for this purpose, involving franchise changes and biennial elections, among much else, was introduced into the 1679 Parliament (44b, *53–4*; 96, *19*). Exclusion, however, was the heart of their programme, and it was the element of fusion provided, under Shaftesbury's generalship and organising genius, by the heavy concentration on this one central, relatively simple issue which largely explains why they were able to keep up their strength and momentum for so long.

The cauterising power of Exclusion was the more important to the Whigs because they represented a coalition of such heterogeneous interests (44b, *10–16*). The Country opposition of 1674–8 may have supplied much of the hard core of Whiggery in both Houses, and in the Lords, especially, a striking continuity of policy as well as personnel between the two periods can be traced.[6] But as already noted, by no means every Country member, or indeed peer, of that vintage automatically voted for Exclusion (dissentients on the first bill included Powle, Cavendish, Clarges, Littleton and Sir William Coventry), while Shaftesbury himself observed that no less than half of his potential supporters in the Commons which met in March 1679 were members new to Westminster.[7] To the Country core, old and new, however, there adhered, firstly, the remnants of the Old Presbyterians of the 1650s and 1660s, long since nominally Anglican but still utterly opposed to the persecution of non-Anglican Protestants; secondly, the genuine Dissenters, who had been hounded by Danby and the bishops in the mid- and late 1670s (Ch. 10). They were mostly a non-parliamentary force, but they did number more than fifty members and five or six peers in the Exclusion Parliaments (38, *374–475*; cf. 25, *I, 53*). Thirdly, there was one overwhelmingly external group, the radical element in the City of London, which had some counterpart in several provincial centres of commerce and industry. The radicals alone carried into the Whig ranks something of the levelling, republican traditions of the Interregnum, which stood in sharp contrast with the views of most aristocratic Exclusionists. One major reason for Shaftesbury's dominant, though not wholly unchallenged position among the first Whigs was that he fully appreciated the value of Exclusion in fusing all these diverse elements into a formidable weapon, since every section saw in 'the bill' the surest way to remedying its own special grievances. What else could have made the London radicals probably the staunchest supporters of the patrician earl?

By contrast, on the Court side – the 'Tory' side, as it gradually came to be called – the key figure throughout the crisis was not a parliamentary politician. Admittedly, Danby's shattered Court party of the 1670s did re-form to some extent after March 1679 and from its much reduced ranks subsequent Tory leaders did emerge to prominence and grow in stature as a result of their opposition, sooner or later, to Exclusion. Notable among them were Clarendon's son, Lawrence Hyde earl of Rochester, Lord Chancellor Finch's son, Daniel (later to be 2nd earl of Nottingham), and two of the solid Anglican gentry of the shires, Sir Christopher Musgrave and (a convert from the Country party) Sir Thomas Clarges. But from neither Court nor former Country quarter did an authentic party leader emerge *at the time*. The loyalty of the Anglican clergy, with their still unquestioning commitment to Divine, Hereditary Right and to Passive Obedience, was vital both to the Yorkist cause and to the rise of a Tory party. Archbishop Sancroft worked with passionate involvement throughout the crisis to keep his brethren firm to the rights even of a Popish successor, convincing them, and through them the country gentry, that their Church was in far greater danger from the triumph of a Whig-dissenting alliance than it was from James (14, *173–4, 66–7* [Beddard; Jones]). But Sancroft was in no sense the key figure on the Tory side. The focus of all opposition to the Whigs, in fact, was the King himself. Faced with the biggest threat of his reign, and convinced that Exclusion threatened not only the succession but the power and status, and perhaps the existence, of monarchy itself, Charles II, for once in his life, shook off his natural indolence and allowed his political talents full scope. Except during his serious illness in August 1679, it was he, time and again, who determined the aims and above all dictated the tactics of the Tories. After the initial blunder of dissolution, he rarely put a foot wrong, but especially instrumental in deciding the final outcome of the crisis after many alarms along the way were four features of a masterly campaign.

To begin with, Charles managed to recover his ground and restore his tarnished prestige with the many High Anglicans who, during the autumn of 1678 and the following winter, had wavered in face of the apparent horror of the Popish threat. He did this by readiness to compromise, or temporarily appease, on almost every other issue except the fundamental one of the succession. A variety of such ploys in 1679 all played their part in the eventual creation of a solidly-based Tory party out of a beleaguered Court rump and some Country secessionists. Three days before the first Exclusion Parliament met (above, pp. 10–11), he sent his brother James into temporary exile until the political temperature should cool; though called back in early September by ministers thrown into panic by the King's illness, James was soon packed off again – this time to Scotland where, to clucks of approval from the English clergy, he worked off his frustrations by persecuting the Covenanters (above, p. 11). Three weeks after James's first departure (for Brussels), Charles had also agreed to accept Danby's resignation and, having ensured his minister's ultimate protection by granting him a pardon under the Great Seal, was not too unhappy to see the parliamentary hounds (to Shaftesbury's annoyance) delay the introduction of the Exclusion bill while spending weeks pursuing their old quarry. The King further anticipated the bill's arrival by a tactical master-stroke in April 1679, when he admitted to his Privy Council leading members of the old Country party who were now thought to favour Exclusion. Prominent among them were Shaftesbury's nephew, Halifax, the subtlest politician of the day; the earl of Essex (as head of the Treasury Commission which replaced Danby); Lords Russell and Cavendish, two of the most distinguished Whig patricians in the House of Commons, and even Shaftesbury himself, who, somewhat to his embarrassment, became for six months Lord President.

Two aspects of the King's compromise tactics, in particular, paid handsome dividends. Right through the 1679 session, and indeed as long as the crisis lasted, Charles sought to underline his apparent goodwill and concern for a settlement by regularly talking about his willingness to look for 'expedients', as he allusively called them: conditions or 'limitations' which would make it impossible for James, if he came to the throne, to subvert the constitution or attack the Established Church. Unlike many of his later Tory supporters, and some erstwhile Whigs, there is no real evidence that, so far as the prerogative was concerned, he was sincere in these hints (contained, for example, in all his speeches to Parliament), but his professions widened the gap among his initial opponents between the small 'limitations' party and the full-blooded Exclusionists, so that by April 1679 Halifax, Clarges and others[8] had already begun to edge away from Shaftesbury on this score, and they were another essential factor in helping to rally an Anglican Tory party against Exclusion. His guarantees of support for the Church were also effective in this respect: 'I will not be for lessening it', he assured the waverers in 1679, 'and if I do, I know I less my crown, for we must march together.'[9]

The other factor of the greatest importance in recovering and holding the loyalty of thousands of Anglican gentry was Charles's attitude towards the treason trials: the ghastly trials of the Catholic priests and lay men who were charged with treason and convicted, almost all on grotesquely perjured evidence, between November 1678 and December 1680. Charles's position here was an unenviable one. It is quite possible that he believed that only Coleman, of the twenty-four Catholics who suffered the full barbarity of being hanged, drawn and quartered, was genuinely guilty. And yet he knew that to stay afloat, especially during the high tide of the Plot down to the summer of 1679, he had to allow the Crown's prosecutions to continue and make ritual sacrifices periodically to a hysteria which had infected even the monarchy's natural supporters. Kenyon has shown, however, that much of this bloodletting caused Charles deep disgust and remorse and it could explain the peculiar harshness (which has puzzled historians) of the vengeance he took on his enemies after 1681 (45a).

A second feature of the Tory campaign in addition to placatory gestures – and again it was essentially a personal aspect – was the coolness with which Charles played for time. For this purpose the most effective weapon in the King's armoury was his right to prorogue and dissolve Parliaments at times of his choosing. Thus the third Exclusion bill, like the first, had not even gone through all its stages in the Commons when Charles nipped the session in the bud. He prorogued the second Parliament no fewer than seven times before its first meeting, so that when the most dangerous of the three bills eventually reached the Lords (November 1680) Charles was able to engineer its defeat with surprising ease. It is true that the Crown had a natural advantage in the Upper House, where so many Court and government officers sat as well as the bishops. But with James once again in Scotland, having been blackballed by the Privy Council (42b, *590–1*), and a number of the King's ministers, notably Secretary Sunderland, convinced that Exclusion would have to be conceded in the end and prepared to vote for it (45b, *52–7*), few at the start of the session had regarded the Lords' verdict as a foregone conclusion. Far from buckling under pressure, however, as he often had in the past, Charles gave his potential supporters the clearest of leads to reject the bill. All the same, a Tory majority of 33 in the Lords (above, p. 11) could never have been achieved twelve months earlier. And it is significant that the King waited until this late stage in the crisis before allowing himself the luxury of frontally resisting Exclusion. For twenty-one months he had been content with the unheroic rôle of stalling and procrastinating, gambling on the fact that as long as he could stave off an early parliamentary defeat, anti-Popish hysteria would eventually die down and moderate opinion on the opposition side would swing over to the Crown and the Tories. He believed this to be all the more likely because, in order to preserve their own impetus in face of delaying tactics, the Whigs would grow in militancy and forfeit much of their initial popularity. In all these assumptions Charles was completely vindicated by events.

Thirdly, the King made skilful play with the most serious long-term weakness of the Exclusionist cause. The Whigs were unanimous on the need to debar the duke of York from the throne but far from agreed over which Protestant successor should be nominated in James's place. There were only three serious possibilities. The first was Princess Mary, the duke's eldest daughter by his marriage with Anne Hyde. It was her right which the second Exclusion bill apparently (though not by name) upheld, but as an unknown quantity and a woman, who (it was generally felt) would be too easily influenced by her husband, William of Orange, she was supported equivocally and without enthusiasm. The Prince of Orange himself had his advocates among the Whigs. He was a man of proven ability and of international stature, and, as the King's nephew, he had a blood claim of sorts. On the other hand he had little personal popularity and was too wary to commit himself. The Whigs in general seemed to William to have much in common with his own Dutch republican opponents and for Shaftesbury, in particular, he felt the deepest distrust – a feeling which the earl fully reciprocated. Although the rift in the opposition leadership in 1679 between Halifax and Essex, on the one hand, and Shaftesbury on the other, was primarily over 'limitations', it also reflected disagreements over the proposed Protestant heir. Halifax, who ideally would have liked William to succeed if the King ever agreed to Exclusion, was totally opposed to Shaftesbury's policy of keeping Whig options open and meanwhile making what capital he could out of the popularity of a third candidate, the duke of Monmouth. But it was this policy that was adopted [F(i)].

Monmouth was Charles II's favourite bastard son. He had all the charisma which Mary and William patently lacked, and his great personal appeal made him a tempting proposition for some of the more reckless Whigs. The 'adventurer' element which J.R. Jones has detected in the Exclusionist ranks, typified by the piratical Harbord and Montagu and the rakish Colchester (44b, *13–14*), made Monmouth their particular favourite. But he could never hope to win united Whig backing, let alone persuade both houses of Parliament to accept his claims, unless the King chose to remove the millstone of illegitimacy from around his neck, and this Charles blandly refused to do, exposing the suggestion that he had been secretly married to Monmouth's mother, Lucy Walter, as mere wishful thinking, and eventually dismissing him from his offices. Shaftesbury never committed himself irrevocably to the duke's cause. Nevertheless, the fact that the third Exclusion bill was the first to omit even a carefully veiled, unspecific reference to Mary's claim, and therefore appeared to leave the door ajar for Monmouth, was indicative of the growing frustration and extremism which he, and the Whigs in general, had been exhibiting for some months past.

'It is time for the tide to turn', a Tory peer had written in December 1680.[10] Even while the second Parliament was still in session, Halifax, 'the Trimmer', had conclusively gone over to the Tory camp, contributing appreciably to the scale of the Whig defeat in the Lords by brilliantly out-arguing Shaftesbury in the dramatic debate on the bill.[11] As the winter of 1680–1 drew to a close, it became fairly clear that a significant, though not yet overwhelming, body of moderate opinion in the country at large was following his example. Many discerned the spectre of a new civil war advancing dangerously close as a result of Whig intractability, and they feared such a prospect more than that of any Catholic king. The City, however, from the Corporation down to 'the crowd' on the London streets (but cf. Harris, 93, *219–20, 227*), still remained staunch, the ace of clubs in Shaftesbury's hand: only a trump could take the trick and finish the game. But Charles had just such a card in reserve, and at the psychological moment he played it. When the Whigs came up from their constituencies for the third Exclusion Parliament in March 1681, it was to Oxford, that traditional centre of loyalism, that they were called, and not to Westminster, where they could have looked to enjoy the comfort of a Protestant mob at their backs.[12]

Aware that the King had drafted a contingent of some 500 Guards into Oxford for the occasion (139a, *229*), the Whigs arrived in force, many attended by armed bands of friends, retainers and other party activists. It was an understandable sign of nervousness and frustration, but one that inevitably made their own position the more dubious.

The moral advantage had now plainly shifted to the King and the Tories. Charles was confident that the huge Commons majority which electoral energy and organisation had again secured for the Whigs [E.1] no longer reflected the true *vox populi*. Furthermore, with the firm promise, if not the actuality, of a new French subsidy in his pocket as his coach took the Oxford road (Ch. 5, above), Charles found himself in the almost unprecedented position of being able to open a session without having to ask for money at the outset. Consequently, having made plain his determination to use, if necessary, this small but serviceable and now thoroughly loyalist standing army, he was able to throw the Whigs completely off balance by a snap decision to dissolve the new Parliament a mere week after it had met, convinced that if his opponents were tempted to react by open defiance their remaining support would melt away. For Shaftesbury, however, the time for armed rebellion had not yet arrived, and the presence of the Whigs in a hostile environment effectively damped the ardour of other militants. It might have been a different matter if the Whigs had been utterly desperate rather than angry. But most of them, we should bear in mind, were quite unaware that this was the end of the road for Exclusion. They saw the premature end of the Oxford Parliament as just another frustrating setback, another instance of royal duplicity and evasion.

To historians, however, it is quite clear that by the end of March 1681 Charles II had safely weathered the Exclusion storm and had won, for the first time in his reign, a conclusive victory over his parliamentary opponents. Triumph did not come overnight; indeed it was to be some time before either side grasped the full implications of what had taken place. The fact was, however, that the comparative strength of his financial position after 1681 enabled Charles this time to clinch his victory by governing without Parliament for the rest of his reign, and without a Parliament to buttress them the Whigs were to find themselves frighteningly vulnerable, once they were exposed to the full force of the Stuart reaction (Ch. 11).

---

1. Andrew Marvell [MP Hull], *An Account of the Growth of Popery and Arbitrary Government in England* (Amsterdam, 1677), p. 14. Cf. p. 16 on Louis XIV, 'the Master of Absolute Dominion' and 'the declared Champion of Popery'.
2. Paper in Lord Shaftesbury's hand, 6 March 1679, printed in W.D. Christie, *A Life of Anthony Ashley Cooper, First Earl of Shaftesbury* (1871), II, p. 314.
3. Shaftesbury, 6 March 1679, loc. cit. (my italics).
4. Marvell, *An Account of the Growth of Popery and Arbitrary Government in England*, p. 3.
5. *Lords' Journals*, XIII, 333: 2 Nov.
6. A. Swatland, 'The House of Lords in the Reign of Charles II' (Birmingham Ph.D. thesis 1985), pp. 239–73.

7. J.R. Jones, 'Shaftesbury's Worthy Men', *BIHR*, **30** (1957) (cf. 25, I, pp. 27, 78).
8. Including at this stage the earl of Essex, who joined Halifax in outvoting Shaftesbury on the issue in the Privy Council (29 April, see Haley 42b, *517*), but who by 1680 had changed his mind again.
9. Beaufort papers (Marquess of Worcester's account), quoted Feiling (46), p. 187.
10. Add. MSS 28051, f. 94: Lord Maynard to Danby, 29 Dec.
11. H.C. Foxcroft, *Character of a Trimmer* (Cambridge, 1946), pp. 115–19.
12. Though ironically the local Westminster 'crowd' itself was possibly the most loyalist in the capital during the crisis of 1679–81. Harris (93), p. 219.

CHAPTER 9

The first political parties

I

The emergence between 1679 and 1681 of two major groups of politicians, claiming support nation-wide as well as in Parliament and recognised by historians as Britain's first genuine political parties, gives the Exclusion Crisis exceptional long-term, as well as immediate, significance. The main purpose of this chapter is to examine more closely than has so far been possible both the early development and organisation of parliamentary parties before 1679 and the machinery, platforms and ideologies which sustained the wider two-party division of the political nation after the spring of 1679. But in a brief postscript we shall also see how far these distinctions persisted during the years of the Stuart reaction which followed the dissolution of the Oxford Parliament, and with what implications for the political nation.

Whether it is justifiable to refer to 'parties' at all before 1679 is open to debate. It can be argued that in a representative political system parties exist to fight elections as well as simply to dispute control over the legislature, and that the absence of any General Election in England for eighteen years after 1661 prevented the efforts to organise members of the Cavalier House of Commons from producing more than factional groupings or 'interest groups' (44a, *49, 53, 59, 70*). Yet as we are already aware (Chs. 7, 8), there were significant developments in both Houses of Parliament between 1661 and 1678, especially after 1673, which cannot be dissociated from what happened during the Exclusion crisis. Clearly, no discussion of the origins of the first Whigs and Tories should ignore them, any more than it should neglect certain ideological threads prominent in the politics of the 1670s.

In the House of Commons, throughout the 1660s and for at least half the following decade, most of the initiatives aimed at imposing some measure of organisation on members appear to have stemmed from the ministerial rather than the opposition side. Although there were isolated exceptions, for example the determination to revise the Triennial Act in 1664 (above, p. 4), the overriding pressure came from the Court's constant need to extort supplies from a tight-fisted House. Such identity and cohesion as the Country opposition acquired down to 1675 developed largely in response to the progress of organisation on the Court side; only occasionally, as with the campaign for the Irish Cattle bill (which in any case was partly orchestrated by anti-Clarendonians within the ministry) (39a; 44a, *51*) did the opposition show the way. By 1670–1 Clifford was effectively marshalling a battalion of well over 100 government supporters in the Commons, and their cohesion on finance votes so dismayed their opponents that on one occasion it provoked a protest walk-out of 80 country gentlemen from the chamber, who 'left the rest to vote as they pleased'.[1] Nevertheless, it is very doubtful whether this Court interest deserves to be labelled a genuine parliamentary 'party', if by party we understand a group of men who shared some common interest, other than self-interest. This is why, despite the scathing denunciations of Marvell and other contemporary critics, Danby's 'Court party' of 1675–8 marks a significant step forward, looking towards 1679 and after. It was in essence a different case from Clifford's creation because, for all his manipulation of patronage and his willingness to descend to bribery through systematic use of secret service money (43b; 25, *I, 35*), Danby did seek to build up support for the King on the basis of certain policies (Ch. 7), and not simply on the basis of 'influence' alone. Moreover, behind some of these policies lay ideological assumptions which are hard to distinguish at certain points from the tenets of early Toryism. A striking example is the attempt made in 1675 to compel members of both Houses to subscribe to a declaration accepting the central Anglican dogma that resistance to legitimate kingly authority, in any circumstances, was unlawful. Danby's 'Non-Resisting Test' had had its precursors, in 1665 and again in 1669 (39a, *36*). But what was new in 1675 was the fact that the measure was promoted not by Cavalier backbenchers but by an organised Court party. The failure of the attempt does not detract from its clear significance in helping to prepare the ground for the emergence of a Tory party.

Although the Country party of 1674–8 had similar – indeed, stronger – ideological links with the Exclusionists (see below), it did lag far behind both the later Whig party and Danby's Court party in effective organisation in the Commons. Ministerial manoeuvres such as the snap adjournment of July 1677, for example, cruelly exposed its vulnerability.[2] A basic obstacle was the ingrained resistance of country gentlemen to organisation of *any* kind. Any ties which appeared to impose restraints on their liberty to speak and vote exactly as they thought fit were considered sinister. To Shaftesbury it seemed self-evident that the Court's opponents should aim to beat the Court at its own game. But this was an idea hard to implant in the minds of individualists like Sir Thomas Meres and Henry Powle. They and other leading Country spokesmen in the Commons – William Garraway, Sir Thomas Lee, William Sacheverell or Lord Cavendish, for example – would occasionally meet together, and act together. But they acknowledged no leader among themselves, and were understandably most reluctant to have either leadership or organisation imposed on them from the Upper House, where the 'malcontent' lords frequently achieved an impressive degree of concert.[3]

All the same, among Country members, as among opposition peers, there were some symptomatic developments in the years from 1674 to 1678, as the need to resist partisan initiatives from the Court party grew ever more pressing. One such development was the formation of the Green Ribbon Club in 1674. Even from the start, political consultations by some, at least, of the leaders of the parliamentary opposition appear to have taken place at its meetings, although the club's influence as an organising group was as yet relatively slight. Secondly, there was a tendency, which probably became marked as time went by, for the more committed opposition members to sit together in the Commons' chamber in St Stephen's Chapel. For instance, in 1673 the Country spokesman Sir Thomas Meres 'was something sharply reflected upon by Secretary Coventry, as if [he] . . . often used the words "of this side of that House, and that side", which was not parliamentary . . .'. Yet in 1674, when there was an attempt to introduce into a bill for securing the Protestant Religion a prophetic clause, which would have excluded from the succession any prince of the blood royal who followed the example of the duke of York and married a Catholic without Parliament's consent, the move was unapologetically attributed by Sir Gilbert Talbot, a courtier, to 'a combination betwixt the discontented and turbulent Commons on the south-east corner of our House and some hotspurs in the Upper (the earl of Shaftesbury, the Lord Halifax, earl of Salisbury and the Lord Clare being the most forward)'.[4] This latter incident throws important light on the rise five years later of the first Whig party, for it shows that one thing, at least – the explosive force of anti-Popery – did have the power to break down the Country MP's antipathy to organisation and his distrust of Shaftesbury's and other efforts to dictate tactics and policies.[5] It also warns us that by concentrating too heavily on the development of 'management' one can easily obscure the *atmosphere* of parliamentary politics in the mid- and late 1670s, which under the pressure of divisive issues was often virulent and passionate. At the climax of the 1675 session, after a division in the Commons on the recall of English troops from French service [one member vividly recalled], 'both parties grew so hot that all order was lost. Men came running confusedly up to the table, . . . every man's hand on his hilt'.[6]

It is in the field of issues and policy, where certain generally agreed priorities began to take shape in the mid- and late 1670s, that we can detect a third link between the Country party of the Cavalier Parliament and the Whig party of the Exclusion Crisis. Acute concern for the security of the Protestant interest; solicitude for the independence of Parliament against the encroachments of Danby and the Crown; an irreverent attitude to the prerogative; willingness to entertain limited statutory toleration for Protestant dissenters[7] – in all these respects, Country politicians lit a torch which it was to be natural, later, for the Whigs to take up. In March 1677 Lord Cavendish uttered pure Whiggery when he roundly attacked the High Anglican-Cavalier arguments for Passive Obedience and Non-Resistance towards erring monarchs; declaring himself '[not] of the opinion of the worthy Serjeant [Charlton] that if the Prince were a Mahometan we ought to obey him; for the protection of our liberties and properties and religion is what ties and acquires our allegiance, and [I] believe a Prince not of the established religion would be but uneasy here.' Even on the largely tactical issue, so dear to Shaftesbury's heart, of forcing a dissolution, Country members in the Commons showed themselves capable of considerable cohesion and 'labour[ed] hard to make proselytes'.[8]

Finally, symptoms of burgeoning party development began to appear outside Parliament, in the City of London, and indeed far beyond. Although the Country party was denied any major electoral opportunity until 1679, in the numerous by-elections of 1673–8 interests began to emerge in the constituencies (usually in counties or open boroughs) which bore a marked similarity to the conflicting Country-Court interests in Parliament. Cambridgeshire, Northamptonshire, Shrewsbury, Norwich and Grantham afford a few of the clearest examples of such partisan elections.[9] While, therefore, it would be fair to say that as late as December 1678 England had still to experience political parties full-blown, the lines of parliamentary division were already sharp enough, and there were already sufficient signs of organised partisanship beyond Westminster, to make the transition that took place in 1679 rather less startling than it has often seemed.

II

The effect of the crisis of 1679–81 was to create an intense, hot-house atmosphere in which the first genuine political parties produced rapid and exotic growth, though on somewhat fragile stems. Most modern parties in a democratic state possess certain essential features in common. Each normally has a leader who, with the assistance of some form of central committee, directs its activities. Each has an organisation at local level, capable of marshalling its electoral support, as well as at the centre. Each controls or relies upon organs of propaganda; can be identified, at any given time, with a broad political programme or platform; and can normally relate such policies, however they may change in detail or emphasis, to some kind of political philosophy. Jones's work on 'the First Whigs' (44b) has shown that they satisfy most of these tests. The early Tories, for their part, measure up well to some of them, though they lacked a clear-cut leadership (Ch. 8) and failed to overhaul their opponents in effective organisation until after the crisis was over.

The Whigs indubitably had their leader in Shaftesbury. His authority did not go wholly unchallenged, even after the lurid events of 1678 had seemingly vindicated all his grim warnings of the previous four years, but over those who put their faith from first to last in Exclusion, Dryden's sinister Achitophel towered head and shoulders in political, if not physical stature. It used to be thought that by 1679 the Green Ribbon Club, in its now permanent rooms at the *King's Head*, Chancery Lane, was fulfilling many of the functions of a party HQ on the Whig side. Modern scholarship has cast some doubt on this, and it is possible that its prime function remained a social one. But it can be firmly linked with the subsidisation of the Whig press and with financing and staging the Pope-burning processions and other London propagandist demonstrations during the Exclusion Crisis, and it is probable that some Whig bills and election petitions were drafted in its premises as well as in more informal 'coffee-house' clubs.[10] As for Whig party organisation, in London, in the county communities and in the borough corporations, it was developed with remarkable speed and efficiency through three successive General Elections fought out on partisan issues, the last two of which were all-out campaigns, for and against Exclusion (44a, 56–7). How far this organisation had progressed after the two 1679 Elections alone is illustrated by the huge petitioning campaign of 1680 to pressurise the King into allowing the second Exclusion Parliament to meet. The London petition alone was said to have been a hundred yards long; in the provinces scores of thousands of signatures were obtained on county and borough petitions, both by local organisers canvassing house-to-house and by peripatetic Whig agents sent out from London. The Tories made a creditable response with their own counter-petitions, whose subscribers were known as the 'Abhorrers'. Moreover, in some county constituencies, where the territorial influence of the gentry and the Crown's deliberate manipulation of lieutenancies and commissions of the peace (126b, *45–52*) gave them a natural pull, Tories were beginning to match Whigs in organisation by the final winter of the crisis (though not many election results in February 1681 reflected the fact).

Shaftesbury was an inspired propagandist and, helped initially by the lapsing of the Licensing Act (*The Age of Oligarchy*, Ch. 12) at the dissolution of the Cavalier Parliament, the Whigs of 1679–81 used polemical literature to woo the electorate on a scale without precedent. In addition to a torrent of pamphlets, a number of Whig newspapers appeared in the course of the crisis, like the *Protestant (Domestick) Intelligence* and the *True Protestant Mercury*, presenting strongly slanted versions of events. None was more effective than *Smith's Protestant Intelligence*, the work of a zealous Baptist bookseller and pamphleteer (38, *115–16*; 98). Again the Tories were forced to reply in kind, and by 1681 they had their own party news sheet, the *Loyal Protestant*, as well as L'Estrange's *Observator* and the official *Gazette*. The last two apart, such publications enjoyed only brief lives, but as the forerunners of the spate of politically-committed newspapers and newsletters which was to flood London, and finally spill over into the provinces, in the twenty years after 1695, their place in the history of party in England is assured.

That the two parties of the Exclusion period were ranged against each other on two opposing platforms, presented to the public in blunt contradistinction, was not in doubt, although we can now see that the Whig platform was more unstable than most of its supporters realised (Ch. 8). Yet one open question remains, to cast a measure of doubt on the authenticity of these first parties. Had either party developed even by 1681 a distinctive ideology, a genuine political philosophy which would entitle us to consider the struggle a conflict of party principle, as well as a conflict of parties? J.R. Jones has argued that since most of the political thought and writing of the period was produced in response to specific and urgent practical needs, it was largely improvised and superficial. Up to a point his case has to be conceded, and the same may be said of Miller's partially related argument, that the speeches of Whig MPs in the Commons debates of 1679–81 reveal rather more ideological uncertainty than conviction (44b, *214–16*; 41a, *18–23*). On the other hand there were some ideological developments of these years which went a lot deeper than the ephemeral offerings of the pamphleteers (313, *Chs. 1, 2*; 310b, *Ch. 5*). One was the publication in 1680 of Sir Robert Filmer's *Patriarcha*, a substantial work of political theory, written but not printed in the late 1640s, which justified the rights of kings to absolute obedience, and even hereditary succession, in the context of the accepted conventions of seventeenth-century social and family relationships, as well as with the biblical arguments beloved of Anglican theologians.[11] Weighty replies to *Patriarcha* came in 1681 from James Tyrrell and Henry Neville, both of whom based part of their anti-monarchical case on the history (as they saw it) of the 'ancient' English constitution.[12] Much more notable was the fact that John Locke, Shaftesbury's friend and devoted lieutenant, wrote the first of his *Two Treatises of Government* during the Exclusion Crisis in direct refutation of Filmer, and completed the bulk of his *Second Treatise*, articulating the creed of the more extreme Whigs, in the months that immediately followed the dissolution of the Oxford Parliament. Like Algernon Sidney's scarcely less radical *Discourses concerning Government*, also written in 1680–1, the *Treatises* were not to be published until William III's reign. But it seems fairly clear that the ideas of both men had a fairly wide private circulation among Whig activists before the end of 1681, even if the full sophistication of their contrasting theories of 'contract' and of their ideas on resistance was not revealed by the time the third Exclusion Parliament met (8, *intro.*; 310a; 310b). Furthermore, as Richard Ashcraft has now conclusively shown, even at the humbler level of hundreds of lesser tracts and pamphlets published in the Exclusionist cause from 1679 to 1681 – some attributable (for example to Somers, Bethel, Hunt and Settle), but most anonymous – there are important common denominators between the arguments advanced and those of the weightier political thinkers (310b, *185–6, 190–1ff.*).

While it could not be claimed, therefore, that the ideological positions of Whigs and Tories had been defined with clinical sharpness during the Exclusion controversy, both sides could and did muster very powerful theoretical and philosophical artillery, as well as a hail of small-arms fire, to support their respective platforms and actions. What can we deduce from this barrage, as well as from the public utterances of the party politicians?

In the first place, few on either side can have doubted by 1681 that one of the fundamental tenets of radical Whiggery was the idea of the sovereignty of 'the people', though it was certainly not a matter of Whig consensus how that term should be defined. Even in 1679, after Shaftesbury had accepted the Lord Presidency of the Council, he told his City friends that he would stay in the ministry 'only to be a tribune for the people there' (42b, *530*). After the opening of the Oxford Parliament, when Court spokesmen like Sir Leoline Jenkins opposed a motion to print the 'Votes' of the Commons, deploring it as 'a sort of appeal to the people', Whigs enthusiastically pressed it on those very grounds, and 'Mr Secretary . . . was soundly mumbled for his pains'. By far the commonest Whig argument in support of the third Exclusion Bill was now simply that the popular will, as successive Elections on the issue had shown, was unmistakably in its favour. 'The weight of England is the people', declaimed Sir William Cowper, 'and the world will find that they will sink Popery at last.'[13] Not that the first Whigs, or at least the great majority of them, bore much resemblance to Levellers. Most of their theorists were anxious enough to defend themselves, as Henry Tyrrell did, from Tory jibes that by 'the people' they meant 'the rabble' or 'the mob'; Locke was a rare bird in refusing to compromise on this question (310b, *302–12*). Of course the Whigs were happy enough to reap the benefits of Shaftesbury's exercises in populism, such as his stage-managing of Monmouth's 'progresses' through the West Country and elsewhere. But to all but a small minority of radicals among them, at least in the period from March 1679 to March 1681, a Parliament whose Lower House was elected by fewer than 300,000 adult males, 'men of property', on however small a scale, was unarguably the voice of the people. Not even those who called for franchise reform or more rational constituencies appear to have very seriously doubted that 'the sovereignty of the people' meant, in effect, the sovereignty of Parliament, even of an unreformed parliament. The author of *Vox Populi*, one of the most impressive Whig pamphlets of 1681, sensed no irony in giving that title to a closely reasoned justification of Parliament's central rôle in England's government and constitution, one that, by natural law, had to be *regularly* re-enacted to guarantee the 'fundamental rights and liberties' of the nation. Indeed he chose as his subtitle, *the People's Claim to their Parliaments* [sic] *Sitting*. Only when it was brought home to the Exclusionists, in the spring and summer of 1681, that Charles II was determined not to call Parliament again, was it necessary for them to re-think their position. It was then that extreme Whigs like Ferguson and Hickeringill began to write of an 'appeal' to the people outside the framework of the constitution, and it was at this period that John Locke, in his *Second Treatise*, firmly equated 'the people' with 'every man' (310b, *305, 311, 317–8*).

To all claims for popular, or parliamentary, sovereignty the Tories opposed their conviction that the royal prerogative was not merely supreme but sacred. And fundamental to that prerogative was the right of the Crown to call and dispense with its Parliaments as and when it pleased. As the coining of the word 'Abhorrers' plainly showed, the notion of an appeal to the people's will on *any* issue – from the right of a parliament to sit, to the unthinkable extremity of Exclusion itself – was anathema to the thinking Tory, as it was to the instinctive one. There could be no intellectual half-way house towards this position in the years 1679–81. To concede even a share of sovereignty in the current crisis was the recognition of its right to dictate the succession to the throne itself if the national interest, *salus populi*, required it.

By 1680 all Whigs, even moderate 'Country men' such as Winnington and Capel, were prepared to argue that no prince had a *jure divino* claim to a throne. An intrinsic part of the Exclusionists' whole political position was now (as logically it had to be) to reject the traditional, strictly religious view of the basis of authority in favour of the secular view that all civil government, including the authority of kings, rested in the last resort on consent. And some of the most influential Whig writers carried this idea a critical stage further by advancing the theory that consent presupposed an original man-made contract between those who governed and those who were governed. Opinions vary on how far the contract theory, in the distinctive form propounded by Locke, ever took an unquestioned place in Whig ideology. But the idea that all political societies rest on *some* kind of 'pact', 'agreement' or 'contract', involving 'mutual obligations' 'voluntarily entered into' is so commonplace in Whig writing of the early 1680s (310b, *190–1*) that it surely took root widely among influential members of the party. That it did so is indeed clear from the formula devised by their leaders in the Convention Parliament in January 1689, to clear the way for the disposal of the English crown after James II's flight (Ch. 13). This formula, embodied in a vote declaring a 'vacancy' of the throne to which both Houses had willy-nilly to agree, included the explicit charge that King James had 'endeavoured to subvert the constitution of this kingdom by breaking the Original Contract between King and people'. It is true that this phrase, unlike the rest of the motion, was left out of the Declaration of Rights a fortnight later. But this was because the circumstances in which the Declaration was presented demanded consensus (Ch. 13), and the Tories in the House of Lords, particularly the bishops, would never have swallowed the inescapable secularism of admitting that monarchy was contractual. The first Tories in 1680–1 almost to a man concurred with the orthodox Anglican clerical view that kingship, so far from being based on consent or any man-made bargain, was ordained by the law of God – a law which, following Filmer, they now asserted to be wholly consonant with 'the Law of Nature'.[14] When the University of Oxford pronounced its celebrated anathema of 1683 against *Pernicious Books and Damnable Doctrines*, the first two such 'doctrines' condemned were that 'all civil authority is derived originally from the people' and that 'there is a mutual compact, tacit or express, between a prince and his subjects.' And because they accepted that monarchy was a divine institution it followed inexorably that Tories, from the time of the Exclusion Crisis until confronted by the very moment of truth in January 1689, overwhelmingly subscribed to the doctrine of a divine hereditary right of succession, an 'indefeasible' right which could never be alienated or interfered with and which logically could not admit that the throne could become vacant.

The notions of consent and contract led naturally on to a third crucial assumption of Whig philosophy, one that again had to wait until the Revolution against James II for its classic manifestation. This was the claim to a right of resistance, hitherto warily explored, but made graphically explicit during 1681 by Locke, Ferguson, Samuel Johnson and others. If the people's consent was forfeited by the ruler (or if the contract was broken), the government of the country, and with it the obligation of obedience to the king's authority, was 'dissolved'. He could therefore be legally resisted and even dethroned by force. This claim the anti-exclusionists rejected. They took their ideological stand on two Tory theories as dear to the Anglican clergy of their day as the idea of divine right: the doctrines of non-resistance and passive obedience. To a legitimate sovereign acting within the law any form of resistance was sinful as well as unlawful. Even the illegal exactions of a tyrant must be *passively* endured, for, as the clergy taught, and as some Cavaliers argued in Parliament before as well as during the crisis,[15] it was God's responsibility, not man's, to mete out justice to erring monarchs. These doctrines reached their apogee in the Oxford decrees of July 1683, declaring the subject's duty of obedience 'clear, absolute, and *without exception* . . .' (46, *201*; 309, *113–14*), though it is likely that numerous lay Tories, even in the ultra-loyalist climate of Charles II's last three years, already made mental reservations to that unbending rule, lifelines some of them gladly seized hold of in 1688.

In the course of the Exclusion struggle most Whigs came to champion religious toleration for Protestant dissenters, not just as an expedient to appease a powerful group of their supporters but as a principle. This was underlined on the last day of the second Exclusion Parliament, in January 1681, when the Commons voted that the persecution of the dissenters under the penal laws was 'grievous to the subject' and a weakening of the Protestant religion (15, *II, 606*; cf. 42b, *818–19*). Shaftesbury, like his friend Locke, was a convinced protagonist of toleration. To the typical Tory, on the other hand, the established Church and the Crown were indivisible, twin interdependent props not merely of the political and religious order but of the social order as well. Therefore the Tory mind of the late seventeenth century recoiled from the prospect of allowing independent sects to practise their religion legally outside the establishment. Yet it was also during the Exclusion crisis that some enlightened Tories, clerics such as Lloyd and Stillingfleet and laymen such as Daniel Finch, Edward Dering and Thomas Clarges, revived in Parliament the cause of 'Comprehension', largely under wraps since 1668 (Ch. 10),[16] as an acceptable alternative to toleration.

Finally, it was Whig writers and theorists who in the early 1680s upheld most vigorously rights of private property against state encroachment. For all his use of demagogic methods and dubious allies, Shaftesbury believed firmly in vesting political power in the hands of men of property, but it was not only those who owned *large* or purely *landed* property whose rights Shaftesbury, and still more Locke, contended for. Whig apologists wrote extensively on the subject of property during the Exclusion Crisis (310b, *249–85*); their opponents, by contrast, 'said surprisingly little' about it (310b, *253*). The Tories were to show in 1688, when under pressure themselves, that they would be as jealous of property rights as their opponents were, but because of their enmeshment in absolutist theories, and because of their association with purges of the magistracy and the attack on the borough charters (Ch. 11), they were at first sorely vulnerable on this score.

Attempting to isolate the basic distinctions of principle between the first Whigs and Tories can, of course, serve to disguise how hazily some (though by no means all) of them were defined at the time, and how imperfectly grasped by many of the rank and file. Nevertheless, both sides were fully aware of the ideological context of the Exclusion struggle at the time, and the divisions we have just surveyed were to exercise an even more fundamental influence later, particularly on the Whigs. Between 1682 and 1685 the Whigs, stripped of parliamentary protection, saw their leadership broken up and their organisation comprehensively smashed (Ch. 11). After the landslide of the 1685 Election, when a mere 57 Whigs out of over 500 members were returned (25, *I, 47*), and once Monmouth's rebellion had ended in fiasco, it was natural that even on the Tory side much of the electoral machinery and most of the propaganda organs which the crisis of 1679–81 had produced should be allowed to fall into disrepair. Yet even when the ostensible fabric of the original parties seemed temporarily to have crumbled, the rival ideologies persisted. They, more than anything, ensured the survival of the parties' separate identities down to the time of the Glorious Revolution, in spite of such potential solvents as James II's Indulgence policies. They made it possible for the Whigs, in particular, to keep the faith during the black years of foreign exile or domestic ostracism, 1683–7, and to rediscover their cohesion in the crisis of 1688, since those events seemed so completely to vindicate much that they had preached seven or eight years earlier. And once the temporary bipartisan accommodation of the winter of 1688–9 had ended, powerful ideological reasons remained – inevitably modified but not fundamentally changed by the Revolution – why Whig and Tory would re-assert their dominance over the world of politics for at least a generation thereafter.

---

1. Add. MSS 36916, f.167.
2. H. Margoliouth, ed., *Poems and Letters of Andrew Marvell* (1971), II, pp. 353–4: Marvell to Sir Edward Harley, 17 July 1677.
3. A. Swatland, Birmingham Ph.D. thesis, pp. 239–40.
4. B.D. Henning, ed., *The Parliamentary Diary of Sir Edward Dering, 1670–1673* (New Haven, 1940), pp. 128–9; W.D. Christie, ed., *Letters . . . addressed from London to Sir Joseph Williamson . . . 1673 and 1674* (Camden Soc. N.S. 9, 1874), II, pp. 156–7: Talbot to Williamson, 28 Feb 1674.
5. See also, e.g. Christie, op.cit., II, pp. 55–6, for the organised 'union' of country gentlemen which in Nov 1673 had carried an address against the consummation of York's marriage with Mary of Modena.
6. Andrew Marvell to William Popple, 24 July, *Poems and Letters*, II, p. 342.
7. *Diary of Sir Edward Dering*, pp. 119–26.
8. Add. MSS 28091, f. 59; Add. MSS 29556, f. 94: 'R.L.' to Lord Hatton, 4 Jan 1677.
9. Henning (25), I, *passim*. J. H. Rosenheim, 'Party Organisation at the Local Level; the Norfolk Sheriff's [Country Party] Subscription of 1676', *HJ*, **29** (1984) explores an interesting repercussion in party political terms of two such by-elections, those for Norfolk county in 1675.
10. J.R. Jones, 'The Green Ribbon Club', *Durham Univ. Journ.*, **49** (1956); D. Allen, 'Political Clubs in Restoration London', *HJ*, **19** (1976); K. H. D. Haley (42a), pp. 48–9; R. Ashcraft (310b), pp. 143–5.
11. P. Laslett, ed., *Patriarcha and other Political Works of Sir Robert Filmer* (Oxford, 1949), especially pp. 231–5; cf. R. Ashcraft (310b), pp. 250–1 and n. 91 for revised dating of *Patriarcha*.
12. C. Robbins, ed., *Two English Republican Tracts* (Cambridge, 1969).
13. Anchitell Grey, *Debates* (1759), VIII, p. 293; Locke to Thomas Stringer, Oxford, 26 March 1681, printed Christie, *Shaftesbury,* II, App. VII. Cf. Shaftesbury to Lord Russell *et al.*, 30 Jan 1680: 'As our affairs stand, we have no hopes of a good composure but by *the weight of the nation* in a manner compelling us . . .', ibid., II, p. 357; also ibid., p. 310, Shaftesbury, 6 March 1679: ' . . . *the universal mind of the nation*'.
14. For example, Robert Brady, *The Great Point of Succession Discussed* (1681).
15. For example, Add. MSS 28091, f. 59: Hales, 20 Mar 1677.
16. The bishops in the House of Lords had, however, promoted a Comprehension bill, which had made only limited progress in 1674.

CHAPTER 10

Reason, authority and dissent:
science and religion, 1662–1687

Behind the opposed secularist and religious views of monarchy in the decade before the Revolution lay a deeper debate about religion itself. In two respects the authority of religion was under pressure between the 1660s and the 1680s. For one thing, in both Charles II's British kingdoms the supremacy of the re-established state churches fell well short of completeness. In Scotland, helped by a deep split among the Presbyterians throughout the 1650s between 'Resolution-ers' and 'Protesters', the makers of the Restoration ecclesiastical settlement had attempted to enforce an episcopalian church order on an unreceptive nation. They had also put an end to the election of ministers and restored lay patronage over benefices (see above, pp. 3–4). Although in some respects more hybrid and moderate than its Cavalier-Anglican counterpart in England, especially when Lauderdale was pursuing conciliatory policies from 1669 to 1674 (above, pp. 6–8), the Scottish settlement was also more alien (281). Over two decades after 1661 it provoked widespread nonconformity and two Covenanting rebellions (1666 [Pentland] and 1679) before the rising of the Cameronians in 1680. The challenge to the Church of England restored by law in 1662 was less serious to the security of the kingdom. Nevertheless, the Church's authority was rejected by a dedicated minority of dissidents in both the Puritan and Catholic camps. State-sanctioned repression reduced the scale of dissent but, as we shall see, could not eradicate it. There was, however, another threat, less overt than defiance of the established churches but a source of mounting disquiet by the 1680s. The authority of the Christian religion itself was beginning to seem less than wholly secure in the face of certain intellectual and scientific currents of the day which had patently grown in strength since 1660. These currents were not (with very few exceptions) anti-religious in inspiration, but their effect was to disturb the roots of some long-standing Christian assumptions.

I

In the second half of the seventeenth century England experienced the climax of what has been justly termed her 'scientific revolution'. This must not be viewed out of context. It was not exclusively English, or 'Protestant'; neither was it narrowly confined to a few decades after 1660, or even after 1650.[1] A number of intellectual giants had bestridden the Continent of Europe since 1500. Coperni-cus, Galileo, Kepler, Brahe and Descartes had challenged the centuries-old biblical interpretation of nature and the cosmos, and despite condemnation by the Catholic Church had won widespread acceptance for their ideas – such as placing the sun, not the earth, at the centre of the planetary system – among (what we should nowadays call) Europe's tiny intelligentsia (302b, *12–17, esp. 13*; 302a, *Ch. 2*). The Frenchman, René Descartes, in the years from 1637 to 1644, had made an especially basic contribution to the whole conduct of science in the later seventeenth century. He did this both by bequeathing the 'Cartesian System' of philosophy, with its insistence on deductive method, profound scepticism about what was known, but confident optimism about what the human mind was capable of knowing, and by using that system to argue that all natural processes were susceptible to explanation by mechanical laws (302a, *Ch. 7*; 303b, *58–63*). Meanwhile, although late Elizabethan and early Stuart Britain had produced no scientific thinker of the same herculean stature, it did possess in men such as Francis Bacon, William Harvey, discoverer of the circulation of the blood (1628), William Gilbert, author of a pioneering work on magnetism, and the Scotsman John Napier, who invented logarithms, scientists of independence or particular distinction. Among these it was Bacon, an eminent lawyer and politician who personified the eager lay interest in matters scientific in early seventeenth-century England, who exercised the greatest general influence. His advocacy of an inductive, empirical method for the investigation of all natural phenomena and his insistence on a firm religious and social framework for scientific advance profoundly affected the thinking of the next two generations of his countrymen.

As their vigorous, and in large part Bacon-inspired, activity during the Interregnum plainly shows, English savants of the pre-Restoration generation were fully conscious of the wider intellectual climate of their day. It was not, therefore, freakish that it should have been in England, between the Restoration and the opening years of Anne's reign, that a great European movement achieved its most brilliant flowering. Genetic accidents must have had some bearing on that extraordinary burst of creative genius which over the course of a few decades yielded the work of Boyle, Hooke, Newton and Halley. Yet even the transcendent gifts of Isaac Newton, which seemed to bemused contemporaries to be almost beyond mere human agency,

> Nature and Nature's laws lay hid in night:
> God said, Let Newton be! and all was light[2]

could never have achieved all they did but for the richness and liberating power of the ideas he imbibed before 1670, while still in his late teens and twenties. Most Newton scholars have stressd what he owed, both specifically (for example, to the calculus as exploited by John Wallis, to the theories of Kepler, or to the Baconian insistence on experiment) and in general, to that basic premise of Descartes's thought, that all nature is explicable in terms of laws derived from mathematics – even though in his mature work Newton was to depart a long way from the rigidly mechanistic Cartesianism which remained so much in vogue on the Continent (302a, *Ch. 12 cf. Ch. 24* below).

The realisation that mathematics, physics (or 'natural philosophy') and astronomy, to say no more, would never be the same again after the late Stuart scientific revolution is not the product of historical hindsight. By Queen Anne's reign thousands of educated Britons were well aware that they stood the other side of one of the great intellectual watersheds in man's experience. Most of all were they conscious of the seemingly limitless possibilities of mathematics. Almost all the great scientific breakthroughs of the years 1660–90 – for instance, Hooke's theory of light, Halley's law of atmospheric elevation, part of Boyle's work on gases and the entire synthesis of Newtonian physics – were dependent on mathematical reasoning. Newton's *Principia* (1687), embodying his three laws of motion and his epic theory of gravitation,[3] was a triumph of sheer mathematical genius over mind-bending problems. The English title of his masterpiece, *Mathematical Principles of Natural Philosophy*, speaks for itself; as, to modern eyes, does Newton's insistence that most of the intellectual groundwork for it had been done over two decades earlier, when he was a stripling of 23 and 'in the prime of my age for invention' (*quoted* 302a, *307*).

There were, therefore, three dominant features of the scientific revolution which guaranteed it boundless influence, an influence far beyond the confines of what *we* think of as 'science' (a term which, in our restricted twentieth-century sense, was significantly unknown to contemporaries). One was the use of mathematical formulae to express a rationalistic, 'mechanical' view of the universe and the interdependence of natural phenomena. The second was the acceptance that in every susceptible branch of knowledge the approach to problems must be based on close observation and experiment. The third followed naturally from the second – an attitude of mind, common to all the great thinkers of the age and to most of its lesser luminaries too, that was not merely questing but questioning. If the title of Newton's greatest work is wonderfully revealing, so is that of Robert Boyle's, *The Sceptical Chemist* (1661). It is hardly surprising that a revolution with such characteristics should have had far-reaching effects in many fields, or that in some – in philosophy, political thinking and 'political arithmetic' (Ch. 2), and not least in religion – these effects were swiftly experienced. And it now seems equally predictable that in those areas, in spite of what Mr Briggs has justifiably called the 'profoundly religious' aims of Newtonian science (303b, *78*; 302b, *31–2*), the underlying drift and *ultimate* logic of the scientific revolution should have been secularist.

The apparent paradox requires some explanation, for it has been a frequent source of misunderstanding. To begin with, there can be no question that the bonds between the restored Church of England and the new science after 1660 were many and firm. They are self-evident in the membership and proceedings of the Royal Society (Ch. 5), that unique forum in which experimental and theoretical scientists, inventors and the forerunners of our modern 'technologists' could meet together and share their interests with 'laymen', whose involvement was none the less keen for being dilettante (305a, *12–17*). A striking feature of its fellowships was the number of Anglican divines of the first rank who were elected. Among them were Thomas Sprat, who wrote the Society's *History* in 1667; Edward Stillingfleet, distinguished author of the *Origines Sacrae* (1662), and two future archbishops of Canterbury, Tillotson and Tenison. One of the Society's founder members was John Wilkins, who became bishop of Chester; he was one of the few clergy who was a first-rank scientist in his own right, though

Bishop Seth Ward was reputed a fine mathematician. Much more significant than the rôle of the clerical fellows in the Royal Society, however, were the intellectual links which these and other clergy forged with the true men of science, above all with Newton. Naturally it was not until the 1690s that the full impact of the *Principia* on Anglican thinking became apparent: in that decade Stillingfleet, Richard Bentley, in his brilliant Boyle Lectures of 1692, and Newton's friend John Craig, Canon of Salisbury,[4] mounted a formidable defence of Christianity round Newton's view of the natural world as a divinely-inspired masterpiece of symmetry and order. But Margaret Jacob has explained how long before this an influential group of clergy whom she labels 'the Newtonians', including active fellows of the Royal Society, had appreciated the great potential of the new science as a weapon to combat irreligion and promote the Christian ethic. Personal friendship, like that of Tillotson with Halley, helped to underpin their faith in it (306, *16–17, 28ff.*).

The trouble was, the weapon was double-edged. It was some years after 1690 before the full realisation dawned on Anglicans that it could be every bit as damaging in the wrong hands as it was efficacious in the right ones; yet there was deep unease on this score in more traditionalist quarters well before the Revolution (319b, *42–3*). So strong was the reaction in the restored Church against the dogmatism and 'fanatic enthusiasm' of the Calvinistic Puritans that the appeal of the natural philosophers, with their stress on calm deduction and reasoned proof, was all too insidious. If science adopted as a firm rule that all accepted orthodoxy must be regarded *a priori* with scepticism, should not religion, too, be prepared to justify itself in the cold light of reason? In an intellectual climate in which 'all forms of traditional authority were suspect' (318, *2*) it became hard to see a convincing rôle in future Anglican teaching either for revelation or the teaching of the Fathers. By the 1680s patristic learning was under siege, and while revelation remained an integral part of the *theology* of Tillotson and his 'Newtonian' friends it had little place in their Christian apologetics. As one scholar has written of the Boyle Lecturers, 'the logic of the apologists' situation made it imperative for them to address their infidels in terms upon which both sides might agree.'[5] Two of the basic assumptions of the rationalist theologians of the eighteenth-century Church – that the essentials of Christian belief were few and simple and that men could and should be intellectually convinced of their truth – were classically expounded in John Locke's *The Reasonableness of Christianity* (1695). But they had been anticipated well before that, for example by Wolseley and by Cudworth and the 'Cambridge Platonists'.[6] For Newton, a truly religious man with a horror of atheism (and very much a man of his time, as his obsession with millenialist numerology clearly demonstrates), it was not only implicit but explicit that, while natural philosophy could 'unfold the mechanism of the world' it could not presume to explain 'the very first Cause, which certainly is not mechanical'.[7] Yet he was to be grieved over the thirty years which followed the appearance of *Principia* to find how many who claimed to be his disciples distorted his message, and how the God who for him was still a personal redeemer became, at best, a *deus ex machina* in the hands of the Deists and the exponents of 'natural religion' (Ch. 24).

II

In the period 1660–87, however, open dissent from the Christian religion itself was still of insignificant proportions compared with dissent from the authority of the state Church. In theory deviancy of the latter kind was harshly discouraged. We have already examined the circumstances which had effectively put paid by 1662 to Charles II's hopes of a compromise religious settlement, marked by that spirit of easy-going tolerance which characterised his personal attitude to matters of faith and practice (Ch. 1). Only five and a half years after the Restoration there were penal laws capable, if fully enforced, of bearing down almost as heavily on Protestant nonconformists as on Catholic recusants [N.2].

How coercive the Acts, and how fixed the lines of division cleft out in 1662–5, would prove to be in effect depended on a variety of factors. On the one hand, as well as some residual sympathy for the dissenters among politicians (Chs. 7, 9), there was also an influential moderate element among the clerical establishment, often indiscriminately lumped together under the derogatory label of 'latitudinarians' or 'latitude-men'. It lacked the coherence of a party and cannot be made to fit many of the stereotype associations (for example, with science and rationalism) which historians have sometimes foisted upon it (159; *cf*. 306). But many of its original members had conformed both to the Interregnum regime and to the restored ecclesiastical order of 1662; although united mainly in their rejection of Puritan 'enthusiasm' and extreme predestinarian doctrine, and opposed to the tolerationist designs of the Court, they were unconvinced by the path of coercion, and they included high-profile clergy, such as Wilkins, Stillingfleet and Edward Fowler, who continued to work for an ultimate accommodation that would bring all moderate Protestants inside the pale (159). There was, for instance, a surprising degree of minority support among the bishops in the House of Lords for the Comprehension bills of 1668 and 1674. On the other hand, it seems clear that a majority of the Anglican hierarchy took its lead from Archbishop Sheldon in insisting after 1663 on the strict letter of the Clarendon Code. Even so, the rigour with which these and later penal laws, like the Second Conventicles Act, were enforced was not in practice a matter which either hardline bishops or liberal Anglican divines could alone determine. It depended partly on the will or whimsy of central authority and its agents in the judiciary, but partly also – and perhaps most tellingly – on the sympathies of county and borough justices.

The picture of Protestant dissent from 1662 to 1687 thus tends to be a two-dimensional one: in the foreground, a complex tracery of local variations, while through and behind it we can glimpse the persecution of dissenters ebbing and flowing like the waters of a tidal estuary. For example, the advent of the Cabal (1668) and the lapsing of the first Conventicles Act signalled two years, down to the spring of 1669,[8] in which nonconformist worship went largely unscathed and the General Baptists even held a national assembly (160b, *115*). This interlude was succeeded, first by stern repression (May 1670–April 1671), then by a period of relief culminating in the Indulgence of 1672–3 (Ch. 7), then by mounting pressure under Danby, reaching a peak around 1675–6. The freer rein which nonconformists enjoyed during the anti-Popery scare and the Exclusion Crisis eventually gave way to the harshest reaction of all from 1681–5.

The fluctuating personal attitude of Charles II had been a highly important factor from the start in controlling the movements of the tide. It was never more decisive than in the last phase of the reign. The total commitment of the dissenters to Exclusionist Whiggery had destroyed Charles's goodwill totally. Anglican bishops found the King's courts of law more amenable than ever before to their efforts to re-enforce uniformity. The Tory gentry, too, would not easily forget the electoral indignities they had suffered at nonconformist hands since February 1679. 'After this', wrote Sir John Reresby of the electoral revolt of the sectarian cutlers of South Yorkshire, 'I concerned myself very little for the Sheffieldians'.[9] The Rye House assassination plot, in which Baptists and ex-Cromwellian officers were plainly implicated, aroused all the old fears of Puritan subversion and recoiled on the heads of the pacific Presbyterians and Quakers no less than on the tiny extremist minority. Charles II's reign closed with the nonconformists (as one of the brethren put it) 'all in expectation of ruin' (38, *163*).

However, expectation had been confounded before and it was to be so again. We have seen how, although persecution followed a certain broad national pattern, local situations were rarely stereotyped. The key variables here were the discretionary power of JPs and the influence of local corporations. The road which *could* end for a dissenter in prison or destitution invariably began with an appearance before magistrates. Everything therefore depended initially on how the latter reacted to each case brought before them. Although many county magistracies were comprehensively purged in 1660 (Ch. 1), justices often declined to prosecute under the First Conventicles Act, on such grounds as lack of seditious intent. It was probably the 1670 Conventicles Act, that 'quintessence of arbitrary malice' which Charles II and the Cabal grudgingly accepted as 'the price of money',[10] which did most to tighten the screws against nonconformity. Under it a single JP (instead of the two required in 1664) was empowered to act, on informer's evidence. The great lawyer Sir John Maynard protested that there was 'more power by this bill on one Justice of the Peace than in all the judges'.[11] Yet the sharp edge of this Act could cut both ways. Justices were often well represented on the larger municipal corporations, and there were urban Puritan strongholds which in consequence were the bane of hard-line Anglicans. In such towns as Newcastle-on-Tyne, Taunton, Great Yarmouth and Norwich crowded dissenting meetings continued to be held, often with little more than token subterfuge, even in some of the darkest years of persecution nationwide. In London, too, it was said within two months of the passing of the 1670 Act that 'the fanatics most every Sunday here [are] as numerous as ever'.[12] Much depended on how far local corporations could be infiltrated by non-Anglicans, circumventing the barrier of the 1661 Corporation Act [N.2(ii)]. Down to the years 1682–3 this was certainly not an impossibility for determined men, although, once again, the variety and inconsistency of local experience must be stressed. After 1665 less than half the members of Yarmouth corporation were conforming churchmen and when the King visited the port in 1670 the Anglican clergy were prevented from paying their respects. After a conciliar *coup* in 1678 Yarmouth's dissenters became less aggressive but their congregations remained intact down to the time of James II's first Indulgence in 1687 (Ch. 12; 160b, *381, 385, 391, 400–2* [for Newcastle]). In Bristol, staunch friends among the city fathers stood the large dissenting population in good stead down to 1681, but could not save them from savage repression thereafter; whereas in Exeter, whose bishop comforted himself even during the 1672 Indulgence that 'the government of this city stands as firm as ever . . . in the behalf of the Church and the laws', there was some relief for the place's 2,000-odd nonconformists in the late 1660s, but very little after 1673.[13]

For one sect, the Quakers, harassment became in many districts a regular fact of life. Against them, the Quaker Act of May 1662 proved a potent weapon to reinforce the rest of the armoury of penal statutes; for if local justices were minded regularly to tender the oath it prescribed – one that no conscientious Quaker could swear – a Friend could face an almost indefinite prospect of imprisonment (unless he was well-to-do enough to go on disgorging fine after crippling fine) (160a, *51, 43*; 150, *225*). Quakers were as much anathema to most Presbyterians as they were to Anglicans, and their socially insubordinate habits and 'plain speech' were likely to alienate gentlemen magistrates no less than their religious views and practices. 'For more than twenty years', writes Dr Whiting, 'the Quakers endured a storm of persecution such as no other religious body endured'. This view has been endorsed by respected authorities such as Braithwaite and Watts, and relatively speaking it is indisputable: after all, it has been estimated that 15,000 Quakers, all told, were put in prison during the persecution and that 450 died there. Yet the unpublished work of Richard Clark has revealed how even in dealing with Friends zealous magistrates were usually outnumbered by those unwilling, or unable, to act. They might be restrained by humanity, or legal scruples, by distaste for informers' evidence, or most commonly, by the failure of constables and other petty officials to present offenders; whatever their cause, these restraints were widespread.[14]

Just how important local favour was to the survival of Dissent between 1661 and 1687 can be best appreciated in the light of the havoc which truly hostile authorities *could* wreak under the new laws. Financial ruin was the chief cause of desertions from the Good Old Cause. There were implacable magistrates who could and did impose with numbing frequency, on both ministers and their lay patrons, the £20 maximum fine payable under the 1670 Act – half the annual income of a small farmer. One London pastor incurred the staggering sum of £840 in cumulative fines in one year (150, *231–2*; 160a, *56*). Reduction to bankruptcy or abject poverty was not the only hazard to be run. Inability to pay fines led regularly to confiscation of goods. Hundreds of meetings over the years of persecution were violently broken up, mob violence being at times more terrifying than the savagery of the official bully boys. It is clear that at high points of Anglican frenzy – after Venner's Rising, for instance (Ch. 1), or in the winter of 1670–1, or during 1683–4 – the shadow of imprisonment loomed over thousands. More than 200 of the ejected ministers of 1662 tasted prison at some time. In March 1661 there were 535 Yorkshire Quakers in gaol, and during a five-week period in 1664 Newgate received 797 new inmates from London Quaker meetings alone (150, *236*; 160a, *90–1*). Prison conditions were in general appalling. And yet, while dissenting resistance to authority was frequently battered, it was never broken. In issuing his Declaration of Indulgence in 1672 [N.1(iv)], the King rightly observed that it was evident 'by the sad experience of twelve years that there was very little fruit of those forcible courses'. When the second Conventicles Act was re-enforced after 1673, it caused much suffering but, even in black spots, no mass exodus to the churches. Only in the last three and a half years of the reign, the years of Tory-Anglican ascendancy following the failure of Exclusion, when they were left utterly naked of protection from Whig parliaments and justices and when Puritan councillors were purged from borough corporations (Ch. 11), did England's dissenters begin to lose numbers quite heavily – and, not surprisingly, here and there, lose heart as well. At one stage Lord Paget confessed to the Revd. Philip Henry that he could see 'no hope but upwards'.[15] Even so, most of the larger congregations contrived somehow to retain their identity, as events after March 1686, when James II issued his general pardon to English dissenters and emptied the gaols, were clearly to reveal (Ch. 12; 150, *257ff.*).

How then did they do it? Lay patronage was one factor of great importance. Despite the exodus of many Whigs to the Continent after 1681 such support remained influential right down to the late 1680s. Puritan peers like Holles, 'Bible' Wharton and Delamere showed the way, and despite the Test Act of 1673 [N.5A(i)], there were prosperous and powerful gentlemen in almost every county, men of the stamp of Sir Charles Hoghton in Lancashire, Sir John Fagg in Sussex and Sir John Gell in Derbyshire, who kept up their protective shield whatever the climate. The loyalty and resilience under persecution of such pillars of urban Dissent as Thomas Crispyn, the Exeter fuller, were likewise indispensable. Another important factor of a different nature was that nonconformists, laymen and clerics alike, learned to fight back against the law. The Quakers gave a lead with their 'Meeting for Sufferings' (1675); the growing determination of Friends to resort to legal advice, and its not infrequent success (as with the prosecution of informers for perjury), was a lesson not lost upon both Presbyterians and Independents.

By the mid-1680s, however, about half the ejected ministers of 1660–2 (Ch. 1) had died. Had the sects been unable to replace them, Anglican uniformity must still have triumphed between 1681 and 1686. The two things needful were education for the ministry, now that the doors of Oxford and Cambridge were closed to potential recruits, and a procedure for ordination. During the 1670s both problems found a solution. Of the new generation of pastors many received their divinity training in Holland, but the key factor in the long run was the ability to study at one of a group of dissenting academies which, illegally but effectively, began to sprout up in various parts of England. At just one of the best of them, Rathmell Academy in North Yorkshire, Richard Frankland took 303 pupils between 1670 and 1698, despite much early trouble with the authorities, and 110 of them became either Presbyterian or Congregational ministers

(160b, *455–9*; 160a, *188–9*). Secondly, during the brief interlude of Charles II's Indulgence policy the Presbyterians took a decisive step by initiating their own ordinations. In 1681 Dean Edward Stillingfleet reflected that it was those years, 1672–3, which saw the final transmutation of the old Puritanism into the new Dissent.

Although few of the senior Presbyterian leaders had given up hope at that stage of ultimate reconciliation with the Established Church, the vast majority of other sectarians both accepted and desired a permanent schism. Five sects by the 1670s overwhelmingly outnumbered all the others combined: Presbyterians, Independents (Congregationalists), Particular Baptists, General Baptists and Quakers. The Fifth Monarchists, along with other survivors of the anarchistic 1650s, had become a fringe sect. Archbishop Sheldon had already gathered some statistics on Dissent to prepare the ground for the second Conventicles bill (161 [Thomas], *206*). In 1676, now a frail old man, he instructed Bishop Henry Compton of London, at Danby's behest, to organise a complete religious census of England and Wales.[16] Full returns for the province of York were never made, but the 'Compton Census' [N.6] revealed for Canterbury province (which included every diocese except York, Durham, Carlisle and Chester) just over 93,000 Protestant nonconformists of communicant age – 16 and over. As an accurate gauge of the position across the country at large the census had serious shortcomings on several counts: not, as has often been claimed, because of deliberate distortion – Dr Whiteman has now disposed of the notion that many vicars 'cooked the books' so as to place their own parish situations in the most favourable light – but primarily because 'partial conformity' to the services of parish churches was still so widespread among Presbyterians and Independents that they were frequently left out.[17] In addition, the estimates produced for the northern counties (15,525) were arbitrarily contrived and well below the mark.

None the less, the returns serve to underline two things which are very relevant to the concerns of this chapter. They partly explain why for the next twelve years most Tory politicians and Anglican divines felt secure enough in their bastions to reject any calls to placate Dissent by new legislation. But they also reveal that, however much its outer shell might be chipped away by further persecution, Dissent had a solid nucleus of those who, as Sheldon put it, 'either obstinately refuse, or wholly absent themselves from the communion of the Church of England',[18] a nucleus that would prove indestructible even when the savage blasts of the 1680s were smiting it. Indeed, it can be argued on the basis of some local studies such as Brockett's on Exeter, that the determination of the hard core of dissenters to brave out the penal laws was if anything stiffer by 1685 than in 1665; and by the years 1685–7 there were signs of an increasing acceptance by the established clergy themselves that uniformity was now no longer an attainable dream and that continued persecution for conscience sake was likely to be counter-productive. In particular, by 1687 many Anglicans had convinced themselves that it was folly for Protestants to consume their energies attacking each other while a far fiercer wolf was at the door.

151

III

The indigenous Catholic community in England and Wales during Charles II's reign was appreciably smaller than the combined strength of the Protestant sectaries. Two modern scholars, using data mainly from the years 1676–87, have arrived at an estimate of roughly 60,000, a much lower figure than previously accepted (40b, *9–12*; 151, *188–9*; cf. *278–9, 282*). Professor Bossy, however, while suggesting that 'the nadir of the community's fortunes' may have been reached under the restored monarchy, attributes this to poor clerical leadership and inadequate missionary endeavour. Lay adherents did not fall away significantly, their numbers remaining roughly constant between 1660 and 1685: no higher than in the early seventeenth century and less than in the first half of the eighteenth, but stable enough to stand up to all the storms of the two decades after 1670 (Ch. 8). There were two keys to this situation, the near-total dependency of English recusancy on the sustenance of those landowners who remained faithful to the old religion, and the live-and-let-live attitude which had developed between them and their Protestant landed neighbours. Only in the North-East of England, Lancashire, parts of the Welsh border and, above all, in London, whose 2,000-odd practising Catholics included many tradesmen, shopkeepers and artisans (40b, *24–5*), can one think in terms of 'popular recusancy'. Catholics may have constituted little more than one per cent of the entire population, but their representation among the aristocracy and landed gentry was far higher. Moreover their lay leaders were politically conformist as well as socially respectable. They respected the jurisdiction of local magistrates no less than the authority of the King and the validity of parliamentary statutes – even those very statutes which laid such heavy penalties on themselves. The consequence was that they enjoyed more practical toleration from their neighbours – except at moments of the most acute phobia – than did the dissenting Protestants.

It is surely revealing that even in the hysterical atmosphere of 1679–80 only one peer (Lord Stafford) and not a single recusant gentleman of landed family was convicted of high treason by a jury. Admittedly some found it prudent to take a trip abroad and several noblemen were lodged in the Tower by order of Council; all the same, the contrast with the carnage among Roman Catholic priests is remarkable. The attitude of their Protestant neighbours towards the Catholic gentry is most clearly seen in the lax enforcement of the penal laws over the greater part of Charles II's reign. To twentieth-century eyes, surveying the ferocious array of anti-recusant and anti-missionary statutes produced by the Parliaments of Elizabeth I and James I, the wonder is that the old faith survived at all, except behind the locked doors of a few isolated mansions and manor houses. Yet by the 1660s there were still around 700 Catholic priests in England, seculars and regulars, including 150 Jesuits, and in spite of the terror of 1679–81, resulting in 17 executions and many more flights or deaths abroad, those numbers had been made good again by 1695 (151, *209, 217–19*). When modern Parliaments pass statutes it is normal to presuppose the existence both of the will to enforce them and of the means of enforcement. Yet in seventeenth-century England the former was frequently lacking and the latter, at best, defective. As early as December 1660 the King had made his own attitude towards the penal laws privately known, and it was only from 1673–5 and for rather more than three years after Oates's revelations that his Council put any serious pressure on JPs and Lords Lieutenant to turn the screws on the recusants – and not always successfully even then.

As we know, it had not been hostility to the native lay community but other factors which led to the great phobias of the 1670s (Ch. 8). When the crisis was over, the clergy of the Church of England, who had instinctively rallied to defend the hereditary right of a Catholic successor, soon found their joy at the triumph of Anglican political principles alloyed. The Roman religion still flaunted itself at Court, and the duke of York began again to participate formally in government (50, *117*; above, p. 12). Abroad, Louis XIV's ambitions now threatened Germany (Ch. 6), while his persecution of the Huguenots was fast coming to a climax. And even the most bigoted anti-Puritan divine must have found it ironical that by 1684 the recusancy laws were being principally used to flay Protestant dissenters (40b, *191*). In the winter of 1684–5, just before Charles's fatal illness, 730 pardons were granted to Catholics imprisoned during the Exclusion crisis (45a, *236–7*). But Anglican clergy were most of all disturbed by rumoured plans to admit Catholic officers to the King's army in Ireland. It was not much more than forty years, after all, since a bloody Catholic rising there had produced a turmoil so violent as to bring their Church very close to extinction. Thus when in February 1685 English churchmen learned that their new King had instructed his judges that persecution of his Catholic subjects must cease forthwith, they may have been dismayed but they can hardly have been taken aback. As James rightly implied, his late brother, had he lived, would very likely have done the same.

And so, for all their formal expressions of loyalty and prayers of thanksgiving for James's peaceful accession, many Anglican clergy were already extremely nervous about the further advance of Romanism, and some of the established Church's ablest preachers and controversialists were soon at work setting the defences of Anglicanism in order. From early in 1686 began to appear a stream of writings which, as Bishop Burnet later wrote, 'examined all the points of popery with a solidity of judgement, a clearness of arguing, a depth of learning . . . far beyond anything that had before that time appeared in our language' (1, *III, 104*). The campaign was led by John Tillotson, dean of Canterbury, and by an exceptionally gifted group of London clergy, including Stillingfleet, dean of St Paul's, and two later archbishops, Tenison and Sharp. A young chaplain named William Wake – also destined in time to become primate – crossed swords with considerable aplomb with the great Bossuet; in May 1686 John Sharp, rector of St Giles, responded to the proselytising activities of Roman priests in his parish by a course of fifteen uncompromisingly anti-Catholic sermons, the second of which was to be indirectly responsible for bringing James II and the Church of England into head-on collision (Ch. 12).

IV

The energy with which the champions of Anglicanism engaged in anti-Catholic controversy in the late 1680s reflected the extent to which the Church of England had grown in strength, influence and self-esteem since the Restoration. Its progress had bred confidence without as yet encouraging complacency. And indeed there were no grounds for complacency. Catholicism was not the only threat in 1685. Only two years before he turned his fire on Rome John Sharp had warned both Anglicans and nonconformists that their 'unnatural separation' from each other, apart from being sinful, was 'giving occasion for a deluge of atheism and profaneness and impiety'.[19] As Redwood has explained, the term 'atheism' in late seventeenth-century England was by no means as limited in its connotation as it is today (317, *11–15, 29–30*). At a time when Godfearing men were acutely aware that long-accepted systems of belief were under attack and traditional assumptions about the physical universe were crumbling they were prone to label as 'atheists' all who appeared to threaten the old order damagingly: not just the man who denied the existence of God or who scoffed at Christianity, but the Deist [A], who accepted God as an impersonal creator while rejecting any concept of a personal and redeeming deity, or those Socinians [A] whose 'evil doctrine and schism', rejecting belief in the Trinity, was beginning to preoccupy a number of London preachers between 1679 and 1685.[20] Nevertheless, the Church which was beset by these anxieties could confront them boldly, aware that it had done much since 1660 to put its own house in order.

For one thing much of the physical damage to its fabric suffered during and after the Civil Wars had been made good, while twenty-three of Wren's City parish churches, completed in the two decades after 1670, elegantly underlined the vigour of the Anglican response to the ravages of the Great Fire of London. Like the rapidly rising walls of the new St Paul's or (to take only one great provincial achievement) the huge sums raised privately for the restoration of the war-battered Lichfield cathedral, they reflected manifest pride in the Anglican inheritance. Meanwhile, after the recovery of its lands at the Restoration, the Church's revenues had been steadily repaired. It has been suggested that in counties where agricultural productivity was rising and enclosures going forward between 1660 and 1689, glebe and tithe yields improved in many county parishes. It was doubtless galling for the Church that much of the profit of improvements there, and on episcopal and chapter estates, went into the pockets of gentry impropriators and lessees – as it would continue to do until the adoption during the eighteenth century of more realistic leasing and entry fine policies (158a, *100–08 passim*; Clay, *P&P*, **87**, 1980). Yet the value of physical and practical achievements was as much symbolic as material. A dilapidated and indigent institution, unable to keep up appearances at least as successfully as the pre-war Laudian Church, would have been as fatal to the clergy's self-respect as to their hopes of re-establishing loyalty to Anglicanism in the hearts of the faithful.

As the Anglican hierarchy was well aware, the repair of the Church's discipline was just as vital to its hopes of influencing the laity as that of its buildings and revenues. 'There is nothing but discipline that keeps societies in order', wrote Archbishop Sheldon in 1669, 'and good order is what makes them continue and stand.'[21] How were he and his episcopal brethren to impose 'good order', high standards of decency, uniformity and conscientious discharge of duty on more than 10,000 conforming clergy, many of whom initially were reluctant or politic conformists? It cannot be overstressed what a formidable task this was, not least enforcing the rubric of the 1662 Prayer Book. For instance, it took Ralph Josselin, the vicar of Earl's Colne, five years to swallow the traditional Easter communion service and almost twenty years to reconcile himself to the use of the surplice,[22] and well beyond James II's reign visitors to former Puritan strongholds such as Hull and Taunton were startled to find large parish churches where the Lord's Table, instead of being railed off at the east end, still stood unabashed between chancel and nave 'in the good old manner' (3). Nevertheless, by the 1680s ecclesiastical discipline was *in general* more rigorous and successful than at any time since Elizabeth I's last years. Discipline over the laity, which entailed chiefly the clergy's ability to secure attendance at services and, among plebeians, to combat moral laxity, presented still greater difficulties. Yet by the 1680s, with business in the church courts running at higher levels than for many decades and JPs more ready than ever before to lend secular muscle to the Church's own disciplinary arm, it was beginning to seem for the first time by no means impossible of ultimate achievement. In Cheshire, for example, the number of secular prosecutions alone for non-attendance at church rose from 310 to 718 between 1681 and 1684 (162; 17 [Bennett]; 14 [Beddard], *174*).

The effectiveness of the Restoration Church's parish ministry was damaged initially by the exodus of the Puritan divines in 1662. But wherever there was a reforming episcopal presence, as in Exeter diocese under Ward and Sparrow (1662–76), the beneficial effect on clerical standards was soon felt; over the last dozen years before the Revolution the quality of the parish clergy in general gave little cause for serious concern, except in a few dioceses such as Durham, Carlisle, or Lichfield under the scandalous Wood, where untypical bishops conspicuously failed either to lead by example or to support their archdeacons in cracking the whip over offenders. London had become the show-piece of the Church by the 1680s, but more typical of the national picture was probably the situation in Leicestershire, the only county whose parish clergy have been systematically studied over the whole later Stuart period. Dr Pruett concludes that 'the great majority of the clergy [from 1660 to 1714] apparently managed to live up to their parishioners' expectations'. Most of the laity had opportunities to take communion thrice yearly or quarterly – monthly in Leicester and a few of the larger market towns – and less than 5 per cent of the county's clergy before 1688 were complained against for neglecting services (158a, *132–3*). One suspects, however, that Pruett's evidence has not allowed him to detect all the backsliding that took place during the Barlow regime in Lincoln (1675–91), for in 1686 Archbishop Sancroft was so appalled by reports of negligence in this great diocese, of which Leicestershire was a part, that he ordered a metropolitan visitation.

Pluralism soon presented as big a problem to the post-Restoration Church as it had before the Civil Wars. But three-quarters, at very least, of the pluralists were parsons in poor or modest circumstances, combining livings which separately were too small in value to ensure a reasonable livelihood; thanks to the employment of stipendiary curates, far fewer parishes than is often thought (only 20 per cent of those in Leicestershire in 1712, for instance) were served by clergymen who were non-resident. The educational standards of the Anglican clergy, too, were causing little complaint by the 1680s. Except in a few remote and inhospitable dioceses almost all vicars and rectors by the time of the 1688 Revolution held Oxford or Cambridge degrees. In the immediate aftermath of 1662, when there was a pressing need for new ordinands, bishops were not always careful enough in ascertaining candidates' knowledge of divinity before ordaining. By 1670, however, 66.5 per cent of Leicestershire clergy already held a master's degree, normally a guarantee of some theological training; a further 5 per cent held divinity degrees; most kept adequate or good libraries (158a, *43* [Table], *42* for MA degree). The exceptions were usually victims of poverty rather than idle wastrels.

It has been argued that the influence of the Anglican clergy over the conforming laity, at least in rural parishes and country market towns, had never been as strong (nor was to be again) as in the late 1670s and 1680s. Certainly, if church attendance is used as a yardstick the case seems a strong one. Parsons struggling in King William's reign to stem a swelling tide of defections from their congregations (Ch. 23) recalled with nostalgia the years before the Revolution as a halcyon period of full churches, crowded communion rails every Easter and biddable flocks (17 [Bennett], *157*). Pruett has shown that the picture can be too idealised (158a, *116–20 passim*). Nevertheless, there was one respect in which the power of the post-Restoration Church was unequivocal. This was a church with a social and political as well as a spiritual mission. There was remarkable unanimity among its bishops and priests as to what that message was and they preached it with regularity and conviction. It was virtually an article of faith that as well as being ministers of the gospel of Christ they were also bound to do all in their power to promote the service of the King, as head of both church and state, for was it not the Church of England's special glory to be (in the memorable words uttered by Clarendon's chaplain in 1666) 'the truest friend to kings, and to kingly government, of any other church in the world'?[23] Again and again Anglicans were told that Christian obedience to kings, as the fathers of their peoples, was as necessary to a healthy body politic as the obedience of children to parents and servants to masters was requisite for the coherence of the social order. As for the doctrines of Divine Hereditary Right and Non-Resistance, they were commended to congregations more fervently in the 1680s – especially after the Rye House Plot and the Monmouth Rebellion (Ch. 11) – than ever they had been in Laud's time.

Ironically, the Church of England's impressive recovery from the disasters of the Puritan Revolution owed less to the support of the Crown than so loyal a state church deserved. For fifteen years Charles II displayed a tolerant view of Dissent, a barely-disguised sympathy for Catholics and an amused contempt for the Church's moral teachings, which persisted despite the affront of being once turned away from the communion table for scandalous immorality. Cumulatively these attitudes did his harassed friends of the Anglican establishment grave disservice. A lengthy quarrel between Charles and the restored Church's indomitable defender, Archbishop Sheldon, came to a head with the 1672 Indulgence (Ch. 7), which had grievous effects, in the short term, on ten years' episcopal work in the dioceses (14 [Beddard], *169*); 156c, *1010*). Not until 1675, when Danby urged Charles to call Sheldon and two more bishops to his Council and when Anglican leaders cooperated closely with Court supporters over the 'Non-Resisting Test' (Ch. 7), did Church and Crown begin to approach an accommodation truly helpful to the former. This was cemented by the clergy's unwavering opposition to Exclusion, and when the idea of comprehension resurfaced, with some Tory support, in 1680 (Ch. 9) Charles for once set his face against it (48, *29*; 161 [Thomas], *225–30; 14* [Beddard], 174). From 1681–5, though continuing to irk the Church by his indulgence to Catholics, the King fully encouraged the use of the secular arm against the dissenters.

In the final reckoning most of the credit, first for the survival and then for the revival of Anglicanism in the quarter-century following the Restoration, must go to the Church's own leaders. The quality of the episcopate for much of the period 1662–88, once the creaking gates of the early 1660s had been replaced, was high. Naturally, under a system where intriguing courtiers could influence appointments, there were weak links in the chain, none frailer than the soporific Barlow at Lincoln (1675–91) and Thomas Wood, scandalously elevated by the King to Lichfield in 1671 under pressure from the duchess of Cleveland. But a bench which contained at the same time such fine scholars as Morley, Gunning, Wilkins and an outstanding theologian in Bishop Pearson of Chester must be rated intellectually distinguished; and most dioceses at some stage felt the presence of a vigorous administrator, a man such as Cosin, Hacket, Ward, Compton, Mews, Lloyd or Frampton, who carried out visitations regularly, ordained discriminatingly and confirmed the young with diligence (152, *8–16* passim). Above all, the debt such prelates owed to the encouragement and example of two outstanding metropolitans, Gilbert Sheldon and William Sancroft [N.3], would be hard to exaggerate. Sheldon, tough-fibred, pugnacious, inquisitorial and fiercely determined to uphold the authority, legal rights and revenues of the Church,[24] was the chief architect of the alliance between the clergy and the Cavalier (later Tory) gentry. And not only the events of the early 1660s but those of 1681–7 were to vindicate to the hilt his belief (and later that of Danby) in the enormous potential power of this parson-squire concert. He was also the driving force behind the movement for order and uniformity after 1662, based unwaveringly on the revised Prayer Book, the jealous guardian of clerical standards and the scourge of 'the scandalous and faulty'.[25] Yet behind this stern face lay compassion, shown for instance in his prodigious charitable giving and the concern he showed for augmenting the incomes of poor incumbents. The latter was a cause in which he tirelessly exhorted his lay friends, a matter of the head as well as the heart, for he knew how vulnerable the Anglican recovery would be in the long run to the bane of persistent and widespread clerical poverty (14 [Beddard], *170–1*; 156c, *1013–17*).

Sancroft, his successor, was equally dedicated to achieving the lofty ideal of a purified, ordered and disciplined Church, but much more so to forging unbreakable links between 'the altar and the throne'. His success in keeping his clergy united behind the monarchy and the Yorkist succession in the crisis of 1679–81 left him with immense prestige. Sancroft had little sympathy with the new-fangled churchmanship of the 'latitude-men', and little time for the new science or the devotees of 'natural religion'; but despite an ascetic life and a conservative outlook he possessed – even more than Sheldon – the gift of inspiring his troops.[26] His was the driving force behind the revitalisation of the church courts in the 1680s. His schemes for improving the quality and incomes of the parish clergy bore the hallmark of an original mind. For years he was a persistent foe of nonconformity and opponent of comprehension; but to his credit, in the drastically changed circumstances of 1687–8 (Ch. 12) he had the flexibility to concede the case long made by Stillingfleet and his friends, that the surest way to 'the better and more perfect establishment of the Church' lay not in holding tenaciously to the ground recovered by 1662 but in broadening its extent and appeal without sacrificing its essential character (152, *34, 84–6*).

Despite its anxieties on the score of Dissent and Popery, therefore, and its apprehensions about the growth of rationalism and the creeping menace of 'atheism', the way ahead for the Church of England early in 1685 was in the main a path of hope. How the extreme policies of James II soured this sweet promise and forced even Sancroft into a posture towards the monarchy which he would have found unthinkable in the early months of the new king's reign we shall see in Chapter 12.

---

1. Cf. C. Webster, *The Great Instauration: Science, Medicine and Reform, 1626–1660* (1976) for the argument (1) that the years between the Civil Wars and the Restoration were of critical importance to scientific advance and achievement; (2) that Puritanism, not post-Laudian Anglicanism, provided the ideal climate for the revolution. For an excellent brief critique of these views (which were foreshadowed in C. Hill, *Intellectual Origins of the English Revolution* [1965]) see A.G.R. Smith, *The Emergence of a Nation State: the Commonwealth of England 1529–1660* (1984). For a magisterial book-length discussion of the European scientific revolution which sets the 'Protestant ethic' thesis firmly in context see A.R. Hall (302a).
2. Alexander Pope, 'Epitaph intended for Sir Isaac Newton' [1727].
3. A.G.R. Smith (303a), pp. 129–32, provides a lucid, brief summary for the layman.
4. In his consciously-titled *Theologiae Christianae Principia Mathematica* (1699).
5. G.V. Bennett, 'Patristic Tradition in Anglican Thought, 1660–1900', *Sondedruck aus Oecumenica: Jahrbuch für Ökumenische Forschung 1971/2* (Minneapolis, 1972), pp. 72–3; R.L. Emerson, 'Latitudinarianism and the English Deists', in J.A.L. Lesmay, ed., *Deism, Masonry and the Enlightenment* (Newark, Delaware, 1987), p. 27.
6. Sir Charles Wolseley, *The Reasonableness of Scripture Belief* (1672); Ralph Cudworth, *The Intellectual System of the Universe* (1677).
7. Isaac Newton, *Opticks* (Bell edn. 1931). (For whole passage which provides context see Briggs, [303b], pp. 78–9).
8. Add. MSS 36916, ff. 134, 151.
9. A. Browning, ed., *Memoirs of Sir John Reresby* (Glasgow, 1936), pp. 1, 87.
10. A. Marvell to Wm. Popple, 21 Mar 1670, in A. B. Grosart, ed., *The Complete Works . . . of Andrew Marvell, MP* (1875), II, p. 316.

11. Anchitell Grey, *Debates*, I, pp. 227–8: 9 Mar 1670.
12. Add. MSS 36916, f. 186: Newsletter to Sir Willoughby Aston, 12 July 1670.
13. Whiting (160b), pp. 370–7; A. Brockett, *Nonconformity in Exeter, 1650–1875* (Manchester, 1962), p. 338.
14. Whiting (160b), p. 186; Watts (150), pp. 227–8, 244–6; W.C. Braithwaite, *The Second Period of Quakerism* (2nd edn., Cambridge, 1961), p. 115; R.I. Clark, 'The Quakers and the Church of England, 1670–1720', Lancaster Ph.D. thesis, 1987, Ch. 2.
15. M.H. Lee, ed., *Diary and Letters of Philip Henry* (1882), p. 316: 23 Aug 1682.
16. A. Whiteman, ed., with M. Clappinson, *The Compton Census of 1676* (1986), pp. xxiv–v; Browning, (43), I, pp. 197–8.
17. Whiteman, ed., op.cit., xxxvi–xli.
18. B.L. Harleian MSS. 7377, f. 61: Sheldon to [Compton], 17 Jan 1676.
19. A.T. Hart, *The Life of John Sharp, Archbishop of York* (1949), p. 89.
20. E. S. de Beer, ed., *Diary of John Evelyn* (Oxford Standard Authors edn.), pp. 666, 772, 785, 805.
21. Bodl. Add. MS. c. 308: to William Piers, 14 June 1669, quoted in V.D. Sutch, *Gilbert Sheldon . . . 1640–1725* (The Hague, 1973), p. 161.
22. N. Sykes, (152), pp. 27–9; A. Macfarlane, ed., *The Diary of Ralph Josselin* (1976): Easter Day, 1665.
23. Quoted Beddard, in Jones (14), p. 167.
24. E.g. his circular letter 'to several deans', 29 July 1670, BL Harleian MSS 7377, f. 16.
25. Ibid.
26. This brief picture of Sancroft owes a debt to the late G.V. Bennett's 4th Birkbeck Lecture, 'Revolution and Toleration'; see above, p. 43, n. 13.

CHAPTER 11

The threat to 'Liberty and Property', 1681–1687

I

In the *Declaration* he issued to vindicate his invasion of England in 1688, William of Orange accused James II's counsellors of inflicting 'arbitrary government' on all Englishmen, and on those who had opposed their policies 'the loss of their lives, liberties, honours and estates' (11a, *11, 13*). These last words bear a striking similarity to those written by John Locke in the famous passage in his *Second Treatise of Government* (published at length in 1689; cf. Ch. 9 above) in which, having defined 'the great and chief end . . . of men's uniting into commonwealths' as 'the preservation of their property', he proceeds to explain that what he 'call[ed] by the general name, property' was 'the mutual preservation of their lives [i.e. 'persons'], liberties and estates'.[1] The near-interchangeable vocabulary is very significant, because William was addressing the whole political nation [A] in his *Declaration*, and he seems to have been persuaded that even if that nation, from church-and-crown Tories at one extreme to radical Whigs of Locke's stamp at the other, could find common ground on little else in the autumn of 1688, they could at least agree that Englishmen's 'liberties and properties' were, and had been for some time, as 'greatly invaded' as the legal preserves of their established Church.[2] How long they had been at risk was another matter. It would have been hard to find a Tory prepared to concede that any coherent threat had existed before James's accession (though this is not to say that all Tories were overjoyed at the *quo warranto* proceedings [A] of the early 1680s or at the recall of the Tangier regiments [below, pp. 170]); but to the Whigs, who had had to endure systematic proscription, and in many cases worse, from 1682–5, the differences between King Charles, in his final years, and his brother seemed much less clear-cut – matters of degree or artifice rather than of essentials. To them Charles had simply been working by stealth towards what his brother had tried to achieve openly, the institution of an absolutist, Catholic state.

Historians have found it impossible to agree on how much political continuity to ascribe to the last seven years or so before the Glorious Revolution (e.g. cf. 45b, *90–1 et seq*; 28; 52; 59a; 310b, *Chs. 7–10*; and 54a, *Ch. 7*, on the one hand, with 53a; 42a; and at the farthest extreme, with 14 [Miller]; 41b). But one thing at least is clear to us which was not so swiftly discerned at the time. When Charles II dissolved the Oxford Parliament (Ch. 8) he was opening up political possibilities which only the duke of York and his friends had seriously envisaged earlier. There was now a definite prospect that the constitutional tensions which for almost a decade past had increasingly destabilised the state might be resolved by a resounding and permanent victory for authority and monarchy. Not that Charles himself saw the future in such terms at first. For many months in the aftermath of Oxford he seems to have looked no further ahead than seizing a golden tactical opportunity of crushing his Whig opponents and if possible revenging himself on their leaders. Only two things could have frustrated this aim: a relapse by the King into political indolence and a serious deterioration in his financial position. Neither happened.[3] In particular, the Crown's revenue went from strength to strength, through a combination of good luck and the efficient management of Hyde (created earl of Rochester, 1682) and later Godolphin (110a; [D.1]; cf. Ch. 5). This proved the master key to the situation, since on it turned the question of when, if at all, Charles needed to call a new Parliament. In the event the reign ended with four years of non-parliamentary rule; within little more than two of these years the Whigs slid first from defeat into retreat, and then from retreat into a rout so nearly total that it enabled the Crown to look well beyond the short-term objectives of 1681.

The loss of parliamentary protection proved critical to a party faced not just with a vengeful Court but with a hostile judiciary (below, pp. 168–9) and with a magistracy so extensively purged of its known supporters by the autumn of 1681 that Burnet exaggerated little in writing that: 'none were left either on the bench or in the militia that did not with zeal go into the humour of the court' (126b, *53–5;* 1, *II, 285*). The fate of the Whig press graphically illustrates this vulnerability. As long as Parliaments were meeting, with Whig majorities in the Commons, while in London Whig sheriffs and Whig-packed juries held sway, Chief Justice Scroggs's judgements in the case of Harris and Carr (1680), which made seditious in law any writings or publications critical of the government, had only limited effect, and Scroggs was impeached for his pains. But in 1681–2 seizures by the Secretaries of State of the authors and printers of 'seditious libels' had such devastating repercussions that by November 1682 not a single Whig newspaper was left in business (15, *II, 515–16*; 297, *271, 299*).

Inarticulate at Westminster and with their journalists increasingly muzzled, the Whigs had no effective means of resistance to the attacks on their remaining centres of power, in the borough corporations and constituencies, which were systematically begun in 1682 (below, pp. 167–8). The loss in this year of their main extra-parliamentary stronghold, the corporation of London, was a shattering blow; one aspect of it especially, the Court-rigged election of two Tory sheriffs, left many leading Whigs at the mercy of hostile juries as well as hostile judges in the courts (42b, *700–4*). An exodus to the Continent to forestall prosecution had begun in the winter of 1681, and in November 1682 Shaftesbury himself was forced to join the exiles. He had already escaped one treason charge with the aid of a friendly Middlesex grand jury, but now faced near-certain conviction and death if he remained in England: by a sad irony he died in Holland a few months later, of natural causes. There is strong evidence that at the time of his flight Shaftesbury had been at the heart of some rather inchoate exploratory plans for an armed Whig rising (42b, *707–23*; 310b). Of those Whigs who stayed behind, a reckless minority in desperation contemplated further violence, not least on the persons of the King and his brother. But the revelation of the Rye House assassination plot (above, p. 12) merely completed their ruin, bringing two of their leading champions, Russell and Algernon Sidney, to the scaffold, along with Sir Thomas Armstrong and other notable Exclusionists, and driving Essex to suicide. By the end of 1683 not only the monarchy but all those who had identified themselves with its cause and that of the hereditary succession were enjoying an almost unqualified triumph. When a General Election was called soon after Charles II's death, the Tories won a staggering 468 seats [E.1(i)].

Some historians would argue, however, that while they were luxuriating in the downfall of their opponents, the Tories were making themselves parties (in the main unwittingly) to a far more momentous political change – nothing less than the building of a new kind of state in England. That was certainly how it seemed to the Whigs of the 1680s. Throughout the Exclusion Crisis they had persistently claimed that the threat of 'arbitrary government' would become a reality if a Papist succeeded Charles II on the throne. Afterwards they became convinced that the reality was already materialising in Charles's own last years, as government, with Tory connivance, became appreciably more authoritarian. By 1688, after three years of James II, most Tories were only too aware of the danger of England's succumbing – as Scotland in effect already had since 1680 – to an 'arbitrary government' which imperilled liberty and property; yet for as long as Charles lived, and for perhaps a year thereafter down to early 1686, they had dismissed such a notion as the scaremongering of a thwarted republican faction. But were not the Whigs right all along? How much evidence is there to substantiate their claim that as long as it was overwhelmingly Whig 'liberties' and Whig property rights which were being invaded, Tories had been willing to acquiesce after 1681 in an insidious subversion of the constitution; that even under Charles they had cheerfully countenanced a steady drift towards an autocratic style of monarchy on the Continental model, as long as they themselved enjoyed its patronage?

Even John Miller, who among modern authorities has been the most dismissive of an 'absolutist' interpretation of the 1680s, has said of Charles's last four years that 'the Tories were quite content that the King should bend the law, provided he did so in their interests' (14 [Miller], *45*). However, to test the validity of the 'Whiggish' view of the Stuart Reaction of the 1680s, which is the purpose of the remainder of this chapter, the most instructive approach is to examine the period *as a whole*, and with certain questions in mind which can be applied both to the years before and after February 1685. What were the political intentions of the two kings, so far as they can be divined? What opportunities existed to encourage a more autocratic style of monarchy and government, and how far were they exploited by each king? How strong did English monarchy actually become in the 1680s, and how genuinely did that strength place 'liberty and property' in jeopardy? Not least, what chance of permanency had the Stuart regime of the 1680s, down at least to the time in 1687 when James II began to undermine its supports by a series of gross political and religious miscalculations?

II

Any assessment of the intentions of the Stuart brothers hinges largely on two matters – how we read their characters, and what interpretation we place on their motives in the light of the opportunities that offered themselves. In both cases James II presents a more straightforward problem than his predecessor. He was an autocrat by temperament and conviction, and by the yardstick of his previous record. He had urged a military solution on his brother as early as June 1679 and had seen the Rye House plot as a golden opportunity to make the monarchy absolute (52, *84*).[4] In between times he had cowed Scotland. Autocratic convictions were greatly fortified in his case by a high religious view of kingship. His beliefs taught him that he had solemn obligations to his subjects in all his kingdoms, and that these ought to be matched by those subjects' unswerving obedience to him. But his most powerful incentive to redraw the constitutional map of England in both state and church was his Catholicism. It has often been said that James's dearest wish after he came to the throne was to catholicise England in his lifetime. But it is now generally believed that this was a pipe-dream, and that, however lacking in realism he often was, James was not such a complete fantasist as to convince himself that he could eradicate over a century and a half of ingrained prejudice in a few years (and he believed, almost fatalistically, we should note, that he would not live long – indeed, he had never expected to survive his brother) (54a, *124*). His overriding priorities, therefore, were to make England absolutely secure for the Faith; to assure his co-religionists an equal footing with Anglicans in society and government service as well as in freedom of worship; and to prepare the ground for what he hoped and prayed would be mass conversions in the future (52, *189*; 40b; 50, *127, 128*; 54a, *126*).

Swiftly disappointed in his hopes of cooperation from a loyal but not pliant first Parliament in its eight weeks of business in 1685 (above, p. 13), James soon concluded that even these interim religious ends could not possibly be accomplished without an autocratic approach to government and an exaltation of the prerogative backed by enhanced material and military resources. Miller has suggested that there is no evidence in the King's correspondence that he ever saw himself as a subverter of the laws and the constitution or that he consciously worked towards a French-style absolutism (50, *128*; 41b). Yet other historians have put a very different construction on his words, especially those spoken in many a private conversation with the French ambassador, Barrillon. In any case, it is his actions which speak most eloquently of James's attitudes and intentions. It soon became clear, for instance, that what his *subjects* believed to be their constitutional and legal rights and what *he* conceived them to be were poles apart. And such evidence as his determination to reintroduce imprisonment without trial through repeal of the Habeas Corpus Act in 1685 (53a, *62*; 54a, *125–6*), or his deliberate attack (clearly anticipated by his brother in 1684) on colonial liberties, and in particular on the charters and autonomy of the New Englanders,[5] speaks volumes and exposes the frailty of claims that his authoritarian actions were never more than means to the end of attaining his religious objectives (41b, *197*).

No one has doubted that there were very marked differences of temperament between James and his elder brother. But while recognising that Charles II was not a natural autocrat, we should not underestimate the extent to which the cynicism which had coloured his attitude to politics for the greater part of his reign was reinforced after 1681 by a new ruthlessness. Self-indulgence and self-preservation were more powerful instincts down to 1679 than his liking for the French way of government and his growing distaste for the annual sparring bouts between Crown and Parliament. But Charles was a much changed man after the bitter experiences of 1679–81. That 'time and opposition began to sour his blood' was recognised even by supporters (see above, p. 87). In such a mood he had little compunction about stretching either his prerogatives or the laws to the very limit of their flexibility in favour of the Crown's authority: he needed only to be convinced that the time was opportune and that this route, and not the old path of conciliation, was the best way to ensure himself a quiet life in the future. The extent of the Whig collapse before the strong-arm tactics of 1682 provided Charles with the clearest possible pointer. Quite apart from the plight of Whiggery, however, other opportunities presented themselves in the 1680s, which had not existed before, enabling both monarchs to regard an autocratic reaction as a practical possibility. The most important were the ideological climate of the decade; the eclipse of Parliament; the favourable financial position of the Crown; and the build-up of its military power.

In the first place, the Stuart reaction could never have been carried as far as it was without the support or acquiescence, for six years or so, of much of the political nation [A], and it is not possible to understand why this was so without appreciating the ideological climate which prevailed in England for much of the 1680s. Among the country's propertied classes, and with particular intensity among those Tory-Anglican men of property who found themselves in the ascendant in central and local government from 1681–7, an emotional monarchist reaction of peculiar intensity set in after 1680. It was inspired by a mixture of guilt, at the excesses perpetrated during the Popish Plot hysteria; thankfulness at the peaceful resolution of the Exclusion Crisis; and most of all, fear of a future relapse into anarchy. The shadows cast over the whole island by the events of 1642–60 were very long. Rightly or wrongly, many believed that the horrors of renewed civil war had been only narrowly averted in 1681. To run such a risk again seemed unthinkable: even to the republican Henry Neville, it was a 'remedy . . . worse than the disease'.[6] It was not difficult, therefore, in the early and mid-1680s to convince any but the most dedicated Whigs that enhancing the authority of the Crown and the state was the firmest guarantee of future stability and order.

Such assumptions lent powerful support to a parallel religious reaction post–1680, in favour of those Anglican doctrines which traditionally bolstered monarchical prerogative and the idea of the Christian responsibility of obedience (Ch. 9). By the middle years of the 1680s the commitment of a Sancroft-led Church to the tenets of Divine Right, Non-Resistance and Passive Obedience was being preached throughout England with a fervour and conviction which easily surpassed their previous high-water mark, in the heyday of Laud. Three times in succession the recent march of events had given them particular point. The conclusive triumph of the monarchy after the Oxford Parliament, the deliverance of the royal brothers from the assassination conspiracy of 1683, and James's peaceful and popular accession, in such sharp contrast to his earlier troubles: each in turn supplied ammunition for a thousand pulpits. The comparative ease with which the rebellions against James were then snuffed out – the earl of Argyll's small force disintegrating in the Clyde valley in June 1685 and the army of the duke of Monmouth, with its numerous respectable artisans and small farmers,[7] slaughtered in Somerset soon after (above, p. 13) – heavily underscored the parsons' message to a politically troubled people. The futility of trying to keep a divinely-ordained heir off the throne, and of seeking to resist him when he had achieved his crown, appeared to have been amply demonstrated.

The logical corollary of the injunction 'passive obedience *in all circumstances whatsoever*', instilled by Oxford dons after 1683 into every trainee for the ministry, was authoritarian kingship. And the logic, we should remember, was not only the product of domestic pressures. All over Europe in the later seventeenth century, in every major power except the United Provinces (and, to a far lesser extent, Sweden), as well as in most minor states, autocracy was the firmly-established norm. Parliaments and Estates were either in decay or in total eclipse. Centralised bureaucracies had developed extensive, though not invariably effective, local tentacles. The amateur local officialdom of England and Scotland, representing the traditional working partnership between the Crown and the aristocracy and gentry, was an isolated freak. Judges and courts of law were in most states subservient to central authority: occasional frail gestures of independence notwithstanding (as with the Parlement de Paris,) the judiciary was normally expected to buttress and certainly not to trammel absolutist regimes. Most states had standing armies that were large in proportion to their populations, available not only to fight their rulers' dynastic wars but to suppress rebellions. And because apprehension of Louis XIV's France, the archetypal continental autocracy, was widespread in England in the second half of Charles II's reign, it should not be assumed that French methods of government (somewhat idealised for export) did not command a certain grudging admiration on the English side of the Channel, especially among professional royal officials.[8]

In recent years loyalist Englishmen had had their fill of Parliaments. In the climate of opinion which now prevailed, an institution which had so often taken an obstructive attitude towards the Crown's financial needs, chivvied the prerogative, and since 1679 asserted unprecedented claims to sovereignty, seemed to most Tories at best a mixed blessing. They were content that it should be enjoyed (or suffered) as infrequently as possible. Perhaps the most significant of all the pointers to the strength of the tide which began running for the monarchy in Charles II's last years is that the King was allowed to break the law with impunity in March 1684, when he failed to call a new Parliament in accordance with the terms of the 1664 revised Triennial Act. It had been part of his secret pact with Louis XIV in April 1681 that he would not call another Parliament – an undertaking known to, and tacitly approved by, his high Tory minister, Rochester, and while Charles had failed to honour similar agreements in the 1670s because of financial necessities, he was determined if humanly possible to keep this one (14, *21*; 41b, *204, n.73*). His Lord Privy Seal, Halifax, vainly reminded him in January 1684 that 'his Majesty had promised upon the last dissolution to observe the laws', and added 'that he feared an ill construction might be made of his not doing accordingly'.[9] Yet twelve months later the prospect of a new Parliament was still not on the horizon, and hardly a murmur of protest was being heard. Had not Charles's sudden death compelled the holding of new elections – for the life revenues granted to one king could not be legally assumed by the next without fresh parliamentary sanction – the electorate might have remained untroubled indefinitely. The Parliament which James was compelled to call was treated by him with scant respect. Having satisfied the King's early financial expectations, but then disappointed his main non-financial hope from it (that it would agree to an early repeal of the Test Act [above, p. 13]), it was rebuked and sent packing in November 1685 after two short sessions, the second being of derisory brevity; in July 1687, without further meeting, it was dissolved. Indeed, during the period of almost eight years from March 1681 to January 1689 there was a sitting Parliament for less than two months. It is true that James began issuing writs for the election of a new Parliament in the autumn of 1688; but they were later recalled (Ch. 12). He had made his own attitude to Parliament's place in the constitution clear enough in the first three months of his reign, when he authorised his officials to collect *all* his late brother's revenues – including the excises and the hearth tax, for which there was no precedent – without waiting for formal legal sanction. And he was to underline that attitude far more blatantly, as we shall see, by his cynical manipulation of the borough electorate.

The long periods of rule without Parliament in the 1680s did much to facilitate the adoption of more arbitrary methods of government. But like the growth of a standing army, a point to be discussed later, they would not have been possible but for the healthy financial position in which the Crown now found itself. Without doubt the most important single political asset of the Stuart monarchy from 1681–7 was its financial strength. When Sir Thomas Meres grimly reminded the Commons in 1677 that ''tis money that makes a Parliament considerable and nothing else', he would surely – could he have looked ahead from five to ten years – have added the words 'and necessary' after 'considerable'.[10] It has already been shown what a striking difference the improvement in King Charles's finances made to his freedom of action in the last four years of his reign (Ch. 5). His ordinary revenue and a small French subsidy were together yielding some £1.45 million by 1684–5. By 1686, however, the Crown had reached a more promising financial position than at any time since Henry VIII had enjoyed, and squandered, his bountiful windfalls from the Church and the monasteries. James's total revenue from all sources from Michaelmas 1685 to Michaelmas 1688 averaged no less than £2.06 million a year (110a, *260*) – over £800,000 more than the amount Parliament had (reasonably) judged necessary for the monarch to 'live of his own', from 'ordinary' sources, in 1660. By far the most important factor in this remarkable transformation is one that applied to both reigns (though with more dramatic effects after 1685): the great economic expansion of the 1680s, and in particular the unprecedented boom in the colonial and East Indian trade (Ch. 3). But although the basic cause, it was by no means the only one. An increasingly efficient Treasury administration and a drastic overhaul of the machinery of revenue collection, culminating in the abandonment of the farming of the excise and the creation of the Excise department (1683), did much to maximise returns (118, *100–3*). More economical government and less Court extravagance, together with a cheese-paring, neutralist foreign policy (Ch. 6), significantly reduced these heads of expenditure. And once again, in each case, Charles reaped some of the benefits, although James – a harder-working, austere King and a much more efficient steward of his assets – clearly profited more. James alone, however, benefited in the 1680s from parliamentary generosity: a largely unwitting generosity on the part of the 1685 Parliament in the first weeks of the Monmouth Rebellion (110a, *256–9*; 110b) but one which, through failure to appreciate how fast the yield of both customs and excise was currently appreciating, dangerously over-endowed the new monarch.

III

It remains to ascertain in what other ways the authority and resources of the Crown were significantly advanced during the years of the Reaction, and how seriously 'liberties' and property rights were endangered and the constitution sabotaged. In the first place, quite apart from the obvious determination of both monarchs to keep the Westminster Parliament under wraps, there is much evidence pointing to a sustained, conscious attempt in the 1680s to undermine permanently English representative institutions. It is well known that Charles began, and James continued, a concerted attack on the borough corporations by enforcing the surrender and re-issue of their charters, in order to remodel their membership in the Crown's interest: the main instrument of this policy being the threat, or reality, of *quo warranto* [A] proceedings and, finally, the use by James II of a 'Board of Regulators' [A]. But it is equally clear that the purpose of this campaign was not simply to curtail municipal liberties but to destroy freedom of parliamentary election in a decisive number of borough constituencies by giving the Crown power to determine, directly or indirectly, who should vote in any future election (53a, *430–50 and Ch. 6 passim*). It has been claimed, on Charles's behalf, that he was concerned primarily with destroying the Whigs' main power base in London and the provinces, or rooting out Dissent, and that, unlike James in 1685 and 1688, he had no sinister short- or long-term intention of reducing Parliament to docility – if or when it did have to be called – by 'packing' the Commons.[11] But such partial innocency of motive is a matter for assumption or deduction, and not for proof. The most plausible interpretation of the complex evidence must be that the first three years of the charter campaign, after February 1682, had both local government and broader electoral objectives. Certainly it would have been improbably naïve of these local Tories, whose pressure was clearly a factor in some of the charter surrenders, to take no thought for the future parliamentary representation of boroughs where they had so recently been humiliated; John Locke, for one, was so convinced that Charles's moves against the boroughs were intended to pervert the electoral process 'contrary to the interests of the common people' that he added a final chapter to the *Second Treatise* making such an abuse of power a further ground for resistance (310b, *323*). Neither Charles nor his ministers, after all, could ever rule out the necessity for a fresh General Election, if 'we were compelled to it [as Halifax told Reresby] by a foreign cause'.[12]

What can be said emphatically is that when the test at the polls did come, early in the next reign, the message of many of the results was startling. Of the 99 parliamentary boroughs 'remodelled' by new charters between the 1681 and 1685 elections, Charles dealt with 51, mostly the larger urban constituencies, and the 104 MPs they returned in 1685 included only one clearly identifiable Whig (25, *I, 40*; 53a, *46–7*). Even James II's own manipulation of 48 smaller boroughs in the run-up to the election, the purpose of which none doubted, could not produce returns quite as remarkable as this. Recent analyses of the 1685 election make it plain that even if not a single writ of *quo warranto* had been issued the Tories would still have won the Election handsomely, if not quite so crushingly (25, *I, 40*; 54a, *44–6*). Nevertheless, to James and his ministers, especially Sunderland, a devastatingly effective precedent appeared to have been set, and it was one that was self-evidently followed in the King's still more blatant attempt to rig a projected election through borough 'regulation', in 1688 (Ch. 12).

One implication of those policies can easily escape the modern student. To the seventeenth-century mind any local office that carried some measure of status, however seemingly trivial, was regarded as a piece of property: it had prestige value and, quite likely, commercial value, too. Membership of a common council, and *any* corporation dignity, from town clerkships and treasurerships down to mace-bearerships and the variety of posts held by other 'under officers', was property of no mean value. By the same token, the right to vote in parliamentary elections, whether it was conferred by possession of a freehold, by a burgage tenancy, by being a ratepayer, or by membership of a privileged municipal élite, was also a cherished little piece of 'property' under an electoral system whose vagaries excluded so many male adults from the privilege (28, *26–9*). To disfranchise any man by a dubious legal device or by even more arbitrary forms of state action, was therefore an attack on property rights. It is true, very few Tories saw it this way when they were the beneficiaries, as was the case with the corporation purges of 1682–6. But when at length they became the victims of the same process (Ch. 12) the result was a widespread sense of outrage.

The English system of courts of Common Law (King's Bench, Common Pleas and Exchequer) and Equity (Chancery), with justice dispensed both centrally and through local assizes, frequently caused complaint during the seventeenth century, yet few Continental judicial systems had afforded better protection for the property of the individual or a better guarantee of the preservation of the legal liberties of the subject.[13] Its importance was all the greater when Parliament was inactive. Seen in this light, the use of the prerogative in the 1680s to make an increasingly unscrupulous attack on the independence of the judiciary represented another dismaying shift of the wind in the direction of an authoritarian state. Once again it was Charles II who showed his brother the way; his attitude towards the bench of judges in his later years displayed all his old native cynicism together with a new fixity of purpose. He removed two judges in 1672 for lack of pliancy and no fewer than eleven between 1675 and 1683, and after 1679, especially, the political motives were usually transparent. The case of Sir Francis Pemberton is a bizarre example of the way the King played ducks and drakes with the legal profession: dismissed from the King's Bench in February 1680 for suspected lukewarmness in supporting royal policies; brought back as Lord Chief Justice in 1681 to preside over some of the earliest trials of the Whigs, which he did with rigour; transferred nevertheless to the Common Pleas in 1682 because Charles thought Edmund Saunders a safer bet to judge the vital case of the London charter; and finally removed entirely in 1683. Some of the judges appointed in the last two years of Charles II's reign, notably Sir George Jeffreys and Sir Robert Wright, were violent partisans,[14] who continued their notorious careers under King James. Yet James still thought it necessary to dismiss half the entire bench of twelve common law judges in 1686 because he was not certain he could rely on them to approve royal dispensations on behalf of Catholic officers and officials in the key test case of *Godden v Hales* (7, *420–4*; 120a, *86–8*; 52, *56–8*). By the mid- to late 1680s dispassionate observers, some within the government itself, had begun to profess serious alarm at the effect on the administration of justice of plummeting respect for the judiciary. As Halifax put it in 1685: 'when such sacred things as the laws are not only touched but guided by profane hands, men will fear that out of the tree of the law, from whence we expect shade and shelter, such workmen will make cudgels to beat us with'.[15]

The high-handed treatment by the monarchy of 'the twelve men in scarlet' and the Crown's barefaced and generally successful attempts to bend the law-courts to its own political purposes illustrate well a point made in an earlier chapter (Ch. 7): namely, that in some areas of the post-Restoration constitution genuine confusion reigned, which a determined king, given the right circumstances, could exploit. Judges in the 1670s and 1680s had no security of tenure because the form of their commissions had never been determined by statute. For eight years after the Restoration Charles II, honouring a promise made by his father in 1641, had made appointments *quamdiu se bene gesserint* [A.]; but when in 1668 he chose to go back to the old and dangerous practice whereby judges held their commissions *durante bene placito* [A.] – a formula which was then maintained until 1689 – there was no legal obstacle in his path.

The events of James II's reign, however, were to expose a still more serious element of ambiguity in the unwritten rules of the constitution. What power did the King have through his prerogative to circumvent statutes? Under Charles II Parliament had twice condemned the royal suspending power, most unambiguously in 1673 (Ch. 7), and after that Charles never attempted to revive it, although neither did he concede its illegality. On the other hand, the royal *dispensing* power, used very rarely and with great discretion by Charles (Ch. 7), had never been directly challenged by the legislature.[16] There was no difficulty in finding several judges of most respectable credentials, among them Lord Chief

Justice Edward Herbert, to declare for the dispensing power with conviction in 1686. It was this decision which gave the King the green light to begin infiltrating Catholics into Household and public office. And, what was more sinister in the eyes of those to whom Popery and absolutism were indistinguishable ideas, it seemed to portend a campaign to catholicise the commissioned ranks of the large army which remained in the royal pay after the collapse of Monmouth's rebellion. We now know that these particular fears were based on a misapprehension: there were insufficient Catholics of good family to constitute more than a small minority of the English officers James needed. There were at least 141 Catholic officers already in his English army in December 1685, nearly all of them commissioned during the rebellion under an emergency clause of the Test Act, but subsequently (despite patent unease in Parliament) confirmed by temporary dispensations. What *Godden* v *Hales* did do, however, was to make such dispensations effectively permanent (139b, *19–22*), and it was this the framers of the Bill of Rights were to have in mind after the Revolution when they declared the dispensing power unlawful 'as it hath been assumed and exercised of late'. By contrast the same Bill pronounced the suspending power 'illegal' without qualification (Ch. 13). When James first invoked this power in 1687, by the Scottish and English Declarations of Indulgence (February–April), he acted, as we shall see, to further his broad political and religious aims rather than with purely military ends in mind; the effect was to discharge Catholics and dissenters alike from the penalties of around forty statutes in England alone. The King's Attorney-General was highly uneasy about the suspending power, as he had admitted during the hearing of Godden *versus* Hales (11b, *261*). But with Parliament in abeyance the voice of protest was muted, and even when the Seven Bishops had the courage to challenge the legality of the power when it was used to promulgate a further indulgence in 1688, most of the lawyers involved in their subsequent trial (Ch. 12) preferred to duck the issue.[17] Politically, James II had committed acts of gross imprudence, which to his opponents smacked of absolutism; legally, in 1687–8 he was still arguably within his rights (120a, *75–7*; 54a, *141–52*).

Exactly the same could be said of his military policy. Although there were 209 known Catholic officers in his English army seven months after the Second Declaration of Indulgence, that was still only 11 per cent of the total number (139b, *22*). It was the size and disposition of that army rather than its religious complexion which had been so intimidating, especially since November 1685. We should remember that even Charles II's army in his last years was far from negligible. True, after the tardy disbandment of the forces raised in 1678 (above, pp. 10–11) the forces available to him in England in 1681 amounted to no more than the 6,000 men ('guards and garrisons') conceded by Parliament without objection at the Restoration. However, the returned veterans of the Tangier garrison (above, p. 12) brought the strength of the English establishment to nearly 9,000 from 1683–5; had there been a sudden domestic emergency there were a further 9,700 troops on the Scottish and Irish establishments (well over 6,000 of them in Ireland) on which the Crown could have drawn. The major transformation, however, took place as a result of Monmouth's Rebellion. James was able to raise his English forces by the end of 1685 to almost 20,000 men. More crucially, thanks to the buoyancy both of his ordinary revenue and of the supplementary duties granted by Parliament on account of the rebellion, he managed to keep the establishment at that level until March 1688, and then to increase it by another 14–15,000 troops between March and October (139b, *2*; 110a, *258, 260*). Childs tells us that with the aid of 5,700 men from Irish and Scottish regiments, 'when James issued the orders [in November 1688] for his army to rendezvous on Salisbury Plain he was able to count on the services of between 29,000 and 30,000 trained soldiers in his field army, some 5,000 in garrison, and another 5,000 readying themselves for service' (139b, *4*).

That even the overwhelmingly Tory Parliament of 1685 was deeply concerned at James's refusal to disband his Monmouth regiments was plainly shown by its objections to granting enough money to keep all these troops on emergency footing. 'I had rather pay double [to the militia], from whom I fear nothing', Sir Edward Seymour told the Commons, 'than half so much to those of whom I must ever be afraid'.[18] For once such apprehensions of a standing army were not misplaced. Units were soon being moved obtrusively about the country, instead of being quartered as usual in a handful of garrison towns. If it was too small to engage seriously in Continental warfare, James's army was 'more than adequate', as Angus McInnes has pointed out, for his domestic purposes: to police and overawe 'a nation with one of the weakest military traditions in Europe' (59a, *385*). For three years the King greatly improved his army's standards of training and efficiency and until his ill-advised purges in 1688 of officers whose loyalty he doubted, cemented its allegiance to the Crown and made it the chief prop of his regime. Indeed his whole attitude towards the army, including the undisguised pride he took in it, the *carte blanche* he gave it to lord it over civilians, the protection he gave it against the Common Law and the use he made of it in his campaign against certain recalcitrant corporations, all underline the judgement of one recent scholar about his political intentions: 'an authoritarian monarchy supported by a loyal army' (139b, *112*).

Continental autocracies in the second half of the seventeenth century were becoming more and more dependent for the exercise of their authority on large professional bureaucracies. A marked feature of the 1680s in England, too, was that government officialdom became more visible and more professionalised. The presence in the provinces of some 1,300 excise officers and hundreds more revenue men (hearth-money collectors and customs officials) by the time of the Revolution was one aspect of this; the appearance at the heart of the executive of a small nucleus of career officials – proto-civil servants – of great dedication and ability, among them Pepys, Bridgeman, Blathwayt and Guy, was another. It has been said that these developments took place 'with the consent of the political nation' (41b, *199*). But this overlooks the conviction that the exciseman, in particular, with his right to enter, inspect and search, was un-English and invasive of freedom and property, a feeling which grew as collection became more efficient under the direction of a zealous Excise Board after 1683, and also the fact that the Hearth Tax became so unpopular, for not dissimilar reasons, that it failed to survive the Revolution Settlement of 1689. At the time, however, it was not easy to ventilate such resentments. Walpole's notorious Excise Scheme of 1733 was to create an anti-executive storm of hurricane proportions, provoked by the most vituperative anti-government press campaign yet seen in Britain (*The Age of Oligarchy*, Ch. 5). At the height of the Stuart reaction, however, printed protest about *any* government measure was well nigh impossible. Most revolutionary propaganda in 1688 had to be printed in Holland and smuggled into the country (297, *299–300*; 53a, *226ff.*). Not the least of the 'liberties' under attack from the Crown in the 1680s was extra-parliamentary freedom of protest, even within the circumscribed limits (varying much according to the temper of the times) which seventeenth-century licensing laws and periodic government harassment had allowed to writers, printers and publishers.

IV

The conclusion that the policies of both the Stuart brothers after 1681 did pose a real threat to 'liberties' and rights of property is therefore inescapable. Parliamentary government, free elections, judicial independence, corporate rights, and liberty of the press were all put under pressure; from the winter of 1685–6 an unpopular army battened on the land; and the 'balanced constitution' was, even by 1687, in danger of crumbling in face of a determined thrust towards a brand of prerogative monarchy that was recognisably Continental. It is true, by and large, that things got worse after Charles II's death in February 1685. Except in one respect – the threat to liberty of conscience and the pressure on the Protestant dissenters (Ch. 12) – the reaction became still more pronounced in 1688 than it had been before. But even on the evidence of the years 1685–7 it hardly seems 'wildly implausible', as Dr Miller has suggested, 'that James should have tried to create an absolute monarchy in England' (40b, *197*) – unless by 'absolute' (a word deliberately eschewed in this chapter) something far more unqualified is meant than 'authoritarian' or even 'autocratic'.

However, this is not to go quite so far as Angus McInnes, in suggesting that 'by the 1680s England was . . . fast approaching the condition of an absolute monarchy, a country different only in detail from the classic absolutist states of continental Europe' (59a, *387*) (though if it were possible to imagine a *Protestant* James II it would be more difficult to quarrel with this remark). By the winter of 1687–8 much had certainly been achieved by the Crown. But the portents for any long-term success for the Stuart Reaction were not all favourable, and indeed, warning lights were already flashing in 1687 which a less blinkered ruler than James would have taken heed of. However accommodating the climate of opinion was to the Reaction, it would persist only so long as a more authoritarian monarchy could be seen to be respecting two vital elements in the *status quo*. One was the established property rights of the landed governing class, which after 1682 meant in effect the Tory aristocracy and squirearchy: much would be conceded to achieve the political stability for which they yearned, but not their own local predominance nor the social supremacy on which it rested. The other was the privileged position of the Anglican Church. Of the main obstacles still remaining in James's path by the end of 1687, the strength of Anglican feeling in England was the one to which he had thus far shown himself least sensitive.

Whatever Charles II's private religious sympathies, he had been more clear-headed in his closing years than at any stage of his reign about the impossibility of changing the balance of the constitution in both Church and state simultaneously. The Anglican Tories who had supported him and who welcomed James's untroubled accession were well aware that *some* concessions would have to be made under a Catholic king to that king's co-religionists. But there were the clearest possible indications from both Parliament and pulpits in 1685 that they were not prepared to be pushed too far or too fast, above all as regards the religious tests required of office-holders. In the teeth of this evidence, James, apart from some initial caution in exploiting the favourable verdict in the Hales case, ploughed ahead with his pro-Catholic measures with bull-headed lack of tact and finesse. The setting up of the Ecclesiastical Commission in 1686 may or may not have been illegal (as the revolutionaries were to claim) under the Act of 1641 (Ch. 1; see 54a, *143–4, 151*); the more immediate point at issue was that it at once assumed not merely control over Crown patronage but harsh disciplinary powers over the clergy and the universities which were widely resented. The suspension by the Commission of Bishop Compton of London (Ch. 10) suggested that one of its main aims was to gag Anglican clergy who engaged too vehemently in anti-Catholic preaching and also those who lent support to such activities. The dismissal of Lord Treasurer Rochester that winter seemed to presage the beginning of the end for Tory-Anglican influence at the centre of government and the triumph of the pro-Catholic faction headed by Rochester's bitter rival, Sunderland (50, *163*). Lord Belasyse, one of the four Catholic peers added to the Privy Council the previous summer, now became head of the new Treasury Commission (above, p. 13) [D.1]. Alarm mounted with James's first Declaration of Indulgence just over three months later. The expulsion in the autumn of the President and twenty-five Fellows of Magdalen College, Oxford for their refusal to accept either of two royal nominees, including the Catholic Anthony Farmer, as head of the College, was followed by their gradual replacement by a set of Roman Catholics with the blessing of the Ecclesiastical Commissioners. 'It is difficult [as Bennett reminds us] to overestimate the shock and anger which these events caused' (296b, *V, 18*), for fellowships were legal freeholds in which, in Magdalen's case, the ownership and administration of rich estates was vested. Thus the attack on the College was regarded both as the most serious invasion yet of the property rights (in a seventeenth-century sense) of Tory gentlemen and as part of a naked campaign to undermine the universities, the training-grounds of the Anglican clergy, by Catholic penetration. Sidney Sussex College, Cambridge had already been compelled to accept another recent Catholic convert as its Master (50, *169–70*); and when they heard that the Commissioners had debarred the ousted Magdalen dons from holding any future Church preferment, the Cambridge Fellows could have been forgiven for feeling that their docility had been justifiably prudent.

Although, therefore, James II was materially stronger at the end of 1687 than at the start of his reign, the sense of bitterness and betrayal he had already created among his one-time Anglican supporters had begun to shake the moral foundations on which his hopes of an authoritarian, pro-Catholic regime rested. Other hazards, too, lay ahead. The judiciary had so far proved pliable but might not be so indefinitely: Herbert, for instance, had declared for the dispensing power, but as an ecclesiastical commissioner had opposed expelling the Magdalen Fellows (7, *423–4*). Financially, too, James's position, though powerful, was not impregnable. The clouds of a Continental war or a new rebellion seemed low on the horizon in December 1687; yet any sudden emergency *might* prove too much even for James's plentiful resources and force him to call a Parliament when he least wished it. And even if a Parliament was not needed to vote extraordinary supply, there would certainly come a time – conceivably within the next twelve months – when it would be no longer sufficient, nor perhaps safe, for the Crown to depend on prerogative expedients to bring both Catholics and dissenters into full enjoyment of civil rights as well as freedom of worship. James would have to risk at least one session of Parliament and go all out for repeal of the Test Acts, and if possible of the other penal religious statutes. In fact, to this end his supporters and agents were already at work in the constituencies before the end of 1687 (see above, p. 14), and their efforts would have to continue, in the knowledge that growing Tory disenchantment was making many of the loyalists who had been inserted into remodelled corporations from 1682–6 no longer amenable.

Finally, there remained the intractable problem of county government, still firmly in the hands of the propertied classes. Despite the expansion of the professional civil service which had taken place since 1683, dependence on the traditional local amateur bureaucracy of the county élites was still unrelieved. In this respect, above all, the way England was ruled in the 1680s differed fundamentally from the contemporary model of Louis XIV's France. 'Centralisation', as Professor Jones has stressed, 'ran counter to the basic principles of English government' (14, *19*; 21 [Glassey], *passim*), a fact powerfully underlined by the Restoration Settlement and illuminated in 1687 by the hostility which greeted the two special centralised agencies which were set up, the Ecclesiastical Commission, with its visitorial powers and the Board of Regulators, with its paid peripatetic agents touring the towns. James had no equivalent of *intendants* or *Steuerräthe* to preside over the counties and no prospect in the immediate future of acquiring or affording such officials. He therefore needed somehow to be assured of the cooperation of the men who not only dispensed petty justice, but administered statutes, officered the county militias, and at the same time wielded considerable electoral influence *ex officio*. As 1687 gave way to 1688 such considerations as these were to become, month by month, more inescapable.

---

1. J. Locke, *Two Treatises of Government* (ed. P. Laslett, 2nd edn., Cambridge, 1967): *Second Treatise*, paras 123–4. Although the words had been penned years before in very different circumstances, they were published following a revolution justified by the need to ensure such a 'preservation'.
2. See, for example, the Invitation to William, 30 June 1688, in Sir J. Dalrymple,

Memoirs of Great Britain and Ireland (2nd edn. 1773), II, Appx. pt. 1, p. 229, repr. Williams (11a), pp. 8–10.

3. If there *was* appreciable relaxation on Charles's part in the years 1682–5, as J.R. Jones has claimed – and that is debatable – it was more than counterbalanced by the vigorous rôle of his brother, James. A. Browning, ed., *Memoirs of Sir John Reresby* (Glasgow, 1936), pp. 329, 338: Jan, May 1684.

4. D.J. Milne, 'The Results of the Rye House Plot and their Influence upon the Revolution of 1688', *TRHS*, 5th ser., **I** (1951).

5. P. Haffenden, 'The Crown and the Colonial Charters, 1675–1688', *William and Mary Quarterly*, **23** (1958); see also R. M. Bliss (37), pp. 46–7.

6. C. Robbins, ed., *Two English Republican Tracts* (Cambridge, 1969), p. 177.

7. Monmouth's rebellion had caused alarm before the final *débâcle*. For two important recent scholarly studies, see R. Clifton (51); P. Earle, *Monmouth's Rebels* (1977).

8. J.H. Shennan, *The Parlement of Paris* (1968), pp. 278–83; G.A. Jacobsen, *William Blathwayt* (New Haven, 1932), *passim*.

9. *Memoirs of Sir John Reresby*, p. 327.

10. *Grey's Debates*, IV, p. 115.

11. Recent interpretations along these lines have owed much to the unpublished Oxford D.Phil. thesis of R.G. Pickavance, 'The English Boroughs and the King's Government . . . 1681–1685' (1977). See also J. Miller, 'The Crown and the Borough Charters in the Reign of Charles II'. *EHR*, **100** (1985).

12. *Memoirs of Sir John Reresby*, p. 327: 10 Jan 1684.

13. Comparisons with the Dutch are difficult owing to the great variety of jurisdictions in the United Provinces.

14. G.W. Keeton, *Lord Chancellor Jeffreys and the Stuart Cause* (1965) vindicates at great length Jeffreys's abilities as a lawyer without denying that in political trials these were often perverted by gross partiality.

15. 'The Character of a Trimmer' (*c.* 1685), in J.P. Kenyon, ed., *Halifax: Complete Works* (1969), p. 53.

16. See, however, J. Carter (120a), pp. 75–6, for parliamentary attempts to ensure it would not be abused, either in religious or economic matters.

17. There were odd exceptions, notably John Somers, the future Whig leader, and Mr Justice Powell: Costin and Watson (11b), I, pp. 258–71.

18. Anchitell Grey, *Debates*, VIII, p. 357: 12 Nov 1685.

CHAPTER 12

James II and William of Orange:
the providential revolution

'One of the strangest catastrophes that is in any history.' So wrote Gilbert Burnet, the most knowledgeable contemporary historian of the events of 1688, about the 'unexpected Revolution' that overthrew James II. That a monarch possessed of such formidable assets, with a full treasury, a large army and fleet, and the most powerful ally in Europe, should have 'his whole strength, like a spider's web, . . . so irrecoverably broken, with a touch' seemed to him an event inexplicable in terms of mere human agencies (1, *III, 1*). The Lords and Commons of the Convention Parliament in 1689 seemingly agreed when they described the revolution as a 'miraculous deliverance from popery and arbitrary power' and later enshrined in the Bill of Rights a reference to God's 'marvellous providence and merciful goodness to this nation'.[1] Once the swift drama was played out, in fact, the word 'providence' was invoked again and again, the common coinage of the bemused as well as of the devout. Burnet himself had caught the mood as early as anyone when, just a few days after King James's flight to France, he called on his London congregation, including William of Orange, to 'consider the steps of Providence . . . the prodigies and miracles of Providence, that have attended our deliverance'. One example, singled out for special veneration, was that easterly 'Protestant Wind' which in the early days of November blew Prince William's task force ships at high speed down the Channel, and at the same time prevented the English battle fleet from intercepting them. But looking back a year later, Dean Tillotson saw the whole revolution in the same light – 'a thing which cannot be paralleled in History' for suddenness and bloodlessness, 'and which can only be resolved into the over-riding Providence of God.'[2]

It is instructive to read such comments in the light of modern scholarship. Few historians today can accept either the old 'Whig' interpretation, which saw the 1688 Revolution as a virtually inevitable part of England's national destiny, or the contrived – almost stage-managed – phenomenon represented by one of the first of the post-Whig revisionists, Lucile Pinkham.[3] Inhabiting a God-centred world, in which the human condition was beset by appalling uncertainties, the seventeenth-century Briton found no difficulty in reconciling extremes of chance or hazard with a divine pattern or purpose. We may find it hard to appreciate his belief in the workings of Providence: but we must accept that there was much that was unpredictable, and some things in retrospect barely credible, about the events of 1688: 'so many visible and apparent accidents', as one politician put it soon after the Revolution, 'any one whereof had they happened, the whole design must certainly have miscarried.'[4] No excuse is needed, therefore, if such 'accidents' figure prominently in this chapter.

On any reasonably informed assessment of James II's position in December

1687, it would certainly have required a prophet of uncanny prescience to foresee that within twelve months he would in effect have lost his throne. A few Whig exiles, cut off from reality and a prey to wishful thinking, looked into their crystal ball and saw 'violent fermentation' ahead.[5] But to most observers on the spot it was James's strength and the bleak prospects of any domestic opposition to him which seemed self-evident. Although the King had made enemies among the Anglican Tories, they were some way yet from being wholly alienated. Recent events at home had, of course, left them puzzled and resentful. Even more alarming was the news from Ireland, where the earl of Tyrconnell, Lord Deputy since January 1687, had been flagrantly bent on extending his former policy of catholicising the army (the Irish army was now effectively Catholic-officered) to every area of civil government. His policies 'seemed to expose the implications of a Catholic monarchy in their starkest form' (268a, *264*; 271), as the arrival of a flood of Huguenot refugees in England since the Revocation of the Edict of Nantes had exposed them in France (above, p. 13). Despite some Catholic penetration of the county magistracies and lieutenancies, however, the Tories' hold on the English localities was still largely unbroken at the end of 1687. In any event, in an England obsessed with dread of a new civil war it was Tories and churchmen who, of all James's subjects, remained most averse by conviction and instinct from any thought of rebellion.

The Whigs, on the other hand, had less compunction about resisting a bad king by force, but the prospect of their doing so after the Monmouth disaster seemed to James negligible. He knew of course that there were dangerous recalcitrants and plotters among those who had fled abroad. But how were they to raise an answering spark among those left at home? With only a few exceptions the surviving front-line activists of 1679–81 seemed content to lie low. And their contacts with their old supporters, whose proscription from local positions of influence remained almost as bleak a reality in December 1687 as it had been for the past five or six years, had withered still further since the 1685 election. In any case, James believed that his toleration policy would enable him within a few months to neutralise any risk from the Whigs, by offering to nonconformists a tempting share in those local offices which Tories who continued to resist this policy would forfeit. Indeed, in some corporations the Board of Regulators was already employing former Exclusionists among its agents.

Despite everything he was to do to alienate his subjects in the first six months of the new year (below, pp. 181–3), it is hard to find evidence that even in the midsummer of 1688, let alone in the spring (56, *231*), James was faced with the threat of a *rebellion*. As late as 27 August his chief Secretary of State wrote to Paris:

> Men are not to judge of Englishmen by their talk in coffee houses, nor by what idle, beggarly knaves that go into Holland say . . . to make their court. All the Dissenters are satisfied, and the Church of England's principles will keep them loyal . . . In short, I believe there never was in England less thought of rebellion'[6].

Certainly conspiracies existed, more indeed than Sunderland's spies were aware of: small groups of desperate men who aimed, as we shall see, at spreading disaffection at home while recruiting foreign arms for the purpose of either overthrowing James or enchaining him. But there was no major uprising brewing. The King had no fears on that score, and though he and his ministers were proved wrong about so much in the last year of his reign, they were right about this (139b, *138, 161*). There were few parallels, we must note, between the internal situation in 1688 and that which had existed in 1641–2. No Parliament was in being at Westminster (or in Edinburgh) to provide a focus for mounting discontent, still less raise an army against the King, and however many great nobles and squires might have contrived to raise their tenantry in 1688 and stiffen them by county militia, they could not conceivably have been a match for a standing army of at least 20,000 trained troops, their numbers rising week by week (Ch. 11).

James could only have been defeated militarily, therefore, by an invasion from the Continent, backed by as much domestic support as could be mustered, including defectors from the royal army and navy. Even in the spring and summer months – generally assumed to be the only feasible period to launch it – the prospects facing such an invasion would never be better than doubtful (53b, *128–9*; 139b, *177*). His army apart, James had the biggest fleet in Europe, in numbers of ships if not in fire power;[7] and the labours of Pepys at the Admiralty had done much in recent years to imbue its officers with high professional standards (47; 226a, *Ch. 9*). And if called on to face such an invasion, the King seemed in the summer of 1688 to have a good prospect of support from his mighty French ally, whose pension he was pocketing. In practice there was only one base, the Dutch Republic, from which an invading expedition could come to the aid of James's opponents, and only one major European figure who was at all likely to plan and lead it. William of Orange, stadholder of Holland, Zealand and other provinces, was both the King's nephew and son-in-law. Until the birth of a male heir to James in June 1688 Princess Mary, William's wife, was first in the Protestant line. Although active in turning English political opinion against Charles II in 1672–4, William had conducted himself with caution in his dealings with England between then and 1685, and by and large had continued to do so down to December 1687. When, for reasons we must examine later, the Prince at length determined to make his gambler's throw, it was essentially he, and he alone, who made possible one of the few great revolutions between the seventeenth and the twentieth centuries which was first and foremost an invasion and only very secondarily a rebellion.

Leaving aside the Whig and Covenanter exiles and the 3,000 professional soldiers of the Anglo-Dutch brigade who came over with William's Dutchmen, Brandenburgers and Swiss, the number of Englishmen who took up arms against James between the landing on 5 November and the end of the month, that is, while the issue was still open, was small; and the number of Scots who did so north of the border was negligible. The active English rebels, some of whom rose by design and others (like the Harleys in the Welsh borders and Sir Edward Seymour and his followers in the South-West) spontaneously, could boast some notable leaders (below, p. 186) and their contribution was psychologically, though not militarily, important. It is also indisputable that the outcome of the whole enterprise would have been very different had not a passive majority of both political nations – in England an overwhelming majority – resolved to do nothing positively to *aid* their stricken king when the blow was struck against him. The fact remains, however, that while the English rising had many sympathisers among the nobility and gentry, most of them remained fence-sitters until it was patently safe to jump down on the winning side (55), and that in Scotland the only violent demonstrations were confined to mob attacks on Episcopalian and Catholic priests and property. Although, to their credit, the Scottish Estates, so supine in 1685, had held out against the subsequent attempt to bully them into repealing the anti-Catholic Tests (above, p. 13), memories of Stuart repression were too fresh and bruising in the minds of Presbyterian lords and gentlemen for them to be tempted into precipitate action in response to William's offer of 'deliverance'. Despite the withdrawal into England of the bulk of James's Scottish forces in the autumn of 1688, not even the King's most committed enemies among the Scottish ruling class (apart from those in exile) made any overt move against him until the issue was decided hundreds of miles away (18, *170–5, 263–6*).

Since it was 'the descent on England' which conjured a glorious success out of what could so easily have been a catastrophic failure, nothing could be more distorting historically than to treat the Revolution of 1688 as an insular phenomenon.[8] In outlining and analysing the main stages whereby the English scenario underwent such an extraordinary transformation between December 1687 and December 1688, some of the most important questions to be addressed therefore concern the European context: the Prince of Orange's relations with his uncle; his Continental preoccupations, and above all, the motives and timing of his momentous decision to intervene in Britain. Likewise, the circumstances which determined that his expedition would be unopposed by the power of France had a vital bearing on his success. That said, there would have been no revolution but for the disastrous policies pursued by James II during 1688. Why he attempted, and ultimately failed, to turn Whigs and dissenters from political pariahs into reliable allies is of relevance here, but the key domestic question concerns his relations with the Tories: how and why did he contrive to put these under such intolerable strain that the great majority of them were prepared to stand by at the last and see him humiliated, while some were drawn into conspiracy and even into revolt? The part played in events by the conspirators and rebels themselves is another essential part of the mosaic: the rôle of the Whig exiles; the significance of the famous 'Invitation' to William of Orange and of its signatories – often misunderstood; the scale of the conspiratorial iceberg of which those signatories, the 'Immortal Seven', were the tip; the precise extent of disaffection in James's army and navy on which both the conspirators and William pinned so many hopes. Finally, there remain for the historian of the Revolution intriguing questions concerning the climactic events of November and December 1688, many questions which together add up to one: how can we explain why the invaders and their rebel collaborators achieved, against most reasonable predictions, a success that was swift, overwhelming and accomplished (in England) with comparatively little bloodshed?

As we have seen, the central figure in the entire drama, apart from James himself, was William of Orange. An appropriate starting-point, therefore, is to establish what his attitude was towards developments across the North Sea between 1685 and the end of 1687 and what pattern the Prince's relations with his uncle had followed. Periodically since the early 1670s[9] the head of the house of Orange had found himself a focus for the hopes of those in England and Scotland who were opposed to the policies of both Charles II and his brother. In general he had trodden very warily, especially during the Exclusion Crisis (Ch. 8) and at the time of the ill-fated expedition of the duke of Monmouth. For some two and a half years after Monmouth's execution William's attitude to James and his kingdoms was governed by three principal considerations. Foremost were his Continental preoccupations: his continued conviction that Louis XIV's aggressive ambitions were unappeased and that another attack on the United Provinces, a repetition of 1672, was only a matter of time, combined with a growing belief (partly the result of wrong diplomatic advice) that James would engage his forces alongside those of Louis in a Catholic alliance. The second consideration was the great difficulty the Prince experienced in persuading the Dutch estates of the reality of these threats (50, *158–63*). The third factor was his expectations of controlling the entire British inheritance, through his wife's right of succession, so long as James continued to be unable to produce surviving male heirs by his second marriage. Even the news that Queen Mary Beatrice was pregnant again, which broke officially in December 1687, did not at once affect these expectations, for Mary had either miscarried or given birth to short-lived infants eight times since 1674, inauspicious foundations for Catholic hopes. Thus the counter-arguments against William intervening by force in England remained overwhelming for over three years of James II's reign. This is not to say relations between the two were warm. On the contrary, they deteriorated markedly. An early straw in the wind was the negotiations which the Prince began with Brandenburg in 1686, with a view to engaging the Elector's troops to defend the United Provinces if a substantial Dutch army was committed elsewhere (53b, *78–80*). Also, from 1685 to 1687 he and James were at loggerheads over the officering of the Anglo-Dutch brigade (English and Scottish regiments serving in the Dutch army under semi-permanent loan from the Crown), James trying to insist on the removal of Whig undesirables and their replacement by loyalists, and the Prince thwarting his wishes (139b, *Ch. 5*). (This brigade was ultimately to be the spearhead of the invasion force). An especially provocative step was taken by William in 1687 when he announced, via his envoy Dijkvelt, that he would never acquiesce in a repeal of the English Test Acts and the admission of Catholics to public offices or to Parliament. James would have been still angrier had he known that the Prince was also using Dijkvelt's visit and a later mission by Zuylestein to establish and maintain a whole network of undercover contacts with friends and potential friends in England, using his closest adviser, Bentinck, as linkman (53a, *222–3 et antea*). Nevertheless, with a Catholic succession still far from certain and James's own health suspect, William remained committed to non-intervention early in the following year. As Professor Baxter has put it, 'no sane man prefers a risk to a certainty' (56, *225*).

There is not a shred of evidence that William began to think at all seriously of taking such a risk before the spring of 1688, and he did so then only in the light of radically changed circumstances. Since many of these circumstances were created by James II's own policies in the early months of this year, and the upheaval in his relations with the English parties, it is to this part of the road to revolution that our attention must now turn.

Some time in the early autumn of 1687 James was persuaded by some of his closest advisers, in particular by Sunderland (45b, *171*) and probably by Lord Chancellor Jeffreys, that by refining, and also extending to the counties, those techniques of manipulation which had been so successful in the boroughs in the 1685 election, a packed Parliament of loyalists could eventually be secured which would agree to remove the civil disabilities of Catholics and dissenters. To this end James naively determined to put the loyalties of his natural allies, the Tories, to the most searching test yet by ordering the 'three questions' to be put to all justices of the peace and militia officers. Each was asked (1) whether he would support 'the taking off of the penal laws and the tests' if he were elected an MP; (2) whether he would work for the election of members known to favour such a policy; and (3) whether he would support the recent Declaration of Indulgence 'by living friendly with those of all persuasions'. The returns from some three-quarters of the counties have survived; and while it is possible to reduce them to some kind of statistical tabulation (53b, *Appx. A*) it is only by reading individual answers that one can appreciate both the irritation and the embarrassment which the interrogation caused the Tory gentry and the infinite variety of mental and verbal expedients (or, alternatively, collusion to produce stereotyped formulae) to which hundreds resorted to avoid giving a blunt refusal.[10] It has been suggested that the government *might* have interpreted the results, when it reviewed them in January-February 1688, in two ways: either that some three-quarters of those questioned had indicated by various shades of dissent or doubt, or by large-scale abstentions, that they were unlikely to support repealing the Tests (in contrast to a more cooperative attitude over the penal laws); or that a majority might acquiesce in the results of such a policy if a Parliament was prepared to do the dirty work (53b, *242*; 52, *221–2*). James, unfortunately for him, put the worst construction on the evidence. Between February and April 1688 wholesale changes were consequently made in the county commissions of the peace (126b, *82, 84*). With few exceptions, only those justices who had given firm indications of support (roughly half of them Roman Catholics introduced on to the benches since the 1687 Indulgence) were spared the unprecedented purges which now ensued. Norfolk and Wiltshire may be taken as not untypical examples. Between them they had 143 JPs in the first commissions of James II's reign, Tories almost to a man. Only eighteen were still officiating in the summer of 1688. Over the country as a whole the heads of hundreds of the leading county families in the land, the natural rulers of their shires, were publicly disgraced (for so they interpreted their 'putting out') in the upheaval of February–April 1688. Among the victims were many ultra-loyalists – men such as the Lancashire squire, Sir Thomas Stringer – whose ejection (Dr

Glassey has written) 'surely carried tactlessness to the point of imbecility' (in 21, *156*). To add insult to injury their replacements – some of them scraped from the very bottom of their county barrels – were either Catholics of distinctly lower standing than the families already insinuated, or Protestant dissenters. Meanwhile, seventeen out of the thirty-one lords lieutenant, all peers, had either resigned or been replaced, either for refusing to put the 'three questions' or for putting their own gloss upon them (52, *214–15, 222*).

These massive changes in the magistracy were carried out from lists drawn up by the Board of Regulators, the same body, headed by Sunderland, Jeffreys and Sir Nicholas Butler, and advised and serviced by local agents organised by Robert Brent, that had been set up in November 1687 to remodel the corporations. Between then and the end of March 1688, sixty-five boroughs were 'regulated' (sixty of them towns placed in Tory hands by the new charters of 1682–6) and more than 1,200 councillors or local officials were purged (53a, *148–9*). For replacements the commissioners had fewer Catholics to call on than in the counties, so the government had no option but to place its main reliance on Whigs and dissenters, wherever possible men of influence who were expected to cooperate, on religious grounds, in the subsequent election campaign. From April, when the King was assured that he could expect a subservient Parliament in the autumn, all the efforts of the Regulators and their agents were devoted to procuring one: for example, through the re-issue of charters and the selection and priming of suitable candidates, pledged to secure full civil rights and freedom of worship for religious minorities, and the inevitable picking off of most of the still surviving Tory burgesses and officials (21 [Glassey], *154–5*). Well before September, when James, under threat of invasion, put his whole policy of building up a pro-toleration alliance into sudden and screeching reverse (see below, pp. 187–8), his relations with the Anglican Tories were beyond repair.

This was all the more the case because that summer had seen his most damaging clash yet – nothing less than a head-on confrontation – with the Church of England. As we noticed, strains developed early between the Catholic King and the state Church whose rights he had undertaken to protect. These had been intensified subsequently by the setting up of the Ecclesiastical Commission, by the suspension of Compton, the attack on Magdalen, and above all by the first Declaration of Indulgence (Chs. 10, 11). For as Dr Bennett has explained, whatever disagreement there might be among the clergy about the treatment of dissenters, a state of general toleration, 'which would shatter the whole disciplinary machinery of the national church', was anathema to all of them (162, *274*). Clerical and lay Tories naturally drew together as the 'property' rights of both came under attack. What finally forged their alliance, and annealed it in a fire of popular enthusiasm, was the most astonishing miscalculation of even this reign of royal blunders, the prosecution of the Seven Bishops.

In April 1688 the King issued his second Declaration of Indulgence [N.1(vi)]. His first Declaration had been dismaying enough to Archbishop Sancroft and his episcopal lieutenants, especially to dedicated Yorkists like the outstandingly able Francis Turner, bishop of Ely. They had been prepared to see a relaxation of the penal laws against Catholics on the understanding that the King would countenance their coercive policy towards Protestant dissenters. Even before the expected formal declaration of freedom of conscience was published, however, churchmen had been forced to look sadly on in the early months of 1687 as the efficacy of the Church courts as instruments of religious uniformity collapsed, along with that of the Anglican magistracy, before the rampant royal dispensing power, increasingly used on behalf of dissenters. In the twelve months which followed the first Declaration, the Anglican clergy responded vigorously by stepping up their anti-Catholic preaching and propaganda. It has been plausibly argued that the King's fateful decision to reissue the 1687 Indulgence, followed by an explicit command to the clergy to read it aloud in their churches (above, p. 14), was a deliberate bid to bring the clergy hard to heel before the November elections for a Parliament committed to 'liberty of conscience', which the new Declaration explicitly promised (162, *268–77*).

The effects were to achieve the very opposite. James had no expectation that the clergy would defy him; they had little positive encouragement to do so from leading Tory laymen they consulted, such as Nottingham (the former Daniel Finch), Rochester and Danby, yet defy him they did. Bishop Turner orchestrated the opposition of London, whose attitude was crucial to the attitude of the provincial ministry. He even engaged the support of the Presbyterian pastors of London, having apparently persuaded Sancroft – to the joy of the 'latitude-men' (Ch. 10) – that the achievement of a common Protestant front on this issue was so important that the dissenters should be offered renewed hope of a comprehension. Hence when the historic protest of Sancroft and six of his episcopal colleagues was presented to James, it contained not only a flat refusal to instruct their clergy to read the Declaration and a direct questioning of the legality of the suspending power,[11] but an insistence that their stand was not to be attributed to 'want of due tenderness towards Dissenters, with whom we shall be willing to come to such a temper as shall be thought fit when the matter comes to be settled . . . in Parliament.'[12] The bishops can have had no inkling that from this commitment was eventually to stem, after many twists of fate, the growth of partial religious toleration in England in the form enacted by Parliament in May 1689 (Ch. 23). Still less did they foresee that their protest would play its part in bringing about a revolution; indeed, five of them were to repudiate that revolution subsequently by refusing to take the oaths to King William and Queen Mary. What the bishops hoped to do was to jolt James into abandoning his pro-Catholic and Indulgence policies and returning to his initial alliance with the Church of England. They certainly shook, and deeply shocked him, and shock turned to anger in face of the subsequent defiance of the lower clergy. The outcome, however, was not a reappraisal of royal policy but a prosecution of the seven bishops for seditious libel. Both their imprisonment in the Tower and their eventual trial and triumphant acquittal (above, p. 14) released a great emotional wave of loyalty to the Church and of protest against the excesses of the Crown, a reaction which appeared to embrace the whole range of London society from 'prentice-boys to dukes.

*

The seven bishops were acquitted on 30 June. That evening another seven men, later to be dubbed 'the immortal Seven', including the suspended Bishop Compton and assorted aristocrats representing both political parties (p. 14), were emboldened to take the extreme step of penning a letter to Prince William of Orange, inviting him to invade England. The sequence of the two events was not wholly unconnected. But it would be hopelessly wrong to represent them as simple cause and effect. If William had not already taken the decision to intervene by force, provided some such invitation was forthcoming, not even the Church of England's singular triumph over Popery and the prerogative would have been sufficient to prompt it. Furthermore, though an 'Orangist conspiracy' against James had already been afoot in England for at least two months before midsummer 1688 (54b; see also below, p. 186), it had proved very difficult to draw into it the weightiest lay figures in the 'Church party', the Tories, with the exception of the earl of Danby. Although Nottingham, for one, acknowledged that William had just cause to defend his wife's interests, neither he nor Rochester and Halifax could be persuaded to join in inviting him over. Disappointing though this may have been to the Prince, it was hardly surprising. Even fiery Whigs such as Thomas Wharton and Lord Delamere, both of whom were quick to rise in arms when the invasion came, found it prudent not to put their names, even in code, to a document which Nottingham tersely described as 'high treason'.[13] The same was true of the small group of malcontent army officers, notably Churchill and Trelawney, of whom William had hopes (54b, *456–7*). It is no coincidence that at least five of the seven who did 'sign' were men whose desperation was heightened by personal grudges against James: Devonshire, for instance, had recently been fined the colossal sum of £30,000 and exiled to Derbyshire, while Russell and Sidney were close kinsmen of the Rye House martyrs (Ch. 11). Thus, for all their euphoric assurances to the Prince that 'nineteen parts of twenty of the people' were 'desirous of a change', and their predictions that support from some of the most 'considerable' landowners and significant desertions from James's army and navy were 'almost certain' (11a, *8–9*), the Seven could only in the end make an *explicit* commitment of their own services if William invaded. When and why, therefore, did the Prince of Orange decide to abandon the caution of the previous two years and begin actively to prepare for an audacious enterprise in which the risks, as well as the stakes, were so high?

The 'Invitation', so-called, gives a vital clue to the timing. The signatories recall that the first intimation that William was prepared to assist the conspirators openly had been brought to them by the naval captain, Edward Russell. We know almost exactly when that was. On 19 April William wrote to his most trusted adviser, William Bentinck: 'Mr Herbert [Arthur Herbert, later to command William's invasion fleet] and the two Russells have been here; I will not tell you what they said to me, since that can be better done by word of mouth, hoping to see you soon . . .'[14] What William was told, in short, was that if he was ever to intervene effectively in England it must be soon, or not at all. Gilbert Burnet, who was in the know, records his answer, the answer that was to change the history of Britain decisively: 'that, if he was invited by some men of the best interest . . . who should both in their own name and in the name of others who trusted them, invite him to come and rescue the nation and the [Protestant] religion, he believed he could be ready *by the end of September*' (1, *III, 241* [my italics]). There were perhaps five main reasons for his decision. Firstly, the Queen's pregnancy had now run almost eight months of its course without mishap: the prospect of a male Catholic heir who might survive to manhood and take England and Scotland indefinitely out of the Protestant camp could no longer be written off. Secondly, the possibility that James would assemble a packed Parliament before the year was out was now a very real one, and alarmed the Prince on dynastic as well as religious grounds (53a). Thirdly, he became convinced as a result of the Russell mission (or so Baxter has surmised) that, without his own armed intervention, James's subjects would very probably rise in revolt anyway, with the outcome either the obliteration of his potential English support or the setting up of a republic (56, *231*). Fourthly, Dutch opinion had recently moved sharply against James as a result of the latter's demand that the regiments of the Anglo-Dutch brigade should be returned to England, so that for the first time there was some prospect of the Prince's getting together the troops and ships he would require for an invasion. Finally, at the time of Russell's mission William's hopes of a Brandenburg alliance, dormant since 1686, had just risen sharply with the fatal illness of the old Elector and the imminent succession of his son, who was heir to the Orange estate.

If these were the reasons for the Prince's decision to invade, what were the motives behind it? Ostensibly these were set out in his 'Declaration' of 30 September 1688, the manifesto in which he justified his impending invasion. To admit to any intention of dethroning his father-in-law would have stamped him as a piratical adventurer in the eyes of Europe and offended the majority of his potential Tory supporters. Consequently he promised to redress the crimes of James's 'evil counsellors'; and while he declared his wife's interest in the succession, accusing the baby Prince of Wales (born in June) of being an imposter, he was careful to add that his expedition was 'intended for no other design but to have a free and lawful Parliament assembled as soon as possible', to rectify abuses, confirm the religious tests and reach an amicable settlement of the problem of Dissent (11a, *10–11, 15–16*). The Prince's sincerity has, of course, often been called in question (e.g. 56, *236–7*; 54a, *74–5*). But however we judge the balance of probabilities, there is no conclusive evidence that William's *overriding* motive for invading was to seize the crown for himself. His primary objective (as all were agreed) was to ensure that the wealth and power of England were thrown into the Protestant side of the scale in the impending struggle with France which he had long foreseen.[15] It is quite possible that he thought a freely elected Parliament might so far shackle James as to be able to push him into the anti-French coalition. But there was certainly no guarantee that such a 'free' Parliament would conspire in his dethronement, provided James accepted military defeat without entirely throwing in his political hand; and this, it must be stressed, still seemed to many the likeliest outcome when William presented his terms for a settlement to the King's commissioners on 9 December.[16] Historians who have portrayed William as hell-bent on usurpation have indeed given him too little credit for realism and pragmatism. After all, he must have known full well – for his intelligence was excellent – that not even the signatories of the Invitation of 30 June were agreed on how they, as individuals, wished to see the crown disposed in the event of a successful *coup*.[17]

In the early summer of 1688, however, the Prince of Orange was not even assured of military success in the coming trial of strength, let alone assured of the crown. He viewed with reserve the airy promise of the Seven that his landing would attract substantial civilian support and treated the, for him, far more crucial inducement of widespread disaffection in James's army and navy with a mixture of hope and circumspection. He therefore made preparations to bring over a much larger army than the 7,000-odd troops the English revolutionaries thought would suffice. It was just as well he did. Through his envoys, Dijkvelt and Zuylestein, the Prince had encouraged groups of his well-wishers in both English parties to keep up contacts during the thirty months of Personal Rule which followed the prorogation of James II's first Parliament (54b, *453–4*). But little that was directly treasonable took place until the Queen's pregnancy was well advanced, and even by June 1688 the scale of the conspiracies active in England, though growing, was still small. Six of the seven who despatched the invitation had been members of a larger group, mostly civilians, which had been holding meetings at the Whig earl of Shrewsbury's house since the spring of 1687 and which became more numerous and active after April 1688 (56, *230*). The seventh, Henry Sidney, the former commander of the Anglo-Dutch brigade and a close confidant of the Prince, acted as the link between this caucus and two distinct opposition groups among serving or former serving officers: the members of the Rose Tavern Club and the so-called 'Tangerines', former military and naval veterans of the Tangier Service. During the summer of 1688 both these latter groups, perhaps thirty men in all, became actively concerned in sowing the seeds of defection in the armed forces (139b, *Ch. 6*; 54b). In the event, the scale of the desertions in the army proved much smaller than had been hoped for; but because, as we shall see, they were shrewdly timed, and because they involved several senior officers, such as Trelawney, Kirke, and above all Churchill (later duke of Marlborough), who had firmly committed himself to William in August, they played a more important part in undermining King James's will to fight than the small magnate-led risings which took place in Yorkshire, Cheshire and Nottinghamshire. On the other hand, there is evidence that the tentacles of the naval conspiracy reached wider and that its influence has been underestimated. James was to pay a heavy price for dismissing Admiral Arthur Herbert – another Tangier veteran – from his command in 1687, not only because he was to carry the Seven's invitation to William and then to command the latter's invasion fleet, but because he had such an extensive connection among serving officers of the Royal Navy, many of whom were indebted to him for their promotion. In fact, the record of a council of war held by Dartmouth, commander of James's Channel fleet, on the very day of William's landfall, reveals so general a disinclination to assist the King among the ships' captains that this cannot be ruled out as a more important factor than the weather (see below, p. 188) in Dartmouth's earlier inability to intercept the Dutch armada.[18]

*

It remains to determine what other factors gave Providence a helping hand in translating William of Orange's gamble and the leap in the dark of a few thousand rebels into a 'Glorious Revolution'. Of great importance was the fact that when the invasion took place James was denied any help at all from his ally, France, and this in a situation so finely balanced that even a limited French contribution might have proved decisive. Lack of French aid was attributable partly to James's own folly, down to late September, and partly to the preoccupations and miscalculations of Louis XIV. James fell victim to a combination of poor intelligence and totally unrealistic deductions about the reality of the threat from his Dutch son-in-law. When Louis first became aware of William's naval preparations he sent the marquis de Seignelay to London with an offer to transfer sixteen French ships from the Mediterranean to the Channel. He renewed the offer (how sincerely is a matter of some dispute) through his envoy Bonrepos in August. Both initiatives were politely spurned[19] (53b, *142, 162*; 45b, *208–10*). But Louis, too, was guilty of gross misjudgement. When no invasion had been launched by the end of August he concluded that, since it would be suicidal (in his view) to risk putting a great expeditionary force to sea at the time of the equinoctial gales, he had a free hand to commit his own forces elsewhere until the spring of 1689 (45b, *212*). For his part, James, even at the beginning of September, could still not believe that William would take so 'unnatural' a step as to attack his own father-in-law; or that, at a time when Western Europe stood on the brink of a new war, after months of crisis generated by the death of the Archbishop Elector of Cologne, the Dutch would be so apparently irresponsible as to allow a significant part of their army to be diverted away from the United Provinces. James was not to get a third chance; on 14 September [O.S.] Louis launched 70,000 troops into Germany, most of them concentrated against the Palatinate fortress of Philipsburg, about as far from the Dutch frontier as the situation made possible. James heard the news with incredulity and for the first time, it seems, with a sense of foreboding; even so, it was not until the 20th that he recognised that an invasion of England was completely inevitable (45b, *215*).

James's long sojourn in cloud-cuckoo land had the effect of intensifying the political confusion in his own kingdom which now ensued. This confusion was to make a significant contribution to the dramatic collapse in November of the King's military resistance. Having finally convinced himself that the unbelievable was really going to happen, he took a rapid series of political and religious decisions which, taken together, bore the mark of panic. By mid-September his agents had sent in reports suggesting that the Commons' majority towards which his government had been working for almost a year was within his grasp: claims which modern research has shown cannot be dismissed as wildly unrealistic (53a, *169–72*). Yet on the 28th the writs for a new General Election, which had just been issued, were withdrawn on the King's orders. This was followed by a brief interlude of standstill obduracy, which reduced Sunderland, James's ablest minister, to despair and evoked from Lord Chancellor Jeffreys the sardonic comment that 'the Virgin Mary was to do all' (46, *228*). Then, over the course of the next three weeks came a frenetic rush of concessions to the very party – the Anglican churchmen – which the King had been so sedulously depressing: the

Ecclesiastical Commission abolished; the fellows of Magdalen re-instated; corporation charters and county commissions and lieutenancies once again thrown into the melting pot, with many Catholics and dissenters on whom James had for months pinned his hopes now consigned to the wilderness (53a, *263*; 126b, *95–7*). There was no time now for a planned campaign, only for wild improvisation. The result was chaos. It demoralised the Catholics and re-united the Whigs without evoking a spark of gratitude from the Tory gentry, who attributed to this eleventh-hour capitulation as much sincerity as a shotgun marriage. Furthermore, as J.R. Jones has written, it 'severely damaged James's reputation for determination . . . by showing that he would give way in the face of danger' (53a, *264*).

William could draw some comfort from all this as he kicked his heels for weeks in Holland, waiting for the westerly gales to abate. But he was well aware that if his expedition failed to make a successful landfall all other advantages would be wiped out. Historians have almost universally agreed with the general contemporary view that the Prince's decision to put his troops ashore in the South-West of England vastly increased his chances of success. It is certainly true that a landing on the Yorkshire coast, which had been strongly urged by Danby and other prominent Northern and Midland rebels, would have been more difficult to accomplish safely in rough autumnal weather; also, James's fleet, under Dartmouth, had been stationed in the Gunfleet with a northern attack primarily in mind. It is also the case that just about everything went right for the invaders even after the 'providential' change of wind which made their initial three-day unimpeded dash down the Channel possible. Torbay offered a safe anchorage (5 November) from the same storm which forced the tardily pursuing Dartmouth to take shelter in the Downs. Devonshire provided friendly territory in which William could rest and organise his army of 14–15,000 before preparing for the anticipated battle; while the King's field army, stationed near London, was forced to make a wretched march in appalling weather into Wiltshire, giving potential defectors both the time and the conditions in which to begin their drift over to the enemy (139b, *Ch. 7, passim*). It has to be stressed, however, that chance, and especially climatic chance, rather than careful calculation was the prime mover in all this.[20] There is little if any concrete support for the theory (55, *12–13*; *rptd* 139b, *173–4*) that William deliberately chose a point of disembarkation as far removed from Yorkshire as possible so as to limit to the minimum his obligation to the Northern rebels, or one equally far away from London. Indeed a careful study of the maritime planning and execution of the invasion[21] reveals circumstantial evidence which indicates that William's first and abortive attempt in October (above, p. 14) may well have had the North as its prime target. It is also clear that even in his second, November venture the Prince did not rule out such a strategy if the weather – the great imponderable – made its adoption unavoidable, and that while he clearly preferred by now a landing on the south or south-west coast, places such as Cowes or Southampton water were at least as high on his short list as anywhere in Devonshire. In the end, the on-the-spot judgements of William's English advisers, plus the 'Protestant Wind', had much to do with the ultimate, supremely fortunate choice.

In the final reckoning, however, it is to a fourth factor, the actions of James II himself after the invasion, that we have to look to understand the sheer rapidity and totality of his collapse. With any lead at all from their king, the soldiers on whom he had lavished so much of his revenue would certainly have fought at Salisbury, and with their at least 2–1 superiority in numbers it is likely that, despite the serious thinning of the senior commissioned ranks by desertion, they would have given a good account of themselves. They were a professional army, and while their morale might have been higher, there is nothing to suggest that initially they were demoralised or lacking in basic professional loyalty. In the event the only 'lead' they got was one that committed them to a miserable retreat when no more than a few shots had been fired. That James, a former soldier and sailor of proven bravery and by reputation, over the years, a man of resolute, not to say wilful character, should have acted so completely out of character in the final crisis of his reign may seem not the least strange feature of Burnet's 'strangest catastrophe'. With hindsight we may claim to detect pointers to the subsequent breaking of his nerve in his panicky moves before the invasion. It is also clear that during his stay in camp James was physically ill, in great discomfort with a nasal infection, and therefore in poor condition to resist the psychological blows which rained on him there: by the time he reached Salisbury (19 November) the earliest defections of officers had already taken place, and these were followed by still more serious losses, above all by the defection of Lord Churchill. Even so, the decision less than three weeks after William's landing to sanction the abject withdrawal of the royal forces from Wiltshire back to London was a disaster (above, p. 14). Far from preserving the army, it precipitated its almost entire disintegration. It can only be explained as the act of a man suffering not just from physical debility but from a complete collapse of character, marked by depression and paralysis of will.

Back in London, with his world crumbling round him and even his daughter, Princess Anne, now among the defectors, James sent commissioners to negotiate terms with William. And the Prince, though in complete command of the military situation, remained cautious enough politically to stick by the letter of his pre-invasion Declaration: his principal demand, apart from the removal of all Catholics from office, was still that the King should concede the summoning of a freely-elected Parliament, a demand James had already anticipated by re-authorising the issue of writs for a new General Election. Why, then, a mere three days after his commissioners had made contact with William, did James decide to leave the country rather than pursue negotiations further? He still had some cards to play. The strongest was the crown itself: William might now desire it, but James held it and by clear hereditary right. The events of the next two months, beginning with the Guildhall meeting of peers on the very day of the King's secret departure from London, were to show that there was a very large loyalist element among the Tory landed classes, not to mention the Anglican clergy, who, while happy enough to see James checkmated, had no wish to see him dethroned. Furthermore, there was still a reservoir of *popular* sympathy for him, even in London – a fact clearly demonstrated by his almost festal street reception when he returned to the capital after the fiasco of his first attempt at flight. And before that attempt (though not after it) he still had an army of sorts, gathered at Uxbridge, a bargaining counter, if no longer a credible asset in the field. In the coming debates on the disposal of the crown both Whig and Tory MPs were to agree that 'the King might without molestation have stayed if he had pleased'.[22]

That James chose to throw away his hand is probably to be explained mainly by his continuing disillusionment and depression, mixed now with fears for his own physical safety, as well as that of his wife and son. Yet there may also have been an element of calculation in his decision. The fact that as parting gifts to his people he destroyed the parliamentary writs not so far sent out, threw the great seal of England into the Thames and gave his commander-in-chief, Feversham, an order tantamount to disbanding his army suggests that he had every intention of leaving behind him the maximum possible state of confusion and a breakdown of legal authority, from which, with French help, he might profit before long. If that was his reasoning, he miscalculated badly. R.A. Beddard has made it clear how far the projected 'counter-revolution of the loyalists', organised by the Hyde brothers, by Bishop Turner of Ely and Archbishop Sancroft, was frustrated from the start by the overwhelming fear of a breakdown of public order, common to Whig and Tory alike, which James's instructions to Feversham and abandonment of the capital had directly fomented.[23] From now on James, as both loyal and not-so-loyal Tories were soon to discover, was wide open to the charge that he had deserted his sacred office and had therefore 'abdicated' the throne (Ch. 13).

By mid-December William alone had the means at hand to guarantee the protection of life and property, and avert the threat of a Catholic backlash, in London at least. When the city authorities, acting independently of the 'provisional government' (Beddard's phrase) at the Guildhall, invited him to enter the capital, he accepted with alacrity. All initiatives, political as well as military, now lay unequivocally with him. Not surprisingly, when James made his second bolt for France soon afterwards, the Prince of Orange's connivance made very certain that this time it would be a successful exit. Whereas in Scotland a rebellion, instigated by Viscount Dundee, had still to be raised and suppressed before the crisis could be properly regarded as 'over', while in Ireland, controlled by Tyrconnel, a bloody and bitter road lay ahead, in England, at least, the political nation could focus all its thoughts from Christmas 1688 on the settlement which a providential revolution had made necessary.

---

1. G.M. Straka, 'The Final Phase of Divine Right Theory in England', *EHR*, **77** (1962); E.N. Williams (11a), p. 30.
2. Burnet (1), 23 December 1688; Tillotson, 5 November 1689, both quoted in G.M. Straka, loc. cit.
3. L. Pinkham, *William III and the Respectable Revolution* (Harvard, 1954); cf. the apogee of the Whig interpretation, in G.M. Trevelyan, *The English Revolution, 1688–9* (1938).
4. Sir John Lowther, *Memoirs of the Reign of James II* (ed. T. Zouch, York, 1808), quoted in W.A. Speck (54b), p. 71.
5. H.C. Foxcroft, *A Supplement to Burnet's History of My Own Time* (Oxford, 1902), p. 261.

6. PRO State Papers Foreign, France, Entry Book 19: Sunderland to Bevil Skelton, 27 Aug, quoted in Kenyon (45b), p. 208.

7. See J. Ehrman, *The Navy in the War of William III* (Cambridge, 1953). (For seasonal reasons, however, at the time of the Dutch invasion in November James's battle fleet was slightly outnumbered).

8. A pioneering work in this respect is Carswell (53b).

9. K.H.D. Haley, *William of Orange and the English Opposition, 1672–4* (1953).

10. See Sir G. Duckett, *Penal Laws and Test Act*, 2 vols (1882–3). A good selection of examples is given in Western (52).

11. Misleadingly referred to in the Petition as the 'dispensing power'.

12. Bodl. Lib. MS. Rawlinson C.798, f. 368b.

13. Finch MSS. Paper in Nottingham's hand [June 1688], quoted in Horwitz (48).

14. N. Japikse, ed., *Correspondentie van Willem III en van Hans Willem Bentinck* ('S-Gravenhage, 1927–8), I, p. 36: 19–29 April 1688 (original in French).

15. Childs (139b), p. 173, quoting journal of Hopp, the Dutch envoy at Vienna, Nov.1688.

16. Printed in J. Miller, *The Glorious Revolution* (1983), document 18, pp. 107–8. Dr Miller comments: 'These make it clear that William was prepared to agree to a settlement whereby James remained king.'

17. See A. Browning (43a), I, p. 422 and Henning (25), III, p. 185 for Danby and Bishop Compton. The little we know about Danby's friend, Lord Lumley, an ex-Catholic, suggests that he too was no out-and-out Williamite.

18. P. Le Fevre, 'Tangier, the Navy and the Glorious Revolution', *Mariner's Mirror*, **73** (1987), p. 189 & n. 22.

19. For a more sceptical version of the second offer, see Miller (50), p. 194.

20. But see the different interpretation in Professor Speck's recent account of the events of 1688 (54a), pp. 85–6 and n. 21.

21. C. Jones, 'The Protestant Wind of 1688: Myth and Reality', *Eur. Studies Review*, **3** (1973).

22. Sir Henry Capel (Whig), 28 Jan 1689, in 'A Jornall of the Convention', repr. in D.L. Jones (6b), p. 236; cf. Gilbert Dolben (Tory): 'No-one can deny that he might have stayed if he would . . .', ibid., p. 235.

23. R.A. Beddard, 'The Guildhall Declaration of 11 December 1688 and the Counter-Revolution of the Loyalists', *HJ*, **11** (1968); *idem* (6a), pp. 36–57; W.L. Sachse, 'The Mob in the Revolution of 1688', *JBS*, **4** (1964).

PART TWO

Revolution, war and change, 1689–1722

1689   General Election in England, Whig but not radical majority [E.1 (i)] (Jan); rebellion of Irish Catholics led by Tyrconnel and Hamilton; Convention meets (22 Jan); debates on settlement of Crown begin (28th); proposal for a Regency defeated in Lords by 3 votes (29th); Declaration of Rights and joint sovereignty in England offered to William and Mary by Convention, and accepted (13 Feb); Louis XIV refuses to recognise titles of William III and Mary II; Dutch declare war on France (Feb).

    James II lands in Ireland with French troops to support Catholic rebels; mutinies in some of James's former regiments in England – Mutiny Act passed; William's opposition to the Tests for Protestants rouses Tory alarm. Scottish Convention meets in Edinburgh (March); approves Claim of Right and invites William and Mary to accept Scottish crown (11 Apr); Graham of Claverhouse (Dundee) calls on Scottish Jacobites to fight for James; bill of Rights introduced at Westminster; both Houses of Parliament resolve to support William in a war against France and to jettison a bill for Protestant comprehension, referring matter to Convocation; all-Whig Treasury Board (apart from Godolphin) approved (Apr).

    William (for England) declares war on France (5 May); William and Mary become joint rulers of Scotland (11th); attempt to build a Hanoverian Protestant Succession into Bill of Rights causes storm in Parliament; English Toleration Act becomes law (24 May); Irish Jacobite forces advance into Ulster, Herbert's fleet defeated by French at Bantry Bay (May). Formation of Grand Alliance against France by England, United Provinces, Empire, Spain, Savoy and many German states (May–June).

    Act abolishing 'prelacy' passed by Scottish Parliament (July); victory of Scots Jacobite rebels at Killiecrankie, but death of Dundee; siege of Londonderry (since April) by Irish Catholic army raised (30 July). Scottish Parliament – in disarray – and English Convention Parliament both prorogued (2, 20 Aug); crippling defeat of rebel Highlanders at Dunkeld; English relieving army under Schomberg arrives in Ireland (Aug).

    Second session of Convention Parliament (Oct). £2 million war supply voted. Mounting dismay at heavy losses of merchant shipping to French and prospect of prolonged struggle in Ireland. Convocation meets: lower clergy strongly oppose Comprehension (Nov). Bill of Rights passed; Convocation adjourned (Dec) – not to meet again for business until 1701.

    Locke's *Two Treatises of Government* and first *Letter on Toleration* published.

1690   Whig Corporations bill lost after Commons defeat the vindictive 'Sacheverell clause' (Jan). William, weary with Whig partisanship, prorogues (27 Jan) and dissolves (6 Feb) Parliament. Archbishop Sancroft deprived for refusing the oaths to William and Mary; Halifax disappoints King by resigning as Lord Privy Seal (Feb). General Election (Feb–Mar): bitterly fought with 106 contests and Tory gains [E.1 (a) (b)]. Sir J. Lowther (T) heads remodelled, bi-party Treasury Board; new Parliament meets; grants William and Mary excise for life but customs for four years only – partial defeat for Danby's Commons management (Mar).

    Abjuration bills – to compel MPs and office-holders to abjure allegiance to ex-James II – fail narrowly in Commons, blocked in Lords; John Tillotson made Archbishop of Canterbury (Apr); Westminster parliament prorogued (May). Second session of Scotland's post-Revolution Parliament opens (Apr); it abolishes Committee of Articles (May) and restores full Presbyterian church government in Scotland (June) and patronage to heritors and Kirk sessions (July). Jacobite remnant under Buchan routed at Cromdale (May). Whig Shrewsbury resigns as a

Secretary of State, leaving High Tory Nottingham (for 6 months) sole Secretary (June).

William leaves for Ireland; Mary in nominal charge of government. Decisive French naval victory at Beachy Head: many Anglo-Dutch ships destroyed or crippled – French control Channel – acute fear of invasion (June). Battle of the Boyne: heavy defeat for James's Franco-Irish army (1 July); French victory over allied armies at Fleurus, Netherlands; James leaves Ireland for France (July). Duke of Savoy's army defeated by French at Staffarda; Tourville's fleet returns to Brest – invasion fears subside (Aug); William returns to England (Sept).

Second session of 1690–5 Parliament opens; Commons accept King's request for army of 69,000 and vote £2.3 million to pay for it (Oct). Difficulties in Parliament over ways of raising army and navy supply; Godolphin returns to Treasury Commission as First Lord, but still with a Whig Chancellor (Nov). Big naval building programme approved; passage through Commons of bill establishing first salaried parliamentary Commission of Accounts; Whig Henry (Lord) Sidney given vacant Secretaryship of State (Dec).

Locke's *An Essay concerning Human Understanding* and *Second Letter concerning Toleration* published.

1691   Public Accounts Act passed and session ends (5 Jan). William in Netherlands commanding greatly-increased English army (Jan). Commissioners of Accounts begin work (Mar) and continue until autumn: Paul Foley (W) and Sir Thomas Clarges (T) leading members. Sunderland allowed to return from exile (May). Robert Harley, a new Whig MP, begins to make his mark in Commission of Public Accounts (June).

Battle of Aughrim, Ireland: St Ruth's Catholic army of 25,000 defeated by allied army under Dutchman Ginkel (July); surrender of Limerick to Ginkel (3 Oct) – end of war in Ireland. Conciliatory Treaty of Limerick (Oct), subsequently to be heavily undermined by Irish Protestant Parliament.

English Parliament reassembles (Oct) for third session; naval estimates cut on the motion of Harley, backed by Tories and Country Whigs; Commons pass a Trial of Treasons bill, favoured by Tories as giving fairer hearing to accused (Nov), amended bill fails when sent down from Lords; the younger Whigs John Somers and Charles Montagu earn King's favour by opposing it (Dec).

1692   Churchill (now earl of Marlborough) dismissed from all his commands, probably on suspicion of Jacobite intrigues (Jan); this results in breach between Queen Mary and her sister, Princess Anne. Massacre of the Macdonalds of Glencoe (13 Feb). King vetoes bill giving judges complete security of tenure and prorogues Westminster Parliament (24th). Rochester admitted to the new 'Cabinet Council' without portfolio; moderate Tory earl of Pembroke, Lord Privy Seal; Seymour joins Treasury Board, but so does the Whig Henry Montagu (Mar); Somers promoted from Solicitor- to Attorney-General (May).

French invasion expedition prepared (Apr–May); success of Anglo-Dutch fleet under Russell at Barfleur and La Hogue (19–23 May) ends danger of invasion. Fall of the fortress city of Namur, 'the greatest stronghold in the Spanish Netherlands', to the French (June); William's army, attempting to recapture Namur, defeated at Steenkirk (July).

Fourth session of Parliament opens (Nov); Somers's bill making it treason to deny William and Mary's title and imposing abjuration oath on office-holders defeated in Commons, 200–175; Place Bill, supported by Tories and Country Whigs, narrowly lost in Lords (Dec).

Henry Purcell's opera *The Fairy Queen* performed in London. First of the Boyle Lectures (1692–1714) 'for proving the Christian religion against notorious infidels' given by Richard Bentley. Witch-hunt in Salem, Massachusetts.

1693   Bill for a '4 shilling Aid' approved, marking arrival of a permanent Land Tax; Tontine Loan Act passed, inaugurating the long-term National Debt (Ch. 17); bill 'for frequent meeting and calling of Parliaments' (Triennial bill) sent by the Lords to the Commons (Jan). King vetoes Triennial bill and brings to an end a stormy session (Mar). Two leading Whigs promoted: Somers, of the 'Junto', made Lord Keeper of the Great Seal and Sir John Trenchard, prominent Exclusionist, Northern Secretary of State, breaking Nottingham's monopoly (Mar).

Sunderland, James II's disgraced and officially unpardoned minister, begins to exert a major political influence on the Court from 'behind the curtain' (June). Attack by French Mediterranean fleet on Anglo-Dutch Smyrna convoy in Lagos Bay, S. Portugal: Levant Company alone loses £600,000 in ships and cargoes (June) – leads to 1694 decision to base an allied fleet in Mediterranean, and to fierce criticism of the Admiralty and the war. William's army routed by Marshal Luxembourg at Neerwinden [Landen], with *c.* 16,000 casualties out of 50,000 (July).

Nottingham, chief butt of opposition criticism, dismissed from Southern Secretaryship; William's second Parliament assembles for its fifth session (Nov).

Opposition to Court in Scottish Parliament over Glencoe and other issues.

Thomas Rymer, historiographer royal, commissioned to collect and edit England's treaties with foreign states; Locke's *Some Thoughts concerning Education* published.

1694   New Place bill, permitting re-election of office-holders, vetoed by William (Jan). Through Sunderland's influence, Shrewsbury returns to Cabinet as Northern Secretary (Mar). Conditional creation of Bank of England through Montagu's 'Tonnage Act' (see Ch. 17); end of parliamentary session – a notable success for Sunderland's management (Apr). Important ministerial changes in favour of Whigs (May): Falkland replaced as First Lord of Admiralty by Russell of the Junto; Treasury Board remodelled – Montagu Chancellor of the Exchequer *vice* Hampden (resigned), Seymour dismissed and replaced by a Junto follower, John Smith; Rochester no longer called to the inner Council.

Attempt to capture Brest fails; death of General Talmash; Russell proceeds with main English fleet to Mediterranean; protracted quarrel begins between Tory Godolphin and Junto Whigs (June); Bank subscription [£1.2 m.] opened and filled in ten days and Bank formally incorporated (June–July). So-called 'Lancashire Plot' (Jacobite) uncovered, several Lancashire and Cheshire gentry arrested (July).

Russell ordered to keep his ships in the Mediterranean and winter them at Cadiz. Lancashire 'plotters' acquitted of treason at Manchester Assizes after the defection to the accused of the key witness (Oct). Final session of 1690–5 Parliament opens; Secretary Trenchard incapacitated by fatal illness; death of Archbishop Tillotson (Nov). New Triennial bill [F(v)] passes both Houses and given royal assent (22 Dec). Death of Queen Mary from smallpox (28th).

Mary Astell publishes *A Serious Proposal to Ladies*, advocating establishment of an Anglican all-female academy of learning. Temple's *Essay upon Ancients and Moderns* (see Ch. 24) and Davenant's *Essay upon Ways and Means of Supplying the War* published.

1695   Junto increase pressure on Court by briefly cooperating with Country Whigs in attack on official corruption – Guy, Secretary of Treasury, dismissed and imprisoned, and Speaker Trevor expelled from Commons, for bribery (Feb–Mar); death of Trenchard (Apr) and appointment (May) of Sir William Trumbull, Tory client of Sunderland, as a Secretary of State. With prorogation of Parliament (3 May) Licensing [Printers] Act expires – landmark in press freedom; the *Flying-Post*, first of the permanent tri-weekly newspapers, launched. Leeds (formerly Danby/ Carmarthen) ceases to attend Council, though retaining post of Lord President (May).

Key fortress of Namur recaptured by William's army (Aug). Electioneering begins (Sept) in anticipation of dissolution of Parliament (Oct); General Election [E.1(ii)] – substantial Whig gains and success for the Court (Oct–Nov). Meeting of new Parliament (22 Nov); the Recoinage bill, prompted by serious devaluation of silver coinage through 'clipping', rushed through; piloted by Montagu, backed by Locke-Newton 'think-tank' (Dec).

Grain shortages throughout Scotland due to poor harvest – the beginning of 'King William's Ill Years'. Act of Scottish Parliament establishes 'The Company of Scotland trading to Africa and the Indies', which incurs King's hostility.

Death of Henry Purcell. Publication of Locke's *The Reasonableness of Christianity*.

1696 Parliamentary attacks begun on East India Company and on King's grant of Crown property to the Dutchman Bentinck, earl of Portland; William dismayed by Tory/ Country Whig proposal to set up a new Commission of Trade, with members nominated by Parliament; Recoinage Act becomes law and Trial of Treasons Act passed: convictions for treason now need more than one prosecution witness. Mediterranean fleet, now under Rooke, recalled because of renewed invasion threat (Jan).

Duke of Berwick's mission to England to coordinate French invasion with Jacobite rebellion (Feb); plot to assassinate William III [Fenwick Conspiracy] revealed (22 Feb) – Robert Charnock, Sir William Perkins, Sir John Friend and over 300 other suspects arrested, Fenwick and Barclay escape; both Houses – with some important dissentients – adopt Whig proposal for an 'Association' of men pledged to defend William, their 'rightful and lawful King' and to support his government (26–7 Feb), a great boost to political influence of Junto against both Tories and Sunderland. Board of Trade bill dropped (Mar – but see below). Trials and executions of leading Jacobite conspirators begin (Mar); French invasion plans abandoned (Mar–Apr).

Parliament authorises a 'Land Bank' to raise £2.5 million for the state; 'Act for the better security of His Majesty's person' passed – Association declaration to be tendered to all office-holders and members of both Houses; end of first session of William's third Parliament (Apr). Resignation of Godolphin as 1st Lord of the Treasury: succeeded by the senior Commissioner, the courtier Sir Stephen Fox (May). Sir John Fenwick, Jacobite conspirator, arrested (June); his confession (July) implicates Godolphin, Marlborough, Secretary Shrewsbury and Admiral Russell in negotiations with ex-King James.

Savoy, exposed by withdrawal of English fleet, makes peace with Louis XIV (Aug); Emperor concedes defeat in Italy and starts to withdraw his troops (Oct).

Parliament reassembles; Paul Foley, Country Whig leader and ally of Harley, chosen Speaker (20 Oct); Fenwick's allegations voted 'false and scandalous' by the Commons, and leave given for bill to attaint him of treason (6 Nov) – only one prosecution witness available; attainder bill passes Commons, 189:156 after great debates (13th–25th), with many Country Whigs as well as Tories opposing.

Collapse of Land Bank project acknowledged by Commons. Lords pass Fenwick attainder bill by only 7 votes, 68:61 (Dec).

Royal Board of Trade set up, with Locke one of its first paid (£1,000 p.a.) commissioners; Isaac Newton appointed Master of the Mint; Gregory King writes, and distributes in MS. his 'Natural and Political Observations upon the State and Condition of England'; John Toland's *Christianity not Mysterious* published; also (Nov) Atterbury's *Letter to a Convocation Man*, launching a four-year Anglican–Tory campaign for recall of Convocation. Second theatre opens in London, doubling the demand for plays.

1697   Fenwick executed (Jan). Privileges of Bank of England extended; failure of Malt Lottery Loan, underlining urgent financial necessity for peace; end of parliamentary session (Apr). Sunderland, back in control, made Lord Chamberlain and a privy councillor (19 Apr); his deal with Shrewsbury thwarts the Junto's first campaign to install Wharton (unacceptable to William) as a Secretary of State. But Somers promoted Lord Chancellor (22nd) and raised to peerage; and Montagu becomes First Lord of the Treasury (1 May).

Peace congress opens at Ryswick, Holland (May); Treaty of Ryswick signed by France, United Provinces, England and Spain (Sept), and by Emperor (Oct) [H(viii)].

James Vernon, Shrewsbury's Whig secretary, replaces Trumbull (T) as Secretary of State; third session of Parliament opens – 'Country' criticism of the administration renewed (Dec); Harley first proposes to the Commons major reduction of the Standing Army (10th). Sunderland, faced with Whig hostility and parliamentary criticism, resigns and later retires from politics.

Dryden publishes *Alexander's Feast*. Beginning of the great British famine (1697–9): wheat prices in England reach second highest peak (after 1693) since the Restoration; existing famine in Scotland compounded by another poor harvest.

1698   Commons vote pay for only 10,000 troops on English peacetime establishment (Jan); parliamentary attack on Montagu fails, but ministry has increasing difficulty in controlling Commons (Jan–Apr). Fresh Junto proposal to have Wharton made a Secretary rejected by the King (Apr). Civil List Act passed (May–June) [F.(vi)].

Parliament dissolved under terms of Triennial Act (July). King leaves England for Holland while elections in progress (20th) and begins secret negotiations to partition Spanish Empire on death of Carlos II. General Election results (July–Aug) [E.1(ii)] affected by 'the most dangerous division of a Court and Country party' [Somers].

After unavailing protests by Junto ministers First Partition Treaty signed by William III, France and Dutch (11 Oct O.S.): Joseph Ferdinand, Electoral Prince of Bavaria, to be chief beneficiary [H(ix)]. Standing Army pamphlet controversy renewed – Trenchard's *Short History of Standing Armies* bitterly critical of William's present establishments (Nov).

William returns to England; fourth Parliament opens – Whig Speaker, Littleton, elected against a divided opposition; resignation of duke of Shrewsbury on purported grounds of ill health – Vernon now sole Secretary; Commons opposition carry further reductions of standing army, on Harley's motion, to 7,000 'native-born' troops (Dec).

'New' East India Company chartered, on making loan to government of £2 million. Scottish expedition, sponsored by the Company of Scotland, sails for Darien in hope of establishing a colony (Caledonia) on Isthmus of Panama. Harvest again fails in Scotland; deaths due to starvation occasion widespread depopulation. Molyneux's *Case of Ireland* published. Jeremy Collier's *Short View of the Immorality and Profaneness of the English Stage*, an attack on the English theatre, attracts widespread support.

1699   Treaty of Carlowitz brings peace at last between Habsburgs and Ottoman Empire; Turks suffer huge territorial losses. Death of Electoral Prince of Bavaria (Jan – see Oct 1698). Disbanding bill passes Commons, 221:154, and accepted by William under protest (18 Jan–1 Feb). King's regiments of Dutch Guards forced to return to Holland (Mar) – William blames Junto for failure to protect his interests in Parliament. Prorogation of Parliament (May).

      Jersey (T) made a Secretary of State, with Vernon (May); Orford's sudden resignation from the Admiralty, against William's wishes (15th), followed by all but two of his colleagues on the Board; Pembroke (moderate T) succeeds Leeds [Danby], ending latter's ten years in office (18th) – but cf. May 1695.

      Resignation of Montagu (cr. Lord Halifax 1700) from the Treasury (15 Nov); succeeded as First Lord, 1699–1700, by Tankerville (W), but retains seat in Cabinet. Parliament reassembles (16th). Commons attack on Somers over Captain Kidd affair defeated, but naval estimates reduced, on Harley's motion, to provision for only 7,000 seamen (Dec).

      Fourth year of poor/failed harvest in Scotland: the last of 'King William's Ill Years'; up to one-third of population deceased or fled by the end of the year.

      Richard Bentley's *Dissertation on the Letters of Phalaris*, decisive contribution to the '*Moderns* v *Ancients*' controversy (Ch. 24).

1700   Poland's attack on Swedish Livonia begins the Great Northern War (1700–21) among the Baltic states (Feb). Second Partition Treaty, agreed by William III with France and the Dutch, autumn 1699, concluded 3 Mar O.S. [H(x)]. Bill to resume to the public all forfeited Irish lands granted by the Crown since 1691 completes stormy passage through Commons (Dec 1699–2 Apr): constitutional crisis threatened by Lords' opposition, averted when William accepted political necessity of Resumption Act. Parliament prorogued (11 Apr). Somers resigns Lord Chancellorship (17th); Sir Nathan Wright, Tory lawyer, appointed Lord Keeper (May); dismissal of Lord Jersey (June).

      Terms of Second Partition Treaty published in England and widely condemned (July); Princess Anne's son, duke of Gloucester, dies (30th), acutely reviving the succession problem; Carlos II signs a will leaving whole Spanish Empire to duke of Anjou, Louis XIV's grandson, on condition French and Spanish inheritances never united (Sept).

      Death of Carlos II brings Spanish succession crisis to a head (21 Oct) – Louis endorses Anjou's succession to whole inheritance (as Philip V) by virtue of Carlos's will; Sunderland's political advice again sought by William III (Oct). Charles XII of Sweden defeats the Russians at Narra – first major battle of Great Northern War (Nov). Sir Charles Hedges, Nottinghamite Tory, appointed to vacant Secretaryship, to partner Vernon (5th); Tory complexion of King's new ministry confirmed by appointments of Godolphin as First Lord of Treasury and Rochester as Lord Lieutenant of Ireland (Dec). Parliament of 1698–1700 dissolved (19th), after two sessions.

      Survivors of Darien colony evacuated. Great bitterness in Scottish Parliament over alleged sabotaging by England of the Company of Scotland and Darien expedition. John Dryden dies; Congreve's *The Way of the World* performed.

1701   General Election in England [E.1]; in Spanish Netherlands French troops occupy Dutch 'Barrier Fortresses' and begin to seize key cities and ports (Jan). William's fifth Parliament meets; Tory-Court majority in Commons elect Robert Harley as Speaker; Convocation assembles (for first time since 1689) – Upper and Lower Houses quarrel (Feb). Slow progress into law (1 Mar–22 May) of 'bill of Settlement', providing for a Protestant Hanoverian succession to English throne and imposing many new restrictions on royal prerogative [F(vii)].

William's Dutch confidant, Portland, and Somers, Halifax and Orford of the Junto impeached by Tories over Partition Treaties (Apr); 'Kentish Petition' urging prompter financial action to prepare for war rejected by Commons, but reinforced by Defoe's 'Legion Memorial' (May); impeached peers acquitted by House of Lords; earl of Marlborough restored to full favour – appointed plenipotentiary at The Hague to negotiate new anti-Bourbon alliance (June).

Treaty of Grand Alliance [H(xi)] signed (27 Aug O.S.). Death of ex-King James II (5 Sept); his son James Edward recognised by France as James III and VIII of England and Scotland; embargo on British goods imposed by France and Spain (Sept).

Sunderland and Somers advise William to turn to the Whigs again; Godolphin resigns after King's decision to dissolve the new Parliament (Nov); second General Election of the year (Nov–Dec), producing even balance of parties [E.1]; dismissal of Hedges; Whigs, Carlisle (27 Dec) and Manchester (4 Jan) appointed to Treasury and Southern Secretaryship; Harley re-elected Speaker of new House of Commons, but by only four votes (30 Dec).

1702   Rochester dismissed. Outbreak of unofficial warfare in Italy between Austria and France (Jan). Abjuration bill (compulsory oath repudiating Pretender) passes through Parliament; King recommends negotiations for Union between England and Scotland (Feb).

Death of William III, accession of Anne (8 Mar). Queen's first ministry formed under Godolphin, Lord Treasurer, and Marlborough, Captain-Gen; Cabinet includes main High Tory leaders, Rochester, Nottingham and Seymour, and only two lay Whigs (Apr–May). Declaration of war on France and Spain by England, Scotland, Emperor, Dutch (4 May). Parliament prorogued (23rd), later dissolved. Sacheverell's Oxford sermon against dissenters (June). English General Election (July) – decisive Tory victory [E.1]; Scottish convention Parliament, first elected 1689, finally dissolved (Aug).

Benbow's unsuccessful naval action in W. Indies: court-martial of Kirby and Wade; opening of Marlborough's first campaign of Spanish Succession War in Netherlands – early timidity of the Dutch (Aug); Bavaria enters war on side of France and Spain (Sept); French troops expelled from fortresses on the Maas and Lower Rhine (Sept–Oct); failure of Cadiz expedition (Sept) but victory at Vigo Bay, N. Spain (Oct).

Anne's first English Parliament opens – Harley re-elected Speaker (Oct); first bill against Occasional Conformity (by dissenters) passes the Commons; English and Scottish commissioners for Union meet in London (Nov); Anne's proposed life grant to Marlborough opposed by High Tories, led by a Cabinet minister, Seymour, in Commons (Dec).

The *Daily Courant*, world's first daily newspaper, and first volume of Clarendon's *History of the Rebellion and the Civil War* (with partisan preface by Rochester) published.

1703   Occasional Conformity bill amended by the Whig peers and dropped; Parliament agrees to finance a 10,000 increase in Marlborough's army of 40,000 in Flanders (Jan). Rochester, disgruntled, resigns his Cabinet office (Ireland); Union commissioners break up without agreement; Lords reject charges of financial malpractice against Lord Halifax (Feb). First session of Parliament ends (27th) and Convocation prorogued with 'the two houses . . . fixed in an opposition to one another' [Burnet].

First Methuen Treaty with Portugal signed 5 May, [H(xii)] – Portuguese alliance and naval bases secured, but at a price of British commitment to 'No Peace without Spain' – and to future campaigns in the Peninsula. New Scottish Parliament meets for first session (May): Act of Security passed, asserting Scotland's right to choose own successor to Anne [F(viii)] – denied royal assent (Aug). Dutch refuse to support Marlborough's plans to attack the 'Lines of Brabant' and 1703 Flanders campaign ends in recriminations and disappointment (Aug); Franco-Bavarians defeat Imperialists at Höchstadt (Danube) – Austria under threat (Sept).

Savoy adheres to Grand Alliance (Oct). Westminster Parliament reassembles; Tories introduce new Occasional Conformity bill (Nov). Second Occasional Conformity bill narrowly defeated in Lords (Dec). Second Methuen Treaty (commercial) with Portugal – port and madeira wines and English cloths secure favoured markets (16 Dec).

Daniel Defoe pilloried for his satire *The Shortest Way with the Dissenters*; released from Newgate and recruited by Harley as the government's chief propagandist. 'The Great Storm' devastates Southern England and Channel shipping, destroys first Eddystone lighthouse (26–7 Nov). Isaac Newton's *Opticks* published.

1704   'Queen Anne's Bounty', for the relief of poor clergy, proposed to Parliament (Feb); parliamentary enquiry into the 'Scotch Plot' (of 1703) – Secretary Nottingham accused by Whigs of protecting Jacobite agents (Feb–Mar); Bounty Act receives royal assent; Parliament prorogued with two Houses in deadlock over *Ashby* v *White* (3 Apr). Fall of High Tory ministers, Nottingham, Seymour and Jersey (Apr); Harleyites given office: Harley, Secretary for North, St John, Secretary-at-War, Harcourt, Attorney-General (Apr–May); Queensberry dismissed as Queen's Commissioner to Scottish Parliament – replaced by Tweeddale, head of the 'New Party' or 'Squadrone' (May).

First Anglo-Dutch troops arrive in Peninsula (Mar); battle of the Schellenberg, Bavaria – victory for Marlborough's army, despatched from Flanders (June); Gibraltar captured from Spain (July); Franco-Bavarian armies crushed by Marlborough and the Emperor's general, Prince Eugene, at Blenheim (2 Aug); naval battle of Malaga – French Mediterranean fleet withdrawn to Toulon (Aug); Bavaria occupied by Austrian troops and knocked out of war; French troops driven west across Rhine (Sept); Trier and other key fortresses fall to Marlborough (Oct).

New Scottish Act of Security [see Aug 1703] passed; receives royal assent on Godolphin's advice (Aug). English Parliament reassembles (Oct); attempted High Tory 'tack' of a third Occasional Conformity bill to Land Tax bill – defeated by Whigs acting with government office-holders and moderate Tories, organised by Harley (Nov). Ministry's Scottish policy attacked in Lords – Godolphin saved from censure only by Junto Whig support and Wharton claims to have 'Lord Treasurer's head in a bag' (Dec); Lords again throw out Occasional Conformity bill (15th).

Death of John Locke; Defoe's *Review*, 'the first unofficial ministerial press organ' [Downie, 300], begins publication (to 1713); first of 20 volumes of Rymer's *Foedera* [1704–35] appears; Samuel Clarke, great Newtonian theologian, delivers his first Boyle Lecture (Ch. 24).

1705   Aliens Act passed, putting economic pressure on Scotland to negotiate for a Union of Parliaments; constitutional and party conflict between Lords and Commons comes to a head (Mar); Parliament prorogued prior to dissolution (Apr). The Whigs begin the long haul back into government – Newcastle replacing Buckingham as Privy Seal; with Scottish 'New Party' in disarray, Argyll replaces Tweeddale as Queen's Commissioner (Apr).

General Election in England (May–June) – Whig gains leave parties almost equal in Commons [E.1]. Marlborough abandons attempt to invade France along Moselle (June); forces Lines of Brabant but is again checked by Dutch political deputies (July); fall of Barcelona to Peterborough's army supporting Habsburg claim to Spain – Catalonia declares for Habsburgs (Oct).

Scottish Parliament votes to leave choice of Union commissioners to Queen, not to its own Estates (Sept); Junto forces Cowper, as Lord Keeper, on a reluctant Anne (Oct); opening of Anne's second Parliament (25th), record first-day attendance, Whigs win a famous victory for the Speakership (John Smith *v.* Bromley). Failure of High Tory 'Hanover motion' in Lords, designed to embarrass Whigs by inviting over Electress Sophia, ostensibly to safeguard succession; Whig tit-for-tat – introduction of Regency bill [F(ix)]; bill introduced to repeal Aliens Act (Nov); Lords' debate on 'The Church in Danger' ends in crushing defeat for High Tories and gravitation of moderate bishops to Junto (6 Dec).

The *Memorial of the Church of England*, openly condemning Godolphin for betraying the Church in dealing with Whigs, published and causes uproar (July). Wren's new St Paul's Cathedral used for Thanksgiving Service for Blenheim; Haymarket Theatre opened.

1706   Agreement on Church affairs between Godolphin and Whig Junto; struggle between Court and Country (W and T) MPs over the 'place' provisions to be inserted in Regency bill – 'whimsical clause' – (Jan–Feb). Regency Act, embodying much modified place clause, passed; Convocation silenced (for four years) after Anne insists on 'maintain[ing] our Supremacy and the due subordination of presbyters to bishops' (Mar). English Commissioners, including all five Junto lords, appointed (Apr); Treaty of Union – 25 articles [F(x)] – concluded (July).

Triumph of Marlborough's army at Ramillies (12 May): Spanish Netherlands (May–Oct) swept clear of French forces. Capture of Madrid by Anglo-Portuguese army under Galway (June) but advantage sacrificed by Lord Peterborough and the Habsburg Archduke Charles ('Charles III'); retreat of the allies from Madrid to Valencia (July–Sept); decisive Austrian victory at Turin destroys French hold on N. Italy.

Articles of Union begin stormy passage through the Edinburgh Estates (12 Oct–Jan); 'Act for Securing the Protestant Religion and Presbyterian Church Government' [Kirk Act] passes Scottish Parliament (Nov); English troops posted on Scottish border (Dec). Anne, after five months' resistance prompted by Harley, agrees to appoint [Charles, 3rd earl of] Sunderland of the Junto Secretary for the South; and opens second session of her second Parliament (3 Dec).

1707   Treaty of Union finally ratified [110:67] by Scottish Parliament (16 Jan); Church of England Security Act – concerted between ministry, Junto and bishops as part of Union package (Feb); debates on Union at Westminster – Tory opposition crumbles (Feb–Mar); royal assent to Act of Union (6 Mar); English Parliament prorogued (Apr).

Allied army in Spain disastrously defeated at Almanza (Apr); Emperor's forces defeated by Villars at Stolhofen (May); attempt to capture Toulon by pincer attack of Austrian-Savoyard troops and Anglo-Dutch fleet: failure of land attack, scuttling of French Grand fleet (Aug).

Third session of Parliament (but first of the Union Parliament) opens at Westminster (Oct); parliamentary enquiry into Admiralty mismanagement – causes Whig divisions (Nov); Whig-Squadrone attack in Commons on surviving (Court-dominated) Scottish Privy Council (Nov–Dec); Tories attack conduct of war in Spain in Lords: Somers's motion for 'No Peace without Spain [for the Habsburgs] carried (19 Dec). 'Bishoprics crisis' causes further stress between Junto and court.

Brief financial panic in the City; Bank of England resiliently survives run on its funds. Farquhar's *The Beaux' Stratagem* first performed.

1708   Compromise settlement of Bishoprics crisis: Tory clerics appointed to Exeter and Chester, Low Church Whigs to Norwich and Oxford Divinity chair; Greg (Harley's clerk) charged with treason; first Commons debate on Almanza disaster – some Whig backing for Tory attack (Jan). Bill to abolish Scottish Privy Council passes Lords – severe ministerial defeat (Feb); fall of Harley and resignation of St John and other Harleyites (8th) after their attempts to urge a 'moderating' Tory scheme of government; Boyle and Walpole ('Treasurer's Whigs') promoted; Ministry rescued by the Whigs from final censure of its Spanish policies (24 Feb). Franco-Jacobite attempt to invade Scotland fails (Mar). Anne vetoes Scottish Militia bill. Parliament dissolved; quarrel between Queen Anne and her erstwhile favourite, the duchess of Marlborough, Groom of the Stole, becomes irreconcilable (Apr). General Election (May) – Whig majority [E.1].

Battle of Oudenarde – Marlborough's third famous victory (30 June); abandons his plan to drive on to Paris (July) and begins to invest great French fortress of Lille (Aug). Sardinia conquered for 'Charles III', with aid of British fleet (Aug); Stanhope captures Minorca, with its valuable base at Mahon (Sept); fall of city of Lille (Oct) and citadel of Lille, after bitter siege (Nov). Demoralised French army retreats to N. France (Dec).

Death of Queen Anne's husband, Prince George (28 Oct), weakens her long resistance to Junto. Opening of new Parliament (Nov); triumph of Junto – Somers and Wharton enter Cabinet (Nov–Dec).

First of two appalling harvests in succession [K.1].

1709   Thames freezes over (Jan); onset in Europe of most savage winter in memory; famine ensues in France and lasts throughout 1709.

Whig Naturalisation bill – to facilitate settling of foreign Protestant refugee immigrants – passes both Houses (Feb–Mar); Treasons bill likewise, bitterly opposed by Scottish representatives as a breach of the Union. Parliament prorogued (21 Apr). With France desperate for peace, negotiations begin at the Hague (27 Apr); Marlborough and the Whig Lord Townshend arrive to represent Britain (13 May); talks break down after Louis XIV had accepted all preliminaries except the notorious demand regarding Spain in Article 37 (22nd – see below p. 239).

Army of Charles XII of Sweden, weakened by the previous winter, defeated by Russians at Poltava (Ukraine) – the decisive battle of the Great Northern Wars (June). New, raw French army assembled under Villars to renew the war against the Grand Alliance (June); fall of Tournai to allies (Aug); battle of Malplaquet (31 Aug) – technically 'won' but at unacceptable cost to allies; Dutch (8,000 dead, against 2,500 Germans and 600 British) become anxious for peace. Townshend negotiates 'Barrier Treaty' with Dutch (Oct) – Marlborough refuses to sign and concessions made to keep Dutch in the war anger Tories.

Henry Sacheverell preaches at St Paul's against 'false brethren in Church and State' (5 Nov). Last surviving moderate Tory in Cabinet resigns; Orford of the Junto becomes First Lord of the Admiralty; second session of Parliament begins (Nov). Whigs vote to impeach Sacheverell (Dec).

Bank of England's charter and privileges extended for 21 years beyond August 1711: bank agrees to circulate Exchequer Bills and doubles its capital with a £2.2 million subscription (Feb); Old and New (1698) East India Companies unite, and make a handsome loan to government. Abraham Darby I of Coalbrookdale devises method of coke smelting ore to produce workable iron (perfected 1712). Richard Steele's *The Tatler*, thrice-weekly satirical periodical, begins publication (to 1711). Regular records of horse-races first kept.

1710　Marlborough threatens resignation in protest against influence of Anne's new favourite, Abigail Masham, in the affair of Essex's regiment (Jan). Trial of Sacheverell opens (27 Feb); Sacheverell riots in London (1–2 Mar); Lords find Sacheverell guilty by a majority of 17 – but his light sentence shocks the Whigs (20th/21st).

Fresh peace negotiations open at Gertruydenberg (Mar), but soon stall. Parliamentary session ends; duchess of Marlborough leaves the Court after traumatic final meeting with Anne; Shrewsbury, now Harley's Whig ally, appointed Lord Chamberlain – first step in Harley's phased overthrow of the Godolphin–Junto administration (Apr). Sunderland dismissed from Southern Secretaryship: replaced by moderate Court Tory, Dartmouth; crisis of public credit – Bank directors advise Queen against change of ministry (June). Victories of Stanhope at Almenara and Starhemberg at Saragossa briefly revive Habsburg cause in Spain (July–Aug).

Lord Treasurer Godolphin dismissed (8 Aug) – replaced by a Harleyite Treasury Board (Harley Chancellor of Exchequer and in Cabinet); Harley puts out secret peace feelers to France, through earl of Jersey (Aug); dissolution of Parliament and fall of the Whigs: Somers, Cowper, Wharton, Orford, Devonshire and Boyle dismissed or resign Cabinet offices; St John (Southern Secretary) and veteran High Tories Rochester and Buckingham come in (Sept).

General Election – crushing victory for Tories [E.1]; Harcourt (Harleyite) appointed Lord Keeper (Oct). New Parliament meets and the Commons choose a High Tory Speaker – Bromley (Nov). Convocation again meets to do business – Francis Atterbury elected Prolocutor of its Lower House. Defeat and surrender of the British forces in Spain at Brihuega (Dec).

Nova Scotia (Acadia) captured by British marines and New England militia (Sept). G. F. Handel visits England (settles, 1712); Berkeley's *Principles of Human Knowledge* published. Revd Jonathan Swift takes up authorship (Nov) of a new political periodical, *The Examiner* – anti-Whig and anti-Marlborough.

1711　Duchess of Marlborough dismissed from her offices; Whig control of House of Lords disturbed by censure of conduct of war in Spain (Jan). Tory 'October Club' begins campaign in Commons against the moderation of Harley's ministry; Place and Naturalisation Repeal bills killed in Lords by tacit Court–Whig alliance; [Landed] Qualifications Act [for MPs: F(xi)] passed (Feb). Guiscard's assassination attempt sends Harley's stock soaring (Mar). 'Fifty New Churches Act' for London passed (Apr).

Sudden death of Emperor Joseph I: Archduke Charles ('Charles III of Spain' succeeds as Emperor Charles VI; St John, anti-Dutch, intrudes himself in secret peace negotiations during Harley's illness (Apr); Harley triumphs with South Sea

Company scheme for dealing with floating Debt – created earl of Oxford and Lord Treasurer (May) – reasserts control over peace talks (June). Parliament prorogued (12th). Convocation prorogued – with Atterbury and the High Church party bitterly frustrated.

Cabinet changes completed as result of deaths of Rochester, Newcastle and Queensberry – no Whig or Godolphinite now remaining (June–Sept). Marlborough's last great feat of arms – forcing of the 'Ne Plus Ultra' lines; failure of naval–military attack on Quebec – St John's pet project (Aug).

Franco-British peace preliminaries signed (Sept); leaked by Austrian envoy to *Daily Courant* and published; Bothmer's Memorial conveys Elector of Hanover's disapproval (Oct); Nottingham, most important Tory still out of office (cf. 1704), breaks with ministry over peace; Swift's masterly *The Conduct of the Allies and of the late Ministry* prepares ground for Parliament's reception of preliminaries and for Marlborough's fall (Nov).

Second session of parliament opens. Shock government defeat in Lords on the sell-out of Spain to the Bourbons (7 Dec); major political crisis, resolved by creation of 12 Tory peers and dismissal of Marlborough (31st). Hamilton peerage case puts further strain on Anglo-Scottish relations; Fourth Occasional Conformity bill (cf. 1702–4) – agreed between Nottingham and Junto – becomes law without opposition (Dec).

Steele and Addison launch *The Spectator*; Shaftesbury's *Characteristics* and Thomas Madox's *History of the Exchequer*, landmarks in philosophy and medieval historiography, published.

1712 Peace Congress opens at Utrecht; Marlborough and Walpole censured by Commons for alleged peculation – Walpole sent to Tower; repeal of Whig Naturalisation Act of 1709 (Jan). Townshend's Barrier Treaty and conduct of the Dutch since 1702 condemned in Commons; Act of Toleration for Scottish Episcopalians passed (Feb). New and more moderate Grants Resumption bill fails by one vote in Lords; fresh deadlock in Convocation (Apr–May).

St John sends 'Restraining Orders' to Ormonde, new commander of British continental forces, commanding him to refrain from action: orders kept secret from allies, communicated to France (May). Parliament informed of Philip V's renunciation of rights to French succession: decisively endorses Oxford's peace policy; prorogued (June). Most remaining Whig MPs in office weeded out (June–July).

Dutch badly defeated by Villars at Denain (13 July) – forced to accept inevitability of peace. France accepts that Philip V must cede Sicily to duke of Savoy; cause of the pro-Habsburg Catalans given up by St John in Utrecht negotiations (Aug). Serious clash in Cabinet between Oxford and St John [now Viscount Bolinbroke] (Oct).

Stamp Act passed, imposing 'censorship by price' on newspapers and periodicals; last judicial trial for witchcraft in England.

1713 New Treaty of Succession and Barrier [see also H(xv) (1715)] agreed between Britain and United Provinces (Jan). Treaties of Peace and Commerce signed at Utrecht between Britain and France (31 Mar); all Grand Alliance partners except Austria and Hanover adhere to Utrecht peace settlement [H(xiv)] (Mar–Apr). Final session of 1710–13 Parliament opens (Apr). Attempt to extend malt tax to Scotland (May) leads to pressure for dissolution of Union – Oxford ministry survives resulting crisis in Lords (1–8 July). Government defeated over French Commerce bill in Commons by Whigs and 80 rebel Tories (including many pro-

Hanover Tories), led by Hanmer; 'Lorraine motion' against Pretender passes in Lords (June). End of session: dissolution of Parliament (July).

Treaties of Peace and Commerce concluded (July) between Britain and Spain (*Note*: *Assiento* conferred on Britain in March Treaty with France). Oxford defeats Bolingbroke in struggle for control of the ministry: Speaker Bromley made a Secretary of State (Aug). General Election (E.1) – Whigs lose heavily again in England but not in Scotland (Aug–Sept). Oxford quarrels with Anne over dukedom of Newcastle for his son (Sept). Serious illness of the Queen at Windsor – Oxford, staying in London, charged by his enemies with 'neglect' (Dec).

Bishop Gilbert Burnet completes his epic *History of My Own Time*; Atterbury made bishop of Rochester, with great reluctance, by Anne.

1714 Queen's illness arouses acute fears for the succession; Oxford tries to persuade Pretender to renounce Catholicism – and sends his brother on mission to Hanover; Steele's *The Crisis* declares the Protestant Succession in danger (Jan). Bolingbroke begins separate negotiations with Pretender (Feb). Anne's last Parliament meets – Hanmer chosen Speaker. Treaty of Rastatt finally brings peace between France and Austria (23rd O.S.).

Steele expelled from the Commons – but some worried Tories support him; Pretender's rejection of change of religion becomes known to Oxford and Bolingbroke (Mar). Lords' debate on the state of the nation: ministry attacked by both Whigs and Hanover Tories (Mar–Apr). Tories badly split as both Houses, by narrow majorities, vote the Protestant Succession not in danger under the present administration; rift between Oxford and Bolingbroke factions in Cabinet becomes irreconcilable (Apr). Death of Electress Sophia of Hanover (May).

Schism bill, devised by Atterbury and Bolingbroke to stamp out dissenting schools and academies (privately deplored by Oxford) passes Commons (May) and the Lords, narrowly (June); £100,000 reward voted for capture of Pretender 'dead or alive' (24 June). Whig attack, with Oxford's connivance, on Bolingbroke's friend Arthur Moore cut short by Queen's prorogation of Parliament (9 July). Oxford dismissed (27th); Shrewsbury appointed Lord Treasurer (30th); Queen Anne dies and Elector of Hanover peacefully proclaimed George I (1 Aug).

Government by – mainly Whig – Regency Council (Aug–Sept). Sweeping government changes in favour of Whigs (Sept–Oct): Treasury in commission under Halifax, rest of Junto in Cabinet, Townshend and Stanhope Secretaries of State, Walpole, Paymaster-General. Nottingham the only Tory in Cabinet but Bromley and Hanmer decline offer of non-Cabinet posts. George I's coronation (20 Oct) accompanied by some pro-Jacobite disorders.

Bernard Mandeville's *Fable of the Bees* appears and Atterbury publishes virulently anti-Whig, anti-German *English Advice to the Freeholders of England* as Election propaganda [see Jan. 1715].

1715 Parliament of 1713–14 dissolved (5 Jan); General Election (Jan–Feb): a great Whig majority returned [E.1]; Parliament meets (Mar). Bolingbroke flees to France (6 Apr); serious pro-Jacobite riots in London (23rd–29th), spreading to the provinces and intensifying (May–July). Deaths of Wharton and Halifax (Apr–May) effectively dissolve the Whig Junto.

Report of Commons' secret committee investigating conduct of Oxford's ministry presented by Walpole (June); motions to impeach Bolingbroke and Oxford (9 June) and Ormonde (21st) carried. Bolingbroke joins the Pretender's service as his Secretary of State; Oxford committed to Tower to await trial (July); Riot Act passes the Commons (18th), given royal assent (20th); news reaches

London of planned descent by Pretender (20th); Habeas Corpus immediately suspended; Ormonde flees to France – he and Bolingbroke attainted by Parliament.

Death of Louis XIV (21 Aug O.S.) afflicts prospects of Jacobites; Regency established in France under duke of Orléans; Abbé Dubois foreign minister. Arrest of Jacobite suspects in England, including leading MPs (Sept); Pretender's standard raised in Scotland by earl of Mar but attempt to seize Edinburgh Castle fails (6th–9th). Walpole appointed First Lord of the Treasury; Ormonde's attempt to land a force in Devon fails (Oct). Thomas Forster's Northern rebels take Preston but then surrender to the forces of Wills and Carpenter (Nov); battle of Sheriffmuir – technically indecisive but a moral victory for outnumbered royal army in Scotland (13th); second Barrier Treaty signed with Dutch.

Death of Archbishop Tenison; succeeded by Wake, bishop of Lincoln (Dec). Pretender lands at Peterhead (22nd).

Alexander Pope begins publication of his *Iliad* [1715–20]; Addison launches his new periodical *The Freeholder* and Steele, part II of *The Englishman*. New Treaty of Commerce signed with Spain (Dec). Total eclipse of the sun – accurately predicted by the astronomer, Edmund Halley.

1716 Pretender and Lord Mar leave Scotland for France (4 Feb). Nottingham, his brother Aylesford (Chanc. of the Duchy) and the lesser Tory Finches dismissed for appealing for clemency toward captured Scottish Jacobite peers; Dutch renew Treaty with England guaranteeing troops to protect Protestant succession (Feb).

Remnants of rebellion in Scotland suppressed (Apr). Septennial bill, extending maximum life of *present* and future Parliaments to seven years [F(xii)], introduced into Lords; gets a second Reading in Commons, 248:162, and passes (26 Apr) – 30–40 Whigs having opposed it. Septennial Act becomes law; Treaty of Westminster signed with the Emperor and revised Assiento Treaty with Spain (May). Parliament prorogued (June).

George I departs for Hanover, with Secretary Stanhope, leaving Prince of Wales as Guardian of the Realm, without full powers (July). Preliminaries of an Anglo-French alliance signed by Stanhope and Dubois (Aug); intrigues by Stanhope and Sunderland at Hanover against Townshend and Walpole (Sept); Dual Alliance treaty with France formally signed in Hanover (28th O.S.). Dutch adhere to Anglo-French alliance to form Triple Alliance (28 Dec) [H(xvi)]. Beginnings of 'the Whig Schism': Townshend dismissed as Northern Secretary – succeeded by Stanhope – but persuaded to accept Lieutenancy of Ireland (15 Dec).

Lord Somers – greatest lawyer-politician of his day – dies, after three years of physical and mental decrepitude.

1717 Arrest of Count Gyllenborg, Swedish minister in London, and Goertz at the Hague, for Jacobite plotting (Jan–Feb). Parliament reassembles (Feb). Hoadly, Whig bishop of Bangor, preaches extreme erastian sermon ('My Kingdom is not of this world') before George I – sparks off the 'Bangorian Controversy' (31 Mar). Details of Swedish Plot put before Parliament; climax of the Whig Schism and remodelling of the Cabinet – Townshend is dismissed and Walpole resigns after opposing supplies for possible war against Sweden; Stanhope goes to the Treasury and Sunderland to the Northern Secretaryship; Townshend and Walpole followed out of office by leading associates, Orford, Devonshire, Pulteney and Methuen (Apr). Walpole and his supporters start to harass Stanhope–Sunderland ministry in the Commons; Oxford, still in Tower, petitions for speedy trial (May). General Lord Cadogan, ally of Sunderland and the Churchills, survives by only ten votes an attack on his alleged corruption by dissident Whigs and Tories; same combination stifles further Commons' proceedings against Oxford (June). Oxford acquitted by Lords (1 July); Parliament prorogued (15th).

Mediterranean crisis begins: Spanish expedition invades and overruns Habsburgs' island of Sardinia (Aug). Britain and France attempt to mediate in Austro-Spanish dispute at Hampton Court conference – Stanhope tries to entice Emperor Charles VI into Triple Alliance (Nov). Parliament meets for its third session (21st); Convocation prorogued after violent High Church attacks on Hoadly's sermon (22nd); Will Shippen, leading Jacobite MP, sent to the Tower (4 Dec). Prince George ordered by King to leave St James's Palace – leads to setting up of rival court at Leicester House (Dec).

Diving-bell invented by Halley; Handel composes the first of his Chandos Anthems.

1718   Army estimates successfully attacked by the Walpole Whigs (Jan). Parliament prorogued; Stanhope and Sunderland exchange offices, Sunderland becoming First Lord of the Treasury (Mar).

Sicily invaded and Palermo captured by Spanish fleet (June). Secret convention signed by Britain and France to force Charles VI to adhere to Triple Alliance as price of assistance in Mediterranean crisis – which he did (Quadruple Alliance, 22 July) [H(xvii)]. Spain rejects terms of Quadruple Alliance settlement (July–Aug) despite Stanhope's readiness to make separate deal over Gibraltar; Sir George Byng destroys Spanish fleet off Cap Passaro (31 July), effectively ending Philip V's first Mediterranean adventure.

Parliament reassembles (11 Nov); strong opposition criticism of Stanhope's foreign policy. Death of Charles XII of Sweden, hastens end of Great Northern War (Nov). Stanhope introduces in the Lords a bill to repeal the Occasional Conformity and Schism Acts (13 Dec). Britain declares war on Spain (17th).

Society of Antiquaries revived; secret talks begin with South Sea Company (Nov) over the settlement of the National Debt.

1719   Great struggle in Commons on Second Reading of Occasional Conformity and Schism Repeal bill: government carry committal by 243:202 (7 Jan); bill passed (10th). The ministry's Peerage bill, a constitutional and political bombshell, introduced into Lords (Feb). With opposition mounting in Commons, Stanhope postpones the third Lords' Reading of the bill – (14 Apr) – it lapses with Parliament's prorogation (18th).

After Spanish landing in Western Isles, General Wightman defeats combined Highland-Spanish force at Glenshiel (June). Bremen and Verden, coveted by George I as spoils of Northern War, guaranteed to Hanover by a treaty with Prussia (Aug).

Parliament begins its fifth session (23 Nov). Peerage bill reintroduced into Lords and passed (30th). Commons' opposition, organised by Walpole, succeeds in defeating the bill by 269:177 (18 Dec). Philip V's chief minister Alberoni dismissed and banished (Dec).

Defoe's *Robinson Crusoe* published; two radical Whigs, John Trenchard and Thomas Gordon, begin publishing their 'Cato's Letters' in the *London Journal* (cf. 1723).

1720   Aislabie, Chancellor of the Exchequer, outlines to Commons (final) South Sea Company scheme for dealing with unfunded National Debt (22 Jan); accepted (2 Feb). Spain accepts Mediterranean settlement under terms of Quadruple Alliance (Feb) [H(xvii)]. Declaratory Act [Ireland] passed (Mar – cf. *The Age of Oligarchy*,

Ch. 16) [F(xiv)]; opposition of Bank of England to South Sea bill defeated (23 Mar); bill passed (2 Apr); South Sea stock soars – from 183 [15 Mar] to 610 [1 June].

Negotiations opened for Townshend and Walpole to rejoin ministry – boosted by formal reconciliation between George I and Prince of Wales (Apr). Bubble Act against unauthorised companies passed and Parliament prorogued (June); Walpole and Townshend return to office as Paymaster-General – a demotion – and Lord President respectively. South Sea stock rockets from 610 to almost 950 in the month of June (peak of 1050 on the 24th). Slow fall of South Sea stock (175 points), July–August, followed by bursting of the Bubble in September: collapse from 775 (1 Sept) to 290 (1 Oct); Sword Blade Company – bankers to South Sea Co – cease payments (24 Sept). Widespread losses and bankruptcies. Proclamation by Pretender (Oct); George I hastens back from Hanover (Nov). Parliament meets (8 Dec); outraged Commons demand to see the Company's books; Walpole lays his (or his banker, Jacombe's) rescue package before Commons (21st). Birth of Charles Edward Stuart, 'the Young Pretender' (31st).

1721   Commons' select committee appointed to investigate South Sea Company; escape to France of Knight, Company's cashier; expulsion of four directors from the House (Jan). Sudden death of Lord Stanhope after a stroke (4 Feb); Townshend returns as Northern Secretary (10th); death of James Craggs, Jun., Southern Secretary, from smallpox (16th); nine Commons' resolutions condemning South Sea Company directors (18th); Charles Stanhope, against balance of evidence, acquitted of corruption by three votes, 180:177 (28th).

Carteret, former Tory and ally of Sunderland, appointed Southern Secretary; Aislabie expelled from Commons, sent to Tower (8 Mar); Sunderland cleared of corruption after long debate, 233:172 (15th); death (suspected suicide) of Postmaster-General, Craggs, Senr (16 Mar).

Sunderland accepts 'closet office' as Groom of the Stole; new Treasury Commission – Walpole First Lord and Chancellor (3 Apr). Parliament prorogued (29 July) but recalled for short session (31 July–10 Aug) in order to pass the 'Act to restore the Public Credit', i.e. settling affairs of South Sea Company, mainly according to Walpole's prescription (cf. Dickson, 113a); Walpole raises loan of £0.5 million at 5 per cent – marking beginnings of a return of confidence (July).

Treaty of Nystad ends the Great Northern War – Peter the Great annexes Eastern Baltic provinces to Russia (Aug). Parliament of 1715 reassembles for its eighth, and last, session (Oct). Act passed to protect woollen and silk manufactures from competition of painted calicoes – beginning of a further 'rise of protection' under Walpole.

1722   George I's first Parliament dissolved (Mar). General Election (Mar–Apr): Whigs increase majority over Tories to *c*. 200, even before hearing petitions [E.1]. Dubois reveals Jacobite plot to Walpole; death of Sunderland; Congress of Cambrai, planned to settle outstanding international problems in Western and Southern Europe, begins informal sessions (Apr).

News of the Jacobite conspiracy ('Atterbury Plot') made public (8 May); arrest of bishop of Rochester's secretary (15th). Patent granted to William Wood for minting a new copper coinage in Ireland (July), sparking off three years of Irish 'Patriot' opposition to 'Wood's Half-Pence'. Bishop Atterbury arrested (Aug); his release under Habeas Corpus refused (Sept).

Parliament meets (9 Oct). Habeas Corpus Act suspended, after defeat of Opposition amendment – supported by some Whigs – to limit suspension to 6 months (16th). Jacobite Christopher Layer condemned to death for treason (Nov).

Emperor grants by charter right to Ostend Company (Austr. Neths.) to trade with East and West Indies – early alarm in Britain and Holland (Dec).

Duke of Marlborough dies. Defoe's *Moll Flanders* published.

1723   Walpole fails to oust Carteret from the ministry [cf. 1724] (Jan). Bill of Pains and Penalties against Atterbury passes Commons with huge majorities (Apr); Atterbury's stout defence in Lords (11th–13th May), but bill passes there by 83:43 (15th); execution of Layer; Bolingbroke pardoned and returns to England (25th) but excluded from House of Lords; Parliament prorogued (28 May) – not to meet again this year, and with Walpole's 'interest so strong that he has nothing to apprehend, unless it be from the too great majority of Whigs in Parliament, for it is impossible to satisfy them all . . .' [George Baillie, MP, Treasury Commissioner, July 1723].

Bishop Atterbury goes into exile (June). Nationalist agitation in Ireland: Irish Parliament meets (Sept) and votes to address the King that the patent granted to William Wood [cf. 1722] was 'prejudicial to the revenue, destructive of trade, and dangerous to property'. Deaths in France of Dubois (Aug) and Regent Orléans (Nov).

Workhouse Test Act passed. Trenchard's 'Cato's Letters' in the *London Journal* end, after viciously attacking the Anglican charity school movement for encouraging Jacobitism and social insubordination. Deaths of Sir Christopher Wren and Sir Godfrey Kneller, the painter; birth of Adam Smith.

CHAPTER 13

The settlement of 1689 and the forging of 'the Revolution Constitution'

No one who studies British history before and after the years 1688–9 should fail to be aware that in passing from one period to the other we are crossing one of the great divides on the entire landscape of 'early modern' and modern times. Britain under William III and Queen Anne was so indelibly marked by two influences that it is impossible to conceive of the British state for many years thereafter without almost constant reference to them: the influence of the Revolution which brought William, along with his wife Mary, to the thrones of England and Scotland, and the influence of the great wars against Louis XIV's France which the new king inaugurated. So pervasive were their repercussions well into the eighteenth century that many of the chapters in Part Two of this volume can appropriately be seen as a variety of elaborations on a single theme – the importance of revolution and war together as instruments of fundamental change in the history of Britain.

Frequently in the course of these chapters the effects of war will appear to bulk larger than those of the Revolution. This is probably a fair reflection of the changed priorities of many present-day historians. For some forty years, down to the early 1980s, the Revolution of 1688–9 slid down the revolutionary league table, even its traditional right to be called 'the English Revolution', once so confidently assumed by Trevelyan and others, being denied by students of the mid-seventeenth century crisis (59a). More significantly, it lost its halo. That special aura and mystique which the Glorious Revolution held for at least three generations of scholars reared in the old Whig tradition has left present-day historians by and large unimpressed. Alongside scepticism about the character of the events of November 1688-February 1689 grew a conviction of their basic conservatism. In particular historians became less mesmerised than their predecessors by the whole question of the legacy to posterity of the Revolution, and of the settlement which followed it. Like most reactions in historiography, however, this one was taken too far. Because the effects of the Revolution and of the 1689 settlement – and most of all their short-term consequences in the constitutional field – have been over-valued in the past, we must not be beguiled into undervaluing them now. A series of decisions were taken in the year 1689 alone, in the aftermath of James's flight and William's victory, which were crucially to affect the future history of Britain, not only in the rest of the Stuart period but right through the eighteenth century: that century when 'Revolution principles', though in some respects hazily defined (321, *47–8*), remained something more than a mere shibboleth to which the Whig oligarchs paid cynical lip-service.

The most important of these decisions resolved the two most urgent problems facing James's subjects in January-February 1689: how, and where, to dispose of the thrones which the King by departing had (according to party viewpoint) either 'vacated' or 'deserted', and on what terms, if any, the disposal should be made. Common sense demanded, and the terms of the Prince of Orange's pre-invasion manifesto virtually ensured, that the crowns of both England and Scotland would be disposed of through the votes of a Parliament. It is true that in England, where the settlement of the crown preceded that in Scotland by about two months, there were a few uncompromising Whigs who advocated that William, already in charge of the interim administration, should exercise his 'right of conquest', on the precedent of Henry Tudor, and declare himself king. There were likewise a handful of Tories who were prepared to argue that King James's flight amounted to a 'legal demise', giving his daughter Mary of Orange the right to assume the crown by hereditary succession. But neither view commanded significant support. A Parliament there must be, therefore, before any constitutional decisions could be taken. *How*, exactly, it was to be procured when there was no king to issue writs and no Great Seal under which to issue them, was not a matter of consensus (57a). In the event, early in the New Year, following the 1660 precedent, a Convention was elected for the whole of England and Wales by authority of Prince William's letters of summons. In this body, which first met on 22 January, the Whigs made an astonishing recovery from the disasters of 1685: in combination with some Williamite Tories and neutrals they commanded 319 seats, a majority of almost 90 [E.1(ii)]. In the House of Lords, by contrast, loyalists appear to have enjoyed initially a slight advantage.[1]

I

By the time formal debate on the settlement of the crown began the options had narrowed down to three, one Whig and two Tory. During the next fortnight the outcome came to depend on whether enough non-Whig peers could be brought over from their original opposition to the essentially Whig solution proposed by the Commons, and on how far the latter would have to be modified to make its acceptance by the Lords, and by William, possible. Once the Commons had been stampeded on 28 January into declaring the throne 'vacant' on James's so-called 'abdication' – 'a great vote', one Puritan radical rejoiced[2] – the Whigs planned to offer the crown preferably to William alone but, failing that, to William and Mary jointly, with regal power vested in the former. Furthermore, it was their intention to do so in such a way as to give maximum emphasis to the sovereignty of 'the people' and, as radical Whigs at least desired, to the contractual and even elective nature of the new monarchy. As one hard-line Whig pamphleteer put it at this time, to enthrone William alone would be a singularly 'clear asserting of the people's right, firm evidence of a contract broken, and a sure precedent to all ages'.[3] To this extreme solution the loyalist Tories countered with one at the opposite pole, an idea propounded in the Lords on 29 January and defeated there by a mere three votes: James was to retain the nominal title of King, even in exile, while William would exercise the royal powers as 'regent' on his behalf. By contrast the 'Maryites', a group of Tory commoners led by Sir Edward

Seymour, recently leader of the West-Country rebels, and a much smaller but tactically important squadron in the Lords led by Danby, were resolved to have no more truck with James or Catholic monarchy, yet hoped to preserve the hereditary principle and as much of Tory ideology as they could. Their plan was to have Mary declared sole sovereign by her own hereditary right, in succession to a father who could be regarded either as having abdicated or as being legally 'demised'.

By 31 January, when the two Houses had finished firing their opening salvoes across each other's bows, it was already clear to any realist that neither extreme solution was in the realm of practical politics. In particular, the legitimist pass had been conclusively sold when the Lords concurred with surprising unanimity in a Commons vote that it was 'inconsistent with the safety and welfare of a Protestant kingdom to be governed by a popish prince' – a more extreme *principle* than any of the Exclusion bills had enunciated (57b, *24–6*). By 7 February the 'Marian' Tory compromise, too, had been torpedoed: partly by William's explicit refusal to be his wife's 'gentleman-usher', and partly by the breaking of the deadlock between the two parties and chambers sufficiently to accommodate what was, in essence, a moderate Whig *via media*. This assumed that the Princess as well as the Prince of Orange would be named as joint sovereigns, but on the initiative of the Commons provided for the vesting of real authority in William alone. In the Lords it needed not just the switching of the handful of Danbyite votes but significant defections or abstentions by hitherto loyalist peers to persuade that House to abandon the notion that James had merely 'deserted' his regal responsibilities and to acknowledge not just the compromise fiction that he had 'abdicated' but (worse) that a 'vacancy' of the throne now existed (cf. 43, *I, 430–1* and 46, *252–4* with Cruickshanks, Hayton and Jones [p. 227, *n*.1, below]). Neither the concept of a vacant throne nor the solution of a joint monarchy was reconcilable with the theory of a divine hereditary succession (59a, *388*). In the Commons the more pragmatic Whigs, for their part, persuaded their radical brethren not only that Mary must be part of the bargain but that to seal that bargain securely all talk of James's 'deposition' or 'forfeiture' must be dropped. Indeed, in the end, probably in the closing stages of the committee discussions which prepared the list of grievances against James for embodiment in the Declaration of Rights (see below), even the charge of 'breaking the original contract between King and People', which the Lords had seemed reluctantly prepared to stomach, quietly disappeared (58a, *230–1*).

We should not lightly disregard the fact that much of the agonising which took place in the first fortnight of the 1689 Convention (and would doubtless have lasted still longer if William's patience had not run out) was centred on words and formulae as much as on political expedients. For these men were not playing semantic games. They were wrestling with fundamental matters on which, as they well knew, the future ideological credibility of both political parties, as well as the future of the constitution, depended.[4] For many Tories, for example, the last ditch which could not be surrendered, as Lord Nottingham explained at a conference of the two Houses, was that 'the ancient lineal succession be altered' so far that England would become 'an *elective* kingdom'. And after the decisive

Lords' vote which followed that conference, Lord Thanet, confessing to his neighbour, Clarendon, that 'I look upon this day's work to be the ruin of the monarchy in England, for we have made the crown elective' added nevertheless: 'But there is an absolute necessity of having a government, and I do not see a prospect of any other than this; we must not leave ourselves to the rabble'.[5] There is therefore no ground for the assumption that formulae shaped in large measure by circumstances and reluctant second thoughts had few important implications of principle. Ideologically neither party would be the same again in William III's reign, or thereafter, as it had been in the decade before 1688 (70, *xxx–xxxviii* and *Ch. 3*) (cf. Ch. 9 above). For the Tories – for whom the Revolution could so easily have been an unmitigated disaster – the changes were to be less in the end than they had cause to fear; for the Whigs, somewhat less than they had reason to hope (Ch. 24). For both sets of partisans, however, adapting to their new post-Revolution habitat was made much easier because the settlement of 1689, far from stopping short at changing England's rulers, went on to change the nature of the monarchy itself: not by fine phrases, but by a typically English mixture of law and practice.

In consequence, the Tories during the 1690s were to find nothing impossibly incongruous in the rôle of constitutional opposition to a king whose title was plainly not hereditary and whose powers, however jealously he guarded them, could no longer be regarded as a sacred trust. As for the Whigs, they may have sacrificed their theoretical assertion of a 'contract' in February 1689 but they were soon to have three more solid guarantees that England would not again succumb to authoritarian, non-parliamentary government in which personal prerogative could put law, liberty and property at risk. One such guarantee was the hard-headed financial settlement with which the English parliamentarians rewarded their 'Great Deliverer', the constitutional implications of which will be noticed in due course (Ch. 17). A second was the new coronation oath, taken by William and Mary, which solemnly bound them, in a pointedly contractual phrase, to govern 'according to the statutes in Parliament agreed on' – the first time any reference to Parliament and statute law had figured in this ancient ceremony (120b, *40–1*; 59a, *388*). The third, and by a long way the most important, of these guarantees was the passing into law of a new and comprehensive constitutional statute, the Bill of Rights, which provided England with the nearest approach to a written constitution she had yet possessed.

II

Although the Bill of Rights, as such, did not become law until December 1689, it was essentially an embodiment, with some important additions, of the *Declaration of Rights* [F(ii)] which was presented to William and Mary at Whitehall at the same time as the offer of the crown. Historians have not always agreed that the coincidence of those two events, together with the substance of the Declaration itself, did in effect signify the sealing of a contract between Parliament and the new rulers; or even whether the Whigs intended the happenings of 13 February to be viewed in this light (Cf. Trevelyan [above, p. 190 *n*.3]; *140* with 313, *75* and 58b, *270*). In general the balance of opinion in recent scholarship has leant towards J.P. Kenyon's dismissal of the contract interpretation of the celebrated Whitehall ceremony as 'untenable Whig myth' (314, *40*). However, the most detailed modern study of the genesis of the Declaration of Rights is at pains to stress the contractual nature of the offer and acceptance of the crown (58a, *esp.* Ch. 15). It does, of course, take two to make a contract; and William's attitude to the Declaration is illuminated, first, by his letting it be known beforehand 'that he would not take the crown upon conditions',[6] secondly, by the studied exclusion from his brief speech accepting the throne of any explicit reference to the Declaration, and thirdly, by his undisguised hostility to subsequent attempts to give it binding force in statute. On the other hand, a premeditated ordering of the February ceremony, in which the reading of the list of grievances and rights was given priority; the conjunction in a single document of a formal claim of rights with an equally formal offer of sovereignty; and not least, the tone and language of the Commons' debates and discussion on the preparation of the Declaration, all suggest strongly that by the Whigs at least, and by some Tories too, these rights *were* seen as conditions by which William would be expected to abide. In 1693 the earl of Warrington, who as Delamere had raised Cheshire for the Prince of Orange, was to remind the county grand jury that 'the king and queen received their crown from the hands of the people upon such terms as they gave it', while John Hampden, too, recalled 'that new contract made by King William with this nation' in 1689. Both admittedly were radical Whigs; but it was by no means only Whigs of such a stamp who shared their perspective.

To radicals the one disillusioning feature of the settlement of the Crown was that the restrictions imposed on royal freedom of action by the Declaration and later confirmed in the Bill of Rights were neither numerous enough nor tough enough. There had been days in late January and early February when the outcome had promised to be otherwise. Although Thomas Christie's call from the Tory benches for 'a Magna Charta' to be drawn up by the Convention *before* the settlement of the Crown was opposed by some influential Whigs, on the grounds that such a grandiose scheme would involve unacceptable delays and arouse William's distrust, there was a clear Commons majority on 29 January for the setting out of numerous conditions which the next monarch would be expected to accept. With the previous day's dire warning of Sir William Pulteney, that this could be a once-for-all opportunity, still ringing in their ears, members had responded with enthusiasm to the pleas of such veterans as Garraway and Boscawen to 'consider what terms must be made to provide really and effectually for our own safety' and, before filling the throne, to 'provide such things as are absolutely necessary for securing our religion, laws and liberties'.[7] Yet the impressive twenty-eight 'heads of grievances', drawn up by 2 February, had been whittled down by the 8th to a mere thirteen by the deliberate removal of all items which would require new laws to be passed. Among the casualties which fell by the wayside before the final draft of the Declaration was completed were clauses which, had they had legal force, would have limited the royal power of prorogation and (anticipating the Act of 1694) prevented 'the too long continuance of the same Parliament'; ensured ecclesiastical comprehension, as well as Protestant toleration; safeguarded the independence of judges by security of tenure; and reformed the treason laws. Other major proposals axed were the restoration of 'ancient rights' to boroughs which had had new corporations imposed on them by the Crown since 1682; the abolition of royal pardons to persons impeached and of the sale of offices; the reform of Chancery and other courts; and the remedying of abuses in the hearth tax and excise collection (58a, *299–300, Appx.*). A further setback for the supporters of drastic constitutional reform came when the Lords successfully insisted that the surviving articles should be presented to William and Mary as a *preamble* to their proclamation as King and Queen – a timely reminder of their obligations but not a document requiring their formal assent (58b; 57a). Various theories have been advanced to explain the emasculation of the Declaration of Rights, but it is virtually certain that the decisive factors were William's ill-concealed anger at moves to encumber his future power with a complex web of limitations,[8] and the fear that protracted constitutional arguments might imperil the swift settlement of the Crown itself, and consequently the maintenance of order.

All the same, the grievances ventilated in the Convention between 29 January and 13 February 1689 were not aired in vain. In the first place, the final Declaration was something of a confidence trick. Despite all protestations to the contrary – assurances which William at the time was prepared to accept – it went significantly further than the simple re-statement of 'ancient rights', requiring no new laws to implement them, that it purported to be [F(ii)]. To illegalise the suspending power and the Ecclesiastical Commission, render the dispensing power nugatory, and above all declare that the king could not maintain a standing army in peacetime without parliamentary consent, were no mean achievements, and these were but the most important of the seven articles in the Declaration which went beyond the confirmation of undisputed rights. In effect, they 'made new law in the guise of declaring the old' (54a, *162*; see also 58a, esp. *283*). Little wonder that, once William had had time to reflect on the document's full implications, not least for England's future military effectiveness (below, pp. 232, 247), he should jib at the Convention's stubborn determination to give the whole package legal effect. In the second place, some major demands aired during the February debates leading up to the Declaration but not pursued at the time were embodied in the final Bill of Rights; in fact, they do much to explain why discussions on that measure which began in April were not resolved until December, well into the Convention's second session. In the biggest constitutional landmark of all, the line of the Protestant succession to the throne was spelt out by Parliament, not yet as far as the House of Hanover, as many Whigs even now desired, but at least as far as Princess Anne and her heirs, thus setting the clear precedent for the 1701 Act of Settlement [F(vii)]. Roman Catholics and any persons married to Catholics were explicitly excluded from a right to the throne. And the dispensing power received its *coup de grâce*. Thirdly, although some of the more cherished objectives jettisoned in February 1689 failed to struggle into law during the rest of William's reign,[9] a number of critical ones were achieved through later statutes. Foremost among them were freedom of worship, though not civil equality, for Protestant dissenters, as early as May 1689 (Ch. 23); a three-year limit on the lifetime of any Parliament, which was imposed in an Act of 1694 (Ch. 21); a reformed treason trial procedure (1696); and the independence of the judges, secured by the granting of their commissions *quamdiu se bene gesserint* (legislation in 1701, but not technically in force until 1714) [A; F(vii)]. Moreover, although this last eventually became mandatory by a clause of the Act of Settlement, an earlier bill to the effect having been vetoed in 1692, William's own practice had already made it an established convention of the constitution.

III

The Revolution settlement in Scotland appears, superficially at least, to have been more definite and straightforward than its English counterpart, imbued with Scots logic, and certainly more unequivocally Whiggish. The resolution of the Scottish Convention, with only five contrary votes, that James VII had *forfeited* the crown by his misgovernment, quite unlike the 'abdication' fiction concocted by English parliamentarians, fudged no embarrassing issues. Both here and in the Claim of Right ([F(iii)] the Scottish equivalent of the Declaration of Rights), also voted in April 1689, a strong contractual flavour is easily detected. In listing James's misdeeds in uncompromising terms, and wasting little breath on feeble English palliatives, it concluded, equally boldly if somewhat unhistorically, that he had invaded 'the fundamental constitution of this kingdom and altered it from a legal limited monarchy *(sic)* to an arbitrary despotic power'.[10] When they embodied in their Claim the resolution that William and Mary be declared King and Queen of Scotland, the Estates were saying to them plainly enough that Scotland would expect to be ruled hereafter by limited monarchs, bound by the laws of the land. There is no question that the Scottish Convention expected the new rulers to subscribe to the specific conditions laid down in the Claim: that the monarchy was to be Protestant; its prerogatives subject to the overriding rule of law; all its financial supplies dependent on parliamentary consent; its Estates entitled to frequent meetings and to freedom of debate. (This last was an oblique attack on the malign influence of the Lords of the Articles [see Ch. 1 above], an attack that was promptly unveiled in the accompanying 'Grievances' of the Estates and was to result in 1690 in the outright abolition of this hated committee.) What is more, since the Claim of Right also included a blunt condemnation of prelacy [F(iii)], concluding that it 'therefore ought to be abolished', William, when accepting it along with the crown of Scotland in May 1689, was deemed to have implicitly anticipated the exclusive Presbyterian religious settlement in Scotland which was to follow (July 1689 – July 1690) (above, p. 195) (6b, *57–65*; 277a, *5–6*; 18, *266–7*; 104, *34–5*).

However, much of this would have been hard to anticipate at the time the Convention first assembled in Edinburgh (above, p. 195). The full-blooded 'Williamites' and 'Jacobites' at the two extremes were both relatively small groups. The Presbyterian zealots among the former were certainly 'aggressive and vocal' (283a, *8*), yet a majority – possibly a large majority – of all three estates, despite Westminster's example, were uncertain how to act. They looked for a clear lead from the great lay magnates, who were themselves at this stage divided (for example, loyalist Episcopalians at odds with Catholics). It is true that even in March there was a strong religious tide outside the Parliament-house flowing the Presbyterian way. Episcopacy itself had been undermined, perhaps fatally, by the uniform association of all Scotland's nine bishops with the late Jacobite regime, a fact of which the Convention was starkly reminded at its first meeting, when the Bishop of Edinburgh prayed 'for God to have compassion on King James and to restore him' (6b, *51*). Nevertheless, it was only after a month of often confused debate that a consensus was achieved for a strong Whig-Presbyterian approach to the Scottish Revolution settlement. For this four things were mainly responsible. The first was the sharply contrasting tones of the two letters read to members on the third day of the Convention: William's, tactful and laced with anodynes; James's typically hectoring. The second was the latter's landing in Ireland and the news which reached the Scots (25 March) that tens of thousands of Irish Catholics had rallied to his standard. The secession from the Convention a week earlier of Graham of Claverhouse, Viscount Dundee, the ablest and most feared soldier among the committed Scottish Jacobites was held (quite rightly) to presage rebellion in Scotland, involving at least the loyalist Highland clans. The fourth, and decisive, factor was the emergence of the determined Presbyterian minority as the dominant (self-styled) 'Revolution interest', with the help of an organisation as successful at recruiting powerful Whig friends in London as at outmanoeuvring their opponents in Edinburgh (268b, *246, 250*; 283a, *8–20*).[11] By April parliamentary opposition to this 'interest', already weakened by Jacobite secessions, had crumbled away.

The Revolution settlement in Scotland produced a remarkable change in the distribution of power between the Crown and Parliament. It was a more dramatic transformation than took place in England, because since the Restoration the constitutional scales had been weighted in favour of monarchical authority far more heavily in Edinburgh than at Westminster. William lacked both the time and the understanding needed to master Scottish affairs, and was inclined to take the docility of his Scots subjects too much for granted once Dundee's rebellion had failed (above, p. 195). But in the thirteen months beginning in June 1689 he was to have his first taste of just how recalcitrant the parliamentary representatives of those subjects could be. Both the King's main recommendations to the estates, conveyed through his first commissioner, the duke of Hamilton, ran into rough water; and it is clear that the waves owed much of their turbulence to the closely co-ordinated activities of the 'Club', an alliance of convenience between zealous Presbyterians and various malcontent groups (283a, *31–2*; see also note 11). The fate of the first recommendation – that the Committee of Articles be retained – has already been alluded to. The second, which commended a form of religious settlement 'most agreeable to the nation' but hinted strongly at the need for a measure of conciliation with the Episcopalians, was capsized by an inexorable succession of Acts from July 1689 to July 1690 (see above, p. 195). The extinguishing of 'prelacy' and reinstatement of Presbyterian ministers and church government caused grave disquiet to English Anglicans of all persuasions, whose own religious settlement in May 1689 had afforded far greater protection to minority institutions and beliefs (Ch. 23); while the final Act, abolishing lay patronage in the Church of Scotland, especially dismayed the King (he was, of course, less alarmed than the leaders of the Church of England when the first General Assembly of the Kirk to meet since 1653 adopted a statement of doctrine that was relentlessly Calvinist). Scotland's ecclesiastical settlement ended for good the various Stuart attempts to bring their British kingdoms into some kind of religious harmony. Even so, the 1690 parliamentary session was less of a shambles than that of 1689, when the supply bill was logjammed and, because of a dispute between Parliament and the Crown over nominations to judicial offices, no business was done in the Scottish law courts (277a, *9*). In retaliation the King had withheld his consent from all but three of the many Acts passed during that stormy session.

Plainly, William and the Scots were interpreting the 'contract' of April 1689 in very different ways. Although patronage and manipulation were used in the years ahead to bring about temporary periods of cooperation (283a, *86–8*), the new-found 'muscle' of the Edinburgh Parliament was to create difficulties for the Crown not only for the rest of William III's reign but into the early years of his successor. They were to become particularly serious at times of undue stress – following the massacre of the Jacobite Macdonalds of Glencoe in 1692, for example, or the disastrous fate of the Darien venture in 1699–1700 (Ch. 19). In short, the Revolution settlement posed constitutional problems and problems in Anglo-Scottish relations which in the end only a parliamentary union of the two kingdoms could solve. Ironically, a proposal for just such an arrangement, after being commended by William in March 1689,[12] was endorsed by the Scottish Convention the following month, together with a commercial union. But at this time the English could see little benefit for themselves in the scheme, and it earned no serious attention from a much-preoccupied Westminster (285b, *179, 183–4*). Ultimately, what was arguably the most fruitful of all the constitutional changes which stemmed *indirectly* from the Glorious Revolution, the Treaty of Union of 1706, was only to come about through the exigencies of the greatest war either kingdom had ever fought, the War of the Spanish Succession (Ch. 20).

IV

The 'Revolution constitution', which was to become such an object of veneration for the ruling classes of Hanoverian England, took far longer to evolve than its admirers commonly conceded. Crucial as the 1689 settlement itself was in determining the course that would be taken, there were other essential features of the system under which eighteenth-century Britain was governed, as well as the Union of Parliaments, whose links with that settlement were less palpable or even remote. Steady and organic – rather than sudden – change remained the natural order of things. A revolution whose rationale had been to *preserve* everything that, by general consent, was best in the restored constitution of 1660 and whose supporters saw King James and his henchmen, not themselves, as the dangerous innovators, was never likely to lead to loud clamour for basic structural changes in the major institutions of government or in the way the law was made and administered. The tiny republican fringe which still existed among the Whigs never attempted any serious challenge to the central constitutional dogma of 1660 – that the government of England 'is and ought to be by King, Lords and Commons'; their few parliamentary representatives confined their efforts in 1689, and after, entirely to trying to clip the wings of the prerogative (312).Thus the traditional courts of common law and equity, however much they fell short of perfection through abuses in their operation, were still almost universally seen as bulwarks of liberties and property rights (Chs. 11, 18). The rôle of the King's judges on assize, and of the justices of the peace acting through Quarter and Petty Sessions, as essential instruments of justice and of the rule of law in the provinces, was never seriously questioned in the aftermath of the Revolution, nor indeed at any time before the 1790s (264b; 126a). When the makers of the Declaration of Rights declared 'that elections of members of Parliament ought to be free', they were far from contemplating anything savouring of radical change; they meant, of course, 'free' from those sinister new methods of borough manipulation which had threatened to produce a puppet House of Commons in James II's reign. So the electoral system itself was never in serious danger. It had been unchanged between 1660 and 1688 except for some altered – usually widened – franchises and the addition of six new seats through the enfranchise-ment of County Durham and of two new boroughs (25, *I, 104–5*). Yet little was heard in 1689, and still less thereafter, of the demands for reform which some Whig exclusionists had raised a decade or less earlier: the Whigs had, after all, handsomely won four of the last five General Elections on the strength of the old system, and doubtless they hoped to win many more. And so, despite its manifest irrationalities (Ch. 21), the established electoral order comfortably survived what subdued criticism it received between the Revolution and the Wilkite radical upsurge of the late 1760s. That the system had a heavy built-in bias, though not yet an overwhelming one, in favour of the influence of large landed proprietors did it little harm in the eyes of post-Revolution legislators. And once assured that the Crown no longer had the power to rig elections across the board, they were not averse to preserving for it a certain legitimate measure of influence, for example, through boroughs such as Rochester, Portsmouth and Harwich, in which the government had a strong direct interest.

V

Yet for all the powerful pull of post-Revolution conservatism, the British constitution of the 1720s, already well on the way then to becoming the sacred cow of the 'Old Corps' Whigs, did differ appreciably from that of the early 1690s. One powerful agency of change proved to be the wars against France. Another was the precariousness of the Protestant succession, which on at least four occasions after the passing of the Bill of Rights (1701, 1706, 1707 and 1716) created the necessity, or at least the excuse, for further major constitutional legislation [F(vii),(ix),(x),(xii)]. Nor should one overlook the personal factors that were at work on the day-to-day practice of the constitution, the strengths and shortcomings, abilities and ambitions of particular rulers and politicians. Few of them were predictable with confidence in 1689, but cumulatively, over the span of two generations, they had a very considerable influence.

By the 1720s the British system of government could reasonably be defined as a limited parliamentary monarchy: that is to say, the prerogatives of the Crown were circumscribed by a large body of both statutes and conventions which had not applied before 1688, and they could be exercised only within the framework of an established parliamentary system in which the annual presence of a bicameral legislature had become automatic. The pious injunction of the Declaration of Rights that 'Parliaments ought to be held frequently' was soon given sharp teeth by the convention's early refusal to grant William ordinary life revenues; so far as ensuring annual sessions was concerned, the almost immediate onset of an expensive war, in which loans were raised on parliamentary credit, and the passing of the Civil List Act in 1689 (Ch. 16) [F(vi)] did the rest (120b; 112a). The events of 1689, culminating in the passing of the Bill of Rights, did take both the English and the Scots past some notable milestones along the road to limited monarchy. For instance, of the discretionary powers exercised (however controversially) by the pre-Revolution English monarchy in relation to legislation, only one – the ultimate power of veto – remained by 1690. And while William used it on a number of important occasions early in his reign (to kill the Triennial bill, for example, in 1693; see above p. 197), for a Crown or a ministry forced, willy nilly, to seek a smooth, working relationship with Parliament it was a provocative device (62a, *114*), and increasingly an anomalous one. After 1708 it was never resorted to again. There was also a further important constraint. Whereas earlier Stuarts could always resort, if absolutely necessary, to prorogation in order to suffocate unwanted legislation (as in March 1681), William's hands, and those of his successors, were much more tied in this respect by the sheer volume of fiscal business which had to be transacted in the average session.

And yet, while William III, even in his earliest years, ruled as a parliamentary king, as well as a king with a parliamentary title, his kingship was by no means as 'limited' as that of George I was to be. We have observed (above, pp. 217–18) how some of the major legislative landmarks passed in the middle and last years of his reign can well be seen as the completion of some of the unfinished business of February 1689. But the two most important of them, the Triennial Act of 1694 and the many restrictive clauses tacked on to the Act of Settlement in 1701, are deeply revealing in a different sense, for they also reflect the great dissatisfaction which English politicians of both parties felt at the way William had used, or abused, the many prerogatives still left to him after 1689. The Triennial Act, which passed at the third attempt and much to the King's disgust (above, p. 197), was the first-ever statutory invasion of the royal prerogative of dissolution. Because of apprehensions that the King and a ministry now containing Carmarthen (the former Danby) might be tempted by the example of the Cavalier

Parliament, first to tame the House of Commons through patronage, and then keep it in being indefinitely, an absolute limit of three years was placed on the life of every Parliament. The effect of this measure on politics as well as government over the next twenty-two years was dynamic (Ch. 21), too dynamic eventually for the early eighteenth-century Whigs, who repealed it after the 'Fifteen rebellion and forced through a Septennial Act instead [F(xii)]. And the fact that most eighteenth-century Parliaments lasted a *full* seven years, by virtue of what has been called 'the septennial convention', and that George III in 1784 provides the sole spectacular example of a Hanoverian king dissolving a Parliament well within the statutory limit to gain a political advantage for a minister of his choice, tells us much about how far the 'Revolution constitution' had evolved by the 1720s since the aftermath of the Revolution itself. By contrast, before 1714 William III and Anne had thrice asserted their prerogative for political ends against the 'triennial system' (see above, pp. 200, 201, 205).

Historians have often taken the view that the 1701 Act of Settlement, passed after three years acutely disturbed by constitutional tensions, asserted the independence of Parliament over the influence of the Crown much more stridently than the Bill of Rights had done. Certainly the battery of anti-prerogative clauses in the Act represented a massive implicit indictment of William's style of government. But in fact its bite was never as fearsome as its bark [F(vii)]. Ostensibly it was designed to hobble whoever eventually succeeded to the throne of England from the autocratic background of the electorate of Hanover. Only one important clause had immediate force – that no pardon under the Great Seal was to be pleadable to an impeachment – and this had a lengthy pedigree. Nearly all the remaining clauses were technically designed to become operative either on William's demise or after the death of William's sister-in-law, Anne. In the event, however, some never came into force at all, notably the doctrinaire exclusion of all placemen and pensioners from the House of Commons, on which Parliament fortunately had second thoughts in 1706 (above, p. 203; F(ix)); and one, the clause prohibiting any monarch after William's death from leaving his dominions without Parliament's consent, was repealed after the Hanoverian succession. The notorious 'place clause' of 1701 had reflected the fears of the 1690s that the rapid growth of bureaucracy and the armed forces during the Nine Years' War might enable the Crown to flood the Commons with 'officers', military and civil – who were all assumed, quite wrongly, to be lobby fodder for the administration of the day (Chs. 14, 16, 22). However, the far soberer place clauses of the 1706 Regency Act re-focused 'Country' thinking on a selective, rather than a blanket approach to exclusion (71); and this enabled the Revolution constitution, discarding a separation of powers on the later American style, to preserve a valuable lubricating function for patronage (now in any case, more ministerial than monarchical) in the working of the future partnership between Parliament and the executive.

Having made these reservations about the Act of Settlement, and granted that its primary purpose was to regulate the Protestant Succession, the Act was nevertheless responsible for several notable lasting extensions to the statutory fabric which had been erected in 1689 and added to from 1694–8. As well as guaranteeing the freedom of the Common Law judiciary from royal or ministerial gerrymandering, it was the first statute to place an explicit limitation on the Crown's prerogative in foreign affairs, through requiring parliamentary consent to any declaration of war involving the defence of foreign territory. And in a further significant limitation, activated after Anne's death, it curtailed the King's right to appoint freely to offices and to make grants of Crown land to individuals, though only where foreigners were involved [F(vii),(6)].

The years between 1689 and the early 1720s were marked by four other salient constitutional developments, whose direct links with the Glorious Revolution were even looser than those of the anti-prerogative clauses of 1701. The end of the old distinction between ordinary and extraordinary revenue, finally reduced to utter nonsense by King William's war with France, is a matter more appropriate to 'the New Finance' (Ch. 17). But the period also witnessed the emergence of a prime minister in something approaching a nineteenth-century sense, in the person of the head of the Treasury – a change consummated by Sir Robert Walpole but anticipated successively by the earls of Godolphin and Oxford between 1702 and 1714; it likewise saw the establishment of a clear responsibility, at last, for the conduct, if not the formulation, of foreign policy, in the office of the Secretaries of State (cf. Ch. 6), and the evolution of a Cabinet or 'Cabinet Council'. The first two changes stemmed directly from the special circumstances of Queen Anne's reign, from the Queen's wretched health and the fact that her grasp of public business, though not derisory, was unarguably more limited than William's had been. Both circumstances were thrown into all the sharper relief by the fact that her reign was overshadowed almost from beginning to end by a war of unprecedented scale. In William's reign, after all, the King himself had been very much his own prime minister, and equally his own foreign minister when the chips were down, as during the Ryswick and Partition Treaty negotiations of 1697–1700 (Ch. 15). George I was better equipped than Anne to preside over the administration and was to enjoy brief flurries of self-assertion in the first half of his reign, notably in 1717, when one observer commented approvingly that 'the Prime Minister is the King';[13] in his later years, however, his own indolence and the advent of Walpole were to change that situation decisively. As for the Cabinet, this had some pre–1688 antecedents but it properly originated in the winter of 1691–2, as a body meeting as required in the monarch's presence. It developed later in William's reign, and even more in Anne's, as a regular and vital organ of government, its function made imperative by the need of co-ordinating both the conduct and the diplomacy of two wars; and it finally met in formal session without the King's presence in the course of George I's reign (70, *Ch. 6*; 32, *I*; 123; 76a, *Chs. 7, 9*).[14]

VI

It is customary to say that the great conflict over sovereignty in seventeenth-century England was resolved in post-Revolution Britain by locating sovereignty in 'the King-in-Parliament'. The generalisation is harmless enough but it tells us little about the realities of power distribution within the Revolution constitution, or about how that distribution changed over the three to four decades after the flight of James II. The Crown institutionally, and even the monarch personally, still had freedom of action in the 1720s; and the gradual acceptance of the need for governments at the top level to be constituted by men of the same party complexion (Ch. 25) reduced the frequency and seriousness of friction with Parliament. The conduct of foreign affairs remained theoretically an area of almost unfettered prerogative, except for the legislation of 1701; but in practice George I and his ministers, like Anne and her advisers before them, were much more accountable to Parliament for their actions in foreign policy than William III had been. The scope for personal royal policies, though certainly not for personal diplomatic initiatives, was by 1720 effectively removed (145b; 140; 76b; 147). And again, it was not the Revolution directly, but rather the irresponsible way William was judged to have exercised his powers after the Revolution which explains these changes (Ch. 15). In theory, too, there remained only the single limitation in the Act of Settlement to impair the monarch's complete freedom of choice in the appointment of ministers and no restriction at all on his freedom of dismissal. In practice, even William found it difficult to follow his own inclination unreservedly when faced with the need to reconcile the management of Parliament with the pressures of party ambition and prejudice; Anne and George I had even greater problems.

It was difficult to hold on to ministers who could no longer command the confidence of Parliament and of their Cabinet colleagues, even though they still had the full confidence of the monarch. The fall of Robert Harley (the later Lord Oxford) and his friends, St John, Harcourt and Mansel from high office in February 1708 illustrates this better than anything.[15] It was difficult too to resist the clamour for office of those who did have great parliamentary leverage. Anne's enforced capitulation to the three Whig Junto lords, Somers, Wharton and later Orford, in the aftermath of their party's electoral victory in 1708, and George I's reluctant readmission of Walpole and Townshend to his government in 1720, after three years in which they had caused him and his ministers acute parliamentary embarrassment, are telling cases in point (see above, pp. 204, 208–10; 69, *283–4*; 79a, *248–92*). On the other hand, all rulers in this period had the capacity to fight long delaying actions and to make it extremely difficult for parties or factions to establish a complete stranglehold over the administration, as Queen Anne proved conclusively before and after 1710; while the monarch's personal prejudice against individuals, if deep-rooted (as with Anne's positive refusal to re-employ the High Tory leader, Nottingham, after he had deeply offended her in 1705) was very hard to overcome (70, *200–5*). It is therefore going too far to claim, as Professor Roberts has done, that party captured patronage from the monarchy after the Revolution (67, *196–205*), although if one substitutes 'Walpole Whigs' for 'party' that situation was very close by 1725.

There was one traditional sphere of the prerogative, with very important constitutional implications, which was not invaded at all after the Revolution, although an assault on it was attempted and beaten off in 1719. This was the monarch's rôle as the fount of honour. The right to create new peers or promote within the existing peerage obviously strengthened the Crown's natural pull over the loyalties of the House of Lords, the more so because a high proportion of peers in every Upper House of Parliament held Household office or pensions by royal grant, no fewer than eighty-three of them by 1720 (21, *96*). This could theoretically have disturbed the cherished balance of the constitution by giving the Crown a too-powerful counterweight against the influence of the Commons. But although the House of Lords was never more influential politically than in the years between the Glorious Revolution and 1720, its support for the administration could at no time be complacently taken for granted (see Ch. 21). One reason for this – though not the only one, as we shall later see – was that all post-Revolution monarchs had to be very careful not to offend the susceptibilities of the governing élite by bestowing peerages carelessly or too obviously 'to serve a turn' in Parliament. William III incurred some criticism from the Tories on this account; the English peerage increased by twenty between 1689 and 1700 (242a, *14–15*) and he was certainly more lavish with non-royal dukedoms than his predecessors had been. But Queen Anne trod very carefully in this field until her passionate desire for peace persuaded her to agree to the creation of Lord Oxford's 'dozen' – twelve new peers in the space of two days at the end of 1711 – a palpable manoeuvre to force the peace preliminaries through an otherwise uncertain Upper House (above, p. 206). The sense of constitutional outrage which this aroused (1, *VI, 94–5*) had not died down by 1719 and helped to create a body of support in the Commons for the Peerage bill.

This measure, the brain-child of the Stanhope-Sunderland administration of 1717–20, would have had the effect of placing a statutory limit on the freedom of the Crown to grant peerages at will. The motives of the bill's promoters were self-evidently far from altruistic. In 1717 the new Whig supremacy, built up since Anne's death, was threatened by a combination of personal rivalries and foreign policy disagreements which split the ministry asunder. Almost half the Cabinet departed, mostly resigning, and a bevy of talented ministers of the second rank associated with the chief defectors, Townshend and Walpole, also left office, leaving the rest of the ministerial Whigs, headed by Stanhope and Sunderland, uneasily in charge of the field, and the Tories in hopes of revival (see above, p. 208). In the year that followed, down to March 1718, the rump ministry, though often discomfited in the Commons, found its previously secure majority in the House of Lords in even more serious danger. With the bishops and the Prince of Wales's supporters, as well as the dissident Whigs, no longer to be relied on, one tight division followed another; and since a war with Spain was clearly imminent and controversial religious legislation was planned (Ch. 23), it seemed on the cards that the administration would lose control of the House altogether, without emergency recovery measures – and an absolute certainty that it would do so if George I died (70, *xiv n.15*; 83a and c).

Hence the ingenious provisions of the Peerage bill [F(xiii)]. Stanhope himself conceded privately that in his view 'we must carry it now or never, since it will probably never happen again that a king and ministry will be for it';[16] but after a classic debate the measure was defeated in the Commons by the votes of a combination of Country or disaffected Whigs and Tories and the oratory of

Robert Walpole, who in a speech of 'genius' warned his fellow members that the bill would totally disturb the balance of the constitution by forming the peerage into 'a compact, impenetrable phalanx'.[17] However, George I, while strongly favouring Whigs in the new creations he did make, did little more *in toto* throughout his reign than make good the gaps in the hereditary peerage created by death (242a, *14–15, 26*).

The defeat of the Peerage bill did not save the House of Lords from relative decline in the next decade. For this decline there were various reasons. A long-term factor was the greatly enhanced rôle of the Commons in the whole conduct of government business as a result of the revolution in public finance between 1689 and 1720: it needed an exceptional constellation of political stars in the Upper House to counterbalance this, and by the 1720s many of these stars were extinguished. A freakishly large crop of new episcopal appointments in the early 1720s also accelerated this decline (see *The Age of Oligarchy*, Ch. 7). The reduction of Tory strength in the House to something near impotence in the course of George I's reign led inevitably to a loss of vitality (81a; 68a). If the forging of the Revolution constitution on the anvil of Augustan politics upset decisively the balance of power between Parliament and the Crown which the men of 1689 contrived, it had also, by the last years of George I, crucially changed the balance within Parliament itself. Signalling this change in a remarkable way was the, at the time astonishing, decision of Walpole in 1723 to decline a peerage and to continue in the House of Commons as First Lord of the Treasury and undisputed first minister for the next nineteen years. Although rarely noticed by traditional constitutional historians, this decision now seems in retrospect one of the most significant landmarks of our whole period in the evolution of the British system of government.

---

1. B.R. Henning (25), *I*, p. 47; E. Cruickshanks, D. Hayton and C. Jones, 'Divisions in the House of Lords on the Transfer of the Crown and other Issues, 1689–94', *BIHR* **53** (1980), pp. 59–65.
2. Add. MSS 40621, f. 20: Sir Edward to Robert Harley, 9 Feb 1689. There is a vivid account of the stampede at the end of a passionate debate in D.L. Jones (6b), pp. 244–6.
3. *Reasons humbly offered . . .* in *An Eighth Collection of Papers relative to the Present Juncture of Affairs* (1689), quoted J.P. Kenyon (314), p. 8.
4. See the contemporary parliamentary debates in G.L. Jones (6b), *passim* and the historiographical debate in N. McKendrick, ed. (179), pp. 43–69 [Kenyon – 'Resistance and Contract']; J.P. Kenyon (314), pp. 7–11; T.P. Slaughter, '"Abdicate" and "Contract" in the Glorious Revolution', *HJ*, **24** (1981) and '"Abdicate" and "Contract" Restored', *HJ*, **28** (1985); J. Miller (315b).
5. Cobbett (2), V, p. 92: 6 Feb; 'Notes of a Noble Lord', printed in D.L. Jones, (6b), p. 86.
6. Add. MSS 40621, f. 22.
7. 'A Jornall of the Convention', in D.L. Jones, ed. (6b) p. 256: Pulteney, 28 Jan; 'Notes [by Somers] of what passed in the Convention', *Hardwicke State Papers* (1778), II, pp. 414, 415, 416: Garraway, Christie, Boscawen, 29 Jan; repr. Jones (6b), pp. 218–20.
8. Add. MSS 40621, f. 20: Sir Edward Harley MP to Robert Harley, 9 Feb 1689. In a

later letter of the same date (ibid. f. 22), Sir Edward claimed that the extent of the King's displeasure had been exaggerated by those wishing to wreck the settlement, and that William 'told some the power was sufficient for an honest man and too much for a knave'.

9. A bill for restoring corporations foundered in 1690; Chancery reform was frustrated on no fewer than 8 occasions; and there were 5 unsuccessful bills to prohibit the sale of offices.
10. *Acts of the Parliament of Scotland*, IX, pp. 38–40.
11. J. Halliday, 'The Club and the Revolution in Scotland, 1689–90', *Scot. Hist. Rev.*, **45** (1966).
12. *Acts of the Parliament of Scotland*, IX, pp. 8–13.
13. Add. MSS 1013, f. 216: White Kennett to S. Blackwell, 2 Feb 1717.
14. See also J. Carter, 'Cabinet Records for the Reign of William III', *EHR*, **78** (1963).
15. G. Holmes and W.A. Speck, 'The Fall of Harley in 1708 Reconsidered', *EHR*, **80** (1965).
16. Add. MSS 32686, f. 156: Stanhope to duke of Newcastle, 27 Oct 1719.
17. HMC *Onslow MSS.*, p. 459; J.F. Naylor, ed., *The British Aristocracy and the Peerage Bill of 1719* (Oxford, 1968), pp. 264–9, for Walpole's speech.

CHAPTER 14

The struggle with France and the birth of a great power, 1689–1713

I

It has been suggested (Ch. 13) that a major compensation of the historiographical reaction against the Whig interpretation of the 1688 Revolution has been a heightened awareness of the decisive part played by war as a catalyst at this juncture of Britain's history. From first almost to last the reigns of the last two Stuarts were dominated by wars or the threat of war, and this warfare was to have widespread and far-reaching domestic consequences (Chs. 16–22). But its most fundamental effect was to transform Britain's European status. England in 1688 was still a second-class power – one which for the past fourteen years, especially, had been either unwilling or unable to affect the mainstream of European relations. This may not have been her natural position, but the three decades following Oliver Cromwell's death had certainly made it seem so (Ch. 6). Scotland, sharing England's king, had not threatened once since 1660 to play a Continental rôle that was remotely independent of her neighbour, except in trading relations. By the end of the Spanish Succession War in 1713 England and Scotland had for six years fully merged their political identities and the new state of Great Britain had become, and was to remain, a formidable force to be reckoned with in the calculations of all the major Continental powers.

This chapter must begin, therefore, with a summary sketch of the course of war and foreign relations during the twenty-five years preceding the peace settlement of Utrecht. The narrative of events is amplified elsewhere (see pp. 195–207 above; [I.1, I.2; H]). But what follows should provide an adequate backcloth for the subsequent analysis of some of the main problems posed for the historian by Britain's prolonged struggle against France, her erstwhile ally, and by her entry during the course of it into the ranks of the Great Powers.

When William of Orange landed at Torbay on that (for Protestants) propitious day in 1688, the anniversary of the discovery of the Gunpowder Plot, it was already clear to every statesman of any pretensions in Europe that the United Provinces, Spain, the Austrian Habsburgs and many of the lesser states of Germany were on the brink of their second great effort of arms to contain the overweening power of France. Louis XIV's fearsome armies had just overrun and devastated the Rhenish Palatinate, and he had made it very plain that this time his determination to dominate Germany and subjugate the Dutch was not going to be baulked by mere diplomatic obstacles. There were acute apprehensions, too, that France was only waiting for the death of the Spanish king, Carlos II – a man as feeble in health as he was in mind – to pounce on the vast and wealthy Spanish empire and swallow up a hefty portion of it. William of Orange ever since 1672 had been Louis's most committed opponent. In the previous war of 1672–8 he had saved Holland, and probably Germany too, not so much by his military skill as by bravery, sheer pertinacity and force of character allied to diplomatic acumen. The Prince's desperate gamble in 1688 of committing himself to lend armed support to the would-be English rebels is a fair measure of his absolute determination to draw the island kingdoms into the massive further confrontation with France that was imminent. William was convinced that without England's sea power and her now much augmented commercial and financial strength (Chs. 3, 11), the League of Augsburg (as the anti-French coalition called itself) would have little, if any, chance of ultimate success.

Whether William believed he could harness England to that alliance without turning James II off his throne remains an open question (Ch. 12). He must have been well aware, however, that his task would be vastly eased if the Revolution did end in James's deposition. And it is very significant that no sooner had the King fled the country, some seven weeks before the settlement of the Crown had been thrashed out in Parliament, than the Prince gave clear notice of his intentions by ordering the French ambassador to leave the country. Even so, Louis XIV (not for the last time) played into his hands. It was understandable that he should offer shelter to ex-King James. But his flat refusal to recognise William's and Mary's titles was bound to give offence to both English and Scots. And his prompt decision to lend James arms, money and even men to strengthen the latter's attempt to invade and recover Ireland, as a springboard for the later recovery of his other two kingdoms, furnished William with the strongest argument possible to rally his new subjects' support for a declaration of war on France. Little more than a month after James and his French troops had landed at Kinsale (12 March), to reinforce an Irish Catholic rising of alarming proportions which had erupted in January (above, p. 195), the English House of Commons was ready to vote its support to William III in a war against France.

However, when England adhered to the anti-French alliance in 1689 [I.1; cf. H (vii)] most Englishmen probably thought they were embarking on a relatively short, sharp struggle, which for them would essentially be a war of the English Succession. The war they envisaged was one designed partly to force Louis to draw in his horns on the Continent; even more to compel him to back off from Ireland, so that that kingdom could be wrested back again from James II and the Catholics; but most of all to safeguard the Protestant Revolution Settlement at home and the prospects for a Protestant succession from a French-supported counter-revolution and counter-invasion. When Scotland followed England into the conflict, those Scots who approved the Revolution – especially the Presbyterian Lowlanders – found their priorities not markedly dissimilar from those of the English. Fear of the Irish situation and fear for the security of the new Revolution establishment in Scotland (Ch. 13) proved far stronger than any sentimental attachment to the 'auld Alliance' with France or than the distaste for increased taxation, which was even more powerful north than south of the border. However, William's supporters in both kingdoms would have been very much less enthusiastic about his commitment to the League of Augsburg – in fact many of them would have been incredulous – had they guessed that instead of being involved in a two- or three-year defensive war they were embarking on nothing less than a struggle for mastery between Britain and the greatest military power the world had seen since the days of imperial Rome: a struggle which was to involve two great wars and nineteen years of actual fighting and was not to be resolved for twenty-four years.

The first war – we shall call it the Nine Years' War, although this is by no means the only label which has been stuck on to it[1] – lasted until 1697. It saw the recovery of Ireland (1691), though only after early humiliations and much hard campaigning both before and after the emotive victory at the Boyne (above, pp. 195–6). It also achieved the frustration of French designs for an invasion across the Channel, in 1690, 1692 and 1696. Even on the Continent Louis XIV was eventually denied the decisive military breakthrough which the outstanding successes of his armies in both Flanders and Italy from 1690–93 had seemed to presage (above, pp. 195–7). But it was a bloody, unprecedentedly costly and controversial war; and the peace which ended it, the Treaty of Ryswick [H(viii)], while it included a paper guarantee by Louis of William's British titles (proved four years later to be worthless), still left unsettled the crucial issue of the Spanish empire and therefore the whole question of the Balance of Power in Europe. For England, the disposal of this empire was not just of dynastic and political significance, as it was for France, Austria and Germany (and to a large extent for William III, too, as Stadholder-King). In the light of her Commmercial Revolution, of the great expansion in her commerce with Spain and the Mediterranean ports since 1660 and in the illicit but lucrative trading of her merchants with the Spanish American colonies,[2] it was above all a matter of acute economic concern. And so indeed it was for the Dutch, whose capacity for self-defence through their new barrier fortresses in the Spanish Netherlands [H(viii), *note*] was also much at stake.

There was peace from 1697 to 1702, but it was a precarious peace almost from the start. Within a year William had embarked on secret negotiations with the other major powers concerned, including France, in the hope of arranging a partition of the Spanish Habsburg possessions by treaty (above, p. 199) and after the death of the principal beneficiary of the first 'Partition Treaty', the Electoral Prince of Bavaria, these efforts were renewed and produced a second treaty in 1700 [H.(ix, x)]. But in October of that year the whole situation took a decisive turn for the worse when Carlos II of Spain at last did what had confidently been expected from him at almost any time for the past three decades, namely, died. Louis XIV at once tore up the second Partition Treaty and put his Bourbon grandson, Anjou, on the Spanish throne, as Philip V and heir to the entire inheritance. This he did by virtue of the will of the late king, signed a mere month before his death. Louis made plans to invade the Low Countries, to put French troops in key ports such as Antwerp and Ostend and to wrest back from the Dutch the protective fortresses granted them in 1697. These plans were all implemented early in 1701, and meanwhile Louis had already begun systematically to corner the wealth of the Spanish Indies for French merchants.

This time many of William's British subjects, especially the Tories among them, took a good deal more persuading than in 1689 that the crisis could only be resolved by force. The Nine Years' War had imposed grievous strains on England; not as ruinous as Tory economists and political arithmeticians such as Davenant and King were prophesying by 1695–6 (227; repr. 16), but serious none the less. For landowners, swingeing taxation had coincided with a run of bad years for agriculture [K.1(i)] and the depression of rents. The war had taken a heavy toll of English trade, especially in the early 1690s (Ch. 19), and the worst of the major maritime disasters, the loss of a hundred ships of the Smyrna convoy to a French fleet (above, p. 197), had led to bitter recriminations. After Ryswick, concerted parliamentary attacks by Tories and some Country Whigs underlined their suspicion of further Continental adventures by cutting down William's standing army to minimal levels (above, p. 199). Tories were incensed by the secret negotiation of the Partition Treaties (Ch. 15) and were initially predisposed in favour of the principle of hereditary right which the late king of Spain's will arguably upheld. It was only after it became clear in 1701 that Louis would not respect the will's stipulation that the two Bourbon crowns should never be united (18, *460*), that English trade could be more effectively defended by war than without it, and that France would continue to support the Jacobite cause even after ex-King James's death in September, that attitudes changed. By the time William died in March 1702, his life's work still incomplete, he had at least made it certain that his British kingdoms would once more stand shoulder to shoulder with Austria, the United Provinces, and ultimately many lesser states, in a new Grand Alliance [I.1; H(xi)].

And so in May 1702 England and Scotland entered the Spanish Succession War, the greatest either nation had ever engaged in. But if the English, by and large, did so willingly, if not in many cases enthusiastically, the Scots – whose economy had suffered much more disastrously from the Nine Years' War – were, one recent historian has claimed, 'virtually hi-jacked into war', their Estates deliberately left unsummoned in order to give the courtiers on the Scottish Privy Council a free run in the declaration of war (104, *72–3*; 282, *67–71, 245*). In this way and in others, as we shall see, the Spanish Succession War was to prove part of that chain reaction which produced the Union of Parliaments in 1706–7 (Ch. 20). Nevertheless, before as after the Union, Scottish officers and regiments played a notable part in the many victories of a war which was waged ferociously against both France and Bourbon Spain from 1702 until the autumn of 1711 (above, pp. 201–6). By that time a majority of Britons were sated with un-accustomed military glories, weary of high taxation, and, from Queen Anne downwards, not a little sickened by the seemingly endless bloodshed – not least the tens of thousands of lives unavailingly squandered in the efforts to recover Spain for the Austrian Habsburgs. Secret and separate peace negotiations between Britain and France, begun a year earlier when a Tory ministry came to power in Britain under Robert Harley, had by October 1711 produced a set of preliminary terms which were to be the basis for the final treaties of Utrecht in 1713, treaties which sealed beyond question Britain's arrival as a Great Power [H(xiv)]. The Emperor and the Dutch, together with other states in the Alliance, fought on; but in order to put pressure on her allies to make peace, the British government, having first cleared its path by sacking the Queen's brilliant Captain-

General, the duke of Marlborough (Dec 1711), withdrew its troops from the field (May–July 1712), thereby exposing the Austro-Dutch army to a painful and costly defeat in the final major battle of the war, at Denain (above, pp. 205–6). The cry of 'perfidious Albion' which echoed round the Continent after this disaster left the British with an unenviable reputation for betraying their allies which persisted right down to the twentieth century. Yet at the same time it was a backhanded admission of a fact which the history of the hundred years after Utrecht was repeatedly to confirm: that without Britain's firm support no European alliance aimed at containing France and maintaining the Balance of Power was likely to prosper.

The diplomatic framework within which the struggle with France took place from 1689 to 1713 cannot, of course, be divorced from the more general principles and considerations underlying foreign policy, from the Revolution through to the age of Walpole and the Pelhams. These we shall examine subsequently (Ch. 15; *The Age of Oligarchy*, Ch. 4). Here we make no attempt to pursue the course of the Nine Years' and Spanish Succession Wars in any detail. But in order to arrive at some understanding of their far-reaching domestic repercussions we must at least know something about the scale of these wars, their geographical scope, and their cost. Furthermore, against the background of the strategy of Britain's wars against Louis XIV – a matter of much contention at the time – it should be possible to judge how successfully, by and large, they were conducted and briefly to illustrate how fortunes in the struggle for mastery ebbed and flowed over nearly two decades of fighting.

II

In the first place, the psychological impact of these two great wars of the reigns of William III and Anne was immense. To appreciate this we have to set the wars in their seventeenth-century perspective. How, for example, would a well-informed member of the governing class of the vintage of John Evelyn, the diarist, have regarded them in the final years of his life? Evelyn was approaching 70 at the time of the Revolution and did not die until 1706. Yet until 1689 men of his generation had gone through their entire lifetimes without experiencing any protracted warfare other than the civil broils of the 1640s. Certainly, seven foreign wars were waged in the eighty-five years after 1604, the year when the long Elizabethan conflict with Spain came to an end. But of these seven only two had lasted more than two and a half years, and not one had involved any large-scale land commitments against a European power. The biggest English army, mercenaries apart, to fight on Continental soil between 1604 and 1690 was probably the detachment of 6,000 men of the New Model Army which fought at the Battle of the Dunes in 1658 (paid for, mostly, by the French). So to all Englishmen, old as well as young, the two-act drama in which their nation was pitted against the power of Louis XIV after 1689 was a startling contrast in every respect. Not only was it long-drawn-out and, in contemporary eyes, unimaginably expensive, it also marked a complete break with any wars since the mid-fifteenth century in that it saw from 1691 onwards large British armies campaigning year after year on the Continent.

What is more, the geographical breadth of the conflict, in its second phase especially, defied comparison, not simply with seventeenth-century experience, but with all earlier wars. Under Anne troops from the home kingdoms, together with a substantial stiffening of foreign soldiers in the Queen's pay and uniform, campaigned regularly in the Low Countries, for a while in Germany and for many years in the Iberian peninsula. They fought in smaller numbers in the West Indies, and they took part in combined operations as far apart as Cadiz, Toulon in the south of France and Quebec, via the St Lawrence river, in Canada (above, pp. 201, 203–4, 206). As for the Navy, while its activities were at first mainly confined to the Channel, the North Sea and the Irish Sea, their range later expanded to take on the full extent of the Mediterranean from west to east, and much of the North Atlantic, from the French, Iberian and West African coasts to the North American seaboard and the Caribbean. From 1694–6, in the wake of the Smyrna convoy disaster, there was a prolonged English naval presence in the Mediterranean, and from 1703 this became a permanent presence in wartime (and ultimately in peacetime, too). It became a key factor in the strategy of the two Grand Alliances, as it was to be in later wars against France, right down to Nelson's time, sustaining the Savoyards and Austrians, bottling up the French southern fleet and, of course, protecting vital trade routes. And it was a presence that was guaranteed for the future during the Spanish Succession War, by the acquisition of two invaluable bases, Gibraltar and Minorca (above, pp. 202, 204).

As daunting to the average Briton of the day as the geographical scope of the struggle with France was the size and scale of the forces involved [I.2]. It will be recalled that although James II's standing army never reached the numbers or approached the quality of Cromwell's in the mid-1650s, the fact that he could put some 30,000 English, Irish and Scots troops into the field in November 1688, with some 10,000 more in reserve or in garrisons, was regarded as an intolerable threat to English liberties. The Stuart navy, despite interludes of neglect, had expanded considerably between 1660 and 1689, its strength boosted by the Thirty Ships programme of 1677 (47, *243*) and much cossetted later by James II. By the time of the Revolution the latter had some 160 ships of all kinds, about 100 of which on paper were capable of standing 'in the line of battle' (although many of these were small and lacking in the fire-power of their French and Dutch counterparts, so that some authorities have put the number of true battleships at 59). At any rate James had spent half of his total English revenue, on average, on his armed forces. His army had disintegrated, however, in the winter of 1688–9 so that in that respect William III had to start building from ground level. The first expeditionary force sent to the Continent in 1689 contained only 11,000 British troops, with another 9,000 engaged in Ireland. By the last three years of the Nine Years' War, however, the Westminster Parliament was voting for service abroad, quite apart from the home reserve, over 68,000 men, of whom 48,000 were British [cf. I.2]. After an initial cutback, the military commitment to the Spanish Succession War became even greater, so that eventually the army in the Low

Countries reached 65,000, with a further 40,000 troops fighting in other overseas theatres, many of them in Spain and Portugal. From 1706 to 1711 the *total* army, excluding officers, maintained an average strength of 120,000; throughout the war from beginning to end the average number under arms annually was 92,708 [I.2] (133, *30–1*). It is worth bearing in mind that there were no more than 1.3 million adult males in the whole of England at this time: there may well have been fewer.

The expansion of the navy after 1688, to reach 225 ships by 1714, including 131 genuine line-of-battle ships, was just as decisive and much more permanent, since not a few of the vessels built under William and Anne were still in service in the 1740s and 1750s. More important than increase in mere numbers, however, was the improvement in tonnage, armament, general quality and flexibility. Tonnage increased by 60 per cent between 1689 and 1697 (142a). Twenty of the battleships of 1714 were the formidable new three-deckers with their massive fire-power of 96 or 100 guns, needing 15,000 officers and men to man them. There were also by the end of Anne's reign 42 large third-raters of 70–80 guns, demanding over 19,000 officers and men, and 65 'cruisers' (5th- or 6th-raters, the rough equivalent of the later frigates and sloops, and used greatly for commerce protection).[3] In 1688 there had been a mere eight ships of this latter type in service. Well before the end of the 1702–13 war, therefore, the Royal Navy was not only the largest but by far the strongest in Europe.

It goes without saying that this wholly unprecedented effort of arms, culminating in 1711 when 186,000 men (far from all, it is true, natives) were serving in the two armed forces together, entailed a war budget that would have been inconceivable in Charles II's reign. By 1706 the army budget alone had reached £2.75 million, some four and a half times the average yearly cost of maintaining Cromwell's New Model Army in the 1650s, and the war in Flanders swallowed up about half that sum. The Spanish Succession War proved roughly five times as expensive annually as the Dutch War of 1665–7 had been. The total cost of the entire struggle with France, taking 1689–97 and 1702–13 together, was around £140 million.

Yet although the outlay of both men and money on these two wars dwarfed all previous military and naval commitments in Englishmen's experience, it was no more than commensurate with the task in hand. For the power and resources of Louis XIV's France were awe-inspiring. Her population was well over three times that of England and Scotland put together. She had an army which rarely fell below 250,000 and occasionally topped 400,000 men,[4] and, in the 1690s at least, a fine navy, the legacy of Colbert. Louis was served by some outstanding generals, in the best tradition of Condé. Luxemburg, whom it was William III's misfortune to oppose in the Netherlands until the Frenchman's death in January 1695, was the most brilliant, but others such as Villars, Marlborough's wiliest adversary, and Berwick, the bastard son of James II, whose masterly campaigns ruined the allied cause in Spain in the middle years of Queen Anne, were not far behind him in ability. In addition France could boast the greatest experts in both siegeworks and the fortification of towns that the world had ever seen. In the Nine Years' War she stood virtually alone against her enemies, though receiving valuable indirect support from the Turks. But after 1701 French power was supplemented by that of the greater part of Spain, and this meant not only Spanish manpower and sea power but, most opportunely, the swelling of the Bourbon revenues by the treasure fleets from Spanish America. Bullion worth 180 million livres, much of it Peruvian silver, was said to have flowed into France between 1701 and 1709 alone.[5]

In the circumstances it was hardly to be expected that Britain's struggle for mastery with France should have been a continuous success story. And the reasons for this were by no means all connected with the formidable assets of the French themselves. There were times when England was ill-served by her allies, disagreements with the Dutch in the Spanish Succession War proving particularly costly. But far more important were her own failings, especially in the war of 1689–97. Sheer inexperience and lack of preparation lay at the root of many of them, the fruit of thirty years of singular lack of achievement, diplomatically and militarily since 1658; even Pepys's navy had still to be put to the test in 1689. The political direction of the Nine Years' War, down to 1694 at least, was often deplorable, frequently undermined by party rivalries and personal vendettas; matters were made worse by the fact that neither many of the politicians nor the nation at large were mentally prepared for the uncompromising war which King William and his more bellicose Whig supporters found themselves committed to. What is more, even those who did accept, with varying degrees of enthusiasm, that the struggle must continue once Ireland was reduced and the main threat of invasion had passed, and again, that it must be renewed in 1702, faced a strategic dilemma. And even by the early years of the Spanish Succession conflict that dilemma had not been wholly resolved.

From the early 1690s the precise rôle which England should play in the strategy of the alliance became the subject of fierce disputes, in the government, in Parliament and in the political nation outside Westminster. William III, while fully aware of the value of sea power and regarding the naval encirclement of France after 1692 as a strategic necessity, insisted that there must also be a land commitment on the Continent of major proportions. With no seventeenth-century precedent to guide them, many Englishmen naturally found this argument very hard to accept. Initially, distrust of a large army of redcoats heavily coloured their attitude: memories of Hounslow Heath in 1688 were still vivid, and far more important, the scars left by the New Model remained angry even after thirty years. Later, however, there developed a less emotive conviction, rooted deep in bitter experience by 1693 and 1694, of the expensive futility of large-scale Continental campaigns, especially in the Spanish Netherlands or near the north-east frontier of France, a region bewebbed by fortified towns. Most Tories, especially, came to argue, and continued to do so in the early years of the war of 1702–13, that even in alliance with the Dutch and the Imperialists and stiffened by German mercenaries, English and Scottish troops would never beat the French at their own game. In Flanders, so the High Tory leader, Lord Rochester, wrote in 1702, the enemy 'by the strength of his numerous garrisons, must be, for many years at least, invulnerable'.[6] Even if successes were achieved, it was argued that they would advance Dutch rather than English interests, and anti-Dutch feeling ran high at times in both these wars. Instead the 'blue-water' school contended that the only effective contribution Britain could make to the defeat of the Bourbons was to build up an unchallengeable naval supremacy and use it to concentrate heavily on a maritime, or at most a 'mixed', strategy. In this the army would be used mainly to make colonial gains from the French, or in what today would be called 'combined operations' against certain specially-selected Continental and Mediterranean targets; although in Anne's reign some supporters of this school did work up enthusiasm for Spain, with its opportunities for more fluid campaigning, as an appropriate field of military activity for the British.

Although King William suffered a string of disappointments, and mounting criticism persisting at least until 1695, they did not deter him. As far as land strategy was concerned he stuck to his guns right through the Nine Years' War. More decisive for the ultimate outcome of the struggle was the fact that the powerful alliance between the duke of Marlborough as Captain-General and Lord Godolphin as Lord Treasurer, which managed all Queen Anne's ministries – Tory, Whig and hybrid – down to 1710, held firm to what was basically the same Williamist strategy. It is true, they did vary it with a scattering of small colonial expeditions, such as the seizure of St Kitts, and with several major combined operations, the most ambitious being the attacks on Cadiz, Gibraltar and Toulon in the years 1702–7. But of the latter, the first was a fiasco and the third an expensive disappointment which scarcely seemed to justify the faith which the maritime school placed in such ventures. Not only did the 'duumvirate' maintain the scope of the land war, so far as Britain was concerned; with Whig backing, and initially with some Tory support (especially that of Nottingham) in the Cabinet, they greatly extended it. The landmark here was the signing of the Methuen Treaties with Portugal in 1703 (above, p. 202; [H(xii)]). The Portuguese had originally been allies of France in the Succession War. But in persuading them to change sides in 1703 Anne's ministers committed the British people to war aims far beyond those laid down in the Grand Alliance Treaty of 1701: nothing less than an undertaking to eject Philip V from the Spanish throne by force in favour of the Emperor Leopold's second son, the Habsburg Archduke Charles. Within less than three years this commitment had involved the presence of a large British army in Iberia, first under Peterborough, later under Galway and James Stanhope.

It was just before the opening of the second front in the Peninsula that the Williamist strategy of squeezing France on land from the north-east and the east, as well as from the south through an alliance with Savoy and by naval strangulation, began for the first time to command fairly general approval. The trouble from 1691–7 had been that it had needed a commander of superlative ability to demonstrate that William was right; William himself, though a good and brave soldier, had neither the tactical brilliance nor the temperamental ballast for the task. He was defeated at Steenkirk in 1692 and at Neerwinden, where his army was crushed by Luxemburg, a third of its number were killed or maimed. William's only positive success of note in the Netherlands theatre was the recapture of the key fortress town of Namur in 1695. For the rest, his military achievement was the essentially negative one of preventing the French from completely overrunning Flanders, thereby preserving the United Provinces from devastation. Although Louis XIV's armies ended the Nine Years' War triumphant on the Italian and Spanish fronts, they were denied total victory by the stalemate in the North-East, which William had ground away to achieve. By 1696 the rival forces there had battered each other into a state of mutual exhaustion.

Marlborough, the former General Churchill (Ch. 12), who had spent much of William's reign under a cloud, changed all that, for he was that rare phenomenon, an English military genius. As a tactician he was not a startling innovator: rather he had absorbed and mastered all that was best in the practice of the previous three-quarters of a century. But as a strategist he was supreme in his day, and his qualities of generalship were enhanced by a combination of organising abilities and diplomatic gifts rarely found in any soldier in any age.[7] Yet not even Marlborough was able to find full scope for his talents until the French themselves opened up the Spanish Succession War in 1703–4 by striking with their Bavarian allies into the very heart of the Empire (above, pp. 201–2). This was no gratuitous flight of whimsy but a bold and imaginative stroke which by the spring of 1704 had brought Louis very close indeed to capturing Vienna, eliminating Austria from the struggle and thereby winning the war in Germany. In the end, one controversial, highly risky decision, and that alone – the decision to transfer Marlborough's British army from the Netherlands theatre to the Danube to reinforce Leopold I's stricken forces – stood between France and a spectacular triumph. To transfer an army of 40,000 troops with all their guns, baggage and horses halfway across Europe in six weeks, while maintaining its morale and fighting trim and keeping the enemy guessing as to its true intentions, in itself posed problems which probably no other contemporary general could have solved: roads were, after all, primitive and desertion an endemic disease in every seventeenth- and eighteenth-century army. To get these troops to the Danube in time to link up with the imperialist forces under Prince Eugene and at Blenheim destroy Marshal Tallard's army, killing or capturing 30,000 out of 50,000 Frenchmen and Bavarians, smacked almost of sorcery. Blenheim was not just a major battle. It was a 'famous victory' in every sense of that much-abused term. It saved Austria; it enabled the allies to sweep Germany clear of French forces; it was the first serious land defeat inflicted on France since Louis XIV had assumed regal powers in 1661; it made Marlborough overnight a national hero, and it made the fortunes of the Churchill family.

In the course of the next four years the duke was to demonstrate that what he could achieve in Germany he could do again in the most taxing theatre of all, the North-East. A tremendous victory at Ramillies in 1706 made the Netherlands virtually untenable by Louis's armies, and among the many fortified towns which fell to Marlborough in the wake of that triumph was one, Menin, over the French border. At Oudenarde in 1708 he repeated the dose, and that year's campaigning season ended with a psychological master stroke, the reduction after a long and bitter siege of the reputedly impregnable French fortress town of Lille. Yet so far as the ultimate outcome of the war was concerned, what had happened in between these two epic battles was as significant as the battles themselves. There is good reason to think that Marlborough could have ended the war in 1706–07, after Ramillies, with a successful invasion of France and the capture of Paris. But two things prevented that: the first being the jealousy of his Dutch allies and a lack of co-operation from both the generals and political deputies of the States, which was not new in itself (cf. above, pp. 202, 203), but which in the changed circumstances of 1706 seemed to the British so blinkered and bizarre as to defy reason; the second being the impossibility of Marlborough's reinforcing his Flanders army with the extra 20–30,000 British troops that might have made all the difference because of the insistent demands of the Spanish theatre. There the Bourbon-Habsburg struggle at this juncture hung in the balance. Despite two abortive early attempts to invade Spain from Portugal, the war in the Peninsula began well enough for the allies, and for the British, with some airy flourishes from Peterborough (until he departed in a fit of pique) and with Philip V expelled, if only briefly, from Madrid in 1706. However, a humiliating defeat at Almanza in 1707 at the hands of Marshal Berwick transformed Spain into the disaster-area of the British war effort; in the same year Marlborough's cherished plan of catching the French in a pincer grip from the south as well as the north-east, greatly encouraged in 1706 by Eugene's victory at Turin (above, p. 203), came to grief before the walls of Toulon. Almanza, we can now see, virtually doomed the Habsburg cause in Spain, and the *coup de grâce* would not have been delayed for three and a half years, nor would Stanhope and Starhemberg have been permitted their fleeting hope-reviving victories at Almenara and Saragossa (1710), had Louis not been so hard-pressed elsewhere as to be unable to spare his grandson decisive reinforcements (above, pp. 203–5).

Within a matter of months after Oudenarde and Lille, however, the French were desperate for peace. Their representatives went to the Hague negotiations of April-May 1709 in the knowledge that their country was bankrupt, its economy in ruins, its population, weakened by the most savage winter in memory, facing the certainty of a second successive catastrophic harvest (Bromley, ed., (24a): chs. by Dickson and Meuvret). They would undoubtedly have settled then for terms much more favourable for the allies as a whole than those finally agreed at Utrecht and Rastadt in 1713–14 if Britain's by now Whig government had not insisted on turning the screws too hard. Carrying the policy of 'No Peace without Spain' to unrealistic extremes they demanded not only that Louis XIV should abandon all Bourbon claims to the Spanish Empire – which he was ready to do – but that he should assume the responsibility for 'persuading' Philip V to leave Spain within two months, which was both offensive to Louis's pride and beyond his power (143a, *II, 511–50*). So France fought on. And although later that summer, Marlborough, after leading the allied army across the French frontier, won one more field victory, at Malplaquet, it was much less clear-cut than his earlier triumphs. What is more, it was only achieved at the cost of bloodshed so heavy on the allied side[8] that British public opinion was sickened by it (19, *III, 8–19*). From then on the duke's genius was always fettered by the mounting pressure for peace at home, pressure for which he himself could feel a measure of sympathy. In 1710 he extended his hold over France's north-east frontier territory and in 1711 accomplished what in his own opinion was his greatest military feat, breaching Villars's 'Ne Plus Ultra' defence lines at Bouchain, after a brilliant feint (143b, *181–3*). But by now he was being deliberately starved of the resources he needed to finish the war by pressing on to Paris, and in December 1711 the Tory ministry of Robert Harley, which had come to power after the fall of Godolphin in 1710 (above, p. 205), found a trumped-up pretext for dismissing him. The way was then open for the issuing of the infamous 'Restraining Orders' to his successor, Ormonde, and the calculated isolation of the Dutch and the Imperialists designed to force their plenipotentiaries at the Utrecht congress, along with those of Prussia, Savoy and the other allies, to agree to 'a general peace' (24a, *461–7*; 144).

As we saw, Marlborough's opponents, like William III's before him, had often claimed that England's own aims in the struggle with France could be gained more effectively, and a great deal less expensively, at sea. The Royal Navy, with well over 40,000 seamen and petty officers to be paid each year, and the largest ships of the line costing £41,000 or more to build, always had a generous budget: Parliament saw to that (133, *31, 34*; [I.2]). Yet in fact the conflict at sea, like that on land, was a chequered one, and there was not a little trial and error before the Navy was able to translate its steadily growing superiority into decisive command of the sea-lanes. Both wars began with naval setbacks. Admiral Torrington was so badly beaten by Tourville off Beachy Head in 1690 that the French for a while commanded the Channel, and had Louis felt able to spare the necessary troops from the Netherlands and Italy he could have invaded England with excellent prospects of success. Not without reason were there panic stations for many weeks in London (above, p. 196). The start of the Spanish Succession War, too, was blighted by a naval setback, less serious than Beachy Head but especially galling to the advocates of 'blue-water' policies, with their stress on colonies and trade. Admiral Benbow, commanding the English fleet in the Caribbean, was betrayed by four of his captains (two of whom were later shot for cowardice) and failed lamentably to destroy a weaker French squadron, the remnant of a forty-ship armada which had recently departed with the Spanish silver fleet; Benbow died of his wounds into the bargain.

The Navy's basic problem, however, from the time of Admiral Edward Russell's decisive victory off La Hogue in 1692 (above, p. 196), which more than avenged Beachy Head, was that it found very few other opportunities in the next twenty years to bring a major French fleet to battle. In the whole of the Spanish Succession War, it is astonishing to note, there was only one full-scale engagement, that at Malaga (1704). A few dangerous sallies apart, one of which put paid to the Levant convoy, the French preferred to keep their line-of-battle ships safe under the guns of Brest and Toulon. There were long periods in the war of 1702–13 when it seemed that their only mission was to provide escorts for the annual treasure ships from the Indies. Instead France chose to concentrate on commerce destruction, mainly through privateers based on Dunkirk and other Channel ports. And a highly successful, and for the privateer captains a highly profitable, job they made of it for many years. The ravages of Duguay Trouin and others became legendary; the insistence of British negotiators in 1711–13 that the fortifications of Dunkirk must be destroyed as part of the peace settlement can be seen as a reflection of a new kind of maritime warfare which the Royal Navy found it very hard to counter. The Navy and those in political charge of it, came under severe parliamentary and press criticism, both in William's reign and in Anne's, for failing to prevent massive losses of English merchant ships: indeed, around 6,000 were lost between 1689 and 1708, although many of them were subsequently bought back by their owners.[9] Eventually a Whig Board of Admiralty in Anne's middle years got control of the situation by organising more efficient convoy systems and by giving top priority to the building of more 'cruisers', or frigates. By the closing years of the Spanish Succession War the Navy was able not only to sweep the seas clear of enemy ships but to point to the capture of over 2,200 prizes of its own.

III

It may well seem highly ironic that the dénouement of the thirty-year struggle for mastery with France which has been the subject of this chapter found two enemies actually in collusion with each other in an attempt virtually to dictate a settlement to Britain's allies. And in the end, after fifteen months of negotiation at Utrecht, all except Austria were brought to accept it [H(xiv): *note*]. But if the situation was ironic, it was also historically appropriate, for at the end of the struggle Britain alone, of all the major participants, had succeeded in achieving her original war aims – and a few more besides [H(xiv); Chs. 15, 19]. A new Great Power had been born. And if she had not yet succeeded in establishing a clear-cut mastery over France, she had at least demonstrated to the whole world her right to co-exist with France as a complete equal, a status unthinkable in her client days of the 1670s and the 1680s. At the same time she had shown herself both determined and able to frustrate France, or any other state, threatening the balance of power in Europe. Britain's unilateral abandonment of the policy of 'No Peace without Spain', which made possible the conclusion of the secret Anglo-French peace preliminaries of September 1711 (above, pp. 206, 232–3), represented not only an acknowledgment of military reality but the recognition that it was no longer France which threatened to achieve an unhealthy preponderance but the Habsburg Empire, after the Archduke Charles – titular Carlos III of Spain – had in April succeeded his brother Joseph I (1705–11), as Emperor Charles VI. In the next chapter we shall begin to examine the fuller implications of these momentous years of war in transforming Britain's position in Europe and her relationship to Europe well into the eighteenth century. Thereafter we shall consider the vital importance of these same years in transforming Britain herself.

---

1. Alternatives from British historians have been 'the War of the League of Augsburg', 'King William's War' and 'the War of the English Succession'.
2. J.O. McLachlan, *Trade and Peace with Old Spain, 1667–1750* (Cambridge, 1940).
3. R.D. Merriman, ed., *Queen Anne's Navy* (1961), pp. 365, 369–71.
4. D.G. Chandler, 'Armies and Navies', Ch. 22 of 24a, p. 741.

5. French official memoir, quoted in H. Kamen, *The War of Succession in Spain 1700–15* (1969), p. 175.
6. Rochester's preface to Lord Clarendon's *History of the Great Rebellion*, I (1702), pp. viii–ix.
7. Correlli Barnett, *Marlborough* (1974), pp. 263–4 – the best popular life. But see also Burton (143b), Ch. 9; Chandler (143c), *passim*.
8. The Dutch, and to a lesser extent the Germans, bore the brunt of the fatal casualties. British losses were much exaggerated by Tory propaganda. See above, p. 204.
9. J.S. Bromley, 'The French Privateering War', in H.E. Bell and R. Ollard, eds, *Historical Essays, 1600–1750* (1963).

CHAPTER 15

The transformation of foreign policy, 1689–1714

I

An inevitable consequence of Britain's involvement in two major wars after May 1689 and of her rise to Great Power status was a radical reappraisal of her relations with her European neighbours and of the foreign policy which governed them. In Chapter 6 we examined that depressing phase of disengagement from Europe which had disfigured much of the 1670s and 1680s, a period of inward-looking policies which had isolated England and seriously lowered her European stock. In 1714, when the first of the Hanoverians succeeded the last of the Stuarts, the new state of Great Britain once again stood isolated from her neighbours. But now it was a very different sort of isolation from that of the Restoration years. For one thing, it soon proved to be a purely temporary period of estrangement from old allies – an interlude between the breakdown of one great alliance system and the construction of a new one, beginning in 1715–16. More significantly, British isolation in 1714 was a product not of weakness but of strength. The recent peace settlement had been brought about, in effect, because by 1711 Britain was so indispensable to the coalition pitted against the Bourbons that she was able, more or less unilaterally, to make her own terms with France and Spain, leaving her allies with no alternative in the end but to fall into line.

The terms hammered out by Strafford and Robinson at Utrecht in 1712 and 1713 [H(xiv)] had been epoch-making in themselves. They were negotiated at a cost, in terms of faith broken (as with the effective abandonment of the pro-Habsburg Catalans to the tender mercies of Philip V [H(xivb) 4] and of goodwill sacrificed, but they nevertheless spoke eloquently of the complete transformation which had taken place since 1688 in Britain's international position and outlook. Largely on the basis of the Treaty of the Hague (Grand Alliance) of September 1701, England had committed herself to a second war against France with several objectives paramount [H(xi)]. It was hoped to force Louis XIV, this time beyond all evasion, to abandon his support for the exiled Catholic Stuarts. But this was also to be a war to ensure that the crowns and successions of Spain and France remained separate, with 'equitable and reasonable satisfaction' for the Austrian Habsburgs in lieu of the Spanish throne; to establish the freedom of the Netherlands from Bourbon control, whether French or Spanish, and (a point on which William III insisted) make the area an effective buffer in the future defence of the United Provinces;[1] and to guarantee that Italy should not be dominated by a strong maritime power but rather provide the main pickings for the compensation of Austria. Finally, it was understood (though not stated explicitly) that the fighting would, at the very least, restore the commercial status quo in the Spanish Americas, where the French had rudely disturbed the illicit trading prospects of English and Dutch merchants, and it was agreed that any West Indian conquests made by either England or Holland should be retained at the peace. By 1713–14 all these original objectives had been achieved; in two vital respects, overseas acquisitions and commercial concessions, Britain had advanced well beyond them. As well as making the relatively minor annexation of half of the Caribbean island of St Kitts, she was confirmed in her possession of two Mediterranean bases and of extensive, if not very prepossessing, tracts of French North American maritime territory [H(xiva) 4], and she acquired for the first time legal rights of trading with the Spanish Indies, including the coveted *Assiento* contract ([H(xivb) 3]; Ch. 19; *The Age of Oligarchy*, Ch. 4). When the ink dried on the treaties of Utrecht, therefore, Britain was left indisputably a major power in two continents, as well as on the oceans.

It is true that the peace settlement could not have been made without some retreat on the part of the Harley ministry from the more extravagant of the revised aims with which the Godolphin administration had become identified after 1702. Of these fresh commitments, all a result of the diplomatic exigencies of the Spanish Succession War, the three most important were the policy of 'No Peace without Spain', first foreshadowed in the Methuen alliance treaty with Portugal in 1703 [H(xiia)] and finally enshrined in a Whig parliamentary vote of 1707 (Ch. 14); the obligations incurred (1703–9) to Victor Amadeus II of Savoy, in return for his invaluable military support in Italy, and the over-generous terms of the Whig Barrier Treaty with the Dutch, negotiated by Townshend in 1709 [H(xiii)].[2] All three stemmed originally from the need to offer baits to foreign powers, either to change sides in the war (in the case of Portugal and Savoy) or to keep on fighting (as with the United Provinces). Otherwise British interests were in no case *directly* advanced by the new war aims, and in the case of the commercial advantages promised to the Dutch in 1709, it could well be said (and was so at the time by the Tories) that these interests were sacrificed. Nevertheless, it was only the commitment to place a Habsburg on the throne of Spain that was totally abandoned at the peace, and this, as we have observed, had become first a military impossibility, and then, in 1711, a dynastic minefield (above, p. 241). As regards the Dutch, no attempt was made to gain for them the parity in the Spanish American trade or the privileged economic position in the southern Netherlands which they had been led to expect since 1709. On the other hand, British influence procured for them a better string of barrier fortresses than they could reasonably have hoped for in 1701, including Tournai, at Lord Oxford's insistence, albeit one more 'agreeable to the English nation' than Townshend's lavish hand-out (144; 69, *335*). For Savoy British negotiators extracted the kingdom of Sicily from Spain. This was not merely a handsome prize for an ally but (since Austria had expected the territory) a calculated check to Habsburg, as well as Bourbon, influence in the peninsula. While Britain was thus busy re-drawing the map of western and southern Europe, in conjunction with France, her powerful bargaining position was further advertised by her success in extracting specific advantages for herself from the allies whose future she was manipulating. A unilateral agreement with Victor Amadeus in 1712 guaranteed her new naval bases and trading privileges in Sicily, while in the second Anglo-Dutch treaty (January 1713) the States, in return for the Oxford ministry's barrier promises, renewed the undertaking they had made in 1709 to supply Britain with 6,000 troops in the event of a Jacobite invasion. That undertaking was duly discharged in 1715.

The making of the settlement of 1713, as well as bearing unanswerable witness to Britain's arrival in the front rank of European powers, also signalled her *commitment* to the affairs of the Continent. She had become a guarantor of one of the most ambitious blueprints yet devised for the reconciliation of international differences and the preservation of future peace. Having been largely instrumental in designing the building, she could hardly now shuffle off responsibility for its stability – especially as she inhabited part of it. Here was arguably the most momentous of all the changes which revolution and war had wrought on Britain since 1689. Events abroad, which for much of the seventeenth century had never evoked more than a spasmodic response from English governments, and only rarely an effective one had, well before 1714, become for informed Britons a regular source of interest or concern. By the same token, foreign affairs, not long since an esoteric indulgence among most British politicians, had become one of their most important preoccupations.

II

What G.C. Gibbs has called 'the revolution in foreign policy'(140) after 1688 was thus a revolution in English attitudes towards Europe as well as in relations with Europe. What made this remarkable change of outlook possible? Many things contributed to it, of course. But a fundamental prerequisite was the very rapid development, over two decades round the turn of the century, of an informed opinion in England on Continental issues, a degree of political education which had simply not existed for most of the seventeenth century. In this educative process, again, various developments played their part. The influence of the Huguenot immigrants, many thousands of whom came over from France after 1685, could well have been a factor of importance. The return of the Whig political exiles from Holland after November 1688 was certainly so. One can also point to the maintenance of a larger and more specialised diplomatic corps under William III and Anne, in contrast to the often gimcrack arrangements of the Restoration monarchy.[3] Most far-reaching of all was the influence of a partially liberated Press after 1695. The lapsing of the Licensing Act (above, p. 198; *The Age of Oligarchy*, Ch. 13) encouraged, among other things, the mushroom growth by the early years of the eighteenth century of nearly a score of privately-owned London newspapers, and also of the earliest provincial ones. Such papers as the *Daily Courant*, the *Post-Boy* and the *Flying Post*, like the official *Gazette*, purveyed to the reading public a steady stream of foreign news. One of the oddities of Augustan journalism, in fact, was that news from abroad was relatively cheap to come by and bulked a lot larger than domestic items in 'the prints' (141, *117–29* [de Beer]; 299).

The gradual adoption during the 1690s of distinctive party standpoints on Europe (Ch. 22) was another reason for, as well as a reflector of, the magnitude of the change which took place. The year 1701, as we shall see, was an especially vital one in the country's progress towards full European commitment, and not least because it was during that year that the attitudes and opinions of the English partisans inside and outside Parliament firmly crystallised. Slowly and painfully since 1689 a substantial body of English opinion, much of it concentrated within the Whig party, had at length come to accept the 'Williamist' view of the kingdom's destiny. This essentially was the outward-looking view that the only real safety for the English nation and for her Protestant religion lay not in disengagement from the affairs of the Continent – as many Tories and a fast dwindling number of 'Old Whigs' continued to believe – but rather in involvement; not in ignoring the expansionist aims of great Catholic autocracies but in opposing them. And as a new century dawned this could only mean, as it had done for almost three decades past, not pandering to France, as the Stuarts had been too ready to do from the late 1660s, but cooperating with other threatened states to maintain some system of what contemporaries called 'mutual security' (as we should say, 'collective security') against her. For it was clearer by the end of 1701 than it had ever been before that the same state which sheltered and succoured a Popish Pretender to the English and Scottish thrones was also the state threatening to dominate Europe; adding now the menace of economic hegemony, through its new links with Spain (Ch. 14), to its long-standing ambitions for political domination.

To describe the emphasis on positive involvement and cooperative security as the 'Williamist' view of Britain's rôle in Europe is surely right. For whatever else contributed to the transformation of her foreign policy and outlook on her neighbours in the generation after the Revolution, almost everything had its origins in the events of 1688. It stemmed from the fact that Britain's 'Great Deliverer' was a Dutchman, whose whole understanding of Continental politics and experience of Continental diplomacy exceeded by far that of any English king since the Plantagenets. When the Convention offered the crown to William in February 1689, it was in effect offering the supreme direction of English foreign policy to a prince who, from his vantage point in the Low Countries, had seen in England a kingdom of great potential capacity, much of it still unused and unrealised: not only making no effective contribution to the Protestant cause but in serious danger of being lost to the contrary cause he most abominated, that of Catholic absolutism. From the day he accepted the crown, therefore, he set out single-mindedly to ensure that this new kingdom of his would at last fulfil its potential, by taking on the European rôle for which he, at least, could see that it was fitted.

It is easy enough now to see how right he was. England was in many ways admirably equipped for a more active part on the European stage, and certainly for a pivotal rôle in the opposition to France. Her militant Protestantism – a tradition which stretched back to the 1560s – and her growing wealth, her unique strategic situation and of course her sea power were ideal qualifications. But all this was less than transparent at the time. In 1689 relatively few Englishmen shared their new King's vision or even understood the full implications of the war into which he promptly drew them (Ch. 14). He himself made the task of conversion more difficult by his 'take it or leave it' approach and his deliberate preference for using foreign instruments, such as Hopp and Bentinck, in the conduct of important negotiations (when he was not handling them in person). So for a long time the new policies, even when they were comprehended, were not generally popular; and neither was William. There were times when he despaired of success, and never more so than in the years immediately after the Treaty of Ryswick when he was preoccupied with the world-wide contingencies that were to be anticipated when King Carlos II of Spain died. In 1698, for instance, William wrote to the Grand Pensionary of Holland: 'the people here are now so foolishly engrossed with themselves, that they do not pay the least attention to what is going on in foreign countries'; it was, he added, as if 'this island is the only thing on the face of the earth'.[4] In fact, sheer frustration brought him soon after this to contemplate abdication. But he battled on, and in the end, with a great deal of gratuitous help from Louis XIV, who in the crisis of 1701 played his cards with singular recklessness and arrogance (140, *71–2*), William achieved his goal. We at least can see what he himself, sadly, had no means of knowing on his death-bed in March 1702, that from that time on Britain would never again, for any length of time, contract out of Europe. There would be brief interludes of isolationism or partial withdrawal. One of the most striking was to occur in the mid–1730s, during Walpole's hegemony; another was to follow in the 1760s. But there would never again be any protracted period when Britain would turn her back completely on her international responsibilities.

Responsibility was what Restoration foreign policy had, most of all, lacked (Ch. 6). In objectives, at least – though not, to begin with, in method (below, pp. 255–6) – responsibility was the hallmark of the new foreign policy of post-Revolution Britain. All states must consider, and to a large extent pursue, self-interest in their relations with their neighbours; Britain from 1689 to 1714 was no exception. 'Responsibility' in foreign affairs begins, first of all, at the point where *national* self-interest begins to replace the selfish aims of a ruler, a family or a governing clique. Charles II's policies had been governed to an unhealthy degree by personal ends. William III's worst enemies could not have claimed that this was true of him (however much some might accuse him of pro-Dutch bias), and although under Queen Anne Marlborough was charged by his more inveterate opponents with perpetuating war for his own enrichment, the accusation was unworthy and unjust. However, to follow a truly responsible foreign policy entails more than the substitution of public for private selfishness. It means the replacement of narrow, blinkered national self-interest by *enlightened* national self-interest as the chief motivator: the recognition that with most problems in foreign affairs there are a number of different responsibilities, obligations and opportunities which have to be reconciled, and that, for example, it may be prudent as well as morally respectable not to ignore responsibilities to one's allies. That Britain moved some way along this road under the last two Stuarts, in step with her growth in political maturity, can be seen by looking at the particular national interests which the policies of post-Revolution governments towards Europe sought to serve in the first quarter of a century after 1688.

Three such interests eventually came to override all others; and we shall observe in another work (*The Age of Oligarchy*, Ch. 4) how their extension into the decades after 1714 lend a basic continuity and coherence to British policy over a much longer period. One was the need to preserve a balance of power between the great dynastic forces of the Continent; for all English political leaders with any pretensions to statesmanship came to recognise over the first twenty-five years after the Glorious Revolution that their own country had nothing to gain and much to lose from an unhealthy concentration of territory and influence in the hands of a single power in any major quarter of Europe. There were also commercial objectives which pressed insistently for attention: the necessity of protecting from foreign threats the country's existing trading markets, merchant shipping and sources of supply and, beyond that, of promoting by treaty or war new commercial opportunities and making fresh colonial acquisitions advantageous to British trade. (To a generation still steeped in the mercantilist assumptions underlying the Navigation Acts (Ch. 3), it was still axiomatic that to bring economic benefit to the Mother Country was solely what colonies existed for.) Of higher priority still for many was the acceptance that Britain's influence abroad must be used to secure the Protestant succession at home. For quite apart from the unthinkable domestic repercussions of a successful usurpation, with foreign aid, by another Catholic king, it was taken for granted that such a calamity must bring about the inevitable reduction, if not destruction, of Britain's independence of action in her relations with her neighbours.

The notion that it was vital in the ultimate interests of Britain herself to ensure that a power-equilibrium be maintained on the continent of Europe was the toughest of all the lessons taught by that stern schoolmaster, King William. And it was one that was only instilled into the average parliamentary politician by the hard experience of the years from 1698 to 1702, when the vast dominions of the last Habsburg king of Spain at last came on to the table. Down to 1697 it would be more accurate to say that the concept of the Balance of Power played a dominant part in William's personal thinking (these being the years when *his* foreign policy and England's were largely synonymous) without being a conscious priority with most of his subjects, save a minority of leading Whigs. It was the threats which France represented to English security and to her Protestant line and religion, rather than any generalised fear of the destabilising effects of French penetration of the Low Countries, Germany or Italy, that enabled William to get unstinting financial support for his war policy from the three Parliaments of 1689–97. After 1702, however, the Balance of Power became a prime concern of every Whig regime, from the Junto under Queen Anne to the Pelham administration of 1746–54, and of every Whig foreign secretary (or principal Secretary of State) in the line from Sunderland (1706–10) through Stanhope and Townshend to Carteret and Newcastle [D.2]. But it is also important to take note that this same 'balance of Europe', as the then Tory ministers called it, had been laid down as a basic platform of *their* foreign policy after the settlement of Utrecht, in one of Anne's last Speeches from the Throne. In the draft prepared for her by her chief minister, Oxford, she claimed to

> have set before me for my rule the example of those of my predecessors who have been most renowned for their wisdom . . . They made it their practice and their maxim to hold the balance between the contending powers of Europe, to be the peace-makers, and by managing of it so that where Britain cast in the weight, that gave the preference.[5]

Although the 'balance of Europe' was still thought of primarily in terms of western, central and southern Europe, involving most obviously the rival interests of Habsburg and Bourbon, British governments already had to be aware of, and prepared to react to, conflicts or the danger of disequilibrium in two other parts of the Continent, the North and the South-East. The latter in its turn was closely linked with the situation in Asia Minor. In the North there were four leading powers: the Swedish Empire of Charles XI (d. 1697) and Charles XII; Peter the Great's Russia; Denmark-Norway; and Brandenburg-Prussia under the Hohenzollerns. Russia was a large but in 1689 largely unknown quantity, still thought of far more as a part of Asia than of Europe, whereas Brandenburg-Prussia had been the rising star in Germany in the second half of the seventeenth century, and for his support of the Habsburg cause its Elector, Frederick III (1688–1713) was to secure from the Emperor in 1701 the title of King *in* Prussia (as Frederick I) and have that title formally endorsed by his grateful Grand Alliance partners at Utrecht. To the South-East the Ottoman Empire still enveloped as recently as 1683 the entire European as well as Asian coastline of the Black Sea (except for Circassia), and the whole of the Aegean coast, extending also up the east shore of the Adriatic to Croatia, within less than a hundred miles of Trieste. The Turks, in fact, then occupied more European territory than the areas of France and Spain combined. They had swallowed up over the centuries not only the Balkans, Greece and virtually the whole of present-day Albania and Yugoslavia, but Transylvania and Hungary, where in the North-West they had a frontier only a few days' march from Vienna, and much of the land between the rivers Dniester and Dnieper to within some 30 miles of Kiev. Only the Emperor had the resources to resist a renewed Turkish advance into the heart of Germany and Bohemia, and since 1684 Austria had been the core of the 'Holy League', whose other members, shored up by Papal subsidies, were Venice, Poland and (from 1686) Russia. The League enjoyed success in the 1680s, until the war against the Ottomans was overtaken and overshadowed by the mightier conflict in the West. Even so, there was still a huge imbalance of power in the South-East in 1689, and although, at the Peace of Carlowitz in 1699, the Turks lost most of Hungary, Transylvania and Podolia for ever, that only partially redressed the territorial scales. It is also worth remembering that as yet the 'Eastern Question', in its later-eighteenth- and nineteenth-century form, did not exist. It was only in 1700 that Russia gained a foothold on the Black Sea (at Azov) for the first time, and even that she lost again in 1711. Russia's main external concerns under Peter the Great were elsewhere.

During the seventeenth century England had acquired a tangible commercial stake both in the rivalries of the northern powers and in the course of Euro-Turkish relations. The effects of prolonged military activity and political uncertainty in these areas were viewed to begin with primarily in the light of their effects on the Baltic and Muscovy trade or the Levant trade (Ch. 3). But after 1689, during the long struggle with France, it also became an interest of William III, Anne and their ministers to minimise the drain from these distant theatres on the resources of vital allies whose efforts were badly needed in the West. Austria presented the biggest problem, since she remained at war with the Turks down to 1699; even thereafter, right through the Spanish Succession War, she continued to be at some risk of further embroilment in the South-East, especially from 1711 when the Porte began to manifest a dangerous bellicosity once again. There was a problem of a similar kind with Prussia, too, after the outbreak of the Great Northern War in 1700. It was no coincidence that English mediation between the Emperor and the Sultan helped to bring about the Carlowitz settlement in 1699, a time when anxiety was running high in the West at the possible effects of Carlos II's imminent death, and William III was patently fearful that Leopold I might continue to have his attention distracted south-eastwards. Likewise, British subsidies and the arguments of British diplomats at Berlin were influential in keeping Prussian eyes fixed after 1702 more or less firmly westwards, with only the occasional hungering glance at the North German outposts of the Swedish Empire. In the case of the Ottoman Empire, specifically, there was a religious, as well as a commercial and military motive for the makers of post-Revolution foreign policy to take account of. The traditional English prejudice against the Turk as a Mahommedan as well as a barbarous alien was active still: witness the spontaneous joy with which England greeted the news of the relief of Vienna from its Turkish besiegers in 1683. It would be small exaggeration to say that for many Englishmen the main (and, for some, the only) recommendation of the Catholic and absolutist Austrian Habsburgs as allies against Louis XIV's France after 1689 was the immense kudos they acquired in the 1680s and 1690s as defenders of Europe against the Ottoman menace. There was, therefore, a predisposition in London throughout this period to regard with approval any successes by the Imperialists and Venetians in striving to redress the grossly uneven balance between Christian and Muslim power in south-east Europe. And this attitude was further hardened from 1689 onwards by the knowledge that France was the natural ally of the Porte in the West, by a tradition going back to the sixteenth century, and that, as England's chief competitors in selling cloth to the Levant, French merchants derived great advantage from the complicity of Turkish officials there (132, *361*). Nevertheless, it was in Britain's interests to remain in good diplomatic standing at Constantinople, as the maintenance of an ambassador permanently there from 1687 onwards indicates; it is significant that, just as one ambassador, Paget, played a key part in the Carlowitz peace negotiations, so one of his successors, Sutton, mediated at Passarowitz at the end of the next Austro-Turkish war, in 1718 (*The Age of Oligarchy*, Ch. 4).

In the North, British policy had to respond to a far more fluid situation, especially after 1700. Sweden had built up a very powerful position in the Baltic in the course of the seventeenth century. On the northern seaboard the Swedes held Finland; to the west, the four provinces of Karelia, Ingria, Esthonia and Livonia, which blocked Russia's outlet to the sea; and in Germany, the important ports of Stralsund and Stettin and the two secularised bishoprics of Bremen and Verden, which controlled the mouths of the Elbe and Weser rivers. But the Baltic was not a Swedish lake – Denmark, for instance, still controlled Norway, and therefore the Sound – and after the Glorious Revolution Britain's traditional friendship with the House of Vasa, stimulated by the latter's militant Protestant-ism and Sweden's value to England as a source of iron imports and naval stores (her economic links with seventeenth-century Scotland were even closer), was strengthened by Charles XI's cooperative attitude to William of Orange's invasion in 1688. Anglo-Swedish relations cooled in the 1690s, after William failed to coax Charles into the anti-French alliance, but at least he had the satisfaction of seeing the Baltic powers remain neutral in the Nine Years' War and no threat posed either to peace or to English trade in the North during that period.

It was the accession of a 14-year-old king, Charles XII, in 1697 which, by rousing the greed and stirring up the desire for revenge of Sweden's neighbours, threw the whole Baltic situation into turmoil. The Great Northern War which broke out in 1700 was not to end until 1721. The rout of the Russians at Narva and the early triumphs of Sweden's brilliant young soldier-king over the coalition of Denmark, Poland/Saxony and Russia (events which coincided with the advent and early years of the Spanish Succession War) appeared to have made nonsense of the ambitions of Sweden's enemies. To these victories an Anglo-Dutch fleet contributed, in fulfilment of treaty obligations to Sweden, by helping to put Denmark effectively out of the war for nine years; and they encouraged British diplomacy to concentrate on coaxing Charles XII into making peace on moder-ately favourable terms and turning his attention to the war against Louis XIV. But this aim was thwarted by Charles's own rising ambitions, and after his invasion of Russia, culminating in catastrophic defeat at Poltava (1709), and his four years of virtual captivity in Turkey, British policy inevitably switched its emphasis (24a [Hatton], *670* and *passim*). Whigs and Tories alike now sought, mostly by diplomatic means but also through one (unsuccessful) threat of force in 1714, to prevent the threatened collapse of Swedish power and the partition of her Baltic empire. And it seemed to the leaders of both parties particularly undesirable that the unpopular Russians, who had taken an uncooperative attitude, to put it mildly, towards British trade in the North, should be the principal beneficiaries of Sweden's plight. Such was the situation in August 1714, when the accession of a Hanoverian king in Britain introduced into it a new and very disturbing element (*The Age of Oligarchy*, Ch. 4).

It is interesting to observe the reaction of the Tory ministers of 1710–14 to 'the balance of the north',[6] because it reminds us again that between them and their Whig predecessors, as between them and Godolphin and Marlborough, there was more common ground over the *aims* of foreign policy than is usually supposed. And this was true even of western, central and southern Europe, where concern over the balance of power was most pressing. Here it was not

William's objective of preserving an acceptable equipoise between Bourbon and Habsburg interests which divided opinion, but rather the Williamist *method* of effecting it, by a 'mutual security' policy – by bringing Britain into the very heart of a Continental alliance system on the grand scale, as he did in 1689 and again in 1701. In the political nation at large it would not be far wrong to say that, outside the Whig party, 'Grand Alliances' only here and there commanded ungrudging support for at least thirty years after the Revolution (141, [M.A. Thomson], *Ch. 15 passim*). And this, of course, was mainly because for so long after 1688 a collective security policy had to be directed towards containing the overweening power of France, and events proved that this could only be done by a prolonged effort of arms. It seemed to commit Britain not only to ambitious Continental combinations, as such, but to becoming the linchpin, and paymaster, of great war coalitions. This was a rôle which she was destined to play out again and again before the final defeat of Napoleon in 1815. But in the eyes of a generation wholly unprepared by past experience for such binding and continuing commitment, it was inevitably a controversial rôle. Had either of the Partition Treaties of 1698 and 1700, William's most resourceful exercises in balance of power diplomacy (Ch. 14), achieved their ends and succeeded in staving off the Spanish Succession War, conversion might well have come more quickly; though not inevitably so, for the Italian terms of the second Treaty [H(x)] proved highly contentious on economic grounds, and the way they were negotiated by William also gave much offence.

It may be that only the experience of a long period of peace could have reconciled Britons as a whole to their country's regular participation in a network of treaty compacts, with their complex of interlocking commitments. But to Whigs, at least, such ambitious constructions, and the diplomatic balancing-acts they usually entailed, had become part of political second nature by 1714, and on coming back to power they soon revealed that it was to be an integral part of the diplomacy of post-Utrecht Europe, as it had been of the war years down to 1711. By 1718 they had even managed to resurrect 'the Old System' of alliances between Britain, the United Provinces and Austria, which five years earlier had appeared to be destroyed beyond repair (*The Age of Oligarchy*, Ch. 4); (141 [Thomson: 'Self-Determination']; 146a). The conversion of the Tories was inevitably slower. Yet it is important to remember that even Bolingbroke, the principal Secretary of State in Anne's last ministry, who went on record as having 'looked [in 1710] upon the political principles which had generally prevailed in our government from the Revolution in 1688 to be destructive of our true interest',[7] never contemplated unduly prolonging Britain's self-inflicted isolation once the Utrecht treaties were signed. The evidence is clear that, if he had had his way, new alliances would soon have been negotiated, with France, Spain and possibly Savoy, to replace the old Austro-Dutch 'system' which he, even more than the earl of Oxford, had so rudely dismantled. As for Oxford himself, this first, and last, Tory prime minister of the eighteenth century claimed with genuine pride in 1717, in reply to the impeachment charges against him, that his administration had left 'the balance of Europe . . . upon a better foot than it has been for an hundred years past'. And indeed most Whigs would have conceded after the event, if not in the bitterly charged atmosphere of 1711–12, that there could have been no real balance in a settlement which had left Spain in the hands of a man who had now become Emperor.

The Tories of 1710–14 were much more open in advertising their commitment to the second major objective of post-Revolution policy, the pursuit of commercial and colonial advantage. It was their boast that Tory peacemaking, preceded by a final flourish against French North America, would secure greater benefits for British trade and more colonial concessions than the Whig insistence on fighting on after 1711. In the event, because of the failure of the Quebec expedition and the rejection of the Anglo-French Commerce Treaty by Parliament (above, pp. 206–7), the harvest proved rather less bountiful than Bolingbroke had hoped. None the less, it was still an impressive one. Commercial calculations had played next to no part in involving England in the Nine Years' War, and catastrophes such as the loss of the Smyrna convoy, as well as the heavy depredations of the Dunkirk privateers (Ch. 14), were hardly likely to endear Williamist policies to merchants, Whig or Tory. To many the old commercial rivalry with the Dutch was at least as live an issue at this stage as that with France (140, *69–70*); although ironically, some of the strongest opposition to the Second Partition Treaty of 1700 was generated by those who felt that, if it took effect, it would jeopardise the valuable English Mediterranean trade by handing too great an advantage in Italy to the French. The events of 1701, however (Ch. 14), finally awakened the legislators, as well as the merchants, of a country whose life-blood was trade to the vital importance to English interests of the disposal of every part of the Spanish Empire. For the first time, 'a danger of French economic predominance was added to that of political supremacy in Europe' (129b, *157*). It is a striking fact that from then on commercial or colonial terms figure in most treaties of alliance, and in every peace treaty, which Britain concluded in the next sixty-two years. In the short run we see this in the terms of the Hague Treaty of 1701, the second Methuen Treaty and the first Barrier Treaty [H(xi–xiii)], as well as in the two treaties of commerce negotiated as part of the final settlement with France and Spain in 1713–14. Whether it was, in the last resort, *worth* fighting great wars to achieve economic ends – wars likely in general to be infinitely more costly than the seventeenth-century mercantilist wars fought against the Dutch – was a question still wide open as Britain moved from the Stuart into the Hanoverian age. And it was to remain a matter for active, and sometimes furious, debate until almost the end of Walpole's ministry (*The Age of Oligarchy*, Ch. 4).

Even given the dangerous threat to English trade which a Bourbon succession in Spain posed by 1701, it is improbable that William III could have carried a united nation into a new war in 1702 if Louis XIV had not, in September 1701, recognised Prince James Edward Stuart as the rightful King of England and Scotland. He did so, moreover, a mere three and a half months after the Westminster Parliament, by the Act of Settlement, had determined that the crown of England would descend after Princess Anne's death to the Protestant house of Hanover. Securing international guarantees of the titles of William and Anne to the crowns of the post-Revolution monarchy, and thereafter maintaining and safeguarding the future Protestant succession, together constituted the third great priority of British governments of this period in conducting foreign affairs. It was also the objective most generally understood and supported, not only in Parliament itself, but through the entire island, south of the Highland line. The question of William's own right inevitably figured in the Grand Alliance treaties of 1689 and in the Ryswick settlement [H(vii, viii)]: not for nothing has the Nine Years' War acquired as one of its alternative labels that of 'the War of the English Succession' (above, p. 241 n.1). The Protestant Succession was an absolutely key point in the amended Hague Treaty of 1702, re-defining the renewed war aims of England, Holland and the Emperor [H(xi.6)]. The military safeguard clause written into the Townshend Barrier Treaty with the Dutch in 1709 has been referred to already. Finally, without a secret French guarantee to renounce support of the Pretender in 1711, Queen Anne's last Tory ministry would never have dared – indeed would never have contemplated – carrying forward the separate negotiations which were to end round the tables of Utrecht. To what extent the Jacobite threat continued to play a prime part in the foreign policy of George I and his ministers long after the 'Fifteen Rebellion had come and gone is a matter for another work.

The frightening cost in money and lives of the Spanish Succession War affected every politician of any maturity who emerged from it. It had in truth, as Bolingbroke said with real passion in 1713, been 'such a war as I heartily wish our children's children may never see'.[8] And this was not only a party view. When we reflect that the events of 1702–13 were enough to turn even a fire-eating young Whig like Robert Walpole into a confirmed pacifist for the rest of his days, it is no very difficult matter to appreciate the revulsion against Britain's new relationship with Europe which both the wars against Louis XIV provoked among some thousands of backwoods gentry, among men who were not pro-fessional politicians, who were instinctively Little Englanders and frequently xenophobes, but also taxpayers. We can relish the absurdities of the kind of archetypal squire satirised by Addison in 1716, who 'declared frankly that he had always been against all treaties and alliances with foreigners' and who even 'expatiated on the inconveniencies of trade, that carried from us the commodities of our country', which 'would be the happiest . . . in the world, provided we would live within ourselves'.[9] Yet the satire was close to the bone, and we must still bear in mind that it was with the votes and interests of a host of country gentlemen, not so many miles removed in mentality and outlook from Addison's bucolic companion, that the Tories were returned to power with thumping majorities in 1710 and 1713.

Was the Whig supremacy after 1714, therefore, utterly essential to the long-term preservation of the revolution in British foreign policy? One of the arguments of this chapter has been that it was not: that Tory governments would certainly have embraced commitment to Europe with less enthusiasm, and would have tried to evade some at least of its implications which they most disliked and distrusted; but that there were other implications – and basic ones – which they could not have escaped. Some changes had gone too far already by 1710, and still more by 1714, to be reversible. And because of them, it is not credible that responsible Tory critics of Williamist and Whig policies towards Europe, as opposed to their blinkered, ill-informed supporters in country manor houses and parsonages, could seriously have allowed the tail for long to wag the dog. Indeed, Linda Colley reminds us that in the late 1730s the small but active Tory opposition in the House of Commons could be as critical as the dissident Whigs of Walpole's phase of pacifist neutralism (81a, *223–4*; cf. *94*).

Possibly the decisive reason why no ministry after the Peace of Utrecht, whether Whig or Tory, could for long have pursued a thoroughly irresponsible foreign policy is that it was not only the course but the whole conduct of policy which had fundamentally changed since the Revolution. By the early eighteenth century both the influences which shaped relations with European powers and the methods of carrying policies out had undergone as great a transformation since the 1680s as the policies themselves. In two revealing essays Mark Thomson and G.C. Gibbs have explained how these alterations came about: partly, as we would expect, as a result of the Glorious Revolution, but mainly as a consequence of the storm which erupted in 1701 over William's Partition Treaties and the impeachments of his Whig ex-ministers for their acquiescence in agreements in which their direct involvement had been nil (145a; 140). The resulting crisis in Parliament and orchestrated outcry in the country gave the death blow to that brand of secret royal diplomacy which had plagued England since Charles II's day (Ch. 6). From now on no monarch, and no minister, would dare to involve the country in a basic re-routing of foreign policy without attempting to carry first the Cabinet and then Parliament with him. Closely linked with this in its effects was the extent to which a more educated public opinion outside Westminster could now be mobilised and brought to bear on the politicians. The early eighteenth century furnishes many examples of such influences being exerted on policy, whether through the press (as with the pamphleteering of Defoe in 1701 and of Swift in 1711–12) or through influential pressure-groups, such as the merchants engaged in the Mediterranean trade or the East India interest (145b).

All these changes, together with the regular involvement after 1701 of at least one of the Secretaries of State in the making of foreign policy and the growing formalisation (pre-Walpole) of Cabinet government (Ch. 13), not to mention the much greater use of orthodox diplomatic channels,[10] meant that the aims of British foreign policy in the eighteenth century simply had to bear a far closer relation to national aspirations and interests than was the case before the Revolution. It is probably fair to say that every major line of policy pursued under Queen Anne (as later under the first two Georges), including the shifts which followed changes of ministry, could command, for a period at least, a reasonably substantial body of parliamentary and public support. Conversely, whenever this solid base of support began to crumble, and became no more than the opinion of a minority, it always led before long to a change of policy, and sometimes to a change of administration in the process. The setbacks suffered by the Tories in 1701–2, after their prevarications over the Spanish Succession and, more spectacularly, the loss of power in 1710 by the Whigs, who had appeared to be favouring a policy of war to the last guinea to enforce total surrender on the Bourbons, soon illustrated how drastic the effects of the new accountability could be.[11] When Walpole in 1739 was forced by a great parliamentary and popular outcry to abandon his policy of conciliation with Spain (*The Age of Oligarchy*, Chs. 4, 5), he was bowing before a wind that had first begun to blow nearly forty years before. Perhaps he had forgotten the warning words of his more experienced Whig Cabinet colleague, Lord Sunderland, as long ago as 1716: that it was folly to toy with reactivating the 'notion [which] is nothing but the old Tory one, that England can subsist by itself whatever becomes of the rest of Europe, which has been so justly exploded ever since the Revolution'.[12] From any reasonable historical perspective Sunderland was right. For by the time George I succeeded Anne, Parliament, the press and public opinion had all played their part, along with other far-reaching political and constitutional developments since 1688, in decisively laying the ghost of Little England.

---

1. No specific fortress towns were earmarked for possession by the Dutch, but it was stipulated that the southern Netherlands 'should serve for a dyke, rampart and "barrier", as had been the case in the past . . .': P. Geyl, *The Netherlands in the 17th Century, Part Two, 1648–1715* (1964), p. 278. For the First Barrier Treaty, see also H(xiii), especially cl. 3.
2. G. Symcox, 'Britain and Victor Amadeus II: or, The Use and Abuse of Allies', in S. B. Baxter, ed., *England's Rise to Greatness, 1660–1763* (Berkeley and Los Angeles, 1983); Geyl, op. cit., pp. 294–5, 317–18.
3. It should be noted that envoys and resident ministers corresponded unofficially with private individuals as well as with the Secretaries of State and their officials.
4. R. Grimblot, ed., *Letters of William III and Louis XIV and their Ministers* (2 vols, 1848), I, p. 184: William to Heinsius, 15 Feb 1698. Towards the end of another 'miserable session of Parliament' in 1699, William lamented 'the impossibility of finding a remedy'. Grimblot, op. cit., II, p 324.
5. BL Loan 29/7/6: draft speech, 19 Feb 1714. See further in Holmes and Speck (5), p. 96.
6. Lord Townshend's phrase, to James Stanhope, 16 Oct 1716: W. Coxe, *Memoirs of . . . Sir Robert Walpole* (1798), II, p. 119.
7. Henry St John, Viscount Bolingbroke, *A Letter to Sir William Wyndham* (1717/1753), p. 20.
8. *Letters and Correspondence of . . . Viscount Bolingbroke* (ed. G. Parke, 1798), IV, p 19: to earl of Shrewsbury, 29 March.
9. Joseph Addison, *The Freeholder*, no. 22, 5 Mar 1716 (ed. J. Leheny, Oxford, 1979) pp. 133–4.
10. See D.B. Horn, *The British Diplomatic Service, 1689–1789* (Oxford, 1961).
11. This, however, was not the only factor in the Whig *débâcle* of 1710. For the belief that the Whigs were pursuing a vendetta against the Church of England at that time, see Ch. 23 below.
12. W. Coxe, *Memoirs of . . . Walpole*, II, p 128: Sunderland to Lord Townshend, [31 Oct] 1716.

CHAPTER 16

The fruits of war: I – The New Executive

The ultimate accountability of the Crown to Parliament and its growing responsiveness to public opinion, which were such important features of the transformation of British foreign policy between 1689 and 1714, have to be understood in relation to the wider constitutional framework within which Britain was governed and conducted her politics by the early eighteenth century. Three parts of that framework which helped to mould the more responsible foreign policies of Queen Anne's reign and George I's – the genesis of the Cabinet, the evolution of a prime ministerial office, and the more formal development of Secretarial responsibility – have already been identified as crucial by-products of the two uniquely demanding wars of the post-Revolution period (Ch. 13). Furthermore, the regular sessions of Parliament at Westminster, which were utterly basic to the new institutional context in which foreign policy was thereafter made, can be seen in much the same light. While Parliament might conceivably have established its permanent, annual rôle in the system of government after the Glorious Revolution even if William III had never taken England to war, it was unquestionably the exigencies of twenty years of war finance [see G, *passim*] which *guaranteed* it that rôle.

However, the overriding need for post-Revolution governments to direct, organise and, not least, pay for the two most complex and costly wars in England's experience had repercussions which went well beyond even such vital constitutional changes as these. Two of the most fruitful developments which late seventeenth- and early eighteenth-century Britain experienced, and from which future generations profited, can be very largely traced to the stimulus of those same pressing necessities. Firstly, in the period between the last years of Charles II's reign and the end of George I's, a great change came over both the working and the personnel of executive government, much of it being called for because the administrative machinery of the Restoration monarchy was too primitive and too inefficiently manned to be capable of coping with the war demands of 1689–1713. Over a rather shorter period, beginning in the 1690s, both public and private finance were so far transformed in their institutions and in their methods that we still live today with the consequences of some of the innovations made then. In this chapter and the next we shall consider each of these developments in turn and assess some of their implications for eighteenth-century Britain.

In the thirty years between 1683 and 1713, but most of all after 1688, the machinery and methods of executive government in England were drastically overhauled and reformed, and after 1707 some of these changes began to affect the Scots as well. Of course, we must get them in perspective. The basically

Household government of the Middle Ages had undergone reorganisation in the 1530s, under Thomas Cromwell, although many of its features proved impermanent. A similar fate, though for different reasons, overtook the next important period of experiment and expansion in administration, that associated with the English Republic in the 1650s.[1] Of more direct relevance to what took place after 1688 is the fact that Restoration England had also witnessed some very important, and in this case durable, administrative changes (14 [Tomlinson]; 110a; 122). The 1670s and 1680s had, for example, seen the end of tax farming, as one by one the collection of the customs, excises, hearth tax and postal revenues ceased to be put out to contract and became direct government responsibilities. In the two decades after 1667 there had also been a great extension of Treasury control over both the revenue and the spending departments, and important reforms of the Treasury office itself and its procedures (111b). Two able and energetic Secretaries of the Treasury, Downing (1667–71) and Guy (1679–89), played influential parts here, but the dominant figure was Lawrence Hyde, earl of Rochester, the political head of the Treasury for much of the 1680s [D.1] and the chief inspiration behind the efficiency campaign of that decade. This campaign left only a few areas of the executive untouched in a major effort to improve the financial viability and the naval and military capability of the monarchy during the Stuart Reaction. Two very significant by-products of these post-Restoration administrative developments must also be noted. For one thing, they involved an expansion (at the least, a doubling) of the personnel required to service the reformed executive, and in the process the creation of by far the two biggest government departments yet seen in England, the new-modelled Customs (1671) and the Excise (1683). At the same time they fostered a new ethos in government, rudimentary as yet but recognisably bureaucratic. This was inspired by a small élite of public servants of high ability and dedication, among whom Samuel Pepys and William Blathwayt, as well as George Downing and Henry Guy, were perhaps the most influential. Under Guy's regime in the 1680s, for example, Treasury clerks who showed their mettle were for the first time allowed a fair prospect of security.

On the eve of the French wars, therefore, England had already had an executive, staffed by some 4,000 officials at all levels (122), which had progressed a great deal since the antiquated regime of Clarendon and Lord Treasurer Southampton in the mid–1660s. Conversely, much still remained to be done after 1713 before a system which aspired to *overall* efficiency and economy as ends in themselves could come into being. For rather more than a decade following the Peace of Utrecht the wind of change of the war years continued to blow, at least as a stiff, bracing breeze. Under both the Treasury regimes of Sunderland and Walpole the Excise department grew larger still and further extended its field of activity, acquiring responsibility for the leather duties and for Walpole's innovatory bonded warehouse scheme of 1723 (*The Age of Oligarchy*, Ch. 5). Customs administration benefited from the rationalisation measures of the years 1721–5, for which Walpole supplied the political drive and Charles Carkesse, the long-serving secretary to the Customs Board, the nuts and bolts in the form of a comprehensive revision of the 'Book of Rates'. At the same time, in an attempt to staunch the ceaseless loss of revenue from Scottish customs frauds, substantial progress was made towards greater administrative uniformity between England and Scotland (283c, *275–83*). After 1725, however, there ensued a long period of relative quiescence, and by the 1730s – the decade in which the violent opposition to Walpole's controversial Excise Scheme finally cooled his ardour for reform (*The Age of Oligarchy*, Ch. 5) – signs of complacency and stagnation in the executive, and of some misuse of patronage for political or self-interested ends, are becoming increasingly apparent. Not until the failures of the American War of 1775–83 had shocked the political nation into anxious scrutiny of its institutions (*The Age of Oligarchy*, Ch. 22) was there a sustained, determined attempt at rehabilitation.

Nevertheless, the period of the wars against Louis XIV, prefaced by the reforming surge of the 1680s, still stands out in retrospect as a period of sea-change in the process of central government, the most important to take place before the nineteenth century. There are four distinct aspects of the late Stuart transformation of the executive to concern us in this chapter: physical growth; a more scientific approach to government; committee rule, and the advance of professionalism.

The physical growth of the administration was indeed striking. Nothing remotely comparable had been experienced before (28, *112ff.*). This is true whether one measures growth structurally or in terms of personnel, where even between 1688 and 1714 there was, on a rough calculation, a trebling of men employed by the executive in civil fields (and this in spite of the abolition of the Hearth Tax in 1689 and the disbandment of the numerous officials who had collected it). Looking back at the pattern of all this growth, our first impressions may be of some unevenness and even irrationality. For instance, among the traditional departments of state, the Treasury and the offices of the Secretary of State had to carry a tremendously increased load of work in wartime with only modest increases of staff, whereas the 175 men employed by the Ordnance Office in 1667 had grown to nearly 450 by 1704.[2] The government's representation abroad, near negligible in Charles II's reign, also expanded substantially and by Anne's reign such specialists as Stepney, Whitworth, Stanyon and Henry Davenant had emerged as recognisable prototypes of the career diplomat. The oldest department of all, the Exchequer, presented a bizarre contrast in itself: conservative to the point of fossilisation in carrying out most of its ancient functions, yet forced to come to terms with the new world after 1689, when it acquired an office for managing Exchequer bills, an Annuity Teller's office and eventually, between 1710 and 1714, 51 new officials to manage – of all things – state lotteries.

However, there is a much more clear-cut pattern in the way war ensured the continuing and vigorous growth of the younger departments set up in the few decades before 1688: the Post Office, the Navy Office, the new Customs department, and the great creation of the 1680s, the Excise. By 1708 the number of regular employees on the Customs had risen to around 1,900, and the Board also employed a large body of 'extraordinary men' (roughly 1,000 in London alone) who were taken on strength whenever weight of business required. Some idea of the scale of the expansion of the permanent establishment between

James II's reign and the middle of Queen Anne's can be gleaned by looking at just two of the important outports. Between 1687 and 1708 the staff at Bristol doubled, from 57 to 115, and that at Plymouth increased from 33 to 56. The employees of the Post Office probably quadrupled in the years from 1650 to 1714, much of the increase coming after 1685. As for the Excise, Defoe wrote in the 1720s of the head office of the department, housed in what had formerly been a large private mansion in the Old Jewry: 'in this one office is managed an immense weight of business, and they have in pay, as I am told, near four thousand officers' (3, *I, 340*). This is sometimes discounted as a typical flight of Defoe's journalistic imagination, but in fact research reveals that the estimate was commendably close to the mark (122, *256*; but cf. 133, *66* for the year 1726). The meticulous John Chamberlayne, in his periodic review of government establishments, had estimated the number of 'common' excise officials or gaugers – that is, those in the bottom grade of the service alone – as 'near 2,000' in the middle of Anne's reign and at some 2,700 fifteen years later.[3] The army of excisemen that was to become the bogy of Robert Walpole's opponents was palpably on the march well before the end of the wars against Louis XIV.

Almost equally important to the physical growth of the executive was the way the wars themselves threw up a crop of completely new government departments. The office of Trade and Plantations, under the Board of Trade, was the most prestigious; the Transport Office one of several destined to be wound up when hostilities were over. The most remarkable of the *arrivistes* was a complex of new revenue departments. Seven in all came into being during the French wars, although one of them, the Glass Office, disappeared in 1700. The largest of the newcomers were the Salt Office, the Stamp Office and the Leather Office. Those three departments alone may well have accounted for 1,500 additional civil servants by the end of the Spanish Succession War.

Even more significant for the future than physical growth was the fact that in this period an attempt was made in some earnest to adopt a more scientific approach to the problems of government. The progress made in the 1650s towards producing order in the administration of the English Republic and modernising its civil service[4] had been largely abandoned after the Restoration. Small wonder, then, that in the new steps taken towards more methodical, rational government after 1680 there were some glaring inconsistencies and not a few stumbles along the way. While on the one hand the greatest scientific genius of the seventeenth century, Sir Isaac Newton, was presiding over the Royal Mint and supervising reforms there, certain sectors of the executive remained stubbornly anachronistic. The Exchequer, for one, was still cluttered with sinecurists when peace arrived in 1713, less, perhaps, for political and patronage reasons (at this time) than is often thought; the main factor was the sheer lack of time under wartime pressures for the planned reform of the drawing-board. And yet, reform, systematisation and rationalisation did take place. For one thing, in all the new departments created during the wars, as in those established since the 1650s, realistic salaries replaced the traditional method of remuneration, passed down from Tudor and early Stuart times, based on fees and perks. Furthermore, the Treasury quite frequently approved increases in salaries to match heavier workloads or new responsibilities. Thus many emoluments in the Customs were rightly held to be too low in the 1680s and were duly adjusted, while the Commissioners of the Stamp Office were awarded a rise of 33.5 per cent after the imposition of new stamp duties in 1712. Another advance lay in the introduction of contributory pensions. In the Excise department, always in the van of rational progress, a superannuation scheme was brought in shortly before the Revolution, by which all revenue officers and clerks paid in at the rate of 3d in the £ and received retirement pensions scaled according to grade. The Salt Office adopted essentially the same scheme for its employees in 1702, and the London staff of the Customs followed suit with a pensions fund of their own in 1712.

Two further examples may be given of the reforming spirit at work. One, most fitting for the age of Newton, was a greater emphasis on the application of mathematical techniques to government, as with complex actuarial calculations which made it possible from 1693 onwards for the Treasury to float an impressive series of public loans through the offer of annuities to investors, just as private insurance companies offer them today (Ch. 17). At a much humbler level, manuals of instruction were issued to excise gaugers and customs collectors and from the 1680s the mathematical ability of the former was carefully scrutinised.[5] Finally, the impact of the scientific revolution on the executive can be seen in the call made by the governments of the period for statistics of a wide-ranging nature, and in particular for data that was relevant to the formulation of fiscal policy. There is some evidence that in the 1680s the ministers of Charles II and his brother placed a good deal of faith (some of it misguided) in the 'political arithmetic' of Sir William Petty. Of more value, despite their flaws, were the copious statistics on population, on national wealth and consumption, and on trade, compiled in the 1690s not only by Gregory King, whose 'Natural and Political Observations' were 'received' by the Board of Trade in September 1697, but by two distinguished civil servants, Charles Davenant and William Culliford (Chs. 2, 4). Culliford, for instance, as a high official in the Customs department, was the first man to supply English governments with regular annual import and export figures, something he began to do in 1696.[6] Without statistics, one could well argue, truly scientific government is not possible (227; 173, *Ch. 11* ['Political Arithmetic and Social Welfare']). By the 1720s there was still a mountain to climb in this respect. But the last two decades of the seventeenth century had unquestionably seen the first strides over the foothills.

Just as the years from 1680 to 1720 saw, after the Revolution, the first experiments with Cabinet government, culminating in a system of regular, minuted meetings both of full Cabinets and of their chief working members in committee (Ch. 13), so they also witnessed a powerful trend towards collective forms of executive government. This was a notable change of approach for England, where, except in a few departments such as the Ordnance Office, the emphasis had traditionally been on the individual responsibility of ministers to the King, and it was a change that was to influence the working of the administrative system profoundly for much of the eighteenth century. It is true that one can trace its origins back to the committee-conscious years of the Civil Wars and the Interregnum. Yet after 1680, and particularly after the outbreak of

King William's War, the pace of the change was very much quickened. As new departments were created they were all put in the charge of boards (in the contemporary phrase, 'put in commission'), from the start. This was as true of the most important charges, like Excise and Trade, as it was of the tiniest office of all, that set up to handle the duties on London hackney coaches, presided over by a board of five whose members were paid just £100 apiece for their services. There were three revenue boards in 1693; by 1711 there were eight (plus one sub-board within the Treasury), each administering a different 'branch', except for the Excise commissioners who were responsible for collecting the lucrative malt tax as well as the duties on a variety of liquors.

No doubt the governments of the day were not entirely innocent of patronage motives in some of these cases. The Scottish 'Commission of Chamberlainry and Trade' (1711) was the most glaring case in point (283c, *174–85*). But there were other factors too. In administering the raising of revenue, shared responsibility was seen as the most effective safeguard against peculation. The Excise and Salt Offices had a system of 'visitations' for supervising the various regional collections, and experience proved that a team effort at the highest level was the most effective way of working it (119). Most of all, the trend towards committee rule reflects wartime pressures. One sees this most clearly in the tendency of some of the oldest offices to follow the suit of the newest ones by going into commission. In the war years such great offices as that of Lord High Treasurer and Lord High Admiral carried so heavy a burden of responsibility and were so vulnerable to parliamentary criticism that, even when the Crown was ready to bestow them on individuals (which William, by and large, was not), only a handful of politicians were prepared to take them on. The massive burden which Godolphin carried at the Treasury in the first eight years of the Spanish Succession War – a burden which probably shortened his life and certainly shortened his temper – was very much in the duke of Shrewsbury's mind when he was offered the Treasurer's white staff in 1710, and prudently turned it down 'for ten reasons, every one strong enough to hinder my doing it'.[7] An even more striking incident had occurred the year before, when Lord Orford of the Whig Junto, formerly Admiral Edward Russell and a man unrivalled among politicians in his experience of naval administration, refused point blank to take the Admiralty unless it was put in commission, with shared responsibility. And it is a fact that after 1714 neither the Treasury nor the Admiralty was ever again officially run by one man [D.1,D.6].

Before turning to what, in the long term, proved the most far-reaching change of all experienced by the executive, the growth of professionalism, we must take into account Sir John Plumb's contention that the late Stuart revolution in government was, essentially, a revolution without reform. 'It is vital to remember', he writes, with the whole question of the eighteenth-century patronage machine in mind, 'that although . . . offices were created in abundance, next to none, except at Court, were abolished' (28, *101*). It cannot be denied that in this period, outside the royal household (77), very few redundant offices were done away with. So, for example, the Clerk of the Green Wax, the Foreign Apposer, the Clerk of the Pells, and the Chamberlains of the Exchequer (a number of gentlemen whose job was to look after the Domesday Book and who charged an inspection fee of 6s. 8d. [*c.* 33p] and a transcription fee of 4d. a line) – these officials were still there, and still going through their antique motions, in George I's reign; and many more besides. Also, the time-honoured practice of appointing deputies to do the actual work of many of the more ancient offices, in such departments as the Customs and the Exchequer, leaving the formal holders, as 'sleeping' incumbents, to enjoy the bulk of their emoluments, was left virtually undisturbed. But all this is hardly surprising. The three outstanding Treasury ministers of the years 1689–1714, Montagu, Godolphin and Harley, were all hard-pressed statesmen, whose overwhelming concern was to ensure that, somehow, an unheard-of range of new government responsibilities was effectively discharged. Of course their preoccupations were with adaptation and invention, with additions rather than with subtractions. They saw no reason to challenge the attitude of most of their contemporaries, that a reasonable supply of sinecures and offices discharged by deputies, which 'provided outdoor relief for the lucky families that held them' (28, *114*), was more benign than pernicious. As for Walpole after 1721, *quieta non movere* was a maxim that in his eyes was as applicable to the institutions and personnel of the administration as to politics and religion.

What was not lacking, as late as 1733, was the *will* to reform, wherever it was deemed both necessary and possible. The instances given earlier of the trend towards more rational, scientific government surely bear this out. One further example is worth our notice. It is highlighted by a new regulation issued by the Customs commissioners in 1705: to the effect that local Collectors of Customs were to be appointed only 'out of such persons as had been bred to clerkship and other business *in the Customs*, and that the Collectors of the lesser ports should be preferred according to their merits to the greater ports.'[8] The fact that this regulation was frequently evaded in the Hanoverian period should not disguise its significance at the time. In the first place, it reflects the conviction of a growing number of senior civil servants by Anne's reign that protracted warfare had made demands on efficiency which only reform could satisfy: expansion alone would not be enough. But equally, it underlines the advance of professionalism within the late Stuart executive, and that growing sense of professional identity which is detectable in the government service even before the Revolution and which increasingly pervaded it thereafter (122, *245–53*).

Such professionalism was by no means confined to the revenue departments. It was to be found in the Treasury itself, where William Lowndes, whose career there stretched from 1675 to 1725, and who became the most distinguished bureaucrat of the post-Revolution generation, continued the work of his predecessor, Guy, in promoting *esprit de corps* as an essential condition of efficiency. It was also manifest in the Navy Office, where Pepys eventually found a worthy successor in Charles Sergison, and to a high degree in the Post Office. But the revenue was the life-blood of the war effort, and its collection made special demands on technical expertise. On both counts experience and continuity of service were at a premium. Edward Hughes has underlined this point by telling how at the end of Anne's reign the Excise Department sacked a certain Mr

Ferryman, one of its Welsh Collectors, 'for intermeddling in an election contrary to law and repeated orders'. A new Treasury Board, Whigs to a man, tried to replace him with a candidate who, reading between the lines, was primarily a political nominee. The Excise Commissioners promptly objected, concluding a long memorial with these words: 'that the placing of persons who were never concerned in the Revenue, at the first step into the Office of Collector will not only be a discouragement to those in that service, but to all other officers who have served long and faithfully in the revenue.' There was some huffing and puffing from the Treasury, but in the end it concurred (119, *272*).

Over the previous twenty years it had come to be recognised by those with the interests of good government at heart that even for the very top posts in the revenue departments a long experience in at least some branch of the service was the ideal qualification. And so we find, among others, John Danvers, having served a long apprenticeship as a Searcher of the Customs in the port of London and established a reputation as a martinet and efficiency expert, being appointed an Excise Commissioner for several years in the mid-1690s, in the hope that his presence would help to remedy some major defects which that department had begun to display during the Nine Years' War. In 1702, when the Treasury was looking for someone who could play a leading rôle in getting the new salt duties off the ground, Danvers was their choice; as chairman of the Board, surviving every change of ministry between then and his death in 1716, he had a major share in ensuring the Salt Office's undoubted success. When, by a series of Acts of Parliament passed between 1694 and 1701, all revenue officials, including eventually commissioners themselves, were excluded from sitting in the Commons, one result was a considerable spur to the growth of the kind of specialised professionalism which officials like Danvers, Thomas Everard and George Townshend exemplify (122, *243–4, 251*). The revenue service called for full-time commitment at all levels, and it was necessary to get away from the position which still persisted in the Excise Board in 1698, when William Fleming wrote to his father, Sir Daniel, complaining of 'it being hard duty to attend our office from 8 to 11 or 12 and then the Parliament to 4, 5, 6 and today to 7 at night'.[9] That state of affairs was neither good politics nor effective government.

The key factor, however, in the development of what can be rightly called a permanent 'civil service tradition' was not place legislation but the attitude of the two outstanding political managers of post-Revolution Britain, Godolphin and Harley [D.1]. These statesmen did not always see eye to eye, but they did agree in recognising two closely-connected priorities for the achievement of a well-oiled machinery of government in wartime. One was that there should be some continuity of executive policy and administrative methods between the lifetime of one administration and the next. The second was that there must be a permanent store of professional expertise at the service of successive political heads of departments, especially in those departments most closely concerned with running the Spanish Succession War and with financing it. As a result, at a time when party chiefs of the stamp of Wharton and the third earl of Sunderland, or Nottingham and St John, would gladly have engrossed *all* patronage for their own henchmen, however specialised the job, non-partisan career bureaucrats not merely survived the furious tempest of party but, as a body, grew very considerably in numbers and stature.[10] In 1688, as we saw, they were still a handful. By 1714 there was a large and impressive squadron of senior civil servants – men who had made themselves indispensable to government in the course of two wars; below them, at the levels of what we would now call the 'executive', 'clerical' and 'technical' civil service, the principle of security for those of proven competence was still more firmly implanted. Not even the Walpole regime, probably the most patronage-conscious in the entire eighteenth century, more than partially disturbed its roots (122, *245–7*). It was largely for this reason that the executive of mid-Hanoverian Britain, although it had to wait until the 1780s for a renewal of the current of reform, managed to cling on to much of the ground gained in the period 1680–1725, so that for all its flaws it proved adequate to the task of servicing the winning of an empire in the last years of George II.

---

1. See G.R. Elton, *The Tudor Revolution in Government* (Cambridge, 1953); G.E. Aylmer, *The State's Servants: The Civil Service of the English Republic, 1649–1660* (1973).
2. H.C. Tomlinson, *Guns and Government: The Ordnance Office under the later Stuarts* (1979), pp. 14–15; J.C. Sainty, *Treasury Officials, 1660–1870* (1972); id., *Officials of the Secretaries of State, 1660–1782* (1973).
3. John Chamberlayne, *Magnae Britanniae Notitia* (1708 and 1723 edns).
4. Aylmer, *The State's Servants*.
5. BL Harleian MSS. 5020, 5022–3 *passim*.
6. Sir G.N. Clark, *Guide to English Commercial Statistics, 1696–1782* (1938), Intro; see also C. Brooks, 'Projecting, Political Arithmetic and the Act of 1695', *EHR*, **97** (1982).
7. Longleat MSS. Portland Papers, VI, f. 28: Shrewsbury to [Robert Harley], 22 July 1710 (by courtesy of the Marquess of Bath).
8. PRO, Treasury Out-Letters, Customs, XIV, p. 406, quoted in E.E. Hoon, *The Organization of the English Customs System* (2nd edn, 1968), p. 204. My italics.
9. Cumbria RO (Kendal), WD/Ry 5388 (Le Fleming MSS.), W. to Sir D. Fleming, 2 May 1698.
10. One of the grateful survivalists, Whitelocke Bulstrode of the Excise, subsequently paid a glowing tribute to Harley's 'gentle usage of mankind' in the public service, and to his resistance to the pressure of 'violent hot men'. BL Loan 29/128: Bulstrode to Lord Oxford, 21 Aug 1714.

CHAPTER 17

The fruits of war: II – The New Finance: from the credit revolution to the South Sea Bubble

The struggle against France after May 1689 compelled post-Revolution governments not merely to extend and modernise their administrative mechanisms but to transform the system of finance inherited from the Stuart past. In a masterly study (113a) P.G.M. Dickson has described the most spectacular of those changes as 'the Financial Revolution'. He has shown how the need to raise sums of money that were completely without precedent in the 1690s, and again after 1702, dramatically affected the facility with which English governments could borrow from those they governed. But the new finance in late seventeenth- and early eighteenth-century Britain was no one-dimensional phenomenon. It involved not a single 'financial revolution' but three: two in the public theatre and one in the private. To miss this point is to miss much of the significance of a process of immense consequence, one with far-reaching implications for society and for the economy as well as for government, politics and foreign affairs.

In the first place, the tax structure of Britain was drastically remodelled between 1689 and 1714 to produce a fiscal pattern which then persisted, with little more than minor changes of emphasis, for most of the eighteenth century (117). Simultaneously there took place the great public credit revolution, with which Dickson is primarily concerned. The origins of the English National Debt and the establishment of the Bank of England were the two most conspicuous developments which set it in motion and did most to govern its course. Thirdly, however, radical changes overtook the arena of London big business and *private* finance in the generation after 1688. Unless one is aware of the latter, the startling new departures in government finance remain only partially comprehensible, and it becomes impossible to appreciate the magnitude of the South Sea crisis of 1720, in which the worlds of public and private finance came for a few terrifying months into violent and potentially disastrous collision.

I

In the period between the Restoration and the Revolution the credibility of the time-honoured distinction between ordinary and extraordinary revenue had been seriously undermined by the erratic yield of the duties allocated to the ordinary revenue in and after 1660 (Ch. 5). This had first imposed a stringency on the Crown so severe that it was almost forced into constitutionally irresponsible policies, and then in the 1680s produced a revenue glut for James II which was even more dangerous than the earlier dearth. After the Revolution the most pro-William MPs were sufficiently cautious to shy away from giving the new king the same financial freedom of manoeuvre as the old. The less well-disposed appear to have been determined only to vote permanent life revenues that were deliberately too small to enable him 'to live of his own' in peacetime, thus obliging him to have regular recourse to Parliament when the war ended. Sir Joseph Williamson, while professing that 'a revenue for the King to live with honour and comfort upon' was the wish of the whole House of Commons, articulated the unease at the back of nearly every member's mind when he reminded them that 'when Princes have not needed money they have not needed us'.[1] The Convention came and went with no more than interim provision made for one year. The new 1690 Parliament voted the King a revenue that, at £1.2 million, was patently too small *in toto* for 'ordinary' purposes; only half of it (the Excise) granted for life, and the customs voted for a grudging four years. But up to and during 1695, when Parliament resumed its cat-and-mouse game with the old hereditary customs, the French war was making arrant nonsense of the old system anyway. And the need to keep on foot even a small standing army after the Peace of Ryswick in 1697, plus a still considerable navy, finally laid bare its total irrelevance (112a and b).

Thus from 1698, the year of the Civil List Act [F(vi)], dates a completely new principle which was to remain constant from now both in peace and war. The distinction between ordinary and extraordinary revenue was formally abandoned. The King was given a 'civil list', comprised of revenues voted for life (it was fixed at £700,000 in the first instance), and from this he was expected to pay only the expenses of his household and his civil government. All military and naval expenditure became from now on, even in peacetime, the regular, automatic responsibility of Parliament. Historians have not been slow to direct attention to the constitutional importance of this arrangement: as yet another firm step along the road from prerogative kingship to limited, parliamentary monarchy. But the passing of the Civil List Act also signifies the fact that Parliament by 1698 had at its disposal a tax structure to service the new system, and in particular to discharge its own obligations within it, a structure at once more sophisticated and more reliable than anything which had existed before the Revolution.

Every year between 1689 and 1714, including the years of peace, the administrations of William III and Queen Anne had to raise, on average, £5 million in taxation. At the height of the Spanish Succession War (1706–11) that average was nearer £6 million [see also G.2(v)]. It is sometimes imagined that Britain owed her endurance in the 1690s and her victories in the succeeding war to the superiority of her financial credit over that of her enemies, and it can certainly be argued that this was the factor that tipped the balance. The fact that the large and far-flung forces committed to these wars so rarely ran seriously short of supplies, munitions and, above all, pay is mainly attributable to the country's capacity to raise heavy loans with such relative ease. Yet loans as such did not pay for the wars. Loans of all kinds met only roughly one-third of total expenditure calculated over both wars. And as for those long-term, funded loans which were the special hallmark of the new system of public credit initiated in the 1690s, their contribution was slight before 1702: they provided only £6.9 million out of a total expenditure since 1689 of £72 million. They bulked much larger in Anne's reign, yet even in the 12 years down to 1714 they still accounted for well under 40 per cent of the £99 million bill (113a, *47–9, 79 & n.2*). Meanwhile, taxes had soared to a peak level almost three times as high as even Oliver Cromwell's regime had achieved.

The new fiscal strategy which made this possible (if 'strategy' is not too elevated a word for policies towards which the politicians initially groped rather than planned their way) (116) had three essential features. Duties on overseas trade were exploited to an unheard-of degree for revenue purposes: many new commodities were caught in the Customs net, and there was a steep rise in the general level of duty paid, eventually to as high as 20 per cent and in some cases 25 per cent (114) [G.2(iii,a-b)]. Still more striking was the growth in both the range and yield of excise or excise-type duties. Thanks partly to the levying of the first stamp duties from 1694, but mainly to the targeting of three basic items of popular consumption, salt, malt and leather, which joined a rich variety of liquors as plump prey for the taxmen, the point was reached where during Anne's reign inland duties had become by far the more lucrative branch of indirect taxation [G.2(v)]. If this was innovatory, equally so was the third aspect of the new strategy, the levying of the Land Tax. Although its origins, in the '4 shillings Aid' of 1693, came half way through the Nine Years' War, this imposition still accounted for roughly a third of the total tax revenue of £122 million pounds which came into the Treasury under William and Anne.

The novelty of the Land Tax did not lie principally in its conception. For despite the intention of its initiators to tap many kinds of income, and not least income from offices,[2] by 1698 it had firmly become in practice a quota tax, county by county, levied primarily on the rents and produce of land and real estate; as such it followed a more traditional trail, beaten out by the extraordinary taxes of the Interregnum and most of the crisis years of Charles II's reign – the so-called 'assessments' (110a, *Ch. 5*; 116, *286–90*). What was new about the Land Tax was its combination of flexibility and permanence. It was flexible in that, depending on pressure of need, it could be levied at a rate of four, three or two shillings in the pound – a sliding scale of from 20 down to 10 per cent [G.2(ii)]. But above all it was the first high-yield direct tax in English history which came to be levied and collected year in, year out, regardless of war or peace, changes of ministry or of sovereign: not without grumbles, admittedly, but without any serious protest or evasion. Everyone recognised that it was not ideal (115a). But though the sufferers groaned, they paid. The institution of the Land Tax marked the English taxpayer's coming-of-age: the acceptance by him and his parliamentary representatives that liberty, property and the Protestant religion were worth paying for permanently. Two important aspects of the administration of the tax must also be stressed. Some latitude was allowed – as in Cumberland, Westmorland, Durham and Hampshire – for the operation of local customs and variants. Moreover, apart from the receiver-general in each county, the local administration of the Land Tax was in the hands of local men, supervised by commissioners (themselves nominated by local MPs) whose membership was often almost equatable with that of the county magistrates' bench. It has been convincingly argued that both features contributed to the acceptability of the tax, and that the latter (which was in marked contrast to the rôle of centrally-controlled and salaried government functionaries in the collection of the customs and excise duties) did so to a very significant degree (115b).[3]

At all events, for the war-ridden post-Revolution generation this 'flower of the funds' became utterly indispensable. Although it sometimes took more than a year for all the proceeds to come in, the ultimate predictability, from 1698 onwards, of its yield of around £2 million per annum at maximum rate [G.2(ii)] meant that short-term loans could regularly be raised on its security. For the future, however, one major question of fiscal principle was still to be resolved. Excises were unquestionably a more efficient, as well as a more equitable, long-term bet than the Land Tax, since they touched the whole population. What is more, even more than the graduated poll taxes raised (with no great success) in the early 1690s, they did so in rough proportion to the subject's capacity to pay, reaching down even to the poor (and Sir William Petty and others had long argued against 'a fallacious tenderness towards the poor').[4] The question was, could they, for all these advantages, overcome their unpopularity? If public opinion could come to terms with the bureaucratic, frequently inquisitorial methods their collection entailed, might they not gradually take the place of the Land Tax as the bedrock of the whole tax structure in post-war Britain? The answer to this problem and the resolution of a protracted contemporary debate (116, *300ff.*), did not become known until the 1730s, the decade of the Excise Crisis (*The Age of Oligarchy*, Ch. 5).

If the revolution in taxation was in general accepted with remarkable phlegm by a country which for so long had been accustomed to having government on the cheap, the developments in public credit initiated in the 1690s proved more astonishing and a good deal more disturbing. Reactions to them ranged from wonder and pride to bewilderment and downright hostility. The bewilderment is not hard to understand. Few informed Britons could have failed to be aware by the later years of Queen Anne that a new financial world had come into existence. How could they be ignorant of it when, by this stage, the political prospects of every ministry were often discussed in terms of the state of its credit and the fluctuations of the stock market. But being aware of a new phenomenon was a very different matter from understanding it, enshrouded as it was by 'such an unintelligible jargon of terms . . . as were never known in any other age or country in the world'.[5] The terminology of credit finance and 'Change Alley in the bemused ears of unsophisticated squires, yeomen and tradesmen sounded, as one historian has put it, 'like baffling incantations, chanted by a strange new sect . . . while the mechanism of the system appeared to be a diabolical machine for creating wealth out of thin air' (66, *136*).

'The mechanism of the system' essentially had two generators. One was the product of substituting for the hitherto royal debts a *National* Debt, along with relatively minor Civil List debts. For the old *royal* debts, except in the exceptional case of the Stop Debt of 1672 (Ch. 5), Parliament had taken no formal responsibility. For the National Debt Parliament, on the nation's behalf, now assumed full responsibility by underwriting loans to the King's government. (It also recognised an obligation to bail the Crown out periodically when the Civil

List proved inadequate.) The other great source of power in the generation of public credit came from the foundation of a state bank in the City of London. The Bank of England not only became a major creditor of government itself but an indispensable agency for oiling the wheels of public borrowing in other quarters.

The origins of a true 'National Debt' are usually traced back to the third winter of King William's War, that of 1692–3. It was then that the Treasury lord, Charles Montagu, the financial expert of the Whig Junto, induced Godolphin and his other colleagues on the Treasury Commission to float a loan of £1 million, for which the main bait would be the offer of annuities to investors. He then persuaded the Commons to guarantee the interest needed to pay out those annuities into the distant future by setting up a *fund*, to be fed from the yield of new excise duties which were specifically imposed for this purpose for 99 years. Hence the genesis of the new term 'funded debt'. The 1693 loan proved reasonably successful,[6] although possibly only because the Act gave investors the option (which the majority took up) of switching to an annuity for one life at a very high and, from 1694, tax-free rate of interest (14%). Nevertheless, down to 1704 the National Debt remained more an accumulation of short-term or 'floating' debts of the old style, repayable within limited terms, than a long-term, funded debt of a new model (113a, *48–9, 60–1, 344*). It was only in Anne's reign that the great change took place. Confidence in public credit increased by leaps and bounds, so that at the Queen's death the great bulk of the National Debt was funded and many tax revenues had been mortgaged for up to a century ahead to service it. A whole new *rentier* class was created in the process.[7] Hundreds of people received steady incomes for much of the eighteenth century on the strength of money lent to the government in their youth or infancy during the wars against Louis XIV. Charles Duncombe, the classical scholar, enjoyed 77 annual payments from 'the Funds', thanks to the foresight of a relative who invested £100 in his name in 1693, when he himself was three years old.

Investment in the British government had thus by 1714 become permanent and secure instead of, as in the past, temporary and speculative. The growing strength of the credit system can be gauged by the much lower rates of interest at which Anne's ministries were able to borrow, compared with the governments of William III. In William's reign, when confidence was slow to develop and suffered a severe setback in a serious financial crisis in 1696–7, some long-term loans had to be floated at as high as 14 per cent and the average rate for the whole reign was 8.39 per cent. By contrast, on the huge long-term debt of £35 million incurred between 1702 and 1714, the average rate of interest was down to 6 per cent. How was the money raised for these long-term loans? Essentially it was done by devising three expedients and ringing the changes among them. There was, of course, the method pioneered in 1693–4, and renewed to raise a further £9 million between 1704 and 1710 – the sale of annuities, either for one or more lives or for terms of years. These were sometimes loosely called tontine loans, though in fact only the original measure of January 1693 was a genuine tontine.[8] A second method, first explored in 1694, involved the creation of state lotteries, managed either by the Exchequer or the Bank of England. Lottery loans reached their peak of popularity from 1711 to 1714, raising a total of £9 million – a crucial contribution in the final years of the war when other sources were drying up (113a, *48–9, 71–5 and Table 6*). Thirdly, great sums were raised by procuring major loans from one or other of the three great financial and commercial corporations of post-Revolution England. These were the Bank, the East India Company (for a while two separate companies, the 'Old' and the 'New', each ready to bid for government favour), and, from its foundation in 1711, the South Sea Company. And because of the increasingly heavy public indebtedness to them, amounting by 1714 to no less than £15.7 million, these companies and their directors acquired great influence.

The most prestigious of the three, and of course the most innovatory, was the Bank of England. It was founded in 1694 through a combination of three elements: the ingenuity of William Paterson, the Scottish farmer's son with one of the most brilliantly inventive financial minds of the age, who hatched the idea; the foresight and political courage of Montagu (now Chancellor of the Exchequer) in backing it, and the willingness of a group of leading Whig businessmen, most notably Michael Godfrey, John Houblon and Gilbert Heathcote, to stake a good deal of their own personal fortunes on the initial success of the venture. It was a gamble at the start. The main backers of the corporation had to promise to lend half its subscription capital of £1.2 million to the government in return for the charter as a state bank. In 1696–7 the Bank had to survive the desperately serious financial crisis and a run on its reserves, including an unsuccessful challenge from a new Land Bank, projected by Hugh Chamberlain (above, pp. 198–9). After 1697, however, the Bank of England went from strength to strength. Its stock became the most coveted commodity on the market, and its backing became the most vital asset any post-Revolution government could have. As well as making crucial long-term loans itself, the Bank also became the key agent in facilitating short-term government finance; in particular, from 1707–8 it undertook to cash on demand the greater part of Exchequer bills in circulation.[9] In 1713, when the Bank made yet another of its handsome loans – this time to Harley's Tory government – it secured a continuation of its charter until 1743, and this effectively guaranteed the institution in perpetuity.

The Bank of England, of course, transacted a vast amount of private as well as public business, and its notes, though not strictly legal tender, were widely circulated as such. In Scotland too at this time the Bank of Scotland (established 1695) was issuing notes, much needed in a country where informal paper tender was already in wide use owing to the shortage of specie. It had a monopoly of Scottish banking until the incorporation of the Royal Bank in 1727. No chapter on the New Finance of this period would be complete if it left out of account the revolution in private finance after the Glorious Revolution; like the transformation of the machinery of public credit, it was spectacular.

A remarkable case in point was the joint-stock boom of the early 1690s. Alongside the public financial measures of this decade, and to some extent integrated with them, went a sensational upsurge in the popularity of the joint-stock company (cf. Ch. 3) among men with spare capital to invest (167 [K. G.

Davies]). By 1695 the shares of at least ninety-three English joint-stock companies, with a paid-up capital totalling £4 million, were being marketed. These companies promoted a wide range of home as well as overseas enterprises, among them industrial ventures such as copper mining, linen manufacture and the gunpowder industry, and the overwhelming majority of them had materialised since 1689. With forty-four joint-stock ventures of her own by 1695, Scotland had her full share of the prevailing euphoria; in 'the Company of Scotland trading to Africa and the Indies' (1695), by far the most ambitious of those ventures, English investors too showed strong interest, contributing in good measure to its final share capital of £600,000 (70, *482 n. 10*; 277a, *26–7*). Long before the Company of Scotland was wrecked by the ill-fated Darien Scheme (Ch. 19) scores of the new companies so hopefully founded in both countries from 1689–95 had been swept away in the financial crisis of 1696. John Houghton's *The Price of the Stocks*, the first regular published guide to the London market, was quoting only seven major securities by 1697; three years earlier, it had been publishing quotations for fifty-eight. But while the small fry went under, the bigger battalions, and a few that were not so big, survived. In England they included the East India Company ('Companies' from 1698), the Africa Company, the Bank of England, and the Million Bank, alias 'the Million Adventure', which had been founded with a total stock of £200,000 in 1695 and was to remain an important institutional creditor of the state for a quarter of a century (94b, *108*; 113a, *270*); among lesser enterprises, the New River Company and the Hudson's Bay Company also emerged intact. By 1714 these survivors, notwithstanding the slow strangulation suffered by the Royal Africa Company (Ch. 19),[10] had been formidably strengthened by the appearance on the scene of the South Sea Company and had increased their combined share capital to £20 million. The stage was already being set for another mushrooming of joint-stock enterprises six years later, which would prove more hectic even than that of the 1690s.

Although after 1700 government securities usually outnumbered private stocks on the market, it is clear, nevertheless, that the years from 1689 to 1720 saw a vast increase in the total volume of private, as well as public, investment. Even in the late 1680s, investment openings in the city had failed to match the large capital accumulations which the Commercial Revolution had made possible (167 [K. G. Davies]). And it is worth reiterating that a lot of the abundant new investment after the Revolution remained outside the field of foreign trade, where in the 1690s especially the element of risk in wartime seemed to many abnormally high. 'A great many stocks have arisen since this war with France', Houghton wrote in 1694, 'for trade being obstructed at sea, few that had money were willing it should lie idle'.[11] Habits which became ingrained in years when merchant shipping was extremely vulnerable to enemy action were not easily thrown off when hostilities ceased, so that in 1701, after four years of peace and commercial revival, one MP (with the usual dash of political licence) was still complaining bitterly at Westminster that 'our trading is now dead; . . . for [a] merchant finds a better return between the Exchequer and the Exchange, than he make[s] by running a hazard to the Indies'.[12] We must bear in mind this substantial diversion of merchant capital into both private and public channels.

Although it was predominantly colonial, Levant and Iberian merchants who were involved in it (94b, *136–53*; 246 [D. W. Jones]), it became a contributor of some importance to that growth of hostility towards the London business community *as a whole* which, as we shall see, developed in the 1690s and persisted at least until the dust of the South Sea crisis of 1720 had finally settled (Ch. 18).

In the thirty years or so before 1720 this City business community became far more sophisticated than ever before. If the joint-stock boom was one notable feature of the revolution in private finance, this growth in complexity and sophistication was surely another. From this period, for instance, date the Sun Fire Office, founded in 1710, and the London Assurance and Royal Exchange Assurance Companies (both with an initial emphasis on marine insurance) in 1720. At the same time new techniques and media came into regular play to facilitate and speed up all manner of business transactions. The magic of paper was exemplified not only by Bank notes and Exchequer bills but by bills of exchange for international transactions. A 'Stock Exchange' emerged, in practice if not in name, in William III's reign: based partly on the old Royal Exchange, but more effectively on two large coffee houses in 'Change Alley, Jonathan's and Garraway's, which became recognised haunts of London financiers and merchants. Here a new breed of stockjobbers and licensed brokers could be found every weekday bidding for business, and soon developing, in a highly competitive process, a new vocabulary. Terms like 'bull' and 'bear' and many others made up a sort of verbal shorthand without which, as a later observer wrily remarked, 'it would be impossible for their lungs to hold out'.[13]

Along, therefore, with the development of novel techniques and media, and of an 'unintelligible jargon' to match them, the personnel of the London business world also acquired a new dimension. The City had had its 'monied men' of a kind earlier in the seventeenth century: men whose prime business concerns lay neither with overseas trade nor with manufacturing, wholesale or distributive trades. It had had its scriveners and money-lenders, and of course its private bankers (usually goldsmiths) – there were forty-four of them in 1677 (94b, *158*). But now it acquired by the score its brokers and its stockjobbers, too. 'Stockjobbing' became one of the most emotive words of the age. Even in Anne's reign it had come to be associated in the minds of thousands of country gentlemen with huge, ill-gotten, parasitic gains at the expense of unsuspecting clients. After the 'Bubble' of 1720 it carried for many years the mark of Cain – 'a trade which once bewitched the nation almost to its ruin' (3, *I, 336*).

The truth is, even among those stockbrokers who did manage to stay in business throughout all or much of this period (and many succumbed to the troubles of the mid-1690s); the bulk were part-timers who made relatively small profits out of broking or 'jobbing' alone. The analysis of investment lists of William's and Anne's reigns has revealed that there were more 'plums' (i.e. fortunes of £100,000 or more) being made by substantial merchants or private bankers, using all the new financial opportunities now open to them, including broking, than by men who were solely dealers in stock (113a, *495–505*). Nevertheless, by 1715–20, leaving aside dozens of freelance operators, there were about eighty dealers who specialised in handling either East India or Bank stocks, and among them were a small handful who did make fortunes out of stockjobbing: the notorious John 'Vulture' Hopkins, for one, or William Sheppard, who in one year alone handled transfers of Bank stock totalling £500,000. It was inevitable, however, that many of the élite merchant-financiers, those City 'all-rounders' who accumulated exceptional wealth in the years 1689–1720, would become experienced in playing the market themselves for profit. Prime examples of such magnates were Sir James Bateman, a naturalised Fleming who had his finger in many a pie, including a brace of the major directorates; Sir Henry Furnese and Sir Theodore Janssen, the supreme experts of the day in international finance, and much in demand for organising the payment of Britain's armies abroad, and Sir Gilbert Heathcote, the dominant figure in the Bank by Anne's reign and the special bugbear of the Tories. Heathcote, who had been a rising star of the West Indian and wine trades in the 1680s, made a killing of £60,000 by dealings in Bank stock alone on a rising market from 1697 to 1700.

Bateman and Janssen both became key figures in the South Sea Company, the only giant corporation other than the Bank and the short-lived New East India Company to be created in this period. It was conjured up in 1711 on the initiative of Robert Harley's ministry to deal with the worrying problem of the 'floating' National Debt. Harley, then on the eve of his elevation from Chancellor of the Exchequer to Lord Treasurer [D.1], persuaded Parliament that £9 million of this debt, currently in short-term securities, could be effectively 'funded' by being converted into the stock of a new company. To lure existing government creditors and attract further support the new creation was allotted a monopoly of Britain's trade with Spanish America, which was expected (wrongly, as things turned out) to become very lucrative when the war was over. Even from the start the South Sea Company was mainly a financial corporation, with only a precarious trading base. But it was one in which Whig as well as Tory businessmen soon eagerly invested and competed for directorships, in which politicians on both sides bought shares, and which hardened speculators like James Brydges, Paymaster-General, who made half a million in his career by a variety of honest and dishonest means, quickly saw as by far 'the best way to lay out money in hopes of a great and sudden profit'.[14]

II

It was 'hopes of a great and sudden profit' from trafficking in stocks and shares which in the years 1719–20 produced the biggest public scandal of the age, an outrageous drama in which, as the revolutions in the public and private sector became locked together, driving the New Finance, like a careering railcar, clean off the rails, the South Sea Company found itself cast as the chief villain of the piece. After the end of the French wars and the fall of Harley (Oxford) in 1714, the size of the remaining National Debt [G.1] caused the Whig Treasury regimes of Halifax, Carlisle, Walpole, Stanhope and Sunderland continuing (though, as we can now see, exaggerated) anxiety. The idea of a *perpetual* debt was not one the country would be easily reconciled to for some decades yet. In September

1714 the long-term debt alone stood at over £40 million, on which the government had to meet a formidable annual charge of £2.5 million (113a, *80, Table 7*). In the next few years, schemes of conversion and consolidation and the inauguration of a Sinking Fund, mostly at Walpole's instigation, did a good deal to contain and rationalise the problem; but the Jacobite rebellion and successful conversions of short-term securities into the 'Funds' or Corporation debt combined to inflate the long-term National Debt still further, and by the autumn of 1719 it stood at close on £50 million. Early in 1720, therefore, the South Sea Company, by now already the biggest single public creditor (at £11.74 million), made a deal with the Stanhope-Sunderland administration, which amounted in effect to a take-over, at low interest, of potentially a further 80 per cent of the remaining Debt. Since the least tractable sector of the Debt, the £5 million annuitants' debt or 'irredeemables', was one of the two elements in question, it is not hard to see why the government of the day found the proposal seductive.

Unfortunately, the Company's directors, concerned by the recent slump in the Spanish American trade, were not content to let their scheme stand on its inherent attractions alone. They reinforced them by lavish bribes to ministers, courtiers, royal favourites and other interested parties. For example, John Aislabie, Chancellor of the Exchequer since 1718 [D.4], was able to acquire no less than £77,000 worth of stock in five months and sell out quickly for a profit of almost 100 per cent. Also, in order to persuade the existing private creditors to exchange their safe and profitable government annuities for company stock, as well as ensuring massive profits for themselves, the directors had to hold out the bait of capital gains far beyond normal expectation. This they did partly through the publicity value of the deal itself, but mainly by engineering a rapid rise in their own share prices through a whole gamut of ingenious but deeply shady manoeuvres.

On 1 June 1720 the Company's stock (par value 100), which five months earlier – before the deal – had stood at 128, was selling at 610. But it was over the next three weeks that the rush to buy, already reckless, acquired a lunatic momentum. By 24 June South Sea shares were changing hands in Exchange Alley for £1,050 a piece. By this time scores of investors had already sold out with dizzying gains on the soaring market. But hundreds more held on to their stock, or scrambled for the new June issue of a further £5 million, marketed at 1,000. The British casino mentality could not resist the prospect of limitless progress which the Company still seemed to offer. Not only that, the incredible euphoria of the business world at the time is illustrated equally vividly by the flotation inside a mere six months (January-June 1720) of 174 new joint-stock companies, soon to be fatally dubbed the 'bubble companies'. Some, like the insurance and fishery companies, were genuine; some, honest but over-optimistic; some – like the companies for furnishing funerals throughout Britain, importing broomsticks from Germany and establishing chains of pawnbrokers – unashamedly bizarre, and a proportion (though how large a proportion is hard to say) downright fraudulent.[15]

In mid-August, however, market confidence began visibly to sag. The 'Bubble Act', passed by Parliament in June, and technically in force by Midsummer Day, was generally held, despite much confusing verbiage, to have illegalised unauthorised joint-stock ventures and to have made their promoters subject to the penalties of praemunire.[16] On 17 August the South Sea directors, fearful lest some of these upstart rivals might undermine the shaky foundations of their own paper empire, persuaded the government to start legal proceedings against three of the more successful new companies for illegal dealing. The unease this aroused before long turned to panic. At the same time, a crucial amount of foreign capital which had been invested in South Sea stock was lured back abroad, particularly by the appearance of a crop of new speculative ventures in Holland, and within weeks a great deal of English money followed it. These were the darts which punctured the grotesquely inflated South Sea Bubble. Between 1 September and 14 October 1720 the price of the Company's stock plummeted from 775 to 170 (see also above, pp. 209–10).

The effects of the crash on hundreds of individual investors who were overtaken by the collapsing market, both in South Sea and bubble companies' stock, were undoubtedly shattering. Six London banking houses stopped payments. The Company's directors suffered huge, though in some respects selective, forfeitures under the later 'South Sea Sufferers bill'. The many bankrupts included Sir Justus Beck, a pillar of the Exchange for years, and Lord Hillsborough, who went down bravely gambling to the last at Newmarket races. The duke of Portland came so near to ruin that he found it expedient to go to earth for the rest of his life in Jamaica. Even the King, who was abroad when disaster struck, lost £56,000. More lowly victims ranged from country squires to civil servants and from hapless widows to no less gullible university dons. 'The rage against the government was such', Arthur Onslow later recalled, '. . . that could the Pretender then have landed at the Tower, he might have rode to St James's with very few hands held up against him'.[17]

For all the anguish, however, and the justifiable anger, the nation's basic prosperity remained unimpaired. The experience was part of the growing-pains of a great power. Certainly a lot of families learned the hard way that Britain's prosperity still rested largely on the old, solid foundations of trade and land, and owed less than many had come to believe to the mysterious wonders of the New Finance. Perhaps Britain needed a trauma like the South Sea Bubble to teach this vital lesson. But private wealth had not been dissipated during the crisis; rather it had been redistributed. And once that wealth had settled into a saner pattern of investment – as it did with remarkable speed once the crisis was resolved – the British financial revolution was able to cut its losses, consolidate its supremely important gains, and pass those gains on to succeeding generations.

---

1. A Grey, *Debates*, X, p. 11: 27 March 1690.
2. H. Horwitz, ed., *The Parliamentary Diary of Narcissus Luttrell, 1691–1693* (Oxford, 1972), pp. 311–54 *passim*: 13 Dec 1692 – 6 Jan 1693.
3. See also J.V. Beckett, 'Local Custom and the "New Taxation" in the Seventeenth and Eighteenth Centuries', *Northern History*, **12** (1976); id., 'Land Tax Administration at

the Local Level, 1692–1798', in M. Turner and D. Mills, eds, *Land Tax and Property: the English Land Tax, 1692–1832* (Gloucester, 1986), pp. 163–4.

4. There was a contrary view, that excises bore down unjustly and inequitably on the poor. An example is John Hampden, *Some Considerations about the most proper Way of Raising Money* (c. 1692), printed in (2), V, Appx. no. VI..

5. Jonathan Swift, *The Examiner*, no. 13, 2 Nov 1710 (ed. H. Davis, Oxford, 1957, p. 7).

6. There was a shortfall of a little over £100,000 which was made up in Feb 1694 by a further small life-annuity loan. It was at this stage that the 'tax-free' concession (see above, p. 270) was reintroduced.

7. A.C. Carter, *The English Public Debt in the 18th Century* (1986); E.L. Hargreaves, *The National Debt* (1930), pp. 16–17.

8. Hargreaves, *National Debt*, p. 6 and n. 3.

9. The Exchequer Bill was first introduced by Montagu in 1695 to provide credit for the government during the stressful period of the Great Recoinage and had since then become the most important departure in short-term securities – the normal way by which 18th-century governments anticipated their tax revenues. See J.R. Horsfield, *British Monetary Experiments, 1660–1720* (1962), *passim*.

10. The Company had its exclusive privileges seriously curtailed by Parliament in 1698 and abolished in 1712. K.G. Davies, *The Royal African Company* (1957), pp. 132–5; G.S. De Krey, (94b), pp. 137–8.

11. John Houghton, *A Collection for Improvement of Husbandry and Trade* (1692–1703), 15 June 1694 (Bradley edn, I, p. 261)

12. Bodleian Lib., MS. Carte 117, f. 117.

13. T. Mortimer, 1761, quoted from Dickson (113a), p. 503.

14. Huntington Library, Stowe MSS. 57, V, f. 121: Brydges to William Benson, 7 July 1711; Cumbria RO Lonsdale MSS: Nicholas Lechmere, MP to James Lowther, MP, 7 July 1711. Under George I Brydges achieved the dukedom of Chandos – we shall encounter him again. [By courtesy of the Lonsdale Estate Trust.]

15. Scott, *Joint Stock Companies*, III, p. 445ff.

16. Cf. Dickson (113a), pp. 147–8 with Carswell, op. cit. p. 157.

17. HMC, 14th Report, Appx., Pt. IX, p. 504.

CHAPTER 18

Revolution, war and property: social change and conflict, 1689–*c*.1725

I

The two great wars of the period 1689–1713 imposed considerable strains on the social fabric of England, a fabric which hitherto had absorbed the measured and relatively uncontentious changes of the post-Restoration years with little difficulty (Ch. 4). To us the strains may be understandable, in part at least, in the light of those governmental and financial developments just examined. Yet they were certainly not foreseen, still less desired, by those socially very conservative men who rebelled against James II. Indeed, they were all the more disquieting because the 1688 Revolution itself had seemed likely in other respects to restore and re-buttress the fabric of society after the rude jars it had suffered in the final year of James's reign.

It was to the Glorious Revolution that David Ogg, with characteristic sagacity, attributed 'the salvation of freehold' in England (18, *72–3*); the divine right of kings gave way after 1688 to the divine right of property-owners.[1] Most revolutions threaten the sanctity of private property; this one established it more firmly than ever. Ideologically, at least, that is hardly surprising. However much some Tories may have helped to make the events of 1688–9 possible, it was Whig ideology that those events essentially vindicated. And a basic tenet of Whig political philosophy, classically enunciated in John Locke's *Second Treatise*, was that 'the great and chief end . . . of men's uniting into commonwealths, and putting themselves under government, is the preservation of their property'.[2] The view that Locke himself intepreted property and its ownership very exclusively, even capitalistically (e.g. 308), has been convincingly demolished by Richard Ashcraft (310b, *256–83*). But ideology apart, there were practical and political reasons of obvious importance why the Glorious Revolution became so pre-eminently glorious for men of *substantial* property. This was a revolution both conceived and carried through by representatives of the propertied classes, and if it was not wholly in the interests of these classes that it was effected, it was not to be expected that those interests would be ignored in its aftermath. For none of James II's actions had so united the political nation against him – Whig and Tory, peer and gentleman, clergyman and lawyer, tradesman and yeoman – as that series of measures in 1687–8 which had seemed to undermine established rights of 'property', in that word's widest seventeenth-century sense (Chs. 11, 12).

Just as significant as the ideology and causes of the Revolution in paving the way subsequently for the triumph of the property-owners was its course. So swiftly was James dethroned that those men of property who led the rebellion against him were never forced to make any appeal for popular support, never in any danger of losing control. It cannot be stressed too emphatically that the radical forces in London which Pym had felt bound to enlist in 1641 and Shaftesbury in 1680–1 left only a minor imprint on the central political and constitutional events of 1688–9. Despite much caballing in the 'commonwealth' clubs and dissenting cells of the City, a fierce burst of radical pamphleteering in January 1689, and a petition to the Convention by the City Whigs, bearing 15,000 signatures, Parliament went its own prudent way undeterred. Its determination to be seen to be resisting popular coercion was underlined by the refusal of both Houses even to receive the February petition; it was only in what has been called 'the Revolutionary crisis in London politics' itself (94b, *45ff.*) that the radicals could find an effective outlet for their populist brand of Whiggery (94b, *56–7;* 312, *200–18;* 310b, *563ff., 593–7*). Significantly, by the mid–1690s the new generation of Whig leaders, epitomised by the members of the so-called Junto, had severed virtually all the old links between their party and its old radical wing (229, *82–3*).

So high, in various ways, was the stake of the men of property in the Revolution that we cannot doubt that two of the most vital constitutional legacies of 1688–9 – a regular parliamentary presence at Westminster and the freedom of the judiciary from unhealthy royal pressure – were seen by men of the post-Revolution generation as guarantees that never again would an arbitrary regime be in a position to imperil property, as James's had done. The peaceful accession of the Protestant house of Hanover in 1714 seemed, to the victorious Whigs at least, to reinforce those guarantees; the poet Ambrose Philips, in a eulogistic ode to Lord Halifax, looked forward not merely to the sanctification of property under the new order but to its deification:

'O Prosperity! O Goddess, English-born!'[3]

Recently, however, historians have focused on another aspect of the legacy of the 'respectable revolution'. They have found it hard to believe it a coincidence that after 1689 the criminal law, as well as the law of the constitution, began to bear down more heavily than ever before on offences against property. There had to be security against the crimes of unregenerate plebs no less than against the arbitrary acts of tyrannical kings. There is no need to follow certain historians of Marxist hue, who in interpreting these trends claim to have sniffed out a conspiracy of the social élite to manipulate the law for their own class purposes. The game laws apart (clearly a special case), most of the victims of larceny in the eighteenth century, and by the same token most of those who brought the private prosecutions necessary to institute actions, were men or women of relatively small property – something of which Locke would not have disapproved (cf. 264b with 265; 258, *148–50*). The facts are, nevertheless, that at the time of the Revolution there were about fifty different crimes for which the death penalty could be inflicted. But between the late 1690s and 1723, when the notorious 'Black Act' was passed, the legislature steadily added to this number a string of offences against property of one kind or another that were made punishable by death. In 1698, for instance, it was made a capital crime to steal, or assist others to steal, goods to the value of five shillings [25p] from any shop, warehouse, coach-house or stable. The Black Act alone created no fewer than fifty new capital offences, among them cutting down young trees, broaching fishponds, even writing threatening letters. In subsequent decades the list was further lengthened, for instance by the Sheep and Cattle Acts of 1741–2. Not one of these capital statutes was repealed until 1808 and by then there were nearly 200 on the book. It is true that a capital crime did not automatically mean capital punishment. The mounting savagery of statute law, in a state whose lack of a professional police system bred a particular sense of insecurity among both its property-owners and legislators,[4] was intended to deter as much as to exact retribution; and there were, in sober fact, far fewer executions by the early and mid-eighteenth century than in the early seventeenth century, and, it would seem, far fewer felonious crimes (263a; 264b; 258, *182–4*; 229; 169, *111*). Nevertheless, as a result of the whole gamut of late Stuart and Hanoverian measures one *could* be hanged just as thoroughly for petty shop-lifting or making off with a sheep as for stealing the crown jewels. And in Surrey from 1736 to 1753 almost fifty per cent of those found guilty on capital property charges *were* hanged. As part of the same process, benefit of clergy was eroded in the early eighteenth century and as a result of an Act of 1718 transportation to the colonies became the commonest punishment meted out to those convicted of 'clergyable' or non-capital crimes against property.[5]

II

At the very time, however, when constitutional and legal constraints together were thus helping to make England safer for men of property in general, economic trends were bringing about changes of the greatest importance in the distribution of property among the bigger property-owners. And it was largely as a result of these changes that the effects of revolution and wars on English society between 1690 and the mid–1720s proved so unpredictable and, in some ways, contradictory.

There were two major structural alterations in post-Revolution society which cannot have been anticipated by the men of 1688 but which were to place a lasting mark on Hanoverian Britain. One was a change within the landowning sector of society: less thoroughgoing, certainly less universal, than students of this period have long been accustomed to think, but basic enough to cause much concern at the time. The second was a remarkable further advance in the economic and social status of certain essentially non-landed elements, partly professional interests and partly business interests. We have already observed the crucial bearing which the wars against Louis XIV's France had on the latter change (Chs. 14–16). And although they were by no means the only phenomenon affecting the fortunes of those who owned land in the late seventeenth and early eighteenth centuries, they were at very least an important aggravating factor here.

During the last two decades of the seventeenth century an essentially new landowning pattern slowly began to take shape in some English counties, and during the next twenty to thirty years this pattern became more clearly defined and gradually extended to other parts. The result was to produce, however unevenly, a significant shift in the balance of landownership, and although in its origins it pre-dated the outbreak of hostilities in 1689, it owed not a little of its subsequent impetus to nearly twenty years of warfare. For over a century before 1660 the proportion of land held in great estates had been shrinking in relation to the share held by the gentry (Ch. 4). From the 1680s, at the latest, this proportion began to increase once again. At first, like most such changes, it was unspectacular. But there are strong grounds for thinking that for a quarter of a century, beginning in the early 1690s, the tide ran more strongly in favour of large landowners than at any time since the mid-sixteenth century, and that right up to 1750, at least, the same trend continued, though less powerfully.

However, neither the new disposition of landed property which resulted nor the reasons why it came about are matters for uncritical generalisation. Essentially we are looking not at the bold effects of a fresco but at the moving pieces of a highly complex mosaic (70, *lv-lxi*; 238b; 242a, *Ch. 5*). That has not always been apparent. In a pioneering essay published in 1940, Sir John Habakkuk established conclusively that in two south midland counties of which he made a close study, Northamptonshire and Bedfordshire, wealthy aristocrats like the dukes of Bedford and Kent, the earl of Sunderland and Lord Rockingham were buying land heavily and prospering in the late seventeenth and early eighteenth centuries, not least during war years. He also showed that most of this land was being snapped up from the many casualties which this period produced among both the gentry class, in its middle and lower reaches, and the 'yeomanry' or small independent proprietors (237). (A subsequent investigation of the fortunes of the latter, on a national scale, was to lead the same authority to the conclusion that low farm prices and [after 1689] high taxation made this same period the most crucial one of all in that long and much-debated process, *la disparition du paysan anglais* (Ch. 4).[6]) As for the buyers of the land which became available, it appeared that in Bedfordshire and Northamptonshire, at least, the big aristocratic dealers had limited competition from successful army officers and lawyers, but surprisingly little from London merchant princes and business tycoons. The latter, in spite of their growing wealth in the 1680s and under the last two Stuarts, figure much less prominently in the South Midlands land market than had been the case earlier in the seventeenth century.

Despite the evident importance of these findings it was to be some thirty years before landownership in other counties in this period began to be put under the microscope in the same comprehensive way, and even now such comparative work has a long way to go. Meanwhile what had started, with Habakkuk, as a hypothesis had already drifted into widely-accepted orthodoxy. The view that there was a nationwide, and not just a local, swing in favour of 'the great lords and the great estates' from the late seventeenth century onwards was weightily endorsed (e.g. 236a, esp. *Ch. 1*), though sometimes with prudent warnings against over-stressing short-term influences on what could be seen as an essentially long-term development (220b). More recent research, however, has illuminated marked variations between region and region and even between counties within regions. It begins to seem very probable that the more peripheral the county, and the more pastoral its agrarian economy, the greater was the capacity for survival of its lesser landowners, whether gentlemen or yeomen. Where, in addition, there was a largely absentee aristocracy, as in Cumberland and Westmorland, it was likely to be the substantial squires who bought most of those estates or holdings of any size which came up for sale (238a; 244). Even in less remote and more prosperous areas it is clear that no iron laws governed landownership and the land market. Rich noblemen or squires buying heavily in one county are sometimes found to be selling in others, in order to consolidate their estates. In the rich grazing county of Wiltshire the government official Sir Stephen Fox (though mostly before 1690) and the London banking family of Hoare were among the foremost purchasers; while in arable Lincolnshire, in the early no less than the later decades of the eighteenth century, native gentry as well as yeomanry bought as well as sold, and with land coming plentifully on to the market there was ample scope too for investment by both merchants and professionals.[7] More striking even than local idiosyncracies are the manifold individual variations on the general theme: personal, often fortuitous circumstances which could devastate the big as well as the small proprietors. Extravagance, bad management of estates, family misfortunes – these were as common between the close of Charles II's reign and the middle of George II's as at any other time. This is underlined by the heavy sales forced on such aristocratic families as the Petres, Fairfaxes, Booths, Cecils (earls of Salisbury) and Cornwallises, and by the disasters which overtook leading commoner families like the Culpeppers of Kent or the Cottons of Leicestershire (70, *lviii-lix*). And in one respect, demographic adversity, and in particular the failure of male heirs leading to the break-up of large agglomerations of land, the generation of parents born to both the nobility and gentry between 1675 and 1725 is known to have been uniquely vulnerable (243a; 233b).[8]

And yet, all reservations made, there are still good grounds for the conviction, even among the revisionists, that 'the equilibrium between the large and small landowners was being upset with particular rapidity' between 1680 and 1750 (240a, *517*); that during the war years from 1689 to 1713, especially, many middling gentry families were hard pressed to hold their own, and that the bulk of the parish and one-manor gentry of from £100 to £300 a year – always a vulnerable group – were subject to exceptionally daunting pressures. It was certainly believed at the time (though it has never been, and can never be, conclusively proved) that families of the lesser gentry were being forced out of landed society altogether in unusually large numbers in the course of the French wars, and probably for some time after. It was in the mid–1720s that Defoe observed that, even when the rigours of taxation had relaxed, 'what with excessive high living, which is of late grown so much into a disease, and the ordinary circumstances of families, we find few families of the lower gentry . . . but they are in debt and in necessitous circumstances.'[9] He went further, and like another popular writer of the day, John Macky, urged on these unfortunates the positive benefits of selling their country houses as well as their land and settling into a cheap but genteel way of life in some congenial provincial town.[10]

It is more than likely that contemporaries over-generalised about the plight of the 'mere' gentry. What is beyond all question is that the victims of the financial and economic pressures of this period, beginning with the many glut years of the 1680s which so depressed agricultural prices, included many hundreds of the less substantial yeoman freeholders in the grain-growing regions of England, whereas their counterparts in pastoral counties – in Cumbria, for example, Lancashire and much of Wales – were much better insulated against adversity. In the North-West, at least, they even enjoyed a marked rise in living standards (244; 239). It is also certain that, while opportunities still existed for wealthy *nouveaux* (including, increasingly, provincial *nouveaux*) to move into landed society from the 1690s onwards (187b, *Ch. 10*), it was mainly the nobility and the élite of the commoners – those with rentals of at least £1,000 a year – who were to be found significantly extending their estates at this period. Moreover, their advantage was preserved well beyond the war years, when for a while land prices were seriously depressed, into the 1720s, when prices reached unheard-of levels after the South Sea crisis. In many southern and midland counties, in particular, there were some extremely heavy spenders among the existing landed élites. The king of the land market in the early eighteenth century was John Holles, first duke of Newcastle, who lived in princely splendour at Welbeck Abbey, Nottinghamshire. Having already inherited in the 1690s a great estate from the last Cavendish earl of Newcastle, as well as the lands of his deceased cousin, Lord Holles, he then proceeded in the last ten years of his life (1701–11) to lay out at least a quarter of a million pounds on yet more land. While his lesser neighbours groaned about the burden of the Spanish Succession War, Newcastle's agents negotiated the purchase of estate after estate in Nottinghamshire, Lincolnshire, Cambridgeshire and Middlesex.[11] Within a year of Newcastle's death the duke of Marlborough had given notice of his intention to outdo him: the £400,000 which Marlborough vested in trustees to buy land for the Churchills was duly disbursed in the twenty years or so after 1712, £150,000 of it on the confiscated estates of South Sea Company directors (233b, *218, n. 45*)).

There seem to have been four main reasons why big fish were able to swim confidently into new and even bigger pools while smaller fish were floundering. In the first place, this was a period, down to 1715 at least, which on the whole was a very difficult one for agriculture: a period of climatic extremes characterised by severe harvest fluctuations (the over-bountiful 1680s, for example, followed by the 'seven lean years' of the 1690s [K.1(i),(ii)]), and by generally stagnant rents, with arrears becoming commonplace. It ended with a time, from perhaps 1707 to 1712, when there was much dark talk of the bottom falling out of the land market (240b). All this put an especially high premium on 'improvements', and to improve estates and make them profitable in such a climate, keep farm premises in good repair so as to attract new tenants, and employ professional agents to maximise returns, made demands on capital which only men of large fortune could normally meet. Secondly, the big landowners, being for the most part men of great family, had built-in advantages in addition to their land. For example, they were ideally equipped because of their rank to compete for the richest prizes in the marriage market. A record of success here was vital for almost any family bent on *sustained* progress, and some marriages, such as the duke of Bedford's with Elizabeth Howland, had a truly dramatic effect on aristocratic incomes. (Not that every fine settlement automatically brought long-term blessings: Richard Beaumont's marriage with the Countess of Westmorland in 1698, for instance, drained the Witley and Lascelles estates of over £30,000 in the next thirty years [240a]). A third reason why the dice were loaded in favour of the existing landed élite was directly connected with the wars against Louis XIV. Over a good deal of England it was only the substantial landlords who were able to shrug off the burden of the new Land Tax. Nothing quite like this tax had hit the English taxpayer before (Ch. 17). For seventeen out of twenty years up to 1713 [G.2(ii)], in much of southern and central England, though not in the favourably assessed northern and far western counties, it remorselessly took four shillings in the pound (20 per cent) off the *real* value of landed rents. Indeed, because of continuing alarms, domestic and international, after the Peace of Utrecht 'there were only four years out of 29 between 1693–4 and 1721–2 in which the rate of the land tax came down to the "peace-time level" of 2 shillings in the pound which was to become the norm under Walpole' (70, *lvii-lviii*). Finally, there is a further war-induced trend to be kept in mind: the diversion of funds from the mortgage market and the higher interest and mortgage rates of the years after 1689. Interest rates were particularly high in the 1690s and it needed an Act of Parliament in 1714 to place a 5 per cent ceiling on private loans. These were worrying times, in particular, for hundreds of landed families who, encouraged by the easy credit available in post-Restoration England, had saddled their estates with new-fangled settlement charges to provide for marriage portions or for the future of sons (233a). And once again, other things being equal, they were problems much more easily coped with by the big landed proprietors than by those with more limited resources.

That contemporaries themselves became aware that a shift of great consequence was taking place in the social distribution of landed property is clear from several post-Revolution pointers. One indicator is the number of promotions to dukedoms between 1689 and 1720. These were on a scale far beyond all precedent. In 1688 there had only been four dukes in the peerage of England, apart from the six royal bastards.[12] By 1719 there were twenty-five English dukes, including a few Scots with post–1707 'British' titles (241a, *486–8*). The dukedom constituted the highest rung of the hereditary peerage. Another pointer to changing attitudes was an abortive proposal made in the House of Lords in 1701 that the minimum qualification for elevation to a place on the lowest rung of the peerage, a barony, should be laid down by law at £3,000 a year. To get this sum in perspective, it was five times the level actually required, from 1711, of a squire or nobleman's son before he was allowed to represent his county in Parliament as a knight of the shire [F(xi)]. But £3,000 was mere pin money compared with the annual incomes being attributed (usually with justice) to some of the great English magnates by the second half of Anne's reign: the dukes of Newcastle (credited with £40,000 by the time of his death), Bedford (£35,000), Beaufort (£30,000) and Ormonde (£25,000, though much of it from Irish lands). Marlborough was thought to enjoy at least as large an income as Newcastle by 1711, and his massive short-term loans to the Whig government after 1718 were the actions of 'one of the richest private citizens in Europe' (113a, *431–2*). Meanwhile, a mere baron, Lord Brooke, could boast a rental and other revenues of over £20,000 a year, and between the £14,000 and £20,000 mark were to be found by 1714 a very sizable group of peers, including Somerset, Devonshire, Rutland, Wharton and Kingston. Equally impressive was the even larger group of commoners who could now boast landed incomes, in an average year, of £10-£15,000. They included many who were to acquire peerages later from the Hanoverians, among them Bromleys of Horseheath, Cokes of Holkham, Curzons of Kedleston, Courtenays of Powderham and Sir Richard Child of Wanstead, heir of the greatest of seventeenth-century East India magnates, Sir Josiah. Of course, even among the peers there was, as always, another side to the coin: not merely families who ran on to the rocks through extravagance or misfortune, but 'poor lords', like Fitzwalter, Hunsdon, Lincoln and the near-destitute Colepeper and Willoughby of Parham, who had more or less permanent difficulty staying afloat and needed pensions as desperately as drowning men need life-rafts. The Scottish peerage claimed some harder cases still, among them the 7th earl of Home, who had to borrow £100 to get to London in December 1711 to take his seat in the Lords.[13]

By and large, however, life at the top in early eighteenth-century Britain was becoming increasingly enviable. The social and cultural standards which the favoured élite could now set were a rising barometer, by which the progress of Britain's wealthiest landlords could be measured. The 1680s and 1690s saw the beginning of the most spectacular period of mansion building England had yet seen, the age of the baroque, its massive monuments throwing into starker relief the painful struggles of financially embarrassed neighbouring gentry. But the great lords now had other status symbols, as well as vast houses and their lavish interiors: in particular, displays of gracious furniture, and collections of fine paintings, porcelain and statuary, for which not only Europe but Asia was eagerly combed (*The Age of Oligarchy*, Ch. 14). An awestruck Daniel Defoe described Wilton House, the seat of the 8th earl of Pembroke, as 'a mere museum, or a chamber of rarities, . . . so prepared, as if built on purpose to receive' the treasures with which that noted connoisseur had filled it (3, *I, 194*). Equally *de rigeur* were those stately parks, beloved of travel diarists, and the new-style landscaped gardens, where nature's work was cunningly improved by the hand of man. Those peers with the more exuberant tastes were never short of fresh ways to mark their one-upmanship. Lord Orford, the victor of La Hogue, set a new fashion in the 1690s as the first peer to pull down most of a village (Chippenham) in order to perfect his park. Walpole later followed his example at Houghton. In 1718 the first duke of Chandos not only installed the eminent Johann Pepush as director of music at Cannons Park, where he ran a successful music school, but furnished him with a permanent orchestra at a cost of £1,000 a year to entertain his house guests (226a, *30, 31*). Handel too was enlisted and composed his beautiful Chandos anthems for the latter's pleasure.

The more ostentatiously or arrogantly the great flaunted their wealth, the more glaring may seem to us the contrast between their sumptuous splendour and the poverty and harsh, uncertain lives of those whose sweat kept them in luxury – servants, wage-labourers, small farmers. And yet to the propertyless of post-Restoration Britain themselves, as McInnes and Cannon have emphasised, such social antitheses were mostly a matter of stoical indifference or passive acquiescence (229; 242a, *169–74*). It may have been improving economic circumstances (Ch. 25) which made it easier for them than for their forebears of the Civil War period to accept implicitly the age-old order of ranks and degrees as something God-ordained (29). Alternatively, it may have been a change in the political climate since the 1650s. Certainly, truly *popular* radicalism, as opposed to bourgeois or 'country' radicalism, was at a low ebb by the early decades of the eighteenth century (21 [Dickinson], *69–83*), and popular protest and disorder, when it occurred, was remarkably conservative in its inspiration (*The Age of Oligarchy*, Ch. 12). When mobs rioted at election times, they did so not in their own interests, but in the cause of one or other of the national political parties, neither of which, ironically, recognised their right to participate in any way in the process of government. Post-Revolution Britons rarely seem to have doubted that this part at least of their social structure, cemented by patriarchalism and deference (321, *78ff.*), had a permanence which could more or less be taken for granted.

And yet, the élite of the political nation after 1688 made no such assumptions about the stability of their society *as a whole*. To many of them that society was developing features that seemed novel and dangerous. Far from being much less mobile after 1700 than before 1660, as we are often prone to imagine (221; cf. 234), the social fabric in the eyes of Augustan Englishmen was being rendered seriously unstable by the unhealthy degree of mobility it allowed. It was not the lower storeys which caused them concern. Rather it was higher up the fabric that the strain was perceived, and even there not in those parts where earlier seventeenth-century experience might well have led them to expect it.

The significant change in the balance of landownership discussed earlier in this chapter might, in other circumstances have fissured the landed classes themselves, just as the violent motions of 1540–1640 (Ch. 4) had done in the two generations before the Great Rebellion. One reason why it did not do so may be that here at least – within existing landed society – upward mobility *was* appreciably diminished by contrast with that earlier situation. Movement from the yeomanry into the ranks of the lesser gentry, and likewise from the latter into the ranks of the squirearchy, did not cease entirely, but it was very restricted. Moreover, the strong resentments undoubtedly harboured by many hundreds of the lesser gentry under William III and Anne prove, under the researcher's microscope, to have been more localised than was once believed. But perhaps the most important reason why these resentments did not cause bitter animosities among landowners themselves is that they were deflected away from aggrandising landlords by what seemed at the time, to the rank-and-file of the landed interest, a more unforeseeable and far more sinister change in the distribution of property. This was the crucial thrust forward made after the Glorious Revolution by interests whose true stake was not in the land at all.

III

The rapid social as well as economic advance made in the quarter century after 1688 by large numbers of essentially non-landed families provided the lower and middling gentry of the country with an alternative and emotionally more satisfying object for their rancour. Passions which might otherwise have been spent in fulminations against the élite of their own class were invested instead in what contemporaries came to call 'the conflict of interests', and through that, in the political warfare between Whigs and Tories. Once again there can be no question that the chief agents of social change, and in this case of social conflict, were the two great post-Revolution wars. In 1709 the most brilliant young Tory politician of the day, Henry St John, told his friend Lord Orrery:

> We have now been twenty years engaged in the two most expensive wars that Europe ever saw. The whole burden of this charge has lain upon the landed interest during the whole time. The men of estates have, generally speaking, neither served in the fleets nor armies, nor meddled in the public funds and management of the treasure. A *new interest* has been created out of their fortunes, and a sort of property which was not known twenty years ago, is now increased to be almost equal to the terra firma [landed property] of our island. The consequence of all [this] is that the landed men are become poor and dispirited . . . while those men are become their masters who formerly would with joy have been their servants.[14]

Social historians who have argued for the 'openness' rather than for the increasingly 'closed' nature of British society in the century before the Industrial Revolution have commonly assumed that this was a mainly beneficial characteristic (183; 226b; 29 [Holmes]). And so it was for at least fifty years before the onset of rapid industrialisation. The frequency of intermarriage between county and City; investment by landowners in business enterprises; the rise of new professions, and perhaps most of all, the extensive land purchases still being made, as for so long they had been, by men whose wealth sprang from commerce as well as professional success – these elements, and others, were from the 1720s onwards vital in keeping the social structure basically stable yet nicely flexible.

Of the decades before then, however, contemporary rhetoric like that of St John and of scores of others equally impassioned if less eloquent tells a more partial but very different story. Its message, if taken at face value, is that there was a long period after the Glorious Revolution when it seemed that such flexibility as did exist in late Stuart society would be insufficient to cope with the exceptional strains produced in that society by war. For had not those bridges which normally carried a heavy stream of two-way traffic between the county communities of England and the City of London become of late precarious and the number of passengers using them atypically low? Only very recently have these assumptions been subjected to searching scrutiny, on the basis of less subjective and less random evidence bearing on the 'mobility' of the London businessmen of 1689–1714. And it would now seem that contemporary perceptions about the 'big bourgeoisie', at least, are not entirely to be trusted (255b,

287

263–96). Not every feature of these years was as novel as it often seemed to war-harassed country gentlemen. Yet at the same time it remains clear that in the exceptional circumstances of the reigns of William and Anne there were justifiable grounds for unease. The proportion of the City merchant and business élite recruited from county families had gone into steep, and as it proved permanent, decline (255b, *284*; 255a). As for the marriage bridge, the heads of many landed families, or their heirs, did still contrive to net well-endowed City brides, but during the wars against Louis XIV a substantial majority of the daughters of London's aldermen – far more than hitherto – married to cement business alliances or partnerships, or elsewhere within the City, rather than to bring their families traditional social kudos. Modern research, furthermore, has confirmed St John's impression that during the French wars 'the men of estates have, generally speaking, [not] . . . meddled in the public funds' (113a, *Ch. 11*). And – the most distinctive trend of all – those London businessmen who, like Sir James Bateman or Sir Thomas Scawen, did purchase *great* country estates with their City wealth between 1689 and 1714, were conspicuously few in numbers (233b, *214–16*). Only a minority of the true plutocrats bought no real estate at all outside the capital. But the pattern already foreshadowed by the 1680s, of making only limited purchases – often within 'commuting' distance of the city – for reasons of status or perhaps to secure electoral influence, thereafter became the norm (3, *I, 146–7, 158–9, 168; II, 2–3;* 255b). With the return on stocks and loans so high, and that on highly-taxed land in the south-east so low, what could be more logical for the 'new interest' in post-Revolution society?

The key to this situation – the wars apart – was that while the Revolution was rightly greeted as a triumph of property and property-owners, 'property', in a seventeenth- and eighteenth-century sense, did not have to be in land, or indeed in bricks, stone and mortar. Traditionally, of course, land had always been regarded as the supreme hallmark of status and citizenship. It gave a man 'a permanent fixed interest' in the country, a special claim to inherit both privileges and the responsibilities that went with them. And with taxation falling more heavily on land after 1689 than it had ever done, this tradition seemed to many existing landowners to have acquired still greater relevance. But the significance of the twenty years which followed the Revolution was to give greatly enhanced value to property of a different kind: to that enjoyed by the new legion of 'civil officers' or career bureaucrats (for their offices, though rarely purchased, were by and large regarded proprietorially); or to the 'property' which the large new corps of army and navy officers enjoyed by virtue of their commissions, and the rich rewards which these investments (literally that in the case of the army) brought to the successful among them. Above all, the post-Revolution years transformed the prospects of those in the business world able and fortunate enough to seize their opportunities, for bank and major company stocks, Treasury bonds, government annuities for life, prizewinning lottery tickets – these were 'property' too, and much of it indeed of 'a sort [in St John's words] . . . which was not known' before 1688.

The Commercial Revolution and the strengthening of the Stuart state had made their contribution to all these processes. But they sent no shock waves through the foundations of propertied society. The developments of the war years, on the other hand, unquestionably did. The unprecedented expansion of both the executive and the armed forces (Chs. 14, 16) caused deep unease in some quarters of the landed classes. But reactions to the new age of government borrowing, which opened up such an alluring field of secure yet profitable investment for men with capital and an eye to the main chance (Ch. 17), were positively alarmist. For thrown up in the process, (and, so it seemed, almost overnight) was a novel social group of great wealth and influence. It was the more resented because it presented a noticeably alien image. The group included wealthy Jews, like Henriquez and Pereira, and a prominent cohort of recent immigrants from France and the Low Countries, plus a great many English merchants native by birth but of dissenting religion. Recent research has identified well over 40 per cent of Bank of England directors from 1694 to 1715 and nearly a third of the directors of the New, and later United, East India Company from 1698 to 1715 as members of English nonconformist congregations (113a, *263–80*; 94b, *109, 99–112 passim*). The 'new interest' of which St John complained in 1709 – contemporaries usually called it 'the monied interest' – was thus an almost entirely London-based body of men, deeply permeated by various brands of socio-religious dissidence. Although not entirely *arrivistes*, indeed overlapping significantly with the pre-Revolution City merchant class, they broke conspicuously with the traditions of that class in one respect above all: in that, as long as the wars lasted, they preferred to keep much – and in some cases all – of their fortunes tied up in the elaborate new mechanism of loans and credit or hard at work in plying the stock and foreign exchange markets. On top of that, however, their wary attitude to the land market (p. 288 above) added a double dose of gall to the country gentleman's cup. For as well as enjoying a far higher return on investment in wartime than they could ever have done from rents, they also effectively evaded the burden of the wartime Land Tax. Sir Gilbert Heathcote (Ch. 17) had a great landed estate and a fortune of at least £700,000 by the time he died in 1733 (26a, *II, 123*). But the great bulk of his land was bought in his old age, in the 1720s, thirty years and more after he had helped to found the Bank of England.

That contemporaries suffered from some delusions about the monied interest is beyond doubt (above, p. 273 ; 70, *xlvi-xlix*). But it had its reality as well as its mythology. It did not escape notice that most of the beneficiaries of its rise were committed Whigs. The Bank of England was overwhelmingly Whiggish from the start and remained so, in both its directorate and its major stockholders. Of the big London corporations with prominent stakes in the National Debt only the Old East India Company, before its dissolution in 1708, had a majority Tory presence. Even Harley's South Sea Company soon succumbed to Whig infiltration (94b, *125, 132*). The obverse of the coin was equally clear. A heavy majority of the sufferers from the system of war finance, certainly among the smaller gentry, were Tories, and their party, especially in Anne's reign, frankly espoused the cause of the hard-pressed 'landed interest'. It was because of these political associations that the so-called conflict of interests became deeply enmeshed in the party politics of the day. To many Tory gentry it seemed, by the middle of

Anne's reign, that the most desperate problem facing their party, in the words of one knight of the shire, was how 'to prevent the beggary of the nation, to prevent the moneyed and military men becoming lords of us who have the lands.'[15]

Even socially the new status and property revolution seemed intolerable to them. Before the start of the Spanish Succession War a Tory squire was already grumbling to the Commons about the 'rich coaches, fine liveries, splendid equipages, luxurious tables and numerous other expensive ways of state' he saw daily in London, professing himself 'certain that some of these gentlemen not many years ago were scarce able to keep a pad nag and a drab coat.' By the end of the war he and his kind were convinced that things were much worse. The Tory MP for Bridport bitterly reflected in 1712 'how many a noble fortune and ancient family have been reduced since this war, and how many of these men that now surprize the Town with their [financial] misfortunes were worth sixpence at the Revolution; nay how many even of those that surprize all thinking men with their riches.'[16] Offensive though the social changes were, however, it was when the City plutocrats, along with some civil officials and many careerist army officers, began in growing numbers to use their property to buy their way into parliamentary seats, and therefore into political power, that the alarm of the landed interest became acute. A climax was reached in the Whig-dominated Parliament which sat while the Hague peace opportunity was squandered and the field of Malplaquet ran with blood. No fewer than eleven directors or ex-directors of the Bank came into the Commons of 1708–10, along with Whig generals like Cadogan, Macartney and Meredith who had been swiftly jumping the military promotions queue, and honest country gentlemen were elbowed out in the process. When just before the end of this Parliament Heathcote, the Governor, and three other directors of the Bank gained an audience with the Queen and warned her that she would destroy public credit if she dismissed her Whig ministers and dissolved Parliament, scandalised Tories cried out that 'the insolence of these fellows is without example'.[17]

At the root of much of the Tory clamour for peace in Anne's later years lay a very real fear that if the war went on much longer not merely the traditional social order, with its priorities based on landed property, but the political establishment might be thoroughly subverted. As well as being voiced in Parliament (for example, in the debates preceding the passing of the 1711 Act imposing a landed qualification on members of Parliament) (above, p. 284; F(xi)), such fears were articulated by the political press, and by no one more effectively than Jonathan Swift in 1710–11, in a widely-read periodical, *The Examiner*, and in a brilliant tract, *The Conduct of the Allies and of the Late Ministry*. By concentrating fire on both the political influence and the inordinate financial profit which war had brought to Marlborough and his protégés, on the one hand, and to 'such whose whole fortunes lie in funds and stocks', on the other, Swift reinforced the deepest apprehensions of the landed interest. The fears were highly exaggerated (29 [Holmes]). Yet they are understandable: after all, it was little more than twenty years since the English nation had dethroned a king largely to preserve the property as well as the 'liberties' of the established governing class.

The political repercussions of the 'conflict of interests', especially in Queen Anne's reign, have received ample attention from historians. The question of how close the conflict had come to flash-point by the time the Peace of Utrecht arrived in 1713 remains an open one (70, *Ch. 5*; 66; 29 [Holmes]). What is clear is that the signing of the peace treaties, by immediately reducing the British government's dependence on the City, and still more by enabling the Land Tax to be halved, took an appreciable degree of heat out of the situation. The cooling process was not uninterrupted, however. The Jacobite rebellion sent the rate of the Land Tax up once again in 1716 to its maximum four shillings in the pound, and with foreign affairs continuing tense the gentry would not have guessed that this would be the last such rise, bar one (1727), in the next quarter of a century [G.2(ii)]. The 'monied corporations' at first obstructed the plans of the Whig Treasury in 1716–17 to consolidate and reduce the interest on the National Debt. The decisive event, both politically and socially, was the bursting of the South Sea Bubble. The collapse of so many joint-stock companies and the loss of so many paper fortunes and nest-eggs (Ch. 17) took away much of the glamour and glitter of the new world of big finance. In conjunction with a steady fall of interest rates it had the effect, as we have seen, of bringing land thoroughly back into favour as a long-term investment, not least for City magnates: the sharply rising land prices of the 1720s leave us in no doubt about this (240b). The seismic shocks of the war years had not in the end produced the earthquake that had been feared, and Walpole's soothing influence, fiscal retrenchment and consensus policies for two decades after 1721 made it finally certain that they never would do (*The Age of Oligarchy*, Ch. 1). The 'monied interest' had come to stay in English society, and by the 1730s it was fast being assimilated, along with the new professional groups, far more painlessly than had seemed possible thirty years before, into a social élite whose culture, values and mores all men of property, irrespective of function, came – as 'gentlemen' – to share (321, *71*; cf. Ch. 4)).

---

1. This phrase, or something very like it, was also coined by Ogg, but I cannot now trace the reference. G.S.H.
2. [John Locke], *Second Treatise on Government* (1681/1689), ch. 9. See R. Ashcraft (310a), pp. 102–3 for the post-Oxford date at which this chapter, and most of the *Second Treatise*, was written in 1681, and Ashcraft and M.M. Goldsmith (311) for the November 1689 date of its publication.
3. Quoted in Trevelyan (19), II, p. 84 n.
4. The uniqueness of the British situation in an 18th century context is stressed in the classic work of L. Radzinowicz (128), pp. 23–35. But cf. J.A. Sharpe (258), Ch. 8.
5. J.M. Beattie, 'Crime and the Courts in Surrey 1736–1753', in J.S. Cockburn, ed., *Crime in England, 1550–1800* (1979). On the leniency of 18th-century courts towards first offenders and men of previously good character, see J.H. Langbein (265), *passim*.
6. I.e. 'the disappearance of the English peasant'. H.J. Habakkuk, 'La disparition du paysan anglais', *Annales E.S.C.*, **20** (1965). For a more recent judgement cf. J. Thirsk, ed. (211), pp. 1–15.
7. C. Clay, *Public Finance and Private Wealth: the Career of Sir Stephen Fox 1627–1716* (Oxford, 1978), pp. 334–5; B.A. Holderness (243b), *passim*.

8. See also C.W. Chalklin, *Seventeenth-Century Kent* (1965), Ch. 2; C. Clay, 'Property Settlements, Financial Provision for the Family, and Sale of Land by the Greater Landowners 1660–1790', *JBS*, **21** (1981).

9. *The Complete English Tradesman*, I (1726), p. 244.

10. Defoe (3), I, p. 46; Macky, *A Journey through England* (1722), II, pp. 153–4, 210–14.

11. O.R.F. Davies, 'The Wealth and Influence of John Holles, Duke of Newcastle', *Renaissance and Modern Studies*, **9** (1965).

12. Richmond, Grafton, Southampton, Northumberland and St. Albans (illegitimate sons of Charles II); Berwick (James II). The remaining four were Norfolk, Somerset, Ormonde and Beaufort. [A. Collins], *The Peerage of England* I (1709), pp. 39–68.

13. Christ Church, Oxford, Wake MSS. Arch. W. Epist. 17: list of Scots peers appended to a letter of R. Dongworth, 11 Nov 1710; HMC *Portland MSS*, V, p. 121; X, pp. 406–7; Holmes (70), p. 394; E. Gregg and C. Jones, 'Hanover, Pensions and the "Poor Lords", 1712–13', *Parl. Hist.*, I (1982), pp. 176–80.

14. Bodleian Lib. MS. Eng. Misc. e. 180, ff. 4–5 (partly printed in Holmes and Speck, (5), pp. 135–6). The italics are mine.

15. Sir John Pakington, MP Worcestershire, in the Bewdley election debate, 1709: (2), VI, 932.

16. Bodleian Lib. MS. Carte 117, ff. 177–8 (19 Feb 1702); Nat. Lib. Wales, Ottley MSS. 2448: Thomas Strangeways, jun. to Adam Ottley, n.d. [*c*. April 1712]. By courtesy of Daniel Szechi.

17. HMC *Portland MSS.*, VII, p. 1: William Stratford to Edward Harley, Oxford, 24 June 1710.

CHAPTER 19

People, trade and industry:
from the 1690s to the 1720s

I

'In relation to the present war', wrote Gregory King in 1695, 'we are to consider that if this nation [of England and Wales] do at this time contain 5,500,000 souls, it did contain, anno 1688, about 50,000 more . . .'[1] The scale of the war, he calculated, was upsetting the normally slightly favourable balance of births over deaths and emigration, not only by increasing mortality but by reducing 'increase by procreation'. King was wrong about the 1690s; he was just as mistaken in 1711 in assuming that the population had fallen by a further 200,000 since 1695, as he was in his conviction that the wars against Louis XIV had seriously impaired national wealth and the English economy (227, *52 and n. 48*). In reality, the late 1680s were the years when England came out of her post-Restoration demographic trough and haltingly embarked on nearly four decades of slow but fairly steady population growth (Ch. 2). According to the most reliable modern estimate, the population of England (without Wales) grew from the low point of 4.86 million in 1686 to 5.48 million in 1727, the bulk of the expansion occurring before 1720 (196, *210, 212 [table]*; cf. B.1 for England *and Wales*). Except in some areas of industrial or commercial growth the birth-rate remained little more than sluggish for most of that period, and unusually low during the second half of the Spanish Succession War (1707–12). But from shortly before the Glorious Revolution until the eve of the South Sea Bubble the death rate fell, as the country enjoyed substantial immunity from epidemic disease on the grand scale [B.4]. In the light of English experience since the mid-1650s this remission is remarkable and difficult to explain, but it undoubtedly took place. The years 1694, when even Queen Mary died of the smallpox which scourged London,[2] 1695, when fever rampaged in the West Country, and 1711–12, were relatively sickly, though not marked by heavy nationwide mortality. Not until 1719–21, in fact, did outbreaks of typhus and other diseases inaugurate what are sometimes seen as the last two decades of 'massacre by epidemic' in English history (194, *32, 92–106*; 192, *28–33)*. The phrase may be over-dramatic. It was only from 1727–31 and from 1741–2 that the death-rate in England at large rose above the danger level of 34 per thousand, and only in 1729 – the year of the 'putrid fever', and much else – that it caused universal alarm [B.4]. Nevertheless, despite a quite striking rise in the birth-rate during the 1720s and 1730s (a crucial pointer to the future) (195b), it was to be 1735 before the population securely recovered the ground it had lost since 1719, and approaching 1750 before England was firmly set on a steeply upward demographic path (*The Age of Oligarchy*, Ch. 9) [B.1].

By then Scotland's case was not dissimilar. In 1755 a Church of Scotland clergyman named Alexander Webster undertook, with the help of his colleagues in the parishes, one of the most ambitious of all private censuses. So thorough were his methods that the total of over 1,265,000 he arrived at is now generally regarded as a secure anchor-point (274, *259ff.*; [B.3.(ii)]). As such it suggests that since the Union in 1707 Scotland's demographic recovery had been at least as marked as that of her neighbour, and probably more so. For, possessed as she was of a more vulnerable economy, and with so heavy a dependence on her oat crop, her experience in the decade after 1688 had not been the same as England's. Scottish farmers, too, had had their 'seven ill years' from 1692 to 1699 (pp. 198–200), but the effects for them and their countrymen had been a famine of Malthusian severity. The Scottish famine of 1696–99 was comparable to those which decimated the French peasantry and urban labourers in 1693–4 and 1709–10, worse than the Irish famines of 1708–10 and 1728–30, and at least as bad as that of 1740–1. Starvation and disease stalked hand in hand, exacting such a heavy toll of the Scots both during and after the famine years that thousands of survivors recalled to their lives' end the sight of 'death in the face of the poor'[3] and of roads swarming with hunger-stricken beggars. If the loss of life was as devastating as contemporaries claimed, it may well have been thirty years after the Revolution before Scotland's population began to get back to somewhere near its level of the 1680s (194; 274, *153–5, 242*).

England was spared these horrors. The poor harvests of the second half of the 1690s caused privation among the poor; real wages in 1697 dropped to their lowest level for forty years [M.2]. But there was no corresponding increase in mortality. Indeed, ironically, England was a much healthier place when bread was dear in the 1690s than amid the plenty of the early to mid-1680s; in the same way, there were to be far fewer deaths in 1709 and 1710, after two appalling wheat harvests, than there had been in 1705, a year of bounty. Why was England now famine-proof? It was not irrelevant, of course, that the rapid population growth of the sixteenth and early seventeenth centuries had been completely checked between the Interregnum and the accession of James II. In addition, there was the fact that, even before the 1690s, which saw the beginning of half a century of unprecedented interest and activity in improving the country's river navigation (218a), she already possessed one of the best systems of internal communications and probably the best marketing network in Europe. But it was the combination of these benefits with the agrarian advances made since 1650 which proved utterly decisive. Post-Revolution England not merely had only a tiny subsistence peasantry by contemporary Continental (and Irish and Scottish) standards; even that backward minority was a peasantry that never starved. In John Walton's view 'a pattern of events which closely resembled a Malthusian crisis' is detectable in some regions of upland Lancashire and even in parts of the south of that county as late as the period of the Civil Wars and the Interregnum, but not thereafter (189a, *30; cf.* ibid., *82*).

Two decades of war in the period 1689–1713, with their attendant taxation and perhaps some labour scarcity (cf. 180), at worst only slightly held back the progress of that ongoing agricultural revolution whose beginnings in England and

Wales we have already observed (Ch. 2). It may be that the pace of non-parliamentary enclosure, which on one estimate had taken in roughly a quarter of the entire land surface of the kingdom during the seventeenth century, began to flag during the Spanish Succession War and after. It was, after all, an expensive process, especially when it required resort to legal action, and there were many other demands on landowners' resources (217a). Nevertheless there were some areas, like the southern Cotswolds, for which these were the very years when enclosures developed their greatest momentum, and travellers in this period were struck by the transformation of both landscape and agriculture which enclosure had wrought in such surprising areas (to them) as South Westmorland and North Yorkshire.[4] In other respects the continuity between the post-Restoration period and the decades of well-documented 'improvement' from the 1720s to the 1780s can be illustrated in a variety of ways. The Agricultural Committee of the Royal Society continued the investigative and educative work it had begun in 1665, and William's reign saw the publication for twelve years, from 1691, of the most influential organ of agricultural propaganda yet to appear, Houghton's *Letters for the Improvement of Husbandry and Trade*; Scotland caught the bug in 1723 (209, *61*). It was near the end of King William's reign that Jethro Tull patented his seed-drill, and in 1714 that he began successful experiments with soil pulverisation to extend fertility. Hoskins has drawn attention to the striking number of substantial William and Anne houses still standing in rural Leicestershire and Northamptonshire, bearing witness to the exceptional prosperity of their successful graziers, and there are other counties which have been studied, open-field Oxfordshire for one, where the evidence of improving productivity in the same period seems incontestable (215a, *66–79*; 211, *Pt. 1, passim*).

II

In those two areas of the English economy which had contributed most to mounting national wealth and prosperity in the 1680s, trade and industry, the year 1689 proved to be a watershed in various ways. For one thing, the final defeat in England of authoritarian ideas of monarchy and the much enhanced rôle of Parliament in the system of government after the Revolution had more important economic consequences than is often realised. For instance, under pressure from various interested parties, who could from now on lobby or petition the House of Commons for anything up to six months in every year, Parliament in William III's reign sanctioned some significant reductions in export duties and lifted long-standing restrictions on sending goods out of the country. Such moves as the total freeing from duties of home-grown corn, the final abolition of the low but irritating duty on exported cloth and the 1694 Act permitting iron and copper to be sold anywhere abroad except France are the more significant because William's government needed high customs duties to meet its pressing revenue needs (Ch. 17; also below, p. 301). They must not be attributed to any widespread doctrinal demand for 'free trade'. In most respects the general trend of the years from the 1690s to the 1720s, like that of

Hanoverian Britain down to 1783, was strongly in the opposite direction: to which, among others, the Acts of 1701 and 1721, giving protection to the native silk industry and the Lancashire 'cottons' industry against the flooding of the home market by East India silks, muslins and calicoes, bear witness (3, *I, 62, 118*). The Westminster Parliament clearly took it for granted, too, that English industries vulnerable to Irish competition should be protected, as with the notorious 1699 Act forbidding the Irish to export their manufactured woollens to any country other than England, where they were subject to crippling duties. Nevertheless there was *some* liberation of the economy, in so far as post–1688 Parliaments were more prepared than Stuart regimes before them had been to look at each trade or industry on its merits, removing restrictions where there appeared to be a strong enough body of opinion in favour.

Furthermore, although the Parliaments of 1689–1714 had no idealistic concept of the benefits to be had from lowering trade barriers between nation and nation, they were interested in promoting freer competition among Englishmen themselves. This they demonstrated most clearly in their hostile attitude towards monopolistic trading companies, some of which had been too closely associated with the Stuart court for their own good. Arguably, most of the older 'regulated' companies, such as the Eastland Company, were dying anyway, so that the enforced reduction of their entrance fees only hastened their end. Much more pointed was the legalisation in 1697–8 of 'interloping' by private merchants on the preserves of the two joint-stock foundations of Charles II's reign. The small Hudson's Bay Company was not seriously damaged but the wealthy Royal African Company fell prey to the freebooting slave and ivory traders of London and Bristol and was then unable to prevent the total abolition of its monopoly in 1712. Even the great East India Company was forced to submit to seeing its chief City rivals incorporated as the New East India Company (1698) and showered with Whig favours. Only the Levant Company's monopoly survived this period intact, although the two East India Companies were reunited in 1709 [J.3.A].

For the economy at large the most influential event in the three decades following the Revolution was the outbreak of war with France in 1689. For twenty out of the next thirty years the trade and industry of both England and Scotland can only be realistically viewed in this context. England, in particular, had never previously fought any war in which the economic stakes were as high as they were between 1702 and 1713. And throughout both the Nine Years' and Spanish Succession Wars the economic life of both kingdoms was subjected to intense shock-treatment. Indeed, for Scottish trade, the arrival of a new political era in 1689 soon proved to be an event of the most basic significance. To the Scots – their economy already damaged by the Highland War of 1689–91 – the protracted French wars brought few benefits and many serious difficulties, compounding by the late 1690s the problems caused by the great famine and bringing home to landowners and merchants alike how precariously-based and backward their economy was. Perhaps the most damaging consequence of both wars was the chronic disruption (ameliorated only by smuggling) of one of Scotland's most profitable branches of trade, the exchange of home-grown (or English contraband) wool for French wines. Even in the 1680s Continental customers had been taking declining quantities of Scottish goods; prolonged warfare made it more difficult still for Scots to sell their salt, coal, fish and other exports. It was out of this mercantile frustration, as well as the joint-stock euphoria of the mid–1690s, that the Company of Scotland (Ch. 17) was born. It seemed imperative for the country to diversify its trade by emulating the English, if only in a small way, by founding a colony in Africa or in the New World and enjoying the benefits of a protected commerce with it. Unfortunately, the choice of territory for the Company's first venture, the isthmus of Darien in Central America, was catastrophic. Quite apart from its climate and terrain, posing desperate hazards to health, Darien was political dynamite. It was legally annexed to the Spanish crown, and this made William III as hostile to the venture as those East India and other London merchants who opposed the new company on self-interested grounds. After three expeditions (1698–1700), involving tragic loss of life as well as of capital that could be ill spared, the scheme collapsed in an atmosphere of gloom, bitterness and Anglophobia (282, *205–53*; above, pp. 198–200).

To offset very partially the many difficulties which the Scottish economy encountered after 1689 were two wartime advantages. One was the safety of the English market for two of Scotland's staple exports, linen and cattle. The other was the remoteness of the Clyde approaches from the French privateering bases on the Channel coast and the consequent opportunities for Glasgow merchants to hold on to a small share of the vital North American tobacco trade (282, *175–8, 213–14, 233–6*). But before 1707 neither opportunity could be properly exploited. Tariffs had been imposed on linen and cattle crossing the border since the 1660s. And as yet there was no more than a toehold, and an illegal one at that, on that ladder which in the mid-eighteenth century was to take the tobacco lords into high realms of prosperity which no Scottish merchant could have dreamed of fifty years earlier. There were some strong grounds in Scotland, as we shall see, for opposing the proposed Union with England in the middle of Queen Anne's reign (Ch. 20), but one argument on the other side, the economic argument, had by then become unanswerable. It was imperative that the northern kingdom be brought both into a free trade union with England herself and – more crucial still – within the protectionist haven of the English Navigation laws (285b).

For the English themselves the economic credit and debit balance by the time both wars were over was much more even. As we know, the success of their commercial revolution before 1689 had largely turned on the rôle of their New World colonies and their Indian and African trading stations. One indisputable gain from the French wars was an important extension of the colonial empire. Those parts of French Canada ceded to Britain at Utrecht [H(xiva) 4] were areas with a valuable trade of their own, in fish and in furs, but they were not the only respects in which the British colonies emerged from the wars with a wider and more flexible economic base than they had possessed in the 1680s, to the home country's benefit as well as their own. As the wars took a heavy toll of English shipping and as, later, the Great Northern War of 1700–21 disrupted the traditional import trade in hemp and tar from the Baltic ports, so New England and other northern American states were encouraged to build many more of their own ships and to produce their own naval stores to meet Britain's needs. To the south, some transatlantic planters had by 1720 already begun to see the possibilities of new crops, especially raw cotton, which was eventually to become of critical importance to British economic growth. Indeed, the fact that by George I's reign the colonial trade had become less overwhelmingly dependent than in the past on the two boom commodities, tobacco and sugar, proved essential to the next stage of Britain's Commercial Revolution (*The Age of Oligarchy*, Ch. 10); because, once St Dominique (acquired by France in 1697) had been cleared for sugar cane planting, French West Indian settlers were able to exploit the greater potential of their Caribbean islands so successfully that by the third and fourth decades of the eighteenth century they had begun to undersell their English sugar rivals (*The Age of Oligarchy*, Ch. 4). Britain's acquisition at Utrecht of the French half of St Kitts was not enough to check this progress.

England had gone to war in 1702 for powerful commercial as well as dynastic and religious reasons, and the settlement of 1713–14 fully reflected those commercial aims. Although English trade had been generally buoyant in the interval of peace after Ryswick, London mercantile, and ultimately parliamentary, opinion became convinced by French policy in 1701 that it would be necessary to fight a fresh war over the Spanish Succession. The stake in the trade with Old Spain and the southern Netherlands, like that in the illicit but profitable commerce with the Spanish American empire, was too vital to be surrendered to France without a struggle (above, pp. 248, 253). In view of the subsequent failure to oust Philip V militarily from Spain, the Anglo-Spanish Treaty of Commerce (1714), which formed part of the peace settlement, appeared to most observers at the time an impressive justification of the economic rationale of the war. Historians now agree that the direct harvest of the *Assiento* contract [A.] and 'annual ship' provision secured in 1714 by the South Sea Company [H(xiv)b.3] proved smaller than had been anticipated. But this should not obscure the value of these clauses to Britain as 'a licence to smuggle' (292, *103*), nor the certainty that British neutrality in the war of 1702–13 would have left France with too many Spanish commercial cards in her hands.

England's lucrative commercial links with southern Europe and the Mediterranean [Ch. 3; J.3.C] also emerged stronger than ever from Queen Anne's war and from the limited conflict with Spain in 1718–19 (above, p. 209). The trade with Old Spain and Italy was secured, and the Levant trade, though doomed ultimately to decline in the face of French competition, was ensured a lengthy stay of execution.[5] The most important beneficiary, however, was the Portugal trade. The Methuen Trade Treaty of 1703, an integral part of the alliance with Portugal, earned English woollen textiles most-favoured-nation treatment in that kingdom, creating new vested interests not only in the cloth industry but among the wine merchants (the port and madeira lobby). Both contributed to the shock parliamentary defeat of Bolingbroke's Anglo-French commerce treaty, signed at Utrecht in 1713 [H(xiv)a.6; see also pp. 206–7 above]. Consequently, exports to Portugal increased by about 150 per cent between 1699–1701 and 1719–21, and in 1713 the value of the Portugal trade from English ports touched £1 million a year in the Customs ledgers for the first time. In 1738 it reached a peak of £1.4 million, and since the Portuguese sent large shipments of bullion in return, the whole traffic was singularly gratifying to the fashionable 'balance of trade' pundits of the day, who had long preached that a less restricted trade with France would produce the very opposite result.[6]

Without the rapid expansion of the merchant fleet after 1660 English merchants could never have capitalised on their post-Restoration opportunities (Ch. 3). During the Nine Years' War there were horrendous shipping losses, as we know, and French privateers continued to take a heavy toll from 1702 until at least 1707. On the Admiralty's own evidence well over 5,000 ships had by then fallen into enemy hands since 1689. Despite the many such vessels subsequently 'ransomed' back by their owners, heavy purchases from America, and the 3,482 foreign prizes brought into English ports by 1713, it is unlikely that the tonnage of the merchant marine by the time of the Utrecht settlement was back to its late seventeenth-century peak of around 350,000 tons. Nevertheless, both the French and the Dutch had done so much worse in the meantime that Britain remained well equipped to consolidate her mastery over the world's carrying trade in the two decades which followed the wars: clearances of English tonnage from English ports could still average 420,000 in the years 1715–17, compared with 330,000 in 1686.[7] The position reached by the end of Sir Robert Walpole's ministry in 1742, when the English merchant marine was carrying fully half the commerce of the known world, was already in sight when Walpole began his premiership [see also J.3.B].

Inevitably, heavy shipping losses, serious trade dislocation in the early stages of both wars, and diversion of merchant capital into other channels (Ch. 17) took a good deal of the steam out of the Commercial Revolution. But it did not lose all its impetus. The fact that there was no Culliford at the Customs prior to 1696 to produce regular trade figures makes it hazardous to attempt statistical comparisons between the years before and after 1689. But such figures as we do have make it clear that the total volume of English trade, without re-exports, increased significantly between the periods 1697–1704 and 1715–24, and that for the next fifteen years the rate of growth further accelerated. By the early 1720s even re-exports, which had sagged during the war years, were touching levels never achieved before the Revolution. In the years 1722–4 England's total *gross* commodity trade, including re-exports, was worth an estimated £14.5 million a year, compared with £7.9 million in the period 1663–9 (168, *133 Table 11*). The patterns of that trade, however, are also of interest. For between the 1690s and the 1720s the progressive diversification of English industry we observed in the post-Restoration period (Ch. 2) was beginning to make its mark more plainly upon them (176, *59*).

III

The wars against France had an unsettling effect on English manufactures. New taxation, disruption of markets, uncertainties affecting raw material imports – all posed problems. Yet if there were difficulties to be surmounted there were also opportunities to be grasped. It has been cogently argued that all the major eighteenth-century wars, down to the Peace of Paris in 1763, were, on balance, beneficial to English industry (182b). And certainly if one examines the foundations of Britain's future industrial greatness, it is difficult to avoid the conclusion that, in England at least, those foundations were more extensive and secure after 1713 than they had been before the Revolution.

Some progress can obviously be seen as a direct response to the requirements of unprecedentedly large armed forces, including the armies of Britain's German allies. Without the French wars Birmingham, which housed the country's main concentration of gunsmiths and swordsmiths, would never have grown so rapidly between 1689 and 1714; neither would the dockyards at Chatham, Portsmouth and Plymouth have expanded into the largest industrial units in the country, in which workforces of up to 1,500 men were subject to organised labour discipline. Without the big army and navy contracts which brought him his wartime fortune and helped to make him Europe's premier ironmaster, it is unlikely that Sir Ambrose Crowley would have developed at Winlaton, County Durham, from 1690 onwards the first great unitary complex of foundries, forges and mills in Britain, the prototype for some of the great works of the mid- and late eighteenth century (206, *21*). The establishment of Sir Owen Buckingham's sailcloth 'manufactory' at Reading, employing many hundreds of hands, can also be directly linked with a coveted war contract; while the building of the first cloth halls in Halifax, Wakefield and Leeds (1708–11) (185, *233*) symbolised the debt of the heavy woollen and worsted industry in the West Riding to the fat orders its clothiers had received for uniforms and army blankets.[8]

It is sometimes argued that of greater importance still for the future was the spur to invention and to technological change. Unarguably there was progress here which can be clearly linked in time with the wars of 1689–1713, though whether the connection was to some extent coincidental is another matter. The assumption that the record number of patents issued in the early 1690s manifested a genuine surge in industrial inventiveness is no longer sustainable.[9] Nevertheless, one invention of the 1690s, the 'Miner's Friend' patented in 1697 by Thomas Savery, a pioneer of steam pistons, foreshadowed one of the most significant innovations of our whole period, Thomas Newcomen's steam pump. The final version of Newcomen's engine (*c.* 1705), produced in partnership with Savery, was put to work in the next eight years in several tin and coal mines, from Cornwall through the West Midlands to the Tyne valley (186a, *227*). Not until Watt's invention of the separate condenser [L.2] could the full possibilities of steam power begin to be realised; but by then over 300 Newcomen engines, incorporating the safety valve devised for them in 1717 and generating up to nine times the original 5½ horsepower, were installed in various parts of Britain, performing a variety of industrial tasks and public works in addition to pit drainage. The second major technological breakthrough of the first decade of the eighteenth century was made by a Quaker ironmaster, Abraham Darby. In 1709 he discovered a method of using coal in the smelting of iron ore in such a way as to produce iron that was both durable and workable. Thus was solved the problem that had baffled the industry throughout the previous century. The secret of coke fuel was admittedly well kept, so that most blast furnaces until after 1760 continued to make do with charcoal from the country's dwindling supplies of coppice wood. Yet however slow its application, a historic discovery had been made at Coalbrookdale. Britain's transformation into the world's first industrial nation could never have begun in the 1780s if, some eighty years earlier during the Spanish Succession War, she had not first begun to learn how to capitalise industrially, through steam and coke, on the richest natural endowment she possessed, her seams of coal.

The effects of the French and Northern Wars on industrial markets was extremely variable. Thus, while some branches of textiles did well after 1702, others, for example the bay and say manufactures of Essex and Suffolk for which Spain was a crucial outlet, received a setback from which they never permanently recovered. Ironically, the south-western serge industry(Ch. 2), having reached the height of its prosperity between 1690 and 1714, when the looms of Tiverton and Taunton were at their busiest, declined thereafter. The Dutch market which had been essential to its success crumbled away startlingly in the eight years after the Utrecht settlement.[10] The effects of war taxation, too, were patchy. The brewing industry was hit in turn by the ale excise, malt tax and hops duty, but few deep inroads were made into the continuing profits of big metropolitan brewers such as Sir John Parsons, Jack Lade and Thomas Crosse (significantly made a baronet in 1713). The new salt duty caused alarm, but it was the discovery of Cheshire rock salt, first seriously exploited in William III's reign, and the proximity of Liverpool to its deposits that probably did more to depress old brine areas such as Worcestershire (119, *225ff.*).

There were some industries, moreover, for which wartime impositions and prohibitions proved a positive boon. In the fifteen years after 1689 the traditional English tariff structure was transformed. Ever since the 1650s it had remained remarkably impervious to the theories of mercantilist economists. At its core was still the simple framework of a 5 per cent duty on most imports *and exports*, a levy designed to raise money rather than to help trade. The change that followed, 'from a generally low-level, fiscal system into a moderately high-level system which . . . had become in practice protective' (114, *307*), was prompted originally by decisions that were essentially non-commercial. In the endless search for revenue expedients to keep the armies in the field and the navy afloat, the Parliaments of William and Anne raised the general duty-level on goods coming into England threefold between 1690 and 1704. By 1708–9 a majority of foreign imports were paying 20–25 per cent, and in some cases more. There are doubtless some minor chinks in Ralph Davis's ingenious argument that at the very time when ideas of freer trade, in some form or other, were first being modestly advertised in print, in the 1690s, there slipped in unpremeditated, by a back door, the system of protection which was to blanket English industry scarcely challenged until Adam Smith's brilliant logic cut through so many of its assumptions in 1776.[11] It is certainly hard to imagine that after two to three decades of very unfriendly tariff policies on the part of the French, Dutch and Germans there was no element whatsoever of tit-for-tat in the ultimate English response. In the main, however, the pattern unfolded differently. Certain English industries which had hitherto struggled to cope with foreign competition were able to establish themselves so successfully under the protective umbrella of the war years that it became inexpedient for any government after 1713 to remove, or even lower, the fiscal tariffs which had sheltered them. In this way a system not planned for permanence became self-perpetuating. Thus two immigrant-led manufactures, silk and white paper, emerged from the wars with their futures assured. There were, for example, around 200 paper mills in England and Wales by 1714 (203, *38*), and neither their recent proliferation nor the higher proportion which now manufactured a quality product would have been possible without protection from French competition. It was a similar story elsewhere. The English linen industry could not fully exploit the high duties levied on Dutch and German fine linens, but the wartime prohibition on French brandies had an electrifying effect on the native distilling industry (as the gin mania of George II's reign reminds us).

One of the most durable myths of eighteenth-century British history is that English industry before the 1780s was overwhelmingly 'domestic' in organisation, and that it was relatively rare for large-scale capital to be deployed in it, at least by specialists. Practically all the industries just mentioned were organised in non-domestic units and most were capital-intensive. Of course in the many branches of cloth manufacture, including the linen industry, cottage spinning and weaving was the quintessential feature throughout the period. Likewise the metal-working of Birmingham and the Black Country, like the cutlery trades of Sheffield, was carried on in the small forges or workshops attached to urban living quarters, and Midlands nail-making was often interspersed with agriculture, at least in the seventeenth century (204). Yet even in textiles, except in a few areas, such as the industrial villages of the Halifax area, where manufacture was organised round numerous small master-clothiers, a great deal of capital was frequently invested by the merchant-clothier in the 'putting-out' and marketing processes of the industry. Capitalists such as the 'gentlemen merchants' of Leeds, who included some of the wealthiest men in the North under the first two Georges, sometimes owned their own fulling mills and dye shops also.[12] Paperworks, though usually small in scale, employed a wage-earning labour force of both skilled and unskilled men and required 'access to credit or capital outside the scope of the small man' (203, *38*). It took much bigger capital and considerable plant to erect and equip a successful early eighteenth-century 'brew-house'. Silk-weaving, in its main centres of Spitalfields and Canterbury, was a workshop industry with ten to twenty looms in each shop, although according to evidence given before the House of Lords in 1694 the 'master throwsters' of London often owned many such shops and some of those capitalists employed from 500–700 men each (189b, *106*). However, it was the spinning side of this industry which saw one of the most remarkable organisational – as well as technological – wonders of the age. In 1719, following a spying visit to northern Italy, the brothers Lombe built a five-story factory at Derby, in which the water power of the river Derwent was harnessed by an ingenious engineer, George Sorrocold, to drive 78 winding engines, 8 spinning mills and 4 twist mills; 300 hands were then set to work the

Lombe mill on a shift system. Sir Thomas Lombe, a wealthy London silk merchant, put £30,000 into this heroic venture. It failed in the 1730s, mainly through the hostility of Derby corporation; but its example was to inspire comparable throwing factories in Cheshire in the 1750s, large-scale concerns in every way and the clearest progenitors of the water-powered cotton mills of the 1770s and 1780s (189b, *304–5*; 192, *14–15*; 178c, *116–19, 180*; cf. *The Age of Oligarchy*, Ch. 11).

Since Tudor times the primary iron industry had absorbed more capital than any other branch of English manufacturing. Its appetite for investment grew in the late seventeenth and early eighteenth centuries, as existing ironmasters, like Crowley, and new entrepreneurs became more intent on consolidating on or near one site as many processes as possible, from smelting through to rolling and slitting. Coalbrookdale was by no means the most ambitious venture of the period, but it cost Abraham Darby £3,500 to establish it in 1708–9 and it was valued at £5,000 by 1715. A single new slitting mill normally required a minimum outlay of £1,200–£1,500. Partnerships, either within or between families, became the order of the day in iron manufacture. They were responsible for a crop of new ventures in the three to four decades after 1690, including those in the Stour valley (the Foley and Knight partnerships), in the Furness region of Lancashire (the Backbarrow and Cunsey companies, which began operations there between 1711 and 1720), and at Pontypool, where works were set up in Anne's reign (186b, *56–9*; 206, *16–19*). The more expensive the plant and equipment involved, the greater was the incentive to rationalise. The success of the reverberatory furnace in tin, copper and brass manufacture (Ch. 2) resulted during the years 1690–1730 in a migration of their smelting works away from the areas where the ore was mined to the most conveniently placed coal seams: in particular, they moved from Cornwall to Bristol and South Wales, where operations were on an altogether more ambitious scale.[13] The result was not only a big increase in the production of brassware and wrought copper for the home market in the first half of the eighteenth century but a near tenfold growth in exports of those commodities between 1700 and 1760 (186b, *127*; cf. above, p. 295).

With large capital in such demand, there was ample scope for members of the aristocracy and upper gentry to play an active entrepreneurial rôle in the metal manufacturing industries. Prominent among those who responded were Lords Dudley and Foley in iron, the Mackworths of Glamorgan in copper, and the Hanburys of Monmouthshire in iron and tin. But it was in the extractive industries that landed capital was most heavily committed. Some of the most successful coalmines and lead mines in the country were owned by great landowners, and their stake in those two rapidly expanding industries was increasing all the time. Some owners were not industrially active, preferring to lease out their mines. But a surprising number retained direct control and took a keen interest in developing their precious resources. Lord Mansel was drawing 'a royal income' from his collieries in Glamorgan by the early eighteenth century, while the productivity of the earl of Scarborough's four Durham pits rose between 1724 and 1727, in money terms, from £4,176 to £4,960 a year. So much capital was pumped into the Whitehaven collieries of the Lowthers, especially by Sir John Lowther's son

James, that pits whose profits had only very rarely exceeded £1,000 a year before 1707 were yielding a clear surplus of £4,589 over expenditure by 1726.[14] Among many other great landlords closely and profitably involved in the post-Revolution period were Lord Paget, in the Cannock Chase coalfield; Lord Middleton (until 1712, Sir Thomas Willoughby), in Nottinghamshire; Sir Richard Newdigate, in Warwickshire, and the great Denbighshire lead-owner, Sir Richard Myddleton of Chirk.

IV

Many coalmines and the vast majority of blast furnaces and forges in early eighteenth-century England were well removed from towns. But the tendency, observed already in the post-Restoration period, for industry to become more urbanised as it diversified became more emphatic from the 1690s onwards. Even in cloth manufacture, the swift advance of the New Draperies since 1660 had made large towns like Tiverton and Colchester, and even the cathedral cities of Exeter and Norwich, into veritable 'hives of industry' by 1700. It has been estimated that 80 per cent of Exeter's 12,000 inhabitants were then engaged in some stage of the city's serge manufacture (173, *189*). Many of the growth industries of the early eighteenth century, including (in addition to those mentioned already) glassmaking, potteries, sugar-refining and stocking-frame knitting, became associated with particular towns, some large, some small. Thus industry, like trade, made a telling contribution to one of the most striking features of the English scene in the decades when the country was making its advance to Great Power status, a rise in the urban population. It was a much more significant rise than in the period 1660–90, particularly at a time when the population as a whole was increasing only slowly. The growth was by its nature uneven, although scores of small towns and industrial villages (for example, the hosiery villages of the North and East Midlands) did have some share in it. London still led the way, though now, it would seem, at a slackening speed [B.2 (i)]. But in certain provincial regions, and at certain points within those regions, urban population in the years from the 1690s to the 1720s increased at a rate that was unusually rapid for pre-industrial England [B.2 (ii)]. A connection between this expansion and the wars against Louis XIV becomes apparent as we identify at least four of the main types of town which shared this experience: west-coast ports, benefiting from their relative immunity from the scourge of privateering; dockyard and shipbuilding towns, presenting the clearest link between war and urban growth, along with the clothing centres in the North and West Country – particularly, though not exclusively, those specialising in the heavier cloths in demand for the armies – and the metalworking towns of the Midlands and South Yorkshire.

Among the first group the biggest leaps forward were made by Bristol, Liverpool and Whitehaven [B.2 (ii)], with more modest progress in a few other places such as Lancaster. Whitehaven's growth was extraordinary; no more than a village at the Restoration, it had more than 5,000 inhabitants by 1730 (191, 7;

254, *14*). At the same date, Liverpool's population was approaching 30,000, and the vigour of its growth at this time was signalled by the building in Anne's reign of the largest wet dock outside London [B.2 (ii)]. The 'spectacular' expansion of the dockyard towns during the French wars – for example in Plymouth, with its appropriately named suburb of Dock – has been observed by several recent urban historians. It should be noticed, however, that Scarborough, which built coasters not warships, also grew fast in the first half of the eighteenth century, as did Sunderland, the main outlet for the Wearside coalfield, which possibly trebled its population between 1690 and 1720 (253, *54*; 193; [B.2 (ii)]). Among the Yorkshire clothing towns, Leeds [B.2 (ii)] and Halifax profited most from wartime orders. Defoe was quite explicit when he wrote in the 1720s of Halifax: 'the trade having been prodigiously encouraged and increased by the great demand of their kerseys for clothing the armies abroad, . . . it is the opinion of some who know the town and its bounds very well that the number of people in the *vicarage* of Halifax is increased by one fourth, at least, . . . since the late Revolution.'[15] Modern research has also confirmed Defoe's impression that the port of Hull, the main external outlet for Yorkshire cloth, shared in the prosperity of the West Riding clothiers.[16] During the wars, though not primarily because of them, some of the main cloth towns of the South West were growing quickly too. Finally, the generally flourishing state of the metal crafts led to a considerable influx into Black Country towns such as Wolverhampton, Walsall and Dudley, and a more remarkable growth, by pre-industrial standards, in Birmingham and Sheffield. Birmingham by 1730 had become the fourth largest provincial town after Norwich, Bristol and Newcastle, while Sheffield parish, which included the industrial chapelry of Attercliffe, increased its population three-fold, to 14,531 (3,111 households), between 1672 and 1736 [B.2 (ii)]. What Attercliffe was to Sheffield, Hunslet and Holbeck were to Leeds and Deritend to Birmingham: by George I's reign it is no longer feasible to appreciate the growth of industrial communities simply by confining one's attention to the mother townships themselves.

The Age of Oligarchy (Ch. 14) will refer to other aspects of urbanisation in this period. Meanwhile, two further points should be borne in mind about the process of urban growth itself, in the four decades or so after the 1688 Revolution. One is that, although economic stimuli were almost always of prime importance wherever growth was appreciable, they might well be *sui generis* and not susceptible to neat pigeon-holing. Thus only individual factors can fully explain the continuing growth of Manchester, well before the post–1750 textile boom began to make an appreciable mark on any other town in South Lancashire, or why Coventry should have strikingly revived between 1695 and 1737, or why the population of Newcastle on Tyne, with its unique combination of the coal trade and the biggest captive urban market in Europe, approximately doubled in the first half of the eighteenth century [B.2 (ii)]. Nottingham replaced London after 1690 as the chief centre of stocking frame knitting, but economics alone cannot explain why the town had 5–6,000 more inhabitants in 1739 than in 1674. Its experience reminds us, secondly, that urban development before the Industrial Revolution often hinged on a complex interplay of functions, in which a town's social rôle, administrative function or place in the communications network might be as influential as its place in the regional or national economy. For such reasons places such as Northampton, Preston, and above all Bath, as well as Nottingham, were already acquiring cachet, enjoying much new building and acting as magnets for 'the better sort of families', in particular. Along with the more flourishing ports and manufacturing centres, these and other towns all shared in an 'urban renaissance' (250), which blossomed from the late seventeenth century to beyond the middle of the eighteenth century: a remarkable phenomenon whose effects on society and culture will be observed in due course (*The Age of Oligarchy*, Ch. 14).

---

1. 'Natural and Political Observations and Conclusions upon the State and Condition of England: 1696', in G. Chalmers, *An Estimate of the Comparative Strength of Great Britain* (1802 edn), p. 43.
2. E.S. de Beer, ed., *The Diary of John Evelyn* (Oxford, abridged edn, 1959), pp. 982, 988–90.
3. Sir Robert Sibbald, 1699, quoted in T.C. Smout (274), p. 155 n. 28.
4. E. Kerridge, 'Agriculture, *c.* 1500–1793', in *VCH Wilts*, IV (1959), pp. 46, 47; C. Morris, ed., *The Journeys of Celia Fiennes* (revised edn, 1949), pp. 190, 192; Timothy Thomas, 1725, in HMC. *Portland MSS.*, VI, p. 136.
5. D. Defoe, *The Complete English Tradesman* (1745 edn), II, pp. 198–200; J.O. McLachlan, *Trade and Peace with Old Spain* (Cambridge, 1940); R. Davis, *Aleppo and Devonshire Square* (1967), Ch. 2, esp. p. 42.
6. H.E.S. Fisher, *The Portugal Trade. A Study of Anglo-Portuguese Commerce 1700–1770* (1971) Chs. 1, 3, 5 and Appx. 1; A.D. Francis, *The Wine Trade* (1972), chs. 5–7; D.C. Coleman, 'Politics and Economics in the Age of Anne: the Case of the Anglo-French Trade Treaty of 1713', in (174).
7. Ralph Davis (198) cautions, however, against the possible short-term distortions that might lurk in such figures.
8. All acquired still more splendid halls, along with Bradford and Huddersfield, in the years 1755–79. Hey (185), p. 233; Corfield (252), p. 26.
9. C. Macleod, 'The 1690s Patent Boom: Invention or Stock-jobbing?', *EcHR*, **39** (1986).
10. A.F.J. Brown, 'Colchester in the Eighteenth Century', in L.M. Munby, ed., *East-Anglian Studies* (Cambridge, 1968); W.G. Hoskins, *Industry, Trade and People in Exeter, 1688–1800* (2nd edn, Exeter, 1968), pp. 70–5; C. Wilson, *Anglo-Dutch Commerce and Finance in the Eighteenth Century* (Cambridge, 1941), p. 37.
11. In his *Inquiry into the Nature and Causes of the Wealth of Nations*. See E.J. Evans, *The Forging of the Modern State. Early Industrial Britain 1783–1870* (1983), pp. 37–40.
12. R.G. Wilson (187b), pp. 31, 95; W.G. Hoskins, op. cit., p. 37.
13. H. Hamilton, *The English Brass and Copper Industries* (1927); W.E. Minchinton, *The British Tinplate Industry* (Oxford, 1957)
14. Defoe, (3), II, p. 55; F.W. Beastall, *A North Country Estate: the Lumleys and Saundersons as Landowners, 1600–1900* (1975), p. 17; J.V. Beckett (191), pp. 234–6.
15. Defoe (3); (my italics – the parish was a very large one, including a cluster of industrial villages as well as the town).
16. G. Jackson, *Hull in the Eighteenth Century* (Oxford, 1972).

CHAPTER 20

The union of Britain:
Scotland and England, 1690–1727

While the Revolution Settlement and the post-Revolution wars were transforming a European offshore island into a great power and bringing about or accelerating the many internal changes we have examined in the previous seven chapters, they were also – slowly, painfully, but decisively – playing their part in the creation of a united British state. If the Revolution had not made a politically volatile out of a politically quiescent Scotland; if the struggle with France had not convinced England that Louis XIV and the Jacobites would at some time exploit this instability, and if, at the same time, the wars had not so seriously damaged the Scottish economy as to push free trade with England close to the top of the Scots' agenda, it is hard to envisage how a 'United Kingdom of Great Britain' could otherwise have come into being by 1707.

Ironically, the fate of the Darien scheme (Ch. 19), while highlighting with cruel clarity the gulf separating the economies of the English and Scottish kingdoms at the end of the seventeenth century, and reinforcing the already strong theoretical case for their closer integration, in some respects seriously set back the chances of such a relationship being brought about. Feeling among the Scots against their southern neighbour, already stirred in the 1690s by an unpopular war into which they seemed to have been dragged on the latter's coat-tails, ran so high after the Darien disaster that few could take a constructive view of their situation. Most of those who could, outside the leading ministers of state, were disposed to look for their country's salvation in terms of a drastic reduction of the Court's power in Scotland and their own greater distancing from all things and influences English. Such was the programme of the 'Country Party' which began to take shape in the Edinburgh Parliament from 1698 onwards – or, more accurately, such was the programme of its non-Jacobite members. Its thinking was little affected by the famine which at this very time was grimly underlining Scotland's lack of economic self-sufficiency. It is striking how far one of the 'Country' leaders, Andrew Fletcher of Saltoun, had swung away by the end of William's reign from the opinion he had held at its outset: that 'we can never come to any true settlement but by uniting with England in Parliaments and trade' (285b, *184*). That was not a popular view in 1700.

On the other hand, the King himself was so dismayed by the violence of the anti-English reaction which had set in by that time in Scotland, and by the inability of his Scottish ministers and Council to contain it, that before his death he had become a firm convert to the principle of Union. The contemporary shorthand for a constitutional arrangement by which both countries would accept, at very least, a common Parliament and free trade was 'incorporating Union'; certainly anything less than that, whether some form of federation or a simple 'union of trade', had no attractions for that cold pragmatist, William III. By the time he came to recommend 'a firm and entire Union' in a special message to his English Parliament, sent only eight days before his death (2, *V, 1340–1*), the case for putting an end to Scottish legislative independence had been further strengthened, to his mind, by the studied refusal of the Scots to follow the English example in 1701 and settle the succession to the crown by statute on the Protestant House of Hanover. When Queen Anne succeeded her brother-in-law in March 1702, her first Speech from the Throne contained a clear echo of William's last message, on 'a matter that very nearly concerns the peace and security of both kingdoms'.[1] This speech was probably drafted by the two men who were soon to become Anne's chief advisers for the first eight years of her reign; which suggests that Godolphin and Marlborough, at least, among English politicians were prepared to grasp the Union nettle. The former, in particular, had been in office long enough under William to be familiar with the background of the Crown's resolve. Not merely since the death of Anne's only surviving child in 1700 (above, p. 200), but since 1689 Scotland had become – from William's point of view – progressively more ungovernable. The various parliamentary commissioners, from Melville to Queensberry, and the different permutations of Scottish ministers and factions on which the King had relied to damp down animosities north of the border and to preserve some harmony between his two kingdoms, had too often failed to deliver the goods.

Only recently has the full extent of William's failure in Scotland been revealed. It was commonly thought that down to the late 1690s, without ever approaching a true understanding of his Scottish subjects, he was tolerably successful in keeping their Parliament in line through English-style management techniques and political balancing-acts (277b, *176, 178*). But detailed work on the politics of the reign has left little of this argument intact. It is now apparent that in almost everything of importance to him in Scotland the King was thwarted. The voting of revenue was a partial exception: payment of the 'cess', Scotland's pitifully unproductive equivalent of the English Land Tax, was badly disrupted in 1689–90 but not thereafter, down to the end of the war. On the other hand, the constitutional and religious acts of the Revolution settlement dealt a humiliating rebuff for the Crown (Ch. 13). The attempted pacification of the Highland clans, even as a cosmetic exercise, was badly scarred by the infamous Glencoe Massacre (1692), a particularly dire example of how ill-served William was by his Scottish managers.[2] And throughout, a hardline Presbyterian establishment, jealously concerned to protect the disproportionate gains of 1690, successfully defended not just its religious monopoly but an effective monopoly of office (283a; 268b, *250–1*). The Kirk had cause for nervousness, for, with a few prominent exceptions, convinced Presbyterianism was hardly a distinguishing characteristic of the Scottish nobility. But the consequences were stark. Especially in the Lowlands, Jacobitism, bolstered by a deep sense of episcopalian grievance and further sustained by economic disaster, was appreciably more entrenched at the end of the reign than at the beginning (104, *55–72*).

King William was not mistaken in seeing the bitterness of Scotland's religious divisions as a root cause of his failure there. But the diagnosis was only partial.

He contributed unnecessarily to his own problems – given the shift in the constitutional balance after 1689 – by taking little direct interest in Scottish affairs himself, relying too heavily on the uninspired advice of his Dutch favourite, Bentinck, and of the former exile William Carstares. Above all, he underestimated the wrecking power exercised in the post-Revolution Parliament by the great Scottish *seigneurs*. Dr Riley has illuminated the self-seeking of that handful of magnates – Queensberry, Argyll, both dukes of Hamilton and the duke of Atholl – whose semi-feudal powers and network of clientages gave them an influence well beyond that of all other Scottish noble houses from 1689 to 1707. It must be doubted whether any stability was possible, either within Scotland or in Anglo-Scottish relations, until the destructive rivalries of these magnates and the influence of a few political entrepreneurs who manoeuvred round and among them, like Ogilvy (Seafield), Mar and the Dalrymples of Stair, were contained and neutralised within a single *British* system.

However, it was by no means sufficient for the Crown to be convinced of the need for a full Union, on these grounds or any other, as long as the bulk of political opinion in both countries remained unreceptive, if not downright hostile. The fact that the old Parliament which met (with dubious legality) in Edinburgh after Anne's accession agreed to her request to appoint commissioners to treat for a Union, and that these took part in negotiations in London in the winter of 1702–3, indicated no fundamental change of mood in Scotland. The appointing Act was entirely the work of the Scottish Court Party, at this time marshalled by the duke of Queensberry, in a rump legislature from which 74 opposition members, led by Hamilton, had seceded.[3] Queensberry and his supporters, who monopolised the membership of the Scottish Commission, were motivated mainly by their desire to preserve their offices. They were well aware that as long as their preferment had to be justified by their ability to maintain control over a separate Scottish Parliament, it would be precarious, perhaps impossible once the new elections, now imminent, had been held. In 1702, however, only a few prominent Scots, including Marchmont and possibly Tweeddale, were convinced Unionists on what might be termed 'principle', believing that the safeguarding of the religious settlement and the Protestant Succession now depended on it and that it was necessary in other ways for the common weal of Scotland.

Among the English political parties there had been some shift by 1702 away from the attitude of total indifference displayed in 1689 towards the idea of Union (Ch. 13). Such support as there was – and much of it was unenthusiastic or tempered by political calculation – came mostly from the Whig side. Leading Whigs in the House of Lords displayed a cautious interest during debates on Anglo-Scottish relations in January 1700 and Whig votes seem to have been largely responsible for the passing of the bill empowering the Queen to appoint Union Commissioners at the start of her reign (2, *VI, 24–5*). But the party grew cooler later in 1702 when Marchmont and other leading Presbyterians were dismissed from their Scottish offices, when a proposal for an oath abjuring the Stuart Pretender was defeated in Scotland, and when the eventual dissolution of the Revolution Parliament seemed certain to favour the Episcopalians or 'Cavalier' party. The Whig Junto (Chs. 18, 22) had no wish to see a united Parliament in which a crypto-Jacobite Scottish contingent would supply additional lobby fodder for the English Tories. The latter, especially their High Tory wing, fearing that any Incorporating Union would lead to the pollution of the Church of England, had reacted to William III's message with a combination of extreme reserve and frank hostility. There were a few open minds, like the earl of Nottingham's, but those of the majority of High Tories were as closed as that of their leader in the Commons, Sir Edward Seymour, who had 'wonderfully exasperated all the Scotchmen . . . in town' in 1700 by contemptuously suggesting that uniting with Scotland would be like marrying a beggar, 'and whoever married a beggar could only expect a louse for her portion . . .'[4] The Tories' dominance of Anne's first ministry was reflected in the fact that Seymour and others of his kidney were cynically nominated to the Union Commission of 1702–3 and that almost every Whig of consequence was excluded from it. It surprised nobody when those negotiations petered out, though not without clearing some useful ground.[5]

Presumably Godolphin and Marlborough were disappointed at the failure of the talks to make appreciable progress, but they were too preoccupied with the problems of a new war to spare them much thought. The Whigs were detached; the Tories satisfied that they had proved a point, the Scots were focusing most of their attention on the new Parliament due to meet in May 1703. That Parliament, however, in which the 'Cavaliers' had increasedtheir strength to 70 and, together with a Country Party of around 60, comfortably outnumbered the Court, was within two years to transform relations between England and Scotland. A situation of stress and aggravation was replaced by 1705 by one of unmistakable crisis, and this crisis led directly, and with what may now seem a certain inevitability, to the Union of 1707.

The revival of Scottish nationalism and the insubordinate behaviour of the Parliament of Scotland, the two most remarkable features of politics in the northern kingdom since the Glorious Revolution, came to a climax in the turbulent sessions of 1703 and 1704. In the 1703 session the new Parliament passed two Acts which caused an alarmed and angry reaction in England. For non-Jacobite Englishmen it had been bad enough that the old Parliament had sidestepped the issue of the Protestant Succession. But it was far worse when the new one proposed to deal with it, as the new bill of Security did [F(viii)], by saying in effect to the English: we will name no successor until after the Queen's death; the Edinburgh Parliament will then make its choice of a sovereign, 'of the royal line of Scotland and of the true Protestant religion'; but that choice will not fall on the house of Hanover unless *in this session* prerogative powers over the Estates are severely curbed, freedom of trade with England and her colonies conceded, and the liberties and religion of the country preserved 'from English or any foreign influence'. The second piece of legislation, the Act anent Peace and War, was almost as shattering in its implications as the Act of Security. When the Queen died, even if the present war was still in progress, the Scottish Parliament would assume the right to a prerogative hitherto sacred to the Crown in both kingdoms, the right to conclude peace and declare war. A third Act of 1703, the Wines Act, went on to add economic provocation to Edinburgh's political defiance. A measure of the desperation to which Queensberry, as Anne's Commissioner, was reduced is that he touched the Peace and War Act with the sceptre while withholding the royal assent from the Security Act, in the hope of a change of heart in the following session. But in 1704 Tweeddale, seduced from the Country opposition and installed as Commissioner with a view to settling the Hanoverian succession and getting the cess voted again, could only achieve the latter – for a grudging six months – at the price of extracting the reluctant consent of the Queen and Godolphin to his passing the Act of Security (though without the free trade clause).

So vivid is the contrast between the strident Anglophobia and self-assertion of the Scottish Parliament in 1703–4 and the comfortable majorities with which, ultimately, virtually the same members accepted the articles of Union in 1707 that, to some contemporary observers, like George Lockhart,[6] as to some modern historians, it could only be explained by allotting a decisive rôle to shameless political jobbery. In fact William Ferguson has branded the Union as 'probably the greatest "political job" of the eighteenth century' (285a, *110*). Certainly the patronage system was fully exploited in the process, and financial sweeteners, mostly of a legitimate kind such as the timely discharge of arrears of salary, were offered to needy peers and lairds. It is difficult, however, to pinpoint any votes gained in this way which are not accountable for in other ways (283b). Even the notorious cementing of the great Argyll interest to the Unionist cause, through the grant of an English dukedom and military promotion to the greedy head of the Campbells, and titles and other douceurs to some of his relatives and clients, looks in retrospect like a work of supererogation. It is hard to envisage Argyll lining up at the last ditch with Hamilton and Atholl, the Cavaliers and the Jacobites, against the Treaty.

It cannot be stressed too strongly that the votes of 1706–7 in Scotland were delivered in circumstances wholly different from those of 1703–4. In Edinburgh, the makeshift anti-court alliance which produced the 1703 Acts had broken down totally by the autumn of 1706, largely because the diverse motives which inspired it had become irreconcilable. The majority of the Cavaliers regarded the Acts of Security and Peace and War as doors through which the House of Stuart could be restored after Anne's death. The Countrymen (mostly staunch anti-Jacobites) saw them as levers which might wrench out of England economic and political concessions for Scotland and, in some cases, office and favour for themselves; a period of confusion, or even of outright hostilities between the two kingdoms, from which only the Pretender could benefit had no place in their scheme of things. When a sham Jacobite conspiracy was 'leaked' by Simon Fraser in December 1703, allegedly implicating the duke of Atholl, among many others, it was a splinter group from the Country Party which took the lead both in Scotland and London in demanding a full enquiry into 'the Scotch Plot'. This group, which included the young earls of Roxburgh and Montrose and George Baillie of Jerviswood, had attracted some 30 Scottish members of Parliament by 1704, and first as the 'New Party', and then under its subsequent label, the Squadrone, it became a serious new force in Scottish politics. Although scarcely more disinterested than other groups, it did become firmly committed to a Hanoverian

Succession, and before the end of 1705, Roxburgh, its most dynamic member, had already convinced himself of 'the risk, or rather certainty, of the Prince of Wales [succeeding] in case of Union's failing'.[7] It was the Squadrone's eleventh-hour decision that support for an incorporating Union was the only way of securing the succession, and at the same time securing their own advantage in the future, that finally tilted the parliamentary balance in Edinburgh towards Union the following winter.

The change in English attitudes and circumstances between 1704 and 1706 was equally decisive. During these years, with the Spanish Succession War coming to a climax, the Scots were confronted by English politicians keenly alive, for the first time since the Revolution, to the deplorable state of Anglo-Scottish relations. A majority of them, in the aftermath of Blenheim, suddenly became determined that neither the outcome of the war nor the fate of the succession in either country should be jeopardised by what they saw as Scottish intransigence and sheer irresponsibility. What is more, the Parliament which met at Westminster in October 1705 after the second General Election of the reign was one in which Godolphin's Court interest (including Robert Harley and his 'New Tory' followers [Ch. 22]), combined with a Whig war party which had just made substantial electoral gains, commanded a clear majority in both Houses; and both elements in this coalition were now in favour of a full parliamentary union of the two countries.

No longer could Godolphin regard Union, however desirable in itself, as a side issue. Following the revolt of the Scottish Estates and the raising of the Scottish militia (by a clause of the Act of Security), the prospect of his friend Marlborough's military efforts being sabotaged by a unilateral withdrawal of Scottish regiments from the fray, combined with a Jacobite *coup*, began to seem uncomfortably real. The Treasurer became so fearful of it that he was fully prepared to back up his commitment to Union with a threat of force. As early as December 1704 Roxburgh, for one, was convinced that he was not bluffing and 'that if we do not go into the succession or an union very soon, conquest will certainly be, upon the first peace'.[8] In addition, Godolphin had been faced in 1704 with certain censure in the Lords, and possibly resignation, for authorising Tweeddale to pass the Security Act, and to extricate himself he had been forced to make a deal with the Whig Junto (70, *85, 110*). It was the latter who proposed to Parliament, as part of this bargain, the Aliens bill as the most effective means of bringing the Scots recalcitrants to heel. This measure, which became law in March 1705, affixed to a recommendation that the Queen should appoint English commissioners to negotiate a Treaty of Union some unpleasantly sharp teeth. If Scotland had not entered into negotiations by Christmas Day, 1705 (or alternatively accepted the Hanoverian Succession by statute), all Scottish estates in England held by non-residents would be treated as alien property in law. At the same time a total embargo would be placed on all the major Scottish imports into England. The Scots nobility, in particular, now had much to lose.

The motives and objectives of the Whigs, at this stage and subsequently, require clarification. Plainly, their tactics of 1704–5 were aimed at securing more than (in Wharton's mordant phrase) the 'Lord Treasurer's head in a bag' (70,

110). But how much more? Although the stipulation about the meeting of Union commissioners was dropped from the Aliens bill before it became law, on the initiative of the House of Commons, this scarcely supports Dr Riley's charge that the Whigs were only interested in securing the succession in Scotland, and that it was very late in the day and *faute de mieux* that they accepted the need for an incorporating Union.[9] The House of Commons in February 1705 was still Tory-dominated, and most Tories remained cold, or at best apprehensive, about a treaty. The Whig Junto, on the other hand, had developed a clear sense of priorities regarding Scotland from the time the Lords had debated the 'Scotch Plot' in March 1704 and had accepted a motion for an address drafted by the Junto's most eminent spokesman, Lord Somers. This concluded by assuring the Queen 'that, when your wise endeavours for settling the succession in Scotland shall have taken the desired effect, we will do all in our power to promote an entire and complete Union between the two kingdoms . . .' (2, *VI, 223*; 1, *V, 134–5*). It is true that the Whigs had no desire, then or in February 1705, to rush into negotiations for such a Union when it still seemed likely that Scottish representation in a united Parliament would initially be biased in favour of Episcopalians, and therefore produce increased support for the Tories. Thus it made sense to deal with the immediate danger by giving precedence to a Scottish Succession Act and to postpone the Union discussions until the Whigs' own influence, in Parliament and in the ministry, was stronger. They wanted, quite simply, to be influential enough to secure a dominant voice among the English commissioners. They also preferred to wait until the Court, rather than the Edinburgh Parliament, had won control over the nomination of their Scottish counterparts. Both conditions existed by 1706. The Whig leaders were not so naïve as to imagine that there could be any lasting security for the Hanoverian succession in Scotland so long as the legislative work of one Scottish Parliament could be undone by the next, hence their utter rejection of any federal approach to a Union (283b, *183*). At the same time, they led a party unremitting in its hostility to France and now undeviating in support of the war, and with the Queen's health always precarious, they could not afford to gamble with such a crucial military, as well as religious, stake as the succession (Ch. 22).

The seriousness with which both the Whigs and Godolphin's war coalition approached the Union negotiations in 1706 is reflected in the handsome concessions made to Scotland to secure the vital point: the surrender of her legislative independence and the absorption of her representatives (16 elected peers and 45 MPs) into a new united Parliament [see F(x)]. These contrast sharply with the grudging approach of the English Tory commissioners in 1702–3 and leave us in no doubt of the determination of both sides in 1706 to make the Union Treaty as saleable a product to their two Parliaments as possible. Economic union was to embrace freedom of trade, not only between the two home countries but between Scotland and the English colonies, and this had been by no means a foregone conclusion. There would be a fiscal union, but with important concessions to the Scots as long as the war lasted. A generous 'Equivalent' (*c.* £400,000) was to be paid by England to discharge the debts on the Scottish Treasury, especially salary arrears, and to compensate the shareholders of the Company of Scotland. Each country was to retain its own legal system – this appeased one of the most important interest groups in Scotland – and, as a particular sop to the Scottish nobility, 'heritable jurisdictions' (an oppressive feudal survival cherished only by those who exercised them) were preserved. On the succession, of course, there could be no compromise: the Hanoverian line was to be uniformly accepted. But it was privately agreed that the distinctive religious establishments of the two countries would be guaranteed by separate legislation in the respective Parliaments, as soon as the Treaty of Union had been approved.

But would the Treaty be approved, even now? No one doubted that if the Edinburgh hurdle could be cleared Westminster would prove a relative formality. Yet the climate in Scotland before the crucial meeting of the Estates in October 1706 was not reassuring. Hostile addresses were submitted, notably from a small majority of the Convention of Royal Burghs, and it was not at all clear whether parliamentarians as a whole would share the attitude of the duke of Argyll in dismissing such protests with patrician contempt as being 'fit only to make kites of' (284, *29*). The Kirk, despite the assurances it received, remained for a long time bleakly disapproving of an Incorporating Union with the 'prelatical' English. Angry mobs took to the streets in a number of towns, especially Glasgow and Edinburgh, and rioting continued in the capital even while Parliament was sitting. In the pamphlet war the pros and cons were more evenly divided, although the former were bolstered by the expert propaganda of an English polemicist, Daniel Defoe, who had been despatched northwards for that very purpose

Defoe put the commercial case with singular eloquence, and to many other pro-unionist pamphleteers the economic arguments seemed the clinching ones. They were aimed, we must recall, not only at the merchants but at the not inconsiderable number of nobles and Lowland lairds who had interests in the cattle or coal trade with England. Whether in the end those arguments *of themselves* swayed many – if any – votes in Parliament has become a matter for strong disagreement (cf. 283b, *197ff.* with 282, *Ch. 12*; 285b). In November 1705, when the earl of Roxburgh's calculations persuaded him that it was 'very probable' that Union would, in the end, be accepted by the Scottish Parliament, he had forecast that 'the motives will be, trade with most, Hanover with some . . . together with a general aversion at civil discords, intolerable poverty and the constant oppression of a bad ministry.'[10] Those who eventually cast their votes the following winter did not leave neat catalogues of their motives for historians' benefit. But what evidence there is does not suggest that Roxburgh was right in backing the economic horse first. It is very likely that most members who supported the treaty, including burgesses sitting for trading burghs, did so from mixed motives, and no less probable that, with most, either party interest or personal ambition was a prominent if not a paramount consideration. Debased though the currency of Scottish politics may have become, however, it is impossible to believe that considerations of public policy and even principle were solely confined to the *opponents* of Union in the various divisions of 4 November 1706 to 16 January 1707. And a recent conclusion that, although 'Union had to be debated in respectable though fictitious terms', trade concerns 'seem to have exerted no influence worth speaking of', smacks as much of over-statement as the same authority's argument that the whole parliamentary process was an elaborate charade, because party dispositions were already known before Parliament met (283b, *281, 272–9*). This most emphatically was not the case, either with the Squadrone, the critical group,[11] or with some individual Presbyterians (276, *135*). The diversity of the subsequent voting pattern is also not without significance; for example, one of the three economic articles of the Union was ratified by a huge majority (156–19). The final vote on the ratification of the entire treaty was carried comfortably by 110 to 69, whereas on the first article, back in early November, the opposition vote had been as high as 83, leaving Godolphin in London still palpably uneasy about the outcome.[12]

In October 1707, seven months after the Act of Union had gone through the last English Parliament (above, p. 203) with only the High Tory hard core resisting its easy passage, the first Parliament of Great Britain assembled at Westminster. If the Union was legally born on 1st May of this year, 23rd October appropriately marks its baptism. While arguments will doubtless go on endlessly about how much was or was not accomplished by the events of 1706–7, one thing is indisputable: they did bring a new state into being. Nor was it solely a political entity that was created. It was no small achievement for the Union's makers to have established, along with it, the biggest free trade area in a Europe bristling with both international protectionism and the jealous defence of local economic privileges. They did not spirit up a new nation; indeed, the negotiators could hardly have recommended their work to most of those who ultimately supported them if they had not deliberately preserved, on both sides, as much of their separate national identities as could be reconciled with the treaty's overriding aims. None the less, they did frame the conditions in which future subjects of the Crown, on both sides of the border, could be conscious of themselves in some respects as being more than simply Englishmen and Scotsmen (cf. *The Age of Oligarchy*, Ch. 15). They sowed the seeds, as Defoe had predicted they would, of 'a new national interest'.

In the early years of the Union, however, the full realisation of these achievements lay well ahead. It still seemed far beyond the horizon in June 1713, when the earl of Finlater (as Seafield, one of the Union's most consistent and convinced champions from 1705 to 1707) moved in the House of Lords for leave to bring in a bill to dissolve it. This was not just a tactical manoeuvre. It was a move that had the backing of almost all the other Scots at Westminster. Not many flattered themselves they were likely to succeed there and then. For most the hope was to attract enough support from the opposition Whig peers, by offering a real prospect of unsettling the Harley ministry, to prepare the way for anti-unionist successes in the forthcoming General Election and for a new attempt in the next Parliament. The six years since 1707 had in fact seen a cumulation of disappointed expectations, and a lot more friction, on a variety of both parliamentary and non-parliamentary matters, than even the cynics had anticipated. As we shall see, it was to be at least twenty years before, to most Scots, the advantages of the Union became, just occasionally, more evident than their own grievances.

For English politicians there had been fewer serious occasions for second thoughts between 1707 and 1713. The existence of a common Parliament and a common focus, in London, for the ambitions of all British politicians, had already shown how much easier it was to draw the fangs of the Scottish magnates, who now found themselves smaller snakes in a much larger pit. Scotland's reaction to the prospect of a Hanoverian succession also seemed reassuring. This was not to be fully tested until September 1715, by which time circumstances had changed considerably (below, pp. 318–19). But down to 1713 there had been distinct indications – seemingly confirmed, for the English, by the pro-Whig Election results of that year in Scotland [E.1(iii)] – that Scottish disgruntlement with the Union had *not* enhanced the prospects of the Jacobites. The value of the Union as 'the strongest bulwark for the Protestant Succession' was what determined an overwhelming majority of Whig peers against giving direct support to Findlater's motion for dissolution. Even the English Tories had found some aspects of the Union, in practice, to their liking. In 1712 it had been the means of bringing to the Scottish Episcopalians a degree of relief from religious disabilities which an Edinburgh Parliament might well have withheld from them for decades (above, p. 206). Indeed Lord Oxford, the head of the Tory ministry of 1710–14 (who had already begun to evolve a method of controlling Scottish patronage directly from the Treasury in ways which anticipated the 'system' perfected by Sir Robert Walpole in the 1720s) scathingly dismissed the dissolution ploy of 1713 as like the act of a man with toothache who was prepared to have his own head cut off in order to cure it.[13]

Yet Oxford was in many ways unfair to the Scots, whose catalogue of grievances was already formidable. Theirs had been the higher expectations in 1707, for in the end it had only been the overt Jacobites, the Cavaliers and the 'constitutional' wing of the old Country Party who had kept up opposition in Parliament to the last, and even the two latter groups were not without their hopes of benefits. Since some of the rosier expectations were unrealistic from the start, and far more hopes of personal advantage were entertained than could ever be satisfied, it need not surprise us that the honeymoon proved the roughest part of the marriage. No ministry and no Parliament in the early years of the Union could have avoided offending some Scottish groups or interests. But English politicians can fairly be accused of dealing out too many ill-considered snubs to Scottish national feeling.

This is not to say every ultimate grievance was universally shared from the start. There may well have been a good case, sooner or later, for abolishing the separate Edinburgh Privy Council, which had been tacitly reprieved in the Treaty of Union. For the new Parliament of Great Britain to do so as early as 1708, to serve the ends of the new alliance between the Whigs and the Scottish Squadrone at an imminent General Election, may seem to us cynically provocative. It was undoubtedly cynical, yet because the existing Council had for years been regarded in Scotland as a tool of the Queensberry faction, its disappearance at the time caused no general outcry. Only afterwards did Scots wake up to the fact that its abolition had left both an administrative and a patronage vacuum. This could have been partly filled if there had been a Scottish Secretary of State permanently and effectively at work. But the chief ministers of both Anne and George I took a long time to decide whether they wanted a third Secretary or not, and if they did, how much responsibility he should be allowed [D.2,5]. When Walpole left the post continuously vacant from 1725–42, following the dismissal of the Squadrone's leader, Roxburgh, he took the decision, like his predecessors, on political rather than administrative grounds. The Privy Council Act was not the only controversial measure of the post-Union years which at the time found willing Scottish accomplices. The Act for the Toleration of Episcopacy (1712) would not have passed without the votes of the English High Tories, but to attribute it, as some historians still do, entirely to the malevolence of the English, badly misjudges the situation at the time. The Scottish contingent of both peers and MPs elected to the Parliament of 1710–13 was very heavily in favour of a Toleration Act, as they were of another Act of the same session restoring lay patronage in Scotland; while both measures offended the Kirk and were denounced by Presbyterians as being contrary to the spirit, at least, of the Union, they significantly found no place in Findlater's indictment in 1713. One step which did, however, was the refusal of the Lords, in the Hamilton case in December 1711, to allow a Scots peer who was given a title in the new peerage of Great Britain to enjoy a hereditary seat in Parliament. Although there was genuine unease among the English aristocracy lest a loophole in the Treaty of Union might be exploited by an unscrupulous ministry to insert dependents into the Upper House, the Scottish nobility felt they were being cheated out of a prospect which, they claimed, had been vital in reconciling them to accepting the system of 'the sixteen' in 1707. So strongly did they feel that for part of the 1711–12 session they withdrew from the House altogether in protest (16, *101–4*).

Unlike the axing of the Privy Council and the rejection of the duke of Hamilton's right to sit in Parliament as duke of Brandon, the passing of the Treasons Act in 1709 was a direct infraction of one of the articles of Union. The measure enforced sweeping changes in Scottish treason procedure, after five lairds charged with high treason following the attempted French invasion of the previous year had escaped conviction in an Edinburgh court. It was pushed through against united Scottish opposition in both Houses (104, *104*; 70, *304–5, 338 & n**); a further blow to Scottish *amour propre*, and to the Edinburgh legal fraternity, followed in 1711 when the House of Lords deemed itself competent to hear an appeal from a Scottish court in the case of the Revd. James Greenshields (105, *86–7*; 283c, *233*). The most general grievance harboured by the Scots in 1713, and the matter which led most directly to Finlater's crisis motion at that time, was also claimed as a breach of the Union. Scotland had been assured in 1707 (article 14) of relief from the malt tax until the war was over. When the House of Commons, under backbench pressure, imposed 6d. a bushel on both English and Scottish malt in May 1713, fighting was indeed over; peace with France had been signed at Utrecht, but Britain was still technically at war with Spain, with whom commercial negotiations had yet to be concluded. The root cause of the trouble, however, was not this technicality but the fact that Scottish barley was so poor in quality that even the levy of 3d. a bushel, unsuccessfully proposed by Oxford's ministry as a compromise, was bound to be bitterly unpopular. No Scottish member hoping for re-election could vote for it. Their cries of pain, and those of their constituents, were genuine enough. Yet although the Whigs combined with the representative peers to try to throw out the bill, and very nearly succeeded, they did so from party interest and not out of undue sympathy. It was generally felt in England, and with some justification, that fiscally Scotland had got off even more lightly in the last six years of the war than the makers of the Union had intended. Thanks to ceaseless duty evasion – the Scottish coastline was, and for years remained, a smuggler's paradise (276, *130*) – and to port officials who were often hand-in-glove with defrauding merchants, little of the country's customs revenue ever reached the Exchequer. Not until Walpole merged the separate customs organisations of Scotland and England under a single Board in 1723 was there a purge of the old officers, and even then the Treasury in London was far from overjoyed by the results. Another English fiscal grievance of the early post-Union years concerned the 'cess': payments of this land tax throughout the years 1707–13 had been regularly below quota.

The Malt Tax Act passed the House of Lords after a great struggle in 1713, in spite of the agitation against the Union. However, the duty was never in practice levied: 'the maltsters refusing to permit the officers entrance into their malt-houses', as Scottish excise officials claimed in 1719, 'and the justices declining to act on account of this duty' (283c, *242–3 n.*). How emotive an issue this remained was seen in 1725 when Walpole's determination to impose a new malt tax on Scotland, at half the English rate, and this time to make it stick, caused an ugly riot at Shawfields, Glasgow. This time, however, the Treasury did not give in. Blaming the Squadrone, one of the two Scottish factions on which the Whigs had relied since 1714[14] for being 'soft' on this and on other issues, Walpole's political answer was to put his trust from now on mainly in the hardliners of the Argyll (Campbell) connection. It was their nominee as Lord Advocate, Duncan Forbes, who was responsible for punishing the rioters, humbling the corporation of Glasgow and, finally, bringing the recalcitrant brewers in Edinburgh and other towns to heel. By the time of George I's death in 1727, despite continued duty evasion on a scale still disturbing to the Treasury, the majority of Scots were slowly becoming reconciled to having to pay more realistically for the greater security which the Union had given them.

The abiding demonstration of this security came not so much with the suppression of the Jacobite rising which broke out in Scotland in 1715 – for this was only achieved after much alarm – but with the government's efficient uncovering and stifling of the subsequent conspiracies to overthrow the Union regime by force down to 1723 (104, *Ch. 8*). The 'Fifteen Rebellion in Scotland and England is dealt with in *The Age of Oligarchy* (Ch.6). What must be stressed here is simply the extent to which it changed the whole context of attitudes towards the Union. By the time the earl of Mar, that least predictable of rebels, had raised the Jacobite standard in the north-east Highlands in September 1715, the Scottish Episcopalians, who had enjoyed some official countenance during the four years of Oxford's ministry, had suffered more than a year of total proscription since Queen Anne's death. Their resentments and despair swelled, far beyond most former predictions, the ranks of those willing to take up arms for the Pretender, especially north of the Tay (104, *126–50*). But after the fighting was over it was all the more unthinkable for the Whigs and for George I to widen the scope of their political patronage in Scotland beyond their own entirely trustworthy allies. And, as Daniel Szechi has so pertinently put it, because 'the new order deliberately excised all effective outlets for political dissent . . . Scotsmen who disapproved of the Whig establishment were confronted with the unenviable choice of acquiescence or treason' (268b, *257–8*). By the early 1720s acquiescence in the Union, much of it still varying from the lukewarm to the apathetic, had become the norm for the great majority of them.

One further question concerns us here. How far did the state of the Scottish economy after 1707 advance or retard this process of acceptance? It is often said that the underlying reason for resentment over the malt tax as late as 1725 was that Scotland had not benefited economically from the Union as she had expected to do. But we must be careful here not to take too much contemporary comment at face value. In the 1720s the Scots still bewailed their poverty as a nation; and they were still right. Eldorado was not just round the corner in 1707, nor indeed in 1725; and it was unrealistic, if understandable, for Scottish merchants and trading landowners to expect dramatic early dividends from their share in a free English market and from the legalising of their colonial trade. But this should not disguise the progress, slow and patchy but perceptible, which Scotland made towards sounder economic health in the twenty years after she became part of 'Great Britain'. These were difficult years for most European economies: even England, with her richly varied commercial and industrial life, had her problems.[15] For Scotland what was vital was that in those two decades, despite setbacks (some of them inevitably ascribed to the Union) (286; 104, *99, 101*), the disastrous downward slide of 1689–1707 was first halted and then reversed. By the 1720s English graziers, factors and butchers as far south as Essex were well aware how much the traffic in Scottish black cattle had increased since the Union; the stimulus to enclosure in the Lowlands in the early Hanoverian period is another side of the same coin. Although the spectacular advance of the Glasgow tobacco trade did not begin until the 1740s, when for the first time Whitehaven, Liverpool and Bristol seriously felt the pinch of its competition, some solid progress had been made earlier, helped by customs evasion on a scale which, to everyone except the Treasury commissioners and the English tobacco dealers, was hilarious. By 1720 over 1 million pounds of duty-free Virginia tobacco, imported via the Clyde, crossed the border, and this was, of course, irrespective of what was consumed in Scotland or sent to Edinburgh for shipment to the Continent. In 1721 the total rose to 1.4 million pounds, causing an outcry in Parliament (283c, *276–7*). Defoe was able to enjoy something of the triumph of a prophet when he wrote in 1726 of the Glaswegians, with their tobacco merchants, new sugar-baking factories and distillery, that 'the Union has answered its end to them more than to any other part of Scotland.'[16] Of the older Scottish industries probably only linen manufacture could be described as being even moderately improved in health before the death of George I, and its best days lay well ahead, but the myth that other industries were seriously blighted by English competition can no longer be sustained (274, *243*; 286).[17] When the 'Second Equivalent' was made available by the Treasury in 1727, and a new

Board of Trustees for Fisheries and Manufactures was appointed in Edinburgh to administer it, the effects were for some years more psychological than material. But in retrospect the Board can be seen as one signal (the founding of the Royal Bank of Scotland in the same year being another) that more prosperous times (above all for Scottish linen) were on the way (276, *141*; 279, *xv, 134ff.*). And in the end it was prosperity, no less than political stability and the system of patronage for Scotland which Walpole and his northern acolytes were at this time busily fashioning (288; 289; see also *The Age of Oligarchy*, Ch. 15), that was to be the key to the full reconciliation of the Scots at large to the Union. In 1727 it could still only be glimpsed, like a distant mountain peak through clouds. Between 1745 and 1770, however, when the English economy moved into higher gear again (*The Age of Oligarchy*, Chs. 10–11, 17), Scotland was no longer left limping along far behind, and the pessimists, albeit late in the day, were finally confounded.

1. *CJ* XIII, 788: 11 Mar 1702.
2. The most recent scholarly treatment and reinterpretation is by P. Hopkins, *Glencoe and the End of the Highland War* (Edinburgh, 1986).
3. The secession was in protest against the Court's failure to hold fresh elections under the terms of the Scottish Act of Security of 1696.
4. E.M. Thompson, ed., *Correspondence of the Family of Hatton*, Camden Soc., NS 23 (1898), II, p. 246: C. Hatton to (?) Visct. Hatton, 20 Jan 1700.
5. C. Jones and G. Holmes, eds, *The London Diaries of William Nicolson, Bishop of Carlisle 1702–1718* (Oxford, 1986), pp. 117, 122–3 and session 1, 15 Dec 1702 – 29 Jan 1703 *passim*.
6. E.g. A. Aufrere, ed., *The Lockhart Papers* (Edinburgh, 1877), I, p. 193.
7. *The Correspondence of George Baillie of Jerviswood* (Edinburgh, 1842), p. 138: to George Baillie, 28 Nov 1705.
8. *Jerviswood Correspondence*, p. 28: to George Baillie, 26 Dec 1704.
9. P.W.J. Riley, 'The Union of 1707 as an Episode in English Politics', *EHR*, **84** (1969).
10. *Jerviswood Correspondence*, p. 138: to George Baillie, 28 Nov 1705.
11. If the Squadrone's decision to jump down on the Union side of the fence was, indeed, already known to the Court before the session opened, making the whole thing a foregone conclusion, as has been claimed, it is (to say the least) extraordinary that Lord Treasurer Godolphin was not in on the secret. See H.L. Snyder, ed., *The Marlborough-Godolphin Correspondence* (Oxford, 1975), II, p. 715: Godolphin to Marlborough, 18 Oct 1706.
12. HMC *Bath MSS.*, I, p. 124: Godolphin to Harley, 15 Nov 1706
13. G. Holmes and C. Jones, eds, 'Trade, the Scots and the Parliamentary Crisis of 1713', *Parl. Hist.* I (1982), pp. 54, 55 and *passim*.
14. The Squadrone had, unwisely as it turned out from their point of view, backed Stanhope and Sunderland against the Walpole-Townshend Whigs in the Whig schism of 1717–20.
15. Much exaggerated, however, in A.J. Little, *Deceleration in the Eighteenth-Century British Economy* (1976). Cf. Szechi, 'John Bull's Other Kingdoms: Scotland' (268b), p. 278 and chapter 15 of *The Age of Oligarchy*, for a rather different view of the Scottish economy in the half century after 1707, or at least of the influence of the Union upon it, from the one taken here. G.S.H.

16. *Tour through the Whole Island of Great Britain* (Penguin edn 1971, ed. P. Rogers), p. 606.
17. There were isolated exceptions, the closure of the Newmills (Lothian) woollen cloth manufactory in 1713 being prominent, (279), pp. 131–2.

CHAPTER 21

The political system and the electorate, 1689–1722

The twists and turns of the road to Union, like the changes in the conduct of war and foreign affairs we have observed and so much else in public policy after the Glorious Revolution of 1689, are only fully intelligible if we remind ourselves that ministers and members of Parliament were not statesmen or politicians acting in a vacuum, with nothing to distort their mature consideration of the common good. Rather they were practical and often ambitious men, whose perception of any major policy issue was almost bound to be influenced by the political system of post-Revolution Britain, within which they all operated and by which they were all imprisoned.

In this chapter and the next we shall try to discover what this system was, in England down to 1707 and in Britain thereafter, and how it worked. Something has been said already of the distinctive place of the Crown and the Court in politics from 1689 to the early 1720s, and of how this was changed significantly by the post-Revolution constitution (Ch.13), as well as being affected by more personal factors such as the succession to the throne of a valetudinarian female in 1702 and of a semi-detached German in 1714. More important still to the workings of the central political mechanism in this period were the distinctive political attitudes of the last two Stuart monarchs. Despite their many differences of temperament and abilities, King William III and Queen Anne shared one thing in common: they both regarded political parties as, at best, necessary evils, and they both tried determinedly, if with differing degrees of success, to evade an undue dependence on either the Whigs or the Tories in making appointments to offices. Never at any time did they concede a *complete* monopoly of ministerial office to a party, although Anne came very close to doing so in the last year of her life (1713–14), when pressure of circumstances, and what she saw as the blind intransigence of the Whigs (never her favourite option), left her with little choice (56; 61; 70, *Ch. 6*; 69). It will be argued in a later chapter that this predilection of the Crown for some measure of (in modern parlance) coalition government, and the struggle to realise that ideal at the lower levels of central administration even when the Cabinet had to be largely conceded to a party, set up tensions in the body politic which were an important cause of continuing political instability. By the same token, therefore, the coming in 1714 of the first Hanoverian king, whose slender objections to bestowing all his favour on one party, the Whigs, were abandoned without compunction after the 1715 rebellion, was a crucial landmark (Ch. 25).

Such success as William and Anne enjoyed in their efforts to prevent one-party government they owed partly to their own resolve, but partly also, from 1693–4 onwards, to the invaluable support of a tiny group of statesmen generally known as 'the managers'. These men – the second earl of Sunderland in the middle years of William III, and under Queen Anne, Godolphin and Marlborough, Robert Harley, and, briefly, the duke of Shrewsbury – were not without their party affiliations: Godolphin and Marlborough and, by Anne's reign, Harley, with the Tories, Shrewsbury with the Whigs. But they 'all shared to some extent the Crown's political ideals and were prepared to defy the party leaders, if necessary, to see them achieved. Their main service to the sovereign was to act as 'brokers' or intermediaries between him and the parties. It was they who supervised the construction of ministries and directed the electoral influence of the Crown, while under Anne (as we know) Godolphin and Harley assumed full responsibility as virtual prime ministers for getting the Queen's business through both Houses of Parliament (5, 7; 63; 45b, *256ff.*; 70, *188–94*). These functions and the way they performed them entitle us to view the managers, by 1702 at least, as 'the "third force" in the working of politics . . ., besides the monarch and the parties' (70, *189*). Their rôle as *parliamentary* managers, in particular, became more and more vital, given Parliament's new, semi-permanent presence on the scene. And in this respect we must bear two things in mind. Firstly, in the absence of any formal system of 'whipping', there was, as Godolphin recognised, 'no such thing as safety' for any ministry in any session 'till Black Rod knocks at the door'.[1] Secondly, the managers had only limited assistance, at least in Anne's reign, from the kind of 'government interest' in Parliament – loyal office-holders, the Crown's electoral nominees and ministerial dependants – which was to be so valuable to the Whig administrations of the post–1722 era (*The Age of Oligarchy*, Chs. 2–3). Although more than a hundred 'placemen' could generally be found in the early eighteenth-century House of Commons, even after the restrictive legislation of 1700–01 (Ch. 16), those who could be depended on, at a pinch, to ignore the tug of their party loyalties were but a small minority (70, *353ff*).

In the House of Lords, on the other hand, the office-holders and pensioners constituted a much larger proportion of the total membership, and there at least the 'Court interest' offered a more viable basis on which ministers could begin to build a system of managerial control (70, *Ch. 12*; 21 [Jones]). Yet it was very far from being invulnerable to 'the rage of party' (see Ch. 22), and this was all the more serious for ministers of the Crown because the House of Lords remained an absolutely integral part of the political system as late as the mid-point of George I's reign. Indeed, the years 1702–1718, in particular, have been described as 'a period when the talents and political importance of the Lords have rarely, if ever, been surpassed'.[2] The impeachments in 1701 of three of the greatest figures in the post-Revolution Whig party (above, p. 201) staked out for the Upper House a place right in the front line of the great parliamentary battles of the early eighteenth century. In 1701, as later from 1702–5, and more frequently still from 1710–14, it acted as a most effective bridle on the rampant power of a Tory majority in the House of Commons; in the process, not only were the parliamentary Whigs saved from possible destruction, at least in the last years of Anne, but an excessive strain was put on relations between the two Houses themselves.[3]

At a time when Whig-Tory loyalties bit deep into the more traditional loyalties of peers to the monarch, and when the Lords contained such a vast majority of the leading political figures in politics and government, there was never the slightest chance of the post-Revolution House of Lords being charged, in common with that of the age of Walpole, with being the administration's poodle. On the contrary, there were many occasions from 1701 onwards when ministries were seriously embarrassed, and even threatened, by an intransigent Upper House. Such was the case over the first Occasional Conformity bill in 1702–3 and the disastrous Sacheverell affair in 1710 (Ch. 23), and over the peace preliminaries with France in December 1711 and the Protestant Succession in 1714. As late as 1718, as we know, relations between the Stanhope-Sunderland administration and the Lords were so fraught that the ministry determined to resort to the unprecedented experiment of the 1719 Peerage bill (68b, *62–9*; 83c; cf. above, pp. 226–7). It is beyond question that without the rapid decline in the stature and independence of the House which took place in the early 1720s both the long supremacy of Sir Robert Walpole and the restoration of political stability in Britain would have been much more difficult to achieve (Chs. 13, 25; 68a).

So far three elements have been identified as major contributors to the distinctive pattern of post-Revolution politics: the novel constitutional position and political ideals of the last two Stuart monarchs, the equally novel rôle of the 'managers', and the exceptional importance and independence in this period of the House of Lords. There were two other features, however, which even more than these set the post-Revolution political system apart both from its immediate predecessor of the decade before 1689 and from the political order which succeeded it in the 1720s and characterised the age of Walpole and the Pelhams up to the late 1750s. One was the emergence of the electorate as a powerful force – at times a decisive force – in politics, and ultimately in government. Its singular contribution will be the theme of the rest of this chapter. The second, to which we shall turn thereafter, was the division, not simply of Parliament, but of virtually the entire political nation by the beginning of the eighteenth century into two parties, locked in an unremitting struggle for supremacy which threatened at times to take possession of English society itself, from top almost to bottom. Although it is convenient to examine them separately here, these two elements were held together by links that were extremely close. In fact, to a great extent they stood and fell as one; when they fell, as they had, as full-blooded phenomena, by the mid–1720s, neither British politics nor British government were ever the same again. Rather more than a hundred years were to pass before conditions recurred that were remotely similar.

The place of the electorate in the political system for more than a quarter of a century after the Glorious Revolution was a unique one. We can best begin to appreciate this by looking first at a concrete situation. In the early summer of 1710 the most powerful Whig administration of the whole period between 1689 and 1715 stood low in popular esteem, partly because the nation was war-weary, but even more because the Whigs had recently been discredited by the notorious case of Doctor Sacheverell (Ch. 23). At this juncture they faced the distinct possibility of a premature dissolution of Parliament by the Queen and of having to fight another General Election, little more than two years after they had won the previous one; the duchess of Marlborough, erstwhile royal favourite and a fervid Whig, consulted two experienced MPs, Hugh Boscawen and James Craggs, to sound out their views on their party's prospects. Boscawen was inclined to be optimistic, but not so Craggs. 'I think he is extremely mistaken [he wrote] when he supposes that, if this present Parliament be dissolved, we shall be able to deal with the adversary in the next elections. I will be bold to foresee, as the common people are now set, [the Tories] will get at least three for one.'[4] The events of the following autumn amply vindicated Craggs's powers of prophecy: he correctly forecast the biggest party landslide victory since 1685 [E.1(iii)], even if he exaggerated its scale. More striking than his prognosis, however, is his diagnosis. *As the common people are now set* seems a remarkable phrase, set in the context of the unreformed electoral system of 1660–1832. This system's many critics and would-be reformers were all to claim later in the eighteenth century that it was the very negation of the national will: that the electors themselves were but a small and grossly unrepresentative sample of 'the people', and that most of their votes were either sewn up or manipulated in one way or another. There was a degree of distortion in this picture even in the mid- and late eighteenth centuries. The student of late seventeenth- and early eighteenth-century English politics, however, would be well advised to discard the stereotype altogether. No one would pretend that there were no attempts to bribe or otherwise corrupt the electorate at this period; that government ministers and officials did not some-times try to influence election results (though they never did so consistently or systematically); that land or property owners did not frequently try to put pressure on their tenants to vote for the candidates they themselves supported; that the 'deference vote' in every county was not an important factor in politicians' calculations,[5] or that pocket boroughs had no place in the system. All these warts existed. But, apart from the influence of the Crown, their effects tended to be self-cancelling: it was not they, before the 1720s, which were decisive in determining the outcome of General Elections.

It will be argued here that it was the electorate itself (or, to be more accurate, that segment of it which was wholly or partly independent[6]) which held the key. It has been vigorously debated of late whether or not the poll-book analyses and other intensive studies of the Augustan electorate over the past twenty years have endowed that body with more independence, greater volatility and a higher degree of political consciousness than it in fact possessed. Readers of this chapter would do well to familiarise themselves with this debate (cf. 81a, *17–20, 118–20;* 321, *15–26* with 99b; see also n. 5, p. 332 below), because what follows is, in large measure, a part of it, rather than an anodyne summary of its pros and cons. The view of the electorate of 1679–1722 which I put forward in 1976 (97b) has not emerged unscathed in every particular from the questions raised by Linda Colley and Jonathan Clark, but its *central* thesis is re-stated here with confidence. It is that, after a brief but impressive preview of its potential from 1679 to 1681, and a perilous interlude under James II, the English electorate emerged in the 1690s and remained for two decades a force genuinely, if crudely, representative of the will of the politically-conscious classes in the country. As such, it showed itself regularly capable of swaying the fortunes of parties and even at times of influencing the composition of governments (as it clearly did from 1698 to 1700, for instance, or in 1708–9).

The origins of the rise of the electorate to its post-Revolution hegemony have been convincingly traced back to before the Civil Wars (97a), and the elections to the Long Parliament in 1640, especially, reflect this.[7] But protracted periods of inactivity between 1640 and 1679 inevitably led to a loss of momentum, although not (as the Exclusion elections were to demonstrate) to widespread atrophy. The momentum was not conclusively restored until after the Glorious Revolution, when it carried the electorate inside a decade to a height of political importance it had never previously enjoyed. General elections in successive years in 1689–90, from which the Court stood aloof, signalled the change, but the true turning-point came in 1694, thanks to the familiar combination of war and the Revolution constitution. To try to ensure the parliamentary cooperation that was so vital to war supply, in sessions that had now settled into an annual pattern, William III and his ministers, following the 1690 election, shied away to begin with from any dependence on party discipline. Instead, they tried to rely on a Danby-like system of 'management' which involved the presence of large numbers of placemen and pensioners in the House of Commons. It was not a success, but this did nothing to still the fears of the Country members of both the Whig and Tory parties that they were in for a repetition of the perpetual Cavalier Parliament of Charles II, fears enhanced by the fact that Danby himself was at this very time rewarded for his services in the Revolution by being brought back into high office as marquess of Carmarthen. Thus the opposition to the preponderantly Tory Carmarthen-Nottingham administration (1690–3), opposition supported for its own ends by a fledgling power group of great ability and ambition, which came to be called the Whig Junto, began to press for a new Triennial Act, which would force the Crown to dissolve Parliament at least every third year (Ch. 13; F(v)). It was this Act, passed at the third time of asking in 1694 and kept on the statute book for the next twenty-two years, which ushered in the true 'golden age' of the unreformed English electorate.

In the course of these twenty-two years six General Elections took place in England, followed by four more (1708–15) in Great Britain. Their frequency was unprecedented over a comparable timespan, and it has never subsequently been paralleled. Half the elections held between 1695 and 1715 were brought about by voluntary dissolutions of Parliament or by the deaths of monarchs. But the other half were the direct result of the Triennial Act. New and more intense levels of activity are also apparent in the number of constituencies which were fought out all the way to a poll. Before 1690 over fifty English Parliaments had already been elected since the coming of the Tudors, but we know of only one General Election in the entire period, that of March 1679, in which more than 100 counties and boroughs in England and Wales were definitely contested. The norm between 1660 and 1689 was around sixty or seventy contests. Beginning in 1690, however, there were undoubtedly two, and possibly three General Elections in William III's reign which saw over 100 English and Welsh contests; under Anne and George I there were possibly six in succession from 1705 to 1722 (1708 being the only doubtful case), with the total rising over 130 in 1710 and again in 1722 (25, *I*; 62a; 99a; 26a). With elections following each other thick and fast, the willingness of candidates (or their sponsors), especially in county seats, to take contests beyond a canvass of the voters to their bitter, and usually expensive, end is the more remarkable. Between the Revolution and 1722, for example, the freeholders of Essex and Gloucestershire were both taken to the polls twelve times.

It has been argued that the extraordinary incidence of elections between 1695 and 1715, one every second year on average, was probably the most important single factor contributing to the domination of post-Revolution politics by the division between Whigs and Tories: a domination which had become virtually total by 1701 (5; 99a) and which remained so until the departure of Walpole, Townshend and their friends from the Whig ministry formed after Anne's death and their migration into opposition in 1717 (Ch. 13). At very least, the combination of frequent General Elections, numerous contested by-elections, and the regular active involvement of the voters in the political process fed what Sir John Plumb has called 'the rage of party' (28, *Ch. 5*) with a non-stop supply of combustible fuel. Further, the rise of the electorate to its zenith in the Triennial era did more than put a unique stamp on the politics of the day; it also greatly intensified the problem of how first England, and then Britain, were to be governed in the aftermath of the 1688–9 Revolution. For the unremitting return of Parliaments with such a strong party bias eventually left the Crown with no alternative, in the interests of government business, but to adjust the *ministerial* personnel of the administration – though not necessarily its entire fund of patronage (cf. 67 and above p. 323) – to the current sympathies of the House of Commons.

It is often said that the standard pattern of political change after the Revolution was for the Crown to initiate the process by making appointments to and dismissals from the ministry *before* dissolving Parliament, and then, in effect, to appeal to the electorate for endorsement, which (we are told) it regularly got (19, *I, 208–10*; *II, 26*; 81a, *19, 120*). Such claims would seem to be supported to the hilt by the words which a distinguished early eighteenth-century Lord Chancellor, Cowper, wrote to the incoming George I in 1714:

> The generality of the world [is] so much in love with the advantages a King of Great Britain has to bestow, . . . that 'tis wholly in your Majesty's power, by showing your favour in due time (before the elections) to one or other of the [parties], to give which of them you please a clear majority in all succeeding Parliaments.[8]

One can, of course, point to General Elections in this period, among them that of 1715, which appear to fit this pattern neatly enough. Yet this is only half the story. The power which the Whig Junto wielded in government in the middle years of William III crumbled away in 1699–1700, not initially because they had lost the King's confidence but because their parliamentary base had been undermined by the 1698 Election. They stormed and captured the ministry again in 1708–9, not because Queen Anne or Godolphin welcomed them in but because the General Election of 1708 had made their claims irresistible. The many gains made at the polls by the Whigs in 1705 and the near-landslide Tory victory in 1710 forced, first Godolphin, later Harley (though after a long delaying-action) to change in favour of these parties the more balanced political dispositions and strategy which they had adopted in remodelling the administration before the elections. The ultimate logic of all this was seen during the second half of the Queen's reign and the first three years of George I's, that is, from 1708 until the Whig schism of 1717. In those years there existed in Britain something very close indeed, not just to a two-party political system, but to a two-party system of government, as we understand it today (70, *378–81*). Robert Harley, the Country Whig rebel of William's reign who became the most politically sophisticated of Queen Anne's 'managers', foresaw this and did his best to stave it off. The Queen herself, he argued, must be the true heart of the political system. He was too much of a realist to believe that government could be carried on without party, but to him it was essential that party leaders, 'without expecting terms' should come 'voluntarily into the promoting of her service'. If they were once allowed to force themselves on the monarch by virtue of a Commons majority it would infallibly 'render the government like a door which turns both ways upon its hinges to let in each party as it grows triumphant'.[9] Yet however much Harley deplored such 'party tyranny', even he in the end, like Godolphin before him in 1708–9, had to come to terms with it, though he would never capitulate to the extreme wing of the Tory party (73a; 105; Ch. 16 above).

The dissolution of the two-party system in post-Revolution politics cannot be pinpointed with total precision. It is reasonable to assume that it continued to operate until the eclipse of the Tories, not as a 'party' *per se* – for this they continued to be for decades after 1714 – but as a force with a reasonable prospect of power. When this happened is not a matter on which historians are universally agreed (Ch. 25; cf. 70, *xiii-xv*; 81a; 60b, *147ff*). *Why* it happened, too, is a complex issue (Ch. 25), but clearly it cannot be determined without some reference to the fortunes of the electorate, and here the repeal of the Triennial Act in 1716 had fundamental implications. The new Septennial Act [F(xii)], with which the Whigs replaced it (Ch. 13), did more than condemn the Tories to frustration in the short run, and in the long run to permanent minority status; by extending the maximum life of the current Parliament and all future Parliaments from three to seven years, it also spelt decline for the electorate. As the heat went out of the fire of party, so too that independence and unpredictability, which had hitherto done much to keep the flames crackling, gradually went out of the voters. In the twelve and a half years which separated the General Elections of 1715 and 1727 the electorate itself was systematically bridled by the combined efforts of a Whig government and Whig magnates who had had enough of its unruliness. The last shadowy semblance of its former power was seen in 1722, at the only General Election to punctuate those twelve years. For although in the end the Whigs won that election easily, thereby increasing the already big majority of seven years earlier, their opponents did at least go into it with almost as many candidates as ever before and forced, in England at least, a near-record number of contests. After that, there were still odd elections – the 'Excise' election of 1734, for instance, and that of 1784 – at which considerable excitement was generated in the 'open' or popular constituencies. But the number of such constituencies had shrunk too much, the financial deterrents against the contesting of seats, especially county seats, had increased too much, and above all the time gap between General Elections had widened too much, to enable the British electorate to recapture its former influence. Not until after the Reform Bill of 1832 did it experience a marked, if constrained, resurgence.

It was suggested earlier that it was not only in its virility but in its ability to represent public opinion that the electorate, in its post-Revolution 'golden' period, contrasts so sharply with its successor under the last three Georges. Since the two features were closely connected, the question naturally arises: why did it have this ability, despite an archaic pattern of seats and franchises? After all, the electoral system of 1690–1720 was already open to criticism on the ground that some of the most thriving centres of recent population growth, such as Manchester, Birmingham, Leeds and Sheffield, returned no members of their own to Westminster. It was also becoming increasingly farcical that, while such towns were denied direct borough representation, forty-four members should still be returned for Cornwall, eighteen of them for decrepit little fishing villages, while thirty-two more MPs sat for the boroughs of another grossly over-represented county, Wiltshire. That places such as Heytesbury, whose 26 holders of burgage tenements were safely in the pocket of the Ashe family, or non-places such as Old Sarum, mostly ruins and sheep runs, should each return (like most boroughs outside Wales) two members – as many as the city of Westminster and half as many as London itself – was likewise indefensible in logic. What has to be borne in mind about such anomalies at this period, however, is not so much the theory of 'virtual representation', which became so beloved of conservatives later in the eighteenth century, nor the actuality (for which there is abundant evidence) that, despite all anomalies, the economic interests of formally unrepresented towns or regions were not neglected in the House of Commons (96, *31–2*; 101). It is rather that the anomalies themselves were not as serious in 1700 as they were to be by 1750, and they were infinitely less glaring than those which gradually undermined the whole system in the period of genuine industrialisation after 1780. This was one reason – though not the only one – why zeal for parliamentary reform proved so hard to rekindle once the alarms of James II's reign were past (above, p. 221). Criticism of some of the tiniest and most corrupt boroughs and of the gross over-representation of certain regions periodically surfaced in print, and occasionally in Parliament. Several attempts were made to curtail by legislation some of the sharper practices which open voting and biased returning officers encouraged. But of changing the electoral system itself, even by the most modest redistribution of seats, scarcely a murmur was heard at Westminster between the session of 1701 and the late 1740s (16, *5–6, 8–9, 25–7*; 96, *Ch. 2*; 99a; 81a).

The fact was that in the lifetime of the Triennial Act the Manchesters and Birminghams of the country represented just a handful of exceptions to the rule that the great majority of England's larger cities and towns, including most of those growing quickly, *were* directly represented at Westminster. This was true of all the main ports, from Liverpool and Bristol to Yarmouth, Hull and Newcastle; of all the county and regional capitals; of two of the three main dockyard towns; of most of the major cloth and hosiery manufacturing towns; even of leading resorts and leisure centres, such as Bath, Scarborough, Bury St Edmunds and Beverley. A few of these places, it is true, had very narrow franchises: Bath, Salisbury, Plymouth, Tiverton and Scarborough are cases in point. But most were quite fairly represented. Another point to remember, usually overlooked, is that even the formally unrepresented 'new' towns were not wholly disfranchised. Their forty-shilling freeholders, of which they had many, had as much right to vote as those of the rural areas in the election of members for their respective counties; surviving poll-books tell us that they did so in considerable numbers, were much courted by candidates, and quite often – as in the case of the voters of Manchester, Leeds and Sheffield – were credited with great influence on the outcome of contests (16, *28–30*).

There is one other respect in which the electorate was far more representative than is commonly imagined. The size of the voting population of England and Wales had been growing steadily since Tudor times (97a), and between 1689 and 1715 this growth continued at a faster pace, easily outstripping in relative terms the slow rise of the population, as more men acquired the franchise and *many* more got the habit of exercising their votes, especially the 'forty-shilling freehold-ers' in the counties. In fact, it has been plausibly argued that much-increased 'turn-out', prompted by local party activists, rather than a great expansion in the total entitled to vote, had much to do with the so seemingly-rapid 'growth' of the electorate in this period (321, *20–1*; but cf. 16, *15–18*); this would square with the otherwise puzzling tendency of the House of Commons, in judging disputed election cases after the Revolution, to uphold narrower borough franchises rather than broader ones.[10] Be that as it may, the 'potential' electorate of England and Wales[11] had by the early years of George I reached between 330,000 and 340,000. At the three elections of 1710, 1715 and 1722 a higher proportion of English adult males voted than at any election held in Britain before November 1868. It is true that in Scotland, where the franchise was in effect restricted to substantial landowners in the shires and to town councillors in the enfranchised burghs, the electorate was a law unto itself, and the whole system a travesty of 'representa-tion': the forty-five Scottish members in the first two decades after the Union were elected by a total of roughly 2,600 voters, divided roughly equally between thirty counties, fourteen groups of burghs and the city of Edinburgh (25; cf. 90, *54–67*). On the other hand, 340,000 English and Welsh voters in 1715 amounted to between one in four and one in five males over the age of twenty-one at that time. This was a higher percentage than were enfranchised between the first two Reform Acts of the nineteenth century. And when one bears in mind that at least half the adult males in the country were either paupers, servants, or the humblest type of wage-labourer or cottager – people to whom even some of the Levellers would have refused a vote – one begins to appreciate why the early eighteenth-century electorate was such a difficult body both for the Crown and the party politicians of the day to control; also why the Whigs, once entrenched after the collapse of the 'Fifteen Rebellion, became so concerned to render it captive or corruptible.

For the pre-Septennial English electorate could not, by and large, be bullied or bought. Certainly this was true of those two elements which did most to determine the dispositions of the Whig and Tory parties in the Commons: the 'floating voters' (between ten and twenty per cent of all electors in an average county), whose presence has been so plainly revealed by the study of poll-books,[12] and the sixty-nine counties and boroughs which I have elsewhere called 'the weathervane constituencies' of the period, the most sensitive independent reflectors of shifts in the opinion of the political nation from one General Election to another (16, 7). This, together with a turnover of voters in almost every constituency, over a two to three year period, which was extraordinarily high, explains why the local leaders and the parliamentary candidates of the two parties had to be prepared to woo, coax and cajole electors in all manner of ways. This is why party managers commissioned such reams of election literature, mostly pamphlet and broadsheet propaganda, before each national contest ('the lampoons fly thick as hail in order to influence the approaching elections', wrote one observer in 1705).[13] This is why so much energy was consumed in getting out the vote, and why, before that could be identified, many candidates had to canvass so assiduously, either in person or through their agents. The diary of Sir Arthur Kay, for instance, shows that before the Yorkshire contest of 1710 he sent his agents into the very depths of Swaledale, to each village, hamlet and farmstead (5, *158–60*). From 1695–1715 alone hundreds of thousands of pounds were spent, not for the most part by organisations, as in our own day, but by individual Whigs and Tories. In this process scores of families were ruined, among them aristocratic families such as the Herberts of Cherbury. The Junto's chief election manager, Lord Wharton (Honest Tom Wharton to his friends and fellow-partisans) had a great income of £16,000 a year after his second marriage. Yet he spent so much on his election campaigns that by 1708 he was close to the brink of bankruptcy, with bailiffs descending on his Dover Street house to distrain the furniture.[14]

That general elections during the whole period from 1690 through to 1715 could, and commonly did, broadly reflect the prevailing political mood of the country cannot be doubted by anyone who has studied all the relevant indicators. If one takes each election constituency by constituency, numerous parts may sometimes seem out of place; yet the sum of the parts, each time, is remarkably convincing. To take only Queen Anne's reign and the beginning of George I's for our examples: the Tories' heady victory in 1702, when polling followed the accession of an 'entirely English' queen and a devotee of the Church, was a genuine reflection of the way public opinion was moving once the uncertainty of the Spanish Succession crisis had been ended. The same party's electoral triumph of 1710 was also, in a real sense, a popular triumph and was celebrated as such; so – though to a lesser extent – was that of 1713, when, as one Tory stalwart put it, he and his friends could 'never go to their elections with more advantage than while the impressions made by the rejoicings at the [Peace] Thanksgiving, and by the Queen's incomparable Speech, are fresh upon the minds of the electors'.[15]

On the other hand, the evenly-balanced result of 1705, like that of December 1701 was, as far as we can gauge from other sources, a fairly accurate measure of the extent to which the recent parliamentary conduct of the Tories had alienated moderate and patriot opinion without deeply eroding the party's bedrock support. And when, just twice after 1701, the popular tide was running very strongly for the Whigs, first in 1708 after the abortive Franco-Jacobite invasion attempt, and secondly in January 1715 after the peaceful accession of the legal Hanoverian heir, it was a Whig majority standing foursquare on a Protestant succession platform which the electorate produced.

By 1722, three decades or more of heavy private expenditure by the great Whig families and by those in the party with strong borough interests, especially in the buying up of burgages or 'vote houses' – and so exploiting the most vulnerable part of an irrational mosaic of franchises – had at long last begun to pay off. The process was helped very considerably, almost certainly crucially, by the Septennial Act and by the ruthless use of government patronage at local level. In the elections of 1710 and 1713 all that zealous commitment and open purses could do for the Whig party was enable it to hold on to a shrinking bridgehead in a House of Commons which, by the last year of Queen Anne, was all but overrun by Tories. But in 1722, for the first time since 1681 (Ch. 8), a party was able to win a majority that was palpably disproportionate to its true strength in the country, and future elections under Walpole would distort 'the sense of the people' even more (16, *32*; 81a, *118–45*). In terms of votes cast the Tories won an empty majority in all three. By George II's reign the days had gone when the English electoral system gave adequate expression to the National Will and when politicians had good cause to be alarmed, as Craggs was in 1710, at the way 'the common people are now set'. And with the loss of this capacity the electorate also lost the ability to mould the pattern of politics, and even influence the colour of government – that unique power which for some twenty-five years had lain within its grasp.

---

1. HMC *Portland MSS.*, IV, p. 81: to Harley, 10 Feb 1704.
2. C. Jones and G. Holmes, eds, *The London Diaries of William Nicolson, Bishop of Carlisle 1702–1718* (Oxford, 1985), p. vii.
3. For a classic example see E. Cruickshanks, '*Ashby v. White*: the Case of the Men of Aylesbury, 1701–4', in C. Jones, ed., *Party and Management in Parliament, 1660–1784* (Leicester, 1984), pp. 90–103. Bitter intercameral quarrels persisted at least as late as July 1717, when the Lords threw out impeachment charges against the late Lord Treasurer, Oxford.
4. *Private Correspondence of Sarah, Duchess of Marlborough* (1838), I, p. 318: 18 May 1710.
5. N. Landau, 'Independence, Deference and Voter Participation: the Behaviour of the Electorate in Early Eighteenth-Century Kent', *HJ*, **22** (1979). But cf. the comment in Holmes, 70, p. xviii, n. 28.
6. It has to be remembered that all but a tiny minority of electors before 1832 had two votes each. It was quite common for one of them to be 'reserved' and for the other to be independent.

7. Derek Hirst, *The Representative of the People?: Voters and Voting in England under the Early Stuarts* (Cambridge, 1975), pp. 104–153 *passim*, pp. 191–3.
8. William, Lord Cowper, 'An Impartial History of Parties', printed in Lord Campbell, *The Lives of the Lord Chancellors*, IV (1846), pp. 428–9.
9. *Huntington Library Quarterly*, **15** (1951–2), p. 39: James Brydges to William Cadogan, 24 Dec 1707 (reporting Harley's views); HMC *Bath MSS.*, I, p. 181: Harley to Godolphin, 10 Sept 1707.
10. See Cannon (96), p. 34. Too much can be read into this trend, however. A lot of the decisions were fortuitous, in the sense that they were determined less by any general prejudice against 'scot and lot men' or 'potwallers' than by the state of party forces, both in the Commons and in the constituencies in question, at the time the cases were heard.
11. I.e. all who *could* have voted had there been contests in every constituency.
12. W.A. Speck and W.A. Gray, 'Computer Analysis of Poll Books: An Initial Report', *BIHR* **43**, (1970); Speck, Gray and R. Hopkinson, 'Computer Analysis of Poll Books: A Further Report', *BIHR*, **48** (1975).
13. Add. MSS. 4743, f. 32: Erasmus Lewis to Henry Davenant, 16 Mar 1705.
14. HMC *Portland MSS.* IV, p. 511.
15. BL Loan 29/201: William Bromley to Oxford, 24 July 1713.

CHAPTER 22

Parliament and 'the rage of party'

At the height of its fury in Anne's reign 'the rage of party' did far more than rouse and deeply divide the electorate. There were many times when it truly seemed to contemporaries that it was threatening to rend apart their whole society. After the turmoil suffered by local government in the 1680s (Chs. 11–12), it was well nigh inevitable that this should remain after the Revolution one of the most bitterly contested of fields. Manipulation of county magistracies and lieutenancies for party advantage, although restrained to a certain extent by practicalities, social conventions, and the need to preserve respect for the bench among the lower orders, became a commonplace of Whig-Tory rivalry under a succession of Lord Keepers and Lord Chancellors, from Somers in 1693 to Macclesfield in the early 1720s. If it fluctuated in intensity, that was largely because the ruthlessness and energy of those who held the Great Seal in that period was also variable (126b, *112–261, Ch. 9*; 126a, *80–95*). The corporations, too, having mostly recovered their old charters, but in an important minority of cases inherited from James II's reign long-running disputes about the validity of either old or new charters, continued to be battlegrounds on which, as Bishop Burnet wrote in 1708,

> the parties are now so stated and kept up, not only by the elections of parliament-men, that return every third year, but even by the yearly elections of mayors and corporation-men, that they know their strength . . . (1, *VI, 224*).

Even in some non-parliamentary boroughs, such as Leeds, things were little better (127, *157–9*; 5, *48*). But nowhere was the strife so fierce – or so anxiously watched by successive governments – as in London. There, from the very aftermath of the Revolution, elections to the Common Council were fought on strict party lines, and the bad blood between the Council and the Court of Aldermen, once the Tories gained control of the former in Anne's reign, became so notorious that it led in the end to Walpole's controversial City Elections Act of 1725 (94a; 95, *181–8*).

It was not only the public lives of Augustan Englishmen, however, that were encroached upon and tormented by their political animosities. They spilled over into such unlikely areas as the administration of poor relief, as well as deeply colouring the religious life, the professional and business life and even the social and recreational life of the age. There were party coffee-houses and taverns; party clubs; and an abundance of party newspapers and periodicals (*The Age of Oligarchy*, Ch. 13). There was party patronage of the stage and party rivalry on the race-track. London even had its Whig and Tory hospitals – St Thomas's and St Barts[1] – as well as its recognised Whig and Tory doctors, its Garths and its

Freinds, to attend the party men in their illnesses or deliver the babies of their often equally partisan wives (5; 70, *Ch. 1*). The marriage mart itself, inevitably, became politicised. With hindsight it is possible to see that, in the passionate closeness of their political involvement, the men of the day could not always appreciate the underlying strength of some of the cements which still held together the shot-torn fabric of their society. Without the elements of restraint and cohesion they supplied, it would have been impossible for social stability to be restored as quickly as it was under the Whig oligarchy in the 1720s and 1730s (Ch. 25). But this is not to say that the broils which so profoundly disturbed the post-Revolution political nation were synthetic or that alarm at their consequences was not entirely understandable.

What kind of phenomena, then, were the Whig and Tory parties of this period? How did they differ in their most distinguishing features from the original parties of the Exclusion period, from which they sprang? What issues and conflicting aims divided them, not only in elections and in the wider society which nurtured the two parties, but specifically in Parliament, their chief forum? And how much room was left there for the survival of the older division of the legislature between the supporters of Court and Country? The nature of political parties in this period gave rise in the 1950s and 1960s to an important historical controversy. Primarily it was a controversy about whether the Whigs and Tories of the early eighteenth century had much in common with our late nineteenth- or twentieth-century notions of political parties as national bodies with a coherent parliamentary presence – a resemblance which most historians down to the 1930s had confidently assumed there to be (46; 19; 143a); or whether, on the contrary, they were more like the miscellaneous coalitions of factions or 'connections' into which the parliamentary Whigs of mid-Hanoverian Britain are known to have disintegrated by the 1760s. In short, ought we to think of politics from 1689 to 1714, if not beyond, being conducted along the traditional lines envisaged by the old 'Whiggish' historians, or did they, as Robert Walcott[2] claimed, conform fairly closely to the 'Namier model', the multi-party model of politics appropriate to the early years of George III? (91). A secondary dimension to this debate, broadly in sympathy with Walcott's interpretation but playing down the importance of family connections, was imparted by Denis Rubini. Concentrating on William III's reign only, Rubini professed to find no coherence and little unity of action among either Whigs or Tories. In every Parliament of the 1690s, he was persuaded, sat a large body of country gentlemen who had no strong sense of party commitment and a positive antipathy to party leadership – not unlike the 'independents' to whom Namier ascribed a major role in mid-Georgian Parliaments. And he concluded 'that most of the important issues [of William's reign] were fought on a court-country basis, that contemporaries usually spoke in these terms, and that the chief exception was in the fight over the offices: that is, when the question was one of men rather than of measures' (65, *259*).

There has been much research into post-Revolution politics during the past twenty years, and the resulting reappraisals, whether of William's reign alone, or of Anne's, or of both [(1) 62a; 61; (2) 70; (3) 28; 60b; 62b] have lent very little support to the Walcott thesis. Neither, with possibly one exception, have they suggested that great confidence can be placed in Rubini's Court/Country interpretation of 1689–1702, except with drastic reservations (59b; cf. 64). These reappraisals have depended much on the answers research has provided to a few key questions. How did men vote at Westminster on those issues for which division lists have survived? In what *terms* did contemporary politicians view their own affiliations, priorities and motives? What part did family relationships or office-holding play in determining political alignments at the centre? The dust of controversy having now settled, the main features of the Augustan high-political landscape can be perceived with some clarity. Some of these features are enduring across the whole terrain between 1689 and the Whig split of 1717; others change in character. Long ago it seemed to the present writer 'sensible to recognise . . . that the pattern of politics after 1701 was not the same in many respects as that which persisted during the 1690s (70, 7). Most modern historians would argue strongly that even in the three Parliaments of 1690–1700, in spite of many cross currents, Whig and Tory remained the two *overriding* facts of political life (e.g. 45b, *248n.*; 62b; 60b). And, taking the reign of William III as a whole, the analysis of voting lists – with due allowance made for the scarcity and imperfections of the evidence – pushes us quite firmly towards that conclusion (62a, *318–19*). Nevertheless, not even that archetypal Whig historian, Lord Macaulay, ever supposed that political life at Westminster in the 1690s – that decade of transition and experiment in so many fields – could be explained in crude two-party terms.

What kind of pattern, then, can help us to interpret the facts of close on three decades of often furious political activity? In the first place, without serious violence to the truth, it would be safe to assume that throughout the years from 1689 to 1717 a four-way division cut across the parliamentary arena. There was a division of almost all Westminster politicians, at virtually all times, into readily identifiable Whigs and Tories; and there was a further division of many of the same men, more intermittently, into the more traditional camps of Country and Court, although the membership of these camps fluctuated considerably according to circumstances. Barely a handful of MPs and a marginally larger proportion of peers supported every administration, whatever its complexion, while a stance of permanent opposition to government *per se* was adopted by no one in either House. The big difference between the years before and after 1701 was that, by contrast with Anne's reign, when (as the Queen herself deplored) 'the detested names of Whig and Tory' were all-pervasive, through the 1690s there were periods when the Court-Country division appeared almost as distinct as that between Whigs and Tories, and even interludes when it overlaid it. One such period lasted from 1691 until the session of 1693–4, a second from 1698 to 1700, and on the latter occasion the change was emphatic enough for the term 'Country party' to come into currency again. But modern scholars are more discriminating. They choose to refer rather to a Country 'platform', a Country 'interest' or a Country 'persuasion'; as Colin Brooks[3] bluntly puts it, 'there was no Country Party in the 1690s', and David Hayton would accept this, if by 'party' we presuppose a group with 'a continuous existence'. The most that the word 'party' meant, even in the late 1690s, was a protracted coalition of Country Tories and a minority of Country Whigs coming together to further a programme of (mainly) anti-prerogative reform, but without losing their primary identities (64, *65*).

Some of the issues which together disturbed the loyalty of Whig to Whig or Tory to Tory in William III's reign have been noticed already: the campaign for triennial Parliaments, for example; opposition to the influence of placemen and officials over the votes of the Commons, which led to a series of attempts at excluding or 'self-denying' legislation (1692–1701) (71), and anxiety over the prosecution and cost of the Nine Years' War. There was also much bipartisan outcry over the alleged spread of corruption in high places (as in the parliamentary attacks on Speaker Trevor and Henry Guy of the Treasury in 1695); linked with this was concern to monitor government spending and probe financial mismanagement through a Commons' Commission of Public Accounts, a highly influential body,[4] which over the years 1691–7 came to supply the nucleus and much of the leadership of the 'New Country Party' (59b). In the middle years of the reign from 1694 until the election of 1698, when Whig and Tory loyalties were re-asserting themselves, new matters of contention which could engage support from country gentlemen of both parties were harder to find and promote. This was especially so in 1696–7, when the Junto came closest, before 1708, to realising its dream of party dominance over both ministry and Parliament (61, *126–7*), and when the hard core of a dozen or so Country Whig members, led by Robert Harley and Paul Foley, were forced ever closer to a permanent amalgamation with the Tory party. But two such issues were the Land Bank scheme of 1696 and bills introduced in successive sessions (1695–7) to impose stiff landed qualifications on MPs. Both were vigorously opposed by the Court and William even went so far as to veto the first Qualifications Bill, though his prerogative was not directly involved. The prerogative, however, was very much under fire again in the two years after the 1698 Election, when the Junto's power was disintegrating and the Country opposition launched devastating attacks (1698–9) on the King's proposals for a peace-time standing army (cut eventually to 10,000 men) (64, *57–60*). William's grants of land to his favourites, especially in Ireland, became the next target, culminating in the Resumption Act of 1700 (above, p. 200). There were also bitter bipartisan denunciations of foreign influences on royal policy, and these were to reach a climax in 1701 when William Bentinck, whom William had created duke of Portland, was impeached along with three of the lords of the Junto.

The parliamentary session of 1701, the first and only session of the most Tory Parliament elected since the Revolution, was the great watershed in post-Revolution politics. Thereafter, until three years into George I's reign, political divisions at Westminster were much less confused than they had been between 1691 and 1700. Even in the 1690s gut sentiment had always had the power to dissolve temporary coalitions of courtiers or 'Countrymen' when issues came up which tugged at old Whig or Tory loyalties. The mutinous Whig could be relied on to rally to the colours when the Revolution Settlement and the Protestant succession seemed under threat. Thus it was no coincidence that in the years before 1701 the Junto came nearest to achieving full support from their party after the Jacobite plot to assassinate William in 1696, and the consequent requirement for all MPs, peers and office-holders to sign a loyal 'Association' acknowledging him as their 'rightful and lawful' king (62a, *175–6*). Similarly, when the Anglican clergy began to sound the alarm bells of 'the Church in danger' in 1697 (Ch. 23), it became clear that, sooner or later, Tories of every hue, 'Countrymen' or office-holders, would respond. Attitudes to France also disturbed temporary alignments along Court and Country lines. The longer King William's War lasted, the more most Whigs tended to solidify in support of it (though many had still to be convinced of the wisdom of Continental campaigns), whereas few Tories were more than lukewarm about it. Thus a great new issue had emerged to divide Tory from Whig – one that was to re-surface more distinctly still in 1702 – just at the time when the two parties were abandoning their traditional stances over another pre-Revolution issue, the defence of the prerogative. It was also significant that throughout the last decade of the century, whatever the parliamentary dispositions of the hour, politicians of both parties invariably sprang to the defence of their leaders when they were seriously under attack from the other side: so it was when Nottingham and Clarges were targets for Whig fire in 1693 and when Halifax and Somers were similarly singled out by the Tories in 1698 and 1700 (62a, *Ch. 13*).

Not surprisingly, therefore, the impeachments of 1701, pressed forward venomously by a large Tory majority against the Junto's Somers, Halifax and Orford after the revelation of the Partition Treaties (Ch. 15), produced a dramatic polarisation. 'This matter', wrote one Tory, 'hath made a feud that I fear will not die';[5] and indeed it was one of four developments during that brief Parliament which helped to re-shape politics for a decade and a half (5). The others were the Spanish Succession crisis, which saw the Whigs unite behind a new Grand Alliance; the settlement of the English Succession through the Act of Settlement (Ch. 15 and below, p. 339); and, outside Parliament, the disputes in Convocation, which split the Church of England into 'High' and 'Low' factions, deeply engaged the prejudices and emotions of the Tories as the Church Party, and compelled the Low Church and moderate occupants of the bishops' bench to look for shelter in the unlikely arms of the Junto. After 1701 it was virtually certain that the Church's problems, and most of all her growing fear of Dissent and of its continuing alliance with Whiggery, would be thrust into the forefront of political action in the next reign. In fact it was to remain there until 1719 (Ch. 23).

Queen Anne's accession to the throne, followed within weeks by the outbreak of another war, guaranteed that the Whig-Tory divide, re-defined and widened in the last eighteen months of William III's reign, would remain the dominant *motif* in parliamentary politics as long as the Queen herself lived. Anne, with her insular outlook, devout Anglicanism, modest abilities and conservative political pretensions, could not possibly be a focus for anti-prerogative sentiment and for Country hostility to un-English influences and policies to the extent that William had been. Politics at the centre now mirrored much more closely what had for years been a more straightforward situation in the constituencies, where it was only in 1698, Somers observed, that the voters' judgement had been seriously confused by 'the most dangerous division of a Court and Country party'.[6] In

Parliament after 1701 the division into Court and Country 'interests' (for the term 'party' in this context now lost all meaning), became a thing of brief spasms and heavily overshadowed by the major cleavage among the politicians (64).

Whigs still voted against Whigs and Tories against Tories on a few important matters, even between 1702 and 1717. Some of these disputes were over genuine Country issues of ripe vintage: for example, landed qualifications for MPs (finally embodied in an Act of 1711 (above, p. 205 [F(xi)]); electoral corruption and malpractice; the frequency of Parliaments, the issue which disturbed the libertarian consciences of many Whigs in the Septennial bill divisions of 1716 (above, p. 208); and, most notably, a prolonged 'place' campaign against the influence of the Crown in the Commons, which made its biggest stir during the passage of the Regency bill in the winter of 1705–6 [F(ix)]. On that occasion a 'Whimsical clause' which would have limited the number of government office-holders in the Lower House to a maximum of forty, only narrowly failed (71). Yet, in contrast with the 1690s, the most spectacular instances of cross-voting in Anne's reign significantly occurred not when Court/Country principles were at stake, but when matters either of conscience or constituency interest split the Tories. The 'tack' of the third Occasional Conformity Bill (see below, p. 340 and Ch. 23), the French Commerce Bill of 1713 and the votes on the Succession in Danger in 1714 (above, p. 207) all exposed the more fissiparous nature of the Tory party in the years before the Whig schism of 1717. It can hardly be overstressed, however, that it was precisely because unity, not division, was the normal habit of both sets of protagonists in Parliament during the period 1701–17 that such dramas as these caused so much stir. Although the great questions of the day occasionally forced Whigs and Tories into uneasy co-operation, they commonly provoked the two sides into fierce opposition.

By 1702 a series of issues had come to the fore, thrown up either by the Glorious Revolution or the French Wars, over most of which the interests and policies of Whigs clashed emphatically with those of Tories. It was these issues which constituted the real meat of controversy in Parliament throughout Anne's reign. Foremost among them was the succession to the throne – a new form of that critical issue which had given birth to the first Whigs and Tories from 1679–81. The Bill of Rights had had the negative result of barring Catholics from the English throne, but had pronounced on the Protestant line of succession no further than Queen Anne and her children. Hence the dismay when the duke of Gloucester, Anne's only surviving child, died in 1700. In June 1701 the Act of Settlement gave the Electress Sophia of Hanover 'and the heirs of her body being Protestants' a statutory title to the throne of England after Anne's death, but not without protests from the Whigs that unenthusiastic Tories had tried to sabotage the measure by 'clogging' it with unworkable constitutional amendments (Ch. 13).[7] Early the following year, after Whig gains in the General Election of December 1701, an Abjuration Act passed, whereby parliamentarians and office-holders were compelled to take or refuse an oath forswearing allegiance to James II's son, 'the pretended Prince of Wales'. But if anxiety about securing the Protestant royal line was relieved by the time of William's sudden death, it was not removed. France's recognition of the Pretender as James III and VIII in

September 1701 was, by itself, enough to keep that an intensely live issue. The leading part it played in the making of the Union, and the contrasting attitudes of the two English parties towards it, have been discussed earlier (Ch. 20). The Regency Act [F(ix)] was the Whig recipe for safeguarding the Hanoverian succession by supplying an interim administration to keep order in the dangerous interval that must ensue between Anne's decease and the arrival from Germany of the legal heir. At the same time, the fact that the Tories in both Houses persistently sought to obstruct the bill's progress (1, *V, 234–9*) demonstrated yet again that, where a question of basic allegiance was concerned, their party still found itself in an uncomfortably ambivalent position: very conscious of the scruples of its Jacobite or crypto-Jacobite wing, unwilling to oppose the principle of a Protestant succession openly, yet unable to identify itself wholeheartedly with practical measures designed to make it a reality or flush out its prospective opponents. As Anne's health grew frailer and relations between Harley's ministry and Hanover between 1711 and 1713 became increasingly strained, so the contrast became all the more stark between absolute Whig unanimity on the succession issue and the divisions and equivocations of their opponents: a Tory dilemma which at the last – after the Pretender refused the final pleas of the Tories, even of the Jacobite MPs, to renounce his Catholic faith – was to drive a disastrous wedge through the party (70, *xxxv-vii, 85–94*; 73a; 105), leaving it indecisive at the Queen's death and still highly vulnerable at the time of the Jacobite rebellion of 1715 (Ch. 25).

However, on most of the big questions dividing them after 1701 the two parties took up their opposing stations with little trimming and heart-searching. From the introduction of the first Tory Occasional Conformity Bill in the early winter of 1702 through to 1719, a subject of bitter, recurring controversy in Parliament was the interpretation of the 'toleration' granted to dissenters in 1689, and the measure of protection to be afforded to an Anglican Church which now felt itself beleaguered. The underlying party loyalties involved were again of pre-Revolution vintage; although the issues were given a series of new twists by events between the Revolution and 1701, these left scope (as the next chapter will explain) for no more than minor variations in the traditional posture of both the lay parties. Only over the question of extending full civil rights to nonconformists, a matter which after 1689 did not surface overtly again until 1719, were the lay Whigs appreciably divided (Ch. 23; but cf. 84). Equally productive of confrontation between Whig and Tory as 'the Church in danger' was a crop of entirely novel issues propagated by the French wars. Even though some of the country members of their party supported a Landed Qualifications Act, Whigs at large looked favourably on the rise of the New Finance and the monied men, while the Tories, who identified themselves closely with the landed interest, were deeply distrustful of these 'complications of knavery' (Ch. 17). The Whigs were passionately anti-French and staunchly pro-Dutch after 1702, and they took a view of Britain's commitment to Europe and of her relations with her allies with which few Tories could as readily identify (Ch. 15). Also, as we know, a running party battle was fought over the strategy of the Spanish Succession War, the need for peace, especially after Oudenarde, and the terms on which the final settlement with France ought to be made (Chs. 14, 15).

It is evident that the ideological content of the party struggle had changed since the 1680s; yet at the same time the elements of continuity remained, and they were of fundamental importance in forming and cementing allegiances. Even the central argument over the nature of government and the rights of the subject, which had underpinned so much Exclusionist and anti-Exclusionist polemic, survived to some extent. The Revolution reduced its intensity and changed its context, but did not, as might have been expected, render it irrelevant. Although most of the leaders of the post-Exclusion generation of Whigs backed away somewhat from Lockean principles, and particularly from the pure milk of the contract theory (313, *74–90*; 314, *Chs. 4, 7–8*; cf. Ch. 24 below), these ideas continued to have wide circulation, and presumably influence, among their rank-and-file supporters in the country. Even the Junto lords and their heirs – a few trimmers apart – stood by the right of resistance (311; 87, *65–9*; 70, *xxxiii-iv, 96–7*).[8] For their part, some of the more sophisticated of the younger Tories – men such as Harley's ally, Sir Simon Harcourt – seized eagerly on an ingenious post-Revolution variant of the old Anglican dogma of obedience. Their postulate was that whereas a king alone, if he acted outside the law, had no unqualified claim on his subjects' obedience, 'the King in Parliament', being truly sovereign and the embodiment of legality, could never be legally resisted. However, when the highflying section of the Anglican clergy, together with Charles Leslie and the nonjurors, began in the middle years of Anne's reign to revive the more orthodox strains of Divine Right, Passive Obedience and Non-Resistance preaching and writing, they struck many a responsive chord among the lay champions of the Church Party (163b, *103–16*; 314, *119–22, 136–8*; 73b, *182–4*). The set-piece debates of the Sacheverell trial in 1710 (Ch. 23) showed very clearly that 'Revolution principles' or 'natural rights' still sat uneasily upon the shoulders of the Tory party;[9] while the flood of loyal addresses which poured in between the end of the trial and the election in the autumn made it equally plain that a party which retained some claim to stand for 'Church and Crown' could still find a common emotional wavelength with great numbers of the Queen's ordinary subjects.

The situation was not without irony, since, in Parliament at least, the Tories since 1689 had certainly shown no more solicitude for the prerogative than the Whigs, and probably less. In fact, one of the most striking differences between the pre- and post-Revolution parties is the degree to which, once the Tories ceased to have a monopoly of royal favour (a shattering experience, which first overtook them in 1687) (81b, *246*), their party succeeded in appropriating the 'Country' clothes of the Whigs. They did so not merely to help to forward genuinely bipartisan backbench measures of the kind already noted; increasingly frequently, too, they used Country shibboleths as a camouflage for the pursuit of essentially partisan ends. Their bringing of exaggerated charges of corruption against their opponents, for instance against Walpole and Marlborough in 1712, illustrates the use of such a cloak very well. And on other important Country issues, such as the Crown's land grants, their motives were, to put it mildly, mixed. Dr Hayton is not far wide of the mark when he writes that 'by Anne's reign Country sentiment seems to have been largely absorbed into backbench Toryism' (70, *xxxvii-xli, Ch. 4*; 64, *65*).

It was not only in certain features of their ideologies, policies and attitudes that the Whig and Tory parties of the reigns of William III, Anne and George I differed from their predecessors of Charles II's day. Their structure and composition, too, had changed in some important respects; their organisation had developed considerably, and a new generation of leaders had also made their distinctive mark on each. Structurally they had one thing in common. Each was built round a core of deeply committed partisans, the men who competed most actively with their opponents for power and office. Likewise each had its Court wing – men of more moderate opinions who would *sometimes* put the government service (or their own places and pensions) before their party principles – and its more numerous 'Country' wing, whose members rarely held or even aspired to office, were usually elected independently, and were not ordinarily bound to the power politicians by any tie stronger than that of common party interest. However, the thirty years after 1679 witnessed a striking decline in the relative importance of the Country element in the Whig party, a decline not decisively reversed until Walpole held power in the 1720s. The Country opposition of 1674–8, in which landed gentry predominated, had been the bedrock of the first Whigs. By Anne's reign, while many country gentlemen up and down the country continued to espouse the Whig cause, those who made their way into the Commons, like other Whig independents, contained few who remained congenitally suspicious of governments of all complexions. In foul weather, if not always in fair, they rallied to their leaders, 'for to be sure', as Sir John Cropley wrote of the Junto in 1710, 'if they are not supported we are gone indeed.'[10] On the other hand, once the Tories became closely identified with 'the landed interest' and, coached by the Country Whigs Harley and Foley, became accustomed in the 1690s to an anti-executive stance in the House of Commons, it was they who became the party of the natural backbencher. Significantly, there was no equivalent on the Whig side at any time in the early eighteenth century to the maverick October Club, which so harassed Harley's Tory administration from the back benches, particularly in 1710–11 (70, *342–4*; 105, *73–84*).

By then, moreover, the Whigs had long since begun to shed their populist image of thirty years before. The urban radical element of old had shrunk, not least in London, where its libertarianism in 1689–90 had seriously alarmed King William (94a; 94b, *39–73*); Whig neo-republicanism had become by 1714 a tiny minority cult, strongest among intellectuals and a few eccentric aristocrats. The startling but brief efflorescence of radical political ideology in the late 1690s, which Pocock has labelled 'neo-Harringtonian' (e.g. 320), by and large accepted a place for monarchy (shorn of the instruments of tyranny, notably a standing army) within a 'balanced' or 'mixed' constitution and had an emphasis decidedly more Country than populist (312; 87, *71*; 70, *xli-xliii*).[11] The increasing suspicion with which Whig leaders regarded wider franchises and electoral reform reflects a more public and practical aspect of this change; so does the fact that there are no parallels after 1701 to the mass petitioning campaigns of 1679–80. As the London mob grew more Tory or even Jacobite in the popular demonstrations of 1710–16 (*The Age of Oligarchy*, Ch. 12) the Whigs were confirmed in their disenchantment with populism. Whig strength in the towns under Anne and George I owed much to the merchants, tradesmen, professional men and urban gentry who supported them – often in larger numbers than their opponents attracted – and relatively little to the artisans and *menu peuple*. At the other end of the scale, the aristocratic dimension of Whiggery undoubtedly bulked larger from 1700–20 than it had before the Revolution. This was part and parcel of the party's access of respectability. The Lords, not the House of Commons, was the chief Whig stronghold at the end of William III's reign and in the dark years of Anne's (Ch. 21). This was the reverse of the situation in 1679–81 and 1689. Appropriately, all five lords of the Junto sat in the Upper House from 1702 until death began to break up their partnership in 1715; and of the front-line figures in the party from 1715–22 only Walpole and (until he was given a viscountcy in 1717) Stanhope were commoners. Yet we should beware of referring to the Whigs as 'the party of the aristocracy'. It is true that by 1720 deaths and defections among the Tory peers had given their opponents complete hegemony in the Lords; but for much of Anne's reign that House was split very nearly fifty-fifty between the parties. Down to 1705 the Whigs sometimes depended at the crunch on bishops' votes to win crucial votes there, and after the creation of Oxford's twelve peers at the end of 1711 (Ch. 13) the party was often worsted in the struggle for control of the chamber by the Treasurer's 'party of the crown' until the spring of 1714. Even then it required a combination with the Hanoverian Tories at the climax of the succession crisis to get them back into the hunt (cf. ch. 21).[12]

The political attitudes of three other important groups, the London merchants, the Anglican clergy and the Protestant dissenters, also require some comment. With the temporary exception of some Quakers, the dissenters in the first two decades of the eighteenth century were as solidly Whig as they had been ever since the Whigs had existed (16, *195–6, 201*; 100, *236, 243, 248*). But whereas in the Exclusion Crisis the 'establishment' figures in the City commercial interest, especially the monopolists of the East India and Royal African Companies, had mostly been Tories, Toryism in the reigns of Anne and George I was much stronger among the smaller independent merchants and the wholesale tradesmen, while most of the big commercial corporations were now Whig-dominated, with a prominent dissenting presence in their directorates (94b, *Chs. 3–4*). Even Harley's South Sea Company did not stay out of Whig hands for long. There had been something of a shift since the 1670s among the Church of England clergy, too. Support for the Tory cause in this quarter had been almost total in the later years of Charles II. Under Anne it remained of vital assistance to the party. But poll books show that up to a fifth of the parish ministers in most counties were voting Whig, while among the bishops and higher clergy, for reasons which we shall explore in the next chapter, the proportion who now found Tory politics distasteful was much higher.

Nevertheless, it was the backing of the great majority of the 'black coats', along with the Tories' further access of strength since 1689 among the landed gentry and yeomanry, which made them, by common consent, the natural majority party in England and Wales by the early eighteenth century. The Tory majorities of January 1701, 1702, 1710 and 1713 in the House of Commons were bigger than anything their opponents achieved between 1681 and 1715; after each of these elections Tory politicians were powerfully entrenched in office and the hopes of their followers sky-high. After Oxford had conceded many more offices to them in the summer of 1711, a depressed Junto lieutenant wrote to a friend: 'You see how things go, not a Whig constable will there be to be found in a 12 months' time'.[13] Yet somehow the Whigs' Armageddon never came to pass. Why did the Tories fail to translate their great advantage into a permanent political supremacy such as the Whigs themselves eventually achieved after 1714?

The ideological strains and policy divisions which did so much damage to the Tory cause in Anne's reign were not the whole story. But historians have rightly stressed the agonising dilemma over the succession which proved so crippling in 1713–14 (Ch. 25); it is also clear that the High Tories who dominated the party in the Queen's early years did it a serious disservice by their inability to agree on a reasonable balance between public and party priorities. In particular, they failed to reconcile the claims of a war which they had not welcomed, but which their leaders in high office were called on to prosecute, with their determination to press forward, even in the teeth of the Queen's disfavour, with divisive policies for countering religious dissent and with partisan demands for a purge of their few remaining opponents from the Cabinet. Nottingham may have persuaded himself that a purged ministry was 'absolutely necessary for the safety of the Church', but he convinced few others (70, *276–7, 376–7*). It was a series of gross miscalculations in assessing these competing claims which led, first, to the resignation or dismissal in 1703–4 of the three most influential High Tories of the time, Rochester, Nottingham and Seymour, and, secondly, to the disastrous attempt of November 1704 to 'tack' the third Occasional Conformity bill to war supply, in a reckless bid to force the House of Lords to accept it. For almost six years thereafter Toryism was in retreat.

As well as the effect of divisions over issues and policies, however, there were two other important reasons why the Tories in the years 1701–5 played an extremely strong hand far less skilfully than the Whigs played a weaker one. One factor has already been mentioned: the centrifugal pull of their large and self-willed Country brigade in Parliament. The other was their marked inferiority to the Whigs in quality and unity of leadership and also in organisation. The Tory party was born as the party of the Crown and of the legitimate succession, and in the crisis years of 1679–81 its true leader was Charles II himself. Among the politicians no clear primacy was established before the Revolution. Rochester, Godolphin, Finch (later Nottingham) and Seymour all enhanced their reputations in the Exclusion struggle, and the first two added to theirs in office during the 1680s, but none emerged with the kind of primacy Shaftesbury had attained among the Whigs by 1681. This posed serious difficulties after 1688 when the monarch's rôle changed to that of arbiter between the parties. Rochester,

Nottingham and Seymour, though all on the right of the party, found each other uneasy bedfellows; the situation was much complicated by Godolphin's transmutation into a centrist 'man of business', prepared to work with the Whigs at a pinch, and still more by the rise to prominence of Robert Harley as the Country champion in the House of Commons. The adopted Toryism of this one-time Whig and dissenter was always equivocal. In 1702 he finally abandoned his Country image and from then until 1708, as Speaker and Secretary of State, and in alliance with Godolphin and Marlborough, he was identified with firm support for the Continental war strategy and equally firm opposition to religious intolerance. Thereafter, not even his hostility to the Junto and his conversion to a peace policy after his resignation in 1708 could make him a truly convincing leader of a Tory ministry: especially as this was not the rôle for which Anne originally cast him in 1710 after Harley, with consummate skill but with his field of manoeuvre limited by his acting essentially as 'the Queen's servant', had engineered the downfall of Godolphin and the Whig cabinet (70, *192–4, 206–9, 265–8, 371–80*). Like his predecessor at the Treasury, he was congenitally averse to unqualified single-party government, especially at 'civil service' level (Chs. 16, 21). His priorities, financial and diplomatic, were those of a statesman, not a partisan. And out of the inevitable tensions in 'the Church party' which resulted, there developed the famous quarrel between Harley and his former lieutenant, Henry St John (Bolingbroke), which compounded the disarray of the Tories in the succession crisis of 1713–14 (73a; 74).

The Whigs suffered no such frustrations. Admittedly, the degree of dominance which the Junto had secured over them by the end of 1701 was not achieved without a long haul. But from then on Junto leadership imparted a cohesion to the parliamentary party, especially in years of opposition, and a focus for the loyalties of its supporters in the country, which the Tory hierarchy could never approach. And when, in the years 1715–17, four of the five lords either died or retired from active politics, they left, along with their sole survivor (the third earl of Sunderland), a new generation of leaders of exceptional talent who had served their apprenticeship in Anne's reign: the most outstanding were Walpole, Townshend and Stanhope. It is true that this early Hanoverian leadership proved to be less solidly united than their famous predecessors; the Whigs were lucky in some ways to survive the traumatic split of 1717–20, when Townshend's demotion, and then dismissal (April 1717), after a violent disagreement over the policy of Stanhope and George I towards 'the balance of the north',[14] pushed four other members of the Cabinet, including Walpole and Orford, and a bunch of junior ministers led by the brilliant William Pulteney, into opposition (79a, *I, 242–5*; Ch. 13, p. 226). But in sharp contrast with some of the Tory leaders, the new generation of Whig protagonists inherited the Junto lords' remarkable combination of total party commitment, administrative gifts, political flair, and organisational talents of a high order. A striking feature of the Junto's own leadership had been the essentially complementary nature of their abilities. Somers, the distinguished lawyer, brought to their partnership a peerless intellect and great moral strength. Halifax (the former Charles Montagu) contributed an outstanding financial brain and brilliance of oratory; Orford (Russell), unrivalled expertise in naval administration, and Sunderland, energy, drive and manipulative skills. Not least, the indestructible Wharton had buttressed the alliance with a formidable debating technique and with the talent for both electoral and parliamentary organisation of the born party manager.

Superior organisation had been a major asset of the Whigs in the first party battles of 1679–81. After the Revolution, and especially under Anne, this superiority was fully maintained. In this respect Wharton and the younger Sunderland – son of the Secretary of State who had master-minded James II's election preparations in 1687–8 – proved worthy heirs of Shaftesbury. Country-house conferences worked out parliamentary strategy in advance of sessions, discussed and formulated policy and planned for general elections. Day-to-day parliamentary tactics were often concerted by the London clubs of the leading Whigs. The Rose (or Rose Tavern) Club of William's reign, and the Kit Cat and Hanover Clubs of Anne's, were in line of descent from the Green Ribbon Club of the 1670s. Great care was lavished on the canvassing and informal 'whipping' of the party's members in both Houses and on marshalling the proxy votes of Whig peers. It was only in ensuring a good attendance at the start of sessions through the use of regional 'whips', and in management of the House of Lords by the earl of Oxford in the last two and a half years of his ministry, that Tory leaders matched their rivals in these essential techniques (70, *300–9 and Ch. 9 passim*; 68a, *92–3, n. 25*).

The configuration of parliamentary politics during the three decades after the Glorious Revolution was thus neither as straightforward nor as wayward as has sometimes been claimed. Yet it did follow a certain pattern, in which Whig and Tory unquestionably provided the basic continuity while Court and Country supplied most of the variations. This chapter has also argued that ideological differences and contentious issues, far more diverse than those of 1679–85, did most to determine that pattern, but that the changing dispositions of some of the major social and religious groupings in the country were also important, as was the rôle of both personalities and developing political techniques. We still, however, need one further key to understanding both the political landscape of the period and the ferocity of the warfare waged across it. It is clear that the overwhelming majority of men involved in central politics at any given time between 1689 and *circa* 1720 bore an acknowledged Whig or Tory identity. More remarkable, and less often appreciated, is the tenacity with which these identities were clung to over time. They regularly overrode obligations of kinship: many important families, among them the Stanleys, Walpoles, Comptons, Berties and Stanhopes, were for years politically divided. Moreover, political identities normally survived, not just the strong cross-currents of Court and Country but the hostile attitude of monarchs and their 'managers' to party monopoly, which gave men on the make every incentive to trim and change sides. Even with politicians of the second and third rank, the evidence is overwhelming that the casting of deviant votes on specific issues was one thing, but that a permanent crossing of the great divide in politics was an entirely different proposition. The number of overt changes of allegiance over the entire period, like the cases of 'Jack' Howe of Gloucestershire, the Revolution Whig who became a firebrand Country Tory (25, *II, 608–10*), and John Aislabie, a Tory in Anne's reign and a Whig Chancellor of the Exchequer in George I's, was astonishingly tiny.

As for the record of the front-line political figures, those with correspondingly more to gain (and lose), it is equally impressive. The great majority came into politics at the start, and remained to the end, committed, consistent party men. The principal 'managerial' politicians of the period (above, pp. 322–3) were very much the exceptions to the rule. 'Compromise', 'mixed' government, and such-like words had little if any place in the vocabulary of the great majority, even though there were times, inevitably, when they had to stomach the reality as an unavoidable means to a more desirable end. The prevailing attitude was graphi-cally summed up in an expression favoured among Tories, that 'you might as well wash a blackamoor white, as a Whig'. The Rochesters, Seymours, St Johns and Bromleys, on the one hand, and the Whartons, Sunderlands, Somerses and Walpoles, on the other hand, sought all or nothing. Tom Wharton, then Comptroller of the Household, expressed this flatly unaccommodating spirit more bluntly than anyone as early as 1689. To William III, who had become dismayed by the vengefulness of many Whigs in the winter of 1689–90 (above, p. 195) and had begun to show more official favour to Tories, Wharton wrote with shattering frankness: '*We* have made you king . . . [and] if you intend to govern like an honest man, what occasion can you have for knaves to serve you.' He was just as unyielding in 1710, when some of his colleagues were toying with the idea of trying to strike some kind of bargain with the man of the hour, Robert Harley. They should have no truck with 'the Trickster', he warned them: for 'he can do no business; will soon break his neck; and [then] all things will be in such confusion as to force the Queen back again into the hands of the Whigs. This is the situation of power we ought to be in; and not to have it in a motley ministry, with such a r[at] as Harley at the head of it.'[15]

However, we must not mistake the mainspring of such commitment. It was not principally, still less wholly, the question of who should be in or who should be out of high office which points to the true substance of the intense post-Revolution struggle between the Whig and Tory parties – however much the disillusioned or the cynical claimed to see it that way. Even the most disenchanted of them all, Lord Bolingbroke, reflecting in bitter exile on the motives with which he and his friends had come to power in 1710, admitted that there had been more to their ambitions than 'to have the government of the state in our hands, . . . great employments to ourselves, and great opportunities of rewarding those who had helped to raise us, and of hurting those who stood in opposition to us.' For 'with these considerations . . . there were others intermingled, which had for their object the public good of the nation, at least what we took to be such.'[16] The party warfare of the entire period from 1689 to the beginning of Walpole's premiership was a battle over measures – and pre-eminently so – as well as over men, *because the two were inseparable*. This was almost as true of the last phase of all, from 1716–21, as it had been of Anne's reign. The biggest parliamentary clashes of those years – over the Septennial Act, Lord Oxford's impeachment in

1717,[17] the new shift of foreign policy direction towards Hanover and the North (76a, *Chs. 7–8*; 83c; 146a), the Peerage bill and the religious legislation of 1719 (Ch. 23) – admittedly found the Whig majority less monolithic than that party's support had been from 1701–15. What is more, the last four of them foreshadowed a new basic pattern of parliamentary politics, the pattern which from the next decade was to characterise the oligarchic years of the Walpole-Pelham era (*The Age of Oligarchy*, Chs. 2–3), and thus signalled the end of the alignments of the post-Revolution age of party (70, *xiii-xv, lxi-lxii*). Between 1717 and 1719, for the very first time, we find significant numbers of 'men of business' in the Whig party, as well as Country independents as in the past, voting with the Tories in Parliament against the measures of a Whig administration. From one angle this may seem to have been very much an alliance of convenience for the Walpole-Townshend Whigs: a series of tactical votes by men determined to fight their way back into office, preferably on their own terms. But viewed from another angle a different aspect appears. All the most divisive issues of 1717–19, like the Septennial Act before them, raised major questions of principle; it was perfectly possible for the Whig rebels to argue, without being totally disingenuous, that they, and not the ministry led by Stanhope and Sunderland, were upholding 'true Whig' principles on these issues – that they indeed were the genuine custodians of the Ark of the Party Covenant.

Of course there was, and always had been throughout 'the rage of party', a struggle for power going on, and at all times between 1689 and the early 1720s there were self-interested men engaged in the struggle. But the rationale of the conflict between Whig and Tory, and not least the attempts of the party leaders to secure control of the Cabinet, once that became the main organ of policy-making (Ch. 13), was ideological. The men of Anne's reign, in particular, usually knew their own priorities, and they were the kind of priorities that the humblest understrappers could appreciate as much as the contenders for the highest prizes in the state. They were tersely summed up by Lord Wharton when he summoned the Whig voters of Aylesbury to what he thought was his deathbed in 1703 (though in fact he had another twelve years' lease ahead of him), and bade each of them 'farewell, and stick to your principles'. They were even more memorably enshrined in a single agonised line written by a Whig War Office clerk in 1710, as he saw the Godolphin ministry beginning to crumble and envisaged the prospect of a new Tory triumph. 'God deliver us', he wrote, 'from such men, *and from such principles*'.[18] Not until the issues, the conflicts of interest but above all the issues of principle, which so sharply divided Parliament and the whole political nation in the early eighteenth century, were either resolved or de-fused would Britain be fully ready for the tranquillising hand of Robert Walpole. And it is with possibly the most divisive of all these issues that the next chapter is concerned.

---

1. I owe this point to an unpublished paper by Dr C.M. Rose.
2. R. Walcott, *English Politics in the Early 18th Century* (Oxford, 1956).

3. C. Brooks, 'The Country Persuasion and Political Responsibility in England in the 1690s', in *Parliament, Estates and Representation*, **4** (1984), p. 136.
4. J. A. Downie, 'The Commission of Public Accounts and the Formation of the Country Party', *EHR*, **91** (1976).
5. Add. MSS 22851, f. 131: Henry Whistler to Thomas Pitt, 20 Dec 1701.
6. *Hardwicke State Papers* (ed. P. Yorke, 1778), II, p. 435: Lord Chancellor Somers to the duke of Shrewsbury.
7. Lord Cowper, 'An Impartial History of Parties' (1714), quoted in Holmes and Speck (5), pp. 23–4.
8. Clark, (321), pp. 45–8, overstates the case for the decline of Lockean Whiggery.
9. Holmes, (73b), Chs. 8–9; M.A. Goldie, 'Tory Political Thought, 1689–1714' (Cambridge University Ph.D. thesis, 1977).
10. Kent Archive Office, Stanhope (Chevening) MSS.: Cropley to James Stanhope, 23 Apr [1710].
11. See also C. Robbins, *The Eighteenth Century Commonwealthmen* (Cambridge Mass., 1959), Ch. 4.
12. C. Jones, '"The Scheme Lords, the Necessitous Lords, and the Scots Lords": the Earl of Oxford's Management and the "Party of the Crown" in the House of Lords, 1711–14', in 27, pp. 123–67.
13. Cumbria RO Lonsdale MSS. D/Lons/W2/3/12: Nicholas Lechmere to [James Lowther MP], 7 July 1711. [Courtesy of the Lonsdale Estate Trust.]
14. See Townshend to Stanhope, 16 Oct 1716, printed Holmes and Speck (5), p. 97, and *The Age of Oligarchy*, Ch. 4. In addition to Walpole and Orford, Devonshire and Methuen resigned from the Cabinet in protest.
15. Sir J. Dalrymple, *Memoirs . . .* (2nd edn, 1771), II, Appx. Pt. II, p. 86: [Wharton] to the King, 25 Dec 1689; Burnet (1), VI, p. 13 n., Onslow's note [tenses altered].
16. Bolingbroke, *A Letter to Sir William Wyndham* (1717, publ. 1753), p. 19.
17. C. Jones, 'The Impeachment of Lord Oxford and the Whig Schism of 1717', *BIHR*, **55** (1982).
18. Add. MSS 33273, f. 37: James Taylor to Henry Watkins, 4 July 1710.

CHAPTER 23

Church and Dissent in the age of party:
the climax of conflict, 1689–1720

Whereas in almost every field of post-Revolution Britain explored above, the period from 1689 to 1720 was one of innovation and change, in politics, as we have just observed, a very different constitutional and European framework after the great divide of 1688 modified but did not destroy an underlying continuity. So it was, too, with religion. Although the Revolution ushered in many religious changes, some of great import for the future, the three decades which followed it in England, down to the big toleration debates in Parliament in 1717–19 (above, pp. 208–9; below, p. 365), were as much the end of an old era as the beginning of a new one. Indeed it could be argued that they saw the climax and final subsidence of that *sustained* religious conflict which had been the warp of English national and political life ever since the meeting of Henry VIII's Reformation Parliament in 1529.

Over the quarter-century after 1688 it may seem, at first sight, that little had altered: that religious ideals, passions and fears were still powerfully and divisively at work. That would be a fair conclusion to draw, for example, from the preoccupations of the press. It is probably the case that under William III and Anne more religious tracts and sermons went into print to satisfy the public appetite than at any time in our history except the 1640s, and this despite an intellectual atmosphere much more inimical to religion in 1700 than it had been in 1650 (Chs. 10, 24; *The Age of Oligarchy*, Ch. 12). One famous sermon delivered in 1709 is thought to have sold at least 100,000 copies, which means it could well have been read by half a million men and women, while the controversy it inaugurated spawned 575 further titles in the next twelve months (73b, *75*; 70, *xix*). Naturally this would not have occurred if the sermon concerned had not been violently provocative and raised weighty political as well as religious issues. But in that it was exceptional only in degree. Religious controversy, much of it in turn permeating politics, was meat and drink to post-Revolution Englishmen. Their avidity reached a peak in Anne's reign, but the flow of polemic did not dry up in 1714. Three years later a sermon preached and printed by the ultra Low-Churchman Benjamin Hoadly, bishop of Bangor, sparked off yet another furious debate, the so-called Bangorian controversy over the relations of Church and State, spilling 'a dreadful deal of ink, black and bitter',[1] and alarming politicians almost as much as it agitated churchmen (above, p. 208; below, p. 365). By 1725, however, the whole temper of the age was changing. The rationalism of the later Stuart period had been excoriating but bracing. But the intellectual air of the 1720s and 1730s was much more enervating. Sermons and religious literature, even meaty works of theology, were still published and read, but the market now was more devotional and academic, the readership increasingly inbred. Religious controversy likewise became more self-absorbed, as with the debate between the Deists and the apologists of the Church of England; for matters of religious substance to cause any significant political excitement, or give rise to parliamentary commotions, as they did in the early and mid–1730s, became an untypical occurrence.

Clearly this was a fundamental change of scene, and in another work (*The Age of Oligarchy*, Ch. 7) we shall investigate it and assess some of its implications, for religion and for the nation. The two overriding impressions left by the evidence of the years 1689–1720, however, are that while religion remained a matter of no less concern in those three decades than it had been earlier in the seventeenth century, at the same time the nature of that concern had changed considerably since the 1660s; and that the Glorious Revolution was the prime, though not the sole, contributor to this change. The object of this present chapter is therefore threefold: to look at the effects of the Revolution both on the Protestant dissenters and on the Church of England;[2] to take brief stock of further serious problems facing the established Church after 1688 which stemmed from causes other than the Revolution, and to ask how, and with what repercussions, the Church tried to cope with its post-Revolution crisis, and especially with the problem of Dissent. These attempts not only involved the clergy in grave internal conflicts; they also tightly entangled them in the strife of secular politics and politicians. And in both cases the consequences were dire.

I

In contrast with the Roman Catholics, for whom the Revolution marked an adverse turn of fortune (*The Age of Oligarchy*, Ch. 6), the Protestant dissenters welcomed it as the herald of more prosperous times. Two aspects of the Revolution Settlement brought them great benefit. In the first place, the statutory settlement, through the Toleration Act of 1689, announced in law that 'the great persecution' of 1662–87 had indeed come to an end. The change was greeted warily by many dissenters, who doubted its permanence, but in the event the clock was not turned back. In the second place, the political settlement after the Revolution proved a boon, because it more or less assured the nonconformists thereafter of at least some powerful friends in high places who would watch over their interests. In the short run their most important ally was probably King William III himself, a convinced Calvinist; a more long-term asset was the support of the Whigs, in their periodic intervals of power from 1689 to 1710 and in their decades of oligarchy under the first two Georges. Not only did they fight against, and eventually repeal, new Tory legislation hostile to nonconformity, but they also made the destruction of meeting-houses – targets for High Church or Jacobite mobs both in 1710 and 1715 – a statutory felony and voted Treasury compensation for the sufferers.

However, it was the Toleration Act [N.5B(i)] that was the great landmark of 1689 in the history of Dissent, as of the Church of England. By it, Protestants who declined to accept the Anglican liturgy and government were allowed to worship unmolested in their own meeting-houses, provided these places were officially licensed and their doors unlocked. One significant qualification was the requirement that their ministers must subscribe to the Thirty-Nine Articles of the Church of England, except for those which related to church government and required infant baptism. The other was that the same clause which excluded Catholics from the benefits of the Act also excluded those Protestants who denied the doctrine of the Trinity [see A. *sub* 'Arianism' and 'Socinianism']. Their views, especially those of the Socinians who cast serious doubt on the divinity of Christ, were widely regarded as heretical, not simply by Anglicans but at this stage by the overwhelming majority of dissenting clergy also. Yet in practice it proved so difficult to weed out Unitarians that the effect of the Act of 1689 was to give virtually *all* Protestant nonconformists legal freedom of worship for the first time, and with this a recognised, if inferior, status in the community. By Anne's reign, at least, it had become perfectly clear that the Act had produced a legally-sanctioned schism in the body spiritual of the nation which showed every sign of becoming permanent.

Ironically, few of the bishops or the Anglican Tory gentry whose voices helped to carry the Act through the Convention Parliament had any thought of bringing about such a revolution in English religious practice. History has labelled this 'the Toleration Act'. But the Act did not repeal the Act of Uniformity of 1662 nor any of the statutes of the Clarendon Code, and nowhere did it proclaim a state of 'toleration'. On the contrary, when the bill was passing through the Commons Sir Thomas Littleton (a Whig) declared explicitly that 'the Committee, though they were for Indulgence, were for *no Toleration*' (2, V, 266 – *my italics*). And this object was fully reflected, both in the frosty official title of the final Act – 'for exempting . . . [the dissenters] from the penalties of certain laws' – and in a grudging preamble which referred to the offer of 'some ease to scrupulous consciences in the exercise of religion'. Only when we are aware of this, and when we realise how little the Act, as it emerged, was the result of forethought or careful planning, can we understand how it can have passed over in total silence issues vital to the future of a separate denomination: why, for example, dissenting education – largely in Presbyterian hands – was left officially in the same state of precarious dependence on episcopal licensing and secular conniv-ance as had existed before either James II's Indulgences or the biting Anglican reaction of 1682–6 which had preceded them.

The clue to all this, as will be seen, is that first, the circumstances surrounding the passing of the Toleration Act conspired to produce not a measure of design but a freak of chance, and that then, the civil powers, from the Crown down to the local magistrates, conspired in their turn not to enforce the new law with anything like the strictness the Anglican clergy hoped for, and indeed expected. The resistance of many dissenters in 1688 to the blandishments of James II had secured them a commitment from Sancroft and the Anglican establishment to a settlement that would end religious persecution for conscience sake, but no more. However, it was not long into William III's reign before many Church of England divines, including even leading moderates like Edward Stillingfleet, the new bishop of Worcester, who had worked to produce such a settlement in the

Convention, began to feel that, almost by an oversight, charity had gone much too far in 1689. To their apprehensive eyes it seemed that in the twenty-five years which followed the coming of the Act into force Dissent was gaining ground alarmingly at the expense of the establishment. They learned of dissenting academies, such as those at Exeter, Stoke Newington and Attercliffe (Sheffield), whose educational prowess was beginning to deflect the sons of some Anglican parents away from Oxford and Cambridge, as well as supplying the training for a new generation of nonconformist pastors. More staggering, and impinging more directly on their own preserves, was the sheer number of licences for meeting-houses being taken out under article 19 of the Act. Just over 3,900 were issued in the first twenty-one years of the Toleration, a figure far in advance of common expectation; and well over 300 of these were for new, or at least permanent structures which furnished striking testimony to the social influence and material prosperity of the new Dissent as well as to its numerical strength. In urban centres many of these meeting-houses attracted great congregations. In a private census taken in 1715 a score of them in the provinces alone were credited with more than a thousand 'hearers' each, rising as high as 2,000 in the case of one Presbyterian meeting at Taunton.[3] If, as seems likely, there were *at least* 400,000 dissenters, including children, in England and Wales by the early years of George I [see N.6], that represents approximately seven per cent of the population at this time and it gives substance to Anglican claims that Dissent had indeed been advancing on a broad front since 1689. The number of nonconformist congregations increased from the 1,200 or so whose meetings were granted licences in the first year of the Toleration to roughly 2,000 in 1718, although it has to be said that in a third of these cases 'congregation' meant a small group of either Baptists or Quakers, numbered in scores rather than in hundreds.

The progress of Dissent under the Toleration attracted the more notice because, increasingly, its adherents were concentrated in certain high-profile areas. By 1715 almost 65 per cent of dissenting congregations met in cities or towns (150, *267*). After London, textile areas proved the most fertile soil: the packed meeting-houses of Exeter, Tiverton and Taunton, of Colchester and Norwich, or of Coventry, Leeds and Manchester, had their counterparts in many smaller cloth-working towns. Nonconformity also flourished in the metal-working towns of Birmingham and Sheffield, and in most of the biggest outports, especially Bristol. One of the main reasons why the Whigs in the first generation after the Revolution, and in many places long afterwards (100), always did much better contesting the borough seats in General Elections than in fighting the counties was the strength of the dissenting vote in numerous boroughs. Of the Colchester electorate of about 1,250 in 1716, dissenters accounted for 442.[4] To the High Church Tories of William's reign and of Anne's, the most aggravating aspect of this was the position in the so-called 'corporation boroughs', where the right to vote was narrowly restricted to the mayor and town councillors, and also in those many freemen boroughs (Colchester was one of them) where the corporation controlled the election of the freemen and therefore, in effect, the electoral roll for parliamentary elections. Strictly speaking, with the Corporation Act of 1661 still unrepealed, dissenters should have been debarred from municipal office. But after the Revolution, with central government either preoccupied or (in Whig hands) only too happy to look the other way, there spread very rapidly the practice of 'occasional conformity'. Once a gesture of Christian goodwill rather than a secular device, it developed during the 1690s into a cynical expedient whereby politically-inclined dissenters took the Anglican sacrament on a solitary Sunday in the twelve months before standing for local office, technically fulfilling the letter of the law, and then repaired to their meeting-houses until the next such occasion arose. In towns such as Coventry, Bridgwater and Tiverton (where a third of the corporation-electorate were non-Anglicans even after the passing of the Occasional Conformity Act in 1711) contempt for the law became flagrant. In Bridgwater's fine new Presbyterian meeting-house, as Defoe found in 1705, seats of honour were installed from the start for mayors and aldermen, 'when any . . . should be of their communion' (3, *I, 270*).

It was in the glaring spotlight of the capital city, however, that the practice seemed to Anglican purists singularly shocking: not surprisingly, since London Dissent flaunted its advance under the Toleration more impressively than anywhere in the kingdom. By 1711 a Tory House of Commons had learned to its consternation that the number of meeting-houses in the suburbs outside the old City already outnumbered the parish churches and chapels of ease by two to one. But long before that it had begun to seem that the dissenters were making a determined bid to take over the greatest municipal corporation in the land. At least two of London's Lord Mayors in King William's reign, Sir Thomas Abney and Sir Humphrey Edwin, had been notorious Presbyterians, and the tide which carried sixty-five known or probable dissenters on to the Common Council and twenty-five into the City magistracy between 1689 and 1715 was already flowing strongly in the 1690s (94b, *Tab III, 4*). Occasional Conformity had become so barefaced by 1697, the year of Edwin's mayoralty, that the Lord Mayor not merely attended services at Mead's meeting-house during his term of office but on two occasions processed there in full regalia, preceded by the City sword-bearer. At least in London dissenters did bother to conform occasionally. In a few provincial boroughs, however, they became too cocksure even for that; at one such place, the small cloth-manufacturing town of Wilton, there was a scandalous election in 1702 which was carried against the Tories by the votes of nineteen burgesses, newly co-opted on to the corporation, few if any of whom were even technically qualified under the Corporation Act (5, *122–3*).

The Wilton case was probably decisive in stiffening the determination of Tory High Anglicans to rid themselves by law of the 'abominable hypocrisy' of Occasional Conformity. But its impact was doubled because it coincided with the most public advertisement yet of the consternation of the Church of England clergy. In 1702 a young Oxford don named Henry Sacheverell launched himself on a career of roaring notoriety by devoting part of an official University Sermon to a vicious attack on occasional conformists: they were branded as 'crafty' and 'faithless' men who 'creep to our altars . . . more secretly and powerfully to undermine us', and Sacheverell called stridently on his fellow Anglicans 'to hang out the bloody flag and banner of defiance' against all dissenters.[5] More will be said later about the parliamentary attack on Occasional Conformity. Meanwhile we need only note that it was the arrival of 'the bloody flag officer' in London in 1709 which would finally bring the cauldron of post-Revolution religious conflict to the boil.

To historians it is now clear that, however important the advance of post-Revolution nonconformity was, its scale was exaggerated by a Church over-obsessed by the threat it presented. Dissenting academies were a case in point. Anglicans too often forgot how dependent most of them were on the reputation of one master and how many folded up when that master died. The *net* increase in the number of academies between 1689 and 1714 was consequently no more than ten[6] (although it is true that many dissenting schools, including grammar schools, were also established in this period) (226a, *Ch. 3*). The taking out of licences for meeting-houses was also misconstrued, for there was no necessary correlation between this and the proliferation of congregations. Certainly the latter did increase in number substantially in the first thirty years of the Toleration, but many individual congregations required three or four separate licences as periodically they moved from one set of temporary premises to another. As for Occasional Conformity, some towns and cities – Exeter, for instance – were relatively unscathed by it, while in central as opposed to local offices the Anglican monopoly stayed largely intact. There were two other less menacing sides to the face of Dissent in the late seventeenth and early eighteenth centuries which have to be borne in mind. For one thing, the outward flush of health, difficult though it was for Anglicans at the time to see behind it, was to some extent misleading. It would be ludicrous to suggest that widespread complacency overtook the dissenters after 1689. So long as the Tories were strong enough to attempt to translate their fear of nonconformity into fresh penal legislation, there was little likelihood of that. Yet there is some evidence that even before Anne's death a greater sense of security and, even more, growing material prosperity, especially among Presbyterians and Quakers, were slowly sapping spirituality and damping down the old Puritan fires.[7] Secondly, the Toleration allowed some of the old disunities, buried during the persecution of the 1680s, to surface and new ones to emerge. Most of the brave cooperative experiments, like the 'Happy Union' of the 1690s, foundered sooner or later and, despite the continuing existence of the Committee of the Three Denominations (1702), Anglican claims that the Church of England was being undermined by a united, coordinated campaign were largely mythical. Most serious in the long run for the dissenters were the doctrinal differences which afflicted them. Quakers and General Baptists both suffered from intra-sectarian squabbles, but far more insidious was the spread of Unitarian beliefs within the Presbyterian ministry, for whom the Salters' Hall conference (1719) proved a fateful parting of the ways (150, *372–7*). It was not possible for the dissenters to insulate themselves against the climate of the times. Even at the most formal level of membership and attendance at services most sects had already passed their peak by 1720.

One further aspect of post-Revolution nonconformity, not always appreciated, is the fresh impetus which the 1689 settlement gave to that remarkable change in the social basis of Dissent which was such a feature of the whole period between 1660 and 1720. Although the practice of occasional conformity did something to mitigate the circumstance, the blunt fact was that the Toleration Act had done nothing directly to break down the statutory barriers which continued to keep the really conscientious dissenters (and there were still many of them) out of state and municipal office, out of the English universities, the civil service and the army, and which made it difficult, though not quite impossible, for them to become physicians or barristers. Even in the party of toleration, the Whigs, there was always *some* support for these civil barriers. After the party shamefacedly acquiesced in the passing of the fourth Occasional Conformity Bill (the result of a deal between the Junto and the Tory earl of Nottingham) in 1711, that body of support grew rather larger, especially in the House of Lords, where after 1714 it was fortified by a varying number of Whig bishops, led by William Wake, who succeeded Tenison as archbishop of Canterbury in 1715. A common front between these Whig conservatives and the Tories succeeded in scuppering an attempt by the Stanhope-Sunderland ministry to reform the universities;[8] it threatened for many months to wreck a bill to repeal the Occasional Conformity and Schism Acts, which only squeezed through in the end, in January 1719, with the aid of delicate government management, assisted by judicious episcopal promotions; in December 1718 it proved quite decisive when the same ministers tried to set aside the most controversial of the measures on the statute-book, the sacramental clauses of the Test and Corporation Acts, and failed embarrassingly.

There can hardly be any doubt that because of the civil disabilities left untouched by the Toleration Act, and the thirty years of legal and political uncertainty which followed, the *landed* gentry, once the great champions of Puritanism, were thoroughly confirmed in their disenchantment with a nonconforming religious allegiance which carried so marked a social stigma. By 1720 the sects, with their increasingly urban image, were still holding adherents among the new pseudo-gentry; but the pattern of the future, with their main strength overwhelmingly based on the middling and lower-middling strata of society, including the yeomanry, and their strong support, lower down, from the 'mechanic trades' and other 'plain people of no education'[9] was already well established. It was not a coincidence that some of the most prominent industrial revolutionaries of the late eighteenth century were descendants of political revolutionaries of the mid-seventeenth.

II

The progress of Dissent under the new Toleration was not the only vital area in which the settlement of 1689 set taxing problems for the Church of England. Complementary to the passing of 'the Act of Indulgence' was the failure of the last serious attempt before the twentieth century at Protestant Comprehension: the last of several moves since 1660 to broaden the base of Anglicanism sufficiently to enable large numbers of dissenters to be comprehended within the official Church (cf. Ch. 10). Even before this, however, the Church had been confronted with another experience as a direct result of the Revolution, one which profoundly affected its future situation and character. In February 1689 the crown had been settled on a man who had no close hereditary claim to it, and the clergy were subsequently saddled with oaths of allegiance to him and to his Queen which had to be taken before March 1690.[10] We shall glance at the repercussions of these events before briefly taking note of other aspects of the post-Revolution Anglican crisis.

To get the matter of allegiance in perspective one need only recollect the remarkable recovery which the Church of England had made before 1687 from the nightmare of the Civil Wars and the Interregnum (Chs. 1, 10). This revival, under the devoted leadership of Archbishops Sheldon and Sancroft, had not merely enabled it to win back great numbers of the faithful, particularly in the 1680s, but had reinvested it with a new sense of purpose and direction (163a). In Sancroft's heyday the Anglican clergy became intensely aware of their unique link with the monarch, God's Vicegerent to whom unquestioning obedience was due, and likewise of their rôle as custodians of an ordered, hierarchical view of society – a view which assumed that social cohesion, like authority in the state, was based on religious obligation. To these churchmen, who had patiently endured all the provocations of Charles II before his surrender to the Church interest in 1679, James II's direct assault on the Anglican supremacy had been nothing short of catastrophic. But William III's accession, even though it saved them from Popery, was hardly less unnerving. That alliance between Church and Crown, between 'the altar and the throne', which had become as distinctive a part of the Anglican creed as any theological tenet, was threatened with destruction. Modern students of political ideas have been at pains to point out that Tory apologists, such as Sherlock and Bohun, devoted much tortured ingenuity to trying to reconcile the facts of the Revolution with the preservation of the notions of Hereditary Right and Non-Resistance.[11] It is also well known that in the course of the High Church revival in Anne's reign there was a renaissance of more traditional Divine Right and Passive Obedience preaching and a frenetic attempt to revive high clerical pretensions. However, it is notable that although this campaign was led by crowd-pulling Anglican parsons such as Milbourne, Higgins and Sacheverell, the main intellectual thrust which lay behind it was provided by clergy or academics who had left the fold of the Established Church through inability to compromise with the Revolution: men of the stature of Jeremy Collier, Henry Dodwell and, above all, Charles Leslie, in his brilliantly written periodical *The Rehearsal*. The fact is, the Church as a whole was grievously disorientated, not so much by the fact of the rebellion against James II (in which, with a handful of exceptions, the clergy's part had been one of passive acquiescence) as by James's 'abdication' and the accession of a Calvinist Dutchman. Many Anglican clergy privately regarded William as a usurper, and very few could feel more than a token *de facto* loyalty to him. Throughout the thirty years following the Revolution, therefore, the Church of England was groping about trying to find a new ideological road in a new direction, having been jostled so rudely from the old track in 1689. It is true that the advent of Anne, James's daughter and a devout Anglican, brought some relief to the searchers. But by 1702 the loss was all but irreparable, particularly as the Queen had no feasible English Protestant heir. And it is worth recalling what it was that had been lost: not simply a *political* theory, something that could be at least partially salvaged and patched up for a while, but an entire concept of state and society, underpinned by a religious view of the social order and its obligations, to which the likelihood of any return was now remote (163a, *159*).

For some, however, there was the more immediate dilemma of being confronted with the oaths to William and Mary. Archbishop Sancroft, six other bishops and just under 400 of the lower clergy refused to renege the allegiance they had sworn to James and the principles of a lifetime, even though the oath devised for them could hardly have been more accommodating. Instead they chose professional exile and, in the least fortunate cases, a future of great hardship. By a supreme irony, five of the prelates concerned had been heroes of the Seven Bishops' Trial of 1688. That the schism caused by these 'Nonjurors' inflicted damage on the Church cannot be doubted, although the extent of the damage should not be overstated. The departure of the nonjuring bishops did not, as used to be thought, open the sluice-gates to let a flood of 'Whig latitudinarians' into William III's episcopate. G.V. Bennett has exploded that myth (163b, *10*; 106b, *15–33* [M. Goldie, 'The Nonjurors . . . ']). Even ideologically the schism was less than a disaster (Ch. 24). It was the loss of individuals, rather than the secession of a group and its continuance outside the pale as a separatist church, which was probably the most serious consequence. By definition almost every Nonjuror in orders was a godly priest with a high sense of calling; many were men of high ability and influence. The deprivation of Sancroft alone was a heavy blow. Tillotson (to 1694) and Tenison, the two Primates who served William III and Anne [N.3], were both energetic and gifted leaders, but, with a question-mark against their legitimacy lingering in many minds, they could never aspire to the firm authority Sancroft had enjoyed at Canterbury nor to the loyal support he had commanded almost universally among the clergy. And at a time when the established Church felt itself to be encompassed about by enemies it was galling to its ministers that many of the most effective ripostes delivered in Augustan England against anti-clericals, heretics and Deists (see below, pp. 360–1) came from men no longer of their brotherhood.

To thousands of Anglican incumbents, however, those were not the antagonists most directly at their gates. What preoccupied them increasingly in the new post-Revolution world was how to hold their flocks together against the marauding of the dissenters and the insidious blight of lay apathy. Although most of them failed to recognise it at the time, the failure to agree on formulae for Comprehension in 1689 had a vital bearing on both these threats. The Toleration Bill has been earlier described as freakish. What made it so was the fact that it was not originally intended to apply to all Protestant dissenters, but only to the irreconcilables who could be expected to reject reunion with the Church of England even on relatively liberal terms. Such terms were indeed proposed, along lines discussed previously by Stillingfleet and the moderates, and even by some Sancroftians, in a Comprehension Bill which the Tory earl of Nottingham (the confidant of many leading divines) introduced into the House of Lords in February 1689: it was an integral part of a twin package (161, *241–7* [R. Thomas, 'Comprehension . . .']). The circumstances in which this Comprehension Bill came to be dropped have often been ascribed to a monstrous piece of political miscalculation and tactlessness on the part of the King.[12] Undoubtedly there were other factors too (152, *85–9*), but what they were matters less than the fact that Nottingham's Toleration Bill was ultimately left to do an unforeseen job: that is, to apply to the whole body of Presbyterians and moderate Independents, many of them the epitome of conservatism and social respectability, instead of to (at most) 150,000 'fanatics' of 'scrupulous conscience'. The consequences were to bedevil the Church right through the eighteenth century, but never more so than between 1689 and 1720. At one stroke she was deprived of an invaluable spiritual leaven and bequeathed a problem, that of 'tolerated' Dissent, which was to assume a scale quite undreamt of in February 1689. To give just one example: few Baptists or Quakers practised Occasional Conformity or cherished local political ambitions; if a Comprehension Act had been passed after the Revolution one of the most divisive issues of Anne's reign, both for clerics and politicians, would never have arisen.

A quite different effect of the failure of Comprehension soon became apparent. Pews which had been comfortably filled in parish churches in the 1680s, especially on communion days, were visibly emptier by 1690 and became more so as William III's reign went on. Had 'the Toleration' only been extended to a few it would have been difficult for lukewarm churchgoers to interpret the new freedom to attend conventicles as freedom to stay away from their local Anglican churches. It was because it finally embraced so many that the apathetic as well as the irreligious were able to claim with some confidence that 'liberty of conscience [was] allowed by the supreme authority'; and from very early in the lifetime of the new Act churchwardens became loth to bring absentees to book, despite the inserting of a clause reasserting the legal obligation of churchgoing on all but bona fide dissenters. Under Anne a good preacher could still fill a town church, but for many ordinary mortals among the clergy declining congregations became a fact of life which spelled first alarm, then growing demoralisation. Parish ministers were not the only sufferers. The decline of the church courts, sharply arrested under the Sancroft regime, resumed with a vengeance. This time, for all the plans of Francis Atterbury and other High Churchmen to revivify them, the decay of the traditional methods of discipline over the laity was to prove irreversible. Although Sancroft's work had already been undermined by James II's Indulgences in 1687–8, it was the dramatic falling-off of presentments for non-attendance after the passing of the Toleration Act which made a further recovery impracticable and left the Church ill-equipped to handle the more serious problem of lay immorality.

The case of ecclesiastical jurisdiction illustrates very well how in so many of the difficulties with which Anglicans had to grapple after 1688, the problems themselves were not novel, but rather took on new forms or acquired more worrying dimensions. Cumulatively their effect was to produce that sense of beleaguerment among the clergy so much in evidence in contemporary writings and sermons. Two more examples from the field of practical affairs are apposite. The Church's administrative as well as its judicial machinery was ill equipped to take additional strains (73b, *Ch. 2*; 152). Dioceses were grossly uneven in size and in the income they yielded [N.4], and not until late in George I's reign did a reforming prelate, in this case Edmund Gibson, have the breathing-space to consider remedies (*The Age of Oligarchy*, Ch. 7). The fundamental weakness, however, was a parish structure which, in spite of some seventeenth-century reorganisation (249, *37*), was still medieval and which required an Act of Parliament for each single modification. The situation seriously inhibited attempts both to counter Dissent and to combat lay absenteeism, and it was undoubtedly aggravated by the late seventeenth- and early eighteenth-century urban population spurt. It was 1712 before Manchester acquired a second parish church and 1715 before Birmingham did so; Liverpool, Leeds and Sheffield had to wait still longer. Another long-standing problem was clerical poverty, with its inevitable companions, pluralism and non-resident incumbency: how bad it had become by 1705 was revealed by the report of the Governors of Queen Anne's Bounty (cf. *The Age of Oligarchy*, Ch. 7)[13]. But in this case it was the French Wars and high taxation which made it so much more acute from 1689 to 1713. Rich pastures were scarce – especially so in the North of England (158a and b) – and increasingly overgrazed by the sons of the gentry. It was hard for the poor man who had education and a sense of vocation but lacked social connections to make even a respectable living, let alone a career, in the Church (although, in spite of this, there was no serious recruitment problem) (226a, *Ch. 4*).

Albeit the Anglican dilemma of these years was partly functional and material, for the majority of parsons it was most of all a crisis of confidence in their own mission. An intellectual challenge to the Church had been mounted between the Restoration and the Revolution, stimulated by the scientific advances of the second half of the seventeenth century, but its influence at that stage was more rejuvenating than hostile (Ch. 10). In the 1690s, however, rationalism became more frequently a high road to freethinking. Deism posed as a socially fashionable creed; Socinianism and Arianism, the two strands of unitarian doctrine, became intellectually respectable. The fact that they infected only a tiny minority brought little solace to the clergy, for it was an influential minority. The idea that even among the unthinking majority Christian belief remained (as Jonathan Clark has insisted) 'almost universal' by the beginning of the eighteenth century (321, *87*) would have been received with scepticism by many Anglican parsons, unless 'belief' were to be understood only in the most superficial and passive sense. The fact that divines of what would now be called 'advanced' theological opinions – men such as Archbishops Tillotson and Tenison and Bishop Stillingfleet of Worcester – began to occupy key positions in the Church itself after 1688 heightened clerical alarm. But above all it was the lifting of Stuart censorship of the press in 1695 which caused the situation to degenerate. The tidal wave which this released seemed to most orthodox churchmen to threaten not merely the bastions of Anglicanism but much of the fabric of traditional Christianity (Ch. 24). Behind their hyperbole, and at times hysteria, lay very genuine fears. When Francis Atterbury, only two years after the end of licensing, issued his famous clarion call for a meeting of Convocation to deal with the crisis, he referred not to a wave but to 'a deluge': it had flooded the country with 'heresies of all kinds' as well as with 'scepticism, Deism and atheism', exposed 'all mysteries in religion' as objects of derision, and encouraged 'a settled contempt of religion and the priesthood'.[14] The latter was not the least disturbing feature. 'Priestcraft' became one of the dirty words of the post-Revolution years; by the middle of Anne's reign Bishop Fleetwood was to single out as the most demoralising of all the Church's problems the clergy's loss of both public and self-respect over the previous ten to fifteen years, in the face of such an outpouring of anti-clerical as well as irreligious literature.

III

What was to be done? Whatever the faults of the Church of England in the first three decades after the Revolution, apathy was not one of them. Faced with a complex of daunting problems, some of which had overtaken them, or worsened, with bewildering speed, few clerics were prepared simply to shrug their shoulders and endure. Overwhelmingly they were agreed that relations with the state must be reappraised, clerical poverty alleviated, discipline over the laity reasserted and church attendances revived. As a matter of high priority heretics and infidels must be confounded, and the place in the religious order of the dissenters – whom even sympathetic Anglicans regarded as sincere but misguided Christians – must be clarified. Tragically, however, agreement went no further. As to what solutions should be implemented, and how, the clergy were soon in sorry disarray. So divided was their response to their problems that in the last years of King William's reign a bruising conflict developed within the Church. This persisted and intensified over the course of Anne's reign and lingered well into George I's; bad became worse when the internecine broils of the clergy widened in the years 1700–20 to become almost inseparable from the party warfare of the laity.

In both creating and politicising their divisions the issue of Dissent played a decisive part. In the minds of nearly all Anglican clergy large question-marks remained after 1689 against a 'Toleration' which had been so adventitious in its origins. Was it to be but the half-way stage in the concession of a comprehensive freedom to dissenters? Or should it be rigidly preserved on the explicit terms of the Act? Or again (as many of the more conservative clergy and Tory politicians came to feel) should it be eroded, so that eventually, when the time was ripe, the 1689 Act could be repealed altogether on the ground that it had never been intended to apply to more than one generation of deviants, that it was never meant (in the contemporary phrase) 'to perpetuate schism'. To resolve its problems of identity *vis-à-vis* the state and society, while combating apathy from the lower ranks of the social hierarchy and intellectual criticism from the upper, the Church of England desperately needed unity and common conviction. The uncertainties enveloping the Toleration would almost of themselves have vitiated such hopes. The High Church and Low Church parties among the clergy which emerged between 1697 and 1702 disagreed violently on other matters too: for instance, High Churchmen bitterly resisted the Low, or erastian [A.] view of the Church's relationship with the state as a subordinate, even dependent, one; likewise the view that moral reformation could be better accomplished by voluntary societies for 'reformation of manners'[15] than by the Church's own courts. But it was their disagreement about how to react to the challenge of Dissent which more than anything else drove the new Church parties into the arms of the lay politicians.

High Churchmen had become convinced by the time of Queen Anne's accession that a political solution to most of the current problems of Anglicanism was the only way ahead. They envisaged a close partnership between a Convocation sitting simultaneously with the legislature and a favourably-disposed Parliament, which would advance their favoured causes via the statute-book. On the other hand, the Low Church bishops, and their adherents among the cathedral and parish clergy, took note of the fact that the Blasphemy Act, passed in 1697, had already proved ineffectual, despite the fact that (as Archbishop Wake later explained to George I) it had been 'very express both in the description and punishment of blasphemy' (321, *286*; 164, *II, 165*); also that Acts of Pardon passed in 1689 and 1694 – which among other things nullified excommunications – had had a withering effect on business in the church courts. Thus they were profoundly sceptical about political action as a universal panacea. They recognised that the state's help would be needed to deal with certain basic administrative and financial problems. For example, they supported Queen Anne's Bounty for the relief of poor clergy in 1704, a scheme originally hatched by one of their own leaders, Bishop Burnet (153, *234* [I. Green]). Nevertheless they held that, by and large, the Church must work out her own destiny in areas where she was free enough from the constraints of establishment to be able to act alone (163a).

The High Church party was particularly elated at the prospect of Tory ministries and Tory Parliaments when Anne came to the throne, for they believed the Queen herself would be well disposed, and the Tories, after all, constantly proclaimed themselves 'the Church Party'. It had been Tory political pressure which in 1701, after four years of campaigning led by the firebrand Atterbury, had forced a reluctant King to revive the representative assembly of the clergy, suspended by the Crown for its unruliness back in 1689. It was certain that Tory-High Church divines would have a built-in majority in the Lower House of Convocation, and for this reason the bishops fiercely resisted their clamour for recall, calling much weighty scholarship to their defence (Ch. 24). Having failed in this, the heavily-outnumbered Low Church forces, marshalled by Archbishop Tenison, were reluctantly forced in self-defence to gravitate towards the Whigs, as the party most committed to the Revolution religious settlement and most likely to protect the authority of moderate bishops against mutinous 'Highflying' subordinates. Highlighting the anguish of a Church rent apart in Anne's reign was the fact that Tenison of Canterbury and Sharp of York, two great archbishops and former comrades-in-arms in James II's London, found themselves *partis pris* on opposite sides of the great Anglican divide of 1701 and after.

The early years of the Queen's reign proved depressingly unrewarding for the advocates of political action. A protracted Commons' campaign over three sessions (1702–04) to stamp out Occasional Conformity by heavy legal penalties was frustrated by Whig strength in the House of Lords. There the Whig-tolerationist cause was crucially reinforced by the votes of the Low Church bishops, as well as by the government's fears (which the Queen came to share) of weakening national unity at a critical period of the war. Moderate votes were also influenced by fear of losing the financial support of the many wealthy nonconformists in the City. When the Commons' supporters of the third Occasional Conformity Bill in desperation planned to force the measure through the Lords by 'tacking' it to the Land Tax bill, dozens of more moderate or responsible Tories, led by the Harleyites, regarded this as a demonstration of 'universal madness'[16] and voted with the Whigs in the Lower House to kill it. Eventually, in the final period of Tory dominance (1710–14), the Highflyers did score some successes. A watered-down Act against Occasional Conformity was finally passed in 1711 [N.5A(iii)] and caused some consternation in Whiggish corporations. The same year saw an Act to build fifty new churches in the London suburbs financed by £350,000 of state revenue – as much a move to counter the dreaded influence of Dissent in the city (see above, p. 354) as to provide for the capital's unchurched masses. The Scottish (Episcopalian) Toleration Act, passed in 1712, caused quite widespread satisfaction to the English Anglican clergy. The Tories' last throw was the Schism Act of 1714. This was beyond doubt a vicious measure, intended to cut the tap roots of Dissent by forcing their separate schools and academies into closure, but it was soon to be thwarted by the refusal of Whig ministers and officials to enforce it when they returned to power after George I's accession. In other respects, however, such as fortifying the Church courts, the politicians were less cooperative. More serious for the established clergy, such success as there was for the High Church party after 1710 was achieved at a heavy cost in terms of animosities aroused.

Taken as a whole, therefore, the entanglement of religion with politics from the late 1690s did the Church a great deal more harm than good. It contributed a great deal to the continual clashes between Upper and Lower Houses which made such a bear-garden of Convocation, and Atterbury's plans to use that assembly as a vehicle for an ambitious reform programme after 1710 ended in bitter abortion (163b, *156*). Convocation quarrels in turn aggravated the personal relations between many bishops and the Tory clergy of their own dioceses. Most damaging of all in the long run was the electoral activity of the clergy. Putting their trust, as they did, in a lengthy period of Tory political supremacy, the High Church parsons felt bound to do all they could to bring this about. The cry of 'the Church in danger' was the leading Tory election slogan in 1705, and again five years later in the fiercest General Election fought under the unreformed system before 1830. High Church clergy rode to the polls like squadrons of cavalry and freely used their pulpits, as well as their parish visits, for electioneering ends; how shamelessly at times we may judge from a corporation sermon delivered at Durham in 1708 when the preacher twisted a text from the Book of Samuel 'by hard straining . . . into the management of elections, on which his entire discourse run' (5, *57*). Given the frequency of elections under the Triennial system, such activities can only have damagingly distracted the clergy from their pastoral mission, and it is certain that they infuriated the suffering Whigs and drove many of them into a hardline anticlericalism which was to cost the Church dearly under the first two Hanoverians (*The Age of Oligarchy*, Ch. 7).

The climax of the Church of England's involvement in post-Revolution party politics came in 1709–10, when that turbulent priest Henry Sacheverell preached another of his explosive sermons and, this time, was impeached by the Whigs for 'high crimes and misdemeanours' (73b). That the Doctor had invited retribution no impartial man could deny. To choose the anniversary not only of the Gunpowder Plot but of the landing of William of Orange at Torbay in 1688 to attack both the Glorious Revolution, obliquely, and the Toleration, explicitly, and to accuse the 'false brethren' in the government of treachery to the state as well as to the Church by cherishing that 'brood of vipers', the dissenters, was monstrously provocative. To do so on a most public occasion, in St Paul's Cathedral before an audience full of City fathers, compounded his offence. All the same, the Whigs were unwise to rise to the bait. Tory propagandists were able to represent the prosecution of this egotistical, bombastic young man as an attack on the very foundations of the Anglican establishment. The trial in Westminster Hall in March 1710 engendered an excitement almost beyond belief. From one end of the land to another the pros and cons of the case, and of the man, set 'husband against wife, parent against child, male against female'.[17] The London mob celebrated the occasion by going on the rampage in the second-worst riots of the eighteenth century, wrecking six dissenting meeting-houses and making bonfires of their contents (261). Sacheverell was in the end found guilty by the Lords, but the margin was so narrow and the sentence so derisory that it was as good as an acquittal. During the summer he strutted in triumph through the country, hailed by delirious crowds, unabashedly milking his popularity for personal gain and in the Tory party interest – for in the current mood the Queen could not resist calls for the dissolution of Parliament.

After the Tories had triumphantly won the 1710 Election, after a campaign dominated even more by pro-Church hysteria than by war-weariness, it was natural enough for the exultant High Anglican clergy to look to the incoming administration and Parliament to dish the dissenters for good and usher in a new golden age for true Churchmen. Even in the short run, as we have seen, they were to experience little but frustration. Until just before his fall, when the Schism Act was passed, prime minister Harley, that congenital moderate and ex-dissenter, either blocked or adulterated nearly all the more extremist schemes in Parliament and Convocation alike. Complementing his political cunning was the devotion of Anne to what she saw as the true interests of *her* Church. For example, since the late 1690s the highest church preferments had been regarded by the party leaders as just spoils for their own ecclesiastical zealots. But Anne and Harley had always resisted this, as the 'Bishoprics Crisis' which preceded Harley's resignation in February 1708 had shown (163b; above, p. 204), and they went on doing so right down to 1714, denying Sacheverell a bishopric and Jonathan Swift an English deanery and succumbing to extreme High Churchmanship only in the case of Atterbury's promotion to the poor see of Rochester.

The long-term penalties of all their politicking, however, were even more serious for the Anglican clergy than its short-term consequences. The association of so many of them with extreme Toryism, and inevitably, when the succession issue resurfaced in 1713–14, with suspected Jacobitism, proved fatal to all their hopes of a revival when the Whigs came into their kingdom under George I. For the latter did not forget their sufferings at the hands of the black-coated army. They had their own answer to the religious problems of early eighteenth-century England, and it was a cut-and-dried and ruthless one. With Convocation, as one Low Churchman put it, 'instead of doing good, we must be satisfied with preventing any harm';[18] the Whigs duly suppressed it in 1717, using as pretext the ugly controversy over Bishop Hoadly's notorious erastian [A] sermon, 'My kingdom is not of this world' (cf. above, p. 350). Two years later they repealed the Occasional Conformity and Schism Acts; though, thanks largely to the influence of Walpole (whose shrewd politician's feel for the susceptibilities of those clergy favourably disposed to the new dynasty led him to foment a rebellion of Whig backbenchers against the extreme policies of Stanhope and Sunderland), the Church's main civil bastion, the sacramental test, was left intact (above, p. 356). Most important of all, backed now by a compliant sovereign to whom Anglican traditions meant little if anything, the Whigs began to subject the clergy to the same remorseless patronage system which they found so effective in controlling politicians. The chance to employ this in a dramatic way at the highest level, that of the bishops' bench, did not occur until the early 1720s (*The Age of Oligarchy*, Ch. 7). But even before Walpole became prime minister it had already become plain that unless a cleric was a good Whig and reliable pro-Hanoverian, all preferment in the Crown's gift would pass him by, no matter how saintly his life or how great his pastoral commitment. Thus, within a decade of Queen Anne's death the Church of England, its most strident and divisive voices stifled, had been reduced to a political quiescence which remained largely undisturbed until 1735–6. In other circumstances, such quiescence might have had as its corollary greater pastoral awareness and effectiveness. But this was not to be the case in the early Georgian age. In the years ahead it would be the gospel according to John Locke, enjoining *The Reasonableness of Christianity* (Chs. 10, 24), rather than Christ's charge to 'feed my sheep', to which the ears of the Anglican clergy would be most readily attuned.

---

1. BL Lansdowne MSS 1031, f. 222: White Kennett, 8 June 1717.
2. Its effects on the Roman Catholics are discussed in *The Age of Oligarchy*, Ch. 6.
3. Dr Williams's Library, London, MS. 34.4 (Evans List).
4. Dr Williams's Library MS. 34.4, p. 36: 'account received [by John Evans] from Mr [Shute] Barrington, 1716'.
5. Henry Sacheverell, *The Political Union: a Discourse shewing the Dependance of Government on Religion . . .* (Oxford, 1702).
6. H. McLachlan, *English Education under the Test Acts* (Manchester, 1931).
7. See, for example, Watts (150), pp. 371–3, for decline of lay discipline in Presbyterian congregations.
8. BL Lansdowne MSS 1031, f. 220: White Kennett to S. Blackwell, 30 Mar 1717.
9. Philip Doddridge, *Free Thoughts on the Most Probable Means of Reviving the Dissenting Interest* (1730), quoted Watts (150), p. 383.
10. The initial deadline was 1 August 1689, but it was extended by grace for a further 6 months.
11. J.P. Kenyon (314); G. Straka, *Anglican Reaction to the Revolution of 1688* (Madison,

Wisconsin, 1962); M. Goldie, 'Edmund Bohun and *Jus Gentium* in the Revolution Debate, 1689–1693', *HJ*, **20** 1977.

12. For William's blundering approach, see Bennett (163b), p. 11.
13. A. Savidge, *The Foundation and Early Years of Queen Anne's Bounty* (1955), p. 9 *et seq*. Returns were made from the parishes in 1705–6 but not published until 1711.
14. F. Atterbury *et al.*, *A Letter to a Convocation Man* (1697), pp. 2–3.
15. For these societies see D.W.R. Bahlman, *The Moral Revolution of 1688* (Yale, 1957); T.C. Curtis and W.A. Speck, 'The Societies for the Reformation of Manners', *Literature and History*, No. 3 (1976); and *The Age of Oligarchy*, Ch.7.
16. BL Loan 29/138: Sir Simon Harcourt to Harley, n.d. [Nov 1704].
17. Register House, Edinburgh, Ogilvie MSS. G.D. 205/4: John Pringle, 21 Mar 1710.
18. BL Lansdowne MSS. 1031, f. 201: White Kennett, 19 Mar 1715.

CHAPTER 24

The ferment of ideas, 1687–*c*.1740:
an English Enlightenment?

I

The siege mentality of the clergy, which became so marked a feature of the post-Revolution Anglican crisis, was a direct product of the ending of effective governmental and ecclesiastical censorship of the press in 1695 (above, p. 198). Although Jonathan Swift, writing his *Tale of a Tub* in 1697, satirically dismissed the recent prodigious output of the printing presses as ephemera, there were many who took a far more alarmist view. The chief cause of their concern was not the effusion of political pamphlets after the lapsing of the Licensing Act (*The Age of Oligarchy*, Ch. 13), deplorable though this seemed to some. Among Swift's fellow clergymen, as also among many serious-minded laymen, it was the dissemination of opinions which in their eyes were either heterodox or irreligious or immoral which aroused the strongest reaction. Such writings appeared to threaten centuries-old foundations of religious, moral and civil authority, and while the secular-minded might tolerate or even delight in their excesses the devout and respectable were appalled. Calling in 1697 for the re-summoning of Convocation, Francis Atterbury contended that 'since Christianity was established in this kingdom' there had never been a graver crisis. 'When such an open looseness in men's principles and practices' prevailed everywhere, he argued; when 'heresies of all kinds, when scepticism, Deism and atheism' were rampant, and 'when the power of the Magistrate and of the Church' was so 'struck at', determined action in the interests both of religion and the state was an urgent necessity (5, *116*).

Even Anglicans who had little sympathy with Atterbury's high brand of churchmanship and were far from sharing his faith in the efficacy of Convocation did not dissent from his assessment of the problem itself. Thus John Harris, a leading moderate, drew attention in the Boyle Lecture for 1697 to 'what vast loads of filth, of all kinds, are to be seen up and down in heaps amongst us. Atheism and Deism, scepticism and infidelity, immorality and profaneness, open contempt of God and of all religion . . .' (306, *193*). In 1705 Bishop Compton of London, echoing these same themes during a great House of Lords debate on the danger facing the Church of England, blamed much on 'the licentiousness of the press' (2, *VI, 484–5*). In retrospect we may think such spokesmen guilty of some exaggeration, but we cannot fairly accuse them of delusion. The five decades or so after 1679 were a period of ideological turbulence, making the first twenty years after the Restoration seem a relatively tranquil interlude by contrast. Down to 1695 the clergy, at least, were partially protected from some of its most disturbing aspects. Then, the vents unstopped, they were suddenly exposed to the pent-up force of a great ferment of ideas; they found to their dismay that the most potent ingredients at work in it were elements directly or indirectly hostile, not simply to many of the basic tenets of Anglicanism, nor even to the clergy as an order, but to the very essence of orthodox, 'revealed' Christianity (cf. Ch. 10).

It is true that few of the ideas and sentiments unchained with such violent effects on the clergy in 1695 were entirely novel. For example, attacks on one of the orthodox Christian's most central beliefs, the doctrine of the Trinity – the idea that God, though One, had three manifestations, as Father, Son (Jesus) and Holy Spirit – had been gathering strength for years. Socinianism [A.], the most radical and fashionable brand of anti-Trinitarianism prevalent in late Stuart England, could trace its roots back to early seventeenth-century Poland, and John Evelyn had noted in his diary as early as 1659 that England was being beset with 'growing heresies, who *(sic)* denied the Godhead of Christ, the Socinians especially'.[1] Arius, the father of the Arian heresy [A.], had been dead for well over 1,300 years. Deism [A.], neatly defined by Redwood as 'that belief which stripped religion of all but a remote Creator who had left a mechanical universe to its own devices' (317, *11*), was of a more recent vintage. Nevertheless its foreshadowings are traceable in England as far back as the 1620s, while in Charles II's reign it had found its first naked exponent in the person of Charles Blount (see below). As for anti-clericalism, this had been a sturdy plant in the early decades of the sixteenth century, and it had put forth vigorous new growths after the Restoration, when a libertine and tolerationist Court found the determined uniformity and the probity of Anglican divines, let alone the suffocating rectitude of the Puritans, highly uncongenial. In the 1660s and early 1670s it became fashionable for courtiers to join in Charles II's sneers at the bishops and in his mockery of stuffy preachers in the chapel royal.

This said, however, anti-clericalism, religious deviationism in all its main intellectual forms, and even bare-faced irreligion all gained ground in the years immediately after the Glorious Revolution. Almost at once the Trinitarian controversy took on a new edge when Arthur Bury [N.8] vigorously attacked the Athanasian creed for its hard-nosed statement of the doctrine of the Trinity, and for his pains he was dismissed from the headship of his Oxford college (163b). William Sherlock wrote a *Vindication of the Doctrine of the Trinity* and was promptly pilloried in some quarters for perpetuating a watered-down heresy of his own – tritheism. Heretic or not, he was made Dean of St Paul's. From 1689 onwards the illicit circulation of Socinian pamphlets gathered pace, much of it being organised by a devout and wealthy London merchant, Thomas Firmin. And while Unitarians and Trinitarians belaboured each other, a small but flamboyant minority of the educated élite grew yearly bolder in denying the existence of any God at all, at least of a God with any meaningful, overseeing function. Two years before the end of formal press censorship a future bishop of Peterborough could already observe with consternation that 'Socinianism *and atheism* drive furiously on.'[2] Meanwhile, even among nominal believers, it was growing increasingly fashionable in the coffee-houses and salons of post-Revolution London to decry what was called, in the vogue word of the time, 'priestcraft'.

Looking back late in William's reign, there were many who saw a link between the Revolution itself and these unhealthy symptoms of the new order, and one too direct to be coincidental. Moreover, those who did so were not all High Church traditionalists. One of the most radical of all Whig clergymen, William Stephens, though an ardent contractualist in politics, thought that the Revolution had 'wonderfully increased men's prejudices against the clergy', who were seen as time-servers for abandoning their Divine Right and Passive Obedience principles and taking the oaths to their new sovereigns in spite of undisguised private reservations. Stephens argued that this anti-clericalism in turn gave 'the old Deists' a marvellous opportunity to make new converts.[3] After William's death, of course, anti-clericalism was plentifully fed from other sources: by the pulpit extravagances of the extreme Highflying divines, epitomised in the lurid sensationalism of Sacheverell, and by the mounting political antagonism of the Whigs (Ch. 23). But the fact that the clergy (as they themselves frequently lamented) had been losing respect long before 1702 was probably to be attributed to, more than any other factor, that 'prostitution of oaths' whereby ninety-five per cent of them had contrived to preserve their livings in 1689–90.

It was a manifest handicap to the clergy, in trying to reburnish their tarnished image, that they were finding it increasingly difficult in the 1690s to keep their own doctrinal house in order. Firmin, for instance, was a leading light of a Church of England congregation in the City (154, *245*). The most prolific Socinian writer, from 1685 right through to 1715 (though he would have rejected the label and called himself a 'Sabellian') was the Hertfordshire vicar, Stephen Nye. Worse still, it became an open secret that Sancroft's successor, Archbishop John Tillotson, and the two most formidable intellectuals among the Anglican laity, Newton and Locke, had private sympathy with some of Nye's views, though the malicious charges that Tillotson was a Unitarian were unfounded and deeply hurtful to that kindly and liberal-minded man (154, *37*; cf. 321, *282*). The riposte to the Socinians, delivered by John Wallis, Charles Leslie and others, was spirited, and from about 1700 there was a brief lull in the conflict. It flared up again, however, in 1708, and for the next decade or so Unitarianism (though now mostly in its older and milder Arian form) had some distinguished and persuasive advocates. William Whiston, Samuel Clarke and Thomas Chubb [N.8] all used their able pens and freedom from prior censorship to propagate their Arian beliefs, although Whiston lost his Cambridge mathematics chair in consequence and Clarke, the brilliant rector of St James's, Westminster, sacrificed his chances of a bishopric.[4] By George I's reign the Established Church was closing ranks, and while the doctrine of the Trinity was still a live issue in the 1720s, it was now a far more damaging one for the Presbyterian churches than for Anglicans.

The most objectionable thing about the Trinitarians, declared one Socinian writer in 1692, was their *unreasonableness*. H.J. McLachlan has argued that by upholding the right of human reasoning to interpret what is or what is not 'revelation' the English Unitarians 'helped to pave the way for the "Age of Reason" in Britain' (319a, *336–7*). However, the plainest possible witnesses to the fact that, in religious thought at least, that age had already arrived were the early eighteenth-century Deists. The first clear pointer after the Revolution to the fact that Deism was on the march was the publication by Charles Blount of a book significantly titled *The Oracles of Reason*. It brought together many of Blount's writings since the late 1670s in which he had argued that the only true beliefs were those derived from experience or from propositions self-evidently demonstrable by reason. While Socinianism and Arianism were Christian heresies, Deism was essentially anti-Christian and, in addition, ruthlessly anti-clerical. Anglicans as unorthodox as Whiston and Nye earned the approbation of Archbishop Tenison for helping the orthodox to combat its advance. The influence of the Deists among men of birth and education was sustained into the early years of George II by the skilfully argued work of Anthony Collins, whose *Discourse of Free Thinking* (1713) sent up many a clergyman's blood pressure, and by the writings of Bernard Mandeville and Matthew Tindal. But there can be no doubt that the point at which Deism came to be viewed by Anglicans and Nonconformists alike as a threat to be taken very seriously indeed was reached with the publication, a year after the end of press censorship, of John Toland's *Christianity not Mysterious*. Blount, who had in any case committed suicide in 1693, might be written off as blasphemous yet lightweight. But Toland's was one of the most sensational books to appear in the entire century following the Glorious Revolution. Although he boasted of his friendship with Locke and claimed that Locke's thought had influenced his own, it has been shown that Locke disowned the relationship and that he wrote his own *The Reasonableness of Christianity* partly as a response to a first draft of Toland's work, which he had seen in manuscript (306, *214–15*; cf. 321, *280*), which exaggerates Locke's proto-Deism. Whereas Locke sought to buttress Christianity by reducing its tenets to the minimum that, he believed, would be perfectly defensible, Toland stripped so much away that there was in effect no Christianity left. He argued that 'whoever reveals anything . . . his words must be intelligible and the matter possible . . ., let God or Man be the Revealer' and he went on to the implacable deduction that if revealed religion contradicted human reason its declared 'truths' must be false.[5] The implications of these theological premises for such fundamental 'mysteries' as the Incarnation and the Resurrection were only too plain.

Christianity not Mysterious caused uproar. Even a liberal as pronounced as Firmin was scandalised and a score of pamphlets soon appeared in refutation. Toland's book was banned by order of a Middlesex Grand Jury, and after Atterbury had made its content part of his platform for a demand for the recall of Convocation both book and author were threatened with persecution in the Convocations of 1701 and 1704. But the Deists were slippery opponents for Christians to corner. This was partly because 'Deism was a temper rather than a creed' (318, *66*), and partly because its advocates relied as much on ridicule as on solid argument. Nevertheless, many Anglican heavyweights as well as a number of nonjuring or dissenting controversialists entered the lists against them: Stillingfleet, Leslie, Atterbury and Clarke, for instance, under William and Anne; Thomas Sherlock (son of Dean Sherlock), Edward Chandler and Arthur Sykes, among many others, under George I. It was, declared a dissenting preacher in 1733, 'the greatest controversy of the present age, and which ever was in the Christian world, where the whole revelation is placed at the bar';[6] it was not until that decade, in reaction to Tindal's supremely provocative *Christianity as old as*

Creation (1730), that orthodoxy produced three champions of such decisive firepower that Deism, as a serious intellectual force, was laid low (*The Age of Oligarchy*, Ch. 7; N.8).

A London preacher of 1700 had seen Arianism and Socinianism as half-way houses, and Deism as a later staging-post, along the road to 'plain Atheism'.[7] The atheism which churchmen of all hues believed to be advancing malevolently in the 1690s was not viewed, like Deism, as the preserve of the well-born and educated: a pamphlet of 1692, for instance, written by one Clement Ellis, was pointedly entitled *The Folly of Atheism Demonstrated, to the Capacity of the Most Unlearned Reader*. But neither was atheism simply equatable with a plain denial of the existence of God (317, *29–30* and *passim*). To Gilbert Burnet, controversial bishop but penetrating observer and recorder of his own time, it was clear that after the Revolution there were 'few atheists but many infidels' (1, *VI, 192*). And infidelism was not thought of solely as an ideological phenomenon: it could embrace blasphemers, or those who scoffed at the Church or at Christianity (and the clergy were as shocked to find themselves becoming targets of derision as much as objects of 'contempt' in the fraught years which followed the Revolution). Even ideologically atheism had, or appeared to have, numerous manifestations. Many post-Revolution Christians would certainly have branded the entirely secularised political thought of Thomas Hobbes as 'atheistical', and likewise the mechanistic philosophy of Descartes, or even theories of the earth's origins which, like those of Thomas Burnet, Blount (1693 [N.8]) and Whiston, rejected the Mosaic account. Dr John Woodward's ingenious *Essay towards a Natural History of the Earth* (1695) was much more conservative in its scriptural implications than any of these, yet it still brought down fires upon his head.[8]

Dr Woodward's dilemma, though in one sense a personal one, does in another sense throw a most revealing light on to the ideological mainspring of so much post-Revolution controversy. At the height of Anglican paranoia, front-line defenders of orthodoxy, whether against heresy, Deism or atheism, not infrequently found *themselves* on suspect ground, and this for the simple reason that they often fought with the same weapons as their antagonists. Theirs too were the accoutrements of rational debate. They too had imbibed the empirical methods of the New Science of Restoration England (Ch. 10). Samuel Clarke was so steeped in the empiricism of the Scientific Revolution that in a much publicised discourse in 1705 he came perilously close to the assertion that man's highest religious duty was to observe and systematically study natural phenomena. And when the Revd. William Derham, F.R.S., vicar of Upminster, published his two Boyle Lectures of 1711 and 1712 he gave them the extraordinary title *Physico-Theology: or, A Demonstration of the Being and Attributes of God from the Works of Creation*.

It is hard for us now to appreciate the intensity of the excitement experienced by the *avant-garde* among late seventeenth-century divines when they were confronted with the scientists' revelation of 'the clockwork universe'. To them it supplied irrefutable evidence of a 'divine clockmaker'. Above all, it was Isaac Newton's theory of gravity which from 1687 onwards supplied the intellectual élite of the Church of England with its brightest and sharpest weapon in repelling 'the atheistical host'. The logical demonstration of working laws governing the mutual attraction of all bodies, terrestrial and heavenly, laws which imparted a harmony and systematic order to the universe that was nothing short of awesome, was like a sign from Heaven itself to the young lions of the Church. To Richard Bentley, perhaps the most dazzling young scholar in Anglican orders in the years immediately after the Revolution, these laws represented (as they clearly did to Newton himself) 'a new and invincible argument for the being of God' (306, *191*). To Clarke they were likewise 'an evident demonstration, not only of the world's being made originally by a supreme intelligent cause; but moreover that it depends every moment on some superior being for the preservation of its frame . . . which . . . does either way give us a very noble idea of Providence.'[9] As Margaret Jacob has shown, the Boyle Lectures (1692–1714), endowed by the scientist Robert Boyle (Ch.10) as a means of vindicating the Christian religion 'against Atheists, Deists, Libertines, Jews, etc',[10] provided the clerical 'Newtonians' with their most influential post-Revolution platform. Once Bentley had inaugurated the series with a stunning performance in 1692, the published lectures year by year became required reading for the man of education (306, *Chs. 4, 5*). From Newton himself and from their other guru, the Master's close friend, John Locke, the lecturers derived their ethos and their method; from the *Principia* not a little of their matter; while from the third patron saint of the eighteenth century Church of Reason, Archbishop Tillotson (*The Age of Oligarchy*, Ch. 7), they took their tone, spurning 'enthusiasm' and cultivating urbanity, cogency and calm moderation.

II

During the years of the Boyle Lectures the British scientific revolution of the seventeenth century was making further notable progress, and both then and through the decades which followed it continued to consolidate earlier gains (Ch. 10) and vastly to broaden its impact. Some aspects of Newtonian physics met with initial resistance from Continental *savants*, especially from Huygens and Leibniz; it was not so much Newton himself as the propagandist efforts of such early eighteenth-century disciples as Clarke which gradually broke it down.[11] Ironically it was Voltaire, one of the least well-fitted of French intellectuals to appreciate the profound religious significance of the *Principia*, who completed the conversion of western Europe to Newtonianism in science. His *Eléments de la Philosophie de Newton* (1736) was widely read, and in *Le Siècle de Louis XIV*, published in 1751, he placed Newton on a heroic pedestal high above such great men of the past as Julius Caesar or Alexander the Great. More than anyone in the past century, more even than Descartes, it was argued – and many French *philosophes* had by now come to accept the fact – Sir Isaac Newton had enlightened and liberated the mind of man, elevating it above the last traces of medieval obscurantism and superstition and carrying it forward from Renaissance and post-Renaissance scepticism and discovery to the achievement of a 'true philosophy' (307).

It is hardly surprising that Newton's ideas needed time to command general acceptance. For one thing, such was the magnitude of his intellectual achievement that only a tiny handful of his contemporaries could live with his argument every step of the way. Furthermore, we must remember that 'Cartesianism' (the philosophical system of Descartes) was well entrenched in Europe by 1687; it was hard for its scientific adherents – including many within Britain itself – to accept that, exposed to the remorseless rigour of Newton's mathematical logic, vital parts of Descartes's explanation of the physical structure of the cosmos and of motion within the planetary system were fundamentally flawed. Newton did start from the same anti-Aristotelean premise as Descartes, that all matter was inherently inert, and likewise accepted his revolutionary theories that all physical phenomena arose from matter in motion and that this motion was capable of being explained by the operation of certain mechanical laws. But in the *Principia* Newton demonstrated that some of Descartes's own laws (for example, the proposition that only *contact* between portions of matter, or atoms, could account for any natural change – a kind of 'dodgem-car' theory of the cosmos) were unempirical and mathematically unsound. So too were the mechanisms Descartes had hypothesised to explain phenomena such as magnetism and the rotation of planets through space. For instance, Descartes believed that some kind of celestial fluid must pervade the universe, keeping stars and planets in motion. This theory, and others no less speculative, Newton totally demolished. It became irrelevant to seek to explain all motion and change in terms of contact or impact if the existence of the force of *gravity*, a force that could operate across distances, however great, were accepted.

Newton propounded, with crushing geometric proofs, several laws of motion which together laid the foundation of all subsequent work on dynamics. But it was his law of gravitation [A], a universal law governing the mutual attraction and interaction of every component in a self-contained solar system, and in other star systems in space beyond it, which first reconciled physics and astronomy. In so doing, it made possible a concept of an organised, harmonised universe which even sophisticated twentieth-century man finds recognisable. The modern scientist, it is true, might well jib at Newton's insistence that since matter itself was inert, its activity in the end rested on divine agency, and certainly at the implication that the 'clockwork' machinery of the solar system would run down or suffer dysfunction without regular divine intervention. Yet to Newton himself this was quintessential to his whole natural philosophy: to him – and to his early disciples, as we have seen – the observable and ascertainable facts of physics and astronomy were in entire harmony with the basic claims of theology (302b, *26–8, 30–1*; 303b, *75–9*; 303a, *130–33*).

By the time Newton was knighted in 1705 his creative career was effectively over. Two years earlier he had been elected President of the Royal Society, a post he held until his death in 1727. The Society had been through a comparatively lean spell in the 1680s and early 1690s, but something of a golden period ensued during the period 1694–1741, for much of which Sir Hans Sloane, distinguished as a botanist and zoologist as well as a physician, held either its secretaryship or its presidency. The number of its fellows increased between 1698 and 1740 from 119 to 301, and a third of the latter were genuine scientific fellows (307, *Table, p. 39*). The Society's image was occasionally tarnished by unseemly internal *fracas*, such as that between Newton (a touchy and, at times, arrogant President) and Sloane, and lack of corporate funds prevented it supporting *programmes* of research. But the sum of the individual achievements of its fellows, including many recorded in its *Philosophical Transactions*, remained highly impressive down to the 1730s, and that owed much to the personal co-operation and interchange of ideas which the Society's meetings facilitated. It is doubtful whether Newton's own greatest work would ever have been published but for the sustained encouragement of Edmund Halley.

It would be fair to say that, with the exception of the brilliant Scotsman, Colin McLaurin (1698–1746), it was France rather than Britain which produced most of the eighteenth century's greatest mathematicians once Newton's creative genius was spent. Neither did Britain rear a chemist of genius for many decades after Boyle's death in 1691. But in physics, astronomy, and in virtually every other branch of the experimental and observational sciences other than chemistry, she remained right in the van of the scientific revolution until at least the early years of George II. Newton's *Opticks* (1704) summed up the results of almost forty years of experiment with and thought about problems of light. Less overwhelmingly cerebral and more empirical than *Principia*, it met with a readier acceptance. The elder Francis Hawksbee and Stephen Gray took tentative steps towards an understanding of electricity. Among astronomers, Flamsteed and Edmund Halley reigned supreme in Europe. The immediate practical benefits of their work for navigation were substantial; indeed, Halley was in international demand as a nautical surveyor. In Edward Tyson, whose *Orang-Outang* (1699) undertook the first comparative study of man and the apes, post-Revolution England had one of the most imaginative zoologists of the day; in Edward Lhwyd and John Woodward, probably the best-known field zoologists before Scheuchzer, and in John Kay, an outstanding botanist and entomologist. The establishment of the Botanical Gardens at Chelsea (1680) and Kew (1730) made their contribution to a notable advance in the knowledge of *materia medica* in this period, as did the private researches of leading apothecaries such as Dale, Sherard and Fothergill. In other respect, too, medical research was energetic, and by no means always misguided. William Hillary, for instance, carried out and published the most serious study to date of tropical epidemic diseases, while the experiments of Drs John Huxham and William Cockburn produced, respectively, tincture of quinine, and a specific for dysentery (226a, *178, 209, 220*).

A striking feature of the early eighteenth-century fellows of the Royal Society was how many active scientists were busily engaged in practical or professional spheres, other than academia. 'The real intelligentsia [of Georgian England]', Roy Porter has written, 'was not chairbound but worked in the market place' (316a, *5*). Among the scientists Halley's case has been noted already; Newton, as we know, became Master of the Mint. Lhwyd was a curator, and more than half the 'scientific fellows' of the Society in the reigns of Anne and George I, among them Sloane, Tyson and Woodward, were professional medical men. Not surprisingly, therefore, British scientific activity after 1689 was characterised by a close interest – closer, perhaps, than in the years 1660–88 – in the practical application of research. It is probably no coincidence that some of the most influential figures in eighteenth-century medicine were surgeons, such as William Cheselden (1688–1752), his pupil John Hunter and Edward Jenner, discoverer of vaccination, rather than physicians.

III

There were few areas of the world of ideas in the late seventeenth and eighteenth centuries which were not permeated, or at least changed in some measure, by the influence of the New Science. The success with which it challenged traditional authority was compelling enough, but perhaps more crucial was the priority it gave to the empirical method. Much has been said already about its impact on theology. In a different field, its capacity to create or stimulate debate can be clearly detected in the often ill-tempered literary exchanges, beginning in the 1690s, between the 'Ancients' and the 'Moderns'. The champions of the latter seized on recent scientific achievements as the strongest evidence that a new enlightenment had displaced the traditionally-accepted authority of Greece and Rome in the arts, as well as in the sciences. An uncritical respect for classical literature was seen (not without reason) as the counterpart of an equally exaggerated scholarly respect for patristic authority in theology or for the great classical masters of moral and natural philosophy. The 'modernists' included Wotton, Dryden, and that rough-hewn Yorkshireman, Dr Richard Bentley, who was, ironically, the finest classical scholar of his generation. The fact that their adversaries, apart from Swift and his patron, Sir William Temple, were spearheaded by a bevy of Christ Church men, including Aldrich and Atterbury, and that this Oxford college was the ultimate bastion of extreme High Church-manship, lent political and religious overtones to a controversy whose centrepiece was the dispute between Bentley and Charles Boyle over the authenticity of the Phalaris Letters. Bentley's *Dissertation upon Phalaris* (1699) was much more than a critical *tour de force*, exposing the letters as forgeries and utterly demolishing 'the gentlemen-wits of Christ Church'; in its whole mastery of cogent argument, supported by detailed evidence and conducted with directness of style, it epitomised the infusion of 'modern' learning and literature with the new scientific spirit (163b, *38–43*; 306, *78–9*). What David Douglas wrote of William Wake's epic work, *The State of the Church and Clergy of England* (1703), that 'it did much more than confound an opponent [in Wake's case, Atterbury] . . . it subordinated controversy to constructive learning',[12] could be said equally of Bentley's *Dissertation*.

Significantly, Wake was both a Low Church bishop and a 'Newtonian', his London house being a frequent meeting-place for scientists, virtuosi and latitudi-narian Anglicans. The scholarly creed of the Wakes and the Bentleys of post-Revolution Britain was best summed up by John Locke, who preached 'the love of truth as such' (24a [McManners], *138*) as the supreme necessity, allowing no historical tradition to be taken on trust without examination and no proposition to be advanced further than its proof would bear. The clever controversialism of an Atterbury or a Swift, of men little touched by the New Science, cleared lesser hurdles with effortless ease but crashed comprehensively at this one. Both before and after his death in 1704 Locke's presence dominated the ideological scene of post-Revolution England like a vast bridge spanning turbulent waters, its massive pillars thrusting down at intervals into different parts of the river bed. In addition to publishing in 1689 the definitive exposition of Whig political theory (but see below, pp. 377–8) and establishing the model in 1695 for all subsequent attempts, over the next half century, to enunciate a rationally defensible Christian theology, he also produced within seven amazing years after the Revolution the most persuasive statement yet of the theoretical case for Toleration, a classic brief treatise on education, and his swiftly and justly acclaimed *Essay concerning Human Understanding* of 1690 (above, pp. 195, 196, 197). In terms of its repercussions the *Essay* was arguably the greatest of all Locke's intellectual achievements. It advanced significantly the frontiers of both metaphysics and psychology in Europe. His approach to philosophy was typified most by his rejection of 'innate ideas' (all that a man can ever know, he argued, he has to *learn*), by his direction of attention towards the sources and transmission of ideas and by his insistence that all thought has 'necessary limits'. For a century and a half after Locke's death, only David Hume (1711–76), whose work in the 1740s and 1750s was in many respects an extension of Lockean principles (*The Age of Oligarchy*, Chs. 7, 15), could match his influence over philosophy in Britain; certainly no other foreign thinker had such a profound influence as Locke upon the later French Enlightenment (316b).

Three qualities permeated virtually all John Locke's work in the field of ideas, all of them products of his intellectual conditioning in the age of Newton. One was his empiricism: all his educational ideas, for example, were firmly rooted in observation, even down to such prosaic matters as the effects of constipation on children (178d, *165*). The second was his liberal and optimistic view of the nature of man; rejecting the Puritan view of human nature as permanently flawed by original sin, he saw it rather as ever susceptible to improvement, whether through religion, education, acceptable government, or other benign influences. This quality of optimism he passed on to his pupil, the third earl of Shaftesbury, whose *Characteristics* (1711) was an important European event in the fields of ethics and aesthetics: both writers anticipated the *philosophes'* view of 'perfectibility'. Locke's third pervading quality was his genius for reconciling and synthesising ideas. Sweet reasonableness generally directed his thinking away from extremes and towards the middle ground. This was yet another reason why Georgian Britain continued to find him a congenial spirit until late in the eighteenth century, his 'individualist prescriptions', as Roy Porter has put it, 'assum[ing] Biblical status for enlightened minds in all walks of life' (316a, *9*).

John Redwood describes the years 1660–1750 as 'The Age of Enlightenment in England' (317). A.M. Wilson has argued more explicitly that while western Europe, and Scotland too (*The Age of Oligarchy*, Ch. 15), enjoyed their Enlightenment in the middle and later decades of the eighteenth century, the calm pragmatism of much English writing and thought from the 1740s to the

1780s is to be explained, not on the hypothesis that she stood outside the Continental mainstream, but by the fact that she had already experienced her own Enlightenment, in the late seventeenth century and early in the eighteenth, 'and with such decisiveness that no further agitation seemed to the English to be necessary or even very desirable' (316b, *20*). 'Have courage to use your own reason!', ran a famous passage of Kant's *Was ist Aufklärung?*, 'that is the motto of enlightenment'. By that general yardstick, undeniably, many of the ideological and scientific developments referred to so far in this chapter would seem to justify the use of a label such as 'the English Enlightenment', even though until recently it has not found great favour with historians. There is no doubt, either, that the ideas of Newton and Locke, Shaftesbury and Toland, or Alexander Pope,[13] to name no more, and even the civilised social tone of the essayists Addison and Steele, proved eminently exportable, especially to the admiring French after *circa* 1740. It may well be that the lack of synchronisation in the whole process can be accounted for, not simply by the singular flowering of scientific genius in late Stuart England, but also by the fact that those political, religious and press freedoms which Frenchmen and Germans struggled for in the middle of the eighteenth century had already been secured across the English Channel between 1688 and 1702 (316a, *1–4, 7–8*).

IV

One critical question about post-Revolution ideologies has still to be asked, however, and it has an obvious bearing on the hypothesis of an anterior 'English Enlightenment'. How close were the parallels between English *political* ideas in the half century or so after 1688 and the political thought of Rousseau, Diderot and the Encyclopedists? It has often been remarked that for two salient features of French pre-revolutionary thought, Rousseau's notion of a contract and the fundamental emphasis which all the politically-minded *philosophes* placed on 'natural rights', there were clear English precedents. And customarily, John Locke's writings have seemed the most obvious candidates to stand *in loco parentis*, especially since Diderot and the Encyclopedists freely and regularly acknowledged their indebtedness to him. Yet there is need for caution on at least two main scores. In the first place, Locke's own centrality in the development of English political ideas – even of Whig ideas – between the Revolution and the mid-eighteenth century has been seriously challenged in recent years. And in the second place, there were other very important strands in English political ideology after 1688, very different from what might be called that of mainline Whiggery; these fit awkwardly, if at all, into any eighteenth-century continuum of recognisably 'Enlightened' western European thought.

Traditional wisdom on the importance of Locke's *Two Treatises on Government* can be conveniently summarised in some words of Sir Ernest Barker: 'It was the political theory of Locke which affected the nation most deeply. Nor did it only affect England. It penetrated into France, and passed through Rousseau into the French Revolution; it penetrated into the North American colonies, and passed through Samuel Adams and Thomas Jefferson into the American Declaration of Independence . . . [Within Britain it] became the creed of a great party, and of a succession of great statesmen . . . who between 1688 and 1832 worked out a system of Parliamentary Government that may justly be called the great contribution of England to Europe'.[14]

Into such sonorous certainty discordant notes must now be introduced. Although John Locke published his classic works on political theory at the end of 1689 it is clear that nearly all his serious thinking on the subject had finished before the Revolution, and very possibly before he left for Holland in 1684 (see Ch. 9 above). Since then, when he had not been dabbling in conspiracy or projected rebellion, he had been working on his *Essay concerning Human Understanding* and his *Letter on Toleration* (310b, *Chs. 9–10*). What is more, because the *Two Treatises* had been conceived in very different circumstances from those in which the 1689 Settlement was hammered out, it has been argued that some of their most controversial ideas had only very limited relevance to the most burning theoretical issues then in debate. For example, because of the concoction of the fiction that James II had 'abdicated' (pp. 213–14 above), it became necessary for Whigs as well as Tories in 1689 to demonstrate that there had not been 'a dissolution of government' in November-December 1688, whereas much of the argument in Locke's *Second Treatise* is based on the assumption that just such a dissolution had taken place; indeed, that point is driven home by a passage deliberately inserted in 1689, before publication (310b, *575*). For such reasons[15] (it is suggested) Locke was forced towards the sidelines in 1689, and his theories made to appear untypical among most other Whig views current at the time, and more extreme than in reality they were. In the decades that followed, as the power politicians in the Whig party became more anxious still to bind all the King's subjects to the Revolution establishment, especially when that king was a Hanoverian, they grew much warier about the more revolutionary doctrines of the *Second Treatise*. They found Locke's lofty disregard for the fashionable historicist approach to constitutional problems bewildering; his distinctive theory of contract too abstract (only two Whig managers, Stanhope and Lechmere, wholeheartedly embraced it in the full-dress political debates of the Sacheverell trial, 1710), and the idea of a right of resistance, in the uncompromising Lockean form, increasingly embarrassing (310b, *578–9*; 313, *123*; 314, *17–19*; 310c). Even the American colonists, we are assured, paid little attention to his political ideas until the 1760s (321, *46–9*).

The bent of all this revisionism, together with other work which has stressed the political abrasiveness of Locke's radical religious views,[16] has been salutary. But it requires some correctives. Even among the post-Revolution Whig establishment, and those who wrote in general sympathy with it, the legacy of John Locke was more substantial and pervasive than recent work – and the near-conspiracy to avoid bringing his august name into contemporary debates – would suggest.[17] The most active propagator of Whig ideas from the early 1700s to the 1730s, Benjamin Hoadly, favoured alike by the Junto and by Walpole, may not have followed Locke into the higher flights of theory, but he was both a firm contractualist and such a vigorous upholder of the people's right of resistance, in

Anne's reign at least, as to cause much trepidation among the bulk of his fellow divines. James Tyrrell's 970-page *Bibliotheca Politica* (1694) lies closer than Locke's *Two Treatises* to the Whig mainstream in its emphasis on English historical precedent, but no one could have mistaken its Whiggery for a new consensus ideology. The striking success of Algernon Sidney (the Whig martyr of 1683)'s *Discourses concerning Government* when they were finally published in 1698 (314, *51*) hardly seems to support the view that the market for radical Whig ideology, even among the ruling classes, was shrinking. Caroline Robbins subtitled her study of Sidney's work 'textbook of Revolution'. There may be a good deal of substance in the view that the Whigs became readier to compromise after the Sacheverell trial than they had been before it. Even so there remains plenty of the pure milk of Whiggery to be found in the early Hanoverian years in the work of Thomas Burnet and the heavily Lockean John Jackson,[18] and it was not until the Whig oligarchy had been established for a decade or so that Burnet, Hoadly and other establishment theorists and apologists began, consciously it would seem, to trim their sails to the new wind.

More important than all this, however, is the evidence that Locke's 'highly theoretical and coherent political ideology with considerable revolutionary potential' (87, *67*) was effectively *popularised* after the Revolution. So much of the maelstrom of political ideas in the early post-Revolution decades is observable only in pamphlets and sermons, as opposed to substantial academic tomes. Thus Ben Hoadly and another leading divine, Offspring Blackall, conducted a crucial debate about non-resistance, Revolution Whig versus moderate Tory, exclusively through these two media in the years 1705–9. And it was through pamphlets, above all, that the essentials of Lockean thought, at times somewhat crudely precipitated from their intellectual solution, permeated down to a far, far wider audience than the *Treatises* would otherwise have reached. Daniel Defoe was one such popular channel, in a number of tracts published between 1700 and 1710. Much less well-known is the fact that large chunks of Locke were purveyed *verbatim* in three of the most successful pamphlets to come on the market in the reigns of William III and Anne: *Political Aphorisms* (1690), *Vox Populi, Vox Dei* (1709) and *The Judgement of Whole Kingdoms and Nations* (1710). The latter, indeed, has been described as 'one of the most important instruments of Whig propaganda to be published in eighteenth-century England'; understandably so, for it went through twelve editions between 1710 and 1717, the first three of which sold 8,000 copies in six months, and its last reprinting was as late as 1771. In *The Judgement* other Whig views are conflated with those of Locke, including those of the more extreme Robert Ferguson, but the pamphlet's chief significance, as Ashcraft and Goldsmith have written, lies in 'the manner in which the ideas of a great political philosopher found their way into a popular political manifesto', which became the embodiment of the most radical Whig 'revolution principles'. But for the preservation of this true radical tradition within 'the alternative political nation' (see *The Age of Oligarchy*, Ch. 3) it would be less easy to explain how Cartwright, Burge, Paine and others were able to take up the torch of natural rights and popular sovereignty with such conviction after 1780 (311; 87, *67–9*).

V

Political Lockeanism – whether in its establishment or its more radical guise – thus occupied, like Newtonianism, a natural and prominent place in the Enlightenment traditions of eighteenth-century Europe. In conclusion, however, we must take note of two very important respects in which the ferment of political ideas in post-Revolution England produced streams of thought that were peculiarly English, and untransplantable to countries which had known no Puritan rebellion, no restored Anglican Church, no political parties and no Glorious Revolution. One was the strain of 'Country' ideology, sustained by some of the ablest political writers of the day, such as Molesworth, Toland, Moyle, Trenchard, Gordon and the Scot, Andrew Fletcher. In origin it was purely 'Old Whig', and very much associated with the group known as 'the Commonwealthmen';[19] but by the middle years of the Walpole era, especially after the recruitment of Lord Bolingbroke to its cause, it became more bipartisan. It stressed the liberties of the subject as against the power of the executive; the danger to every body-politic of becoming infected with corruption; the necessity in a healthy constitution of vesting political authority in men who had sufficient property to ensure their 'independence' and the placing of public good before private gain. Although most 'commonwealth' writers who cultivated the philosophical ideal of the 'community of virtue' acknowledged a debt to Harrington and, beyond that, to Machiavelli,[20] these radical roots yielded over time increasingly conservative fruit. By the early Hanoverian period, for instance, while Country philosophy still embodied occasional ritual calls for annual Parliaments, it showed virtually no enthusiasm even for the theoretical case for root and branch electoral reform, a case which Locke had loftily taken to be axiomatic. The 'community of virtue' was becoming equatable with 'the ancient constitution', and in the process more readily accommodated – though far from completely so – with the stable, oligarchic political system which succeeded the first age of party (313, *190–1 and Ch. 5 passim*).

The second notable feature of the political argument under the last two Stuarts which was largely indigenous was the successful survival of what Dickinson has called an 'ideology of order'. It was an ideology with strong pre-Revolution antecedents and precious little connection with any of the ideals of the Enlightenment. Whig apologists of the 'Old Corps' in the Walpole era eventually subsumed some traces of it, but for at least three decades after the Revolution it was associated almost exclusively with Tory thinkers, preachers and polemicists. The influence of Leslie and other Nonjuring writers upon this process was considerable; but although it is undeniable that 'the years [from 1690] to 1714 saw a great outpouring of Nonjuror and Jacobite polemic' (321, *146*), it would be a mistake to exaggerate the differences between the basic stance of their political ideology and that of conforming Anglican Tories. The point can best be illustrated in relation to the clergy, who supplied most of the pens on both sides. Bennett and Goldie have written tellingly of the brand of illegitimacy stamped on the post-Revolution Church of England by the Nonjurors and of how the conscience of the Church was sorely troubled by these 'confessors who stood in the ancient ways, devout, logical and insistent'. But the ideological gap between those who took and those who refused the oaths of allegiance and supremacy in 1689–90 was not an unbridgeable chasm. Most of those clergy who did conform were just as certain as the Nonjurors that James was still their 'rightful and lawful' prince and they could quote good Anglican precedent for promising obedience, notwithstanding, to the authority *in possession*. Equally significant is the situation after Anne had succeeded William, when many Nonjurors, notably Bishop Ken, seriously considered the possibility of a reconciliation. But in any event, as Goldie reminds us, only a fraction of the profound intellectual influence they exercised over their contemporaries was destructive: 'time after time they traversed the boundary between the conformists and themselves and lent massive scholarly and polemical support to Anglican, Tory . . . causes' (163b, *10*; 106b [Goldie, 'The Nonjurors..']; 314, *Ch. 3*). Despite the undoubted embarrassment the Revolution caused to the Tory party there remained, after all, crucial common denominators on which *all* thinking Tories, clerical and lay, could still agree and which all could defend. Civil government was God-made, not man-made; it should be monarchical, not republican, and hereditary, not elective; it could not be 'dissolved' by the people, or by anyone else; and not least, it existed to preserve order and a social framework which rested on property and deference, not to defend any 'natural rights', still less to fulfil any fictional contract (cf. 321, *Ch. 3 passim*). But to preserve these basics some compromises inevitably had to be made. At times – as, for example, when Charles Leslie, Milbourne, Sacheverell and others were beating the old Divine Right, Passive Obedience and Non-Resistance drums as loudly as ever in the middle years of Anne – it may have seemed that those compromises had been purely temporary. But theirs was but the brazen front of the ideology of order. Behind the polemics genuine concessions to post-Revolution reality were made, in the course of which arguments of considerable subtlety were developed by such as William Sherlock, Bohun, Sharp, Blackall, Atterbury and ultimately Bolingbroke.

Sherlock and Sharp, for instance, showed great resource in persuading Tories, between 1691 and 1700, that obedience was due to the *de facto* authority in the state, and that only thus could order be preserved. Bohun, too, played an important part in legitimising the post-Revolution regime in the eyes of some Anglican sticklers by applying one of the arguments of the great international jurist, Grotius, to the events of 1688–9, namely the idea of a 'just war' which permitted one sovereign to depose another in the cause of the people – the *jus gentium*.[21] Blackall's special contribution was to reconcile Non-Resistance theory with limited monarchy or parliamentary government. It was he who initiated the twin arguments (later taken up by Harcourt and others at Sacheverell's trial) that although all governments were divinely-ordained, God's imprimatur was not – as Filmer had claimed – reserved for absolute monarchies alone, and that where God had decreed that power be shared between a king and a legislature, their joint power was wholly sovereign and could not legally be resisted (313, *48–9*). As the slow transmutation of Tory ideology was worked through, it was inevitable that some of its traditional props – notably Filmer's *Patriarcha* – should finally be discarded as lumber. In Bolingbroke's writings of the 1730s and 1740s the once-revered Filmer had become 'that ridiculous writer', propagator of 'a silly and slavish notion'. The *Patriot King* of Bolingbroke's most important work of political theory (1738)[22] was a new-style, constitutional patriarch appropriate to a post-Revolution world; Locke was met half-way with the concession that civil authority *might* rest in some sort of compact and that consent was a desirable basis of political obligation, though not an absolute necessity to its legitimisation. Yet in one vital respect Bolingbroke remained squarely in the centre of that refined Tory position with which he had identified himself as an active politician in Anne's reign. For him, the first priority of all government was not the protection of rights nor even of property: it was the preservation of that 'authority, subordination, order and union necessary to well-being'.

Bolingbroke's ideology of order did, however, lack one essential ingredient of grass-roots Tory thinking. As befitted the work of a known Deist, it allotted no conspicuous place to the Church. Even when condemned to a permanent opposition rôle under the early Hanoverians, most Tories continued to regard themselves as natural protectors of the Church: a fact they demonstrated in Parliament, not only in 1718–19 but in the years 1730–6 (*The Age of Oligarchy*, Ch. 7) and later, in leading the outcry against the Jewish Naturalisation Bill in 1753. Hence the appeal to Tory intellectuals of John Hutchinson's *Moses's Principia* (1724), which denounced Deists and Unitarians, declared Newton's physics as suspect as his religious principles (and those of his Whig and Latitudinarian disciples), and proclaimed the Bible the only reliable guide both to the making of the earth and the ordering of the state. Its precepts pointed inexorably to a monarchical and hierarchical state in alliance with an established priesthood. The considerable influence which this and later work of the 'Hutch-insonians' exerted, especially over generations of Oxonians down to Pusey and Newman (321, *218–26*), reminds us that while ever there was a 'Church in danger' there would be no lack of ideological justification for a Tory party to defend it. It also shows that, however valid may be the concept of 'an English Enlightenment' in the late seventeenth and early eighteenth centuries, it would be an error to assume that, even intellectually, it carried all before it. And as for the general consumption of its ideas, events in the 1790s would demonstrate how durable some of the old orthodoxies still remained, well after our period's end.

---

1. E.S. de Beer, *Diary of John Evelyn* (abridged edn. 1959), p. 396.
2. BL Lansdowne MSS. 1013, f. 51: White Kennett to Revd Mr Blackwell, 9 May 1693 (my italics).
3. W. Stephens, *An Account of the Growth of Deism in England* (1696), pp. 10–11, quoted at length in Jacob (306), p. 203.
4. Clark (321), p. 284, rightly remarks that the Arians 'contributed powerfully to the destruction of early-eighteenth-century Deism', but Samuel Clarke's association with Arian theology began long after his first great blasts against the Deists in 1704.
5. John Toland, *Christianity not Mysterious* (1696), pp. 41–2.
6. Dr William Harris's preface to Simon Browne, *A Defence of the Religion of Nature and of the Christian Revelation*, p.iii, quoted in Cragg (318), p. 63.

7. De Beer, ed., *The Diary of John Evelyn* (abridged edn.), p. 1056: 26 May 1700
8. J.M. Levine, *Dr Woodward's Shield: History, Science and Satire in Augustan England* (Berkeley, Cal., 1977), ch. 2, esp. pp. 35–47; J. Redwood (317), pp. 124–8.
9. Samuel Clarke, *On the Being and Attributes of God* (Boyle Lecture, 1704), quoted in Jacob (306), p. 192.
10. *Evelyn's Diary*, p. 951: 13 Feb 1692.
11. For example in Samuel Clarke's annotations to his second and third editions (1702/8–1710) of Jacques Rohault's Cartesian *Traité de Physique* (1671).
12. D.C. Douglas, *English Scholars, 1660–1730* (2nd edn 1951), pp. 213–14.
13. Pope's *Essay on Man* (1733) was much in the freethinking tradition of Toland, Collins and of its chief inspiration, Bolingbroke.
14. Introduction to *Social Contract* (ed. Sir E. Barker, World Classics, 1947), pp. xviii–xix.
15. Another example is Locke's seeming indifference in the *Two Treatises* to such matters as the legitimacy of *de facto* kingship.
16. John Dunn, *The Political Thought of John Locke* (Cambridge, 1969); Mark Goldie, 'John Locke and Anglican Royalism', *Political Studies*, **31** (1983).
17. See, for example, J. Nelson, 'Unlocking Locke's Legacy', *Political Studies*, **26** (1978).
18. T. Burnet, *An Essay upon Government* (1716); J. Jackson, *The Grounds of Civil and Ecclesiastical Government* (1718).
19. C. Robbins, *The Eighteenth-Century Commonwealthmen* (Cambridge, Mass., 1959).
20. J.G.A. Pocock, *The Machiavellian Moment* (Princeton, 1975); *Politics, Language and Time* (1972), p. 104ff.
21. M. Goldie, 'Edmund Bohun and *Jus Gentium* in the Revolution Debate, 1689–1693', *HJ*, **20** (1977).
22. But not published, in revised form, until 1749.

CHAPTER 25

The quest for stability:
from the Revolution to the rise of Walpole

For almost ninety years before 1714 England was one of the most politically volatile and precarious countries in Europe. And for even longer than that Englishmen had been vainly trying to re-discover that stable polity which, rightly or wrongly, they associated with the halcyon days of the great Elizabeth. From time to time they had had a fleeting glimpse of journey's end, but, like the desert traveller's mirage, it had always eluded them. Down to the end of James II's reign it is not hard to see why: the constitution had remained in or close to a crisis state for decades and, together with a febrile religious atmosphere, offered little hope of bringing down the political temperature. But even when some of the most basic constitutional problems had apparently been resolved in 1689, instability remained. As we know, neither the later legislation of the Revolution settlement down to 1701 nor the removal from the scene in 1702 of William III, with his determination to strain to the full the prerogatives left to him, removed every outstanding constitutional issue from the realm of politics (Ch. 13). Probably the most fundamental question underlying post-Revolution politics and government was how a new working relationship between the Crown and its ministers, on the one hand, and Parliament on the other could be hammered out at a time when the fury of party and ideological ferment were subjecting the whole system of politics to acute stresses.

One glaring symptom of continuing instability was the fact that only for a short while, in the middle years of his reign, did an able and resolute king succeed in forming a firmly-rooted administration. Except for that period, when he was adeptly aided by the Whig Junto, the composition of William's ministries changed like a kaleidoscope. All of them were in some degree coalitions, but within that frame of reference there were many marked shifts of political complexion, with four lurches to the advantage of the Whigs and four to the Tories [D].[1] In less than thirteen years William employed six First Lords of the Treasury (one of them, Godolphin, in two spells), issued no fewer than fourteen different Treasury commissions and changed his First Lord of the Admiralty seven times. By contrast, he was on occasion so chary of making a false political step that he left important offices such as the second Secretaryship of State [D.2] and the Lord Presidency[2] vacant for unacceptable periods. Under Queen Anne, and in the first half of George I's reign, there was certainly more continuity of personnel and policy at the centre. The presence in key offices for long spells of Godolphin and Harley, and later of Sunderland (1706–10, 1714–22) and Stanhope (1714–21) of itself ensured this. But the whole political scene none the less remained in a state of flux, as first the Tory party, then their rivals, gained the upper hand at Court and in Parliament (Chs. 21–2). Ministerial revolutions put the Tories in the driving seat in 1702 and in 1710 and the Whigs in 1714; there were decisive shifts of balance in 1705–6 and in 1708–9, in both cases to Whig advantage, while government upheavals of a different kind were brought about by serious splits among the Tories in 1704 and among the Whigs in 1717. Tensions were further increased under Anne, especially from 1705–8 and again in 1711, by the Queen's desperate unwillingness to abandon her prerogative right to choose and dismiss her ministers at will and to concede the stern logic of a changed situation in the Commons. The Junto thus became aggressive when Godolphin found it difficult to meet all their claims in the years 1705–8 – claims bolstered by two successful election campaigns; and for a while in 1711 Harley found himself in a similar dilemma confronted by the rampant High Tories of the October Club (70; 105).

Had instability been confined to the narrow orbits of Westminster or the Court men might have viewed it more philosophically, but it was not. When the Stuart line came to an end with Anne's death on 1 August 1714 it seemed to many Englishmen that their country was still, as it had been for years, as bitterly divided by party warfare as formerly by the civil bloodshed of the 1640s. The analogy may appear far-fetched to us, but it did not to them. And as they looked back over the whole 111 years of Stuart rule, there was more to prompt grim reflection than to encourage optimism. In that time England alone had experienced two major revolutions, three civil wars, a number of minor local risings and one serious provincial rebellion (Monmouth's). Twice more, in 1681 and in 1688, she had teetered on the brink of a fresh civil war, but providentially escaped. More recently, in 1708, the new United Kindom had survived a Jacobite invasion attempt which, had it succeeded in making an effective landfall, would probably have triggered a rebellion, at least in Scotland. And as if all this were not enough, the seventeenth century and the first decade of the eighteenth had seen a string of conspiracies to overthrow the established government by murder or by violence, of which just a few of the more notorious were the Gunpowder Plot, the Rye House Plot, and the Fenwick Conspiracy to assassinate William III. And so, while on the Continent in the course of the seventeenth century most countries made marked progress towards civil order and tranquillity, usually through autocracy, for Britons at the end of Anne's reign political instability still seemed in many respects an endemic condition.

They were of course conscious, and very proud, of other and more fortunate legacies from their past, especially those preserved by 'the late happy revolution': liberty, representative institutions, the Common Law – benefits denied to most of their Continental neighbours. And, stable or not, their country had in the past quarter of a century accomplished great things. But the alloy which debased all this fine metal remained. When in 1714 the deep divisions in the Tory party allowed the Elector George of Hanover to succeed to his British thrones without bloodshed, there was great relief. But the remission was a brief one. A rebellion broke out in Scotland in September 1715 on behalf of the Jacobite Pretender, the Chevalier James Edward Stuart. Although prompt action by the Whig government, including the suspension of Habeas Corpus [A], and a healthy sense of self-preservation among the many Englishmen disaffected towards the new dynasty kept the number of active rebels south of the border to between 2,000 and 4,000, a Jacobite advance guard did reach Preston. In Scotland itself between 15,000 and 20,000 men, Lowlanders as well as Highlanders, including 18 peers, rose and it took a bloody battle at Sheriffmuir and the despatch of 6,000 Dutch and Swiss reinforcements to the north before the rebellion was quashed in April 1716 (*The Age of Oligarchy*, Ch. 6). But if the rebellion was over the threat remained, as the Pretender's adherents explored every possibility of foreign aid. In 1717 a Swedish-backed plot was uncovered, and in 1719 there was an invasion attempt with a Spanish fleet which was largely thwarted by a storm, although 600–700 men did land in Scotland (above, p. 209). The new King was still unpopular with his subjects, not least on the ground that he was excessively subject to German counsels (cf. p. 395 below). The Whig party, after asserting its mastery, seemed bent on jeopardising it by fragmenting into factions; no sooner had its quarrels been superficially patched up by the readmission of Walpole and Townshend to the ministry in 1720 than the political world was shaken to its foundations by the scandal of the South Sea Bubble (Ch. 17). With difficulty the regime survived this new crisis, owing a heavy debt in the process to Robert Walpole's acumen and political judgement. When, however, the Atterbury Plot came to light in 1722 it prompted the question, whether the British really were a governable people?

But then came the most startling change. Within the space of half a decade a relatively small number of Whig families so strengthened their grip on the country that the oligarchic political structure they now inhabited was by 1727 already showing signs of solidity. By 1730 stability was no longer a pipe dream but a prosaic reality, and until the 1760s when, as John Brewer has brilliantly shown us, some of its most essential constituents began to crumble (92), it proved impervious to strains. Why its coming was so long delayed, how the way was prepared for it over at least fifty years, from 1675 to 1725, and what was responsible for its final and seemingly sudden achievement – these were the questions which inspired Sir John Plumb's celebrated Ford Lectures of 1965, an interpretative *tour de force* since firmly established as a historiographical landmark (28).

Before turning to these questions it should be noted that subsequent attempts to challenge the basic premise on which they rest – namely, that Britain in the age of Walpole and the Pelhams *was* possessed of an exceptionally stable political system and social order – have been cautionary rather than radical. It is no very difficult matter to demonstrate that between the 1720s and the 1750s there was periodic unruliness in extra-parliamentary politics and at the lower levels of society and occasional excitement at the upper (263a; 86). But this does not constitute an argument for a continuum of instability right through from the early to the later eighteenth century. Plumb's thesis, it should be remembered, assumes that true stability is only achievable in a state where two basic conditions are present: 'a sense of common identity' among those who wield power, not only in politics but over the social and economic fabric of the country; and an 'acceptance by society of its political institutions, *and of those classes of men . . . who control them*' (28, *xvi, xviii* [my italics]). These conditions demonstrably existed between the late 1720s and the early 1760s. By contrast, after 1689 Britain possessed acceptable political institutions, and there was some progress over the next thirty years towards realising a sense of common identity within the governing class (49). But as late as 1720 it would have been futile to pretend that the men who controlled the government of the state commanded anything approaching a consensus in the political nation (cf. 81a, *201*).

In this chapter we shall look afresh at the three questions which Sir John first posed in 1965, taking into consideration as we do, not only the arguments and conclusions originally advanced but the result of further work and thought devoted to them since. The most salient aspects of the Plumb thesis have stood the test of time well. It would be hard to dispute, for instance, that what we might call the raw materials of stability, or many of them, were already present in Queen Anne's reign and that in some cases they had been there appreciably longer; likewise, that this stockpile – the timber, bricks and cement, as it were, out of which a stable political order could in time be built – could not be properly utilised under the later Stuarts because of vitiating factors, counter-productive forces too strong to allow construction to go smoothly ahead. Thirdly, it is plain that some of the main influences which in the end made a decisive contribution to this building work came into play after 1714, when the Whigs were striving to turn a victory into a permanent supremacy, and that Walpole's was the leading hand among them. There is room, however, for important differences of emphasis. It may be urged that the *foundations* of ultimate stability were being increasingly securely laid from the 1680s onwards at the latest – more securely, indeed, than contemporaries themselves realised. Furthermore, it can be strongly argued that much concrete progress had already been made towards the actual *achievement* of political stability before the Hanoverian succession took place; in particular, that there was progress towards the solution of certain intractable problems which the 1688 Revolution left in its wake and towards the discovery of a successful formula for the management of Parliament by the Crown. Such a change of perspective inevitably involves a certain scaling-down of the contribution of the post–1714 Whigs, and of Walpole in particular, essential though this was. Above all, it calls for a heightened awareness of the yearning for stability within the political nation under the later Stuarts, and also of the determination with which some of the leading statesmen of the day pursued the quest for it, before as well as after 1714.

Of the longer-term, preparatory developments three, in particular, were stressed in Plumb's thesis. The first two have been the subject of earlier chapters in this book (Chs. 3, 16). The administrative expansion and reorganisation of the late seventeenth and early eighteenth centuries created a new breed of civil servants with a permanent professional interest in the continuity of firm, efficient government; at the same time it produced a great storehouse of patronage out of which, given the right conditions, the hunger of the governing classes could be appeased. No government before 1688 had had at its disposal nearly as much 'grass for the beasts to feed on' (to quote one of Walpole's favourite bucolic metaphors) as the Crown and its ministers enjoyed in the war years under

William and Anne. This is not to say that patronage was to prove necessarily the decisive weapon in the final battle against the forces perpetuating uncertainty and upheaval in British politics,[3] but without question it was important. The second layer in the foundations of stability was of a totally different nature. The 'Commercial Revolution' of the 1670s and 1680s opened out new horizons of wealth and prosperity, both national and personal, and placed a high premium on a stable constitutional and political system as a necessary guarantee of the preservation of these coveted benefits. Thirdly, and specifically in the political field itself, Plumb drew attention to a significant long-term trend towards electoral oligarchy: a tendency for electoral power to become concentrated in fewer hands than before the Glorious Revolution, thus bringing the eventual subjection of that most volatile of elements, the English electorate, much closer. In this respect he argued, on the one hand, that the cost of fighting and holding parliamentary seats increased steeply, especially over the two decades of the Triennial era from 1695 to 1715, and often became too much for the purses of local partisans, whether squires or provincial merchants. At the same time, changes in the pattern of landownership (Ch. 18) were producing a landed élite of great proprietors who were formidably equipped, given only the right circumstances, to build and maintain secure electoral interests impervious to the oscillations of opinion. That these things *were* to happen, and with those very consequences, in the twenty to thirty years after the 1715 Election is clear enough. How far they already *had* happened by the end of Anne's reign is more debatable. The great inflation of the cost of individual contests, in most constituencies, was still to come, and as the experience of Whig magnates in 1710 demonstrates, the interests of even the biggest proprietors could not at this stage be relied on to deliver the goods against an adverse political tide.

In any event, it is more illuminating to see our problem in a quite different perspective, one which until recently has been neglected. This becomes possible if we try to view the political scene from the 1680s through to the 1720s in its social context, as well as against the background of economic advance already referred to.[4] Augustan society has been labelled 'the Divided Society' (5), and in the sense that much of its social life was overshadowed by party political rivalry (Ch. 21) this is no misnomer. Yet social divisions, as such, were less pervasive. The 'conflict of interests' between the landed and monied sectors after the early 1690s was real enough, but its stresses were chiefly confined to London and those south-eastern and East Anglian counties on which the Land Tax fell most heavily. Elsewhere it was a more superficial problem, productive rather of political propaganda than of a genuine sense of social grievance (70, *xliii–lxii;* cf. Ch. 18 above). The blackest mark against the true 'monied man', as we saw, was that he did not (during the wars, at least) buy land in sufficient quantity, and so share the obligations as well as the privileges of the landed class. But this was not, by and large, true of the most successful merchant families outside London; nor was it true of many of the army and navy officers, or even of some of the new civil servants, whose rise after 1689 also caused discontent among the established social hierarchy. Ambitious admirals, such as Russell, soon ploughed their profits into *terra firma*, as did most of Marlborough's protégés, while some prominent government officials, among them Lowndes, the doyen of the Treasury, also purchased estates. Thus they bought their tickets of acceptance into county society. The advance of the professions, including older professions such as medicine and the law, made a more positive contribution than this to the foundations of stability. As the most active vehicles of social mobility in late Stuart and early Hanoverian England, taking on board recruits from very varied backgrounds (226a), they vitally promoted the development of that 'sense of common identity' within the political nation which, sooner or later, was to subsume and neutralise divisions that were essentially party-induced.

The expanding professions of the day (Chs. 4, 18) had a further contribution to make to the ultimate stabilisation of politics. Without totally dominating any of them, the English gentry, and especially those lesser landed families whose economic position was least viable, found in the professions thousands of congenial homes: habitations above all for their younger sons, but also, in surprising numbers, for heirs and even heads of families. In this way a problem which had been so acute for the English gentry earlier in the seventeenth century, and had manifestly damaged their relations with a clique-ridden early-Stuart court, was solved by a combination of two factors: greatly increased job opportunities,[5] and demographic trends which wrought significant reductions in the size of families (Chs. 2, 19) and therefore in the number of job-hunters of gentle birth. It is feasible to detect in this interaction of circumstances an answer to one of the political conundrums of the period which is otherwise difficult to resolve: why it was that when the Whig gentry after 1681, and the Tories for far longer after 1714, were faced through political proscription with the prospect of permanent exclusion from the lucrative patronage of the Crown (and in most cases from all marks of local distinction as well), they were not reduced to desperation? The meagre, or at best hesitant support which both the Monmouth rebels of 1685 and the Jacobite rebels of 1715 attracted from the English landed classes tells us much about the underlying social equipoise which the country was already attaining. And without social stability, political stability would not have been achievable.

The same also held good lower down the social ladder. Although the barometer of politics read 'unsettled', at best, for most of the period from the 1680s to the early 1720s, a remarkable feature of the climate was that the storms that blew up with such regularity were very largely confined to the high-political ground. The likelihood after 1685 that serious conflicts at the centre would acquire a major popular and radical dimension was always remote. The fears experienced briefly in December 1688 never materialised. Subsequently Whigs and Tories successfully confined their rancorous feuding within the established political nation; so that when, spasmodically, popular elements did become involved in them (for instance, in elections or in the Sacheverell riots) they conformed almost slavishly to the establishment rules of the game, rather than to any disturbing new rules concocted from below. Such developments immeasurably improved the prospects for a settled long-term political climate, especially as they were (not coincidentally) paralleled by an improvement in the living standards of the lower orders.

We are aware already of the demographic reasons why, after 1670 or thereabouts, there was far less pressure on basic food resources than there had been in the early seventeenth century; likewise how, at the very time that the population rise of Tudor and early Stuart times was ending, agrarian improvements were leading to a marked increase in productivity (Ch. 2). The effect on the standards of living of wage labourers, artisans and others of 'the poorer sort' was striking. It was in the later decades of the seventeenth century that the 'English working-man' (to borrow a convenient modern phrase) began to be regarded with growing envy in other parts of Europe. He himself had heard tell of the abject poverty of the peasants of France or Spain or Italy and regarded it with a mixture of pity and contempt, so that, along with his shouts of 'No Popery!' in 1679 and 1680, he bellowed 'no black bread! no wooden shoes!'. In 1694, in *The Present State of England*, Edward Chamberlayne elaborated on these themes:

> There is in England great plenty of excellent leather for all sorts of uses, insomuch that the poorest people wear good shoes of leather; whereas in our neighbouring countries, the poor generally wear either shoes of wood or none at all; whilst the poorest of our labourers have not only shoes, but good strong leather boots too, to preserve 'em from cold when they work in ditches or other wet places.

Chamberlayne also pointed to another striking contrast with the Continental peasantry in the exceptional physical fitness of the English poor in his day, who 'after 12 hours hard work . . . will go in the evening to football . . ., cricket, prison-base, wrestling, cudgel-playing, or some such like vehement exercise for their recreation.'[6] Without an adequate diet, reasonably cheaply come by, such fitness would not have been possible. More than anything else, the amount of meat consumed in late seventeenth- and eighteenth-century England, even by the labouring classes, was a source of wonder to visitors from abroad. It was no coincidence that in the 1720s Robert Leveridge, a well-known bass singer of the day, made a popular hit out of the song 'The Roast Beef of Old England'.

In George I's reign, despite the intervening years of war, disturbing the economy and throwing internal taxation for the first time on absolute necessities of life [see G.2(iii) (b) & (c)], those of the poor who were in employment still boasted their own relative prosperity. Modest though it was, at least it set them apart from their counterparts in all Continental countries of any size, except Holland. More often than not, their wages had risen – in some cases substantially – since before the Revolution [cf. M.2 on *real* wages]. Scarcity of labour, for example in the building trades, was one factor in this rise. The growth of certain key industries or branches of trade (Ch. 19) not only increased the demand for labour in the towns concerned but sometimes stimulated wages in their rural hinterlands. Here and there, too, as in some Devon textile towns, wage rises were helped by the activities of workmen's clubs, early forerunners of trade unions. The naval dockyards paid excellent wages while the wars against Louis XIV's France lasted; afterwards they retained the men they needed and laid off the rest in thousands (167 [Coleman]). That was the way of the early eighteenth-century world, a world where for the lower orders *employment* was everything.

There were, of course, a great many unemployed, at all times, in the England and Wales of William III, Anne and George I: a lot of them seasonal, it is true, but all of them a recurring source of anxiety to those householders who, in addition to all the new state taxation, now contributed in bad years, such as the mid-1690s, more heavily than ever before to the local Poor Rate. But as regards those in work, the comments of Daniel Defoe, penned in 1724, have an obvious bearing on the coming of stability. 'Even those we call poor people, journeymen, working and pains-taking people, do thus: they lie warm, live in plenty, work hard and [need] know no want' (194, *144*). A rose-tinted picture, no doubt, especially if applied to the village labourer of the period with no by-employment. The 'plenty' was but relative. Yet, such as it was, it was a sturdy plant with roots going back four or five decades, and there is strong presumptive evidence that a truly indigenous species of popular politics, at this level, was quite unable to flourish in its shade.

When British politics did once more begin to develop a new subculture, with unsettling effects, in the mid-eighteenth century, it was 'the middling sort' rather than the lower orders who were most actively involved in it. Yet in post-Revolution England, despite their often volatile electoral behaviour they, like the landed classes, were acquiring a strong vested interest in the achievement and continuance of political stability. Admittedly, they too had their economic problems. There was in England between 1690 and the 1720s an unquestioned rise in the cost of many consumer commodities other than basic foodstuffs, a fact which contemporaries unhesitatingly attributed to the New Taxation. Archibald Hutcheson, economist and MP for Hastings, argued in 1721 that if the excise and additional customs duties which had been imposed since the 1690s were to be abolished, the people would be enabled 'to live at least 20 per cent cheaper than they at present do.'[7] And although professional men, tradesmen, shopkeepers and superior craftsmen had not been much afflicted by the Land Tax, they had reason enough to agree with their spokesman, Defoe, in 1726 that 'family expenses are extremely risen'.

> . . . all articles of foreign importation are increased in value to the consumer by the high duties laid on them; such as linen [and] . . . silk, especially foreign-wrought silk. Almost all things eatable, drinkable and wearable are made heavy to us by high and exorbitant customs and excises; as brandies, tobacco, sugar, deals and timber for building, oil, wine, . . . chocolate, coffee, tea.[8]

And yet the same author, to his amazement, noted something else as well. Although the *cost* of living had risen, war and its aftermath had not cut back one iota the much higher *standard* of living which families of the middle rank had come to expect by the later years of the seventeenth century. A more varied agriculture and industrial diversification had both helped to raise their social expectations. The Commercial Revolution had done even more. Not only that; to the mortification of Defoe's Puritan spirit, he found that many such families were actually spending more and more in an effort to raise those living standards still further. There was, he observed, 'a load of pride upon the temper of the nation which, in spite of taxes and the unusual dearness of everything, yet prompts people to a profusion in their expenses';[9] he was particularly shocked at the prodigality of the ordinary London tradesmen and their families, with their wine cellars, tea-tables and silver coffee-pots! Such men were not of the stuff of which true political malcontents would be made. They had, on the contrary, much to gain from a reduction of the political temperature, creating the right conditions for low-budget government and a high-profit economy.

The atmosphere in which such a reduction could take place was thus lightening unobtrusively in various aspects well before Britain entered the Walpole era. To understand why post-Revolution politics was slow to respond to those underlying trends and pressures, one must take account of the strength of the contrary forces at work. The sheer violence of the warfare between Whigs and Tories needs no further comment; we are also familiar with two other destabilising elements closely connected with it: the constitutional stresses which still persisted after 1688–9 and the ideological turbulence which had been so characteristic of seventeenth-century England and showed little sign of subsiding as late as the second decade of the eighteenth. Furthermore, however much contemporaries overplayed the *extent* of the 'conflict of interests', it is not in dispute that social tensions within the governing classes produced by the French wars remained an unsettling influence on politics, at least down to the Peace of Utrecht, and to a limited degree even longer (49, *18–19*; Ch. 18). Then there were those specific problems which remained unsolved by the Glorious Revolution and which, so long as they defied resolution, would put the achievement of lasting political stability beyond reach. By far the most urgent of these in and after 1689 were the interlinked problems of a precarious Protestant succession and of a disaffected Ireland and Scotland, threatening to keep open inviting doors to a Stuart restoration. Finally, there was the more general political problem of how the Crown was to manage Parliament, one that mostly baffled William III, as we have seen. Plumb's analysis of the vitiating factors frustrating the quest for stability gave a particular prominence to the inability of the executive to control the Westminster legislature; he judges it one of the foremost achievements of the post–1714 Whigs, and above all of Walpole after 1721, that they contrived to weld Court and Parliament together into an effective working partnership. At the heart of the quandary for the Crown and its ministers was not only the strength of party passions but, as Plumb sees it, the age-old intractability of the English gentry: the ingrained spirit of independence of those landed families who still dominated the Commons' back benches and who (it is said) persistently defied Court attempts to marshal and discipline them.

The argument is a persuasive one, up to a point, but it is possible to take it too far. In a memorable passage, Sir John suggests that an antipathy to *any* kind of strong government was bred in the bone of the English landed interest, and he sees it as no more than an extension of a 'tradition of conspiracy, riot, plot and revolt among the ruling class that stretched back to the Normans' (28, *19*). Yet even before the Glorious Revolution it is hard to find convincing evidence of such an anarchistic outlook. After all, except in Essex's Rising at the end of

Elizabeth's reign (a highly personal and idiosyncratic affair) no one of any significance had taken up arms against established authority in England in over seven decades from 1570 to 1642. And following the long nightmare of civil dissension between 1642 and 1660 it was not only Charles II's Cavalier supporters who experienced a deep longing for lasting domestic peace and a settled political order. The troubles of the decade from 1678–88 do not constitute conclusive proof that this desire had evaporated. Rather they demonstrate that there were sections of the propertied classes which were simply not prepared to accept the kind of stability which Charles I's two sons by then had in mind, one based on an authoritarian, and ultimately a Catholic-autocratic, solution to the nation's religious and constitutional problems.

Awareness of the danger of drifting into a new civil war, and fears fanned by regular reminders from Anglican pulpits of the sinful horror of the regicide of 1649, remained acute fully seventy years after Charles I's death on the Whitehall scaffold (16, *185*; 314, *Ch. 5*). They offered probably the strongest of all the incentives which Britons had after 1689 to work out their problems peaceably and to continue the search for their secure political anchorage. The storms of the next quarter of a century must not, therefore, be misinterpreted. For contrary to appearances, through all the furious electoral and parliamentary clashes between parties, the party men who engaged in them did hold to their own, perfectly valid ideal of stability. To them it was something that could be achieved constitutionally, by erecting within the framework of their new political system and under a limited monarchy a clear and permanent supremacy for *their own party*. They failed, down to Queen Anne's death at least. But their failure was not implicit in the existence of parties, as such. Things might well have been different, even before 1714, if only the attitude of the two monarchs and of the leading political 'undertakers' of the day – the men who, in effect, constructed most post-Revolution ministries and who managed all of Anne's – had been closer to that of the party leaders (Ch. 21). As it was, however, bitter experience proved over two reigns that the dogged pursuit of coalition government in the interests of stability – even if the balance of forces within them was uneven – could only defeat the ultimate purpose the Crown had in view. Such a strategy made it more, rather than less, difficult for it to control the legislature.

But that is only one side of the picture. One has only to compare relations between Crown and Parliament in the second half of Anne's reign with the parliamentary mayhem committed by the Country opposition to King William's ministers in the early and late 1690s to realise that the Crown and its managers did in time learn from their unhappy experiences. Such is the smoke and fury of the party battlefield, it is easy to lose sight of the crucial fact that throughout the entire joint lifespan of Anne's last three Parliaments, from 1708–14, her ministries suffered only one major defeat (over the 1713 Commerce Treaty with France) in the course of six sessions (see above, pp. 206–7). It was no coincidence that the Godolphin-Junto administration from November 1708, and the Harley administration from the summer of 1711 were, at Cabinet level anyhow, virtually single-party ministries. By 1708 the lesson which Sunderland had tried to teach William III and the politicians in the 1690s, had been sufficiently absorbed by Queen

Anne's managers (though much later, and more reluctantly, by the Queen herself) to make a notable contribution in the next six years to the viability of her last two ministries.[10] Although each ministry, in turn, foundered, it was certainly not parliamentary weakness which was primarily responsible for that. Exactly the same can be said of the first administration of George I's reign (1714–17), which did have a tiny Hanoverian Tory presence down to the time of Nottingham's resignation from the Cabinet in 1716, but which was in essence a party ministry. Significantly, the parliamentary difficulties which its successor, the Whig Stanhope-Sunderland administration, subsequently encountered (Chs. 13, 23) were due not to any trimming between the parties but to the fact that *its* single-party base was too narrow. That fact was duly recognised and rectified by the readmission of Walpole and Townshend in June 1720, less than six months after the sealing of the ministry's fateful bargain with the South Sea Company. And it was just as well that the party closed ranks when it did: otherwise the ministry, and conceivably even that Whig supremacy on which the solidity of the British state was to rest over the next four decades, might not have survived the wave of public anger which followed the collapse of the stock market that autumn (Ch. 17).

Although it was the political events of Anne's reign which first pushed Britain towards the logic of a party system of government, it was the achievement of the post–1714 Whigs to bring the administration of the state into the hands of a one-party oligarchy, thus realising probably the most basic condition of the stable political world of the classic Hanoverian age. It was they, too, who consolidated that oligarchy by eroding and finally taming the electorate, thereby fulfilling a scarcely less crucial condition (Ch. 21). The Junto had striven towards a party lotus land in the mid-1690s, and again from 1708–10; so had the High Tories under Rochester and Nottingham at the beginning of Anne's reign; while the self-confessed aim of Secretary of State St John and those of his way of thinking in the years 1710–14 had, as we have seen (Ch. 16 and p. 347 above) been 'to fill the employments of the kingdom down to the meanest with Tories.'[11] Even so, the heirs of the Junto after 1715–16 would not have succeeded where their predecessors of both parties had been frustrated without three changes in the working of the post-Revolution political system, all of which took place after Queen Anne's death (cf. Ch. 21). Success was contingent on the presence of a monarch prepared to acquiesce in single-party rule, and no less on an end to the 'managerial' approach to ministry-making, which for much of the period 1693–1714 had interposed a few essentially extra-party politicians between the party bosses and their hopes of capturing the full favour of the Crown. Most important of all, it depended on the decline of one of the great political parties to the point at which it could no longer mount serious competition for power. George I, though prepared at the start of his reign to placate those 'Whimsical' Tories who in the interests of Hanover had opposed the Oxford ministry in Parliament in 1713–14, was quite unlike his two predecessors in having no fixed aversion to one-party government. Indeed, after 1716 he was ready positively to abet the creation of oligarchy: a brief flirtation with the Tories before the government reshuffle of 1720 being more a mark of his dislike of 'the Walpoleans'

– alias the Prince of Wales's party (see below, p. 396) – than of any serious conversion to the idea of mixed ministries. Meanwhile, the post-Revolution breed of political brokers and managers, who had manoeuvred so skilfully between the Crown and the parties for a generation, had died out with the fall of Oxford in July 1714 and the resignation later that year of the duke of Shrewsbury, Anne's deathbed choice for the Lord Treasurer's staff. As for the decline of the Tories to a position which condemned them to permanent minority status in Parliament, this did not happen quite so quickly (Chs. 21–2). But by the aftermath of the 1722 Election, if not earlier, it was a *fait accompli*.

For all their impressive parliamentary strength and proven electoral support the Tories found themselves in the summer of 1714, when Queen Anne relapsed into her final illness, a sorely divided party unable to control events. They were distracted by leadership problems, the protracted struggle for control of the ministry between Oxford and Bolingbroke (St John) having only just been resolved by Oxford's dismissal, and even then not conclusively in Bolingbroke's favour. In addition, for over a year they had been racked by mounting disagreements over the succession. In 1714 this issue precipitated not simply two organised factions of Jacobite and Hanoverian Tories but a large and palpably unorganised centre group – in the Commons it numbered well over half the party's MPs – whose members sat uneasily on the fence on the great matter of whether to stand by the Act of Settlement or not; they were neither wholeheartedly ministerialist nor wholeheartedly 'Country'. The Pretender's final flat refusal in March 1714 to change his religion and become even nominally Anglican (105, *188*) was a severe setback to a party whose relations with Hanover had been bad ever since the revelation of the Anglo-French peace preliminaries in October 1711 (above, pp. 205–6). Even the Jacobite party at Westminster had periodically urged on James Edward a politic conversion (105, *47, 102–3*). The split among the rank-and-file was not in itself fatal; in fact, by the time the 1715 Election campaign was under way the Tories at that level were able to put on a surprisingly united front. But while it lasted it was a horrendous political liability. The damage to their leadership, on the other hand, was never repaired – at least, not until it was too late. The fall of Oxford, the flight of Bolingbroke to escape the consequences of impeachment proceedings in 1715, and the apostasy of Nottingham left a vacuum which was never filled as long as the Tories had a realistic chance of breaking the initially-vulnerable Whig supremacy. That chance had already diminished by the end of 1715. The refusal of the party's two most respected commoners, William Bromley and Sir Thomas Hanmer, to accept the King's invitation to take office at the start of the reign was a serious tactical blunder (73a); the tone of Tory election propaganda was off-key, and some of it gratuitously offensive to George I and his German entourage, and the vast majority of English Tories, by failing either enthusiastically to support or robustly to oppose the 'Fifteen, left themselves wide open to an organised Whig campaign of denigration. Nevertheless, the 1715 General Election, though bad for the Tories, was not a total disaster and they were left with numbers in the new House of Commons appreciably larger than the Whigs had been able to muster in 1713–14 [E.1(iii)–(iv)]. By the time the Whig schism took place in 1717 the

Tories' morale had recovered and, further stimulated by a spectacular quarrel between the King and his son and heir, Prince George, who with Princess Caroline set up his own rival court at Leicester House, their hopes of a *renversement* soared (81a, *193*).

Alas for the Tory party, these proved unrealistic hopes. In fact, the blow which, more than any other, was to ruin their prospects decisively had already been struck. The passing of the Septennial Act in 1716 (Chs. 13, 21) gave the Whigs invaluable protection from a resurgent Toryism over a crucial period of four years when their ascendancy was distinctly fragile. By a legislative device they were able to evade the judgement of the electorate, first in 1718 when their own infighting was at its most bitter, and then three years later, when South Sea debris still littered the scene, and when Whig leadership was again in disarray (*The Age of Oligarchy*, Ch. 1). By 1722, when an election at last became legally obligatory, the worst of the danger to the Whigs was passed and the Tories' 170 seats (ultimately – after the hearing of petitions) out of 558 was scant reward for the large number of constituencies they contested then (81a, *199*; cf. E.1(iv)). These lost opportunities were all the more galling to them because they had already, and swiftly, been reduced to ineffectuality in the House of Lords. By 1723 it would have required nothing short of a constitutional outrage to restore their position there to one of parity, let alone supremacy, and the most priceless asset the Whigs had enjoyed after their own crushing electoral defeats in 1710 and 1713 was thus denied to their opponents. Over the next four decades the Tories were to achieve a miracle of survival against the odds but were never able seriously to disturb the 'Venetian oligarchy' of the Old Corps Whigs under Walpole and the Pelhams (*The Age of Oligarchy*, Chs. 3, 5, 18).

The year of 1723, when the Atterbury conspirators were brought to justice and Bishop Atterbury himself was despatched into exile by a Bill of Pains and Penalties (163b, *223–75*), also marks the point at which the succession problem, while remaining a factor in government policy, and in that of hostile powers until after the Austrian Succession War, ceased to be a threat of any substance to the accomplishment of political stability. The likelihood of any further threat from Ireland after the war of 1689–91 was remote: the ruthless Williamite settlement saw to that (*The Age of Oligarchy*, Ch. 16). The problem of Scotland, which by its involvement with the succession issue threatened for a while to capsize the whole post-Revolution ship (Ch. 20), took longer to resolve, but the vital step, the creation of the incorporating Union, was taken in 1706–7 (and it is worth recording, in view of the debate over the timing of the growth of political stability, that the initial making of the Union owed little by and large to that younger generation of Whigs which ruled the roost after 1714). The importance of the legislation regulating and safeguarding the Protestant succession, notably that of 1701 and 1706, has already been stressed. The avoidance of an attempted Jacobite *coup* immediately after Anne's death was arguably the most critical obstacle which had to be surmounted in the long haul towards a politically stable Britain; the Whigs, who in opposition had already begun to make military plans against just such a contingency (78, *142–4*), would certainly have answered force with force. And what did most to snuff out that threat, Tory divisions apart, was the fact that the arrangements made back in 1706 for a regency, to exercise caretaker control over the executive, worked smoothly in the crisis precipitated by Anne's sudden death. The prior nomination of the regency council by the Elector of Hanover[12] ensured, furthermore, that many leading Whigs would be brought back into play at a moment of supreme psychological importance, not only for them but for the prospects of a peaceful transition from one ruling family to another. Of course, no lasting security for the Protestant succession could be even cautiously predicted until after the Jacobite rebellion of 1715–16 had been suppressed. But the fact that by the time the rebellion broke out Hanover was safely installed, and a Whig ministry well entrenched, with its intelligence system in excellent order and adequate forces and war-hardened generals to call on, made the prospects for the Pretender's venture bleak from the start (*The Age of Oligarchy*, Ch. 6).

By June 1723, when HMS *Aldborough* bore off the disgraced Atterbury and with him the last hopes of Jacobite conspiracy before the 1740s, Stanhope and Sunderland – both relatively young men – had also been removed from the scene by death, and Walpole had begun to assert his massive authority over the government and over his party (*The Age of Oligarchy*, Ch. 1). Looking back, it is now clear that, as he did so, the long battle for stability which Britons had been waging since the end of Tudor times was almost won. Almost, but not quite. Walpole yet had his own distinctive contribution to make to the completion and consolidation of that victory. Over the next decade and a half he was to perfect the most sophisticated and systematic patronage system the country had seen, and apply it with complete single-mindedness to cementing the position of the dynasty and of his party and rendering the latter, at least, quite impregnable. More important, he put the coping stone on the edifice of stability by doing what no previous ministry since the end of the Spanish Succession War had attempted: he deliberately adopted policies calculated to conciliate those elements in the political nation which were still disaffected. Except for a serious misjudgement in 1736 (*The Age of Oligarchy*, Ch. 7) he set himself to allay the fears of the Anglican clergy; and he kept steadily in mind the interests of the hard-pressed 'mere' gentry, some 15–20,000 men of strong local influence whose normal political stance was one of gut Toryism. While social and economic trends had already done much to foster that 'sense of common identity' which characterised the British ruling class in the middle decades of the eighteenth century (above, pp. 388–9), it was Walpole's conciliatory consensus policies which sealed the bond. Whether it was a positive consensus he achieved, or rather a consensual indifference, may remain debatable. What is to the point here is that not until his heyday were the great majority of landowners, merchants, financiers and professionals alike enabled to identify their own separate interests with the interests of the government within the framework of a common establishment.

To see Robert Walpole as the sole architect of political stability in mid-eighteenth-century England, however, is unjustified. As this chapter has sought to show, he took over not only a pile of building materials but a largely-finished structure. What is more, the climate of the 1720s and 1730s could not have been much more favourable, in many respects, for bringing the work of his predecessors to fruition. By the time he became indisputably prime minister, the ideological content of post-Revolution politics was already diluted (Chs. 23–4); the fire had largely been taken out of the 'conflict of interests' by nine years of almost unbroken remission from foreign wars; Toryism was deflated and Jacobitism little more than a forlorn hope. Not least, the patronage of the Crown, its value enhanced by Septennial Parliaments, had already been merged with that of the Whig oligarchs into what was virtually a single, comprehensive system. Walpole's achievements over the next twenty years were certainly extraordinary (*The Age of Oligarchy*, Ch. 5). But in many ways he was fortunate in his inheritance.

---

1. The Whigs gained ground in William's ministry in 1689, 1693, 1694, 1697 and 1701–2; the Tories in 1690, 1692, 1699 (slightly) and 1700.
2. Danby (by then duke of Leeds) absented himself from the Council 1695–9, but was not replaced as Lord President until 1699.
3. For example place legislation (Ch. 22), together with post-war pruning of the armed forces and the bureaucracy, significantly reduced the jobs and commissions available in George I's reign.
4. The arguments that follow are more fully developed in G. Holmes (49).
5. New openings in both overseas and internal trade also made some contribution here.
6. E. Chamberlayne, *Angliae Notitia: or the Present State of England* (1694 edn), pp. 45, 52; cf. Mme van Muyden, ed., *A Foreign View of England in the Reigns of George I and George II: The Letters of César de Saussure* (1902), pp. 293–6.
7. *A Collection of Treatises relating to the National Debts and Funds* (1721), quoted in E.L. Hargreaves, *The National Debt* (1930), p. 32.
8. D. Defoe, *The Complete English Tradesman* (1726–7) (1745 edn), I, pp. 76, 77.
9. Ibid. p. 73.
10. Compare, however, the more sceptical view of Oxford's conversion put by Daniel Szechi in (105), p. 196 and *passim*.
11. Viscount Bolingbroke, *A Letter to Sir William Wyndham* (1717/1753), p. 22.
12. The councillors' names had been secreted in the so-called 'black box', opened only after Anne had died.

COMPENDIUM OF INFORMATION

A. GLOSSARY

Arianism: an heretical but moderate revision of the Church doctrine of the Trinity, originating with Arius (*c.* 250–*c.* 336). Arians held that Christ the Son, though divine and created by God the Father before his physical birth on earth, had not co-existed with Him from eternity – he was therefore 'more than man but less than God'. (See also **Socinianism**; for a further, and valuable explanation of these two Christian heresies, see also J.C.D. Clark (321), p. 281).

Armigerous: [of 'gentle'/noble families] having the right to bear coats of arms approved by the College of Heralds.

Assiento: an exclusive contract awarded by the Spanish crown for the supply of slaves [normally Negroes from West Africa] to Spain's New World colonies.

Board of Regulators: or 'Commission of Regulation', instituted 14 November 1687 to supervise the process of purging the borough corporations of members hostile to James II's tolerationist policies and replacing them with loyal councillors and officials; work on the ground performed by local 'regulators' responsible to a sub-committee of the Board, under Robert Brent.

Burgage boroughs: a type of borough represented in Parliament under the unreformed electoral system (pre-1832), distinguished by the limiting of its franchise to either the owners or tenants of ancient pieces of real estate – buildings or plots of land – called 'burgages'.

Deism: a form of 'natural religion' characterised by (1) a rationalist belief in the existence of a Supreme Being, envisaged (on the evidence of the natural world) as a remote and detached Creator, and not as a pervasive, all-powerful judge of men; and (2) rejection of all the elements of mystery and revelation in orthodox Christianity and of the authority of any priesthood.

Durante bene placito: commissions issued to judges *durante bene placito*, i.e. during [the King's] good pleasure, meant that they were dismissible at will: last issued in James II's reign.

Erastianism: the belief that the Church was subordinate to the state and should be subject to ultimate control by the lay authorities.

Gravitation (Newton's Law of): having demonstrated in his *Principia* (1687) that motion was 'the rearrangement of atoms in space during time', and that one of its two most important governing causes was the force of gravity, or 'the action of atoms upon one another at a distance' [R. Briggs (303b, *76*)], Newton propounded his inverse-square law of universal gravitation, which stated 'that every body exerts over every other body an attractive force proportional to the square of the distance between them' [A.G.R. Smith (303a, *132*)].

Habeas Corpus: short title of a writ which could be sued out to procure the release (or bail) of persons imprisoned without charge, or charged but not brought to trial. The Habeas Corpus Act of 1679 made the issuing of such a writ obligatory on the Lord Chancellor and all Common Law judges, except in cases of alleged treason.

'Non-Resisting Test': the declaration and oath provided for in the earl of Danby's bill of 1675 against 'disaffected persons': (1) declaring taking up arms against the King 'on any pretence whatsoever' to be unlawful; (2) swearing not to endeavour to alter the government in church or state. To be taken and sworn by all office holders and members of Parliament. After a protracted and bitter struggle, April–June, the bill failed.

'Political Nation': as used in this volume, a term signifying that part of the population of Britain which was politically-conscious or aware, either through occupying positions of influence, however modest, in public affairs, central or local; or through ownership of property; or through participation in the election of members of Parliament. (For the 'alternative political nation' of the 1760s – the term coined by John Brewer (92) – see *The Age of Oligarchy*, Ch. 3.)

Quamdiu se bene gesserint: commissions issued to judges *quamdiu se bene gesserint*, i.e. 'during their good behaviour', meant that they had effective security of tenure, except on evidence of manifest incapacity or corruption, or on the accession of a new monarch.

Queen Anne's Bounty: the supplementation of the incomes of 'poor clergy' of the Church of England (in practice those holding livings of less than £35 p.a. until 1718 and less than £50 p.a. thereafter) from a fund established by Act of Parliament in 1704. Queen Anne's voluntary surrender of the crown's income from first-fruits and tenths formed the basis of the fund, but disbursements from it were much augmented subsequently by private charitable bequests.

Quo Warranto: writs calling for the surrender and legal scrutiny of a charter of rights. Used by the governments of Charles II and James II especially against borough charters of incorporation. (Because of the expense and difficulty, or futility, of resistance to them, the mere threat of a *quo warranto* would often be enough to frighten boroughs into surrender).

Socinianism: a more extreme anti-Trinitarian heresy than Arianism (see above), named after the 16th-century Pole, Faustus Socinus (d. 1604). Socinians denied the divinity of Christ, asserting that he had had no pre-existence before he was born of the Virgin Mary, and radical Socinians denied that Christ died to redeem, or atone for, the sins of mankind.

B. POPULATION AND SOCIAL STRUCTURE

B.1: Estimated population of England and Wales at decadal intervals and in some other years of interest, 1541–1721

(totals in millions)

	England with Monmouthshire	*England and Wales**
1541	2.774	(2.968)
1601	4.110	(4.398)
1641	5.092	(5.449)
1657	5.284	(5.654)[1]
1661	5.141	(5.501)
1671	4.982	(5.331)
1681	4.930	(5.275)
1686	4.865	(5.205)[2]
1691	4.931	(5.276)
1696	4.962	(5.309)[3]
1701	5.058	(5.412)
1711	5.230	(5.596)
1721	5.350	(5.725)

* The estimate for Wales, without Monmouthshire, has been arrived at by following Wrigley and Schofield's recommended method of calculating 7% of the population of England, ((196), p. 566, note 20).

Notes:
1. 17th-century peak.
2. 17th-century low point.
3. Cf. Gregory King's contemporary estimate (Ch. 2 above).

Source:
E.A. Wrigley and R.S. Schofield (196), Table A3.3, pp. 531–4; estimate reached by back-projection.

B.2: The urban population of England and Wales: estimated growth of some leading towns, 1600–1792

(i) Some recent rough estimates of the population of London

	Wrigley (1967)		*Finlay and Shearer (1986)*
1600	200,000		200,000
1650	400,000		375,000
1700	575,000		490,000
1750	675,000		
1775		[c. 750,000]	
1801 (census)		948,040	

Sources:
1. E.A. Wrigley (188b).
2. R. Finlay and B. Shearer, 'Population growth and suburban expansion', in A.L. Beier and R. Finlay, eds (188a). Their estimates, based on exhaustive study of all surviving parish register evidence, are the most authoritative yet published.

(ii) Provincial urban growth

Year	Bath	Birmingham	Bolton	Bristol	Chester	Coventry	Derby
1792							
1789			11,739*				
1788							8,563*
1786							
1785							
1784							
1781		c.50,000					
1779							
1778		42,350*					
1775	20,500			55,000		c.14,500	
1774					14,713*		
1773			4,568*				
1771							
1762							
1758							
1755							
1752							
1750	9,000	23,688*	c.4,000				
1749						12,817*	
1748							
1740							
1739							
1736							
1730							
1725				c.30,000			
1722					11,000		
1719							
1717							
1713							
1712							4,000
1710							
1700			2–3,000		c.8,000		
1695				19,403*			
1694						6,710*	
1693							
1692							
1690		7,000/9,000‡					
1676		c.4,400					
1673							
1672							
1670							
1665							
1664					c.7,500		
1662							
1660	1,100						

‡ varying estimates
* indicates returns from local censuses
† indicates population of parish (as opposed to township)
$ house-count

Hull	Ipswich	Leeds[2]	Leicester	Liverpool	Manchester (with Salford)	
22,286*						1792
						1789
					c.50,000[3]	1788
				41,600		1786
		12,784*				1785
						1784
						1781
						1779
						1778
13,500		17,121*				1775
						1774
				34,407*	27,246*	1773
		16,380*				1771
						1762
					19,839*	1758
	12,124*					1755
						1752
		12,000	c.8,000	22,000		1750
						1749
						1748
						1740
						1739
						1736
				c.15,000		1730
		c.10,000				1725
						1722
						1719
					10–12,000$	1717
						1713
			6,450*			1712
				8,186		1710
6,000[1]		8,000†		5,145	c.8,000	1700
	7,943*					1695
						1694
						1693
						1692
		6,500		c.4,000		1690
						1676
				c.1,500		1673
						1672
			c.4,800			1670
						1665
						1664
	c.8,000					1662
					c.5,000	1660

Notes to B.2 (ii)
1. The population was 7,500 with Sculcoates.
2. In 1775 the parish population figure was 30,400.
3. The population was 42,821 excluding Salford.

(ii) Provincial urban growth (*cont.*)

	Newcastle-on-Tyne[4]	Norwich	Nottingham	Plymouth[5]	Portsmouth[6]
1792					
1789					
1788					
1786		41,051			
1785					
1784					
1781					
1779			17,711*		
1778					
1775	33,000		16,510*	25,000	20,000
1774					
1773					
1771					
1762					
1758					
1755					
1752		36,169*			
1750	29,000				
1749					
1748					10,000†
1740				c.12,000	
1739			10,720*		
1736					
1730	20,000†				
1725			9,800		
1722					
1719					
1717					
1713					
1712					
1710					
1700	16,000	31,000*	7,000	8,500	7,500
1695		28,546			
1694					
1693					
1692					
1690					
1676			c.5,500		
1673					
1672					
1670					
1665	c.13,000$				
1664					3,500
1662		c.20,000			
1660					

‡ varying estimates
* indicates returns from local censuses
† indicates population of parish (as opposed to township)
$ house-count

Sheffield[7]	Sunderland	Whitehaven	Wolverhampton	Yarmouth	
					1792
					1789
26,538		11,368*			1788
					1786
					1785
				12,608*	1784
					1781
					1779
					1778
	16,000	9,665*			1775
					1774
					1773
					1771
		9,063*			1762
					1758
12,983					1755
					1752
		7,454*			1750
					1749
					1748
					1740
					1739
9,695*					1736
		6,000			1730
					1725
					1722
	6,000				1719
					1717
		4,000			1713
					1712
					1710
3,500				11,000	1700
					1695
					1694
		2,222*			1693
c.2,600					1692
	2,000				1690
					1676
					1673
c.2,100					1672
					1670
					1665
					1664
				c.10,000	1662
		c.200			1660

Notes to B.2 (ii)

4. The 1750 and 1775 figures included Gateshead.
5. The figures include the Dock; in 1740 the population figure was 8,400 excluding the Dock.
6. After 1702 the figures include Southsea.
7. In 1672 the parish population figure was 4,500, in 1736 it was 14,000 and in 1775 it was 27,000.

Note on sources: for B.2 (ii)

The statistics of town growth have to be viewed with some reserve, at least in the first 60–70 years of our period. But with the help of Hearth Tax figures, 1662–88, returns from the Compton census of 1676, returns of population made in response to the Act of 1695 (above, p. 44) and the ever-increasing number of local censuses and house-counts taken from the early decades of the 18th century onwards, urban historians have been able to arrive at figures for most leading towns and cities which are a reliable guide to growth patterns. These patterns can be delineated still more confidently in a few cases with the aid of cartographical evidence and artists' 'prospects' that are precise and valuable. As well as studies of particular towns and counties, the following secondary sources have been used in compiling the above table: C.M. Law, 'Some Notes on the Urban Population of England and Wales in the 18th Century', *Local Historian*, **10** (1972); P.J. Corfield, (a) 'Urban Development in England and Wales in the sixteenth and seventeenth centuries', in D.C. Coleman and A.H. John, eds (174); (b) (252); C.W. Chalklin (254); P.N. Borsay (250).

B.3: Some estimates of the population of Ireland and Scotland, 1678–1801

(i) The population of Ireland, 1678–1791[1] (millions)

1678	2.167	1772	3.584
1712	2.791	1777	3.740
1718	2.894	1781	4.048
1725	3.042	1785	4.019
1726	3.031	1788	4.389
1732	3.018	1790	4.591
1754	3.191	1791	4.753
1767	3.480		

(ii) The population of Scotland, 1700–1801 (millions)[2]

1707	1.048[3]
1755	1.265
1795	1.526
1801	1.608[4]

Estimates of Scotland's population that are based on anything more than guesswork, and solid data on which to base modern demographic 'back projections', are so rare in Scotland before the first (1801) census, that attempts to estimate the size of the population have generally been eschewed by modern Scottish historians. Hence the paucity of figures above. See Ch. 19, p. 294, above.

(iii) Pointers to Scottish urban population growth, 1691–1801[5]

	Hearth Tax 'Paid Hearths', 1691	c. 1700	Webster[6] 1755	Census 1801
Edinburgh (with Leith)	14,745	30–40,000*	57,000	81,600
Glasgow (with Barony)	4,409	12,766[†]	31,700	83,700
Aberdeen (old & new)	3,580		15,600	27,400
Dundee	2,537		12,400	26,800
Inverness	1,099		9,700	8,700
Perth	984		9,000	14,800
	[town only]			
Dunfermline	(?)		8,500	9,900
Greenock	746		3,800	17,400
	[town only]			
Paisley	(over 500)		6,800	31,200
Kilmarnock	(over 500)		4,400	8,000

* virtually all modern estimates are within this range
† magistrates' enumeration

Notes and Sources:

1. K.H. Connell, *The Population of Ireland 1750–1845* (Oxford, 1950), p. 25.
2. R.H. Campbell and J.B.A. Dow, eds. *Source Book of Scottish Economic and Social History* (New York, 1968), pp. 1, 2 and 8f.
3. T.C. Smout (274), p. 258. But cf. M. Flinn, *et al.*, *Scottish Population History from the 17th century to the 1930s* (Cambridge, 1977), p. 4; 'Estimates by earlier historians of a figure of one million or 1.1 millions from the beginning of the eighteenth century are based either on their own or other people's guesses. We must accept therefore that we cannot know what the long-run trends of population were in the seventeenth and eighteenth centuries. We cannot even be sure that the population of Scotland was, say, less in 1690 than it was in 1755, as is commonly assumed.'
4. This is the official census figure, but P. Mathias (178c), p. 166 estimates it to be nearer 1.5 million.
5. Flinn *et al.*, op cit., p. 191; Smout (274), p. 261.
6. See above, p. 294.

B.4: Years of epidemics and heavy mortality in England

		Predominant epidemic disease (where ascertainable)
1657–8	***	influenza
1658–9	**	'the new fever' (regarded by some contemporary physicians as associated with, or a forerunner of, the Plague)
1665–6	***	'The Great Plague'
1670–1	*	
1678–80	* ⎫	influenza in 1679; but in general virulent 'epidemic agues' (including
1680–1	*** ⎭	the 'quartan ague'; 'the New Delight')
1681–3	*	enteric fevers, influenza and agues
1684–5	*	typhus or 'the new fever'; some dysentery
1719–20	*	(?)typhus
1727–30	***	influenza, enteric fever & smallpox; 1729 'relapsing' or 'putrid' fever (probably a new and virulent strain of typhus)
1741–2	***	typhus, in the main; 'spotted fever'
1762–3	**	influenza in 1762
1766–7	*	(?) mainly typhus in 1766; influenza in 1767
1779–80	*	
1781–2	*	influenza; flare-up of smallpox; typhus locally
1783–4	*	probably influenza or 'epidemic agues' in the main; dysentery

Note:
Epidemic years as defined below run from July to June and their severity is graded according to the 'star' system adopted by E.A. Wrigley and R.S. Schofield (196), viz. *** exceptionally severe national mortality crisis ** severe crisis * year of moderately severe, but national, epidemics.

Sources:
Wrigley and Schofield (196), pp. 332—40; J.D. Chambers (194); C. Creighton, *A History of Epidemics in England* (2 vols., Cambridge, 1894; 2nd edn repr., 1965), I. pp. 568–77; II. *passim*; M.W. Flinn (195a).

B.5: Social structure and income distribution in England and Wales, 1688 and 1760: the contemporary views of Gregory King and Joseph Massie*

Rank or occupation	Number of families		Average annual income £		Total income £000	
	1688	1760	1688	1760	1688	1760
Temporal peers	160		3,200		512	
Bishops	26		1,300		33.8	
Baronets and knights	1,400		780		1,094	
Esquires	3,200		450		1,200	
Gentlemen	12,000		280		2,880	
TOTAL Aristocracy & gentry	16,786	18,000[1]		[1]	5,719	8,720

Rank or occupation	Number of families		Average annual income £		Total income £000	
	1688	1760	1688	1760	1688	1760
Higher clergy	2,000	2,000	72	100	144	200
Inferior clergy	8,000	9,000	50	50	400	450
Lawyers & legal officials	10,000	12,000	154	100	1,540	1,200
'Persons professing liberal arts & sciences'	15,000	18,000	60	60	900	1,080
Civil office-holders	5,000 ⎫	16,000	240 ⎫	60	1,200 ⎫	960
Petty civil officials	5,000 ⎭		120 ⎭		600 ⎭	
Army & Navy officers	9,000	8,000	70	85	640	680
TOTAL Professions	54,000	65,000			5,424	4,570
Prosperous freeholders	40,000	30,000	91	100 ⎫	10,240	9,000
Lesser freeholders	120,000	180,000[2]	55	33.5[2] ⎭		
Tenant farmers	150,000	155,000[3]	42.5	51[3]	6,375	7,950
TOTAL Farming†	310,000	365,000			16,615	16,950
Eminent overseas merchants	2,000	3,000[4]	400	466[4]	800	1,400
Lesser merchants	8,000	10,000	198	200	1,584	2,000
Shopkeepers, innkeepers & domestic tradesmen	50,000	184,500[5]	45	54[5]	2,250	9,900
TOTAL Trade & distribution	60,000	197,500			4,634	13,300
Manufacturers, artisans & craftsmen	60,000[6]	308,000[7]	38	26–7[7]	2,280	9,120
TOTAL Manufacturing	60,000	308,000			2,280	9,120
Husbandmen		200,000				
out-servants and wage-labourers in town & country	364,000	220,000	15	14	5,460	5,950
TOTAL Labouring	364,000	420,000			5,460	5,950
Common seamen & fishermen	50,000	60,000	20	20	1,000	1,200
Common soldiers	35,000	18,000	14	14	490	252
TOTAL Common soldiers & seamen	85,000	78,000			1,490	1,452
Cottagers, small ale-house keepers & paupers	400,000	20,000[8]	6.5	20[8]	2,000	400
TOTAL 'Cottagers and paupers'	400,000	–	–	2,000	–	

* While Massie undoubtedly used King as his model, he was of course writing half a century after the Union and it is not crystal clear that his figures were meant to apply *only* to England and Wales.

† excl. wage-labourers and outservants.

Notes:

1. In this (largely) landed hierarchy Massie does not distinguish the number of families or average income within each rank. He assumes 10 families with incomes of £20,000 p.a. or more; 20 of £10,000+; 40 of £8,000+, down to 6,400 lesser gentry families of £2–300 p.a. and 4,800 of £3–400 p.a.
2. Subdivided by Massie into 60,000 at av. £50 p.a.; and 120,000 at av. £25 p.a.
3. Subdivided into 5,000 big tenant farmers at av. £150 p.a.; 10,000 at £100 p.a.; 20,000 at £70 p.a. and 120,000 at £40 p.a.
4. Of whom Massie estimated 1,000 formed a merchant élite of av. £600 p.a.
5. Including 2,500 wealthy tradesmen at av. £400 p.a.; and 12,000 at £100 p.a. av.
6. King did not recognise '[master] manufacturers' as a separate occupational or status group.
7. Ranging from the families of 200,000 artisans earning *c*. £20 p.a. av. to an élite of master manufacturers: 2,500 at £250 p.a. av., 5,000 at £100 & 10,000 at £70 p.a. av.
8. The figures for 1760 in the previous three categories, especially those for artisans and wage-labourers, must be read in the light of the fact that, unlike King, Massie subsumed *all* 'paupers' (those in receipt of poor relief at the time), and presumably some 'cottagers' in other working groups.

Sources:

Second revised version [1698/9] of Gregory King's table of 'the income & expense of the several families of England', printed in G. Holmes (227), Appendix, pp. 66–8; Joseph Massie's estimate of the social structure and income, 1759–60, printed in P. Mathias, *The Transformation of England: Essays in the economic and social history of England in the eighteenth century* (1979), pp. 186–9, Tables 9.1 and 9.3. I have partly regrouped and reworked both sets of statistics to make them more comparable and coherent.

C. MONARCHS AND PRETENDERS

C.1: The Houses of Stuart and Hanover [reigning monarchs are given in bold capitals, Stuart Pretenders in italic capitals]

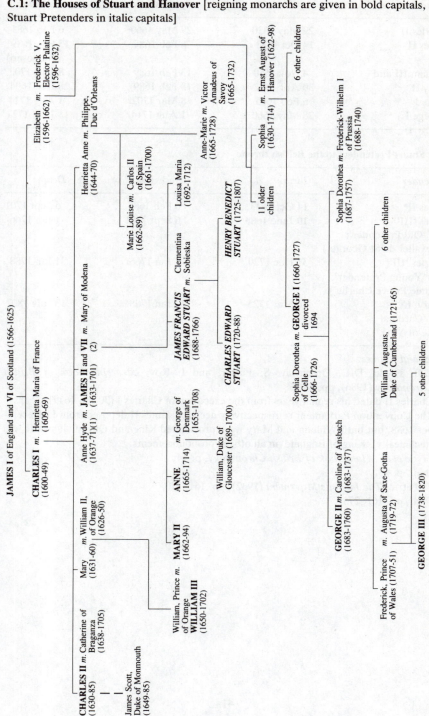

C.2: Reigning monarchs[1]

Monach	Birth	Accession	Death
Charles II	29 May 1630	29 May 1660[2]	6 Feb 1685
James II	14 Oct 1633	6 Feb 1685	13 Feb 1689[3] (deposed)
William III and	4 Nov 1650	13 Feb 1689	8 Mar 1702
Mary II	30 Apr 1662	13 Feb 1689	28 Dec 1694
Anne I	6 Feb 1665	8 Mar 1702	1 Aug 1714
George I	28 May 1660	1 Aug 1714	11 June 1727

C.3: Stuart Pretenders to the British throne

Pretender	Birth	'Accession'	Death
James II[4]	14 Oct 1633	6 Feb 1685	6 Sept 1701
James 'III'[5] (the 'Old Pretender': 'Chevalier de St George')	10 June 1688	6 Sept 1701	1 Jan 1766
Charles 'III'[6] (the 'Young Pretender': 'Bonnie Prince Charlie')	31 Dec 1720	1 Jan 1766	31 Jan 1788
Henry 'IX'[7] (the 'Cardinal Duke of York')	6 Mar 1725	31 Jan 1788	13 July 1807

Notes and sources:
1. E.B. Fryde, D.E. Greenway, S. Porter, and I. Roy, eds, *Handbook of British Chronology* (1986), pp. 44–6.
2. Charles II dated his regnal years from the execution of Charles I (30 Jan 1649).
3. The Convention Parliament retrospectively declared James II deposed from 11 December 1688, but until William and Mary were proclaimed King and Queen, James II was (technically) 'King of England' in all official pronouncements.
4. Fryde *et al.*, *Handbook of British Chronology*, p. 44.
5. Ibid., p. 45.
6. C. Petrie, *The Jacobite Movement* (1932), pp. 161, 270.
7. Ibid., pp. 161, 275.

D. LEADING OFFICE-HOLDERS, 1660–1722

D.1: Heads of the Treasury [First Lord of the Treasury unless otherwise stated]

Note:

Names in capitals indicate acknowledged head or joint heads of ministries/'first ministers'/'prime ministers'

Charles II

Earl of Southampton	Sept 1660–d. May 1667	Lord Treasurer
George Monck, 1st Duke of Albemarle	June 1667–d. Jan 1670	
(no new commission until Nov 1672: Lord Ashley, Chancellor of the Exchequer, cr. earl of Shaftesbury 1672, First Lord by seniority)		
Sir Thomas Clifford		
1st Lord Clifford (1672)	Nov 1672–June 1673	Lord Treasurer
Sir Thomas Osborne, Viscount Latimer (1673)		
EARL OF DANBY (1674)	June 1673–March 1679	Lord Treasurer
Earl of Essex	March–Nov 1679	
Lawrence Hyde, Viscount Hyde (1681)		
cr. earl of Rochester (1682)	Nov 1679–Aug 1684	
Sidney Godolphin, Lord Godolphin (1684)	Aug 1684–Feb 1685	

James II

Earl of Rochester	Feb 1685–Dec 1686	Lord Treasurer
Lord Belasyse	Jan 1687–[effectively terminated by the Revolution]	

William III

Lord Mordaunt, earl of Monmouth (1689)	Apr 1689–March 1690
Sir John Lowther	March–Nov 1690
Lord Godolphin	Nov 1690–May 1697
Charles Montague, 1st Lord Halifax (1700),	
Chancellor of the Exchequer since 1694	May 1697–Nov 1699
Earl of Tankerville	Nov 1699–Dec 1700
Lord Godolphin	Dec 1700–Dec 1701
Earl of Carlisle	Dec 1701–May 1702

Anne

LORD GODOLPHIN, EARL OF GODOLPHIN (1706)	May 1702–Aug 1710	Lord Treasurer
[Earl Poulett	Aug 1710–May 1711 (nominal head only)]	
ROBERT HARLEY, EARL OF OXFORD (1711)	Aug 1710–July 1714	(as 2nd Treasury Comm^r and Chancellor to May 1711; then as Lord Treasurer)

Anne – George I

Duke of Shrewsbury	July–Oct 1714	Lord Treasurer

George I

Lord Halifax	Oct 1714–d. May 1715
Earl of Carlisle	May–Oct 1715
Robert Walpole	Oct 1715–Apr 1717
VISCOUNT STANHOPE, EARL OF STANHOPE (1718)	Apr 1717–March 1718
CHARLES, 3rd EARL OF SUNDERLAND (joint head of STANHOPE–SUNDERLAND Admin.)	March 1718–Apr 1721

George I – George II

ROBERT WALPOLE (SIR ROBERT, 1725)	Apr 1721–Feb 1742

D.2: Secretaries of State

During the whole of this period there were normally two Secretaries of State in office at any one time, to deal with foreign and domestic affairs. (For the third Secretary appointed from time to time between 1709 and 1746 to deal with affairs in Scotland, see D.5.) In a division of duties that was more hard and fast after the Revolution than before it, the Secretary for the Northern Department was responsible for diplomatic contact with the Empire, the United Provinces, Scandinavia and Russia; the brief of the Southern Department embraced France, Switzerland, Italy, the Iberian Peninsula and Turkey. Responsibility for home affairs was shared. In 1782 the old demarcation of duties was to be abandoned in favour of the modern division between Foreign Secretary and Home Secretary.

Charles II and James II

Sir Edward Nicholas	1660–Oct 1662
Sir William Morice	1660–Sept 1668
Sir Henry Benet, Lord Arlington (1665)	1662–Sept 1674
Sir John Trevor	1668–July 1672
Henry Coventry	1672–Apr 1680
Sir Joseph Williamson	1674–Feb 1679
2nd Earl of Sunderland	1679–Feb 1681
Sir Leoline Jenkins	1680–Apr 1684
Earl of Conway	1681–Jan 1683
2nd Earl of Sunderland	1683–Oct 1688
Lord Godolphin	Apr –Aug 1684
Earl of Middleton	1684–Oct 1688
Viscount Preston	Oct 1688

The Revolution

Earl of Shrewsbury	Feb 1689–June 1690
2nd Earl of Nottingham	Mar 1689–Nov 1693
Viscount Sidney	Dec 1690–Mar 1692
Sir John Trenchard	Mar 1693–d. Apr 1695
Duke of Shrewsbury	Mar 1694–Dec 1698
Sir William Trumbull	May 1695–Dec 1697
James Vernon	Dec 1697–May 1702
Earl of Jersey	May 1699–June 1700
Sir Charles Hedges	Nov 1700–Dec 1701
Earl of Manchester	Jan–May 1702

Anne

Earl of Nottingham	May 1702–Apr 1704
Sir Charles Hedges	May 1702–Dec 1706
Robert Harley	May 1704–Feb 1708
3rd Earl of Sunderland	Dec 1706–June 1710
Henry Boyle	Feb 1708–Sept 1710
Lord Dartmouth	June 1710–Aug 1713
Henry St John (Viscount Bolingbroke, 1712)	Sept 1710–Aug 1714
William Bromley	Aug 1713–Sept 1714

George I

Viscount Townshend	Sept 1714–Dec 1716
James Stanhope (Viscount 1717, Earl of Stanhope 1718)	Sept 1714–Apr 1717
Paul Methuen	Dec 1716–Apr 1717
(Whig Schism of 1717)	
3rd Earl of SUNDERLAND	Apr 1717–Mar 1718
Joseph Addison	Apr 1717–Mar 1718
Lord STANHOPE[1]	Mar 1718–d. Feb 1721
James Craggs	Mar 1718–d. Feb 1721
Viscount Townshend	Feb 1721–May 1730
Lord Carteret	Mar 1721–Mar 1724

Note:
1. Stanhope–Sunderland ministry.

417

D.3: Lord Chancellors and Keepers of the Great Seal, 1660–1722

EDWARD, LORD HYDE, EARL OF CLARENDON (1661)	1658 (appointed in exile) –Aug 1667	Lord Chancellor
Sir Orlando Bridgeman	1667–72	
Earl of Shaftesbury	Nov 1672–Nov 1673	Lord Chancellor
Sir Heneage Finch, Lord Finch (1674), 1st earl of Nottingham	1673–Dec 1682	Lord Chancellor
Sir Francis North, Lord Guildford (1683)	1682–d. Sept 1685	
Sir George Jeffreys, Lord Jeffreys (1685) (Seal in commission, 1689–93)	1685–dismissed Dec 1688	Lord Chancellor
Sir John Somers, Lord Somers (1697)	Mar 1693–Apr 1700	
Sir Nathan Wright	May 1700–Oct 1705	
Sir William Cowper, Lord Cowper (1706)	1705–Sept 1710	Lord Chancellor (1705)
Sir Simon Harcourt, Lord Harcourt (1711)	Oct 1710–Sept 1714	Lord Chancellor (1713)
Lord Cowper, 1st earl Cowper (1718)	Sept 1714–Apr 1718	Lord Chancellor
Sir Thomas Parker, Lord Macclesfield, earl of Macclesfield (1721) (Seal in commission, Jan–June 1725)	May 1718–Jan 1725	Lord Chancellor

---

D.4: Chancellors of the Exchequer, 1660–1722

Some notable holders of the office who were not at the same time First Lords of the Treasury include:

Anthony Ashley Cooper, Lord Ashley	1671–72
Sir John Duncombe	1672–76
Sir John Ernle	1676–89
Lord Delamere	1689–90
Richard Hampden	1690–94
Charles Montagu, Lord Halifax (1700)	Apr 1694–May 1699 (First Lord, 1697)
John Smith (1)	1699–Mar 1701
Henry Boyle	Mar 1701–Feb 1707
John Smith (2)	1708–Aug 1710
ROBERT HARLEY	1710–May 1711 cr. earl of Oxford and Lord Treasurer
Sir William Wyndham	1713–14
Sir Richard Onslow	1714–15
John Aislabie	Mar 1718–Feb 1721

418

D.5: Scottish Secretaries 1660–1709: Secretaries of State, 1709–22

Earl of Lauderdale (Duke, 1672)	1660–dismissed Oct 1680
Earl of Moray	1680–8
Earl of Middleton and Earl of Melfort	joint Secretaries 1682–4 and 1684–8 respectively

Revolution

Earl of Melville	1688–91
{ John Dalrymple (1st earl of Stair, 1703)	1691–5
{ James Johnston	1692–6
John Murray, Lord Tullibardine (1696), 1st duke of Athol (1703)	1696–8
{ Sir Jas. Ogilvie, 1st earl of Seafield (1701)	1696–Nov 1702
{ Lord Carmichael, earl of Hyndford (1701)	1698–May 1702
{ Duke of Queensberry	1702–4
{ Visct. Tarbat, earl of Cromarty (1703)	1702–4
{ Earl of Roxburgh	1704–June 1705
{ Earl of Seafield	1704–Mar 1705
Marquess of Annandale	Mar–Sept 1705
{ Earl of Loudoun	June 1705–May 1708
{ Earl of Mar	Sept 1705–Feb 1708
Duke of Queensbury	1709–d. 1711
Earl of Mar	1713–Sept 1714
Duke of Montrose	1714–Aug 1715
Duke of Roxburgh	1716–Aug 1725

D.6: Other civil offices held by important politicians, 1660–1725

[*Abbreviations*: LHA = Lord High Admiral; 1st Lord Adm. = First Lord of the Admiralty; LL Ireland = Lord Lieutenant of Ireland; L. Pres. = Lord President of the Council; LPS = Lord Privy Seal; Comptroller = Comptroller of the Household]

Charles II

James, Duke of York	LHA, 1660–73
Lord Robartes	LPS, 1661–73
Duke of Ormonde	LL Ireland (1), 1662–8
Earl of Essex	LL Ireland, 1672–7
Earl of Anglesey	LPS, 1673–82
Prince Rupert	LHA, 1673–9
Duke of Ormonde	LL Ireland (2), 1677–85
Earl of Shaftesbury	L. Pres., Apr–Oct 1679
Daniel Finch, 2nd earl of Nottingham (1682)	1st Lord Adm. 1681–5
Marquess of Halifax	LPS (1), 1682–5
Earl of Rochester	L. Pres., 1684–5
William Blathwayt	Sec-at-War, 1684–94

Compendium of information

James II

Marquess of Halifax	L. Pres., Feb–Oct 1685
2nd Earl of Clarendon	LPS and LL Ireland, 1685–7
Earl of Tyrconnel	LL Ireland, 1687–9

William III

[Earl of Danby] marquess of Carmarthen, duke of Leeds	L. Pres., 1689–99
Marquess of Halifax	LPS (2), 1689–90
Hon. Thos, Wharton, Lord Wharton (1696)	Comptroller, 1689–1702
Sir Edward Seymour	Treasury Commr., 1692–4
Edward Russell, Earl of Orford	1st Lord Adm. (1), 1694–9
2nd Earl of Sunderland	Ld Chamberlain, 1697
Earl of Rochester	LL Ireland (1), Dec 1700–1
Earl of Pembroke	LHA, 1701–2

Anne

Earl of Rochester	LL Ireland, 1702–3
Earl of Pembroke	L. Pres., 1702–8
Sir Edward Seymour	Comptroller, 1702–4
Duke of Ormonde	LL Ireland, 1703–7
Henry St John	Sec-at-War, 1704–8
Duke of Newcastle (John Holles, 1st Duke)	LPS, 1705–d. 1711
Earl of Pembroke	LL Ireland, 1707–8
2nd Duke of Devonshire	Ld Steward, 1707–11
Lord Somers	L. Pres., 1708–10
Earl of Wharton	LL Ireland, 1708–10
Robert Walpole	Sec-at-War, 1708–10
Earl of Pembroke	LHA, 1708–9
Earl of Orford	1st Lord Adm. (2), 1709–10
Duke of Shrewsbury	Ld Chamberlain, 1710–13
Earl of Rochester	L. Pres., 1710–d. 1711
Duke of Ormonde	LL Ireland, 1710–11
Sir William Wyndham	Sec-at-War 1712–13 (see also Ch. of Exchequer)
Duke of Shrewsbury	LL Ireland, 1713–14

George I – II

Robert Walpole	Paymaster-Gen, 1714–15
Earl of Sunderland	LL Ireland, 1714–17; LPS, 1715–16
Earl of Nottingham	L. Pres., 1714–16
Earl of Orford	1st Lord Adm (3), 1714–17
Earl/Marquess of Wharton	LPS, 1714–d. Apr 1715
William Putney	Sec-at-War, 1714–17 (Cofferer of Household 1723–25
2nd Duke of Devonshire	L. Pres., 1716–17
Viscount Townshend	LL Ireland, Feb–Apr 1717

Duke of Newcastle (Thomas Pelham–Holles)	Ld Chamberlain, 1717–24
Earl of Sunderland	L. Pres., 1718–19
Viscount Townshend	L. Pres., 1720–1
Robert Walpole	Paymaster-Gen, 1720–21
Henry Pelham	Treasury Commr., 1721–4
Henry Boyle, Lord Carleton	L. Pres., 1721–5

Principal sources:

1. E.B. Fryde, D.E. Greenway, S. Porter and I. Roy, eds, *Handbook of British Chronology*, (3rd edn, 1986), pp. 82–195 *passim*.
2. J.C. Sainty, *Treasury Officials, 1660–1870* (1972); id., *Officials of the Secretaries of State, 1660–1782* (1973), pp. 23–5.

E. PARLIAMENT

E.1: Results of General Elections in England (Britain after 1707), 1660–1722

[*Abbreviations*: A = Anglicans; N-A = Non-Anglicans; C = Court/Ministry; O = Opposition; W = Whigs; T = Tories; U = Uncertain; F = Subsequent allegiance fluid]

(i) *1660–89*[1]

								Total classified
1660		A:	262		N-A	286		548[2]
1661		firm C:	297	firm	O:	95	F: 126	
1679	(a)	T:	137		W:	218	U: 167	522[3]
(Mar)	(b)	C:	158		O:	302	U: 36	496[4]
1679		C:	220		O:	310		530
(Oct)								
1681		C:	193		O:	309		502
1685		T:	468		W:L	57		525
1689		T:	232		W & C:	319		551

Notes and Sources:

1. B.D. Henning, ed., (25), I, pp. 31–2, 45–7, 52–4; K.H.D. Haley (42b), p. 500; J.R. Jones, 'Shaftesbury's "Worthy Men"', see 4 below.
2. Figures for 1660–89 embody the results of by-elections held in the years 1660, 1679 (Mar–May), Oct 1679–Jan 1681 (while the second Exclusion Parliament awaited its first meeting), 1685 and 1689. Except in the case of the 1660 Convention, the second Exclusion Parliament and the Convention Parliament of 1689, the number of by-elections concerned was insignificant.
3. Based on division figures for the first Exclusion bill, absentees being counted as 'uncertain'.
4. Based on Shaftesbury's contemporary list of 'Worthy' and 'Honest' Men (O) as against 'Bad' and 'Vile' Men (C), drawn up soon after the March 1679 election; printed by J. R. Jones, 'Shaftesbury's "Worthy Men"', in *BIHR*, **30** (1957), pp. 232–41.

(ii) *1690–Jan 1701*[1]

							Total classified
1690	Tory majority returned, but not possible to estimate its size. With number of placemen up to 119 (from 101), the *Court* vote was now poised to become very significant in the politics of the 1690s						
1695	(a) C:	248	O:	247	U: 9		504[2]
	(b) W:	269	T:	224	C: 1	U: 10	504[2]
1698	C/Army: 241		anti-Army: 227			U: 45	513[3]
1700–1 (Dec–Jan)	Two generalisations possible: (1) Whigs did not lose as much ground as they had feared (2) Tories *with placemen* (many of the latter now of their number) held initially a commanding majority						

Notes and Sources:

1. From sources at present in print it is impossible to attempt *any* numerical assessment of the results of two of the four elections held in these eleven years. The summaries and statistics above are based mainly on information in H. Horwitz (62a) *passim* and on contemporary parliamentary and division lists, notably the three 1696 divisions as analysed in I. F. Burton, P. W. J. Riley and E. Rowlands, *Political Parties in the Reigns of William III and Anne: the Evidence of the Division Lists, BIHR.* Suppl. 7 (1968), pp. 30, 41–51.
2. Burton *et al.*, loc. cit.
3. Anon: contemporary assessment in the papers of Robert Harley, Horwitz (62a) p. 240.

(iii) *Dec 1701–13*

							Total classified
1701 (Dec)	W:	224	T:	289			513
1702	W:	190	T:	323			513
1705	W:	246	T:	267			513
1708	W:	291	T:	222	(English MPs)		558
	W & C:	36	T:	9	(Scots MPs)		
1710	W:	181	T:	332	(English)		558
	W:	17[†]	T & C:	20	U: 8[‡] (Scots)*		
1713	W:	150	T:	363	(English)		558
	W:	29	T:	16	(Scots)		

[†] 2 doubtful
[‡] most in the end probably supported the Tory government
* before hearing petitions

Sources:

1. For England, W.A. Speck (99a), Appx D.
2. For Scotland, P.W.J. Riley (283c), p. 110 (for 1708); D. Szechi (105), p. 151 (for 1713); author's own calculations, based on division lists, etc. for 1710.

(iv) *1715–22*

				Total classified
1715	W: 341	T: 217	(Great Britain)	558
1722	W: 379	T: 178		⎰557
	* W: 389	T: 169		⎱558

* after hearing petitions

Sources:
1. Principal source R. Sedgwick, ed. (26a), I, pp. 19–35. See also L.J. Colley (81a).

E.2: Dates of parliamentary sessions, 1660–1722

Parliament	Sessions	Date of dissolution	Remarks
Charles II			
1660	(1) Apr–Sept		Convention
	(2) Nov–Dec	29 Dec 1660	
1661–79	(1) May 1661–May 1662		'Cavalier Parliament'
	(2) Feb–July 1663		
	(3) Mar–May 1664		
	(4) Nov 1664–Mar 1665		
	(5) Oct 1665		
	(6) Sept 1666–Feb 1667		
	(7) Oct 1667–May 1668		
	(8) Oct–Dec 1669		
	(9) Feb 1670–Apr 1671		
	(10) Feb–Mar 1673		
	(11) Oct–Nov 1673		
	(12) Jan–Feb 1674		
	(13) Apr–June 1675		
	(14) Oct–Nov 1675		
	(15) Feb 1677–July 1678		
	(16) Oct–Dec 1678	24 Jan 1679	
1679	Mar–May 1679	12 July 1679	'1st Exclusion Parliament'
1680–1	Oct 1680–Jan 1681	18 Jan 1681	'2nd Exclusion Parliament'
1681	21–8 Mar	28 Mar 1681	'3rd Exclusion' or 'Oxford' Parliament
James II			
1685	(1) May–July		
	(2) 9–20 Nov	2 July 1687	

Parliament	Sessions	Date of dissolution	Remarks
William III			
1689–90	(1) Jan–Aug 1689		'The Convention Parliament'
	(2) Oct 1689–Jan 1690	6 Feb 1690	declared itself a Parliament,
			20 Feb 1689
1690–5	(1) Mar–May 1690		Technically the second Parliament
	(2) Oct 1690–Jan 1691		of William and Mary until Dec
	(3) Oct 1691–Feb 1692		1694
	(4) Nov 1692–Mar 1693		
	(5) Nov 1693–Apr 1694		
	(6) Nov 1694–May 1695	7 July 1698	
1695–8	(1) Nov 1695–Apr 1696		First 'Triennial' Parliament,
	(2) Oct 1696–Apr 1697		elected under the Act of 1694
	(3) Dec 1697–July 1698	7 July 1698	
1698–1700	(1) Dec 1698–May 1699		
	(2) Nov 1699–Apr 1700	19 Dec 1700	
1701	Feb–June 1701	11 Nov 1701	
1701–2	Dec 1701–May 1702	2 July 1702	
Anne			
1702–5	(1) Oct 1702–Feb 1703		
	(2) Nov 1703–Apr 1704		
	(3) Oct 1704–Mar 1705	5 Apr 1705	
1705–8	(1) Oct 1705–May 1706		Declared by proclamation, 29 Apr
	(2) Dec 1706–Apr 1707		1707, to be 'the first parliament
			of Great Britain'
	(3) Oct 1707–Apr 1708	3 Apr 1708	
1708–10	(1) Nov 1708–Apr 1709		
	(2) Nov 1709–Apr 1710	21 Sept 1710	
1710–13	(1) Nov 1710–June 1711		
	(2) Dec 1711–Jul 1712		
	(3) Apr 1713–Jul 1713	8 Aug 1713	
1714	(1) Feb–Jul 1714		Second session called after Queen
	(2) 1–25 Aug 1714	15 Jan 1715	Anne's death.
George I			
1715–22	(1) Mar 1715–June 1716		First 'Septennial Parliament' – life
	(2) Feb–Jul 1717		prolonged by Act of 1716
	(3) Nov 1717–Mar 1718		
	(4) Nov 1718–Apr 1719		
	(5) Nov 1719–June 1720		
	(6) Dec 1720–Jul 1721		
	(7) Jul–Aug 1721		
	(8) Oct 1721–Mar 1722	10 Mar 1722	

Principal Source:
Fryde *et al.*, eds, *Handbook of British Chronology* (3rd edn, 1986) pp. 576–8.

F. THE CONSTITUTION: STATUTES, BILLS AND PROPOSALS

(i) The Second Exclusion Bill, November 1680
The most important clauses were as follows:

(1) James, duke of York, barred from inheriting any crown in British Isles.
(2) If James attempted to claim lost inheritance, or if he returned to any part of British Isles, he and anyone assisting him by actions, words or writing, to be guilty of high treason.
(3) Indemnification for any actions taken in resisting any invasion attempt.
(4) For purposes of succession to Charles II, James to be treated as if he were already dead (i.e., by implication, Princess Mary to succeed).

[*Note*: In the *Third Exclusion Bill*, introduced into the Oxford Parliament's Commons in March 1681, the question of succession was deliberately left open.]
Source: J.P. Kenyon (7), pp. 469–71.

(iia) Declaration of Rights, 13 February 1689
(Incorporated as Preamble to the Bill of Rights)
Preamble (extracts)

... Whereas the late King James the Second, by the assistance of divers evil counsellors, judges, and ministers employed by him, did endeavour to subvert and extirpate the protestant religion, and the laws and liberties of this kingdom ... [and James] having abdicated the government, and the throne being thereby vacant, his highness the Prince of Orange (whom it hath pleased Almighty God to make the glorious instrument of delivering this kingdom from popery and arbitrary power) did (by the advice of the lords spiritual and temporal, and divers principal persons of the commons) cause letters to be written [summoning the Convention Parliament] ... to meet and sit at Westminster [22 Jan 1689], in order to such an establishment, as that their religion, laws, and liberties might not again be in danger of being subverted: ...

Thereupon the said lords ... and commons ... assembled in a full and free representative of this nation, taking into their most serious consideration the best means for attaining the ends aforesaid; do in the first place (as their ancestors in like case have usually done) *for the vindicating and asserting their ancient rights and liberties* [but cf. Ch. 13], declare:

[a] Declaration (main clauses)

(1) The pretended power of suspending of laws, or the execution of laws, by regal authority, without consent of parliament, is illegal.
(2) The pretended power of dispensing with laws, or the execution of laws, by regal authority, as it hath been assumed and exercised of late, is illegal.
(3) The Ecclesiastical Commission 'and all other commissions and courts of like nature are illegal and pernicious.'
(4) 'Levying money for ... the use of the crown, by pretence of prerogative, without grant of parliament ... is illegal.'
(5) 'It is the right of subjects to petition the King, and all commitments and prosecutions for such petitioning are illegal.'
(6) 'The raising or keeping a standing army within the kingdom in time of peace, unless it be with consent of parliament, is against law.'
(7) The King's Protestant subjects may carry arms for their defence.
(8) Election of members of parliament ought to be free.
(9) Freedom of speech, and debates or proceedings in parliament, ought not to be impeached or questioned in any court or place out of parliament.
(10) No excessive bail; no cruel and unusual punishments.

426

(11) 'And that for redress of all grievances, and for the amending, strengthening and preserving of the laws, parliaments ought to be held frequently.'

[b] The lords and commons confident that the Prince of Orange 'will perfect the deliverance so far advanced by him, and will still preserve them from the violation of their rights, which they have here asserted', resolve 'that William and Mary . . . be declared King and Queen of England, France and Ireland, [with the prince alone enjoying the sole and full exercise of the regal power . . . during their joint lives']. Proposals made for the succession (see below – Bill of Rights).

[c] New oaths of allegiance and supremacy *to be required by law.*
  (1) 'I, A.B. do sincerely promise and swear, that I will be faithful and bear true allegiance, to their Majesties King William and Queen Mary . . .
  (2) 'I, A.B. do swear, that I do from my heart abhor, detest and abjure . . . the damnable doctrine . . . that princes excommunicated by the see of Rome may be deposed or murdered by their subjects . . . And I do declare that no foreign prince, person, prelate, state or potentate hath . . . any jurisdiction . . . or authority, ecclesiastical or spiritual, within this realm.'

(iib) Bill of Rights, 1689 (1 William and Mary sess 2, c.2)
This measure (introduced in April, and made law in December) gave statutory force to the above clauses (as a Declaratory Act) but added these new provisions:

  (1) 'That the entire, perfect, and full exercise of the regal power and government be only in, and executed by his Majesty, in the names of both their Majesties during their joint lives; and after their deceases the said crown . . . shall be and remain to the heirs of the body of her Majesty; and for default of such issue, to . . . the princess Anne of Denmark, and the heirs of her body; and for default of such issue, to the heirs of the body of his said Majesty . . .'
  (2) '. . . whereas it hath been found by experience that it is inconsistent with the safety and welfare of this protestant kingdom, to be governed by a popish prince, or by any King or Queen marrying a papist'; any Catholic, or anyone married to a Catholic, shall be excluded for ever from the succession to the throne (including Ireland); in such a case, the people are absolved of their allegiance; the crown will descend to the nearest protestant heir, as though the Catholic heir were naturally dead.
  (3) Anyone succeeding to the throne must make the declaration against transubstantiation laid down in the Test Act of 1673.
  (4) No dispensation by *nonobstante* to any statute to be allowed, unless specifically allowed by the statute in question.
  (5) Any charter, grant or pardon granted before 23 October 1689, to continue to have full legal effect.

Source: E.N. Williams (11a), pp. 23–33.

(iii) Scottish Claim of Right, April 1689
The main provisions were:

  (1) declared that James had 'forfeited the right to the crown' because of his violation of 'the fundamental constitution of the kingdom';
  (2) laid down that no papist could rule or hold office in Scotland;
  (3) forbade use of judicial torture 'without evidence' or in ordinary cases;
  (4) forbade dragonnades;

(5) laid down that Parliament should meet frequently and freely and must give its consent to raising of revenue;

(6) reversed two Court of Session rulings extending law of treason to include unspoken personal opinions;

(7) condemned prelacy as 'a great and insupportable grievance and trouble to this nation', and advocated its abolition.

Source: A. Browning, ed., *English Historical Documents 1660–1714* (1966), pp. 635–9.

(iv) Treaty of Limerick, 1691
This set out the terms which concluded the war of 1689–91 against the Irish Jacobites:

(1) Catholics to be allowed to practise their religion as they had in Charles II's reign;

(2) Catholics required to take no oaths other than oath of allegiance.

(3) Any Catholics who had fought for James to be allowed to return home unmolested and with full restitution of their property.

(4) Any who wished to leave Ireland (i.e. to fight on in France), to be allowed to go, with families and goods.

[*Note*: The relatively generous paper terms of the treaty were systematically circumvented, against William III's wishes; it had become a dead letter within ten years [*The Age of Oligarchy* Ch. 16).]

Source: Browning, *English Historical Documents*, pp. 765–9.

(v) Triennial Act, 1694 (6 and 7 William and Mary, c.2)
[*Note*: Two triennial bills, having passed the Commons in 1693 as result of backbench pressure against strong royal opposition, had subsequently been lost, one by royal veto, one in the Lords.]

There were three main provisions:

(1) A Parliament must meet 'once in three years at the least'.

(2) This was to take effect with and after the dissolution of the present Parliament [elected in 1690].

(3) No Parliament was to last more than three years, at most, without dissolution [a new provision, not in the Acts of 1641 or 1664].

Source: E.N. Williams (11a), pp. 49–50.

(vi) Civil List Act, 1698 (9 and 10 William III, c. 23)

(1) William to receive £700,000 per annum for life 'on the Civil List', from certain assigned taxes and duties, for maintenance of his personal household and family and to defray normal expenses of civil government. (Parliament tacitly accepted responsibility for upkeep of armed forces.)

(2) Any surplus in yield of taxes assigned to raise this sum was not to be retained by Crown without Parliament's permission.

Source: E.N. Williams (11a), pp. 50–3.

(vii) Act of Settlement, 1701 (12 and 13 William III, c. 2)
'An Act for the further limitation of the crown, and better securing the rights and liberties of the subject.'

(1) Princess Sophia Electress of Hanover to be next in succession to the crowns of England and Ireland after King William and Princess Anne and in default of issue

to them. Succession subsequently to devolve on the heirs of Sophia's body 'being Protestants'. [*Note*: for the many nearer heirs excluded from the succession on the grounds of religion, see A. Browning, *English Historical Documents 1660–1714*, Tables 4, p. 133, and 5, p. 135.]

(2) All future monarchs to be in communion with the established Church of England (operative from William's death).
(3) England not to be involved in any war fought in defence of the monarch's possessions abroad not belonging to crown of England without consent of Parliament (operative from 1714, though evadeable).
(4) No subsequent monarch must leave British Isles without Parliamentary consent (operative 1702; repealed 1716).
(5) Privy Council should transact all government business properly within its remit; all advice given to monarch there should have advisers' signatures appended (to be operative after Anne's death; but repealed 1707).
(6) Only natives of British Isles should be eligible to hold seats on Privy Council, sit in either House of Parliament, or hold any government or household post or receive grants of Crown lands (operative from 1714).
(7) No placeman or pensioner eligible to be an MP (technically with immediate effect, but repealed 1707: see *ix*).
(8) [After death of Anne, *s.p.*], judges to hold office *quamdiu se bene gesserint* [A], and be removable only by addresses of both Houses of Parliament (operative from 1714).
(9) Royal pardons no longer pleadable to bar impeachments by Commons (operative at once).

Sources: E.N. Williams (11a), pp. 56–60; D. Rubini (65), Appendix C.

(viii) Act of Security (Scotland), 1704
[*Note*: This was passed by Scottish Parliament in 1703, but refused royal assent until 1704.]

(1) Scotland's Parliament was to meet on the Queen's death and offer crown to the next heir on condition of his acceptance of Claim of Right.
(2) Heir to be a Protestant, descended from House of Stuart, chosen by Parliament.
(3) *But* (unless suitable terms securing Scotland's sovereignty, trade and religion could be negotiated with England during Anne's lifetime) heir not to be same person as inherited throne of England.

Source: Browning, *English Historical Documents*, pp. 677–80.

(ix) Regency Act, 1706 (6 Anne, c. 41)
[a] The Act's prime purpose was to deal with the interregnum between the death of Queen Anne and the arrival of the Hanoverian successor; to this end:

(1) Parliament was to continue in session for six months, contrary to normal usage.
(2) The Ministers in office on Anne's death to stay in office until removed by the Hanoverian successor to the throne, after his/her arrival in England.
(3) These ministers to be supplemented at once by seven regents, nominated in advance by Anne's heir apparent, names to be kept secret in 'instruments' lodged with the Hanoverian Resident, the Lord Chancellor, and the Archbishop of Canterbury.

[b] Its secondary purpose was to establish provisions designed to strike a decisive blow against the influence of placemen and pensioners in the Commons (see Holmes (16) pp. 41–7).

Most sweeping clauses were eliminated, but the final Act:

(1) Expressly excluded from the Commons all holders of new offices; commissioners for prizes, sick and wounded soldiers, naval out-ports and wine licences; colonial governors.
(2) Stipulated that all members accepting *existing* offices were to resign their seats, but to be capable of re-election (modification of place clause of Act of Settlement).

Sources: W.C. Costin and J.S. Watson (11b), pp. 111–16; M.A. Thomson (108), p. 187.

(x) *Act of Union, 1707* (6 Anne, c. 11)

The terms of the Treaty (of 1706) were embodied in law:

(1) From 1 May 1707 England and Scotland to be united into one Kingdom, 'Great Britain', with a common 'Union' flag, the succession to their joint monarchies settled in the House of Hanover, and a common 'Parliament of Great Britain'.
(2) All subjects of new state of Great Britain to enjoy freedom of trade both internally and with their (in effect, English) overseas 'dominions and plantations'.
(3) Scotland not to be liable to taxation to service the existing English National Debt.
(4) All monies unavoidably so taken to be returned annually in a lump-sum, the 'Equivalent', to be used in first instance to compensate stockholders of the bankrupt 'Company of Scotland' [Darien].
(5) Scotland not to be liable to a malt tax until end of War of Spanish Succession, but *was* to be liable to the English Excise, with exception of that on beer. Scotland to pay £48,000 in Land Tax for every £1,997,763 paid by the English.
(6) Coin to be 'of the same standard and value throughout the United Kingdom', along with common weights and measures.
(7) Scotland to retain her own fully autonomous legal system.
(8) The worship, discipline and government of the [Presbyterian] Church of Scotland to be 'effectually and unalterably secured', and the Kirk to be free of English episcopal supervision.
(9) Heritable jurisdictions, and privileges of royal burghs in Scotland, to be continued and preserved.
(10) Scotland to have 45 representatives in House of Commons of the Union Parliament, elected under existing Scottish electoral system.
(11) Only 16 Scottish peers to sit in House of Lords, elected at each General Election by Scottish peerage.
(12) Otherwise, Scots nobility to have all legal privileges enjoyed by English counterparts.

Sources: W.C. Costin and J.S. Watson (11b), pp. 98–110; G.S. Pryde (284), pp. 83–119.

(xi) *Qualifications [for Members of Parliament] Act, 1711* (9 Anne, c. 5)

(1) Candidates for borough seats in House of Commons must possess unencumbered income from real estate of not less than £300 per annum.
(2) Prospective 'knights of the shire' (i.e. those seeking election for county seats) required a £600 a year real estate qualification.

Source: E.N. Williams (11a), pp. 192–3.

(xii) *Septennial Act, 1716* (1 George I, Stat. 2, c. 38)

Preamble: 'Whereas . . . [the 3-year limit on the life of Parliaments, in force since 1694] . . . , if it should continue, may probably at this juncture, when a restless and popish faction are . . . endeavouring to renew a rebellion within this Kingdom, and an invasion from abroad, be destructive to the peace and security of the government: be it enacted that this present parliament and all [future] Parliaments shall and may respectively have continuance for seven years, and no longer' [subject to the King's prerogative of prior dissolution].

Source: E.N. Williams (11a), p. 189.

(xiii) The Peerage Bill, 1719

The Bill proposed:

(1) that the 16 Scottish representative peers, authorised in 1707, be replaced with 25 *hereditary* peers (the 16 already sitting and 9 others to be chosen by the present King); and

(2) that thereafter, with the exception of creations to replace extinct peerages, no more than six further peerages of Great Britain be created.

[*Note*: By closing off the British peerage while it had a built-in majority favourable to them, the Sunderland-Stanhope faction hoped to be able to thwart any impeachment attempt when the Prince of Wales became King. The bill was introduced twice; the second attempt was defeated in Commons (see above, pp. 226–7).]

Source: D.B. Horn and M. Ransome, eds, *English Historical Documents 1714–1783* (1957), pp. 151–4.

(xiv) The Declaratory Act (Ireland), 1720 (6 George I, c.5)

Sometimes called 'the Dependency of Ireland Act'; this Act followed an attempt by the Irish House of Lords to prevent the execution of a decision of the British House of Lords on an appeal from Dublin. The Act declared:

That the said kingdom of Ireland hath been, is, and of right ought to be subordinate unto and dependent upon the imperial crown of Great Britain, as being inseparably united and annexed thereunto', and that Westminster 'had, hath, and of right ought to have full power and authority to make laws and statutes of sufficient force and validity, to bind the kingdom and people of Ireland.

The House of Lords at Westminster therefore had the right to hear Irish appeals.

Source: Horn and Ransome, *English Historical Documents 1714–1783*, p. 683.

G. PUBLIC FINANCE

G.1: War and the growth of the National Debt, 1693–1722

Year	Size of Debt £ (to nearest 100,000)
1697	16,700,000
1702	14,100,000
1713 (Apr)	36,200,000
1714 (Sept)	40,400,000
1719 (Mich)	49,900,000

Sources:
1. *British Parliamentary Papers*, **35** (1868–9); *British Parliamentary Papers*, **52** (1898).
2. J. Brewer (133), Table 2.1, p. 30
3. P.G.M. Dickson (113a), Tables 7, p. 80 and 9, p. 93.

G.2: Taxation, 1660–1783

(i) *Direct taxation, 1660–88*:
  (a) Hearth Tax, 1662–89
  (b) 'extraordinary' land and property taxes: levied in 1661 (assessment); 1663 (subsidy); 1664, 1665, 1666 (assessments); 1671 (pound rate); 1672, 1677, 1678 (assessments).

(ii) *The Land Tax, 1693–1783*:
levied at 4s. in the £: 1693–7, 1701–12, 1716, 1727, 1740–9, 1755–65, 1770, 1775–83
levied at 3s. in the £: 1698–9, 1717–21, 1728–9, 1750–1, 1766–9, 1771–4
levied at 2s. in the £: 1700, 1713–15, 1722–6, 1730–1, 1734–9, 1752–4
levied at 1s. in the £: 1732–3 (2 years)

(iii) *The growth of indirect taxation, 1689–1714*

(a) *Principal indirect taxes in force, 1688*

Port duties on imports *and* exports: Standard 5% *ad valorem*, i.e. on value of goods as rated in 1660; tunnage on wine; duty on woollen cloth.
Special additional duties of 1685: wine and vinegar; tobacco and sugar; French and Indian linen; brandy; French silks; all wrought silks, imported.
Inland duties (excises): hereditary and temporary, on beer, spirits, cider, mead, vinegar, tea, coffee and chocolate; wine licences.

(b) *Principal new indirect taxes in force, 1702*

New duties on articles of consumption: salt (1694, increased 1698), spices (1695); 'the brewery' (1690), malt (1697); wine – new duties in addition to tunnage and special duties; spirits – 'the distillery' (1690) and further new imposts; tea, coffee and cocoa – 'the new duty' (1694)
Other new duties: timber from Europe (1690); seaborne coal (1695); glass wares, including bottles (1695); whale fins (1698)
General rises in levels of taxation: 25% additional duty on French goods, other than separately taxed wines, brandy etc. (1692); further additional duties on French wines, and brandy, and general level on all other French goods raised to 50% (1695); standard level of duties on *all imports*, and some exports, raised from 5% to 10% (1692, 1698); additional duties on East India and China goods (1690).

(c) *Principal new indirect taxes in force, 1714*

New duties on articles of consumption: salt and spices (additional, 1704, 1709); pepper (1709) raisins (1709); 'the brewery' – increased (1709); malt, additional (1710); hops (1710); spirits – increased (1709); imported tea and coffee – increased (1711).

Other new duties: imported drugs (1704, 1711); wine licences, additional (1710); various domestic manufactures (internal), viz. candles, starch, soap, leather, paper, stamp duties on newspapers, pamphlets, and advertisements in both; printed or dyed silks, calicoes, linens or stuffs (1709–12). Exported coals (1714).

General rises in levels of taxation: standard levels of duties on *general imports and exports* raised from 10% to 15% (1703–4).

(iv) *Further major changes in indirect taxation, 1721–3*

1721–2   Walpole's comprehensive *customs reforms* (8 George I, c. 15, c. 16):

(1) Drawback allowed on wide range of exported silk goods;
(2) import duties repealed on dyestuffs, raw silk and raw materials used in paper and linen manufacture;
(3) additional 20% import duty on drugs abolished; duties on pepper and spices reduced and greatly simplified;
(4) NB all British goods and merchandise to be *exported free*, except alum, lead, tin, copper and some other minerals; tanned leather and hides; white woollen cloth; raw materials for hats.

1723   *Bonded warehousing* for tea, coffee and cocoa nuts: compulsory warehousing of these imports after payment of small duty; could be taken out for re-export without further duty; full tax payable as excise only if taken out for home consumption.

Sources:
1. C.D. Chandaman (110a).
2. J.V. Beckett (116).
3. S. Dowell, *A History of Taxation and Taxes in England* (2nd edn, 4 vols, 1888); D. Pickering, ed., *The Statutes at Large from Magna Carta to . . . 1761*, vols 3–14.

(v) *Changing levels and incidence of taxation*, 1660–1720

Year (5-year average centred on)	Share of national income appropriated to taxation	Excises and stamps		Customs		Direct taxes		Total tax income
	%	£m	%	£m	%	£m	%	£m
1665		0.3	(23)	0.4	(31)	0.6	(46)	1.3
1670	3.4	0.2	(14)	0.2	(14)	1.0	(72)	1.5
1685		0.4	(36)	0.6	(55)	0.1	(09)	1.1
1690	6.7	0.9	(30)	0.7	(23)	1.4	(47)	3.0
1700	8.8	1.7	(35)	1.2	(25)	1.9	(40)	4.8
1710	9.2	1.9	(36)	1.3	(25)	2.1	(40)	5.3
1720	10.8	2.8	(46)	1.7	(28)	1.6	(26)	6.1

Source:
N.P.K. O'Brien (117), pp. 1–32, Tables 2 and 4.

H. FOREIGN POLICY

Treaties of Alliance and Peace, 1661–1722

(i) 1661 Treaty with Portugal (23 June)
  (1) Charles II to marry Catherine of Braganza, Infanta of Portugal.
  (2) England to receive Tangier as part of her dowry – city to be garrisoned, inhabitants to have freedom of religion; Portugal to pay 2 million crowns in two instalments as rest of dowry.
  (3) England also to be ceded Bombay in India and be granted free trade with Portugal and her dominions; undertook to defend Portugal with 2 regiments and 10 ships.

(ii) 1667 Peace of Breda (31 July)
  (1) *Between Charles II and Louis XIV*: Hostilities to cease; navigation and commerce to be open; mutual restoration of islands and territories captured by both sides during the second Dutch War.
  (2) *Between England and United Provinces*: Cessation of hostilities; Dutch interpretation of Navigation Laws, as regards imports from Germany or the Spanish Netherlands, accepted by England; 'the New Netherlands', including New York, on eastern seaboard of North America, to remain in English hands; Dutch acknowledge right of English flag to a salute only in Channel and British seas.

(iii) 1668 Treaty of Triple Alliance: England, United Provinces, Sweden (23 January)
  (1) Defensive alliance between Charles II and States General: each party to supply 40 men of war and 6,400 troops on request.
  (2) Efforts to be made by all three parties jointly to mediate between France and Spain to end War of Devolution, on terms granting Louis some, but far from all, of his 1667 conquests. If France refused, secret clause bound England and Dutch to wage war on France to reduce her to the limits of the Treaty of the Pyrenees.

(iv) 1670 Secret Treaty of Dover: Charles II, Louis XIV (1 June)
  (1) Charles declares himself convinced of truth of Roman Catholic religion and undertakes to make his reconciliation with Rome public as soon as the welfare of his kingdom permits; to receive 2 million livres as a token of French support, half of it within 3 months of ratification – also 6,000 French troops in case of need.
  (2) Both kings undertake to humble the pride of the United Provinces (UP) by making joint war on land and sea, the time to be at Louis's discretion; neither to make peace without the other's agreement. France to undertake main burden of land war (Charles to place 6,000 troops under French command) and England, main burden of war at sea (Louis to place 30 ships under duke of York's command). Every year of war Louis to pay Charles 3 million livres, part of first payment in advance.
  (3) Of the land conquests made from Dutch, England to receive Walcheren and two other islands in Scheldt estuary; efforts to be made to enlist support of, or neutralise, Sweden, Denmark, Emperor and Spain; all previous treaties with the UP to be voided, except the clauses of the Triple Alliance made for maintenance of Treaty of Aix-la-Chapelle (1668).

(v) 1674 Treaty of Westminster: peace between England and UP (19 February)
  (1) Captured territories to be restored; treaty of Breda (1667) to be renewed – Dutch conceding a wider right of salute – and new treaty of navigation to be negotiated; States General to pay an indemnity.
  (2) Secret article: neither party to assist the enemies of the other.

(vi) 1678 Treaty of Alliance: between England and the Dutch (concluded December 1677; ratified 3 March)

Peace and a strict defensive alliance to be established, both sides undertaking to defend the other's territory if attacked; Charles to assist UP with 10,000 foot, UP to provide Charles with 6,000 foot and 20 men of war.

(vii) 1689 Treaty of Grand Alliance: between Emperor, UP and England (19 May: England acceded 19 December)

  (1) France having attacked the Emperor and the UP, involving them in a 'grievous and unjust war', defensive and offensive alliance concluded between them.
  (2) No separate negotiations without consent; no peace to be made until France accepted the territorial limits of the Treaties of Westphalia, Osnaburg, Munster and the Pyrenees.
  (3) Spain and England, along with Lorraine and Savoy, invited to enter the treaty – which they did; England already bound to the Dutch by a naval treaty (Apr), in which they pledged to put 80 ships to sea against France, and subsequently (Aug) concluded a military treaty with them.
  (4) Secret clause of Austro-Dutch treaty pledged UP to support the Emperor in his claims to Spanish succession after death of Carlos II; England adhered to this, too, in December.

(viii) 1697 Peace of Ryswick: treaties between France and England, UP and Spain (10 September), Emperor (10 October)

  (1) William styled in preamble of Anglo-French treaty 'King of Great Britain *by the grace of God*' – a great concession by Louis.
  (2) There was to be 'perpetual peace and friendship' between Louis XIV and William III *and their successors*. (Taken in England as a French guarantee of the English succession as laid down in the Bill of Rights.)
  (3) Louis undertook not to molest William in his British possessions and gave 'his royal word' not to aid, directly or indirectly, William's enemies, nor countenance any rebellions in the latter's kingdoms.
  (4) Restoration of all conquests, colonial and Continental; on Continent, return to status quo of 1688, Louis giving up all his gains since then in Netherlands and Rhineland; but France retained Strasburg (appropriated 1681).
  (5) Commercial concessions by France to the Dutch – return to French tariff of 1664; but *existing* tariffs to remain between England and France.
  (6) Principality of Orange restored to its state of 1678, i.e. after Nijmegen.
  (7) No commitments made about the Spanish succession (to the Emperor's dismay).

[*Note*: After the Peace settlement, but not part of it, an agreement was made by Maximilian Emmanuel of Bavaria, governor of the Spanish Netherlands, with the States-General whereby the Dutch would establish garrisons (25 battalions in all) in eight Netherlands fortresses: Niewport, Courtrai, Oudenarde, Ath, Mons, Charleroi, Namur and Luxemburg. So originated the idea of the Dutch 'Barrier' or barrier-fortresses, which became a key factor in international relations during the next two decades.]

(ix) 1698 First Partition Treaty: Britain, France, UP (1 October [O.S.], 1698)

  (1) Principal heir to the Spanish Empire named as Joseph Ferdinand, Electoral Prince of Bavaria – to receive Spain, the Indies and the Spanish Netherlands.
  (2) French Dauphin to receive Naples and Sicily, with Tuscany and minor territories.
  (3) Duchy of Milan to fall to Archduke Charles, Emperor Leopold's second son.
  (4) Agreement to be communicated later to Emperor and Elector of Bavaria.

(x) 1700 Second Partition Treaty: Britain, France and UP (15 March 1700)

[*Note*: Joseph Ferdinand had died late in January (O.S.) 1699]

(1) Dauphin to receive: Naples, Sicily, Tuscany, duchy of Lorraine (if the duke would accept Milan in exchange) and other Italian territories of Spain.

(2) Archduke Charles to receive: Spain and all the remainder of the inheritance, but the two branches of the House of Habsburg always to remain separated.

(xi) 1701 Second Grand Alliance (Treaty of the Hague): William III, Emperor, UP (27 August/7 September)

(1) 'For the peace and general quiet' of Europe. Emperor to be supported in his claims on the Spanish inheritance, first by amicable means, but by force if necessary.

(2) Participants to endeavour to regain the Spanish Netherlands, in order to act as a barrier separating UP from France; also to recover duchy of Milan and Emperor's territories; likewise Naples and Sicily and the coast of Tuscany.

(3) Lawful for Britain and the UP to seize and hold what territories they could in Spanish West Indies.

(4) No separate treating for peace; no peace to be made until Emperor, Britain and the UP were satisfied that France and Spain would never be united under one government, that France had been excluded from possession of the Spanish Indies, and Britain and UP had secured the right to trade freely with Spanish territories. Defensive alliance to continue after war.

(5) Alliance may be joined by the princes and states of the Empire and any other power wishing to contribute to general peace.

(6) By an additional article of 1702 the three powers bound themselves to fight on until France recognised the Protestant Succession in England and repudiated 'the pretended Prince of Wales' (Hatton and Bromley (141), pp. 241–2).

(xii) 1703 Methuen Treaties

[a] *Political Treaties* with Britain and UP – Emperor adhered later (May 1703)

(1) Portugal committed herself to Spanish Succession war and to the Grand Alliance.

(2) She did so on the crucial condition that Habsburg Archduke Charles (pretended 'Charles III' of Spain) should come to Lisbon and be the focus for a war in the Peninsula.

(3) Portugal to be compensated with Spanish barrier fortresses and frontier territories in Estremadura and Galicia.

[b] *Commercial Treaty* with Britain (December 1703)

(1) Portugal to allow free legal entry into her territory of English cloth.

(2) In return England granted preference to Portuguese wines over French – French wines to pay *at least* one-third more in duty (in practice Portuguese wines paid only half the duty levied on French).

(xiii) 1709 First Treaty of Barrier and Succession: Britain and UP (Townshend Treaty) (18/29 October)

(1) UP were promised right of garrisoning 9 fortified places in the Spanish Netherlands, including Lille, Tournai and Valenciennes, plus 10 others, should they be seized from France.

(2) Dutch promised Britain armed assistance if needed to secure Protestant Succession.

(3) [Article 15] Britain promised to share with UP all the advantages she might secure in any part of the Spanish Empire (this controversial article abrogated Stanhope's unilateral agreement with Charles III for the cession of Minorca and the *Assiento* slave contract).

(xiv) 1713 Treaty of Utrecht
[a] Britain and France: (April 1713)
(1) France recognised the order of succession in Britain laid down by Parliament. Louis XIV undertook for himself and his successors never to acknowledge the Stuart claim to that succession. Pretender never to be allowed to return to France.
(2) Louis renounced any prospect of the French and Spanish crowns being united, and promised to seek no special commercial favours from Spain.
(3) Fortifications of Dunkirk [privateering base] to be rased and the harbour filled in.
(4) France ceded to Britain St Kitts, Newfoundland, Nova Scotia and her pretensions to the Hudson's Bay settlement, but retained Cape Breton and other islands commanding the St Lawrence.
(5) Britain's allies promised 'just and reasonable' satisfaction * by France.
(6) By separate Commerce treaty signed on same day each country granted the other 'most favoured nation' treatment in trade.
(But 8th and 9th articles, dealing with the necessary tariff changes, were rejected by House of Commons.)

[b] Britain and Spain: (July 1713)
(1) Philip V of Spain renounced his claim to French throne and promised not to transfer to France any Spanish-held land or lordship in America (which Philip retained, along with the mother Kingdoms).
(2) Spain recognised the Hanoverian succession in Britain.
(3) Gibraltar and Minorca ceded to Britain; also the *Assiento* contract for 30 years and the right to send an 'annual ship' to 3 specified harbours in Central America.
(4) Catalans (supporters of 'Charles III') to have amnesty and equal rights with Castilians (there was no possibility of enforcing this provision).

[* The Dutch received in 1713 a more limited barrier (Second Barrier Treaty – January 1713): about half the fortresses specified in 1709 [see above], including Ypres, Namur and Tournai, but excluding Lille, Condé and Valenciennes. The Spanish Netherlands, Milanese, Naples and Sardinia allocated to the Emperor (who delayed his consent until Rastadt, 1714); Sicily to duke of Savoy; and Prussia secured international recognition of the kingly title of Frederick I (pre-1701, Elector of Brandenburg-Prussia) along with Upper Guelderland and the principality of Neuchâtel; Portugal drew a blank.]

(xv) 1715 Third Barrier Treaty: Austria and UP (Britain guarantor) (4/15 November.)
(1) Dutch to hold 7 fortresses, as a Barrier in the (now) Austrian Netherlands and garrison 35,000 troops there and in the jointly-garrisoned Dendermonde. Vienna to pay three-fifths of their cost.
(2) Britain, as guarantor, to furnish 10,000 men and 20 warships in case the Barrier was attacked.
[*Note*: In the Second Barrier Treaty, 1713, Dutch had renewed their promise of 6,000 troops to assist Britain against attack from Pretender.]

(xvi) 1717 (N.S.) *The Triple Alliance*: France, Britain, U.P. (24 December/4 January 1716–17)
(1) France confirmed previous engagements made about the English Succession and the Pretender.
(2) France reaffirmed destruction of Dunkirk, except new canal and port at Mardyke.
(3) All powers reaffirmed the settlement of Utrecht. If one attacked, and mediation failed, the other two would come to her assistance: France and Britain with 8,000 foot and 2,000 horse, States-General with 4,000 foot and 1,000 horse.
(4) Each power promised to assist the other two in the event of internal rebellion.

(xvii) 1718 The Quadruple Alliance: France, Britain, Emperor and UP *

(1) Emperor to give up Sardinia [to duke of Savoy] in return for Sicily.

(2) Charles VI to renounce the Spanish Crown unequivocally.

(3) Philip V to renounce reconquest of Spain's former Italian possessions.

(4) Don Carlos's [son of Queen Elizabeth Farnese] right to the Farnese succession (Parma and Piacenza and the Medici succession [Tuscany]) to be recognised and secured by neutral garrisons.

(5) Problems arising from settlement to be dealt with by congresses.

(6) Secret articles committed signatories to use force against Philip V of Spain if he refused to accept terms.

[*Intended and expected to sign, but never did so.]

Principal sources:

1. C. Parry and C. Hopkins, *An Index to British Treaties, 1101–1968*, 3 vols (1970).
2. C. Parry, ed., *The Consolidated Treaty Series* (New York, 1969), vols 6–49.
3. C. Jenkinson, *A Collection of all the Treaties of Peace, Alliance and Commerce, between Great-Britain and other powers from . . . 1648 to . . . 1783*, 3 vols (1785).

I. BRITAIN'S MAJOR WARS, 1660–1722

I.1: Britain's principal allies

War	Allies
Second Anglo-Dutch War, 1665–7	the Bishop of Munster[1]
Third Anglo-Dutch War, 1672–4	France[2]
The Nine Years' War, 1689–97	Hapsburgs[3]; United Provinces; Savoy[4]; Spain[3]; Prussia; Hanover; Denmark
The War of Spanish Succession, 1702–13	Hapsburgs[2]; United Provinces[2]; Savoy (1703); Prussia[2]; Denmark[2]; Portugal (1703)
The War of the Quadruple Alliance, 1718–20	France; Hapsburgs; United Provinces; Savoy

Notes:
1. Ally forced out of war by catastrophic defeats.
2. Ally deserted when Britain made a separate peace.
3. Ally deserted Britain to make a separate peace.
4. Ally changed sides during the course of the war.

I.2: The armed forces and the cost of war, 1689–1783

		Average annual personnel		Average annual	Government expenditure on	Government expenditure on interest
		Navy	Army	Total	expenditure (£m)	forces	payments (%)*

		Navy	Army	Total			
War	1689–97	40,262	76,404	116,666	5.46	79	6
War	1702–13	42,938	92,708	135,646	7.06	72	19
Peace	1714–39					39	44
War	1739–48	50,313	62,373	112,686	8.78	65	25
Peace	1750–55					41	44
War	1756–63	74,800	92,676	167,476	18.04	70	22
Peace	1764–75					37	43
War	1776–83	82,022	108,484	190,506	20.27	62	30

* Balance of expenditure spent on civil government.

Sources:
1. J. Brewer (133), Table 2.1, p. 30.
2. N. P. K. O'Brien (117), Table 1, p. 2.

J. OVERSEAS TRADE AND THE COLONIES

J.1: Legislation

(i) 1660 Navigation Act (12 Charles II, c. 18)

    (1) No goods to be imported to or exported from American colonies or England's Asian and African forts and stations except in ships owned by Englishmen or Irishmen and with crews at least three-quarters English. Penalty: forfeiture.

    (2) No alien permitted to practise as merchant or factor in the Plantations.

    (3) No product of America, Asia or Africa to be imported into England or Ireland except in English, Irish or colonial-owned ships.

    (4) English and Irish coasting trade limited to English ships.

    (5) Naval stores, sugar, oils, wines, spirits to be imported only in ships owned by original exporters [i.e. not by Dutch carriers] and *English-manned* (three-quarters).

    (6) French and Rhenish wines, spirits, naval stores, oil, grain, sugar, potash and all commodities from Russia and the Levant to be deemed 'aliens' goods' and pay double customs *unless* imported in English-owned and -manned ships.

    (7) Goods from Spain, Portugal, Madeira and Azores [wine] and the Canaries to be imported duty-free if carried in English-owned and -manned ships.

NB (8) *'Enumerated' colonial goods*: Sugar, tobacco, cotton-wool, indigo, ginger and dyestuffs of the English Plantations could be shipped directly *only* to England, to Ireland [Ireland was deprived of this privilege in 1671] or to other English colonies. [*Note*: This list was added to periodically later.]

Source: M. Jensen, ed., *English Historical Documents: American Colonial Documents to 1776* vol. IX (1955), pp. 354–6.

(ii) 1663 Staple Act (15 Charles II, c. 7)

    (1) All goods produced or manufactured in Europe and destined for the Plantations to be carried first to England in 'lawful' ships, and there unloaded, before being carried thence in English-owned and -manned ships.

    (2) Scottish and Irish horses, salt for Newfoundland and New England fisheries and wine from Madeira and Azores exempted from (1) above.

Source: Jensen, op. cit. pp. 356–8.

(iii) 1673 Plantation Duty Act (25 Charles II, c. 7)

(This was to prevent abuses arising from the *inter*-colonial trade in 'enumerated' goods allowed by the 1660 Act, provision [8] above)

    A 'plantation duty' of 1d. a pound on tobacco, and other amounts for remaining commodities, to be payable at the colonial port of clearance by any ship's master who could not show a certificate that he had taken out a bond to carry the cargo back to England.

Source: Jensen, op. cit. pp. 358–9.

(iv) 1696 [Second] Navigation Act (7 & 8 William III, c. 22)

    (1) After 28 March 1698 no merchandise to be imported into or exported from any Plantation in America, Asia or Africa, or to be carried from port to port in the same, or to England, except in English-built and owned ships with masters and three-quarters crew English.

    (2) Appointments of colonial governors (made responsible, on oath, for carrying out

the above, and punishable by fine or deprivation) *all* to be approved by Crown, even when appointed by proprietors or corporate companies.

3. Provision for central registration in London of all colonial as well as English shipping.

Source: Jensen, op. cit. pp. 359–64.

Additional sources:
1. J. Thirsk and J. P. Cooper (10).
2. A. Browning, ed., M. Ransome and D.B. Horn, eds *English Historical Documents* vols VIII (1966), X (1957); J.H. Rose, A.P. Newton and E.A. Benians (eds) (291).

J.2: The foundation and annexation of colonies

(i) North America

	Date	Colony	Remarks
(1)	1606–7	Virginia	
	1620	New Plymouth	(later embodied in Massachusetts)
(2)	1628–9	Massachusetts	
(3)	1629	New Hampshire	
(4)	1632	Maryland	
(5)	1636–47	Rhode Island	
(6)	1637–51	Maine	(later embodied in Massachusetts)
(7)	1663	Carolina	(see below, 1713)
(8)	1664	New York	captured from United Provinces; retained 1667 (Peace of Breda) with rest of 'New Netherlands'
(9)	1665	New Jersey	captured from United Provinces; retained at Peace of Breda
(10)	1681	Pennsylvania	
(11)	1682	Delaware	settled from 1664
(12)	1713	North and South Carolina	Carolina split into 2 colonies (see above, 1663)
	1713	Newfoundland, Nova Scotia (Acadia), and Hudsons Bay Territory	annexed at Peace of Utrecht. All partly settled and disputed with France since 17th century
(13)	1732	Georgia	

(ii) West Indies

Date	Colony	Remarks
1624	St Kitts	(part – see below, 1713)
1625	Barbados	
1628–36	Nevis, Montserrat and Antigua (in Leeward Islands)	
1655	Jamaica captured from Spain	
1655–70	Cayman Islands	
1666	Virgin Islands	
1670	The Bahamas	
1713	Remaining part of St Kitts	(see above, 1624) from France

J.3: The seventeenth-century commercial revolution

A *Monopoly trading companies*

(i) Old foundations still extant/active after 1660:

Date	Company	Type	Date of reduction or abolition of monopoly
1486/1564	Merchant Adventurers	Regulated	1621–34; abolished 1689
1555	Muscovy (*alias* Russia)	{originally Joint-Stock Regulated 1610s	abolished 1699
1579	Eastland [Baltic ports]	Regulated	abolished 1673
1581	Levant	{originally Joint-Stock Regulated 1595	abolished 1754
1600	East India	Joint-Stock	temporarily lost monopoly 1698–1709 (see below, 1698, New East India Company)

(ii) Post-Restoration foundations:

Date	Company	Type	Date of reduction or abolition of monopoly
1663/1672	Royal African (reconstituted)	Joint-Stock	restricted 1698 abolished 1712
1670	Hudsons Bay	Joint-Stock	
1698	New East India	Joint-Stock	merged with 'Old' 1709
1709	'United' East India	Joint-Stock	
1711	South Sea	Joint-Stock	

B *Merchant shipping*

Total tonnage English-owned merchant ships	
year	*tons*
1629	115,000
1660	162,000*
1686	340,000
1702	323,000

* L. A. Harper's estimate, *The English Navigation Laws* (New York, 1939), p. 339. [The other figures come from Davis.]

Source:
R. Davis (198), p. 15.

C *Expansion of trade with Southern Europe and the Mediterranean*

(i) Exports (other than shortcloths) by English merchants from London, 1609–1640

	1609	*1640*
% shipped to Northern and North-West Europe	29	22
% shipped to Spain, Africa and Mediterranean ports	46	65

Note:
Number of shortcloths exported from London by natives declined from 127,215 (1614) to 86,924 (1640). Official value of other goods exported from and by same rose from £198,266 (1609) to £609,722 (1640).

Source:
F.J. Fisher, 'London's Export Trade in the early 17th Century' (1940), repr. in Minchinton (197), pp. 66–7.

(ii) Exports of cloths (other than silks) from London 1663/9–1699/1701

		£000	
Years	*Total average p.a.*	*To Northern & North-West Europe*	*To Southern Europe/ Mediterranean*
1663 and 1669	1,512	563	854
1699–1701	2,013	668	1,109
[av. of 1699–1701 for London *and* outports]	[3,045]	[1,544]	[1,201]

Source:
R. Davis (199a).

(iii) Levant Company shipments to Turkey and the Levant

Years	*Cloths per annum*
c. 1635	6,000
1666–72	av. 13,762
1673–77	av. 20,075
1678–83	av. 19,652
1701–05	av. 18,836

Sources:
1. C.G.A. Clay (170b), p. 150.
2. R. Davis, *Aleppo and Devonshire Square* (1967), p. 42.

D *Imports of East India Company textiles*

Years	Average pieces per year imported
1631–40	under 10,000
1664–5	28,000
1663; 1669	240,000*
1671–80	544,692
1683–5	1,250,000 (peak)
1699–1701	861,000*

* These figures, less reliable because based on Customs evidence, are from R. Davis, (199a), p. 82.

Sources:
C. G. A. Clay (170b), p. 167, citing K. N. Chaudhuri, *The Trading World of Asia and the English East India Company* (Cambridge 1978).

E *Imports of colonial tobacco*

	(lbs. weight)	
Years	All English ports	London
1615	50,000	
1619		20,000
1639		1.8 million [valued at £240,000 in 1640 – now leading import commodity]
1662–3		7.4 m.
1672	17.6 m.	
1681		14.5 m.
1700	33.8 m.	22 m.

Sources:
1. R. Davis (199a), p. 80.
2. C.G.A. Clay (170b), p. 168.
3. W.E. Minchinton (197), p. 21.

F *Imports of West Indian sugar*

	cwts. p.a.	Value of sugar and molasses imports (average p.a.)
1625–40	neglible (Barbados not planted until 1640s	
1663; 1669	av. 148,000	£256,000 (into London)
	(Barbados & Jamaica [1655])	
*[1661–1670	av. nearly 200,000]	
1699–1701	av. 371,000	{ £526,000 (into London) £630,000 (into all ports)
*[c. 1700	480,000]	

Alternative series: C.G.A. Clay (170b), p. 169 (using Dunn (201), p. 203).

Sources:
1. R. Davis (199a), pp. 81, 96.

G *Imports from Asia and the Americas as a proportion of total imports*

into London (%)	
1600	NIL
1622	6.5
1634	16.6
1663 and 1669	av. 23.7
1669–1701*	av. 34.7

* The percentage of imports into *all* English ports was 31.8% between these years.

Source:
C.G.A. Clay (170b), Table xx, p. 160.

H *Growth of the re-export trade*

	Re-exports as proportion of all exports (%)	Approx value of re-exported goods
1640	3–4 [?17]*	[£500,000]*
1663–1669	22	£900,000
1699–1701	31	£2,986,000

* The startlingly higher percentage for 1640 and the rough estimated value for that year, derives from D. C. Coleman (203), Table 11, and 'takes into account the Dover re-export trade' (ibid. p. 133).

Source:
R. Davis (199a), p. 92.

K. AGRICULTURE

K.1: The English harvest, 1660–1759

(i) The wheat harvest: years of scarcity, 1660–1759

1657–61	(5)	4 bad or deficient harvests, followed by dearth in 1661
1692–8	(7)	'the seven lean years'; only 1694 average, the rest bad or deficient or, as in 1693 and 1697, years of dearth
1708–11⎫ 1713 ⎭	(4)	bad in 1708; 1709 the worst dearth since 1596; 1710–11 deficient bad
1725–8	(4)	a deficient and an average harvest, followed by 2 bad ones
1739–40	(2)	deficient 1739; dearth 1740
1756–7	(2)	dearth 1756; deficient 1757

(ii) The wheat harvest: years of plenty, 1660–1759

1665–72	(8)	7 harvests either good or (1666–7) abundant; only 1668 'average'
1683–90	(8)	7 harvests either good or (1687–8) abundant; 1684 average
1700–07	(8)	4 abundant harvests, 3 good; 1703 average
1721–3	(3)	all good
1730–33	(4)	4 good harvests in a row
1741–4	(4)	3 good; 1743 abundant
1754–5⎫ 1758–9⎭		4 good harvests, punctuated by the bad years 1756–7 (above)

Source and method of classification:
W. G. Hoskins (214) esp. pp. 15, 28–31.

K.2: Output

(i) English agricultural productivity in the eighteenth century

(a) *Estimated net output of corn (million quarters)*

1700	13.29
1750	14.82
1770	16.70
1790	18.99

(b) *Agricultural output: rates of growth (average % p.a.)*

1710–40	0.9*
1740–80	0.5[†]
1780–1800	0.6[†]

Source:
P. Deane and W.A. Cole
(176a), p. 65.

Sources:
[†] P. Deane and W.A. Cole (176a), p. 78.
* N.F.R. Crafts and R.D. Lee, in R.C. Flood and D.H. McCloskey (181), p. 2, revising Deane and Cole's estimated NIL rate of growth, 1710–40.

Compendium of information

(ii) Grain prices and exports

(a) *Index of grain prices, 1660–1749*
(1641–55 = 100)

Decade	
1660–9	107
1670–9	101
1680–9	89
1690–9	104
1700–9	84
1710–19	104
1720–9	89
1730–9	73
1740–9	77

(b) *Prices of wheat at Cambridge, 1750–83*
(shillings per quarter)

(1740–9	29.6)
1750–9	37.7
1760–9	41.9
1770–83	49.7

Sources:
1. D.C. Coleman (168), p. 112.
2. Calculated from T.S. Ashton, *An Economic History of England: the Eighteenth Century* (1972 edn), Table 1, p. 239.

(c) *Grain exports (wheat, rye, barley, malt),*
  1692–1764: annual average, in quarters

1692–1700	80–100,000
decade	
1700–9	283,000
1710–19	369,000
1729–9	426,000
1730–9	531,000
1740–9	661,000
1750–9	650,000
1760–4	373,000

As a % of all domestic exports
(best year per decade)

1703	9.6
1713	12.2
1722	13.1
1734	18.2
1749	14.8
1750	19.2
1761	10.6
[1765	5.4][†]

[†] Year of prohibition of grain shipments, dwindling and intermittent trade only thereafter.

Source:
A.H. John (216b), pp. 48–9, 64.

447

K.3: Enclosures

(i) Enclosure Acts passed

1604–99	20+
1700–60	208
1760–80	1068

Sources:
1. J.R. Wordie (217a), p. 486.
2. W.E. Tate, *The English Village Community and the Enclosure Movement* (1967).

(ii) Enclosure Rate in England: total surface area

enclosed (%)	
already enclosed by 1600	c. 47
enclosed 1600–99 (overwhelmingly by private agreement)	*c.* 24
enclosed 1700–99 (by agreement and over 1800 parliamentary Acts)	c. 13

Source:
Proportions calculated by J.R. Wordie (217a) p. 502.

L. INDUSTRY

L.1: Industrial output, exports and home consumption in England and Wales, 1700–40*

	Industrial output (£m)	of which: exports (£m)	(%)	Home consumption (£m)	Consumption per capita (£)
1700	18.5	3.8	20.6	14.6	2.77
1705	19.3	4.2	22.0	15.0	2.79
1710	19.2	4.9	25.3	14.4	2.61
1715	20.4	5.1	24.8	15.3	2.75
1720	21.9	5.0	23.1	16.8	2.97
1725	22.6	5.6	22.6	17.4	3.10
1730	23.5	5.4	23.1	18.1	3.24
1735	24.8	6.0	24.2	18.8	3.26
1740	24.2	6.3	26.1	17.9	3.01

* At *c.* 1697–1704 prices.

Source:
Estimates of W. A. Cole (178a), Table 3.1, p. 40 and Note on Sources.

L.2: Inventions and other industrial landmarks

c. 1660–70	'Dutch loom' (engine loom) introduced in Manchester area for ribbon and tape manufacture (Manchester 'smallwares')
1676	Robert Hook: universal joint
1683	William Palin and William Luggins: mill-powered machine for manufacturing ironware
1698	Thomas Savery: steam pump for draining land and mines; supplying water; but many practical problems
1709	Abraham Darby: coke-fired blast furnace for iron smelting
1712	Thomas Newcomen: steam engine (piston) – the first practical pumping engine
1717–18	John Lombe / Sir Thomas Lombe began construction of first genuine silk mill (Derby) with water-powered throwing-machines
1730	Nottingham workmen produced first mechanically-made pair of *cotton* hose (from Indian yarn) on a stocking-frame (*woollen* hose manufactured on frames in Vale of Trent since 1660s)
1733	John Kay: Flying Shuttle: hand-operated machine, enabling broader cloths to be woven more quickly
1733	John Wyatt and Lewis Paul: spinning machine (inventor Wyatt; marketed Paul)
1742	Benjamin Huntsman: invented 'crucible steel' technique – smelting metal at very high temperatures in sealed fireclay crucibles
1743	David Bourne: carding machine, using wire-toothed revolving cylinder
1743	Thomas Boulsover: first produced 'Sheffield Plate'
1760	Job and William Wyatt: screw manufacturing machine
1761	Robert Hinchcliffe: high quantity production of scissors and shears in cast steel

1764	John Hargreaves: Spinning Jenny
1765	James Watt: invented the steam engine condenser (originally a Newcomen engine with a separate condensation chamber)
1768–9	Richard Arkwright: Water Frame (though his first spinning-frame mill [Nottingham, 1771] was in fact horse-powered not water-powered, as subsequently at Cromford, etc.)
1770	Jesse Ramsden: Ramsden's Lathe
1776	Andrew Meikle: threshing machine
1779	'Ironbridge' – cast-iron bridge spanning River Severn at Coalbrookdale
1779	Samuel Crompton: Spinning 'Mule' – combined principle of jenny and frame spinning
1779	James Keir: patented an early version of 'Muntz metal' – capable of being forged or wrought when red-hot or cold
c. 1780	Keir discovered distinction between carbonic acid gas and atmospheric air
1783	Thomas Bell: cylindrical roller process for cotton printing
1784	Henry Cort: puddling furnace (iron)
1785	Edmund Cartwright: power loom

Sources:
1. P. Mantoux, *The Industrial Revolution in the Eighteenth Century* (1928).
2. K. Desmond, ed., *The Harwin Chronology of Inventions* (1986).

L.3: Industrial production and expansion

Coal

Estimated annual production of main coalfields (000s of tons)

Fields	1651–60[1]	1681–90[1]	1700[2]	1750[2]	1775[2]
North-East	65	1,225	1,290	1,955	2,990
Scotland	40	475	450	715	1,000
S. Wales	20		80	140	650
Yorkshire			300	500	850
Lancashire	65	850	80	350	900
W. Midlands			510	820	1,400
E. Midlands			75	140	250
South-West	14	132	150	180	250
Cumberland	6	(?)	25	350	400
Total output: England, Wales and Scotland	210	*c.* 2,900	2,985	5,230	8,850

Total output by 1783: well over 9m. tons p.a.

Notes:
By 1775 the Northumberland and Durham field accounted for less than 34% of total output (cf. 43% in 1700). The contribution of Lancashire and Yorkshire increased in the same period from 12.8 to 19.8% and that of South Wales from 2.7 to 7.3%

1. J.U. Nef (207a), I, pp 19–20.
2. M.W. Flinn, *History of the British Coal Industry*, II (2 vols, 1984), pp. 26–7.

M. LIVING STANDARDS

M.1: Prices in England, 1661–1783

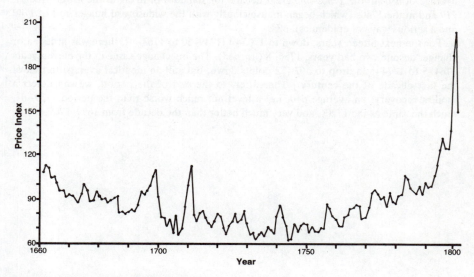

The Schumpeter-Gilboy Price Index

Sources:
Constructed from Indices in B.R. Mitchell and P. Deane (176b) and printed in J.M.
Beattie, *Crime and the Courts in England, 1660–1800* (Oxford, 1986), p. 206, Fig. 5.3.

M.2: The trend of real wages (England), 1660–1783

The most detailed and up-to-date guide to the trend of real wages in our period, year by
year, is provided by E.A. Wrigley and R.S. Schofield (196), p. 643: it is the appropriate
section of the authors' *Real-wage index for England 1500–1912* (Table A9.2). The following
are the more important extrapolations and conclusions to be noted.

In the opening seven years of the period (1659–60 to 1665–6) – characterised by the
last of the hard late-republican years, the economic depression which spilled over into the
early 1660s (Ch. 5), and in conclusion by the Great Plague and the Fire of London – the
index averages *447*. This figure throws a cold light on the 'Merrie England' image popularly
associated with the aftermath of the Restoration, for it is actually lower (by almost 20
points) than that for the years of the Civil Wars and the Interregnum. It does, however,
represent a considerably higher average level of real wages than was achieved in the earlier
Stuart period (it was surpassed in only four isolated years between 1607–8 and 1638–9).

After 1665–6, however, the trend of real wages ran steadily upwards, with only a few
slight and brief dips, notably in 1674–5 and 1684–5, to average *541* on the index in the
1680s (1679–80 to 1688–9) – making that the best whole decade in the seventeenth century
for the ordinary man's living standards. Better still was to come briefly in the opening years
of William III's reign, when over the three years 1688–9 to 1691–2 the Wrigley-Schofield
real wage index rises to an average of *614*.

In any case, in the long-term experience of four generations of wage labourers from the

451

mid-1660s to the mid-1760s, the tightened belts of the middle to late 1690s proved no more than a brief hiatus. Thus for the first decade of the new century (which included the appalling harvest years of 1708–9) the index averages *591*; by the 1720s, it reaches an average of *636*; in the 1730s (*the* great decade for standard of living of the lower orders), *719* and in the 1740s (which began inauspiciously with the widespread hunger riot of 1740 and a serious wave of epidemics), *673*.

For the next fifteen years, down to 1763–4 [1749–50 to 1763–4], there was little major change, despite two bad years, 1756–8 (av. *663*). The big change came in the eleven years 1764–5 to 1774–5, a drop to *591* (72 points down, but still an identical average to that of the first decade of the century.) Thereafter, to the end of the period, we can detect a modest recovery: an average *640*, i.e. a level not much worse than the period 1739–64, much the same as the 1720s, and very much better than the decade from 1699–1709.

N. RELIGION

N. 1: Royal Declarations and Proclamations, 1660–88

(i) Declaration of Breda, 4 April 1660

The most important promises and concessions offered by Charles II were:

(1) a free pardon to all returning to their duty to the king within 40 days of the issue of the declaration, saving only those to be excepted by Parliament;

(2) a solemn promise not to bear ill will against any for their actions during the Civil Wars and Interregnum;

(3) a 'liberty to tender consciences' – religious toleration for all who did not disturb the peace of the kingdom; to be confirmed by act of Parliament;

(4) a land settlement to be set and arranged by Parliament;

(5) all arrears of pay in the army to be met, and those soldiers who were willing to serve the monarchy to be admitted to his service at the same rank and pay.

Source: J. P. Kenyon (7), pp. 357–8.

(ii) Worcester House Declaration, 25 October 1660

Issued following on the deadlock that beset the Worcester House Conference (Ch. 1), the Declaration:

(1) sternly admonished the Presbyterians for not having 'so candidly dealt with [us] as we deserved';

(2) announced Charles's intention to restore episcopacy;

(3) set out what the main features of the restored Church were to be:

  (a) bishops to be chosen for their learning, piety and charity; all unworthy incumbents to be dismissed;

  (b) suffragan bishops to be appointed wherever the diocese was too large for one man to cope with;

  (c) bishops only to ordain and exercise jurisdiction with the advice of their presbyters;

  (d) existing liturgy and Book of Common Prayer to be used in all church services pending revision by a commission of divines to be appointed by the king;

  (e) individual clergymen who objected to specific adiaphorous (non-essential) ceremonies to be dispensed from the need to conduct them, pending a final decision by a national synod on those same ceremonies; likewise from elements of the ritual, use of the crucifix and the wearing of surplices.

Source: A. Browning, ed., English Historical Documents 1660–1714 (1966), pp. 365–70.

(iii) Charles II's 'first Declaration of Indulgence' [so-called], 26 Dec 1662

Declaration designed to include all religious dissenters, Protestant and Catholic alike. Only distinction to be that Protestant dissenters could apply for licences to worship publicly, Catholics restricted to private domestic gatherings. Latter justified on grounds of 'a due sense we have of the greatest part of our Roman Catholic subjects of this kingdom having deserved well from our father of blessed memory, and from us, and even from the Protestant religion itself, in adhering to us with their lives and fortunes for the maintenance of our Crown in the religion established against those who under the name of zealous Protestants employed both fire and sword to overthrow them both'.

Provisions to take effect only subject to Parliamentary approval (cf. Ch. 1).

Source: J.P. Kenyon (7), pp. 403–6.

(iv) Declaration of Indulgence, 15 March 1672
[The Preamble justified the Declaration: 'it being evident by the sad [religious] experience of twelve years that there is very little fruit of all those forcible courses [hitherto pursued]'. Aimed at 'quieting the minds of our good subjects', 'inviting strangers in this conjuncture to come and live under us' and 'preventing for the future the danger that might otherwise arise from private meetings and seditious conventicles'. The last consideration was probably the most important to the king and his government.]

(1) Church of England to be maintained in all its privileges; payment of tithes even by Nonconformists to continue, and no appointments to be made to any benefice where appointee did not exactly accord with doctrinal requirements of Church of England;
(2) execution of all penal laws against Nonconformists and recusants to be immediately suspended;
(3) in order to enjoy the benefits of the indulgence, Nonconformists henceforth required to worship at licensed meetings with licensed ministers, and all such meetings to be open to the public; extra-licensed worship to be severely punished;
(4) Roman Catholics to be allowed to hold services only in private.

Source: J. P. Kenyon (7), pp. 407–8.

(v) James II's first Declaration of Indulgence ('King James the Second his gracious declaration to all his loving subjects for liberty of conscience') 4 April 1687
This takes a different tack from those issued by his brother; there is no mention of services rendered during the Civil Wars and Interregnum. Instead, though clearly influenced by his sincere, pious Catholicism ('We cannot but heartily wish . . . that all the people of our dominions were members of the Catholic Church') it concentrates on advancing pragmatic, ethical reasons for a full religious toleration.
(*a*) Persecution destroys the interest of government by spoiling trade, depopulating countries and discouraging strangers; (*b*) 'it never obtained the end for which it was employed'.

(1) promises to protect clergy and laity of the Church of England 'in the free exercise of their religion as by law established, and in the quiet and full enjoyment of all their possessions';
(2) all penal laws in matters ecclesiastical to be *immediately* suspended;
(3) worship to be permitted either in private houses or in places built for the purpose;
(4) oaths of Supremacy and allegiance under first and second Test Acts no longer to be administered.

Source: J.P. Kenyon (7), pp. 410–13.

(vi) James II's Second Declaration of Indulgence, 27 April 1688
This was a reissue of that of 1687; with addition on 4 May of an order that it be read in all churches of the Church of England on two successive Sundays.

Source: Browning, *English Historical Documents*, pp. 399–400; see W.C. Costin and J.S. Watson (11b), pp. 345–6 for Order in Council of May 4/14, 1688.

N.2: The Restoration Church Settlement and the 'Clarendon Code', 1661–70

(i) Corporation Act, 1661 (13 Charles II, st. 2, c.1)
(1) all persons holding municipal office were to take oaths of allegiance and supremacy, swear that taking up arms against the King was illegal, and abjure the Solemn League and Covenant;

(2) no person could qualify for municipal office without having taken Communion according to Anglican rites during previous year;

(3) special commission empowered until 1663 to root out dissidents on both counts.

Source: J.P. Kenyon (7), 376–8.

(*ii*) *Quaker Act, 1662* (13 & 14 Charles II, c.1): anyone who refused to swear an oath legally tendered, or who met with five or more other Quakers, liable to £5 or £10 fine, 3–6 months' imprisonment and, on a third conviction, transportation.

Source: *Statutes at Large*, VIII, pp. 32–4.

(*iii*) *Act of Uniformity, 1662* (14 Charles II, c.4)

(1) revised Prayer Book (1662) made compulsory for all services in Church of England;

(2) all clergy then beneficed required to have had, or to seek, episcopal ordination; to declare their 'unfeigned assent and consent' to everything in, or prescribed by, the Prayer Book; and to make all the declarations prescribed by Corporation Act (above *i*) – all before the Feast of Bartholomew (24 Aug 1662); those who failed to do so to be deprived;

(3) all clergy subsequently beneficed to make same declarations within 2 months of entry;

(4) all cathedral clergy, chaplains, fellows and heads of colleges, schoolmasters in public or private schools and private tutors to subscribe to a declaration of conformity to the liturgy of the Church of England, of acknowledgment of the unlawfulness of resisting the King and of repudiation of the Solemn League and Covenant.

Source: J.P. Kenyon (7), pp. 378–82.

(*iv*) *First Conventicles Act, 1664* (16 Charles II, c.4):

(1) illegal for any person aged 16 or over to attend a meeting of more than five people for worship ('under colour or pretence of any exercise of religion') without use of Anglican Prayer Book and liturgy;

(2) fines of varying severity or imprisonment for first two offences; fines of £100 or transportation for 7 years for third offence.

(3) Act to remain in force for 3 years after 1664 session [expired 1667].

Source: *Statutes at Large*, VIII, p. 208 (see Second Conventicles Act, 1670, below)

(*v*) *Five Mile Act, 1665* (17 Charles II, c. 2): ministers ejected under terms of Uniformity Act, and other unlicensed preachers refusing to swear to the illegality of resistance and to eschew 'any alteration of government, either in Church or State', forbidden to come within 5 miles of their former parish or of any city or town; forbidden also to act as schoolmasters. Penalty £40.

Source: Costin and Watson (11b), pp. 34–6.

(*vi*) *Second Conventicles Act, 1670* (22 Charles II, c.1): as 1664, except

(1) fines much increased: on laity 5s. for first, 10s. for subsequent offences; on preachers at conventicles, £20 for first, £40 for all subsequent offences; one third of the fines to go to informers;

(2) Act made perpetual, and constables and JPs failing to enforce it made liable to prosecution.

Source: J.P. Kenyon (7), pp. 383–6.

N.3: Leading dignitaries of the Church of England, 1660–1722

Archbishops of Canterbury		Archbishops of York		Bishops of London	
William Juxon	1660–3	Accepted Frewen	1660–4	Gilbert Sheldon	1660–3
Gilbert Sheldon	1663–77	Richard Sterne	1664–83	Humphrey Henchman	1663–75
William Sancroft	1677–90*	John Dolben	1683–6	Henry Compton	1675–1713
(*deprived 1 Feb 1690)		Thomas Lamplugh	1688–91	John Robinson	1713–23
John Tillotson	1691–4	John Sharp	1691–1714	(Lord Privy Seal 1711–13)	
Thomas Lenison	1694–1715	Sir William Dawes	1714–24	Edmund Gibson	1723–48
William Wake	1715–37				

N.4: The Anglian bishops and their annual incomes, 1660–1762

See	pre-Revolution	post-Revolution	1762 ('reputed yearly value')
	(£)	(£)	(£)
Canterbury	4,317 (1681–2)	4,775 + fines etc. (1711–14)	7,000
York	–	2,524 + fines (1692–1704)	4,500
Bath and Wells	850 (c. 1688)	1,400 + (c. 1710)	2,000
Bristol	350 (c. 1688)	400 (c. 1710)	450
(with Residentiary of St Paul's and rectory of Bow *in commendam*,* TOTAL 1,550)			
Carlisle	713 (1688)	800 (c. 1710)	1,300
Chester	744 (c. 1680)	1,000 (c. 1710)	900
(with rectory of Stanhope *in commendam**			TOTAL 1,500)
Chichester	800 (c. 1680)	1,000 (c. 1710)	1,400
Durham	3,500 (1664)	–	6,000
Ely	1,106 (1684)	2,300 + fines (1707–8)	3,400
Exeter	584 (c. 1670)	500 (c. 1710)	1,500
Gloucester	–	600 (c. 1710)	900
(with prebend of Durham *in commendam**			TOTAL ?1400)[†]
Hereford	–	1,000 (c. 1710)	1,200
Lichfield &			
Coventry	1,200 (c. 1660)	1,400+ (c. 1710)	1,400
Lincoln	1,193 (1660)	1,100 (1715)	1,500
London	3,000 + fines (1679)	–	4,000
Norwich	–	1,529 (1692–1706)	2,000
Oxford	–	600 (c. 1710)	500
(with deanery of St Paul's *in commendam**			TOTAL 2,300)
Peterborough	630 (1688)	800 (c. 1710)	1,000
(with vicarage of Twickenham *in commendam**			TOTAL [not known])
Rochester	500 (1663)	600 (c. 1710)	600
(with deanery of Westminster *in commendam**			TOTAL 1,500)
Salisbury	1,920 + fines (1675)	–	3,000
Winchester	3,563 gross (c. 1670)	–	5,000
Worcester	–	–	3,000
St Asaph	800 max (1685)	800 (c. 1710)	1,400
(an archdeaconry and 3 sinecures normally attached)			

See	pre-Revolution	post-Revolution	1762 ('reputed yearly value')
	(£)	(£)	(£)
Bangor	150 (*c.* 1684)	400 (*c.* 1710)	1,400
St David's	*c.* 500 (1684)	700 (*c.* 1710)	900
Llandaff	344 + *commendam.** (1680)	300 (*c.* 1710)	500

* *In commendam*: literally, 'in trust'; used of a benefice which a bishop or other dignitary was permitted to hold along with his own preferment. Usually, in effect, a convenient supplementary source of income for poorly endowed bishoprics.
† my estimate.

Sources:
1. D.R. Hirschberg, 'Episcopal Incomes and Expenses, 1660–*c.* 1760), in R. O'Day and E. Heal, eds, (153), pp. 213–16.
2. Sir J. Fortescue, ed., *The Correspondence of King George III* (1927), I, pp. 33–44: 'A list of Archbishops. Bishops, Deans, and Prebendaries in England and Wales . . . with the reputed yearly value of their respective dignities' (1762).

N.5: Parliament, the Church and Dissent, 1673–1779

A The Anglican Tests, Occasional Conformity and Schism
(*i*) *First Test Act, 1673* (25 Charles II, c.2)
All who held civil office under the Crown and commissions or places of trust in the army and Royal Navy must:

(1) (a) take the oaths of supremacy and allegiance in open court;
(b) sign a declaration repudiating Roman Catholic doctrine of transubstantiation;
(c) receive the sacrament according to the rites of the Church of England before 1 Aug 1673 – or, if subsequently appointed to office, within 3 months of appointment – and produce a certificate to that effect legally attested by the presiding minister, a churchwarden and two witnesses;
(2) in the event of failing to do so, suffer a fine of £500, incapacitation from office and deprivation of legal rights in the courts.

[*Note*: This act explicitly aimed at 'preventing dangers which may happen from Popish recusants', but its sacramental clauses also affected Protestant dissenters unless they practised 'occasional conformity'. Did not apply to members of either House of Parliament.]

Source: J.P. Kenyon (7), pp. 461–2.

(*ii*) *Second Test Act, 1678* (30 Charles II, st. 2, c.1)
(1) no peer of the realm, member of the House of Lords or member of the House of Commons to be allowed to sit in Parliament without first taking oaths of supremacy and allegiance and an anti-Catholic declaration both repudiating substantiation and condemning named 'superstitious and idolatrous' Roman practices;
(2) all refusing the Test to be presumed Popish recusants, subjected to all legal penalties as such and (in all but a few cases) debarred the Court.

[*Note*: (a) the Act excluded Catholics from Parliament until 1829, but because it did not include a *sacramental* test, parallel to that of 1673, did not affect Protestant dissenters; (b) Duke of York excepted from its provisions by an amendment (cf. Ch. 8).]

Source: J. P. Kenyon (7), pp. 465–6.

(iii) Occasional Conformity Act, 1711 (10 Anne, c.6) (repealed 1719)

[*Note*: Three earlier bills to the same purpose, introduced in the sessions of 1702–3, 1703–4 and 1704–5, were either blocked or defeated in the Lords. The first bill prescribed draconian penalties for offenders ((£100 fine plus £5 for every day in office after attendance at a conventicle; disablement from office unless and until they had conformed to the Established Church for a year). The second and third bills were less harsh. The fourth, and successful bill, passed in 1711, was much less severe than the first, and rather less so than the other two.]

(1) Any person who, after appointment to a civil or military office under the Crown, or to a municipal office, or after election to a town council, 'knowingly or willingly' attended a conventicle was to forfeit £40; also to be disabled from holding any such office thenceforward, unless and until they conformed to the Church of England for a year, taking Anglican communion three times during that year;

(2) offenders had to be prosecuted within three months;

(3) the Toleration Act of 1689 (see below), 'which ought to be inviolably observed', was confirmed, and clarified by allowing dissenting pastors and teachers to minister to, and teach *any* congregation regardless of where they were originally licensed.

Source: Williams (11a), pp. 334–7. For first Occasional Conformity Bill, 1702, see W. Cobbett (2), VI (1810), 61–8.

(iv) Schism Act, 1714 (13 Anne, c.7) (repealed 1719)

'An Act to prevent the growth of schism and for the further security of the Churches of England and Ireland as by law established':

(1) No person 'to keep any public or private school or seminary, or teach and instruct any youth as tutor or schoolmaster', unless he had first made a declaration of conformity to the Church of England and obtained a licence from the bishop of the diocese in which he intended to teach.

(2) Licences to be granted only to those who had taken the Anglican sacrament in the previous year, taken oaths of allegiance and supremacy, and made declaration against transubstantiation.

(3) Unlicensed teachers, or licensed teachers who subsequently attended conventicles, liable to 3 months' imprisonment.

(4) *Exceptions*: elementary teachers (of reading, writing and arithmetic); teachers of navigation; teachers and tutors at Oxford and Cambridge universities and private tutors in noble households (exempted from need for episcopal licensing).

Source: Williams (11a), pp. 337–40.

B 'The Toleration', 1689–1779

(i) Toleration Act, 1689 (1 William & Mary, c.18)

This 'Act for exempting their Majesties' Protestant subjects, dissenting from the Church of England, from the penalties of certain laws' had as its original, very limited purpose to grant 'some ease to scrupulous consciences in the exercise of religion' as 'an effectual means to unite their Majesties' Protestant subjects in interest and affection'.

The main provisions were:

(1) [penal statutes repealed].

(2) *Protestant* dissenters relieved of the penalties laid down in certain earlier statutes, notably in the Elizabethan Act of Uniformity (1559), making parish church attendance obligatory, and in the Conventicles Act of 1670 (see N.2(vi)).

(3) Such dissenters could worship without penalty in their own meeting-houses, provided latter were licensed (by church authorities or JPs) and doors left unlocked during services.

(4) Dissenting ministers who took the oaths of allegiance and supremacy and made declaration against transubstantiation were relieved of penalties of Act of Uniformity, Five Mile Act and Conventicles Act (ibid. N.2), provided they also subscribed to 35 of the 39 Articles of Religion of the Church of England (the doctrinal articles); *except* that

(5) Baptists were not obliged to accede to the article relating to infant baptism, and Quakers were not required to swear any of the oaths, but rather make declarations acknowledging allegiance to William and Mary, belief in the Trinity and authority of the Bible.

(6) Papists and Unitarians were explicitly excluded from the Act's benefits.

Source: Williams (11a), pp. 42–6.

(*ii*) [Annual] *Indemnity Acts, et seq.* (1 George II, c. 23)

In the first year of George II's reign an Act was passed 'indemnifying persons who have omitted to qualify themselves for offices and employments [by taking the sacrament and oaths] within the time limited by law, and for allowing further time for that purpose'. Time allowed was one year, until 28 November 1728; it is sometimes said that by passing such acts annually thereafter the Parliaments of the Walpole period and their successors down to 1828 for practical purposes extended the scope of the 1689 Toleration Act by, in effect, suspending the civil disabilities of the Protestant dissenters under the unrepealed Test and Corporation Acts. But *note*:

(1) The Acts were *not*, for many years, an annual event. No fresh indemnity was granted in seven of the 29 years from 1728–57, including 1730, 1732 and 1745. Only from 1758 onwards did these Acts become regular.

(2) The indemnity was not total. The original 1727 Act temporarily nullified penal effects on individuals of 1673 Test Act (*q.v.* above) and of the Act for Further Securing the King's Person and Government (1715), but did not – contrary to common belief – cover Corporation Act of 1661 as well.

Source: Williams (11a), pp. 341–3.

(*iii*) *Dissenters' Relief Act, 1779* (19 George III, c. 44)

Dissenting ministers (and teachers in schools and academies) required only to take the oaths and make a new declaration 'that I am a Christian and a Protestant, and as such, that I believe that the Scriptures of the Old and New Testament, as commonly received among the Protestant churches, do contain the revealed Will of God; and that I do receive the same as the rule of my doctrine and practice'. (This relieved them of the necessity, by law under the Toleration Act, of subscribing to the 35 specified Articles of Religion).

[*Note*: Previous bills to this effect had failed in 1772 and 1773.]

Source: Williams (11a), pp. 345–6.

N.6: The strength of Dissent, 1676 – *c.* 1718

The Compton and Evans Censuses

Three 'Censuses' were taken of 'old' Protestant Dissent in England and Wales between 1676 and *c.* 1715: (1) that undertaken by the Anglican diocesan authorities in 1676 under the supervision of Henry Compton, bishop of London (the 'Compton Census'); (2) that undertaken on behalf of the Committee of Three Denominations by its secretary, Dr John Evans, most of whose information was gathered – from correspondents in every county – in 1715, but some in 1716–18 (the 'Evans List'); (3) the parallel survey carried out at roughly the same time by the Congregationalist Daniel Neal. The results of the first two, warts and all, survive in their entirety and form the chief basis of the analysis below. The manuscripts are preserved respectively in the William Salt Library, Stafford (now printed by Dr A. Whiteman (see Ch. 2, note 4 for title), and in Dr Williams's Library, London (MS. 38. 4). The original returns assembled by Neal are now lost but his lists of congregations in each county survive in a later eighteenth-century copy made by Josiah Thompson (Dr Williams's Library, MS. 38. 5).

Evans's correspondents took scarcely any account of Quakers and their 'census' of Baptists was defective. The figures presented below for 1715–18 are the careful and resourceful estimates made by Dr M. R. Watts (150, pp. 269–70, Appx., p. 491ff.), who augments and refines the Evans totals by using supplementary evidence, *where available*, from Visitation returns, church membership lists, baptismal registers and Quaker burial registers.

(a) *Compton Census 1676*	*Protestant Nonconformists*
Canterbury Province	93,151
York Province (estimate)	(15,525)
Total	108,676

[*Note*: There are many reasons why this total should be treated with caution, and some scepticism, and regarded as a considerable underestimate. (See Whiteman, op. cit., pp. xlvi–xlvii, lxxvi–lxxix). Most important, the returns that came in to the bishops were mainly of 'heads of families' and 'housekeepers'. Most sons and daughters were omitted (virtually all under sixteen) along with all lodgers and servants. By roughly doubling the grand total to *215,000–220,000* the returns can be made to yield rather more sense, but even that estimate incorporates a totally artificial figure for the Province of York, for which the returns were fragmentary, and it builds in some nonsensical under-enumerations even of dissenters of sixteen or more years of age. This was particularly so of the returns from the parishes of Devonshire and from some other parts of the West Country – as we know from the large number of congregations licensed there during the Royal Indulgence of 1672.]

(b) *Evans List, 1715–18* (as defined by Watts, op. cit., see above)
All *native* dissenters (including an estimated 39,510 Quakers):

ENGLAND	338,120
WALES	17,770
Total	355,890*

[* In the text (Ch. 23, p. 353 above) I suggest a figure of *at least* 400,000 for England and Wales at the beginning of George I's reign – a figure which would need to be further increased, by perhaps 20–30,000, if members of foreign Protestant congregations were included. My main reasons for reaching this conclusion are:

(1) interpretation of the very difficult and incomplete Evans data for London and Middlesex, which in Watts's version is made to yield a figure far too low (at *c*. 34,000) to square with other evidence, e.g. that assembled by a House of Commons Select Committee in 1711 (*Commons' Journals*, XVI, 582–3). It is true that the Commons' estimate of 'about 107,500' dissenters 'in and about the suburbs' of the cities of London and Westminster included foreign Protestants, so that it must be scaled down by using a more realistic multiple for average household size – 4½–5 instead of 6; but it also has to be scaled up again to include the many nonconformist

congregations in the City of London 'within the walls', which were outside the Committee's brief;

(2) the fact that Evans's correspondents were in some areas less well informed than those of Daniel Neale. Neale enumerates 99 congregations in England alone of which Evans appears to have no record;

(3) the large number of unnumbered congregations in the Evans record itself (e.g. the vast majority of the 42 [52 according to Neale] in the populous county of Kent; 14 out of 80 in the dissenting stronghold of Somerset) – not all of which Watts appears to have been able to estimate from other sources.]

N.7: The Scottish Kirk, 1660–90

(i) Act Against Separation and Disobedience to Ecclesiastical Authority, 1663
The Act:

(1) directed the Scottish Privy Council to 'call before them all such ministers who, having entered in or since the year 1649 and have not as yet obtained [episcopal licenses], yet dared to preach in contempt of the law, and to punish them as seditious persons and contemners of royal authority';

(2) declared failure to join in regular Kirk services to be 'seditious and of dangerous example and consequence';

(3) laid down fines of a quarter of that year's rent for each 'nobleman, gentleman and heritor', and a quarter of their free moveables for 'every yeoman, tenant or farmer'.

Source: A. Browning, ed., *English Historical Documents*, VIII, pp. 613–14.

(ii) Sanquhar Declaration, 22 June 1680
The declaration by 'the Cameronians' (the most uncompromising faction of Presbyterian nonconformists, followers of Richard Cameron) asserted:

(1) denial of obedience to Charles II in matters ecclesiastical, 'forfeited several years since by his perjury and breach of covenant both to God and his kirk; or civil, because of 'his tyranny and breach of the very *leges regnandi* in matters civil';

(2) declaration of war 'against such a tyrant and usurper, and all the men of his practices, as enemies to our Lord Jesus Christ and His cause and covenants' and ready to deliver 'our free reformed mother-kirk unto the bondage of Antichrist, the Pope of Rome'.

[*Note*: After the savage defeat of the initial uprising, Cameronians resorted to guerilla warfare throughout the 1680s – 'the Killing Time' – and were not finally reconciled to the Kirk until the mid-1690s.]

Source: R. Wodrow, *History of the Sufferings of the Church of Scotland*, III, pp. 212–13, cited in A. Browning, op. cit., pp. 626–7.

(iii) Act Restoring the Presbyterian Ministers who were Thrust From Their Churches Since 1st January 1661, 1690
The Act laid down:

(1) all Presbyterian ministers ejected since 1 January 1661 for rejecting episcopacy to be restored forthwith;

(2) present incumbents (i.e. ministers accepting episcopacy) to be ejected before next Whitsunday.

Source: *Acts of the Parliaments of Scotland*, IX, 111, cited in A. Browning, op. cit., p. 639.

461

N.8: Religious controversy: the debates on the Trinity, Deism and Freethinking: some landmarks, 1680–1736

1685	George Bull	*Defensio Fidei Nicaenae*
1687	Stephen Nye	*Brief History of the Unitarians, called also Socinians* (in fact, an apologia for Socinianism)
1690	Arthur Bury	*The Naked Gospel*
1690	William Sherlock	*A Vindication of the Doctrine of the Holy . . . Trinity*
1692	John Wallis	*Three sermons concerning the Sacred Trinity*
1692	anon	*The Unreasonableness of the Doctrine of the Trinity*
1692	Stephen Nye	*An Accurate Examination of . . . the Divinity of our Saviour*
*1693	Charles Blount	*The Oracles of Reason*
1695	John Locke	*The Reasonableness of Christianity*
*1696	John Toland	*Christianity not Mysterious*
1698	Stephen Nye	*Considerations of the Explications of the Doctrine of the Trinity*
*1706	Matthew Tindal	*Rights of the Christian Church*
1708	William Whiston	*Apostolic Constitutions*
1711	William Whiston	*Primitive Christianity Revived*
1712	Samuel Clarke	*The Scripture Doctrine of the Trinity*
*1713	Anthony Collins	*A Discourse of Free Thinking*
1718	Thomas Chubb	*The Supremacy of the Father Asserted*
*1724	Anthony Collins	*A Discourse of the Grounds and Reasons of the Christian Religion*
*1730	Matthew Tindal	*Christianity as Old as the Creation*

The Attack on the Deists, 1731–6

1731	William Law	*The Case of Reason*
1732	George Berkeley	*Alciphron*
1736	Joseph Butler	*The Analogy of Religion*

* Signifies works of leading Deists or Freethinkers

O. MAPS

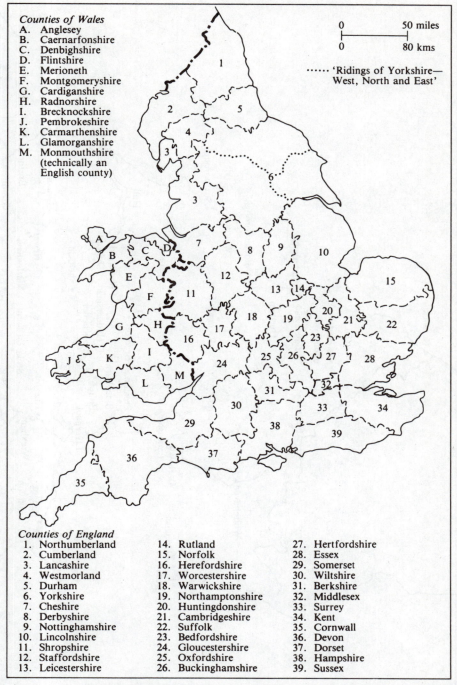

Counties of Wales
A. Anglesey
B. Caernarfonshire
C. Denbighshire
D. Flintshire
E. Merioneth
F. Montgomeryshire
G. Cardiganshire
H. Radnorshire
I. Brecknockshire
J. Pembrokeshire
K. Carmarthenshire
L. Glamorganshire
M. Monmouthshire (technically an English county)

0   50 miles
0   80 kms

······ 'Ridings of Yorkshire— West, North and East'

Counties of England

1. Northumberland	14. Rutland	27. Hertfordshire
2. Cumberland	15. Norfolk	28. Essex
3. Lancashire	16. Herefordshire	29. Somerset
4. Westmorland	17. Worcestershire	30. Wiltshire
5. Durham	18. Warwickshire	31. Berkshire
6. Yorkshire	19. Northamptonshire	32. Middlesex
7. Cheshire	20. Huntingdonshire	33. Surrey
8. Derbyshire	21. Cambridgeshire	34. Kent
9. Nottinghamshire	22. Suffolk	35. Cornwall
10. Lincolnshire	23. Bedfordshire	36. Devon
11. Shropshire	24. Oxfordshire	37. Dorset
12. Staffordshire	25. Oxfordshire	38. Hampshire
13. Leicestershire	26. Buckinghamshire	39. Sussex

Map 1.   The counties of England and Wales in the seventeenth and eighteenth centuries

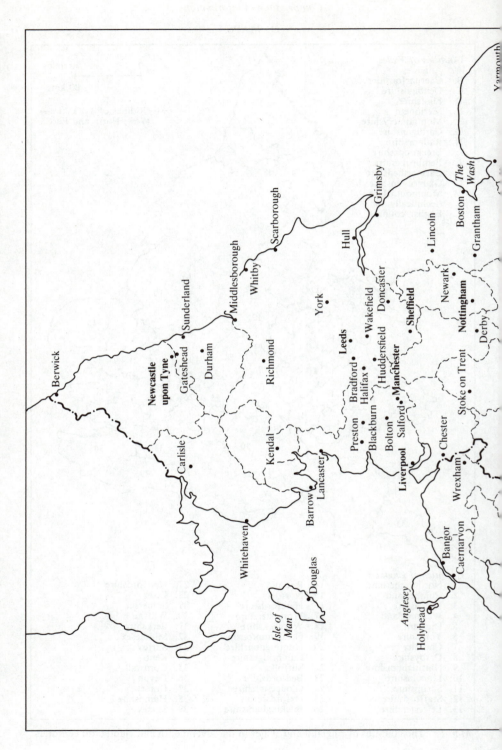

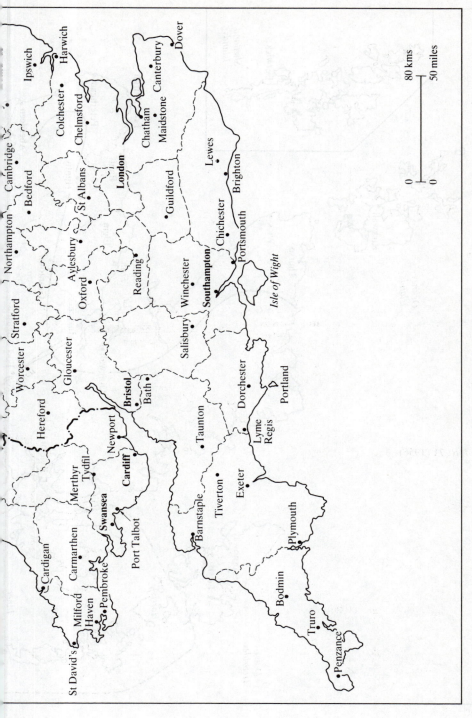

Map 2. England and Wales

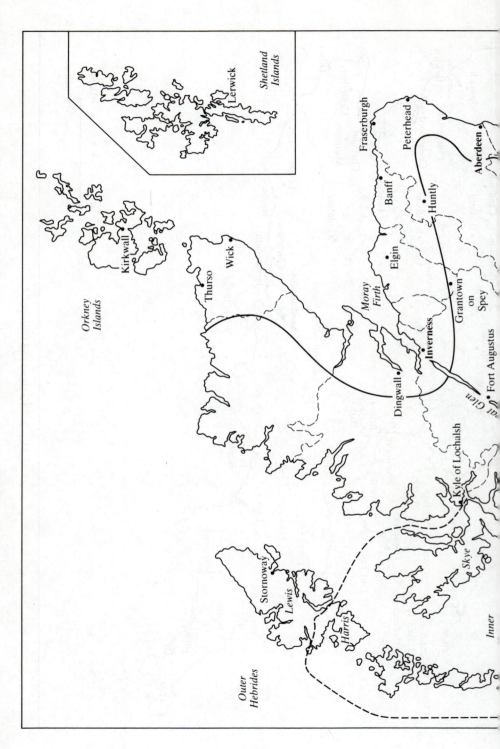

Shetland Islands

Lerwick

Fraserburgh

Peterhead

Banff

Huntly

Aberdeen

Elgin

Kirkwall

Grantown
on
Spey

Moray
Firth

Thurso

Wick

Inverness

Orkney
Islands

Fort Augustus

Dingwall

Great Glen

Kyle of Lochalsh

Skye

Stornoway

Lewis

Harris

Inner

Outer
Hebrides

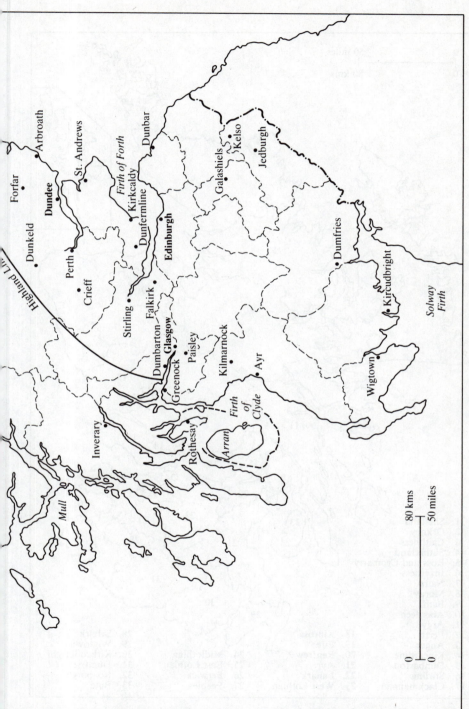

Map 3. Scotland

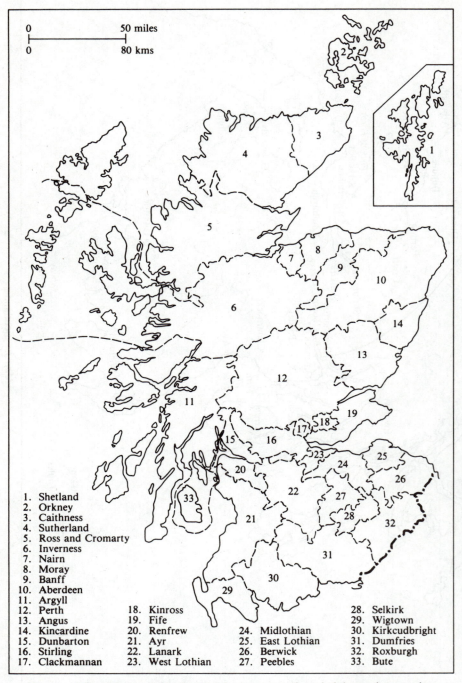

0   50 miles

0   80 kms

1. Shetland
2. Orkney
3. Caithness
4. Sutherland
5. Ross and Cromarty
6. Inverness
7. Nairn
8. Moray
9. Banff
10. Aberdeen
11. Argyll
12. Perth
13. Angus
14. Kincardine
15. Dunbarton
16. Stirling
17. Clackmannan

18. Kinross
19. Fife
20. Renfrew
21. Ayr
22. Lanark
23. West Lothian

24. Midlothian
25. East Lothian
26. Berwick
27. Peebles

28. Selkirk
29. Wigtown
30. Kirkcudbright
31. Dumfries
32. Roxburgh
33. Bute

Map 4. The counties of Scotland in the seventeenth and eighteenth centuries

468

PROVINCES:
A Ulster
B Connaught
C Munster
D Leinster

Boundaries of provinces

County boundaries

0   80 kms
0   50 miles

Map 5. Ireland in the seventeenth and eighteenth centuries

469

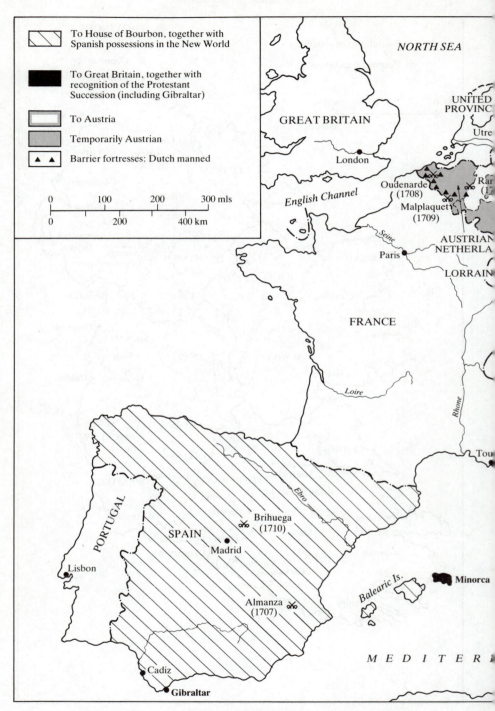

Legend:

- To House of Bourbon, together with Spanish possessions in the New World
- To Great Britain, together with recognition of the Protestant Succession (including Gibraltar)
- To Austria
- Temporarily Austrian
- ▲ ▲ Barrier fortresses: Dutch manned

Scale:
0 — 100 — 200 — 300 mls
0 — 200 — 400 km

NORTH SEA

GREAT BRITAIN

London

UNITED PROVINC[

Utre

Oudenarde (1708)

Ra[

Malplaquet (1709)

AUSTRIAN NETHERLA[

English Channel

Seine

Paris

LORRAIN[

FRANCE

Loire

Rhone

Tou[

Ebro

PORTUGAL

SPAIN

Brihuega (1710)

Madrid

Lisbon

Balearic Is.

Minorca

Almanza (1707)

Cadiz

Gibraltar

MEDITERR[

Map 6.   The Spanish Succession War and the Peace of Utrecht

470

HANOVER

BRANDENBURG
● Berlin

PRUSSIA

POLAND

Elbe

SILESIA

Vistula

T H E

Prague ●

E M P I R E

Vienna ●

Buda/Pest ●

✂ Blenheim
(1704)

BAVARIA

AUSTRIA

HUNGARY

MILAN
(1706)

Belgrade ●

Danube

Y

ONT

OTTOMAN
EMPIRE

A D R I A T I C   S E A

N A P L E S

Naples ●

SARDINIA
(Austrian 1713–20)

Athens ●

*Straits of
Messina*

Palermo ●

A N   S E A

SICILY   (Austrian 1720–35)

Bibliography

Standard bibliographies for the later Stuart and early Hanoverian period include G. Davies (M.F. Keeler, ed.), *Bibliography of British History: Stuart Period, 1603–1714* (2nd edn, Oxford, 1970), M. Pargellis and D.J. Medley, eds, *Bibliography of British History: the Eighteenth Century, 1714–1789* (Oxford, 1951), and W.L. Sachse, *Restoration England, 1660–89* (Cambridge, 1971), though all of these are now showing their age. A welcome, more up-to-date addition, containing helpful assessments, is J.S. Morrill, *Seventeenth-Century Britain, 1603–1714* (1980). The Historical Association also publishes an *Annual Bulletin of Historical Literature*, which is very useful for keeping in touch with important new work in all fields.

The bibliography which follows is considerably longer than that of any previous volume in this series. From the multitude of books available for studying the period and supplying the essential groundwork for the writing of this volume, I have tried single-mindedly to select (except in the brief section 1) only those which a conscientious honours student could reasonably be expected to read in preparing for an essay or seminar on any of the main topics which the book deals with. That my attempted rigour has fallen short in the end of the ruthless hatchet-work and decimation that would have been necessary to slim the bibliography much further is attributable in the main to the almost sinful outpouring of secondary work on both the late seventeenth and the eighteenth centuries during the present decade, i.e. since the first drafts of the earliest chapters of the book were begun. In addition to the items listed below there were, of course, many other more specialised or recondite works which the present author found it necessary to consult; since a zealous, enquiring reader will find these of interest and value, they have been – in accordance with series policy – siphoned off, along with the bulk of the primary source material used and quoted from, into the end-notes which follow each chapter.

To assist the compilation of purpose-designed reading lists the bibliography has been organised into ten subject categories and into further sub-categories, and within each sub-category readers will find entries made in a broadly chronological way.

1. Source material (1–11)
2. General: Textbooks, survey histories and collective studies (12–24)
3. Politics and Parliament; political biographies (25–107)
4. Finance, central and local government, and the Law (108–28)
5. Foreign policy and war (129–48)
6. Religion (149–66)
7. The economy and society (167–266)
8. Ireland and Scotland (267–90)
9. Overseas Territories (291–94)
10. Education and the printed word; science and ideas (295–321)

Note: Place of publication is London, unless otherwise stated.

1. SOURCE MATERIAL

1 G. Burnet, *A History of My Own Time* [to 1713], 6 vols (Oxford, 1833 edn.)

2 W. Cobbett, ed., *The Parliamentary History of England* [debates], 36 vols [to 1803], (1806–20)

3 D. Defoe, *A Tour through England and Wales* (first publd. 1724–6; refs cited from Everyman edn, ed. G.D.M. Cole, 2 vols, 1927). But note also Defoe's *A Tour through the Whole Island of Great Britain* (ed. P. Rogers, Penguin edn, abridged [but sensitively so], 1971)

4 C. Morris, ed., *The Journeys of Celia Fiennes* (revised edn, 1949)

5 G. Holmes and W.A. Speck, eds, *The Divided Society: Party Conflict in England, 1694–1716* (1967)

6 (a) R. Beddard, *A Kingdom without a King: The Journal of the Provisional Government in the Revolution of 1688* (Oxford, 1988)

(b) D.L. Jones, *A Parliamentary History of the Glorious Revolution* (1988)

7 J.P. Kenyon, ed., *The Stuart Constitution* (1st edn, Cambridge, 1966)

8 P. Laslett, ed., John Locke: *Two Treatises of Government* (Cambridge, 1960)

9 R.C. Latham and W.C. Matthews, eds, *The Diary of Samuel Pepys*, 11 vols (1970–83)

10 J. Thirsk and J.P. Cooper, eds, *Seventeenth Century Economic Documents* (Oxford, 1972)

11 (a) E.N. Williams, ed., *The Eighteenth Century Constitution* (Cambridge, 1960)

(b) W.C. Costin and J.S. Watson, eds, *The Law and Working of the Constitution: Documents 1660–1914*, I, 1660–1783 (1952)

The two meaty volumes of *English Historical Documents*, VIII (1660–1714), ed. A. Browning, and X (1714–83), eds D.B. Horn and M. Ransome, remain of enduring usefulness.

2. GENERAL: TEXTBOOKS, SURVEY HISTORIES AND COLLECTIVE STUDIES

12 B. Coward, *The Stuart Age: A History of England 1603–1714* (1980). Of more value pre- rather than post-1660

13 J.R. Jones, *Country and Court: England 1658–1714* (1978). Provides best modern political survey of the Later Stuart period

14 J.R. Jones, ed., *The Restored Monarchy 1660–1688* (1979). Excellent collection of essays in 'Problems in Focus' series

15 D. Ogg, *England in the Reign of Charles II*, 2 vols (2nd edn, Oxford, 1955). Detailed and extraordinarily durable on all aspects of the reign

16 G. Holmes, *Politics, Religion and Society in England, 1679–1742* (1986). Collected essays, pamphlets, etc.

17 G. Holmes, ed., *Britain after the Glorious Revolution, 1689–1714* (1969). For 20 years a student's best introduction to 1689–1714; 'Problems in Focus' series

18 D. Ogg, *England in the Reigns of James II and William III* (Oxford, 1955). Compendious, but not as masterly as (15)

19 G.M. Trevelyan, *England Under Queen Anne*, 3 vols (1930–4). Trevelyan is no longer fashionable, but this work is an epic by any standards

20 J. Black, ed., *Britain in the Age of Walpole* (1984); 'Problems in Focus' series

21 C. Jones, ed., *Britain in the First Age of Party 1680–1750: Essays Presented to Geoffrey*

Holmes (1987). Wide-ranging collection covering politics, government, religion, society, the press etc.

22 W.A. Speck, *Stability and Strife: England 1714–1760* (1977). Companion vol. of (13)

23 J.B. Owen, *The Eighteenth Century 1714–1815* (1974)

24 (a) J.S. Bromley, ed., *New Cambridge Modern History*, VI, 1688–1725 (Cambridge, 1970)

(b) J.O. Lindsay, ed., *New Cambridge Modern History*, VII, 1713–63 (Cambridge, 1957)

3. POLITICS AND PARLIAMENT; POLITICAL BIOGRAPHIES

25 B.D. Henning, ed., *The History of Parliament: The House of Commons 1660–1690*, 3 vols (1983)

26 (a) R. Sedgwick, ed., *The History of Parliament: The House of Commons 1715–1754*, 2 vols (1970);

(b) L.B. Namier & J. Brooke, eds, *The History of Parliament: The House of Commons, 1754–1790*, 3 vols (1962)

27 C. Jones, ed., *Party and Management in Parliament, 1660–1784* (Leicester, 1984)

28 J.H. Plumb, *The Growth of Political Stability in England, 1675–1725* (1967)

29 J. Cannon, ed., *The Whig Ascendancy: Colloquies on Hanoverian England* (1981). First class collection of essays and discussions on politics 1689–1832

30 J.C.D. Clark, 'A General Theory of Party, Opposition and Government, 1688–1832', *HJ*, **23** (1980)

31 P.D.G. Thomas, *The House of Commons in the Eighteenth Century* (Oxford, 1971). Admirable study of the way parliamentary business was conducted

32 H. Van Thal, ed., *The Prime Ministers*, I (1974). Biographies from Walpole to Portland

33 R. Hutton, *The Restoration: A Political and Religious History of England and Wales 1658–1667* (Oxford, 1985)

34 J.R. Jones, *Charles II: Royal Politician* (1987)

35 M. Ashley, *Charles II* (1971)

36 K.H.D. Haley, *Charles II* (Hist. Ass. pamphlet, 1966)

37 R.M. Bliss, *Restoration England 1660–1688* (1985)

38 D.R. Lacey, *Dissent and Parliamentary Politics in England 1661–1689* (New Brunswick, 1969)

39 (a) D. Witcombe, *Charles II and the Cavalier House of Commons 1663–1674* (Manchester, 1966)

(b) D. Hirst, 'The Conciliatoriness of the Cavalier Commons Reconsidered', *Parl. Hist.*, **6** (1987)

40 J. Miller, (a) *Restoration England: The Reign of Charles II* (1985); (b) *Popery and Politics in England 1660–1688* (Cambridge, 1973)

41 J. Miller, (a) 'Charles II and his Parliaments', *THRS*, **32** (1982); (b) 'The Potential for "Absolutism" in Later Stuart England', *History*, **69** (1984)

42 K.H.D. Haley, (a) *Politics in the Reign of Charles II* (Hist. Ass., 1985); (b) *The First Earl of Shaftesbury* (Oxford, 1968)

43 A. Browning, (a) *Thomas Osborne, Earl of Danby and Duke of Leeds 1632–1712*, 3 vols (Glasgow, 1951); (b) 'Parties and Party Organization in the Reign of Charles II', *TRHS*, **21** (1948)

44 J.R. Jones, (a) 'Parties and Parliament' in (14); (b) *The First Whigs: The Politics of the Exclusion Crisis 1678–1683* (Oxford, 1961)

45 J.P. Kenyon, (a) *The Popish Plot* (1972); (b) *Robert Spencer, Earl of Sunderland 1641–1702* (1958)

46 K.G. Feiling, *A History of the Tory Party, 1640–1714* (Oxford, 1924)

47 R. Ollard, *Pepys: A Biography* (1974)

48 H.G. Horwitz, *Revolution Politicks. The Career of Daniel Finch, Second Earl of Nottingham 1647–1730* (Cambridge, 1968)

49 G. Holmes, 'The Achievement of Stability: the Social Context of Politics from the 1680s to the Age of Walpole', in (29)

50 J. Miller, *James II: A Study in Kingship* (Hove, 1978)

51 R. Clifton, *The Last Popular Rebellion* [Monmouth's Rebellion, 1685] (1984)

52 J.R. Western, *Monarchy and Revolution: The English State in the 1680s* (1972)

53 (a) J.R. Jones, *The Revolution of 1688 in England* (1972)
   (b) J. Carswell, *The Descent on England* (1969)

54 W.A. Speck, (a) *Reluctant Revolutionaries: Englishmen and the Revolution of 1688* (Oxford, 1988); (b) 'The Orangist Conspiracy against James II', *HJ*, **30** (1987)

55 J.P. Kenyon, *The Nobility in the Revolution of 1688* (Hull, 1963)

56 S.B. Baxter, *William III* (1966)

57 H. Horwitz, (a) 'Parliament and the Glorious Revolution', *BIHR*, **47** (1974); (b) '1689 (and All That)', *Parl.Hist.*, **6** (1987)

58 (a) L. Schwoerer, *The Declaration of Rights 1689* (Baltimore, 1981); (b) R.J. Frankle, 'The Formulation of the Declaration of Rights', *HJ*, **17** (1974)

59 A. McInnes, (a) 'When was the English Revolution?', *History*, **67** (1982); (b) *Robert Harley, Puritan Politician* (1970)

60 B.W. Hill, (a) *Robert Harley, Speaker, Secretary of State and Premier Minister* (New Haven, 1988); (b) *The Growth of Parliamentary Parties 1689–1742* (1976)

61 E.L. Ellis, 'William III and the Politicians', in (17)

62 H. Horwitz, (a) *Parliament, Policy and Politics in the Reign of William III* (Manchester, 1977); (b) 'The Structure of Parliamentary Politics', in (17)

63 J.P. Kenyon, 'The Earl of Sunderland and the King's Administration, 1693–1695', *EHR*, **71** (1956)

64 D. Hayton, 'The "Country" Interest and the Party System, 1689–*c*. 1720', in (27)

65 D. Rubini, *Court and Country, 1688–1702* (1967)

66 W.A. Speck, 'Conflict in Society', in (17)

67 C. Roberts, 'Party and Patronage in Later Stuart England', in S.B. Baxter, ed., *England's Rise to Greatness 1660–1783* (Berkeley, 1983)

68 (a) C. Jones, 'The House of Lords and the Growth of Parliamentary Stability, 1701–1742' in (21)
   (b) C. Jones and G. Holmes, 'The House of Lords in Early Eighteenth-Century Politics', pp. 62–9 of Intro. to *The London Diaries of William Nicolson . . . 1702–1718* (Oxford, 1985)

69 E. Gregg, *Queen Anne* (1980)

70 G. Holmes, *British Politics in the Age of Anne* (revised edn, 1987)

71 G. Holmes, 'The Attack on "The Influence of the Crown", 1702–16' in (16)

72 P.W.J. Riley, 'The Union of 1707 as an Episode in English Politics', *EHR*, **84** (1969)

73 G. Holmes, (a) 'Harley, St John and the Death of the Tory Party', in (17); (b) *The Trial of Doctor Sacheverell* (1973)

74 H.T. Dickinson, *Bolingbroke* (1970)

75 G. Holmes and C. Jones, 'Trade, the Scots and the Parliamentary Crisis of 1713', *Parl. Hist.*, **1** (1982) [see also section 8]

76 R. Hatton, (a) *George I: Elector and King* (1978); (b) 'New Light on George I of Great Britain' in S.B. Baxter, ed., *England's Rise to Greatness, 1660–1760* (Berkeley, 1983)

77 J.M. Beattie, *The English Court in the Reign of George I* (Cambridge, 1967)

78 B. Williams, *Stanhope: A Study in Eighteenth-century War and Diplomacy* (Oxford, 1932)

79 J.H. Plumb, (a) *Sir Robert Walpole*, I: *The Making of a Statesman* (1956); (b) *Sir Robert Walpole*, II: *The King's Minister* (1960)

80 H.T. Dickinson, (a) *Walpole and the Whig Supremacy* (1973); (b) 'Whiggism in the 18th Century', in (29)

81 (a) L. Colley, *In Defiance of Oligarchy: The Tory Party, 1714–60* (Cambridge, 1982)
(b) L. Colley and M. Goldie, 'The Principles and Practice of Eighteenth-Century Party', *HJ*, **22** (1979)

82 J.C.D. Clark, 'The Politics of the Excluded: Tories, Jacobites and Whig Patriots, 1715–60', *Parl. Hist.*, **2** (1983)

83 (a) W.A. Speck, 'The Whig Schism under George I', *Huntington Library Quarterly*, **40** (1975)
(b) C. Jones, 'The Impeachment of Lord Oxford and the Whig Schism of 1717', *BIHR*, **55** (1982)
(c) J. Black, 'Parliament and the Political and Diplomatic Crisis of 1717–18', *Parl. Hist.*, **3** (1984)

84 B.W. Hill, *Sir Robert Walpole. 'Sole and Prime Minister'* (1989)

85 G. Holmes, 'Sir Robert Walpole', in (16)

86 P. Langford, *The Excise Crisis: Society and Politics in the Age of Walpole* (Oxford, 1975)

87 H.T. Dickinson, 'The Precursors of Political Radicalism in Augustan Britain', in (21)

88 W.A. Speck, 'Whigs and Tories Dim their Glories: English Political Parties under the First Two Georges', in (29)

89 J.B. Owen, *The Pattern of Politics in Eighteenth-Century England* (1962)

90 J. Brooke, *The House of Commons 1754–1790: Introductory Survey* (1968)

91 Sir L.B. Namier, *The Structure of Politics at the Accession of George III* (2nd edn, 1982)

92 J. Brewer, *Party Ideology and Popular Politics at the Accession of George III* (Cambridge, 1976)

London politics

93 T. Harris, *London Crowds in the Reign of Charles II: Propaganda and Politics from the Restoration to the Exclusion Crisis* (Cambridge, 1987)

94 G.S. de Krey, (a) 'Political Radicalism in London after the Glorious Revolution', *Journal of Modern History*, **55** (1983); (b) *A Fractured Society: The Politics of London in the First Age of Party 1688–1715* (Oxford, 1985)

95 H. Horwitz, 'Party in a Civic Context: London from the Exclusion Crisis to the Fall of Walpole', in (21); (see also A.J. Henderson, *London and the National Government, 1721–1742* (Durham, N.C., 1945).

The electorate and parliamentary reform

96 J. Cannon, *Parliamentary Reform, 1640–1832* (Cambridge, 1973)
97 (a) J.H. Plumb, 'The Growth of the Electorate in England from 1600 to 1715', *P & P*, **45** (1969)
 (b) G. Holmes, *The Electorate and the National Will in the First Age of Party* (Lancaster, 1976), repr. (16)
98 D.M. George, 'Elections and Electioneering, 1679–1681', *EHR*, **45** (1940)
99 W.A. Speck, (a) *Tory and Whig: The Struggle in the Constituencies 1701–1715* (1970);
 (b) 'The Electorate in the First Age of Party', in (21)
100 J.E. Bradley, 'Nonconformity and the Electorate in Eighteenth-Century England', *Parl. Hist.*, **6** (1987)
101 P. Langford, 'Property and "Virtual Representation" in Eighteenth-Century England', *HJ*, **31** (1988)
102 L. Colley, 'Eighteenth-Century English Radicalism before Wilkes', *TRHS*, **31** (1981)

Jacobitism

103 G.V. Bennett, (a) see (163b); (b) 'Jacobitism and the Rise of Walpole', in N. McKendrick, ed., *Historical Perspectives: Studies in English Thought and Society in Honour of J.H. Plumb* (1974)
104 B. Lenman, *The Jacobite Risings in Britain 1689–1746* (1980)
105 D. Szechi, *Jacobitism and Tory Politics 1710–1714* (Edinburgh, 1984)
106 (a) E. Cruickshanks, *Political Untouchables: The Tories and the '45* (1979); (b) E. Cruickshanks, ed., *Ideology and Conspiracy: Aspects of Jacobitism 1689–1759* (Edinburgh, 1982)
107 F.J. McLynn, *The Jacobites* (1985)

4. FINANCE, CENTRAL AND LOCAL GOVERNMENT, AND THE LAW

108 M.A. Thomson, *A Constitutional History of England, 1642–1801* (1938). (Still the most wide-ranging and best general survey of its kind on this period. See also 7)
109 C. Roberts, *The Growth of Responsible Government in Stuart England* (Cambridge, 1966)
110 C.D. Chandaman, (a) *The English Public Revenue 1660–88* (Oxford, 1975); (b) 'The Financial Settlement in the Parliament of 1685', in H. Hearder and H.R. Loyn, eds, *British Government and Administration: Studies Presented to S.B. Chrimes* (Univ. of Wales, 1974)
111 (a) H. Roseveare, *The Treasury, 1660–1870* (1973)
 (b) S.B. Baxter, *The Development of the Treasury, 1660–1702* (1957)
112 (a) C. Roberts, 'The Constitutional Significance of the Financial Settlement of 1690', *HJ*, **20** (1977)
 (b) E.A. Reitan, 'From Revenue to Civil List, 1689–1702: The Revolution Settlement and the "Mixed and Balanced" Constitution', *HJ*, **13** (1970)
113 P.G.M. Dickson, (a) *The Financial Revolution in England: A Study in the Development of Public Credit, 1688–1756* (1967); (b) 'War Finance 1689–1714', in (24)
114 R. Davis, 'The Rise of Protection in England, 1689–1786', *EcHR*, **19** (1966). Links closely with war finance

115 (a) W.R. Ward, *The Land Tax in the Eighteenth Century* (Oxford, 1953)
(b) C. Brooks, 'Public Finance and Political Stability: The Administration of the Land Tax, 1688–1720', *HJ*, **17** (1974)

116 J.V. Beckett, 'Land Tax or Excise: The Levying of Taxation in Seventeenth- and Eighteenth-century England', *EHR*, **100** (1985)

117 N.P.K. O'Brien, 'The Political Economy of British Taxation, 1660–1815', *EcHR*, **41** (1988)

118 H. Tomlinson, 'Financial and Administrative Developments in England, 1660–88', in (14)

119 E. Hughes, *Studies in Administration and Finance 1558–1825* (Manchester, 1934). Valuable on 1670s–1730s

120 J. Carter, (a) 'Law, Courts and Constitution', in (14); (b) 'The Revolution and the Constitution', in (17) [on Government and Finance in the 1680s see Western, 52 above]

121 G. Aylmer, 'From Office-Holding to Civil Service: the Genesis of the Modern Bureaucracy', *TRHS*, 5th ser., **30** (1980)

122 G. Holmes, 'The New Men of Government' [chap. 8 of 226a]. Deals with growth of bureaucracy 1680s onwards

123 J.H. Plumb, 'The Organization of the Cabinet in the Reign of Queen Anne', *TRHS*, **7** (1957)

124 A. Fletcher, *Reform in the Provinces: The Government of Stuart England* (New Haven and London, 1986)

125 C.G.F. Forster, 'Government in Provincial England under the Later Stuarts', *TRHS*, **33** (1983). See also A.M. Coleby, *Central Government and the Localities: Hampshire 1649–1689* (Cambridge, 1987)

126 N. Landau, *The Justices of the Peace, 1679–1760* (Berkeley, 1984); (b) L.K.J. Glassey, *Politics and the Appointment of Justices of the Peace 1675–1725* (Oxford, 1979)

127 L.K.J. Glassey, 'Local Government', in (21)

128 Sir L. Radzinowicz, *History of English Criminal Law*, I. (1948) [on Law and Courts 1660–88 see also Carter, 120a above, and Ch. 5 (Lawyers) of 226a below]

5. FOREIGN POLICY AND WAR

General Surveys

129 J.R. Jones, (a) *Britain and Europe in the Seventeenth Century* (1966); (b) *Britain and the World 1649–1815* (1980)

130 J.R. Jones, 'English Attitudes to Europe in the Seventeenth Century', in J.S. Bromley and E.H. Kossmann, eds, *Britain and the Netherlands in Europe and Asia* (1968)

131 P. Langford, *The Eighteenth Century 1688–1815* [Foreign Policy] (1976)

132 D.B. Horn, *Great Britain and Europe in the Eighteenth Century* (Oxford, 1967)

133 J. Brewer, *The Sinews of Power: War, Money and the English State, 1688–1783* (1989)

Periods and Topics

134 J.L. Price, 'Restoration England and Europe', in (14)

135 C. Wilson, *Profit and Power: A Study of England and the Dutch Wars* (1957)

136 R. Hutton, 'The Making of the Secret Treaty of Dover, 1668–1670', *HJ*, **29** (1986)

137 M. Sheehan, 'The Development of British Theory and Practice of the Balance of Power before 1714', *History*, **73** (1988)

138 K. Feiling, *British Foreign Policy 1660–1672* (1930)
139 J. Childs, (a) *The Army of Charles II* (1976); (b) *The Army, James II and the Glorious Revolution* (Manchester, 1980)
140 G.C. Gibbs, 'The Revolution in Foreign Policy', in (17)
141 R.M. Hatton and J.S. Bromley, eds, *William III and Louis XIV: Essays 1680–1720 by and for Mark A. Thomson* (Liverpool, 1968)
142 (a) J. Ehrman, *The Navy in the War of William III* (Cambridge, 1953)
   (b) N.A.M. Roger, *The Wooden World: An Anatomy of the Georgian Navy* (1986)
143 (a) W.S. Churchill, *Marlborough, his Life and Times*, 2 vols (1947)
   (b) I.F. Burton, *The Captain-General: The Career of John Churchill, Duke of Marlborough 1702–1711* (1968)
   (c) D. Chandler, *Marlborough as a Military Commander* (1970)
144 A.D. MacLachlan, 'The Road to Peace 1710–13', in (17)
145 (a) M.A. Thomson, 'Parliament and Foreign Policy 1689–1714', in (141)
   (b) G.C. Gibbs, 'Parliament and Foreign Policy in the Age of Stanhope and Walpole', *EHR*, **77** (1962)
146 (a) G.C. Gibbs, 'Parliament and the Treaty of Quadruple Alliance', in (141); (b) 'Great Britain and the Alliance of Hanover', *EHR*, **73** (1958)
147 J. Black, *British Foreign Policy in the Age of Walpole* (Edinburgh, 1985)
148 J.R. Western, *The English Militia in the Eighteenth Century 1660–1802* (1965)

6. RELIGION

149 K.V. Thomas, *Religion and the Decline of Magic: Studies in Popular Beliefs in Sixteenth- and Seventeenth-Century England* (1971)
150 M.R. Watts, *The Dissenters: from the Reformation to the French Revolution* (Oxford, 1978)
151 J. Bossy, *The English Catholic Community 1570–1850* (1975)
152 N. Sykes, *From Sheldon to Secker: Aspects of English Church History 1660–1768* (Cambridge, 1959)
153 R. O'Day and F. Heal, eds, *Princes and Paupers in the English Church, 1500–1800* (Leicester, 1981)
154 E.G. Rupp, *Religion in England 1688–1791* (Oxford, 1986)
155 D.R. Hirschberg, 'The Government and Church Patronage in England, 1660–1760', *JBS*, **20** (1980–1)
156 (a) I.M. Green, *The Re-Establishment of the Church of England 1660–1663* (1978)
   (b) A.O. Whiteman, 'The Re-Establishment of the Church of England 1660–1663', *TRHS*, **5** (1955)
   (c) R.A. Beddard, 'Sheldon and Anglican Recovery', *HJ*, **19** (1976),
157 R. O'Day, 'The Anatomy of a Profession: the Clergy of the Church of England', in (225)
158 (a) J.H. Pruett, *The Parish Clergy under the Later Stuarts: The Leicestershire Experience* (Urbana, Illinois, 1978)
   (b) E.J. Evans, 'Anglican Clergy of the North of England', in (21)
159 J. Spurr, '"Latitudinarianism" and the Restoration Church', *HJ*, **31** (1988)
160 (a) G.R. Cragg, *Puritanism in the Period of the Great Persecution, 1660–1688* (Cambridge, 1957)
   (b) C.E. Whiting, *Studies in English Puritanism from the Restoration to the Revolution, 1660–1688* (1931)

161 G.F. Nuttall and O. Chadwick, eds, *From Uniformity to Unity 1662–1962* (1962). Especially for 1661–89

162 G.V. Bennett, 'The Seven Bishops: A Reconsideration' in *Studies in Church History*, XV (ed. D. Baker, 1978)

163 G.V. Bennett, (a) 'Conflict in the Church' in (17); (b) *The Tory Crisis in Church and State: The Career of Francis Atterbury, Bishop of Rochester* (Oxford, 1975)

164 N. Sykes, *William Wake, Archbishop of Canterbury* (Cambridge, 1957)

165 E.J. Evans, *The Contentious Tithe* (1976)
(a) G.F.A. Best, *Temporal Pillars: Queen Anne's Bounty, the Ecclesiastical Commissioners and the Church of England* (Cambridge, 1964)
(b) I.M. Green, 'The First Years of Queen Anne's Bounty', in (153)

166 R.A. Knox, *Enthusiasm: A Chapter in the History of Religion with Special Reference to the XVII and XVIII centuries* (Oxford, 1950)

7. THE ECONOMY AND SOCIETY

General surveys or articles and collected essays

167 F.M. Carus-Wilson, ed., *Essays in Economic History*, II (1962)

168 D.C. Coleman, *The Economy of England, 1450–1750* (Oxford, 1977)

169 J. Sharpe, *Early Modern England: A Social History 1550–1750* (1987)

170 (a) C.G.A. Clay, *Economic Expansion and Social Change: England 1500–1700*, I: *People, Land and Towns*; (b) II: *Industry, Trade and Government* (Cambridge, 1984)

171 B.A. Holderness, *Pre-Industrial England: Economy and Society from 1500 to 1750* (1976)

172 J. Wrightson, *English Society, 1580–1680* (1982)

173 C. Wilson, *England's Apprenticeship: 1603–1763* (2nd edn, 1984)

174 D.C. Coleman and A.H. John, eds, *Trade, Government and Economy in Pre-industrial England: Essays Presented to F.J. Fisher* (1976)

175 J. Thirsk, *Economic Policy and Projects* (Oxford, 1978)

176 *For Statistics*: (a) P. Deane and W.A. Cole, *British Economic Growth, 1688–1959* (2nd edn, Cambridge, 1967); (b) B.R. Mitchell and P. Deane, *Abstract of British Historical Statistics* (Cambridge, 1962)

177 P. Clark, 'Migration in England during the Late Seventeenth and Eighteenth Centuries', *P & P*, **83** (1979)

178 (a) W.A. Cole, 'Factors in Demand, 1700–1800', in (181)
(b) N.F.R. Crafts, 'British Economic Growth 1700–1831: A Review of the Evidence', *EcHR* **36** (1983)
(c) P. Mathias, *The First Industrial Nation: An Economic History of Britain 1700–1914* (2nd edn, 1983)
(d) R. Porter, *English Society in the Eighteenth Century* (1982)

179 N. McKendrick, ed., *Historical Perspectives: Studies in English Thought and Society in Honour of J.H. Plumb* (1974)

180 T.S. Ashton, *Economic Fluctuations in England 1700–1800* (Oxford 1959)

181 R.C. Floud and D.H. McCloskey, eds, *The Economic History of Britain since 1700: I, 1700–1860* (Cambridge, 1981)

182 A.H. John, (a) 'Aspects of English Economic Growth in the First Half of the

Eighteenth Century' in W.E. Minchinton, ed., *The Growth of English Overseas Trade in the 17th and 18th Centuries* (1969); (b) 'War and the English Economy, 1700–1763', *EcHR* **7** (1955)

183 H. J. Perkin, *Origins of Modern English Society, 1780–1880* (1969)

Local studies

184 J.V. Beckett, *The East Midlands from A.D. 1000* (1988)
185 D. Hey, *Yorkshire from A.D. 1000* (1986)
186 M. Rowlands, (a) *The West Midlands from A.D. 1000* (1987); (b) *Masters and Men in the West Midland Metalware Trades before the Industrial Revolution* (Manchester, 1975)
187 (a) H. Heaton, *Yorkshire Woollen and Worsted Industries from the Earliest Times up to the Industrial Revolution* (2nd edn, Oxford, 1965)
       (b) R.G. Wilson, *Gentlemen Merchants: The Merchants Community in Leeds, 1700–1830* (Manchester, 1971)
188 (a) A.L. Beier and R. Finlay, eds, *The Making of the Metropolis: London 1500–1700* (1986)
       (b) E.A. Wrigley, 'A Simple Model of London's Importance in Changing England's Society and Economy, 1650–1750', *P&P*, **37** (1967)
189 (a) J.K. Walton, *Lancashire: A Social History, 1558–1939* (Manchester, 1987)
       (b) A.P. Wadsworth and J. de L. Mann, *The Cotton Trade and Industrial Lancashire 1600–1780* (Manchester, 1931)
190 J.P. Jenkins, *The Making of a Ruling Class: The Glamorgan Gentry, 1640–1790* (1983). Comprehensive study: far wider than socio-economic in range
191 J.V. Beckett, *Coal and Tobacco: the Lowthers and the Economic Development of West Cumberland, 1660–1760* (1981)
192 J.D. Chambers, *Vale of Trent 1670–1800: A Regional Study of Economic Change* (Cambridge, 1958)
193 E. Hughes, *North Country Life in the Eighteenth Century: The North-East 1700–1750* (Oxford, 1952)

Demography
(see also end-notes to Chs. 2, 19)

194 J.D. Chambers, *Population, Economy and Society in Pre-Industrial England* (Oxford, 1982)
195 (a) M.W. Flinn, *British Population Growth 1700–1850* (1970)
       (b) E.A. Wrigley, 'The Growth of Population in Eighteenth-Century England: A Conundrum Resolved?', *P&P*, **98** (1983)
       (c) R.D. Lee and R.S. Schofield, 'British Population in the Eighteenth Century', in (181)
196 E.A. Wrigley and R.S. Schofield, *The Population History of England 1541–1871: A Reconstruction* (1981)

Overseas trade (and Empire)

197 W.E. Minchinton, ed., *The Growth of English Overseas Trade in the Seventeenth and Eighteenth Centuries* (1969)

198 R. Davis, *The Rise of the English Shipping Industry in the Seventeenth and Eighteenth Centuries* (1962)
199 (a) R. Davis, 'English Foreign Trade, 1660–1700', *EcHR*, **7** (1954); (b) 'English Foreign Trade 1700–1774', *EcHR*, **15** (1962). Repr. in (197)
200 C. Wilson, *Mercantilism* (Hist. Ass. 1958). Helpful introduction for the uninitiated
201 R.S. Dunn, *Sugar and Slaves: The Rise of the Planter Class in the English West Indies* (1973)
202 R.F. Thomas and D.N. McCloskey, 'Overseas Trade and Empire, 1700–1860', in (181)
See also Section 9 below, esp. (292) and Section 4 above, (114)

Industry

203 D.C. Coleman, *Industry in Tudor and Stuart England* (1975)
204 J. Thirsk, 'Industries in the Countryside', in F.J. Fisher, ed., *Essays in the Economic and Social History of Tudor and Stuart England* (1961)
205 G. Hammersley, 'The Charcoal Iron Industry and its Fuel', *EcHR*, **26** (1973)
206 T.S. Ashton, *Iron and Steel in the Industrial Revolution* (4th edn, Manchester, 1968)
207 J.U. Nef, *The Rise of the British Coal Industry*, 2 vols (1984)
208 M. Berg, *The Age of Manufactures 1700–1820* (1985)
209 P. Mathias, 'Who unbound Prometheus?', in id., *The Transformation of England: Essays in the Economic and Social History of England in the Eighteenth Century* (1979).

Agriculture and communications

210 E. Kerridge, *The Agricultural Revolution* (1967). Makes, but heavily overstates, a case for considering the 'Revolution' as primarily a 16th and 17th century phenomenon
211 J. Thirsk, ed., *Agricultural History of England and Wales*, V: *1640–1750* (parts I and II, 1984)
212 J. Thirsk, 'Agricultural Innovations and their Diffusion', in (211)
213 C.G.A. Clay, 'Landlords and Estate Management', in (211)
214 W.G. Hoskins, 'Harvest Fluctuations and English Economic History 1620–1759', *AgHR*, **16** (1968)
215 (a) E.L. Jones, 'Agriculture and Economic Growth in England 1660–1750: Agricultural Change'; (b) A.H. John, 'Agricultural Productivity and Economic Growth in England'; both in E.L. Jones, ed., *Agriculture and Economic Growth in England 1650–1815* (1967)
216 A.H. John, (a) 'The Course of Agricultural Change, 1660–1760', in L.S. Pressnell, ed., *Studies in the Industrial Revolution*, (1960)
(b) 'English Agricultural Improvements and Grain Exports, 1660–1765', in (174)
217 (a) J.R. Wordie, 'The Chronology of English Enclosure, 500–1914', in *EcHR* , **36** (1983)
(b) R.A.C. Parker, *Enclosures in the Eighteenth Century* (1960)
218 T.S. Willan, (a) *River Navigation in England 1600–1750* (1964); (b) *The English Coasting Trade 1600–1750* (Manchester, 1967)

Society: landed and urban

219 P. Laslett, *The World We Have Lost* (2nd edn, 1971)
220 (a) J.P. Cooper, 'The Social Distribution of Land and Men in England, 1486–1700', *EcHR*, **20** (1967)
     (b) F.M.L. Thompson, 'The Social Distribution of Landed Property in England since the 16th Century', *EcHR*, **19** (1966)
221 L. Stone, 'Social Mobility in England, 1500–1700', *P&P*, **33** (1966)
222 A. Everitt, (a) 'Social Mobility in Early Modern England', *P&P* **33** (1966); (b) *Change in the Provinces* (Leicester, 1969)
223 D. Owen, *English Philanthropy 1660–1960* (1965)
224 (a) D.A. Baugh, 'Poverty, Protestantism and Political Economy: English Attitudes Towards the Poor, 1660–1800', in S.B. Baxter, ed., *England's Rise to Greatness 1660–1760* (1983)
     (b) C. Wilson, 'The Other Face of Mercantilism', *TRHS*, **9** (1959)
225 W. Prest, ed., *The Professions in Early Modern England* (Beckenham, 1989)
226 G. Holmes, (a) *Augustan England: Professions, State and Society 1680–1730* (1982);
     (b) 'The Professions and Social Change in England, 1680–1730', in (16)
227 G. Holmes, 'Gregory King and the Social Structure of Pre-Industrial England', *TRHS*, **27** (1977)
228 R.B. Westerfield, *Middlemen in English Business, Particularly Between 1660 and 1760* (New Haven, 1915)
229 A. McInnes, 'The Revolution and the People', in (17)
230 N. McKendrick, J. Brewer and J.H. Plumb, *The Birth of a Consumer Society: The Commercialization of Eighteenth-Century England* (1982)
231 N. McKendrick, 'The Consumer Revolution of 18th-Century England' in (230)
232 J.H. Plumb, (a) *The Commercialisation of Leisure in Eighteenth-Century England* (Reading, 1973); (b) 'The New World of Children in Eighteenth-Century England', *P&P,* **67** (1976); (c) 'The Acceptance of Modernity' in (230); (d) 'The Public, Literature and the Arts in the 18th Century', in P. Fritz and D. Williams, eds, *The Triumph of Culture: Eighteenth Century Perspectives* (Toronto, 1972)
233 H.J. Habakkuk, (a) 'The Rise and Fall of English Landed Families 1600–1800: I', *TRHS*, **29** (1979); (b) 'The Rise and Fall of English Landed Families 1600–1800: II', *TRHS*, **30** (1980); (c) 'The Rise and Fall of English Landed Families, 1600–1800: III', *TRHS*, **31** (1981).
234 L. and J.F.C. Stone, *An Open Elite? England 1540–1880* (Oxford, 1984)
235 (a) H.J. Habakkuk, 'The Land Settlement and the Restoration of Charles II', *TRHS*, **28** (1978);
     (b) J. Thirsk, 'The Restoration Land Settlement', *Journal of Modern History*, **26** (1954);
     (c) *idem, The Restoration* (1976). Prints documents
236 G.E. Mingay, (a) *English Landed Society in the 18th Century* (1963); (b) *The Gentry* (1976)
237 H.J. Habakkuk, 'English Landownership, 1680–1740', *EcHR*, **10** (1939–40)
238 J.V. Beckett, (a) 'English Landownership in the Later Seventeenth and Eighteenth Centuries', *EcHR*, **30** (1977); (b) 'The Pattern of Landownership in England and Wales, 1660–1880', *EcHR*, **37** (1984)
239 J.D. Marshall, 'Agrarian Wealth and Social Structure in Pre-Industrial Cumbria', *EcHR*, **33** (1980)
240 C.G.A. Clay, (a) 'Marriage, Inheritance and the Rise of Large Estates in England,

1660–1815', *EcHR*, **21** (1968); (b) 'The Price of Freehold Land in the Later Seventeenth and Eighteenth Centuries', *EcHR*, **27** (1974)

241 J.V. Beckett, (a) *The Aristocracy in England, 1660–1914* (Oxford, 1986); (b) 'The English Aristocracy', *Parl. Hist.*, **5** (1986)

242 J. Cannon, (a) *Aristocratic Century: The Peerage of Eighteenth-century England* (Cambridge, 1984); (b) 'The Isthmus Repaired. The Resurgence of the English Aristocracy 1660–1716', *Proceedings of the British Academy*, **68** (1982)

243 (a) P. Roebuck, *Yorkshire Baronets 1640–1760* (Oxford, 1980)
(b) B.A. Holderness, 'The English Land Market in the Eighteenth Century: The Case of Lincolnshire', *EcHR*, **27** (1974)

244 J.V. Beckett, 'The Decline of the Small Landowner in Eighteenth- and Nineteenth-Century England: Some Regional Considerations', *AgHR*, **30** (1982)

245 F.M.L. Thompson, 'Landownership and Economic Growth in England in the Eighteenth Century', in E.L. Jones and S.J. Woolf, eds, *Agrarian Change and Economic Development* (1969)

246 P. Clark and P. Slack, eds, *Crisis and Order in English Towns: Essays in Urban History* (1972)

247 A. Everitt, (a) ed., *Perspectives in English Urban History* (1973); (b) 'The English Urban Inn, 1560–1760', in (247a)

248 R. Grassby, (a) 'The Personal Wealth of the Business Community in Seventeenth Century England', *EcHR*, **23** (1970); (b) 'English Merchant Capitalism in the Late Seventeenth Century. The Composition of Business Fortunes', *P&P*, **46** (1970)

249 P. Clark, ed., *The Transformation of English Provincial Towns, 1600–1800* (1984)

250 P.N. Borsay, *The English Urban Renaissance: Culture and Society in the Provincial Town, 1660–1770* (Oxford, 1989)

251 P.N. Borsay, (a) 'The English Urban Renaissance: the Development of Provincial Urban Culture, *c.* 1680– *c.* 1760', *Social History*, **5** (1977); (b) 'Culture, Status and the English Urban Landscape', *History*, **67** (1982); (*c*) 'Urban Development in the Age of Defoe', in (21)

252 P. Corfield, *Impact of English Towns, 1700–1800* (1982)

253 P. Corfield *et al.*, eds, *Rise of the New Urban Society* (1975)

254 C.W. Chalklin, *The Provincial Towns of Georgian England: A Study of Eighteenth-Century England* (Cambridge, 1984)

255 (a) N. Rogers, 'Money, Land and Lineage: the Big Bourgeoisie of Hanoverian London', *Social History*, **4** (1979)
(b) H. Horwitz, ' "The mess of the middle class" revisited: the case of the "big bourgeoisie" of Hanoverian London', *Continuity and Change*, **2** (1987)

Disorder and crime

256 T. Harris, see (93)

257 M. Beloff, *Public Order and Popular Disturbances, 1660–1714* (Oxford, 1938)

258 J.A. Sharpe, *Crime in Early Modern England 1550–1750* (1984)

259 G. Rudé, (a) *The Crowd in History, 1730–1848* (1964); (b) *Paris and London in the 18th Century* (1970). Collected essays

260 J. Stevenson, *Popular Disturbances in England 1700–1870* (1979)

261 G. Holmes, 'The Sacheverell Riots: The Church and the Crowd in Early Eighteenth-Century London', *P&P*, **72** (1976)

262 N. Rogers, (a) 'Riot and Popular Jacobitism in Early Hanoverian England', in (106);

(b) 'Popular Protest in Early Hanoverian London', *P&P*, **79** (1978)
263 E.P. Thompson, (a) *Whigs and Hunters: The Origin of the Black Act* (1975); (b) 'The Moral Economy of the English Crowd in the Eighteenth Century', *P&P*, **50** (1971)
264 (a) D. Hay, P. Linebaugh and E.P. Thompson, *Albion's Fatal Tree: Crime and Society in Eighteenth-Century England* (1975)
(b) D. Hay, 'Property, Authority and the Criminal Law', in (264a)
265 J.H. Langbein, 'Albion's Fatal Flaws', *P&P*, **98** (1983)
266 J. Brewer and J. Styles, *An Ungovernable People: The English and their Law in the Seventeenth and Eighteenth Centuries* (1980)

8. IRELAND AND SCOTLAND

267 T.M. Devine and D. Dickson, eds, *Ireland and Scotland 1600–1850: Parallels and Contrasts in Economic and Social Development* (Edinburgh, 1983)
268 (a) D. Hayton, 'John Bull's other Kingdoms: Ireland', in (21);
(b) D. Szechi, 'John Bull's other Kingdoms: Scotland', in (21). These form two halves of a joint essay on 'Scotland and Ireland'
269 J.C. Beckett, *The Making of Modern Ireland 1603–1923* (1966)
270 (a) T.W. Moody, F.X. Martin and F.J. Byrne, eds, *A New History of Ireland, III: Early Modern Ireland, 1534–1691* (Oxford, 1986)
(b) T.W. Moody and W.E. Vaughan, eds, *A New History of Ireland, IV: Eighteenth-Century Ireland, 1692–1800* (Oxford 1986)
271 J. Miller, 'The Earl of Tyrconnel and James II's Irish Policy, 1685–1688', *HJ*, **20** (1977)
272 L.M. Cullen, *Anglo-Irish Trade 1600–1801* (Manchester, 1968)
273 J.G. Simms, (a) *Jacobite Ireland 1685–91* (1969); (b) *The Williamite Confiscation in Ireland 1690–1703* (1956)
274 T.C. Smout, *A History of the Scottish People 1560–1830* (1970)
275 G. Donaldson, *Scotland: James V – James VIII* (Edinburgh, 1965)
276 R. Mitchison, *Lordship to Patronage: Scotland 1603–1745* (1983)
277 W. Ferguson, (a) *Scotland: 1689 to the Present* (Edinburgh and London, 1968); (b) *Scotland's Relations with England to 1707* (Edinburgh, 1977)
278 R.H. Campbell, (a) *Scotland since 1707: the Rise of an Industrial Society* (2nd edn, Edinburgh, 1985); (b) *The Rise and Fall of Scottish Industries* (Edinburgh, 1980)
279 H. Hamilton, *An Economic History of Scotland in the Eighteenth Century* (Oxford, 1963)
280 B. Lenman, *An Economic History of Modern Scotland, 1660–1976* (1977)
281 J. Buckroyd, *Church and State in Scotland, 1660–1681* (Edinburgh, 1980)
282 T.C. Smout, *Scottish Trade on the Eve of Union, 1660–1707* (Edinburgh, 1963)
283 P.J. Riley, (a) *King William and the Scottish Politicians* (Edinburgh, 1979); (b) *The Union of England and Scotland: A Study in Anglo-Scottish Politics of the Eighteenth Century* (Manchester, 1978); (c) *The English Ministers and Scotland 1707–1727* (1964)
284 G.S. Pryde, ed., *The Treaty of Union of Scotland and England, 1707* (1950)
285 (a) W. Ferguson, 'The Making of the Treaty of Union of 1707', *Scottish Historical Review*, **43** (1964)
(b) T.C. Smout, 'The Road to Union', in (17)
286 R.H. Campbell, 'The Anglo-Scottish Union of 1707: II. The Economic Consequences', *EcHR*, **16** (1964)
287 B. Lenman, 'A Client Society: Scotland Between the '15 and the '45' in (20)

288 J.S. Shaw, *The Management of Scottish Society 1707–64: Power, Nobles, Lawyers, Edinburgh Agents and English Influences* (Edinburgh, 1983)

289 J.M. Simpson, 'Who Steered the Gravy Train, 1707–1766?', in N.T. Phillipson and R. Mitchison, eds, *Scotland in the Age of Improvement: Essays in Scottish History in the Eighteenth Century* (Edinburgh, 1970)

290 E. Richards, *A History of the Highland Clearances: Agrarian Transformation and the Evictions 1746–1886* (1982)

9. OVERSEAS TERRITORIES

291 J.H. Rose, A.P. Newton and E.A. Benians, eds, *The Cambridge History of the British Empire, I: to 1783* (Cambridge, 1929)

292 J.H. Parry, *Trade and Dominion: The European Overseas Empires in the Eighteenth Century* (1971)

293 C.L. Ver Steep, *The Formative Years, 1607–1763* (I: 'The Making of America')

294 P. Haffenden, 'The Crown and the Colonial Charters, 1675–1688', *William and Mary Quarterly*, **23** (1958)

10. EDUCATION AND THE PRINTED WORD; SCIENCE AND IDEAS

295 L. Stone, (a) 'The Educational Revolution in England, 1560–1640', *P&P*, **28** (1964); (b) 'Literacy and Education in England, 1640–1900', *P&P*, **42** (1969)

296 (a) R. O'Day, *Education and Society, 1500–1800* (1982)
     (b) L.S. Sutherland and L.G. Mitchell, eds, *The History of the University of Oxford*, V: *The Eighteenth Century* (Oxford, 1986)
     (c) L. Stone, 'The Size and Composition of the Oxford Student Body 1580–1909', in L. Stone, ed., *The University in Society, I* (Princeton, 1974)

297 F.S. Siebert, *Freedom of the Press in England, 1476–1776* (Urbana, Illinois, 1965)

298 J. Black, *The English Press in the Eighteenth Century* (1987)

299 G.A. Cranfield, *The Development of the Provincial Newspaper 1700–1760* (Oxford, 1962)

300 J.A. Downie, *Robert Harley and the Press* (Cambridge, 1979)

301 P. Hyland, 'Liberty and Libel: Government and the Press during the Succession Crisis in Britain 1712–16', *EHR*, **101** *(1986)*
     On the Press, *temp*. William III, see also Section 5 above, 141

302 (a) A.R. Hall, *The Revolution in Science, 1500–1750* (1983)
     (b) P.M. Harman, *The Scientific Revolution* (1983)

303 (a) A.G.R. Smith, *Science and Society in 16th and 17th Century England* (1972)
     (b) R. Briggs, *The Scientific Revolution of the Seventeenth Century* (1969)

304 C. Webster, *The Great Instauration* (1976)

305 (a) G.N. Clark, *Science and Social Welfare in the Age of Newton*, (Oxford, 1949)
     (b) M. Hunter, *Science and Society in Restoration England* (1981)

306 M.C. Jacob, *The Newtonians and the English Revolution, 1689– 1720* (1976)

307 A.C. Crombie and M. Hoskin, 'The Scientific Movement and the Diffusion of Scientific Ideas, 1688–1751', in (24)

308 C.B. Macpherson, *The Political Theory of Possessive Individualism* (Oxford, 1962)

309 J.G.A. Pococke and R. Ashcraft, eds, *John Locke* (Los Angeles, 1980)
310 R. Ashcraft, (a) 'The Two Treatises and the Exclusion Crisis', in Pococke and Ashcraft, eds, *John Locke*; (b) *Revolutionary Politics and Locke's Two Treatises of Government* (Princeton, 1986); (c) M. Thompson, 'The Reception of Locke's *Two Treatises of Government*, 1690–1705' in *Political Studies*, **24** (1976)
311 R. Ashcraft and M.M. Goldsmith, 'Locke, Revolution Principles and the Formation of Whig Ideology', *HJ*, **26** (1983)
312 M. Goldie, 'The Roots of the True Whiggism 1688–94', *History of Political Thought*, **1** (1980)
313 H.T. Dickinson, *Liberty and Property: Political Ideology in Eighteenth-Century Britain* (1977)
314 J.P. Kenyon, *Revolution Principles: The Politics of Party 1689–1720* (Cambridge, 1977)
315 (a) T.P. Slaughter, '"Abdicate" and "Contract" in the Glorious Revolution', *HJ*, **28** (1981)
(b) J. Miller, 'The Glorious Revolution: "Contract" and "Abdication" Reconsidered', *HJ*, **25** (1982)
316 (a) R. Porter, 'The Enlightenment in England', in R. Porter and M. Teich, eds, *The Enlightenment in National Context* (Cambridge, 1981)
(b) A.M. Wilson, 'The Enlightenment Came First to England', in S.B. Baxter, ed., *England's Rise to Greatness, 1660–1760* (Berkeley, 1983)
317 J. Redwood, *Reason, Ridicule and Religion: The Age of Enlightenment in England, 1660–1750* (1976)
318 G.R. Cragg, *Reason and Authority in the Eighteenth Century* (Cambridge, 1964)
319 (a) H.J. McLachlan, *Socinianism in Seventeenth-Century England* (Oxford, 1951)
(b) G.E. Aylmer, 'Unbelief in Seventeenth-century England', in D. Pennington and K. Thomas, eds, *Puritans and Revolutionaries* (1978)
320 J.G.A. Pococke, 'Machiavelli, Harrington and English Political Ideologies in the Eighteenth Century', in *Politics, Language and Time* (1972)
321 J.C.D. Clark, *English Society 1688–1832: Ideology, Social Structure and Political Practice during the Ancien Regime* (Cambridge, 1985)

Bibliography Addenda

1. P. Virgin, *The Church in an Age of Negligence: Ecclesiastical Structure and Problems of Church Reform 1700–1840* (Cambridge, 1989)
2. E. Cruickshanks, ed., *By Force or by Default? The Revolution of 1688–89* (1989)
3. C. Jones, ed., *A Pillar of the Constitution: The House of Lords in British Politics, 1640–1784* (1989)
4. G.V. Scammel, *The First Imperial Age: European Overseas Expansion c.* 1400–1715 (1989)
5. P. Earle, *The Making of the English Middle Class: Business, Society and Family Life in London 1660–1730* (1989)
6. R. Hutton, *Charles II King of England, Scotland and Ireland* (Oxford, 1989)
7. B.L. Wykes, 'Religious Dissent and the Penal Laws: An Explanation of Business Success?', *History*, **75** (1990)
8. J. Spurr, *The Restoration Church of England* (Yale, 1991)
9. E. Cruickshanks and J. Black, eds, *The Jacobite Challenge* (Edinburgh, 1988)

Index

Note: Page references in italics indicate entries in the Compendium of Information; those in **bold** type indicate entries in the Glossary. Subentries are arranged in alphabetical, rather than chronological order, for ease of reference.